Consumer Law

**The International Library of Essays in Law and Legal Theory**
*Series Editor: Tom D. Campbell*

*Schools*

**Natural Law, Vols I & II** *John Finnis*
**Justice** *Thomas Morawetz*
**Law and Economics, Vols I & II** *Jules Coleman and Jeffrey Lange*
**Critical Legal Studies** *James Boyle*
**Marxian Legal Theory** *Csaba Varga*
**Legal Reasoning, Vols I & II** *Aulis Aarnio and Neil MacCormick*
**Legal Positivism** *Mario Jori*
**American Legal Theory** *Robert Summers*
**Law and Language** *Fred Schauer*
**Sociological Theories of Law** *Kahei Rokumoto*
**Rights** *Carlos Nino*
**Law and Psychology** *Martin Levine*
**Feminist Legal Theory** *Frances Olsen*

*Areas*

**Criminal Law** *Thomas Morawetz*
**Tort Law** *Ernest Weinrib*
**Contract Law, Vols I & II** *Larry Alexander*
**Anti-Discrimination Law** *Christopher McCrudden*
**Consumer Law** *Iain Ramsay*
**International Law** *Martti Koskenniemi*
**Property Law** *Elizabeth Mensch and Alan Freeman*
**Constitutional Law** *Mark Tushnet*
**Procedure** *Denis Galligan*
**Evidence and Proof** *William Twining and Alex Stein*
**Administrative Law** *Denis Galligan*
**Child Law** *Harry Krause*
**Family Law, Vols I & II** *Harry Krause*
**Welfare Law** *Peter Robson*
**Medicine and the Law** *Bernard Dickens*
**Commercial Law** *Ross Cranston*
**Communications Law** *David Goldberg*
**Environmental Law** *Michael Blumm*
**Conflict of Laws** *Richard Fentiman*
**Law and Religion** *Wojciech Sadurski*
**Human Rights Law** *Philip Alston*
**European Community Law** *Francis Snyder*

*Legal Cultures*

**Comparative Legal Cultures** *Csaba Varga*
**Law and Anthropology** *Peter Sack*
**Hindu Law and Legal Theory** *Ved Nanda*
**Islamic Law and Legal Theory** *Ian Edge*
**Chinese Law and Legal Theory** *Michael Palmer*
**Socialist Law and Legal Theory** *W. Butler*
**Japanese Law and Legal Theory** *Kiochiro Fujikura*
**Law and Development** *Anthony Carty*
**Jewish Law and Legal Theory** *Martin Golding*
**Legal Education** *Martin Levine*

*Future Volumes*

Labour Law, Common Law and Legal Theory, Civil Law and Legal Theory, Law and Society, African Law and Legal Theory, Legal Ethics and Cumulative index.

# Consumer Law

*Edited by*

Iain Ramsay

*Associate Professor of Law*
*Osgoode Hall Law School, Canada*

NEW YORK UNIVERSITY PRESS
REFERENCE COLLECTION

First published in the U.S.A. in 1992 by
NEW YORK UNIVERSITY PRESS
Washington Square
New York NY 10003

**Library of Congress Cataloging-in-Publication Data**
Consumer law / edited [by] Iain Ramsay.
p. cm. — (The International library of essays in law and legal theory)
Essays originally published in various journals from 1970 to 1984.
"New York University Press reference collection."
Includes bibliographical references and index.
ISBN 0-8147-7423-7
1. Consumer protection—Law and legislation. I. Ramsay, Iain.
II. Series.
K3842.C67 1992
343'.071—dc20
[342.371] 91-26750
CIP

# Contents

## PART IV WARRANTIES AND PRODUCT QUALITY



## PART V CONSUMER SAFETY



## PART VI CONSUMER REDRESS

# Acknowledgements

The editor and publishers wish to thank the following for permission to use copyright material.

American Bar Association Journal for the essay: Eric H. Steele (1975), 'The Dilemma of Consumer Fraud: Prosecute or Mediate?', *American Bar Association Journal*, **61**, pp. 1230–4. Reprinted with permission from the October 1975 issue of the *ABA Journal*, the Lawyer's Magazine, published by the American Bar Association.

American Bar Foundation Research Journal for the essay: Susan S. Silbey (1984), 'Who Speaks for the Consumer? Nader's *No Access to Law* and Best's *When Consumers Complain*', *American Bar Foundation Research Journal*, No. 2, pp. 429–57.

The American University Law Review for the essay: Arthur Allen Leff (1970), 'Contract as Thing', *The American University Law Review*, **19**, pp. 131–57.

Donald N. Dewees for the essay: Ronald Hirshhorn (1983), 'The Administration of the *Hazardous Products Act*', in Donald N. Dewees (ed.), *The Regulation of Quality: Product Services and the Workplace*, Toronto: Butterworths, pp. 175–206. Copyright © by Donald N. Dewees.

Harvard Law Review for the essay: Robert Pitofsky (1977), 'Beyond Nader: Consumer protection and the Regulation of Advertising', *Harvard Law Review*, **90**, pp. 661–701. Copyright © 1991 by the Harvard Law Review Association.

Osgoode Hall Law Journal for the essay: Michael J. Trebilcock (1975), 'Winners and Losers in the Modern Regulatory System: Must the Consumer Always Lose?', *Osgoode Hall Law Journal*, **13**, pp. 619–47. Copyright © Osgoode Hall Law Journal.

Stanford University Press for the essay: Jean Baudrillard (1988), 'Consumer Society', in Mark Poster (ed.), *Jean Baudrillard Selected Writings*, *Stanford University Press*, Chapter 2, pp. 29–56. Reprinted with the permission of the publishers, Stanford University Press © 1988 by the Board of Trustees of the Leland Stanford Junior University. Published in Great Britain by Polity Press, Cambridge.

University of Toronto Law Journal for essays: David Cayne and M.J. Trebilcock (1973), 'Market Considerations in the Formulation of Consumer Protection Policy', *University of Toronto Law Journal*, **23**, pp. 396–430 and Iain D.C. Ramsay (1981), 'Consumer Redress Mechanisms for Poor-Quality and Defective Products', *University of Toronto Law Journal*, **31**, pp. 117–52.

Wisconsin Law Review for essays: William C. Whitford (1973), 'The Functions of Disclosure Regulation in Consumer Transactions', *Wisconsin Law Review*, Number 2, pp. 400–70 and William C. Whitford (1981), 'Structuring Consumer Protection Legislation to Maximize Effectiveness', *Wisconsin Law Review*, pp. 1018–43. Copyright © Wisconsin Law Review.

The Yale Law Journal for essays: George L. Priest (1981), 'A Theory of the Consumer Product Warranty', *The Yale Law Journal*, **90**, pp. 1297–352 and William C. Whitford (1982), 'Comment on A Theory of the Consumer Product Warranty', *The Yale Law Journal*, **91**, pp. 1371–85. Reprinted by permission of The Yale Law Journal Company and Fred B. Rothman & Company from *The Yale Law Journal*.

Every effort has been made to trace all the copyright holders, but if any have been inadvertently overlooked the publishers will be pleased to make the necessary arrangement at the first opportunity.

# Series Preface

The International Library of Law and Legal Theory is designed to provide important research materials in an accessible form. Each volume contains essays of central theoretical importance in its subject area. The series as a whole makes available an extensive range of valuable material which will be of considerable interest to those involved in the research, teaching and study of law.

The series has been divided into three sections. The Schools section is intended to represent the main distinctive approaches and topics of special concern to groups of scholars. The Areas section takes in the main branches of law with an emphasis on essays which present analytical and theoretical insights of broad application. The section on Legal Cultures makes available the distinctive legal theories of different level traditions and takes up topics of general comparative and developmental concern.

I have been delighted and impressed by the way in which the editors of the individual volumes have set about the difficult task of selecting, ordering and presenting essays from the immense quantity of academic legal writing published in journals throughout the world. Editors were asked to pick out those essays from law, philosophy and social science journals which they consider to be fundamental for the understanding of law, as seen from the perspective of a particular approach or sphere of legal interest. This is not an easy task and many difficult decisions have had to be made in order to ensure that a representative sample of the best journal essays available takes account of the scope of each topic or school.

I should like to express my thanks to all the volume editors for their willing participation and scholarly judgement. The interest and enthusiasm which the project has generated is well illustrated by the fact that an original projection of 12 volumes drawn up in 1989 has now become a list of some 60 volumes. I must also acknowledge the vision, persistence and constant cheerfulness of John Irwin and the marvellous work done by Mrs Margaret O'Reilly and Mrs Sonia Bridgman.

TOM D. CAMPBELL
Series Editor
*The Faculty of Law*
*The Australian National University*

# Introduction

Consumer protection law has been defined as 'the sum total of the ways in which a state constitutes, defines, and intervenes in markets for the purpose of protecting the ultimate consumer of goods and services'.[1] Although consumer protection has a long history[2] the focus of this book is on contemporary issues. Consumer protection developed significantly in the 1960s and 1970s. During this period there was a growth in public regulation of consumer markets. In many countries, consumer protection policies are now reflected not only in the ground rules of market exchange but also in a variety of institutional frameworks of government which monitor and regulate the market on a continuing basis.[3] It is an established aspect of administration and policymaking in the modern state.

The consumer marketplace is an economic, sociological and cultural form, a site for exchange and the construction of personal identity. It is important to connect discussion of the objectives of consumer law and policy to reflections on these phenomena. One approach is to view consumer law as a method of correcting failures in the market system. The ultimate goal is viewed as that of consumer sovereignty, ensuring that consumer preferences count. In addition, distributive goals, such as the protection of lower-income groups, has been an important undercurrent though there is significant controversy as to the legitimacy and effectiveness of redistributive measures of consumer protection.[4] Paternalism has, it is argued, also motivated consumer protection legislation.[5]

Perhaps under the influence of economic analysis, there has been less attention paid to the source of consumer preferences in the market. In consequence, the equation of a market conception of consumer sovereignty with consumer empowerment neglects the extent to which preferences are socially constructed through advertising[6] and other social forces. It is difficult in any introduction to consumer protection not to be drawn into thinking about questions concerning the construction of tastes and preferences and the broader structural issues associated with the consumer society, such as the organization of city space, separating consumption from production through the development of suburbia. In the chapter by Claus Offe he introduces the idea of 'structurally imposed' consumer needs, for example, medicine caused by poor living conditions or cars in the suburbs. Baudrillard in his essay portrays a structuralist picture of the construction of needs in modern society linking it to the power of capitalist production in its continuing quest for new markets. The internationalization of capital raises in a stark form these structural questions for countries of the South.

If many questions about consumption practices are political, then the issue of consumer influence in the political and administrative process becomes crucial. Trebilcock's chapter, written from a pluralist perspective, draws attention to the difficulties of making the consumer voice heard and the ideological differences within the consumer movement. The period since the Second World War has witnessed the growth of 'new social movements' such as feminist, ecological and urban groups which seek social transformation rather than simply better representation within the existing system. Their social challenge is often to consumerism as an oppressive form of social relations and they differ fundamentally from the 'best buy' model of many middle-income consumer organizations.

The rhetoric of consumer protection is often couched in terms of 'intervention' by public (political) regulation into private (economic) markets, thereby appealing to the liberal public/private distinction.[8] The introductory quotation also mentions, however, the concept of 'ground rules'. It is impossible to establish a market without some rules on such issues as the amount of information which must be disclosed to co-contractants, or the nature of economic pressure which it is legitimate for one party to bring to bear on the other party.[9] Establishing ground rules must be by reference to some theory of distributive justice and human flourishing since economic analysis cannot itself answer this question. The law is therefore constitutive of the market and the issues are not solely about economic costs and benefits but 'part of a continuing process of deciding what sort of society ours shall be – how risk averse, how solicitous of the vulnerable and how willing to allocate resources through markets, or public control'.[10] The market is not a natural pre-political institution and the particular form of market relations reflects a political compromise backed up by state force.

An important aspect of consumer protection has concerned the regulation of unfair and deceptive trade practices. Institutional issues have been much discussed here concerning the relative role of private and public enforcement and the role of industry self-regulation and other forms of 'soft law'.[11] In relation to unfair contract terms the limitations of common law doctrines such as unconscionability and private enforcement are explored in the essay by Leff which also outlines the possible forms of government regulation. Leff's key insight was to draw attention to the misleading conceptualization of consumer contracts as individual bargains. Rather, consumer terms were simply part of the mass-produced product package which might be regulated or not depending on the nature of the particular market, the social importance of the contract, and so on. This essay, which was written in 1970, could also be interpreted as indicating a shift from private law to a public law paradigm concerning consumer terms, a shift underlined by other work of the period which conceptualized standard form consumer contracts as private legislation imposed by business on consumers.[12]

The conservative reaction to this approach came through the law and economics movement which argued, that although consumers might seem powerless individually, they exercised significant power over contract terms through their aggregate market power.[13] This argument is illustrated by Priest's essay on warranties, whose analysis is in turn challenged by Whitford.[14]

The economic approach to consumer terms attempts to turn value judgments into empirical assessments of market conditions. The difficulties of accumulating sufficient data to test economic predictions and the value judgments concealed in the analysis have led several writers to reject efficiency for distributive justice,[15] or paternalism,[16] as the primary rationales for regulating unfair contract terms.

Regulation in this area is a continuing process which requires both technical expertise and political management. These two factors are reflected in the history of regulatory agencies such as the Office of Fair Trading in the UK, The Federal Trade Commission in the USA, and the Consumer Ombuds in Scandinavia. These agencies generally monitor the marketplace, make recommendations for legislation, and exercise rulemaking and enforcement powers. Although often justified in terms of the US 'New Deal' model of a politically-insulated body, rationally developing policy on the basis of 'scientific' expertise,[17] they are invariably an important site of consumer politics.[18] There are various studies of the relative effectiveness of these agencies, the extent to which they go through periods of activism and restraint, their relationship to industry, consumers and other groups.[19] Much of this literature may be placed within the context of general studies of economic and social regulation.[20] A common finding in relation to the enforcement activity of state consumer protection bureaux is that although these agencies may have been established with a regulatory mandate they often become heavily involved in routinized dispute settlement. The essay by Steele discusses the reasons for this approach.[21]

The control of advertising practices has been a central issue in consumer protection. Advertising links the economic and cultural aspects of the consumer marketplace: it is perhaps the icon of the modern consumer society. The essay by Pitofsky summarizes a mainstream view of regulation. In his view the objectives of regulation are to increase the informative nature of advertising messages, thereby making the market work more effectively. He is sceptical of attempts to regulate unfair advertising beyond the protection of vulnerable groups such as children. His position appears to be premised on the difficulties of establishing standards and fears of government paternalism. Yet, over time, commercial advertising may help in shaping popular consciousness so that we associate prestige, security and status with the purchase of commodities[22] and constitute ourselves as consumers rather than workers or members of a particular class.[23]

There is also the economic and cultural impact of advertising on the media. Studies conducted for the Peacock Commission in the UK documented the adverse effects of advertising on the quality of US television and the power of advertisers in ensuring that generally only safe conventional programming was shown.[24] There are also concerns about advertising's impact in countries of the South,[25] resulting in taste transfer from indigenous to multinational products and services.

These questions about the impact of advertising have rarely been addressed by governments and, in those cases where there has been pressure for regulation, have resulted in self-regulatory programmes. This fact is perhaps not surprising if we accept Lindblom's argument concerning the privileged position of business in society. In his view, two consequences of this position are the ability to keep issues off the public agenda and an influence on the perception that certain phenomena such as commercial advertising have a 'taken for granted' status.[26] These questions should however be addressed in any discussion of consumer regulation and they return us to the problems of ensuring consumer influence in the political and administrative process.

Product safety regulation illustrates tensions between economic and ethical values and technocratic and political decision-making. The idea of safety is itself a slippery concept. When is a product safe? Lowrance has drawn a distinction between 'measuring risk, an objective but probabilistic pursuit, and judging the acceptability of that risk (judging safety), a matter of personal and social value judgment'.[27] Others doubt the objectivity of risk measurement.[28] The difficulty of achieving uncontroversial substantive solutions underlines the importance in this area of process issues. Standard setting in the area of consumer safety illustrates the problems. In order to establish standards, governments must often rely on industry information and consumers may not have the information or expertise to match that of industry. There is a continuing search for a model of standard setting which can ensure adequate participation by all affected groups, incorporate expert information and develop standards within a reasonable period of time.[29]

The topic of consumer redress is a large one and overlaps with those of access to justice,[30] the role of private enforcement of public programmes of regulation and the role of law in achieving progressive social change. Consumer problems are one manifestation of the limitations of private litigation in a mass consumption economy, where harm is often small individually but large in the aggregate. Reforms in this area have ranged from attempts to provide greater access to the courts through such devices as class actions, the development of small claims courts and relaxation of costs rules, to the development of alternative informal procedures such as arbitration, or the introduction of consumer ombuds.

The choice of reform will be influenced by ideological perceptions of the importance of consumer claims. To the extent that they are viewed as minor interpersonal injustices, policymaking will attempt to dispose of consumer claims expeditiously without a major commitment of public resources. If, however, we view consumer issues as raising questions of general social concern then we should encourage greater collective action, relaxation of the rules of standing, the facilitation of class actions and so on.[31] This issue is complicated by the fact that the existing system may contribute to particular public perceptions. Indeed, the area of consumer redress is a fruitful area for investigation of the production and reproduction of social norms: the 'normalization' of particular forms of consumer relationships. Ramsay's essay on the norms of the marketplace and Silbey's essay on consumer expectations raise questions such as why and how consumers develop particular expectations of sellers in the marketplace. Clearly, complaint handlers do not solely solve problems but also help to transmit 'proper' norms of behaviour, as do government agencies and other institutions of consumer education.[32]

Recent literature surveying the experience of the past few decades is less optimistic than the writings of the late 1960s concerning the role of private enforcement of consumer law through such devices as class actions.[33] These actions are clearly not a panacea for consumer problems, and in relation to cases of diffuse economic loss as, public regulation will continue to play a central role in regulating and monitoring the marketplace. Class actions were also intended to be a vehicle for politicizing consumer issues, being described by one writer as the 'judicial analogue to the mass demonstration in the streets'.[34] This quotation returns us to the problematic of consumption as a site for political struggle. Campaigns by feminist groups against sexist advertising, consumer boycotts of South African produce, rent strikes and the exploitation of business scandals suggest that there is a need to think through the ambivalent role of law and the state in both sustaining consumption as a way of life and in providing a potential source of rights for the development of opposition to dominant economic interests.[35]

## Notes

1 Bourgoignie, T. and Trubek, D. (1987), *Consumer Law, Common Markets and Federalism*, Berlin: W. de Gruyter.

2 See notes 1–4 in the chapter by Silbey for references on consumer protection history.

3 For example, The Federal Trade Commission in the USA, the UK Director General of Fair Trading and the Swedish Ombuds. A useful discussion of the role and performance of the Federal Trade Commission may be found in Breyer, S. and Stewart, R. (1985), *Administrative Law and Regulatory*

*Policy*, 2nd ed., Chapter 8, especially at pp. 939–1006. For discussion of the Office of Fair Trading see Ramsay, I. (1987), 'The Office of Fair Trading: Policing the Consumer Marketplace', in R. Baldwin and C. McCrudden (eds), *Regulation and Public Law*, London: Weidenfeld and Nicolson. Consumer protection policies have also been developed at the regional and international levels. See Bourgoignie and Trubek above at note 1 and Bourgoignie, T. (1989), *Elements pour une Théorie du droit de la consommation*, Bruylant: Bruxelles, Ch. 4 at 215.

4 See the discussion in chapter 1 by Cayne and Trebilcock and see Kronman, A. (1980), 'Contract Law and Distributive Justice', *Yale Law Journal*, **89**, 472.

5 See Kennedy, D. (1982), 'Distributive and Paternalist Motives in Contract and Tort Law, with Special Reference to Compulsory Terms and Unequal Bargaining Power', *Maryland Law Review*, **41**, 563.

6 For an economic statement of this position see Galbraith, J.K. (1984), *The Affluent Society*, 4th ed.; (1967), *The New Industrial State*; and (1973), *Economics and the Public Purpose*. Also Scitovsky, T. (1976), *The Joyless Economy: An Inquiry into Human Satisfaction and Dissatisfaction*. A useful discussion of these issues is in a special issue of *Theory Culture and Society*, **1** (3), (1983), 'Consumer Culture'.

7 See, for example, Castells, M. (1978), 'Collective Consumption and Urban Contradictions in Advanced Capitalism' in M. Castells (ed.), *City Class and Power*, London: Macmillan; Laclan, E. and Mouffe, C. (1985), *Hegemony and Socialist Strategy: towards a radical democratic politics*, London: Verso.

8 For a critique of the public/private distinction see Kennedy, D. (1982), 'The Stages of the Decline of the Public Private Distinction', *University of Pennsylvania Law Review*, **130**, 1349.

9 For an elaboration of this viewpoint see Kronman, A. (1979), note 4 above.

10 Stewart, R. and Sunstein, C. (1982), 'Public Programs and Private Rights', *Harvard Law Review*, **95**, 1193.

11 See, for example, the special issue of the *Journal of Consumer Policy*, 'Implementing the Consumer-Supplier Dialogue through Soft Law?', 1984, **7**.

12 See Slawson, D. (1971), 'Standard Form Contracts and Democratic Control of Lawmaking Power', *Harvard Law Review*, **84**, 529. A comprehensive discussion of these shifts in thinking about consumer contracts may be found in Rakoff, T. (1983), 'Contracts of Adhesion: An Essay in Reconstruction', *Harvard Law Review*, **96**, 1174.

13 See Trebilcock, M.J. and Dewees, D. (1981), 'Judicial Control of Standard Form Contracts', in Burrows, P. and Veljanovski, C. (eds), *The Economic Approach to Law*, London, Toronto: Butterworth. An economic analysis which is sceptical of the power of consumers to control market terms is Goldberg, V. (1974), 'Institutional Change and the Quasi Invisible Hand', *Journal of Law and Economics*, **17**, 461.

14 For Priest's reply to Whitford see Priest, G.L. (1980–1), 'The Best Evidence of the Effect of Products Liability Law on the Accident Rate: Reply', *Yale Law Journal*, **91**, 1386.

15 See Kronman, note 4 above.

16 See Kennedy, note 5 above.

17 See Landis, J. (1951), *The Administrative Process*, London: Oxford University Press.

18 The politics of consumer protection at the Federal Trade Commission in the 1960s and 1970s is recounted by Michael Pertschuk (Chair of the Commission in the late 1970s), (1982), *Revolt Against Regulation: The Rise and Pause of the Consumer Movement*, Berkeley: University of California Press.

19 For a general outline of theories concerning this phenomenon see Breyer, S. (1982), *Regulation and its Reform*, Cambridge, Mass: Harvard University Press; and see Wilson, J.Q. (ed.) (1980), *The Politics of Regulation*, New York: Basic Books.

20 *Idem* and for a useful overview see Hawkins, K. and Thomas, J. (eds) (1984), *Enforcing Regulation*, Boston: Kluwer-Nijhoff.

21 See also Silbey, S. (1980–81), 'Case Processing: Consumer Protection in an Attorney General's Office', *Law and Society Review*, **15**, 849 and Cranston, R. (1979), *Regulating Business: Law and Consumer Agencies*, London: Macmillan; Hawkins, K. and Thomas, J.M. (eds) (1984), note 20 above.

22 See Ewen, S. (1976), *Captains of Consciousness: Advertising and the Social Roots of Consumer Culture*, New York: McGraw-Hill; Lindblom, C.E. (1977), *Politics and Markets: The World's Political Economic Systems*, p. 216, New York: Basic Books.
23 See Williamson, J. (1978), *Decoding Advertisements: Ideology and Meaning in Advertising*, London: M. Boyars.
24 See *Report of the Committee on the Financing of the BBC* (Cmnd 9824) (1986) and the background paper for the Report by J. Blumler (1986), entitled 'Television in the United States: Funding Sources and Programming Consequences' in West Yorkshire Media Politics Group, *Research on the Range and Quality of Broadcasting Services: A Report for the Committee on Financing of the BBC*, London: Home Office.
25 See Sinclair, J. (1989), *Images Incorporated*, London: Routledge.
26 See Lindblom, note 21 above at p. 204.
27 Lowrance, W. (1976), *Of Acceptable Risk: Science and the Determinants of Safety*, p. 8, Los Altos, Calif.: W. Kaufman.
28 See Douglas, M. (1985), *Risk Acceptability According to the Social Sciences*, London: Routledge.
29 See, generally, Tuohy, C. (1982) 'Regulation and Scientific Complexity', *Osgoode Hall Law Journal*, **20**, 562.
30 See Cappelletti, M. and Garth, B. (1978), *Access to Justice*, Alphen aan Den Rijn: Sijthoff; Sarat, A. (1986), 'Access to Justice: Citizen Participation and The American Legal Order' in L. Lipson and S. Wheeler, *Law and the Social Sciences*.
31 For a discussion of these issues, see Steele, E. (1981), 'The Historical Context of Small Claims Courts', *American Bar Foundation Research Journal*, 293.
32 See further on this topic: Graham, P. (1985), 'Criticalness, Pragmatics and Everyday Life: Consumer Literacy as Critical Practice', in Forester, J. (ed.), *Critical Theory and Public Life*, Cambridge Mass: M.I.T. Press.
33 See, for example, O'Grady, K.J. (1982), 'Consumer Remedies', *Canadian Bar Review*, **60**, 549; Glenn, P. (1984), 'Class Actions in Ontario and Quebec', *Canadian Bar Review*, **62**, 247.
34 Starrs, J.E. (1969), 'Consumer Class Actions', *Boston University Law Review*, **49**, 211.
35 Garth, B., Nagel, I. and Plager, S.J. (1988), 'The Institution of the Private Attorney-General: Perspectives from an Empirical Study of Class Action Litigation', **353**, *Southern California Law Review*.

# Part I
# Frameworks for Consumer Law

# [1]

David Cayne and M.J. Trebilcock*

# MARKET CONSIDERATIONS IN THE FORMULATION OF CONSUMER PROTECTION POLICY†

## *1 Introduction*

Even the most casual observer of contemporary legal literature could not help but note the proliferation of consumer protection rules. The growing importance of consumerism has not yet, however, resulted in a concise statement of the goals which these rules are designed, or should be designed, to achieve. Of what elements are they comprised? What attributes, if any, do they all share? Is there a central theme around which a philosophy of consumer protection legislation can be formulated?

It is our central contention that there has emerged a body of law easy to recognize, but difficult to conceptualize, a series of rules which must, if realistic goals are to be set for them, be capable of justification against a broad conceptual framework. In attempting to suggest such a framework, we propose to examine in detail one particular phenomenon which has elicited or contributed to the enactment of a number of consumer-oriented laws – the costs exacted by poverty in the market-place. We hope that this analysis will provide more general insights about the nature of the options available in the formulation of any consumer protection policy.

We seek first to question the assumption persistently made by commentators that the reason why the poor pay more is lack of effective competition in the low-income market. We then proceed to examine a number of common legal responses to particular 'abuses' in the low-income market, pointing out that in most cases these responses are formulated without an adequate analysis of the structure of the market to which they are to apply, without regard to the real causes of the objectionable phenomena, and thus without regard to the real economic and social consequences likely to be produced. We seek to underline the dangers of succumbing to the momentum of a legislative fashion while avoiding rigorous, hard-headed, and sometimes painful analysis of the real causes of the problems to which

* David Cayne, formerly Associate Professor of Law, Faculty of Law, McGill University, Montreal; M.J. Trebilcock, Professor of Law, Faculty of Law, University of Toronto.

† The authors would like to acknowledge helpful criticisms they received in the preparation of this article from Dr David Bond, formerly Executive Director of the Canadian Consumer Council, Professor Christopher Green, Faculty of Economics, McGill University, and Professor David Beatty, Faculty of Law, University of Toronto.

solutions are sought. We seek to show that to strike out at the symptoms rather than the causes of consumer problems in the market-place is not only worthless, but often actually makes the problems worse. In pursuing this analysis, we hope to develop some concept of what are the possibilities, and importantly, the limitations, of consumer protection laws in controlling problems in the market-place.

## 2 *The Phenomenon: The Poor Pay More*

### A THE POOR DO PAY MORE

In what is perhaps one of the most extensive and well-controlled studies on the subject, the Federal Trade Commission[1] found that consumers purchasing from low-income market retailers pay significantly higher prices than general market retailers command for identical products. The commissioners researched the prices of consumer durables such as television sets, refrigerators, washing machines, freezers, dryers, and the like, and found that, without exception, the highest mark-ups were effected by merchants selling to low-income purchasers: 'The general conclusion that emerges ... is that the low-income market is a very expensive place to buy durable goods. On television sets ... the general market retailer's price is about $130. In the low-income market a customer can pay up to $250 for similar sets. Other comparisons include a dryer selling for $149.95 from a general market retailer and for $299.95 from a low-income market retailer; and a vacuum cleaner selling for $59.95 in the general market and $79.95 in the low-income market.'[2] The FTC study, of course, corroborates in a highly systematic way the findings of Caplovitz who, in *The Poor Pay More*,[3] tirelessly documented the same phenomenon.

Other investigators have found that the same tendency on a reduced level characterizes other commodity markets as well. Goodman,[4] for example, reports that the relatively high percentage of smaller stores in low-income areas of Philadelphia tends to augment food costs, but adds that the poor will respond to lower prices existing in other neighbourhoods. Although less easy to assess than a simple disparity in price, there is no doubt that the inconvenience and cost of transportation would in these circumstances properly reflect the added burden of living in low-income neighbourhoods. In another study effected in the same city, Dixon and McLaughlin[5] found that the cost of a food basket in low-income neighbourhoods exceeds by one

1 *Economic Report on Installment Credit and Retail Sales Practices of District of Columbia Retailers*, US Federal Trade Commission, Washington (1968) hereinafter referred to as the FTC study

2 Ibid, at 16

3 David Caplovitz *The Poor Pay More* (1963)

4 Charles S. Goodman, 'Do the Poor Pay More?,' (1968), 32 *J. Marketing* 18

5 Donald F. Dixon and Daniel J. McLaughlin, Jr, 'Low Income Consumers and the Issue of Exploitation: A Study of Chain Supermarkets,' (1970–1), 57 *Soc. Sci. Quart.* 320

per cent the average price for the city as a whole. Sturdevant reports far more significant disparities illustrating the same phenomenon. He found that a food basket of thirty items will cost from seven to twenty-one per cent more in Watts than in the affluent Beverly Hills area of Los Angeles. And Marcus[6] corroborates the foregoing by concluding that, when food quality is taken into account, Watts shoppers pay more than their Culver City counterparts. Preliminary studies in Canada indicate the same phenomenon.[7]

### B WHY DO THE POOR PAY MORE?

The foregoing studies clearly demonstrate the market-place consequences of poverty. It would be premature, however, to promulgate new legislation on the basis of this evidence without first determining the causes which underlie the plight of the ghetto consumer. Thus it would be pointless to devise additional disclosure requirements if the economic realities of the ghetto dictate that the poor must pay more because they are more expensive to service. Hence, in the analysis which follows, we will initially evaluate the importance of alleged structural weaknesses in the low-income market, and then proceed to assess the extent to which informational deficiencies and cultural characteristics contribute to the burden of the higher prices which afflict the poor.

#### 1/*Structural conditions: competition and the low-income merchant*

Today in Canada, consumer credit outstanding *per capita* of population is almost $600.[8] Clearly, the low-income consumer is frequently unable to purchase a piece of furniture, an appliance, or other consumer durable without recourse to a deferred-payment scheme.

Unlike middle-class consumers, however, the poor are unable to avail themselves of the traditional sources of consumer credit. Whether it be the result of job instability, educational deficiency, insufficient income, or any of the other factors which typically characterize the poor, the regulated lenders, operating within legislatively-determined parameters, often cannot deal profitably with this class of borrower. The consequences are dismally manifest: Caplovitz[9] depicts the manner in which slum merchants subvert rate ceilings by marking up the cash prices of goods sold to reflect the credit risks involved.

6 Frederick D. Sturdevant, 'Better Deal for Ghetto Shoppers,' (1968), 46 *Harvard Bus. Rev.* 130, reproduced in Acker & Day, *Consumerism-Search for the Consumer Interest* (1971), at 390; Burton H. Marcus, 'Similarity of Ghetto and Non-Ghetto Food Costs, (1969), 6 *J. Marketing Research*, at 365–8; but cf Sexton, 'Do Inner-City Chain Stores charge more?' (1973), 7 *J. Consumer Affairs* 145

7 Devine and Hawkins, 'Implications of Improved Information on Market Performance,' (1972), 6 *J. Consumer Affairs* 184, at 187, 188; *The Grocery Store Story Book* (1972); 'A Price Survey of Montreal Area Food Stores,' unpublished student essay, Kenneth Dryden, McGill Law School, 1972.

8 *Consumer Credit* (Statistics Canada, October 1973)

9 Caplovitz, supra note 3, at 82

The extent of the need for credit is undoubtedly a central factor isolating this class of buyer from markets which serve the general community of consumers. This of course does not negate the existence of other contributing conditions. Thus the process whereby the low-income debtor repays the amount outstanding directly to the creditor creates personal relations which, under the circumstances, are difficult to terminate.[10] In addition, there is evidence of fraudulent creditor practices designed to increase existing dependencies. One typical procedure involves the issuance of negative credit reports notwithstanding the debtor's uninterrupted adherence to the contemplated repayment scheme.[11] No less significant are the transportation costs and cultural inhibitions created when the ghetto dweller ventures outside unpleasant but nevertheless familiar territory.[12]

The collective impact of these circumstances frees the slum merchant from the discipline that would otherwise be imposed by chain-store pricing policies. Simply stated, there is no effective competition between these two kinds of retail operations; more precisely, and perhaps more significantly, they cannot properly be said to operate within the same market.

The process of market delimitation will occasionally, but necessarily, involve serious uncertainties. Does a black and white television compete with a colour unit? Are trains and buses to be included within the rubric of 'transportation facilities'? The response to questions such as these must, as a general rule, reflect the extent to which services or goods available at approximately the same price share similar attributes. Hence one could persuasively contend that buses and trains do compete because they are both forms of land transportation, they travel at approximately the same speed, and so on. Conversely, that airplanes are to be classified in a different market is obvious.

On a parity of reasoning it is patently clear that the market which includes the slum merchant, at least insofar as the low-income consumer is concerned, does not extend to the down-town department store patronized by the middle-class buyer. Credit accessibility controls the purchasing power of the poor to such an extent that their decisions are frequently predicated upon the weekly repayment charge, inclusive of credit costs, rather than the absolute price of the object in question unaffected by finance charges.[13] Hence the credit terms available from the chain retailer juxtaposed to the easy credit policies of the ghetto merchant would, in itself and without more, dispose of the matter. There are qualitative differences between the relevant attributes of these two classes of retail operations. This of course does not

10 Milton J. Huber, 'The Poor in the Market Place,' (1968), 2 *Power, Poverty, and Urban Policy* 151, at 167–8

11 Ibid

12 See for example, Sturdevant, supra note 6, at 398.

13 See brief submitted by J.F. Grandy, Deputy Minister of Consumer and Corporate Affairs, to the Special Senate Committee on Poverty (Canada), 29 May 1969, Proceedings no. 8, at 279.

imply that sources of credit which serve the more affluent will never, under any circumstances, extend credit to the poor. There will invariably be a residual class of consumer in respect of whom competition exists between firms participating in otherwise distinct markets. Thus, certain individuals prefer trains to airplanes on the basis of the perceived dangers which the latter involve, or, perhaps, because the former offer downtown-to-downtown service; similarly, the FTC study indicates that some low-income consumers do satisfy the criteria of the traditional lending institutions, but, for reasons which we will canvass later, do not avail themselves of these credit facilities.

It is commonly asserted dogma that legislative policy should be geared to control the exploitative practices of the low-income merchant thus immunized from competition. Ziegel,[14] for example, justifies the regulation of interest rates on this basis; and a body no less prestigious than the National Commission on Civil Disorders[15] has revealed its bias by suggesting that 'exploitative' practices flourish in the ghetto, notwithstanding the modesty of the profits actually earned. This kind of analysis is not only naive; it clouds the relevant issues by framing an economic problem in moralistic terms.

Precisely what constitutes 'exploitation'? Does a creative entrepreneur realizing twenty per cent on invested equity necessarily come within the meaning of the term? Or does it merely contemplate a failure to comply with certain acceptable behavioural norms? If so, is it desirable and legislatively feasible to embody these norms in the law? If General Motors is entitled to maximize profits, is it realistic to expect the low-income merchant to respond differently?

Highly significant in this context is the Federal Trade Commission's finding that low-income retailers earn substantially less on invested capital than general market retailers. The commission nevertheless reasoned that 'the high prices charged by low-income market retailers suggest the absence of effective price competition.'[16] This conclusion is clearly inconsistent with findings that industries characterized by structural weaknesses such as monopoly or oligopoly manifest significantly higher profit levels than those industries where competition prevails.[17]

Theorizing, on the one hand, that insufficient competition amongst retailers underlies the excessive prices which the poor must pay, and faced, on the other, with moderate profit levels, the commission had to rely upon the only analytically acceptable explanation to account for the disparity: high costs, in the form of distribution expenses, bad debt write-offs, and legal fees incurred to collect outstanding loans were absorbing a sizeable

14 Jacob Ziegel, Brief to the Special Senate Committee on Poverty (Canada) 21 October 1970, Proceedings no. 3, at 3.85

15 Report of the US National Commission on Civil Disorders (1968) 274–7

16 Supra note 1, at xiii

17 See Joe Bain *Industrial Organization* (1st ed, 1959), at 411–16.

proportion of revenues. Commissioner Jones[18] has suggested that the expenses which cripple the ghetto merchant result from inadequate managerial skills. According to this analysis, the absence of genuine competition produces an environment in which inefficiency prevails, with the resulting cost increases being ultimately borne by the consumer.

The Federal Trade Commission is to be commended on its extensive and meticulous efforts in collecting and assimilating data relevant to the ghetto consumer. The analysis which the commission applies to these findings and which is reiterated by Commissioner Jones is, however, sorely deficient. It relies upon the assumptions that the merchant lacks the necessary expertise to make rational decisions and, additionally, is too stubborn or stupid to seek managerial assistance. He operates, according to the hypothesis, within a market sheltered from competition and hence consciously or unconsciously dissipates large amounts of money which would otherwise enure to him in the form of profits.

Although the depiction of the ghetto merchant as monopolist or oligopolist is consistent with our analysis that he does not compete with the chain-store retailer, it ignores the possibility of competition within the low-income market itself. Thus it is clearly inconsistent with the retail activity in East Harlem which Caplovitz describes in *The Poor Pay More*: no fewer than sixty furniture and appliance stores serve this particular low-income community.[19] It seems to be equally difficult to reconcile the hypothesis with the finding of the commission itself that nineteen retailers serve the low-income market in the District of Columbia, without taking into account those merchants whose sales do not exceed $100,000. Nor do they jibe with Bain's findings that anti-competitive symptoms only begin to manifest themselves where no more than eight firms control at least seventy per cent of output.[20] Furthermore, the commission fails to explain why structural weaknesses should prevail within the low-income market. It refers to no independent conditions such as high entry barriers or significant economies of scale which might tend to support the hypothesis. Unless and until such evidence is adduced, we think it both unsafe and arrogant to conclude that such retailers do not know how to handle their affairs and survive merely because, through unexplained circumstances, they happen to operate within the parameters of a protected market.

High costs no doubt prevail. In addition to the substantial legal fees and distribution expenses already referred to, Sturdevant[21] contends that the 'mom and pop' stores which serve ghetto dwellers are unable to realize the scale economies which characterize chain retailers. Hence he labels them inefficient and argues that the major retailers should be induced, by means

18 Jones 'The Inner-City Market Place,' (1969), 37 *George Washington L. Rev.*
19 Caplovitz, supra note 3, at 12
20 Bain, supra note 17, at 411–16
21 Sturdevant, supra note 6, at 393

of government subsidies, to participate in this market. Implicit in this analysis is the assumption that increased costs are necessarily co-extensive with inefficiency. The latter cannot, however, be diagnosed *in abstrato*; like any other behavioural standard, it must be determined in the context of surrounding circumstances. Thus it might well be that smaller stores fulfil needs peculiar to low-income neighbourhoods. By way of example, we have already noted the close debtor-creditor relations which prevail in such areas. This closeness may reflect the creditor's need to keep in continuous contact with a debtor whom he regards as unreliable. Alternatively, one might speculate that the borrower who has difficulty in procuring the credit which he so badly needs must time and again return to the one source of credit where he is known and to some extent trusted. In either case, the credit dependencies which characterize the poor would appear to be inconsistent with the emergence of large and impersonal chain retailers. Furthermore, the predominance of smaller outlets is also consistent with the finding that low-income consumers can rarely accumulate sufficient funds to justify an excursion to a supermarket.[22] As a result, they would tend to patronize smaller, more expensive, merchants.

It is not our purpose to justify or explain the existence of small retailers in the ghetto. It is, however, part of our central theme that such businesses are there for reasons which reflect particular needs of the community, whether economic or otherwise. Chain operations were once small outlets which, responding to local conditions, expanded to meet changing needs. Presumptively it seems unlikely that their systematic failure to expand in ghetto areas is unrelated to local conditions. More importantly, it is manifestly premature to label smaller units inefficient in the absence of persuasive empirical evidence suggesting that chain operators could, with lower operating expenses, fulfil the same needs.

Additional research is badly wanting, and should, *inter alia*, be geared to answer the following questions: Is it in fact more expensive to initiate a retail operation in low-income areas? If so, to what extent would additional cost factors tend to discourage potential entrants? Do chain retailers ever participate in these markets? If the latter question is answered affirmatively, what kind of merchandise do they sell? For example, do they concentrate upon consumer durables or upon food? Do they offer credit arrangements or do they typically insist upon immediate payment? Are their pricing policies consistent with those of stores operating in middle-class communities?

It would be equally appropriate to gather similar material relating to smaller retailers. Does their number in fact vary inversely with the average income of the community? If so, is there any evidence of price competition in ghetto areas? Are their pricing policies related to the physical difficulty of consumers, as measured by both distance and transportation facilities, of travelling to a more affluent community? The resulting description would

22 See Grandy, supra note 13, at 282; Thomas Gladwin *Poverty U.S.A.* (1967), at 48ff.

permit the researcher to assess the needs which each kind of outlet fulfils and to make efficiency evaluations in that context. The investigator would then be in a position to effect an empirically justifiable diagnosis of why the poor pay more.

By way of example, the suggested research might well indicate that ghetto merchants emphasize the amount of the monthly payment, rather than total cost. It is of course commonly known that the low-income consumer tends to perceive cost factors primarily in terms of the capacity of his budget to accommodate the contemplated instalments.[23] In his view, 'price' is not the equivalent of total cost, but rather corresponds to the size of the monthly payment.[24] Hence this analysis, premised as it is upon the assumption that merchandising practices in the ghetto are dependent variables responding to needs already existing, would lead to the prediction that it is the monthly, rather than the total, payment which retailers strive to reduce.[25]

Price competition would, of course, extend to all unco-ordinated efforts among retailers to alter either the amount or the modality of payment. Although a 'one-dollar down one-dollar-a-week' payment schedule is not overly pleasing to the middle-class mentality, it might well be the inevitable response of competing merchants to the needs of the low-income consumer. Hence it would be incorrect for researchers to underrate the importance of this form of competition when assessing the structural retail environment which prevails in low-income communities. Indeed, existing predispositions to infer that inefficiencies associated with monopoly or oligopoly characterize the ghetto may in part result from the tendency to discount the structural implications of merchandising efforts geared to minimize the amount of the monthly payment.

In spite of the obvious need for additional research, there has been no shortage of would-be policy makers advocating that structural remedies be applied to the ghetto retail market. Jones, for example, would encourage '... the development of new local entrepreneurs in the inner city market ...'[26] and Sturdevant[27] develops the same theme on a more explicit basis. In his view, exceedingly high insurance costs resulting from vandalism and shoplifting, in conjunction with the serious personnel problems typically experienced in low-income areas, constitute insurmountable entry barriers, thereby allowing existing merchants to prey upon '... a largely captive market.'[28] He favours two modalities of lowering entry barriers: an investment guarantee plan, which would enable a retailer – presumably a chain

23 For an extensive analysis of the importance of subjective factors in the evaluation of cost, see James Buchanan *Cost and Choice* (1970).

24 Supra note 13

25 See Caplovitz, supra note 3, at 15, where the author refers to the predominance of 'a dollar down, a dollar a week' slogan. This comment, although not quantitatively expressed, nevertheless amounts to preliminary support of the stated hypothesis.

26 Jones, supra note 18, at 1028

27 Sturdevant, supra note 6, at 398

28 Ibid, at 399

retailer – to obtain at favourable rates insurance which it would otherwise find uneconomic to procure, and an investment credit scheme to finance construction undertaken in disadvantaged areas.

Although these suggestions are more precise, and hence more palatable, than the vague references which appear in the FTC study to alleged structural deficiencies, they are, in the last analysis, vulnerable to identical objections. They rely upon an unverified assumption that competitive pressures are in fact lacking; more significantly, Sturdevant fails to detail the manner in which the major retailers would pare costs. It is difficult to comprehend how their subsidized presence in the ghetto would eradicate the very conditions he claims frighten them away, namely '... personnel problems, vandalism, and alleged higher incidents of shoplifting in disadvantaged districts.' To the extent that subsidies would enable the chains to absorb these costs and not pass them on, there is no evidence that a similar redistributive effect could not be achieved by subsidizing the merchants already there.

Although not expressly articulated, it is implicit in Sturdevant's analysis that substantial savings would be derived from the practice of selling at the store itself and at no other place. Merchants would thereby obviate the substantial expenses associated with the door-to-door salesman. The extent of these efficiencies, however, remain unverified, and hence it would be difficult to justify legislative action on this basis. Furthermore, it is problematical whether merchandising policies effective in more affluent neighbourhoods would be viable in the ghetto. Merchants rely upon peddlars notwithstanding the costs involved and hence must think the expenditures justifiable. We have no doubt that this mode of distribution merely reflects the nature of the consumer whom it serves. It may well be that the peddlar represents a response to the credit needs of a high-risk class of borrowers; alternatively, one might postulate that it is through this modality that low-income merchants can best exploit the impulsive buying habits of the poor. Whatever the motivation, it is but idle speculation to suggest, in the absence of supporting evidence, that the poor will prefer the lower prices of the chain retailer to the services which the peddlar provides.

To recapitulate briefly, we think that legislative policy must take into account the following three fundamental considerations: First, it should not, in the absence of convincing empirical evidence, be predicated upon alleged structural deficiencies in the ghetto retail market. The assumption that such weaknesses prevail in low-income communities, although made by prominent commentators, remains unverified, and hence it would be appropriate to initiate systematic research geared to test the hypothesis. In the event that it proves to be correct, further studies, designed to answer certain consequential issues such as those which we have raised, would be in order. It is important, however, that future researchers avoid the error made by contemporary commentators of assuming that there is insufficient competition merely because the ghetto merchant does not compete with his counterpart operating in more affluent communities. It is necessary to go further and to determine whether the separate and distinct market comprised of low-income merchants is or is not structurally healthy.

Our second major premise is that, in examining the business decisions of the ghetto merchant, it must be assumed that he seeks to maximize profits and hence has the necessary information to make, and does in fact make, decisions geared to realize this goal. Once again, this assumption is open to evidentiary rebuttal but must stand in the absence of such proof. Finally, it necessarily follows from these principles that all conditions and associated costs unique to ghetto merchandising must necessarily reflect the retailer's attempts to accommodate local needs. Accordingly, it is the requirements and dependencies of the low-income consumer that determine the manner in which his needs are serviced, and hence it is to these characteristics that we now turn.

*2/Informational and cultural factors*

The assumption that workable competition prevails in the ghetto does not necessarily yield the conclusion that low-income consumers actually enjoy the benefits of a market economy.[29] Competition can only ensure that efficiency differences amongst sellers will manifest themselves in differentials of either price or quality. A rational consumer response, however, must necessarily depend upon his having a certain quantum of relevant information.

A whole range of potential causes may underlie specific informational deficiencies relating to price. Consider, for example, the finding which emerges from the FTC study[30] that some low-income consumers who satisfy the criteria set by traditional lending institutions nevertheless rely upon the considerably more expensive credit facilities of the ghetto merchant. Presumably, these persons are unaware of the alternative sources of credit open to them. Their inadequate knowledge may result from the merchant's ability to obviate an interest disclosure requirement by building the credit risk into his price structure, and by absorbing any losses through the modality of higher markups. Alternatively, the merchant may have induced the buyer to believe that his credit was not costing him anything. Once again, it might be that these purchasers lacked the energy and strength of purpose necessary to engage in comparative shopping, or the intellectual competence to

29 The concept of 'workable competition' has been developed with the recognition that, in order to have policy implications, the notion of competition must have functional overtones; that is, it must reflect the particular characteristics of the market which is being described. To illustrate the point, it is noteworthy that one author would, under appropriate circumstances, deem a monopoly to be workably competitive; see Ferguson *A Macroeconomic Theory of Workable Competition* (1964), at 60. For reviews of the significance of the concept, see Clark, 'Toward a Concept of Workable Competition,' (1940), 30 *Am. Econ. Rev.* 241; Knox, 'Workable Competition and Public Policy,' (1962–8), 1 *Antitrust Law and Economics Rev.* 3.

30 Supra note 1, at 43

measure the benefits of seeking financial assistance elsewhere and purchasing from a downtown retailer.

The lesson which emerges from this is that full disclosure legislation and the effective sanctioning of misleading advertising are necessary, but not sufficient, conditions to ensure the realization of the policy objectives which underlie a market economy. They are imperative, quite clearly, because without them the consumer will lack the raw material upon which rational purchasing decisions depend. Yet they are in themselves insufficient, for an inability to utilize information will always subvert a disclosure requirement. The educational inadequacies associated with poverty are relevant in this context, particularly where the consequences of competition manifest themselves in the form of quality differences. Thus a rule that requires a food packager to disclose vitamin and protein content can have little impact if the poor are unaware of the most elementary nutritional principles.[31] Indeed, it would seem a fair generalization that the importance of education to the consumer will closely correspond with merchandise complexity; the uneducated will continue to suffer prejudice from the increasingly complex products which characterize today's market place.

The educational inadequacy which underlies the inefficiency of the poor as producers also accounts in large measure for their inefficiency as consumers.[32] Yet it does not stand alone, for existing evidence suggests that the poor are hopelessly entangled in a complex web of psychological and cultural imperatives which further debilitate an already vulnerable condition. By way of example, some studies suggest that the poor have an unusually strong tendency to exhibit psychoneurotic symptoms[33] while other investigators have found an inability to engage in long-term planning[34] and a correlative predisposition towards impulsive action.[35] The latter characteristic may well underlie and account for the door-to-door method of distribution which depends upon immediate-response purchasing patterns. Caplovitz's case studies in *The Poor Pay More* are corroborative: the most cursory examination reveals the vulnerability of the low-income buyer to high-pressure sales techniques.

We would be venturing beyond both our expertise and the stated objectives of this analysis were we to examine in detail the psychological predisposition of the poor. Ours is an essentially economic perspective, and hence we will leave to others the task of identifying these predispositions in detail. Effective policy will, however, ultimately have to take into account the cultural conditions which underlie the particular needs of the poor, and

31 See Grandy, supra note 13, at 281.
32 Ibid, at 279
33 Ibid, at 280; see also, Beiser, 'Poverty, Social Discrimination and Personality,' (1965), 21 *J. Social Issues* 55 at 55–6.
34 Beiser, supra note 33, at 56
35 Caplovitz, supra note 3, at 64

future policy makers will undoubtedly be charged with the responsibility of determining the relationship, if any, between culture and poverty.[36]

We have attempted to demonstrate that it is the condition of poverty and the attributes of the poor which underlie the prejudice which the low-income buyer suffers in the market place. Paying more is frequently a necessary incidence of poverty and has not been demonstrated to result from weaknesses in the market itself. Hence policy makers, in the light of existing evidence, are unlikely to be able significantly to improve the plight of the poor consumer by attempting to restructure the low-income market.

### 3 A Proposed Model

We have emphasized the impropriety of promulgating consumer protection legislation geared to remedy assumed structural deficiencies in the ghetto market place. Many analysts of the problems that confront low-income consumers have, however, advocated the adoption of other legal rules to deal with specific forms of 'malpractice' or 'exploitation' that they feel can be identified. Accordingly, the analysis which follows proposes to evaluate examples of these rules, with reference to their economic effects, classified under five principal headings: 1/restrictions on interest rates in consumer credit transactions; 2/restrictions on creditors' remedies; 3/rent restrictions and accommodation rehabilitation requirements (examined as an example of the consequences of regulating the price/quality mix of any product or service); 4/restrictions on selling methods; and 5/disclosure and information rules.

Assuming a structurally sound market place, any given rule might give rise to one or more of the three following effects: a rule might be *redistributive* in the sense that it will reduce and reallocate to the consumer excess profits previously earned by the merchant. The contemplated reduction might be consequential upon limitations or reductions in the price which the merchant may charge (eg, control of interest rates), or alternatively, it could be the result of requirements which increase costs (eg, quality controls, restrictions on creditors' remedies). It is axiomatic, however, that significant redistributive effects must necessarily depend upon a rule which controls price, thereby limiting the capacity of the merchant to pass on additional costs to the consumer. Furthermore, it must be consistent with profits sufficiently large to motivate the merchant to remain in business.

An *exclusionary* rule is one which, by imposing additional costs or constraints upon the merchant, causes him to respond with increases in price, with reductions in quality, or by withdrawing from the market. Such effects will clearly result where, without legislating price controls, the policy maker imposes quality standards or other similar cost-increasing conditions. The merchant may conceivably respond with an accommodating price increase;

36 See, by way of example, Valentine *Culture and Poverty* (1968) at 29.

alternatively, where the rule in question does not prescribe minimum quality standards, he might choose to market goods of reduced quality while keeping prices constant. Significantly, the cost increasing rule will produce exclusionary effects varying directly with demand elasticity and, while the merchant's response may determine the form which those effects may take, it cannot alter the reality that it is the consumer himself who must inevitably bear the cost burdens which such rules impose. As a result, some consumers will inevitably be excluded from the market.

*Ex hypothesi*, such adverse effects will be even greater where price controls are annexed to cost-increasing rules. In these circumstances, the seller's response will be limited to reducing quality and marketing an inferior product. Apart from any technical difficulties which he might experience in so doing, the capacity of such cutbacks to accommodate increased costs would soon be exhausted. Without the freedom to reallocate additional expenses, the merchant would face certain and imminent elimination from the market place. The exclusionary effects under these circumstances would extend to all consumers, without regard to demand elasticity.

Exclusionary rules may be labelled *degenerative* where, because of the nature of the commodity to which the rule applies, violators remain mostly unsanctioned. Illegal markets will respond to meet needs which the policy makers have left unsatisfied, thereby leaving the consumer in a weaker position than would otherwise have been the case had normal market processes been left to operate. In the first place, a substantial number of sellers will comply with positive law irrespective of its enforceability, and their consequential withdrawal may result in a structurally impaired market. Potential exposure to the ensuing oligopolistic pricing policies is not the only objectionable consequence, however, for the consumer will also have to bear the additional costs which illicit sellers inevitably experience. Thirdly, and perhaps most significantly, the degenerative rule forces the consumer 'underground' where, by definition, he is dealing with merchants who will ignore law inconsistent with their interests.

It is crucial to note that the assumption of a structurally sound market is not the equivalent of one characterized by perfect competition. The latter is an ideal with important conceptual implications which can be approximated, but never achieved in reality. One such implication is that all sellers competing in any market so characterized earn just enough on invested capital to stay in business and no more. Hence regulatory legislation in this context could only have exclusionary effects, for by definition, there would be no excess profits to be redistributed; by definition, the merchant would be unable, in the absence of price increases exclusionary in nature, to accommodate additional cost burdens legislatively imposed. It is in this context that the notion of workable competition, already referred to, assumes great analytical significance, because it is sufficiently broad to subsume certain market deficiencies.

Hence the notion of a structurally sound market must necessarily be broad enough to encompass circumstances in which imperfections prevail. The extent to which such imperfections are compatible with the concept must necessarily depend upon the criteria against which the policy maker is measuring market performance. Thus, if cost factors are deemed to be the governing considerations, one could hardly label as structurally unsound a market in which new entrants would necessarily bring with them higher prices. If, on the other hand, the social correlates of keeping business small prevail over consequent inefficiencies, the policy maker will be less prepared to accept functional justifications for monopoly and oligopoly. We will not attempt to compare the gains resulting from increased efficiency, on the one hand, and reduced market power on the other. Hence we will not articulate any guidelines relating to the circumstances in which a given market should be said to be structurally unsound. The point which emerges, however, is that every market will have some imperfections and thus there will always be some (however small) redistributive implications to any consumer protection rule. Hence it would be mere pretence to erect a qualitative distinction between the redistributive or exclusionary effects of such rules. Reality requires that the two components blend together to produce the final result, and hence any realistic discussion must necessarily centre upon their relative importance. This is the context in which the analysis which follows must be understood.

It is clear that degenerative rules have little in their favour; as we have already indicated they force the consumer 'underground' to a structurally deficient market comprised, *ex hypothesi*, of illegal operators. The merits of rules essentially exclusionary in nature can only be evaluated by comparing the benefits of protecting the consumer from allegedly unfair practices with the social costs of limiting his freedom to act. Clearly, the policy maker must necessarily engage – consciously or unconsciously – in a delicate ordering of priorities. This evaluative process is fundamental: since they remove the vice by removing the product, exclusionary rules cannot be regarded *per se* as beneficial to the consumer.

In few circumstances, however, should exclusionary rules attempt to protect the consumer from an assumed inability to make rational purchasing decisions. No matter how difficult it may be for him to make effective choices in particular cases, the presumption must be that it is unlikely that the state will be able to choose more rationally for him. Controlling effect should generally be given to the will of the market participant rather than to the dictates of the legislator. Even in cases where low-income consumers become over-committed through the use of credit, it is often difficult for people from another economic class to say that the use of credit is irrational when the alternative to its use is deprivation of necessities of life. This presumption in favour of the market aside, to what guidelines should the policy maker adhere when deciding to exclude a class of consumers from the market? In view of the restrictions which exclusionary rules place upon individual freedom, it is our view that they should only be enacted in the face of compelling humanitarian considerations or where the economic activity at which they are directed involves significant and adverse third-party effects (involuntarily assumed). Certain basic exemptions from seizure and the elimination of debtors' prisons demonstrate the first of these exceptions: society will simply not tolerate the violation of certain fundamental norms, notwithstanding that its sense of moral outrage has the effect of excluding certain borrowers from the credit market. The enactment of safety standards imposing substantial costs upon manufacturers illustrates the second: the state presently controls, and will continue to dictate, the extent to which consumers can, by purchasing defective, but less expensive, merchandise, threaten the safety of their fellow citizens.

The only category of rule which is clearly and in all cases of benefit to the low-income consumer is a redistributive rule which, by definition, will make the poor less poor. As we have already seen, however, redistributive effects are consequential to market imperfections, and hence cannot exceed, without having exclusionary consequences, the excess profits which such imperfections may have produced. Hence they are a poor device with which to redistribute income. If workable competition prevails, their effects would in most instances be small. In the rare case where a tight oligopoly may be said to be workably competitive, however, such rules might have significant effects, although it would be unwise to extend them to markets characterized by greater competition. Even where a redistributive effect is possible, the legislator must consider other, perhaps more effective, ways of transferring income. The graduated system of taxation, for example, could be easily geared to strike at excessive corporate or individual profits, and it has the advantage of producing measurable consequences. In addition, it allows the policy maker to rely upon an administrative apparatus already in existence, and obviates the difficulty of defining precisely what constitutes an excess profit, and that of delineating the markets in which such conditions exist.

The conclusion which emerges is that redistributive consumer protection rules are at best a cumbersome device with which to effect a redistribution of income. Where it is desired to achieve this objective the legislator should rely upon more direct and measurable techniques. Furthermore, the redistributive consequences of such rules will rarely be substantial; indeed, one of the principal points which will be developed in the ensuing discussion is that almost none of the rules commonly suggested for ameliorating the position of the low-income consumer have important redistributive consequences. Whatever else this body of rules may achieve, it does not procure for the great mass of consumers the same package of goods, services, or credit as before but on better, less 'exploitative' terms. The burden of much of the following discussion, which examines these various categories of rules, will be to establish that their effects will be either redistributive, exclusionary, or degenerative in nature, but that in fact the principal consequences of almost all of the rules fall under the latter two categories only.

## *4 The Legislative Responses*

### A INTEREST RATE CEILINGS: THE RATIONALE OF RATE REGULATION

The imposition of interest rate ceilings tends to occupy a central place in the dogma of those who believe that rules prescriptive of a merchant's business policies or practices can protect low-income consumers against problems in the market place. The FTC study recommended regulation of finance charges to 'help low-income as well as other consumers make more rational buying decisions.'[37] Professor Ziegel in his brief to the Canadian Senate Committee on Poverty recommended comprehensive rate ceilings in consumer credit transactions on the grounds that 'a ceiling serves a double function: it protects the unsophisticated and vulnerable borrower against exploitation and it encourages the lender to adopt more prudent credit standards.'[38] The history of usury regulation also, of course, reflects a ready and long-standing disposition in many jurisdictions to regulate interest rates. However, the incoherent pattern of rate regulation in consumer credit transactions that now obtains in many jurisdictions should be enough to raise one's suspicions that clear rationales for rate regulation cannot be as easily identified or sustained as many of its proponents seem to assume. For example, in Canada today, in the lender credit field, banks supply 38 per cent of all consumer credit and are not subject to rate regulation at all. Sales acceptance companies and retailers providing vendor credit facilities, which provide 25 per cent, are also not subject to rate regulation. Small loan companies, which provide 16 per cent, on the other hand are subject to rate regulation under the Small Loans Act.[39] In partial defence of this state of affairs it is said that, because in their inception small loan companies principally provided distress credit, some attempt had to be made to ensure that these companies did not take advantage of a person's distressed circumstances to charge more for their credit than the risk factors present in the situation justified. However, small loan companies are no longer concerned primarily with distress credit; on the contrary a significant portion of their activity is directed toward the consumer credit market, and hence this historical justification is insufficient to distinguish their present position from banks, sales acceptance companies, retailers, and the like. More importantly,

37 Supra note 1, at xiv

38 Proceedings of the Special Senate Committee on Poverty (Canada), supra note 14

39 Stats. Can. 1939, c 23, as amended by 1956, c 46; source of figures, E.P. Neufeld, 'Changing Relative Importance of Suppliers of Consumer Credit in Canada,' at 4; table 1 (Bank of Canada Statistical Summary), in Proceedings of Conference 'Consumer Credit in North America,' School of Business, University of Toronto, May 1970

even if small loan companies were still providing only distress credit, the difficulties rate ceilings create would still be present.

In trying to understand the pattern of rate regulation in Canada, it also must be acknowledged that vendor credit is of much more recent origin than lender credit, or money-lending, which dates back to classical Greek and Roman times. Historically, for complex sociological and religious reasons, money-lenders and usury have attracted an opprobrium that initiated the close regulation of money-lending transactions including, particularly, interest rates. Historical legacies of this kind, however, cannot be permitted to stand in the way of the formulation of rational laws which recognize the operation of present social and economic forces.

The predilection which has persisted both historically and among contemporary consumer commentators towards imposing rate ceilings on money-lending transactions has to be regarded as aberrant from an economic perspective because it violates traditional free-market economic norms which are inconsistent with price control, of which rate ceilings are, of course, an example. Price control has generally only been accorded a 'consumer protection' role in monopoly situations; otherwise, more recently, it has been used for macroeconomic ends as a means of controlling inflation. But taking a consumer protection perspective, and pursuing our present assumption of a competitive market, the central question in relation to rate ceilings becomes the policy objectives, whether economic or social, which this form of price control can achieve. In assessing the extent to which existing laws have met the goals which motivated their enactment, we will incorporate into our analysis the legally important, if economically irrelevant, distinction between vendor credit and lender credit.

*1/Vendor Credit*

In the case of vendor credit, serious problems arise in trying to regulate interest changes without regulating the cash price. These problems are particularly acute in the low-income market where most sales are likely to be on credit and a merchant need not be concerned to keep his cash price competitive in order to attract cash buyers. For example, the FTC study found that low-income market retailers used instalment credit in 93 per cent of their sales compared to 25 per cent for general market retailers.[40] Here, if a ceiling on interest charges is set below the figure at which it is profitable for a merchant to extend credit, the obvious answer is to bury a portion of the credit charge in an inflated cash price. This again is borne out by the findings in the FTC study. Interest rates charged in low-income areas were on their face, on average, only 3 per cent to 4 per cent above those prevailing amongst general market retailers.[41] Yet the average mark-up on goods in low-income areas was about 150 per cent as compared to about 50 per

40 Supra note 1, at ix
41 Ibid, at xii

cent in other areas.[42] Thus, whether as a result of rate ceilings or as a result simply of wishing to conceal the true amount and rate of finance charges, low-income dealers encountered no difficulty in disguising the nature of the charge. The futility of trying to regulate finance charges in vendor credit without regulating prices is not unlike '... trying to regulate the overall height of buildings by specifying that the height of the top floor may not be more than eight feet.'[43]

Presumably in an attempt to meet this difficulty, Caplovitz suggests the enactment of laws regulating prices, on the grounds that low-income area merchants would then 'be unable to offer the "easy credit" plans they now do.'[44] While this conclusion may be well founded, depending, of course, upon the price levels which the regulators deem appropriate, it does not follow that low-income area merchants will deal with their customers on more palatable (and less profitable) terms. On the contrary, existing evidence points to consequences fundamentally different from this. Profit margins are already such that, if one accepts the conclusions of the FTC study, altruism of this kind is unlikely to be forthcoming. Instead the merchant might either go out of business in that area, entirely excluding from the market consumers whom he could only have dealt with at prices not prohibited; alternatively he or other suppliers will be prepared to continue selling the goods to these consumers at the old price, illegally, on the black market. In short, regulation of prices would have only an exclusionary or degenerative effect on the low-income market.

Even in the more affluent vendor credit market, rate ceilings are unlikely to achieve any greater purpose. Here, as elsewhere, the market will establish the operative rate in the event that the prescribed ceiling exceeds the level necessary to ensure an adequate return on capital. Indeed, there exists a substantial body of supportive evidence indicating that, in such circumstances, rate ceilings are superfluous.[45] Where, on the other hand, legislation forces ceilings below economic rates, the credit seller, like the low-income area merchant, will as far as possible try to build part of his credit charge into the cash price of the goods, which has the objectionable consequences of subverting the purpose of the rate ceiling and forcing cash buyers to subsidize credit buyers. Hence rate ceilings governing vendor credit would not appear to be viable policy instruments in either low or high income markets. Even where price controls are annexed in order to render them enforceable, they can only produce consequences essentially exclusionary or degenerative in nature. As we shall see, this fundamental difficulty undermines rules which govern lender credit transactions as well.

42 Ibid, at x, xi

43 Robert W. Johnson, 'The Uniform Consumer Credit Code and the Credit Problems of Low Income Consumers,' (1969), 37 *George Washington L. Rev.* 1117, at 1121

44 Supra note 3, at 191

45 Robert W. Johnson, 'The Myths and Mysteries of Rate Ceilings,' Proceedings of Conference 'Consumer Credit in North America,' supra note 39, at 11

*2/Lender Credit*

A *A ceiling above market rates* If a rate ceiling is set above the level necessary to provide efficient lenders with an adequate return on their capital in the low-income market, rates in fact are going to be set by market forces and not by the ceiling.[46] Once again, the market, not the ceiling, will eliminate inefficient lenders.

B *A ceiling below market rates* Ceilings set below the levels necessary to sustain the efficient lender will eliminate lender credit from the market place; and the processes which the resulting credit squeeze initiates will clearly depend upon the response of the low-income consumer. By way of example, existing evidence indicates that borrowers tend to seek vendor credit from local merchants instead. The availability of vendor credit would clearly undermine any attempt to regulate interest rates in the lender credit market, and hence it is incumbent upon the policy maker to regulate both, or neither. Making the unlikely assumption that both markets are subjected to effective controls, what consequences might transpire? In our view, they may be either exclusionary or degenerative.

It may be true that some consumers who would borrow at a given rate legally would not borrow at the same rate illegally and, to this extent, a rate ceiling may have exclusionary consequences. Notwithstanding this, it would appear a fair generalization to suggest that the demand for money is less elastic than its supply; that is, the imperatives inducing a person to borrow at high rates are more powerful than the forces which impel a person to lend at these rates. Hence it would follow that very serious exclusionary consequences for borrowers would result from the collective withdrawal of lenders from a regulated market place in which they find it uneconomic to operate. Existing evidence underscores the striking inelasticity which characterizes the low-income consumer's demand for credit, and the tendency of this class of buyer to keep using credit despite an inability to qualify for loans at ceiling rates is stronger than for any other class of consumer. In a 1967 study, the Canadian Welfare Council found that most of the 235 families surveyed were indebted notwithstanding gross annual incomes of less than \$6,000. Significantly, those earning under \$3,000 were spending no less than 124 per cent of their income on housing, food, and clothing. Those families in the \$3,000 to \$4,000 bracket were allocating 90 per cent of their income to these basic needs, while those in the \$4,000 to \$5,000 range, 86 per cent. The Economic Council of Canada defines persons in poverty as those families and individuals allocating at least 70 per cent of their income for these needs.[47]

Pursuing the somewhat tenuous assumption that the policy maker has effectively regulated vendor credit, we have noted that the consequences

46 Ibid, at 26

47 Canadian Welfare Council, *Consumer Credit and The Lower Income Family: A legal study and report of a survey of 235 families in Hamilton, 1967*, at 88

might be either exclusionary or degenerative in nature. The inelasticity which characterizes the low-income consumer's demand for credit, will, if this demand is served, place serious limitations upon the exclusionary consequences that might otherwise arise. Simply stated, loan sharks respond to rate ceilings which eliminate the efficient lender. Indeed, there is no shortage of evidence suggesting that degenerative consequences will result where money, so difficult to trace and control, is the commodity being regulated.[48] By way of example, the impetus for the enactment of the Russell Sage Foundation's Uniform Small Loans Law in the United States in the early years of the century came from a recognition that the '6 per cent' usury statutes in force in most jurisdictions prevented legitimate lenders from transacting business with high-risk borrowers, with the result that these borrowers began to rely upon illegal lenders to service their needs. The Uniform Small Loans Law sought explicitly to meet the problem of loan-sharking by permitting licensed lenders to charge rates of interest consistent with risk, and it has been said generally to have accomplished this objective.[49]

The Missouri experience during the years 1946–57 is corroborative. In 1946 the Missouri Supreme Court declared unconstitutional the state's Small Loans Law, thereby renewing that jurisdiction's general usury law which contained an 8 per cent interest ceiling. As a result, law-abiding lenders withdrew from the market, only to be replaced by loan sharks whose activities flourished until new and valid legislation was enacted in 1951.[50] The lobbying activities of illegal lenders affords additional evidence of the degenerative consequences which unrealistically low rate-ceilings produce. It is clearly in their interests to support the enactment of such laws, and it appears that they have on occasion invoked the stratagem of arguing for ceilings fixed at unprofitable levels.[51]

What conclusions, then, can one draw from the foregoing analysis? Can a ceiling, in Professor Ziegel's terms, protect 'the unsophisticated and vulnerable borrower against exploitation and [encourage] the lender to adopt more prudent credit standards'?[52] We think not. Ceilings set above market rates are mere surplusage and those which prove to be uneconomic will in most cases be equally irrelevant because of the difficulty of regulating the vendor-credit market. In the unlikely event that such difficulties can be overcome, an inordinately low ceiling will merely initiate exclusionary or degenerative processes. Although minor redistributive effects may result, the

48 On the incidence of loan sharking, see *The Challenge of Crime in a Free Society: A Report by the President's Commission on Law Enforcement and Administration of Justice* (1967) at 189; and (1969), 5 *Columbia J. Law and Social Problems* 92.

49 F.B. Hubachek, 'Progress and Problems in Regulation of Consumer Credit,' (1954), 19 *Law and Contemporary Problems* 4

50 Harold Johnson, 'Nebraska has no Loan Shark Problem Today,' (1954), 19 *Law and Contemporary Problems* 42, at 46, and notes 7 and 8 therein

51 Hubachek, supra note 49, at 27; B.J. Lenihan, 'Progress in Consumer Credit in Kentucky,' (1954), 19 *Law and Contemporary Problems* 54, at 56

52 Supra, at 411

mass of consumers will not find themselves in the position of procuring credit on more advantageous terms. That result can only be achieved where competitive input is added to a structurally unsound market. Rearticulating the assumption that workable competition prevails, however, the significant policy conclusion is that the most effective small loans law is the one which least interferes with the free flow of market forces. It is competition, not legislation, which protects the low-income consumer's market position.

c *A 'reasonable' rate ceiling*

i THE 'ONE CEILING' APPROACH Admitting, then, that ceilings set above the economic rate are irrelevant while those enacted below that level will produce essentially exclusionary or degenerative consequences, might it be wise policy to legislate a rate which is neither too high nor too low, but precisely that which an efficient lender must charge in order to earn an adequate return on capital? Many of the answers to this suggestion are, of course, to be found in earlier observations. If the argument is that this will eliminate less efficient and more expensive lenders, the market, if properly competitive, will do this anyway, albeit less abruptly. Hence the ceiling will, at best, merely describe the prevailing rate; it will not prescribe it.

If the legislator has complete information, and if economic conditions remain static, such legislation would merely be irrelevant and not harmful. Imperfect knowledge, however, creates a real risk that the legislated rate will be below that which would prevail in an unregulated market; alternatively, an originally appropriate ceiling may, in the context of the dynamic conditions which characterize a real situation, become inappropriately low with the lapse of time. In either case, the effects would be either exclusionary or degenerative in nature, and legislation, once merely irrelevant, would now produce consequences which, in the absence of compelling social reasons to the contrary, should be avoided.

At present in Canada, interest rates amongst commercial lenders in consumer credit transactions range from about 12 per cent, charged by the banks, to approximately 24 per cent, which small loan companies often exact. Spread along the spectrum in between these extremes are, amongst others, retail creditors, variable credit suppliers, and sales acceptance companies. There is obviously substantial overlapping in the areas of business undertaken by these different categories of credit institutions. This is reflected, for example, in the dramatically increased share of total consumer credit business gained by the banks, at the expense of other credit suppliers, since their entry into the consumer credit field in the mid-fifties. It is true that within any particular category of credit supplier, there may be little *rate* differentiation. This is because the institutional differentiations themselves reflect a decision to specialize in particular classes of risks (with the economies that specialization brings), and therefore one would not expect to find large differences among the interest rates charged by, for example, banks. It is also true that, generally, any given lender is likely to charge only one rate to all his borrowers whereas, even within the chosen area of risk specialization, some borrowers are presumably marginally better risks than others. The explanation might well be that it would cost a lender more to investigate all borrowers with the precision needed to establish individual rates than to charge one rate for all borrowers of the class with whom the lender has chosen to deal. Although this failure to discriminate undoubtedly produces a minor subsidization by better risks in favour of inferior risks, the proposition that the rate is fixed by market forces retains its validity.

Thus, neither the lack of rate differentiation within categories of lenders nor the lack of rate differentiation by particular lenders detracts from the fact that there is substantial competition among the different categories of lending institutions. However, if it is sought to give legal effect to this economic reality by setting one rate for this market, the problem arises of where to fix the rate. The hard fact is that one rate cannot possibly reflect the conditions which prevail in an unregulated market. It is too blunt an instrument. Assuming, by way of example, a range of rates from 12 per cent to 24 per cent, what goals might a ceiling fixed equidistant between the two extremes achieve? Presumably, consumers who previously qualified for a rate of 12 per cent (or any rate under 18 per cent) will still qualify for that rate; that is, they are not protected by the ceiling, but by the market. On the other hand, borrowers who present risks consistent only with 24 per cent rates are 'protected' simply by being eliminated from the legal money market. Once again, economic imperatives dictate that a ceiling can at best be irrelevant and at worst will initiate exclusionary or degenerative processes.

ii THE 'MULTI-CEILING' APPROACH One might obviate the rigidity of a 'one-rate' approach by segmenting the general consumer credit market into a number of sub-markets each of which would be subject to a different ceiling. Although this would constitute an improvement for the simple reason that it enables the ceilings more accurately to reflect the variety of market rates prevailing in the field (and to that extent be redundant), it gives rise to the central question of how the sub-markets should be defined. Upon what basis should the policy maker determine that finance companies and credit unions, for example, fall into different sub-markets? Upon what data should he rely?

Irrespective of the criteria deemed most relevant, there is no doubt that lending institutions which are said to fall within different markets might nevertheless, in the absence of rate ceilings, compete with respect to a substantial number of end users. In other words, a variety of rate ceilings artificially segments the market and in so doing introduces structural deficiencies.

By way of example, consider the case of credit unions and finance companies, which are subject to different rate ceilings. One principal effect of the lower rate which presently governs the credit union (1 per cent per month in many provincial jurisdictions) is to eliminate this form of lending institution from the market which serves borrowers who do not qualify for the prescribed rate. Although less harmful than the 'one-rule' approach, it is difficult to perceive the policy considerations which supposedly justify this form of anti-competitive stratification.[53]

### B RESTRICTIONS ON CREDITORS' REMEDIES

Many commentators and policy makers concerned with the protection of low-income consumers also endorse the limitation of creditors' remedies. In particular, they advocate the abolition of deficiency judgments after repossession, and contend that repossession itself should be subject to judicial control, that both salary and property seizures be abolished or that exemptions from seizure be substantially raised and that credit-blacklisting be strictly controlled.

Clearly, the exercise by a creditor of his remedies against a debtor for default are some of the most visible and distressing symptoms of over-commitment and it is natural enough, as a first instinct, to respond to these symptoms by advocating their removal. But, as in many other contexts, the symptoms of a problem are not its cause and to remove the symptoms does not eliminate the cause but more often than not merely gives rise to new symptoms. Once again, policy makers must accept the immutable economic imperative that lenders will only extend credit if they can do so on a profitable basis; and it is equally axiomatic that restrictions on remedies will give rise to correspondingly higher interest rates to the extent that they increase bad-debt write-offs. As a result, a certain number of borrowers, unable to absorb the interest rate exacted, will be excluded from the market. More significantly, degenerative consequences will result where interest ceilings prevent the lender from charging rates consistent with restrictions legislatively imposed. In these circumstances, high-risk consumers whom these lenders would otherwise have served must withdraw from the market place (which, admittedly, some proponents explicitly adopt as their objective), or, alternatively, enter the illegal money market where informal day and night harassment, or even the baseball bat, replace the writ of seizure.

Clearly, the extent to which such legislation initiates exclusionary or degenerative processes will depend upon both the severity of the restrictions imposed and the elasticity or inelasticity of the demand for credit. No one restriction could in itself produce substantially adverse effects and hence one commentator would seem to have taken a rather extreme view in questioning whether '... our economy [would] survive' the abolition of deficiency

53 Since the writing of this article was completed, the US National Commission on Consumer Finance in its report, *Consumer Credit in the United States* (1972), concluded, after a careful theoretical and empirical study of rate ceilings, that 'on balance, rate ceilings are undesirable when markets are reasonably competitive' (at 108).

judgments.[54] Pursuing our assumption of workable competition, market imperfections will always temper the exclusionary consequences of such rules. For example, creditors might respond to the elimination or restriction of deficiency claims and garnishments by relying more heavily on remedies not contemplated by the legislation. Thus, in Pennsylvania, the attachment of a debtor's home became commonplace after that jurisdiction prohibited garnishments.[55] Other potential responses might include greater reliance upon threats of execution against a debtor's personal property as a form of harassment, third-party guarantees, and credit black-listing.

The legislator would be unwise, however, to impose a series of restrictions without regard to their economic effects, for each new limitation imposes additional expenses upon the lender. In the first place, it would seem a fair generalization that the alternate remedies which creditors might invoke are less efficient, and hence more expensive, than the remedies legislatively curtailed. This common cost influence will require all competing lenders to increase the cost of credit in order to compensate for their use of less efficient collection techniques. Secondly, and more significantly, the continuous erosion of remedies will ultimately divest the creditor of any alternate remedies. In these circumstances, he will be compelled to respond with a substantial increase in interest rates giving rise to serious exclusionary or degenerative consequences, depending, as we have seen, upon both demand elasticity and prevailing interest ceilings.

### C RENT CONTROLS AND ACCOMMODATION REHABILITATION REQUIREMENTS

The literature has often assimilated the slum landlord to the ghetto merchant, suggesting that both earn exorbitant profits by exploiting the poor; the commentators have invoked as supporting evidence the poor quality of the accommodation which he provides in relation to the size of the rentals exacted. Here as elsewhere, however, emotion has prevailed over reason with the result that until recently little attempt has been made to analyze and assess the hard economics of housing the poor.

The profitability of slum landlordism has fortunately now become the subject of increasingly rigorous analysis and the picture which has begun to emerge resembles that portrayed in the FTC study of the operations of ghetto merchants. By way of example, Sternlieb has pointed to a whole range of factors which undermine the investment potential of slum property.[56] The difficulties which owners experience in financing low-income housing, their unpredictable resale values, and the ever-present threat of Rental Code enforcement reflect the very substantial risks involved. In addition, the

54 Homer Kripke, 'Consumer Credit Regulation: A Creditor-Oriented Viewpoint,' (1968), 69 *Columb. L. Rev.* 445, at 481

55 See Caplovitz, infra at 429

56 *The Tenement Landlord* (1966), at 95

greater need for repairs arising from overcrowded premises and the difficulty of collecting rentals from insolvent tenants are predictable but nonetheless costly incidents of slum landlordism. In view of the reality that, to prove economic, any venture must generate profits consistent with both risk and the administrative responsibilities involved, one might have thought that slum landlords would earn a substantial return on invested equity, certainly a return above the average for the economy as a whole. Surprisingly, reported studies do not confirm this expectation. In 1955, Grebler published data for low-income area walk-up apartments from the years 1920–4 through 1945–9 which indicated that net income as a percentage of gross income had decreased by one-half during this period.[57] In another study it was estimated that only 30 per cent of the buildings with code violations in the sample surveyed could be brought into compliance and still yield 6 per cent or better on capital at existing rental rates. Another 50 per cent would probably yield a marginal return at best.[58]

For the reasons already given, a 6 per cent return on capital is clearly insufficient to attract substantial private investment into the low-income housing market. Triple A corporate bonds, by comparison, yield 8 or 9 per cent, impose no administrative responsibilities upon the investor, and are liquid assets which can be readily sold or offered as collateral. Hence, it is not surprising that even those commentators with strong pro-tenant biases are now being compelled to recognize the economic realities of the slum landlord's position. For example, in their frontal attack upon government inertia, Sax and Hiestand nevertheless acknowledge that 'standard housing for the poor, adequately maintained, is simply not a sufficiently profitable business to attract investors.'[59] It is against this background that the effectiveness of rent restrictions and rehabilitation requirements fall to be evaluated. Both forms of legislation attempt to distribute the contractual incidents between the parties to a tenancy arrangement in ways other than those that would be produced by market forces. Both attempt to redistribute to the tenant benefits that would otherwise enure to the proprietor.

*1/Rent Restrictions*

In relation to rent controls, a recent study found substantial evidence that rent-controlled buildings in New York city are among the least desirable urban real estate investments in the United States.[60] The return on capital

57 *Experience in Urban Real Estate Investment* (1955)

58 'Tenant Rent Strikes,' (1967), 3 *Columb. J. Law and Social Problems*, at 1–2

59 Joseph L. Sax and Fred J. Hiestand, 'Slumlandlordism as a Tort,' (1967), 65 *Mich. L. Rev.* 869, at 874. However, the dangers of assuming any one prototype of the structure of low-income housing markets are compellingly demonstrated by Ackerman, 'Regulating Slum Housing Markets,' (1971), 80 *Yale L.J.* 1093. Cf Canadian Council on Social Development *Is there a Case for Rent Control?* (1973).

60 'Residential Rent Control in New York City,' (1967), 3 *Columb. J. Law and Social Problems* 30, at 51

is such that 'landlords openly confess that they regularly defer maintenance because of rent control.'[61] Thus, the quality of accommodation progressively deteriorates and the growth of slums is promoted. Conversely, in Los Angeles decontrol was generally followed by a doubling of expenditures for maintenance.[62] Hence the redistributive effects of rent controls tend to be exhausted in the short run. Exclusionary consequences will result when the owner, confronted with maintenance costs rendered critical with the lapse of time, determines that the property has lost its economic value as a housing facility.

These findings have important policy implications, for they indicate that rent control legislation which gives rise to maintenance cutbacks embodies unrealistically low price levels. Hence, where such cutbacks occur, the legislator can obviate exclusionary consequences only by setting the controlled rentals at levels consistent with the economic viability of the property in question. As permissible rental levels are readjusted upwards, they will of course approximate market rates and hence, to that extent, become redundant.

Setting aside for the moment the exclusionary consequences which rent control legislation may bring about, serious objections remain. Even if price levels are imposed which in the short or long run would afford tenants a measure of relief, benefits are conferred upon both high-income and low-income families alike. If it is desired to protect only the latter, the payment of a direct subsidy would achieve this end more efficiently. More significantly, such legislation arbitrarily places the burden of redistribution solely upon the shoulders of the property owner. Society as a whole should clearly underwrite these subsidization costs and hence, once again, direct subsidy payments would be more appropriate.[63]

### 2/*Rehabilitation Requirements*

The other legislative response to poor quality housing has been to constitute legal procedures pursuant to which an owner can be compelled to rehabilitate sub-standard housing at his own expense. Once again, however, existing evidence tends to suggest that legislatively imposed burdens initiate exclusionary processes. Where owners reallocate rehabilitation expenses and exact higher rentals, it appears unlikely that low-income tenants have the resources or motivation to meet these increases.[64] As graphic testimony to this, it has been reported that in jurisdictions where compliance with work requisition orders or code requirements is a prerequisite to rental increases, tenants deliberately create violations in order to forestall impending rent increases and that, at one time, rent inspectors carried cameras to photograph improvements before tenants could vandalize them.[65]

61 Ibid, at 57
62 Ibid
63 But compare Ackerman, supra note 59, at 1157 ff
64 Sternlieb, supra note 56, at 68 ff
65 Supra note 60, at 41

If, on the other hand, proprietors are expected to support rehabilitation costs themselves, either because of the inability of tenants to absorb rent increases or because of rental controls, the economic viability of the housing facility may be endangered. There is also evidence of this: New York City has largely stopped putting buildings into receivership because it does not recover enough from the net rents to repay itself for the repair money advanced.[66] Furthermore, the New York Court of Appeals has often reversed convictions for code violations because compliance is economically impossible,[67] and in 1968 the National Advisory Commission on Civil Disorders reported that in New York 'rigorous code enforcement has already caused owners to board up and abandon over 2,500 buildings rather than incur the expense of repairing them.'[68]

Once again, the familiar economic imperatives apply: markets characterized by workable competition will invariably undermine legislation geared to redistribute wealth by tampering with market processes. Even if monopoly or oligopoly prevails in the low-income housing market there are limits to the extent to which redistribution can be effected, for the entrepreneur can always withdraw from the market place when legislatively imposed burdens render his investment uneconomic. Hence, apart from the injustice of arbitrarily placing the entire burden of redistribution upon property owners, rent control legislation cannot over the long run alleviate a serious housing shortage. The particular problems of the poor in respect of accommodation as well as merchandising stem from their paucity of resources and not from the way in which the market reacts to that fact. Attacking the market mechanism will not make the poor less poor nor the problems that flow from the fact of their poverty less acute.

### D MARKETING METHODS

Commentators have often noted the prevalence of fraud and high-pressure selling tactics which merchants use in low-income areas, and vigorous programs geared to sanction these practices have been widely advocated. We support this form of government intervention, because the community will not and should not tolerate dishonesty, whatever the economic consequences of preventing it. Further, the market itself cannot work efficiently if people are misinformed about the choices open to them. However, even then it must be recognized that the kind of market in which ghetto merchants are operating, and the economic constraints to which they are subject, dictate some of the merchandising policies adopted by them. If they are forced to

66 Albert Rosen, 'Receivership: A Useful Tool for Helping to Meet the Housing Needs of Low Income People,' (1968), 3 *Harv. Civil Rights-Civil Liberties L. Rev.* 311, at 320

67 Judah Gribetz and Frank P. Grad, 'Housing Code Enforcement: Sanctions and Remedies,' (1966), 66 *Columb. L. Rev.* 1254, at 1270

68 Supra note 15

engage in widespread fraud in order to make a living, then presumably if fraud is prevented they will either have to go out of business or raise their prices to cover the number of transactions lost and fraudulent profit margins foregone. Given the relatively inelastic demands of low-income consumers, the latter response would most probably result. How many consumers would be priced out of the market and the consequences of higher prices on those who still elect to buy can only be a matter of conjecture. At least, however, they will know what their real choices are.

Measures to combat high-pressure tactics can probably be analyzed in the same terms. For example, a mandatory 'cooling off' period in door-to-door sales enables consumers to acquaint themselves better with the real proposition being put to them and in that sense assists the market to operate more rationally. Both the outlawing of fraud and the provision of a cooling off period in door-to-door sales have a redistributive effect in that they may enable a consumer to identify a better bargain elsewhere and thus recoup money he would otherwise (unnecessarily) have paid to another merchant. Significantly, this effect is achieved through making the market work more freely, rather than the reverse. It might, of course, be argued that the law should do more, and that most forms of door-to-door selling should be absolutely banned.[69] A proposal such as this could have very serious repercussions for low-income consumers. Ghetto merchants widely use peddlars as vehicles for making sales and, more importantly, for collecting credit as well. With high credit risks, a continuous, person-to-person collection process has to be adopted. As we have already indicated, it would be irrational to presume that ghetto merchants would rely upon such high-cost marketing techniques if they served no purpose. To ban peddling would, in effect, be either to withdraw credit from a substantial number of low-income consumers, to increase the cost of credit, or to encourage the development of alternative collection pressures of equivalent or greater severity.

### E DISCLOSURE LAWS

The great majority of contemporary analysts advocate interest disclosure laws in consumer credit transactions to protect the poor. The FTC pointed out that a significant portion of low-income consumers using credit from ghetto merchants would qualify for credit at lower rates from general market retailers.[70] To the extent that disclosure laws can enable and encourage low-income consumers to utilize their scarce resources more rationally, they clearly are of benefit to them.[71] Disclosure laws may effect a redistribution from a high-cost merchant to a low-income consumer to the extent that the latter is enabled to find cheaper terms elsewhere. *Pro tanto*, the volume of business attracted by the high-cost merchant is reduced. In contrast with

69 See Schrag *Counsel for the Deceived* (1972), at 195.

70 Supra note 1, at 43 71 See Devine and Hawkins, supra note 7.

laws regulating interest rates, restricting creditors' remedies, and controlling rents and accommodation standards, which interfere with market processes, but analogous to laws combatting fraud and high pressure, disclosure laws can be an effective means of protecting the poor but again only because they enhance the operation of free market forces.

The policy maker must, however, recognize the very serious limitations to which such legislation is subject. We have already noted the communication and cultural hurdles which these rules must overcome in order to be effective. They can only be of value if the consumer is intellectually and psychologically equipped to apply the information which disclosure legislation entitles him to have. These difficulties aside, more fundamental limitations remain because, as a general rule, a widespread failure to disclose within any given market will only occur when the withholding of information is consistent with profit maximization. Hence, market participants will only refuse to disclose where the information in question is too complex to be communicated or where there are no price or quality differences worth mentioning. In neither situation will disclosure rules enable the consumer to make more rational purchasing decisions.

Where the complexity of information renders it incomprehensible to the layman or where the costs to him in time or money necessary for comprehension do not justify potential savings, competitors will not waste resources in attempting to communicate material which they know will not affect consumer purchasing decisions. On the contrary, they will direct their efforts to reducing price, which is communicable, or to improving those attributes of the product which the consumer has the competence to evaluate. Hence, incommunicable quality differences will be exposed to anti-competitive processes in otherwise structurally sound markets. It is in this context that government grading procedures take on significance, for they have the effect of simplifying complex information and thereby rendering it communicable to the consumer. The perceived objectivity of a public authority which, for obvious reasons, a market participant does not share, enables it to render credible quality judgments to which the buyer will respond. Government intervention in this way can direct the competitive efforts of market participants.

It is of course true that a consumer who buys a 'grade A' rather than a 'grade B' product selling at the same price is not responding with any greater personal understanding of the product than he would have had in the absence of such labelling. It is also true that any value judgments which form part of the grading process will be incorporated into his purchasing decision, and, to that extent, administrative guidelines will have a substantial impact upon consumer behaviour.

However, one cannot deny the simple reality that the consumer is frequently unable to make effective quality evaluations. Rather than making random choices for irrelevant reasons it is surely preferable that he premise his purchasing decisions upon the evaluations of an independent and impartial tribunal provided that all competing interest groups have a full and fair opportunity to make representations before it.

Hence, by translating incommunicable quality differences into the crude but comprehensible categories which characterize the grading process, such administrative agencies facilitate market processes, and it is for this reason that we support them wherever the estimated benefits to consumers outweigh the costs of the grading process. Nevertheless, the intervention of a human decision-maker, with the correlative value judgments which that entails, distinguishes the administrative process from simple disclosure rules and to that limited extent introduces foreign elements into the operation of market forces. That notwithstanding, such agencies are not fundamentally anti-competitive. Unlike bodies constituted to enact or enforce minimum quality standards (eg, rental rehabilitation boards) they do not attempt to prevent the consumer from entering into transactions in which he would voluntarily participate. On the contrary, their objective is to make quality judgments which the consumer himself would make if he possessed the relevant expertise, and hence their judgments do not initiate substantial exclusionary or degenerative processes. It is crucial, however, that the administrative process comply in every respect with the rules, both substantive and procedural, of natural justice, for the introduction of significant and systematic bias into the decision-making machinery would seriously undermine market processes.

As we have already indicated, market participants might also fail to disclose communicable information where there are no price or quality differences worth mentioning. Uniformity of price and quality may be symptomatic of underlying structural deficiencies; on the other hand it may merely be the end product of competitive processes which have already eliminated inefficient firms. The point is that in neither case can disclosure legislation increase the number of rational alternatives open to the consumer; for where such rational alternatives exist, the profit maximizing merchant will already have made the relevant disclosure. The one exception to this rule, and the only circumstance in which disclosure legislation can make substantial gains, is a situation in which the information withheld would have significant adverse effects upon aggregate demand. Where a market participant fears that such effects will more than offset any potential increase in market share, he will refuse to make the disclosure notwithstanding that it would improve his position relative to that of his competitors. By way of example, a cigarette manufacturer would not be predisposed to advertise that the life expectancy of its clientele is one year longer than that of smokers relying upon competing brands. Aggregate demand will, of course, be in even greater jeopardy where substitute products are available. In these circumstances, the effectiveness of disclosure legislation will vary inversely with cross-elasticity of demand.

These propositions can be tested against experience with legislation for disclosure of interest rates. The possible reasons why at least some credit suppliers did not find it to their advantage to publish their rates relative to those of their competitors, without the compulsion of legislation, and assuming rationality on their part, can, in accordance with the foregoing analysis, be reduced to four. The information is clearly communicable, and hence disclosure would appear to be consistent with the interests of the profit-maximizing credit supplier. Fear of a reduction in aggregate demand for credit is a possible explanation, but it is unlikely that almost all credit suppliers would have found it in their interests to refrain from disclosure on this account. Moreover, even with enforced disclosure, aggregate demand for credit continues to increase significantly.

This then leaves open the possible explanation that, prior to disclosure legislation, there were structural deficiencies either in the consumer credit market generally, or in the various sub-markets into which it may be segmented reflecting the different categories of end-users seeking credit. It is true that, before the growth of bank credit, vendor- and lender-variable credit, and credit unions, there was less competition than there is today. But, nevertheless, it is difficult to point to facts at any time which suggest that it would not have been worthwhile for at least some credit suppliers to disclose their rates relative to those of other suppliers.

This leaves only one other possible explanation of non-disclosure – that, within any given end-user market, that is, category of credit risks, competitive processes had already eliminated inefficient firms and there no longer remained rate differences worth mentioning. Perhaps a sufficiently high consumer sensitivity to *institutional* rate differences had sorted out credit sub-markets to a point where it was no longer profitable for credit suppliers from one institutional category to attempt to attract those borrowers from another category of suppliers who were inadvertently paying more than they need have for their credit.[72] Certainly, experience since disclosure legislation lends some credence to this hypothesis.[73]

Only empirical investigation would enable us to identify which possible reason or mixture of reasons explains the failure of the consumer credit industry to reveal rates without legislative compulsion. However, it is submitted that the explanation has necessarily to be found within the hypotheses advanced above.

## 5 *Conclusion*

The central contention which emerges from this analysis is that consumer protection rules should, in the absence of the compelling social reasons to

72 The empirical study by F. Thomas Juster and Robert P. Shay *Consumer Sensitivity to Finance Rates* (1964), suggested a fairly high level of consumer sensitivity to institutional rate differences even before the advent of disclosure legislation.

73 Cf 1971 Annual Report of the Governors of the US Federal Reserve System.

which we have earlier referred, be limited to remedying the imbalance in bargaining power which frequently characterizes consumer transactions. Such imbalances may be the result of either structural inadequacies in the relevant market or serious informational deficiencies. As we have already seen, these potential causes are to some extent interdependent because, as a general rule, effective competition will ensure effective disclosure. Hence the policy maker might rationally attempt to alleviate consumer difficulties by supporting programs which will make imperfect markets work more efficiently. In this context, it would be appropriate to rely upon anti-trust legislation, tariff reductions, controls upon excessive advertising which gives rise to important entry barriers, rules prohibiting misleading advertising and sales practices, full disclosure requirements, better access to the legal system to enforce existing rights, and consumer education programs.

For a variety of reasons, however, certain markets cannot be rendered truly competitive; scale economies, for example, may be compatible with only one or two market participants. In these circumstances rules which impose restrictions upon the scope or consequences of contractual rights may be rationally relied upon to place excess profits, the correlative of monopoly or oligopoly, into consumer hands. Conversely, legislative attempts to initiate redistributive processes in structurally sound markets where, *ex hypothesi*, there are no excess profits to redistribute, will give rise to exclusionary or degenerative consequences. They will 'protect' the consumer by eliminating him from the legal market place; they will not protect him by remedying an imbalance in bargaining power. We do not object to legislatively imposed restrictions upon consumer freedom per se, and it is for this reason that we have incorporated a caveat into our normative definition of consumer protection rules. The merits of a rule designed to meet the 'compelling social reasons' to which the definition refers must, however, be evaluated in relation to the number of persons who would be eliminated from the market place, and hence the policy maker must engage in a delicate balancing of competing policy considerations. For example, should automobile manufacturers be required to double the existing braking capacity of cars if the consequential costs preclude 50,000 consumers from purchasing a new car? Is it appropriate to increase exemptions from seizure if a substantial number of low-income debtors will thereby be denied access to the legal credit market? Although no hard and fast lines can be drawn, questions such as these, examined within a framework such as that proposed, must be answered when the merits of contemplated legislation are being assessed.

Hence the policy maker must evaluate the prevailing conditions in the particular markets to which a consumer protection rule would apply, if enacted, for in this way only can the effects of that rule be measured. It is true that some of the most sophisticated analysts contend that market processes are increasingly inoperative.[74] It is also true that Canadian markets,

74 Cf J.K. Galbraith *The New Industrial State* (1968).

being significantly smaller than their American counterparts, are characterized by higher levels of concentration.[75] Notwithstanding the correspondingly greater need for redistributive rules in the Canadian context, the extent to which market processes have been undermined is still a matter of considerable debate; furthermore, there is no doubt that intense competition still prevails within many sectors of the economy, and hence specific structural conditions retain an overriding relevance for the formulation of consumer protection policies. Rules producing redistributive effects in certain markets might give rise to exclusionary or degenerative consequences in others where competition prevails, and hence the policy maker will not make substantial gains by superimposing a rule upon a variety of different markets without regard to the economic environment of each. This, of course, emphasizes the difficulty of formulating effective general consumer protection rules.

It is in this context that the central weakness in the thinking of many contemporary commentators emerges: some merely give their unqualified support to any legislation which purports to protect the consumer without so much as a passing reference to its economic effects, while others tend to infer structural deficiencies whenever consumer difficulties of any nature occur in the market place. There appears to be an optimistic but naive assumption that legislation designed to redistribute resources to the consumer will in some undefined manner achieve its purpose irrespective of market conditions. As we have seen, this predisposition is particularly manifest in relation to the problems which beset the low-income consumer.

The unyielding nature of the constraints imposed on policy-making by market considerations are graphically dramatized by the progressive shifts in thinking of Professor Caplovitz, as an acceptance of the stark economic realities emphasized in this article has been forced upon him. In the concluding chapter of his book he advances a number of suggestions for restricting the activities of ghetto merchants. These, and other similar proposals, have been evaluated in the latter part of our analysis. Curiously, in a 'throw-away' paragraph at the end of this chapter, Caplovitz rather laconically acknowledges some apprehensions about his proposals:

> It is possible, however, that even if such laws were feasible, they would not fully accomplish their intended objectives. Instead of forcing poor risks to curtail their consumption because the merchants would no longer extend them credit, such laws might only stimulate deviant patterns worse than those now in effect. For example, as their credit in local stores dried up, more families would probably turn to the peddlars, who depend almost entirely upon personal, rather than legal, controls. Enforcing laws pertaining to peddlars is not an

75 For thorough analyses of the structural condition of Canadian manufacturing industries, see Rosenbluth, *Concentration in Canadian Manufacturing Industries* (1957); Can. Dept. of Consumer and Corporate Affairs, *Concentration in the Manufacturing Industries of Canada* (1971).

easy matter, for these men are highly mobile and not readily apprehended. Also, some families might turn to loan sharks for the money that would enable them to buy for cash. Obviously, there is no simple solution to the ills of the low-income marketing system. But this should not deter efforts to reduce the abuses of the system through legislation.[76]

One would have thought that if legislation may possibly produce deviant patterns as drastically unintended as this, one should not enact the legislation just for the sake of having assumed to have done something about the problem.

Professor Caplovitz seems to have had even more serious second thoughts by the time he came to write the preface to the 1967 edition of his book:

A new printing of a book provides the author with the opportunity to evaluate his own work and to share whatever second thoughts he has with the reader. Needless to say, second thoughts have been prompted by greater experience with the subject matter and the wisdom of hindsight. The first of these has to do with the neighbourhood credit merchant who is cast pretty much as the villain in this book. I think it is a mistake to see the credit merchant only as a notorious exploiter of the poor. A more thorough analysis than I undertook in this book would have to examine the economic constraints that operate on these men. In some respects the local merchants charge more for the simple reason that it costs them more to operate ...[77]

Later in 1967, second thoughts seemed to have crystallized further. That year, before a congressional committee, Caplovitz *opposed* the enactment of a consumer bill abolishing wage garnishments.

... I am not yet convinced that doing away with garnishment is either feasible at this time or would have the desired effects even if it were possible to pass such a law.

For example, garnishment is not permitted in Pennsylvania and yet credit merchants are thriving in that state and consumer fraud is just as prevalent there as elsewhere. The creditors in Pennsylvania do not hesitate to attach both personal and real property and sheriff's sales of furniture and even homes are quite common. To lose one's home because of a consumer debt is certainly as harsh a consequence as losing one's job ...[78]

Caplovitz' intellectual agonizing zig-zagged again in 1970 when in testimony before the National Commission on Consumer Finance[79] he advocated the complete abolition of all creditors' remedies to be accompanied by a free market approach to the granting of credit with no restrictions on the

76 Supra note 3, at 191
77 Supra note 3, at xxv
78 Subcommittee on Consumer Affairs of the Committee on Banking and Currency (1967) H.R. 90th Cong., 1st Sess., Hearings on H.R. 11601, at 662–3
79 22 June 1970

right of entry into the business of credit granting and no restrictions on interest rates, which would be left to be determined by the market mechanism. With poor risks, said Caplovitz, 'an interest rate of say 100 per cent ... does not strike me as particularly shocking.' The sole sanction for non-payment under this system would be an adverse credit rating. This proposal is an intriguing combination of drastic interference with existing creditors' rights and acceptance of a free market in credit. Whether a credit-rating system could ever be made comprehensive enough to cover all creditors and debtors, whether debtors could be adequately protected against inaccurate credit ratings, the relative efficiency of this sanction compared to existing sanctions, which factor may reflect itself in the cost of granting credit, the consequences of receiving an adverse credit rating (exclusionary or degenerative), are all considerations that would need to be evaluated in order to determine the total social and economic impact of this proposal.

However, in the final paragraph of his book, Caplovitz comes close to stating the real truth of the matter:

> In the final analysis, the consumer problems of low-income families cannot be divorced from other problems facing them. Until society can find ways of raising their occupational opportunities, increasing their income, and reducing the discrimination against them – in short, until poverty itself is eradicated – only limited solutions to their problems as consumers can be found.[80]

A principal thesis of this article is that, outside the general social and economic policies elaborated by Caplovitz in this paragraph, few solutions, limited or otherwise, can be found to the consumer problems of the poor by ad hoc restrictions on the flow of market forces. The consumer problems of the poor are an inherent consequence of paucity of resources and can only be remedied by augmenting those resources, that is, by making the poor not poor. They are not for the most part a result of aberrations in the market process and, beyond making it freer, cannot be cured by ad hoc interferences with it. We have attempted to show that to try to solve the problems of the poor, and indeed any class of consumer, in this way in fact usually makes them worse. We have too often in the past yielded to the temptation to look for scapegoats to whom to attribute the unpleasant consequences of poverty. The somewhat unromantic and visible figures of the ghetto merchant, slum landlord, peddlar, and loan shark have proved easy, although irrelevant, targets. Ease of formulation and painlessness of execution (especially for the proponents) should not be the criteria by which solutions to these problems are selected. In framing relevant responses to the costs exacted by poverty in the market place, it is surely time that the myth that the ghetto merchant and his confrères are the major causes of the problems, and that we can escape being part of their solution, was finally buried.

80 Supra note 3, at 192

# [2]

# 10 Alternative strategies in consumer policy*

Most sociologists would agree that the principle of continuous *structural differentiation* both underlies the development of modern societies and constitutes the essence of their 'modernity'. According to one interpretation of modernization, social action that formed part of a (supposed or real) 'original' unity undergoes a division into functionally related structural components. The separation of the domestic household from the sphere of work is an example of this structural separation of formerly integrated patterns of life. The same principle is evidenced in such processes as the division of labour, and in the separation of manual and mental labour, labour and capital, state and society, law and morality, and state and church. As is well known, the fact that spheres of action that were once structurally related become separated from each other involves the important advantage of 'setting free' the elements of a system. The process of differentiation opens up an enormous range of possibilities: the domestic household can consume commodities which it cannot produce; among members of the household, there may emerge moral convictions that are not at all prejudiced by their capacity as citizens of a specific political system; and so on. According to this first interpretation, then, the evolutionary sequence of differentiation/increase in liberty and welfare/further differentiation is celebrated as the crucial advantage of, and the reason for, the superiority of 'modern' societies.

Within academic social science and political movements during the past few years, the question has been raised as to whether continuous differentiation leads to new problems and bottlenecks in development. Some sociologists are already troubled by the

* This paper was first presented to the conference on 'Applied Consumer Research', organized by the West German Federal Ministry of Research and Technology, Bonn, February 1981. It was published as 'Ausdifferenzierung oder Integration – Bemerkungen über strategische Alternativen der Verbraucherpolitik', *Zeitschrift für Verbraucherpolitik*, **5** (1981), pp. 119–33.

possibility that modern society may have been undergoing a process of '*excessive*' differentiation,[1] while others focus upon the concept – and the implicit political programme – of '*de*-differentiation'. This controversy within sociological theory is of great relevance to the study of consumer policy. For only in societies having undergone the process of differentiation does the concept 'consumer' make any sense. In societies such as our own, the concept of 'consumer' designates an array of actions, interests and situations that are clearly delimited from other interests, situations and actions. In so-called primitive societies, but also in medieval societies divided into estates and, therefore, already affected by processes of differentiation, the concept of 'consumer' is simply not meaningful. There, the concept of 'consumer' has no distinct basis in social reality, because the sphere of action related to consumption is not yet clearly delimited from other spheres of action such as work, politics and family life. Only modernized social structures, with their differentiated systems of action, make possible relatively clear-cut distinctions between individuals acting 'as' consumers, workers, voters, heads of the family, and so on.

### Actors and rules in consumer policy

If the 'welfare' of consumers is taken as the normative and strategic reference point of consumer research and consumer policy, it can readily be shown that this welfare is influenced either positively or negatively by three types of actors. These three categories of actors are in a relationship of 'differentiation', in the sense that they are relatively independent of each other. These actors include manufacturers or suppliers of goods and services consumed within the domestic household; the state, especially in its capacity as a judicial and legislative power; and, finally, individual consumers and their organizations.

Each of these three actors pursues certain interests, is subject to certain restrictions and strategic chances, and, in order to improve its strategic position, strives to enlarge its own sphere of action at the expense of other actors. If consumer policy is considered as an empirical process or 'game' that unfolds over time, it is immediately obvious that the respective (provisional) results of this game must be understood as the composite outcome of the interdependent and relatively autonomous actions of the three players. That is to say, not one player alone – be it the consumer, the manufacturer or the state – is in a position to determine outcomes unilaterally. Let us, therefore, try to briefly outline the main characteristics of the three actors participating in the 'game' of consumer policy.

### *Manufacturers/suppliers*

To the extent that they are engaged in the private sector, these actors endeavour to influence the welfare of consumers in manifold positive and negative ways, for instance through market research, marketing policy, product design and voluntary self-regulation of suppliers' associations. However, their economic interest in profits and profitability is a primary goal, and they therefore engage in consumer policy only to the extent that the (positive or negative) influencing of consumer welfare serves this goal of profitability. Only in the case of competitive relationships which favour or even exact a consideration of consumer interests are manufacturers and suppliers compelled to positively take account of consumer welfare. This compulsion is not operative, however, in every relationship of competition. Moreover, by means of a variety of strategic measures (for example, the formation of a cartel), many retailers can escape the conditions of competition which they face within the marketplace. Manufacturers or suppliers of goods and services are in general, therefore, interested in the welfare of the consumer only in an indirect and secondary way. They are in a position to modify, within certain limits, the conditions which might otherwise force them to have 'consideration' for the consumer. In accordance with these facts, an important strategic advantage accrues to the manufacturer/supplier side in the 'game' of consumer policy. This advantage consists precisely in the fact that, to a certain extent, and without prejudicing its interests, the manufacturer/supplier side can afford to be disinterested in the increase of consumer welfare.

### *State/law*

The judicial and legislative powers of the state, together with its regulatory apparatus of public policy, also actively influence consumer welfare through, for example, market regulation, measures of consumer protection, provision of concrete assistance to consumer organizations, and the public promotion of consumer information. Government, political parties and parliaments tend to support consumer welfare for obvious reasons: many consumers are also voters who may well refuse their political support if their interests are not considered to some degree by the organs of state policy. At the same time, the self-interest of state bodies is limited by the fact that no 'unreasonable' demands may be imposed on the manufacturers and suppliers. If this happens, state authorities must reckon with the possibility that manufacturers and suppliers will withdraw their economic activity, which, in turn, may severely encroach upon the specific interest of the state in economic growth, employment and revenue from taxation. In this respect, state policy is caught within a structural dilemma. If it is to avoid seriously infringing its own interests, it may neither engage 'too much' nor 'too little' in consumer policy.

*Individual consumers and their organizations*

It can safely be supposed that consumer organizations have an unlimited, immediate and positive interest in consumer welfare. This interest varies from consumer to consumer, since almost nobody is 'only' a consumer. Individuals perform a variety of different 'roles': at the same time, they may be consumers and employees, or they may be consumers and parents. This implies that individuals may experience conflicts of interest which reduce their determination to exercise their interests as consumers. In addition to this conflict, the collective actors of consumer organizations have to endure a number of well-known difficulties which can only be briefly enumerated here. For instance, these organizations are always at a time disadvantage compared to manufacturers and suppliers, and can thus only respond *ex post* to the already existing supply of goods and services. Faced with enormous variations in the supply of, and demand for, consumer goods, they also find it difficult to formulate and maintain a consistent conception of what constitutes 'the' interest of consumers. Due to the aforementioned fact that hardly anyone is *only* ever a consumer, finally, consumers' associations are faced with the organizational problem of mobilization; that is, with the actual difficulty of stimulating and preserving *motivation* among their potential members, and thus with generating the material and personal resources necessary for the operation of their organization.

If we summarize these considerations, the following picture emerges. Three different groups of independent social actors participate in consumer policy as a political process, namely, suppliers, states and (organized) consumers. Concerning the *intensity of interest* in the welfare of consumers, it can be said that the interest of suppliers is weak and indirect, that of state authority is ambivalent and caught within a dilemma, while the interest of consumer organizations is strong and immediate. The strategic chances of *actually influencing* the welfare of consumers are distributed in precisely the opposite way, however. Manufacturers and suppliers are endowed with considerable and direct chances because of their 'producer's sovereignty'; by contrast, state policy has a limited and indirect capacity to influence consumer welfare; finally, due to their organizational and resource problems and their dependence upon either manufacturers or the state, consumer organizations are endowed with limited and only indirect influence. Within the field of consumer policy, in short, the interested party is weak and the strong party is disinterested.

### Two difficulties concerning consumer 'welfare'

This suggested model of the structural chances of success of consumer policy becomes even more sobering when the concept of consumer welfare is itself examined. According to one approach, consumer welfare is maximized when the *subjectively-perceived* needs of economic subjects acting as consumers are satisfied to the maximum possible extent. However, two objections must be made against such an understanding of consumer welfare.

First, while we certainly 'have' needs, it is often questionable whether they are really our 'own' needs. To indicate this is not merely to allude to the obvious and trivial fact that needs can be 'manipulated' and 'artificially induced'. It is rather to indicate that a large number of needs for consumer goods which consumers express on the market are directly linked with their *living conditions* which, in turn, may not be in accordance with the needs of the consumers.

A hypothetical example of this latter possibility might be the medicaments individuals require in order to ward off illness which would otherwise result from the poor environmental conditions at their place of work or residence. Obviously, these medicaments could only be considered as means of satisfying 'needs' if the need to work or live within poor environmental conditions is itself assumed. The need for medicaments would then be considered as a subsidiary need generated by the satisfaction of the primary need to live and work in exactly these conditions and nowhere else. However, the fact that individuals live and work under conditions detrimental to their health can only be interpreted as being in accordance with their needs if they had the objective possibility of living and working elsewhere. Where this is not the case, it can be said that the choices made by consumers within the market-place are not always actions for the satisfaction of their 'own' needs, but are in fact responses to a situation where certain needs are 'structurally imposed'.

Another example of this 'structural imposition of needs' is furnished by the consumption of automobiles. Consumers often regard automobiles not as a means of satisfying a 'need' (such as the desire for mobility or the pleasure in driving) but, rather, as a response to urban living conditions which often make it 'impossible to live without a car'. In such frequently heard expressions, there is the suggestion that the apparently paradoxical need for an automobile is a need we could, in fact, do without: there is, in other words, a more or less vague awareness of the gap that exists between our needs and the demands forced upon us by the conditions in which we live. While this distinction opens up very difficult theoretical terrain, it is impossible to establish a relatively precise concept of consumer welfare if one simply ignores this phenomenon of 'structurally imposed needs'. In this context, it is interesting to note that steps in this direction have been taken in the recent literature on the theory of the household and in critical studies of consumption.[2]

This point is related to a second objection to the model of subjectively-perceived needs. A concept of consumer welfare which is neither merely naïve nor ideological must not only distinguish between 'genuine' and 'imposed' needs and include the former in the concept of consumer welfare. It should also seriously consider the *ways* in which consuming subjects become aware of their consumption needs; that is, how a need as such stabilizes over time and comes to be permanently associated with an individual. This question can scarcely be avoided by stating that needs simply 'exist'. On the contrary, consideration must always be given to the fact that the acknowledgement or recognition of a need is always a *cognitive* and reflexive process which is regulated by cultural norms and social relations. Not only may needs be objectively imposed; we may also be subjectively *mistaken* about our needs. If such deception is to be avoided, we require a certain degree of knowledge and a capacity to self-reflect which, in turn, are dependent upon socio-structural pre-conditions. The methods of ascertaining one's own needs are quite precarious under modern conditions characterized by a high degree of 'differentiation'. Deluged by 'options',[3] modern consumers find it difficult to choose, recognize and maintain needs *as* their own. This difficulty becomes greater the less recourse can be made to traditional habits and conventional standards of 'normality'. Accordingly, in consumer research there is a growing concern with encouraging the possible 'autonomous determination of needs' and with developing forms of organization and communication which 'help consumers to reflect upon their own desires and needs'.[4]

Considered together, these two objections to a theory of subjectively-perceived needs specify two requirements within a theory of consumer welfare. The first objection points to the distinction between 'genuine' needs and imposed conditions of living and survival, while the second objection emphasizes the need to consider the socio-structural pre-conditions of the autonomous self-determination of individuals' needs. There is much evidence that the proportion of structurally-imposed needs is increasing in complex and highly differentiated societies and that, at the same time, the pre-conditions for the cognitive consideration of individual needs and their integration into personal identity are diminishing. The biases and distortions of a theory of consumer welfare will be the more substantial the more it naïvely clings to the premise that the choices made by economic subjects on the consumer goods market *do* accurately express the real needs of consumers and that these subjects *are* actually in a position to adequately recognize their needs.

On the other hand, these two objections undoubtedly disturb the pillars of liberal economics and psychology by challenging their axiomatic equation of 'empirical' and 'real' needs. Of course, this equation has the unquestionable and essential advantage of resisting political or cultural regimentation and of defending the liberty and sovereignty of the consumer. Today, however, it is an open question whether this liberal equation has exactly the opposite effect, namely, of cognitively 'repressing' and ideologically screening out the numerous and clear indications that many consumer choices have nothing to do with the satisfaction of needs, that they are merely a reflex action to the conditioning of needs by actual social conditions, and that modern social structures restrict the development of the capacity of choosing, establishing and questioning needs.

The arguments briefly summarized above suggest two findings: first, that the structural power and interests of the 'players' involved in the 'game' of consumer policy are distributed in such a way that the chances of realizing consumer interests are very poor; and, second, that our knowledge of these consumer interests, as well as our conceptual tools for investigating consumer welfare are such that severe self-criticisms of conventional economic doctrines and very fundamental controversies are called for. Considered together, these two findings stimulate research into alternatives in consumer policy that might have some chances of success. Two different sets of alternative strategies can be identified.

**Consumer policy as the increase of 'consumer power'**

The first of these can be described as an attempt to increase the countervailing power of consumers. This strategy is based on the idea that consumers' capacity to act must be increased within the framework of the existing differentiation between suppliers, state power and consumers. This can be achieved, for instance, by increasing the right of consumer organizations to participate in the legislative and administrative process. It can also be achieved by improving the information and education of individual consumers, by research into consumer behaviour, and by other ways of providing information as a resource for increasing the power position of consumers. It can also be effected by weakening the dominant position of manufacturers and suppliers through legislative action or policies which regulate economic competition. Or, finally, this goal can be achieved through the development of new models of organization which improve the effectiveness of consumer organizations in activating existing or new members. It is neither possible nor necessary at this point to exhaustively describe the various ideas and concepts usually associated with this global strategy for developing the countervailing power of consumers. However, it can be shown that any strategy of this type meets with at least one of the following two difficulties.

The first of these difficulties is derived from the fact that consumer interests always conflict to a certain degree with interests related to economic growth or, at any rate, with the specific economic interest in profitability. This implies that there is a continual danger of satisfying interests that individuals have *as* consumers at the expense of their interests as *employees*. In view of the worsening conditions in the contemporary labour market, it can be assumed that consumer interests will be weakened in relation to the prevailing interest of both employees and manufacturers in retaining jobs and profits respectively.

The other structural obstacle before which a strategy of mobilizing countervailing power is relatively powerless is the fact that 'consumers' do not constitute a clearly delimitable and organizable complex of individuals. Rather they constitute an abstract category which defines certain *aspects* of the social actions of almost all individuals. Everyone and at the same time no one is a 'consumer'. The concept of 'consumer' does not apply 'segmentally' (i.e., consumers versus non-consumers) but, rather, 'functionally', that is, with reference only to *certain* spheres of action of *all* individuals. It is precisely the magnitude of the clientele of consumer policy – and the 'fuzziness' of the social domain of collective action of consumers – which render the efforts of consumer organizations so difficult and relatively ineffective. At the same time, this problem of size also implies problems of social, technical and temporal heterogeneity. Different individuals consume different goods and services at different times and purchase them from different producers and suppliers. The common denominator of 'consumer' is too abstract to facilitate the development of consumer organizations. Exceptions merely confirm, but do not invalidate this rule. Indeed, in the light of the experience of the Federal Republic and other highly industrialized countries, the general rule is that it is possible to organize consumer interests especially, and usually only, if:

1 the common interest of collectively acting individuals is not increased utility but the *avoidance of (physical) damage*. The relatively great mobilization success of consumer movements and organizations that concentrate on the constructional defects of automobiles or harmful chemical additives in food are examples; the chances of successful consumer mobilization are less if these movements and organizations are concerned with the *price* of goods and services, and especially so if their actions focus upon the *quality*, or positive use value, of goods;
2 the collective action is preoccupied with objects of *homogeneous mass consumption*, especially with such 'basic needs' as communication and transport services, petroleum, housing or rents, and foodstuffs;
3 the collective action is opposed to *highly visible* monopolies or

oligopolies of supply, such as petroleum companies or energy utilities;

4 in addition to their 'exit' option, consumers are provided with the possibility of increasing their influence (or of discrediting political leaders) through *political participation*, especially in state or public monopolies such as postal services, television authorities and public transportation;

5 the consumer movement can identify with political or cultural *symbols of collective identity* (for example, youth or women's movements), so that the consumer interest does not constitute the only point of initiation and crystallization of collective action, but rather merges with other concerns, such as anti-sexist, anti-imperialist or ecological ones.

These conditions probably increase the chances of consumer mobilization and organization in a cumulative way. In the Federal Republic, the only example of the confluence of all five conditions is the uninterrupted mass movement against the further expansion of nuclear energy which, since the middle of the 1970s, has, as a result, been able to develop beyond the scope of a mere consumer movement. The example of the anti-nuclear movement is instructive: besides indicating the very special conditions necessary for the lasting mobilization of consumers, it also still suggests (cf. above) the obstacles encountered by consumer movements in relation to the dominant interests of manufacturers, suppliers and workers in profits and jobs.

### The organizational 'reintegration' of consumption and production

In view of the scepticism generally associated with the strategies of countervailing power, a number of theorists working on 'alternative' models of economic organization and activity have concretely delineated a quite different strategy for the realization of consumer interests. The aim of this second type of strategy is to overcome the structural differentiation between manufacturers and suppliers, the state and consumers, upon which the strategy of countervailing power is based. In other words, the aim is not to strengthen or weaken actors' positions within the 'game' of consumer policy but rather to *reorganize* or reconstitute the game and its actors. This strategy seeks to reinforce the chances of de-differentiation, that is, of remixing or partly *integrating* social functions which have become separated as a result of the differentiation process at work in modern industrial society. The hopes and expectations associated with this conception of de-differentiation in consumer policy rest upon a paradoxical formula: consumers can only acquire the power necessary for the realization of their interests *as* consumers by structurally combining their interests in consumption with productive *and* political functions – and thereby transcending their identities as mere consumers. Theoretically speaking, there are three possible variants of this combination strategy:

1 the fusion of production, administration and consumption into a centralized, regulatory apparatus;
2 the reabsorption of productive functions into the realms of the domestic household and domestic consumption;
3 the incorporation of consumer functions and interests into the sphere of production.

A discussion of the first variant would go beyond the scope of this essay and, in any case, appears to be of little promise in view of the performance and development of Eastern European economic systems. The second variant, which is of greatest interest to proponents of 'alternative' or 'self-help' models of economic organization, pushes consumers beyond the limits of their specialized consumer functions by integrating them with some production functions in the (extended) household domain; for example, in the form of self-help, autonomous craft labour, and co-operative self-support. While the dilemma of consumer policy might be expected to be overcome by this strategy, its proponents often tend to one-sidedly and over-optimistically minimize several of its negative consequences. In the remainder of this discussion, I should like to draw particular attention to the limits and shortcomings of this approach. This will in turn shed light on some of the strategic advantages which, in my opinion, are offered by the third variant which is concerned not with the integration of production functions into the spheres of the household and consumption but, inversely, with the reabsorption and integration of consumer interests into the sphere of production. It may well be, of course, that these two complementary processes of integration can be combined and thereby mutually stabilize each other.

With regard to the shortcomings of the second variant, the strategy of more closely integrating production into the household domain, it is important to emphasize three points. First, the model of productive self-help through the household (or collectives of households) must face doubts about whether the objective and subjective dispositions for 'self-help through grass-roots organization' are actually so widespread – and so evenly distributed throughout the social structure – that production activities taking place within or close to the household domain (for example, the non-market and non-public production and distribution of food, the construction and repair of durable goods, the provision of a wide range of social services) could become quantitatively important. Second, as is generally known, the alternative of self-help is often burdened with losses in efficiency (the key word here is 'self-exploitation') which, in turn, must be considered a real obstacle to the expansion of this form of merging production and consumption at the level of the household. Third, concerning the political motivation and mobilizing potential of self-help activities, one must consider the negative implications of the very compelling argument that, in the final analysis, self-help initiatives (of parents or tenants, for instance) function as stop-gap measures for deficient public service programmes. Supported by cost-saving 'voluntary work', governments strive to control their financial bottlenecks without seriously being interested in the autonomy of the participant consumers or the quality of their services. To sum up, it can be said that self-help initiatives are limited in terms of social and technical resources and that they are frequently of a short duration. They are marked by considerable difficulties of internal organization and unification, and they readily experience severe legitimation problems *vis-à-vis* both the state and their own members. These problems will persist so long as their right to exist, their autonomy, and their resource needs are not supported, acknowledged and guaranteed by public authorities. To appraise self-help initiatives in this sceptical way is not to deny that, as spearheads of social movements, they constitute a form of action which – as the squatters' movement indicates – can fulfil important functions of innovation and protest which signal the need for *political* action and reform. However, self-help will fail to be an effective and permanent institution for organizing 'consumer' interests until its 'informal', 'autonomous' and 'alternative' character is institutionally acknowledged and protected – and thus to a certain extent formalized.

Let us, therefore, consider the inverse solution, that of integrating consumer interests into the sphere of production. In my opinion, a basic problem which must be faced by the theory of consumer policy is the ever-widening gap between the 'institutional' and the 'functional' definition of 'consumption' and 'consumer' in modern, welfare capitalist society. Briefly, according to an *institutional* definition of the consumer, consumption consists of the choices made by private households on the commodity markets. Economic citizens are viewed as acting as 'consumers' whenever they make such choices. This definition suggests that an increase in the rationality of choices can and must have a substantial effect on the 'welfare' of the consumers and domestic households. This 'consumer welfare' is central to a *functional* definition of consumers and consumption, for it includes within the sphere of consumption not just purchase-related acts but all those conditions and actions that have a positive or negative influence on the welfare of households.

It appears that these two definitions are by no means congruent and that the 'overlap' between the phenomena encompassed by each is even diminishing. Nowadays, it is becoming quite evident that private households acquire a high proportion of the goods and (especially) services which are of vital importance for their 'welfare' – regardless of how welfare is defined – not through rational *individual purchases* of goods and services, but through state-regulated provisions, or through such collective 'compulsory purchases' as social security and social services. That is to say, consumer '*welfare*' is only partly, and probably decreasingly, determined by consumer *behaviour* (i.e., choices and purchases); the consumer *as* a consumer is increasingly subject to the decisions and parameters established by the state or large firms and their long-term investment strategies. The consumer movement (for example, Naderism in the United States) and much of the current consumer research have for some time extended and even concentrated their activities and interests on the domain of *public services*; that is, upon those goods which cannot be acquired by way of purchase, but which nevertheless are of great relevance to consumers' welfare.

A further aspect of the fact that the *well-being of consumers* is only partially determined by their *choices and acts of consumption* becomes visible if we look at how the household is related to work. The welfare of the private household depends not only on public services, but also on the conditions encountered by wage earners within the work-place. As is generally known, a special characteristic of the labour market is that – in contrast to all other markets – it depends upon the trading of a 'commodity' (labour power) which, nevertheless, *cannot* be separated from its physical owner and thereby placed at the exclusive disposal of its buyers. In the labour market, in other words, workers certainly exchange income for the work they perform, but they are never fully divorced from the concrete process of the utilization of their labour power by its buyers. It is undeniable that the experience of this utilization process is of considerable relevance in negatively or positively influencing the welfare of working individuals. This holds true irrespective of the amount of household income which they receive from 'selling' their labour power. Because it is impossible to fully separate labour power from its individual owners, the theory of the household must, as it were, project itself into the territory currently occupied by the theory of production. The household is always 'present' and necessarily affected when labour power as a factor of production is set in motion. This seems to suggest that the 'separation' of household and production that is often thought to be *the* dominant characteristic of industrial society is in fact quite incomplete and only apparent. In this respect, it certainly is meaningful to distinguish between the 'investive' and 'consumptive' elements of the labour process. The investive aspects of the labour process refer to the relationship between the energy expended on labour and the income derived from labour, whereas the consumptive elements comprise all the concomitants and side effects of the labour process which positively or negatively influence the welfare of individual workers. However complicated this distinction may at first appear, it has exerted a strong influence on the practice of industrial relations and their development during the 1970s. The whole trade union and political debate on the aims and methods of the 'humanization of work' is concerned to emphasize more strongly the consumptive aspect of the industrial labour process. Similarly, evidence furnished by opinion surveys suggests that, in addition to the investive criterion (i.e., estimates of how 'difficult' or 'well paid' work is), the consumptive criterion (i.e., how 'meaningful' or 'interesting' work is reckoned to be) is gaining in importance.

In so far as empirical evidence suggests that labour power is simultaneously oriented to the goals of business firms *and*, increasingly, to the direct (i.e., non-monetary) securing of the welfare status of household members who work, a new theoretical and political strategy of consumer welfare becomes conceivable. This new strategy would seek to expand 'autonomy' not by integrating production within the household but, rather, through attempts to bring the consumption-related welfare interests of the household into the sphere of production. If consumer research conceptually frees itself from the rigid and increasingly implausible 'institutional' definition of consumption (i.e., consumption = market choices of private households), and provided that it also becomes more willing to focus on those welfare components that are *not* allocated through markets, but instead through state administration, there is no reason why the theoretical frame of reference of consumer policy research should not go one step further by including the consumption aspects of work and production. After all, the latter are at least as relevant for the well-being of consumers as the outcomes of market transactions of private households; the *purchase* of goods and services is only one of several links (and probably a decreasingly important one) that allocate positive or negative use-values to private households. There is, therefore, no reason to restrict the attention of consumer research to this particular institutional link, the market.[5] It is well recognized nowadays that consumers of public goods and services confront the suppliers of these goods and services, i.e., state authorities, in their capacity as voters and bearers of rights and that these consumer-citizens are therefore capable of exerting a considerable influence on the quality, price and safety of these goods and services through appropriate forms of organization, communication and co-operation. The same principle applies to the consumptive dimensions of the production process, in so far as certain steps have been made in the direction of regulating the welfare-related aspects of the work process through enterprise, trade union or state intervention. This development considerably expands the possible scope for stimulating political imagination, which is an acknowledged and legitimate goal of social scientific research on consumption issues. Indeed, three interrelated points of departure of a production-centred consumer policy can be systematically distinguished: work policy, process policy and product policy.

*Work policy* Given that the consumption of such public goods as health or education systems is already the subject of contemporary research on consumer policy, there is no conceivable reason why this research should not also concern itself with the positive and especially the negative (for example, health-related) consequences of the labour process. It is unfortunately true that contemporary consumer research and research on the humanization of work do not yet have a common conceptual frame of reference which might guide their inquiries. Nevertheless, the consumptive interest of workers in improving their working conditions has become a topic on the agenda of labour movements at the firm, trade union and political levels. As the example of 'innovation counselling' conducted by the German Industrial Metal Workers' Union (IG Metall) suggests, there is also a growing awareness that the problem of humanizing work cannot successfully be tackled only at the level of work relations within the business firm, or at the level of the state's promotion of scientific-technical research and development, but that a *third* level – the managerial control over investment – must become an additional point of departure for controlling and improving the 'consumptive' aspects of work. In this strategy, it is essential that the works councils within both the manufacturing enterprises and their customer firms co-operate with each other beyond the level of the single firm. For example, manufacturing enterprises which produce office machinery also 'simultaneously' produce the working conditions within the business firms using these machines, which implies that influencing the product policy of manufacturers of investment goods constitutes an appropriate step in the direction of effective control over the developments of working conditions in the user firms.

*Process policy* Industrial processes of production have (negative) consumptive consequences, not only for the individuals directly involved, but also for all others who do not participate in these production processes. Examples of these negative effects include the pollution of air and water, problems of noise accompanying production, or the ecological and aesthetic degradation of the environment. In many cases, these effects become so important that they begin to have repercussions within the internal structure of the business enterprises as, for instance, when large manufacturing plants have difficulty recruiting senior personnel because the latter hesitate about living within an area negatively affected by the firm's production. Just as poor working conditions and the resulting difficulties and additional costs of hiring labour sometimes tend to stimulate firms' (opportunistic) sympathy for 'humanization' measures, so these problems of recruiting management personnel might be expected to lead to parallel initiatives for the 'restoration of the environment'. Clearly, these 'automatic' corrections within the calculus of the firm will remain limited in their social, technical and temporal scope and highly dependent upon economic developments unless appropriate forms of countervailing power are developed within the enterprise itself. This would facilitate the effective articulation of the consumptive interests of households (including even those not linked directly to the firm through labour contracts). By instituting such organs of countervailing power within the firm, 'consumer protection within the sphere of production' would become a real possibility.

*Product policy* In as much as decisions about the production schedule and the quality, price and side effects of products presently fall outside the sphere of influence of unions, works councils and state regulatory policies, the chances of success of product policy strategies are for the time being uncertain. Nevertheless, Cooley's discussion of the initiatives and successes within the Lucas Aerospace firm suggest a very promising model of product policy controlled by workers and oriented by criteria of use-value.[6] This model of socially useful production is also anticipated in the recent statements of the Industrial Metal Workers' Union on the production and export of armaments ('U-boats for Chile?'). There are also signs of an increasing awareness of the problems likely to be generated as a result of the growing economic concentration of some markets for such durable consumer goods as automobiles and electronic entertainment equipment. The smaller the number of manufacturers engaged in producing a certain product, the greater the statistical probability that the workers of a manufacturing firm will also be the final consumers of the products they themselves have produced. This effect is reinforced by the widespread practice, for instance in the European automobile industry, of companies granting a discount price on products for their own employees, a practice that has even led workers to protest against the reduction of the quality of 'their' products (for example, thinner car-body sheets) because of product or process innovations.

Given the problems associated with process and product policies, there are strong indications that use-value-oriented interests will be pursued only with difficulty and that, in cases of conflict, use-value concerns will be subordinated to that more or less reluctant alliance of labour and capital which reflects the interests of suppliers. Strategies of consumer policy that are based upon the integration of consumptive concerns into production are, however, no more burdened by this difficulty than the conventional type of strategy oriented to increasing the leverage of the consumer within the market-place. This difficulty may even apply less to the former strategy, especially considering that all efforts at consumer organization which focus on the fuzzy identity of 'the consumer' have to face well-known and enormous difficulties – those of overcoming the technical, social and temporal heterogeneity of consumer action by generating the resources and establishing the autonomous forms of organization necessary for collective action. If we compare the two different types of strategy delineated here – defending an 'independent' consumer interest and integrating consumption and production – the strategy of linking together the spheres of production and consumption is evidently more promising because there already exists within the spheres of production trade unions and organizations of workers upon whom consumer interests could depend more strongly than has until now been the case.

In view of the need to overcome the present rather considerable opposition to the type of consumer policies based on the strategy of integration, the further development and securing of an 'autonomous' sector of production and consumption – comprising such household-linked activities as autonomous work, self-help, neighbourhood co-operatives and community work, the co-operative system and squatters' actions – could come to play an important role. As long as they were recognized as socially 'normal' and vital for certain individuals or age groups, these household-linked forms of activity could help break up the power of the individual and collective imperative of wage-labour and 'full employment', an imperative that presently enables the industrial sector to insulate itself against consumer and use-value interests.

## Notes and references

1 N. Luhmann, *Gesellschaftsstruktur und Semantik: Studien zur Wissenssoziologie der modernen Gesellschaft*, vol. 1 (Frankfurt 1980).

2 cf. the critical study of William Leiss, *The Limits to Satisfaction* (Toronto 1976); the distinction between comfort and pleasure introduced by T. Scitovsky, *The Joyless Economy. An Inquiry into Human Satisfaction and Consumer Dissatisfaction* (Oxford 1976); and A. Hirschman's distinction between 'preferences' and 'metapreferences' in his *Shifting Involvements* (Princeton 1982), pp. 70ff.

3 Ralf Dahrendorf, *Life Chances* (London 1979).

4 G. Scherhorn, 'Die Entstehung von Verbraucherproblemen im Spannungsfeld von Konsum und Arbeit', *Zeitschrift für Verbraucherpolitik*, **4** (1980), p. 112.

5 ibid., p. 113.

6 M. Cooley, *Architect or Bee?* (London 1983).

[3]

# 2

# Consumer Society

Today, we are everywhere surrounded by the remarkable conspicuousness of consumption and affluence, established by the multiplication of objects, services, and material goods. This now constitutes a fundamental mutation in the ecology of the human species. Strictly speaking, men of wealth are no longer surrounded by other human beings, as they have been in the past, but by *objects*. Their daily exchange is no longer with their fellows, but rather, statistically as a function of some ascending curve, with the acquisition and manipulation of goods and messages: from the rather complex domestic organization with its dozens of technical slaves to the "urban estate" with all the material machinery of communication and professional activity, and the permanent festive celebration of objects in advertising with the hundreds of daily mass media messages; from the proliferation of somewhat obsessional objects to the symbolic psychodrama which fuels the nocturnal objects that come to haunt us even in our dreams. The concepts of "environment" and "ambiance" have undoubtedly become fashionable only since we have come to live in less proximity to other human beings, in their presence and discourse, and more under the silent gaze of deceptive and obedient objects which continuously repeat the same discourse, that of our stupefied (*medusée*) power, of our potential affluence and of our absence from one another.

As the wolf-child becomes wolf by living among them, so are we becoming functional. We are living the period of the objects: that is, we live by their rhythm, according to their incessant cycles. Today, it is we who are observing their birth, fulfillment, and death; whereas in all previous civilizations, it was the object, instrument, and perennial monument that survived the generations of men.

While objects are neither flora nor fauna, they give the impression of being a proliferating vegetation; a jungle where the new savage of modern times has trouble finding the reflexes of civilization. These fauna and flora, which people have produced, have come to encircle and invest them, like a bad science fiction novel. We must quickly describe them as we see and experience them, while not forgetting, even in periods of scarcity or profusion, that they are in actuality the *products of human activity*, and are controlled, not by natural ecological laws, but by the law of exchange value.

> The busiest streets of London are crowded with shops whose show cases display all the riches of the world: Indian shawls, American revolvers, Chinese porcelain, Parisian corsets, furs from Russia and spices from the tropics; but all of these worldly things bear odious white paper labels with Arabic numerals and then laconic symbols LSD. This is how commodities are presented in circulation.[1]

## Profusion and displays

*Accumulation*, or *profusion*, is evidently the most striking descriptive feature. Large department stores, with their luxuriant abundance of canned goods, foods, and clothing, are like the primary landscape and the geometrical locus of affluence. Streets with overcrowded and glittering store windows (lighting being the least rare commodity, without which merchandise would merely be what it is), the displays of delicacies, and all the scenes of alimentary and vestimentary festivity, stimulate a magical salivation. Accumulation is more than the sum of its products: the conspicuousness of surplus, the final and magical negation of scarcity, and the maternal and luxurious presumptions of the land of milk and honey. Our markets, our shopping avenues and malls mimic a new-found nature of prodigious fecundity. Those are our Valleys of Canaan where flows, instead of milk and honey, streams of neon on ketchup and plastic – but no matter! There exists an anxious anticipation, not that there may not be enough, but that there is too much, and too much for everyone: by purchasing a portion one in effect appropriates a whole crumbling pyramid of oysters, meats, pears or canned asparagus. One purchases the part for the whole. And this repetitive and metonymic discourse of the consumable, and of commodities is represented, through collective metaphor and as a product of its own surplus, in the image of the *gift*, and of the inexhaustible and spectacular prodigality of the *feast*.

In addition to the stack, which is the most rudimentary yet effective form of accumulation, objects are organized in *displays*, or in *collections*. Almost every clothing store or appliance store presents a gamut of differentiated objects, which call upon, respond to, and refute each other. The display window of the antique store is the aristocratic, luxurious version of this model. The display no longer exhibits an overabundance of wealth but a *range* of select and complementary objects which are offered for the choosing. But this arrangement also invokes a psychological chain reaction in the consumer who peruses it, inventories it, and grasps it as a total category. Few objects today are offered *alone*, without a context of objects to speak for them. And the relation of the consumer to the object has consequently changed: the object is no longer referred to in relation to a specific utility, but as a collection of objects in their total meaning. Washing machine, refrigerator, dishwasher, have different meanings when grouped together than each one has alone, as a piece of equipment (*ustensile*). The display window, the advertisement, the manufacturer, and the *brand name* here play an essential role in imposing a coherent and collective vision, like an almost inseparable totality. Like a chain that connects not ordinary objects but *signifieds*, each object can signify the other in a more complex super-object, and lead the consumer to a series of more complex choices. We can observe that objects are never offered for consumption in an absolute disarray. In certain cases they can *mimic* disorder to better seduce, but they are always arranged to trace out directive paths. The arrangement directs the purchasing impulse towards *networks* of objects in order to seduce it and elicit, in accordance with its own logic, a maximal investment, reaching the limits of economic potential. Clothing, appliances, and toiletries thus constitute object *paths*, which establish inertial constraints on the consumer who will proceed *logically* from one object to the next. The consumer will be caught up in a *calculus* of objects, which is quite different from the frenzy of purchasing and possession which arises from the simple profusion of commodities.

## The Drugstore

The drugstore is the synthesis of profusion and calculation. The drugstore (or the new shopping malls) makes possible the synthesis of all consumer activities, not least of which are shopping, flirting with objects, idle wandering, and all the permutations of these. In this way, the drugstore is more appropriately representative of modern consumption than the large department store where quantitative centralization leaves little margin for idle exploration. The arrangement of departments and products here imposes a more utilitarian approach to consumption. It retains something of the period of the emergence of department stores, when large numbers of people were beginning to get access to *everyday* consumables. The drugstore has an altogether different function. It does not juxtapose categories of commodities, but practices an *amalgamation of signs* where all categories of goods are considered a partial field in a general consumerism of signs. The cultural center becomes, then, an integral part of the shopping mall. This is not to say that culture is here "prostituted"; that is too simple. It is *culturalized*. Consequently, the commodity (clothing, food, restaurant, etc.) is also culturalized, since it is transformed into a distinctive and idle substance, a luxury, and an item, among others, in the general display of consumables.

> A new art of living, a new way of living, claims advertising, (and fashionable magazines): a pleasant shopping experience, in a single air-conditioned location; one is able to purchase food, products for the apartment or summer home, clothing, flowers, the latest novel, or the latest gadget in a single trip, while husband and children watch a film; and then later you can all dine together on the spot.

Cafe, cinema, book store, auditorium, trinkets, clothing, and many other things can be found in these shopping centers. The drugstore recaptures it all in a kaleidoscopic mode. Whereas the large department store provides a marketplace pageantry for merchandise, the drugstore offers the subtle recital of consumption, where, in fact, the "art" consists in playing on the ambiguity of the object's sign, and sublimating their status and utility as commodity in a play of "ambiance."

The drugstore is neo-culture universalized, where there is no longer any difference between a fine gourmet shop and a gallery of paintings, between *Playboy* and a *Treatise on Paleontology*. The drugstore will be modernized to the point of offering a bit of "gray matter":

> Just selling products does not interest us, we would like to supply a little gray matter ... Three stories, a bar, a dance floor, and shops; trinkets, records, paperbacks, intellectual books, a bit of everything. But we are not looking to flatter the customer. We are actually offering them "something": a language lab on the second floor; records and books where you find the great trends that move our society; music for research; works that explain an epoch. Products accompanied by "gray matter", this is the drugstore, but in a new style, with something more, perhaps a bit of intelligence and human warmth.[2]

A drugstore can become a whole city: such as Parly 2,[3] with its giant shopping center, where "art and leisure mingle with everyday life"; where each residential group encircles a pool club (the center of attraction), a circular church, tennis courts ("the least of things"), elegant boutiques, and a library. Even the smallest ski resort is organized on the "universalist" model of the drugstore, one where all activities are summarized, systematically combined and centered around the fundamental concept of "ambiance." Thus Idleness-on-the-Wasteful[4] simultaneously offers you a complete, polymorphic and combinatorial existence:

> Our Mt Blanc, our Norway spruce forest; our Olympic runs, our "park" for children; our architecture, carved, trimmed, and polished like a work of art; the purity of the air we breathe; the refined ambiance of our Forum, modeled after Mediterranean cities where, upon return from the ski slopes, life flourishes. Cafes, restaurants, boutiques, skating rinks, night clubs, cinemas, and centers of culture and amusement are all located in the Forum to offer you a life off the slopes that is particularly rich and varied. There is our closed-circuit TV; and our future on a human scale (soon, we will be classified as a work of art by the department of cultural affairs).

We have reached the point where "consumption" has grasped the whole of life; where all activities are sequenced in the same combinatorial mode; where the schedule of gratification is outlined in advance, one hour at a time; and where the "environment" is complete, completely climatized, furnished, and culturalized. In the phenomenology of consumption, the general climatization of life, of goods, objects, services, behaviors, and social relations represents the perfected, "consummated,"[5] stage of evolution which, through articulated networks of objects, ascends from pure and simple abundance to a complete conditioning of action and time, and finally to the systematic organization of ambiance, which is characteristic of the drugstores, the shopping malls, or the modern airports in our futuristic cities.

## Parly 2

"The largest shopping center in Europe."

"Printemps, B.H.V., Dior, Prisunic, Lanvin, Frank et Fils, Hediard, two cinemas, a drugstore, a supermarket, Suma, a hundred other shops, all gathered in a single location!"[6]

In the choice of shops, from groceries to high fashion, there are two requirements: progressive marketing and a sense of aesthetics.

The famous slogan "uglyness doesn't sell" is outmoded, and could be replaced by "the beauty of the surroundings is the precondition for a happy life": a two-story structure ... organized around a central mall, with a main street and promenades on two levels; the reconciliation of the small and large shop and of the modern pace with the idleness of antiquity.

The mall offers the previously unexperienced luxury of strolling between stores which freely (*plain-pièd*) offer their temptations without so much interference as glare from a display window. The central mall, a combination of rue de la Paix and the Champs-Elysées, is adorned by fountains and artificial trees. Kiosks and benches are completely indifferent to seasonal changes and bad weather. An exceptional system of climate control, requiring eight miles of air conditioning ducts, creates a perpetual springtime.

Not only can anything be purchased, from shoestrings to an airline ticket, or located, such as insurance company, cinema, bank or medical service, bridge club and art exhibition, but one need not be the slave of time. The mall, like every city street, is accessible seven days a week, day or night.

Naturally, the shopping mall has instituted, for those who desire, the most modern form of payment: the "credit card." The card frees us from checks, cash, and even from financial difficulties at the end of the month. Henceforth, to pay you present your card and sign the bill. That's all there is to it. Each month you receive a bill which you can pay in full or in monthly installments.

In the marriage between comfort, beauty, and efficiency, Parlysians discover the material conditions of happiness which the anarchy of older cities refuses them.

Here we are at the heart of consumption as the total organization of everyday life, as a complete homogenization. Everything is appropriated and simplified into the translucence of abstract "happiness," simply defined by the resolution of tensions. Expanded to the dimensions of the shopping mall and the futuristic city, the drugstore is the *sublimation* of real life, of objective social life, where not only work and money are abolished, but the seasons disappear as well – the distant vestige of a cycle finally domesticated! Work, leisure, nature, and culture, all previously dispersed, separate, and more or less irreducible activities that produced anxiety and complexity in our real life, and in our "anarchic and archaic" cities, have finally become mixed, massaged, climate controlled, and domesticated into the simple activity of perpetual shopping. All these activities have finally become desexed into a single hermaphroditic ambiance of style! Everything is finally *digested* and reduced to the same homogeneous fecal matter (this occurs, of course, precisely under the sign of the disappearance of "*liquid*" *currency*, the still too visible symbol of the *real* excretion (*fecalité*) of real life, and of the economic and social contradictions that previously haunted it). All that is past (passed): a *controlled*, lubricated, and *consumed* excretion (*fecalité*) is henceforth transferred into things, everywhere diffused in the indistinguishability of things and of social relations. Just like the Roman Pantheon where the gods of all countries coexisted in a syncretism, in an immense "digest," the super shopping center,[7] our new pantheon, our pandemonium, brings together all the gods, or demons, of consumption. That is to say, every activity, labor, conflict and all the seasons are abolished in the same abstraction. The substance of life, unified in this universal digest, can no longer have any *meaning*: that which produced the dream work, the poetic work, the work of meaning, that is to say the grand schemas of displacement and condensation, the great figures of metaphor and contradiction, which are founded on the lived articulation of distinct elements, is no longer possible. The eternal substitution of homogeneous elements alone remains. There is no longer a symbolic function, but an eternal combinatory of "ambiance" in a perpetual Springtime.

## Towards a theory of consumption

### *The autopsy of* homo economicus

There is a fable: "There once was a man who lived in Scarcity. After many adventures and a long voyage in the Science of Economics, he encountered the Society of Affluence. They were married and had many needs." "The beauty of *homo economicus*," said A. N. Whitehead, "was that we knew exactly what he was searching for." This human fossil of the Golden Age, born in the modern era out of the fortuitous conjunction of Human Nature and Human Rights, is gifted with a heightened principle of formal rationality which leads him to:

1 Pursue his own happiness without the slightest hesitation;
2 Prefer objects which provide him with the maximum satisfaction.

The whole discourse on consumption, whether learned or lay, is articulated on the mythological sequence of the fable: a man, "endowed" with needs which "direct" him towards objects that "give" him satisfaction. Since man is really never satisfied (for which by the way he is reproached), the same history is repeated indefinitely, since the time of the ancient fables.

Some appear to be perplexed: "Among all the unknowns of economic science, needs are the most persistently obscure" (Knight).[8] But this uncertainty does not prevent the advocates of the human sciences, from Marx to Galbraith, and from Robinson Crusoe to Chombart de Lauwe,[9] from faithfully reciting the litany of needs. For the economists, there is the notion of "utility." Utility is the desire to consume a specific commodity, that is to say, to nullify its utility. Need is therefore already embedded in commodities on the market. And preferences are manipulated by the arrangement of products already offered on the market: this is in fact an elastic demand.

For the psychologist there is the theory of "motivation" which is a bit more complex, less "object oriented"[10] and more "instinct oriented,"[11] derived from a sort of ill-defined, preexisting necessity. For the sociologist and psychosociologist, who arrived last on the scene, there is the "sociocultural." The anthropological postulate, of the *individual* endowed with needs and moved by nature to satisfy them, or of a consumer who is free, conscious and aware of his needs, is not put into question by sociologists (although sociologists are suspicious of "deep motivations"). But rather, on the basis of this idealistic postulate, sociologists allow for a "social-dynamics" of needs. They activate models of conformity and competition ("Keeping up with the Joneses")[12] derived from the pressure of peer group, or they elaborate grand "cultural models" which are related to society in general or to history.

Three general positions can be identified: for Marshall, needs are interdependent and rational; for Galbraith, choices are imposed by motivation (we will come back to this); for Gervasi (and others), needs are interdependent, and are the result of learning rather than of rational calculation.

Gervasi: "Choices are not made randomly. They are socially controlled, and reflect the cultural model from which they are produced. We neither produce nor consume just any product: the product must have some meaning in relation to a system of values."[13] This leads to a perspective on consumption in terms of integration: "The goal of the economy is not the maximization of production *for the purposes of the individual*, but the maximization of production in relation to society's value system" (Parsons).[14] Similarly, Duesenbury will claim that the only choice is, in fact, varying one's possessions according to one's position in the social hierarchy. In effect, the differences in choice from one society to another, and the similarity of choices within a society, compels us to view consumer behavior as a social phenomenon. The economist's notion of "rational" choice has been changed into the model of choice as conformity, which is significantly different. Needs are not so much directed at objects, but at values. And the satisfaction of needs primarily expresses an *adherence to these values*. The fundamental, unconscious, and automatic choice of the consumer is to accept the life-style of a particular society (no longer therefore a real choice: the theory of the autonomy and sovereignty of the consumer is thus refuted).

This kind of sociology culminates in the notion of the "standard package,"[15] defined by Riesman as the collection of products and services which constitutes the basic heritage of the middle-class American. Constantly on the rise and indexed on the national standard of living, the standard package is a minimum ideal of a statistical kind, and a middle-class model of conformity. Surpassed by some, only dreamed of by others, it is an *idea* which encapsulates the American way of life.[16] Here again, the "standard package" does not so much refer to the materiality of goods (TV, bathroom, car, etc.) as to *the ideal of conformity*.

All of this sociology gets us nowhere. Besides the fact that the notion of conformity is nothing more than an immense tautology (in this case the middle-class American defined by the "standard package," itself defined by the statistical mean of consumed goods – or sociologically: a particular individual belongs to a particular group which consumes a particular product, and the individual consumes such a product because he or she belongs to such a group), the postulate of formal rationality, which in economics determined the individual's relation to objects, is simply transferred to the relation of the individual to the group. Conformity and satisfaction are interrelated: the resulting similarity in the subject's relation to objects, or to a group *posited as a distinct entity*, is established according to the logical principle of equivalence. The concepts of "need" and "norm" respectively are the expressions of this miraculous equivalence.

The difference between the economic notion of "utility" and the sociological notion of conformity is identical to the distinction Galbraith establishes between the pursuit of profit and economic motivation, which is characteristic of the "traditional" capitalist system, on the one hand, and the behavior of identification and adaptation, which is specific to the era of organization and of the technostructure, on the other. The *conditioning of needs* becomes the central issue for both the psycho-sociologists of conformity, and for Galbraith. This is never an issue for economists (and for good reasons), for whom consumers, with their ultimate rational calculation, remain ideally free.

Since Packard's *The Hidden Persuaders* and Dichter's *The Strategy of Desire* (and some others as well),[17] the conditioning of needs (particularly through advertising) has become the favorite theme in the discourse on consumer society. The celebration of affluence and the great lament over "artificial" or "alienated needs," together have fueled the same mass culture, and even the intellectual discourse on the issue. Generally this discourse is grounded in the antiquated moral and social philosophy of a humanist tradition. With Galbraith, however, it develops into a more rigorous economic and political theory. We will therefore remain with him, starting from his two books, *The Affluent Society* and *The New Industrial State*.

Briefly summarizing his position, we could say that the fundamental problem of contemporary capitalism is no longer the contradiction between the "maximization of profit" and the "rationalization of production" (from the point of view of the producer), but rather a contradiction between a virtually unlimited productivity (at the level of the technostructure) and the need to dispose of the product. It becomes vital for the system at this stage to control not only the mechanism of production, but also consumer demand; not only prices, but what will be asked for the price. Either prior to production (polls, market studies) or subsequent to it (advertising, marketing, conditioning), the general idea "is to shift the locus of decision in the purchase of goods from the consumer where it is beyond control to the firm where it is subject to control.[18] Even more generally:

> The accommodation of the market behavior of the individual, as well as of social attitudes in general, to the needs of producers and the goals of the technostructure is an inherent feature of the system [it would be more appropriate to say: a *logical* characteristic]. It becomes increasingly important with the growth of the industrial system.[19]

This is what Galbraith calls the "revised sequence," in opposition to the "accepted sequence" whereby the consumer is presumed to have the initiative which will reflect back, through the market, to the manufacturers. Here on the contrary, the manufacturers control behavior, as well as direct and model social attitudes and needs. In its tendencies at least, this is a total dictatorship by the sector of production.

The "revised sequence," at least, has the critical value of undermining the fundamental myth of the classical relation, which assumes that it is the individual who exercises power in the economic system. This emphasis on the power of the individual largely contributed to the legitimation of the organization; all dysfunctions, all nuisances, the inherent contradictions in the order of production are justified, since they enlarge the consumer's domain of sovereignty. On the contrary, it is clear that the whole economic and psychosociological apparatus of market and motivation research, which pretends to uncover the underlying needs of the consumer and the real demand prevailing in the market, exists only to generate a demand for further market opportunities. And it continuously masks this objective by staging its opposite. "Man has become the object of science for man only since automobiles have become harder to sell than to manufacture."[20]

Thus everywhere, Galbraith denounces the boosting of demand by "artificial accelerators," which the technostructure carries out in its imperialist expansion, rendering the stabilization of demand impossible.[21] Income, luxury goods, and surplus labor form a vicious and frantic circle. The infernal round of consumption is based on the celebration of needs that are purported to be "psychological." These are distinguished from "physiological" needs since they are supposedly established through "discretionary income" and the freedom of choice, and consequently manipulable at will. Advertising here of course plays a capital role (another idea which has become conventional) for it appears to be in harmony with commodities and with the needs of the individual. In fact, says Galbraith, advertising is adjusted to the industrial system: "It appears to place a significance on products only in so far as it is important for the system, and it upholds the importance and prestige of the technostructure from the social point of view." Through advertising, the system appropriates social goals for its own gain, and imposes its own objectives as social goals: "What's good for General Motors ..."

Again we must agree with Galbraith (and others) in acknowledging that the liberty and sovereignty of the consumer are nothing more than a mystification. The well-preserved mystique of satisfaction and individual choice (primarily supported by economists), whereby a "free" civilization reaches its pinnacle, is the very ideology of the industrial system. It justifies its arbitrariness and all sorts of social problems: filth, pollution, and deculturation – in fact the consumer is sovereign in a jungle of ugliness, where *the freedom of choice is imposed on him*. The revised sequence (that is to say the *system* of consumption) thus ideologically supplements and connects with the *electoral system*. The drugstore and the polling booth, the geometric spaces of individual freedom, are also the system's two mammary glands.

We have discussed at length the analysis of the "technostructural" conditioning of needs and consumption because it is currently quite prominent. This kind of analysis, thematized in multiple ways in the pseudo-philosophy of "alienation," constitutes a representation of society which is itself part of consumerism. But it is open to fundamental objections that are all related to its idealist anthropological postulates. For Galbraith individual needs can be stabilized. There exists in human *nature* something like an *economic principle* that would lead man, were it not for "artificial accelerators," to impose limits on his own objectives, on his needs and at the same time on his efforts. In short, there is a tendency towards satisfaction, which is not viewed as optimizing, but rather as "harmonious" and balanced at the level of the individual, a tendency that would allow the individual to express himself in a society that is itself a harmony of collective needs, instead of becoming caught up in the vicious circle of infinite gratifications described above. All this sounds perfectly utopian.

1 Galbraith denounces the "specious" reasoning of economists on the issue of "authentic" or "artificial" gratification: "There is no proof that an expensive woman obtains the same satisfaction from yet another gown as does a hungry man from a hamburger. But there is no proof that she does not. Since it cannot be proven that she does not, her desire, it is held, must be accorded equal standing with that of a poor man for meat."[22] "Absurd," says Galbraith. Yet, not at all (and here classical economists are almost correct in their opposition to him: quite simply, they position themselves to establish the equivalency of satiable demands and thereby avoid all the problems). It is nevertheless the case that, from the perspective of the satisfaction of the consumer, there is no basis on which to define what is "artificial" and what is not. The pleasure obtained from a television or a second home is experienced as "real" freedom. No one experiences this as alienation. Only the intellectual can describe it in this way, on the basis of a moralizing idealism, one which at best reveals him as an alienated moralist.

2 On the "economic principle," Galbraith claims: "What is called economic development consists in no small part in devising strategies to overcome the tendency of men to place limits on their objectives as regards income and thus on their efforts."[23] And he cites the example of Filipino workers in California: "The pressure of debt, and the pressure on each to emulate the most extravagant, quickly converted these happy and easygoing people into a modern and reliable work force."[24] In addition in underdeveloped countries the introduction of Western gadgets is the best form of economic

stimulation. This theory, which we could call economic "pressure," or disciplined consumption, and which is connected to forced economic growth, is seductive. It makes it appear that the forced acculturation to the processes of consumption is a *logical development* in the evolution of the industrial system. An evolution which progresses from the discipline of timetables and everyday behavior (to which workers have been subjected since the nineteenth century) to the processes of industrial production. Once having asserted this, we need to explain *why* consumers "take the bait," why they are vulnerable to this strategy. It is much too easy to appeal to "a happy and carefree" disposition, and mechanically to assign responsibility to the system. There is no "natural" inclination to a carefree disposition any more than there is to the work ethic. Galbraith does not take into consideration the logic of social differentiation. Hence he is forced to represent the individual as a completely passive victim of the system. These processes of class and caste distinctions are basic to the social structure, and are fully operational in "democratic" society. In short, what is lacking is a socio-logic of difference, of status, etc., upon which needs are reorganized in accordance to the *objective* social demand of signs and differences. Thus consumption becomes, not a function of "harmonious" individual satisfaction (hence limited according to the ideal rules of "nature"), but rather an infinite social *activity*. We will eventually come back to this issue.

3 "Needs are in reality the fruits of production," says Galbraith, pleased with himself for having put it so well. Expressed in a clear and demystified tone, this thesis, as he understood it, is nothing more than a subtle version of the natural "authenticity" of certain needs and of the bewitching character of the "artificial." What Galbraith means is that without the system of production a large proportion of needs would not exist. He contends that, in the production of specific goods and services, manufacturers simultaneously produce all the powers of suggestion necessary for the products to be accepted. In fact, they "produce" the need which corresponds to the product. There is here a serious psychological lacuna. Needs are strictly specified in advance in relation to *finite objects*. There is only need for *this or that* object. In effect, the psyche of the consumer is merely a display window or a catalog. Certainly once we have adopted this simplistic view of man we cannot avoid the psychological reduction: empirical needs are the specular reflections of empirical objects. At this level, however, the thesis of conditioning is false. We are well aware of how consumers resist such a precise injunction, and of how they play with "needs"

on a keyboard of objects. We know that advertising is not omnipotent and at times produces opposite reactions; and, we know that in reference to a single "need," objects can be substituted for one another. Hence, at the empirical level, a rather complicated strategy having a psychological and sociological nature intersects with the strategy of production.

The truth is not that "needs are the fruits of production," but that *the system of needs* is *the product of the system of production*, which is a quite different matter. By a system of needs we mean to imply that needs are not produced one at a time, in relation to their respective objects. Needs are produced as a *force of consumption*, and as a general potential reserve (*disponibilité globale*) within the larger framework of productive forces. It is in this sense that we can say that the technostructure is extending its empire. The system of production does not "shackle" the system of pleasure (*jouissance*) to its own ends (strictly speaking, this is meaningless). This hypothesis *denies* autonomy to the system of pleasure and substitutes itself in its place by reorganizing everything into a system of productive forces. We can trace this *genealogy of consumption* in the course of the history of the industrial system:

1 The order of production produces the productive machine/force, a technical system that is radically different from traditional tools.
2 It produces the rationalized productive capital/force, a rational system of investment and circulation that is radically different from previous forms of "wealth" and modes of exchange.
3 It produces the wage-labor force, an abstract and systematized productive force that is radically different from concrete labor and traditional "workmanship."
4 In this way it produces needs, the *system* of needs, the productive demand/force as a rationalized, controlled and integrated whole, complementary to the three others in a process of the total control of productive forces and production processes. As a system, needs are also radically different from pleasure and satisfaction. They are produced *as elements of a system* and not *as a relation between an individual and an object*. In the same sense that labor power is no longer connected to, and even denies, the relation of the worker to the product of his labor, so exchange value is no longer related to concrete and personal exchange, nor the commodity form to actual goods, etc.)

This is what Galbraith does not see and along with him all of the "alienists" of consumption, who persist in their attempts to demonstrate that *people's relation to objects, and their relation to themselves is falsified*, mystified, and manipulated, consuming this myth at the same time as the object. Once having stated the universal postulate of the free and conscious subject (in order to make it reemerge at the end of history as a happy end[ing]),[25] they are forced to attribute all the "dysfunctions" they have uncovered to a diabolic power – in this case to the technostructure, armed with advertising, public relations, and motivation research. This is magical thinking if there is such a thing. They do not see that, taken one at a time, needs are *nothing*; that there is only the system of needs; or rather, that needs are nothing but *the most advanced form of the rational systematization of productive forces at the individual level*, one in which "consumption" takes up the *logical* and necessary relay from production.

This can clear up a certain number of unexplained mysteries for our pious "alienists." They deplore, for example, the fact that puritan ethics are not abandoned in periods of affluence, and that an outdated moral and self-denying Malthusianism has not been replaced by a modern ethos of pleasure. Dichter's *Strategy of Desire* is determined to twist and subvert these old mental structures "from below." And it is true: there has not been a revolution in morals; puritan ideology is still in place. In the analysis of leisure, we will see how it permeates what appear to be hedonistic practices. We can affirm that puritan ethics, and what it implies about sublimation, transcendence, and repression (in a word, morality), *haunts* consumption and needs. It is what motivates it from within and that which gives needs and consumption its compulsive and boundless character. And puritan ideology is itself reactivated by the process of consumption; this is what makes consumption the powerful factor of integration and social control we know it to be. Whereas from the perspective of consumption/pleasure, this remains paradoxical and inexplicable. It can all be explained only if we acknowledge that needs and consumption are in fact an *organized extension of productive forces*. This is not surprising since they both emerged from the productivist and puritan ethics which was the dominant morality of the industrial era. The generalized integration of the "private" individual ("needs," feelings, aspirations, drives) as a productive force can only be accompanied by a generalized extension, at this level, of the schemas of repression, of sublimation, of concentration, of systematization, of rationalization (and of "alienation" of course!), which, for centuries, but especially since the nineteenth century, have governed the structuration (*edification*) of the industrial system.

### *The Fluidity of objects and needs*

Until now, the analysis of consumption has been founded on the naive anthropology of *homo economicus*, or at best *homo psychoeconomicus*. It is a theory of needs, of objects (in the fullest sense), and of satisfactions within the ideological extension of classical political economy. This is really not a theory. It is an immense tautology: "I buy this because I need it" is equivalent to the claim that fire burns because of its phlogistic essence. I have shown elsewhere[26] how this empiricist/teleologist position (the individual taken as an end in itself and his or her conscious representations as the logic of events) is identical to the magical speculation of primitive peoples (and of ethnologists) concerning the notion of mana. No theory of consumption is possible at this level: the immediately self-evident, such as an analysis in terms of needs, will never produce anything more than a consumed reflection on consumption.

The rationalist mythology of needs and satisfactions is as naive and "disabled" as is traditional medicine when confronted with psychosomatic or hysterical symptoms. Let us explain: within the field of their objective function objects are not interchangeable, but outside the field of its denotation, an object becomes substitutable in a more or less unlimited fashion. In this field of connotations the object takes on the value of a sign. In this way a washing machine *serves* as equipment and *plays* as an element of comfort, or of prestige, etc. It is the field of play that is specifically the field of consumption. Here all sorts of objects can be substituted for the washing machine as a signifying element. In the logic of signs, as in the logic of symbols, objects are no longer tied to a function or to a *defined* need. This is precisely because objects respond to something different, either to a social logic, or to a logic of desire, where they serve as a fluid and unconscious field of signification.

Relatively speaking, objects and needs are here interchangeable just like the symptoms of hysterical or psychosomatic conversion. They obey the same logic of shifts, transferals, and of apparently arbitrary and infinite convertibility. When an illness is *organic*, there is a necessary relation between the symptom and the organ (in the same way that in its role as equipment there is a necessary relation between the object and its function). In the hysterical or psychosomatic conversion the symptom, like the sign, is (relatively) arbitrary. Migraine, colitis, lumbago, angina, or general fatigue form a chain of somatic signifiers along which the symptom "parades." This is just like the interconnection of object/signs, or of object/symbols, along which parades, not needs (which remain tied to the object's rational goal), but desire, and some other determination, derived from an unconscious social logic.

If we trace a need to a particular locus, that is, if we satisfy it by taking it literally, as it presents itself, as a need for a *specific* object, we would make the same error as if we performed traditional therapy on an organ where the symptom is localized. Once healed it would reappear elsewhere.

The world of objects and of needs would thus be a world of *general hysteria*. Just as the organs and the functions of the body in hysterical conversion become a gigantic paradigm which the symptom replaces and refers to, in consumption objects become a vast paradigm designating another language through which something else speaks. We could add that this evanescence and continual mobility reaches a point where it becomes impossible to determine the specific objectivity of needs, just as it is impossible in hysteria to define the specific objectivity of an illness, for the simple reason that it does not exist. The flight from one signifier to another is no more than the surface reality of a *desire*, which is insatiable because it is founded on a lack. And this desire, which can never be satisfied, signifies itself locally in a succession of objects and needs.

In view of the repeated and naive confusion one finds when faced with the continual forward flight and unlimited renewal of needs – which in fact is irreconcilable with a rationalist theory claiming that a satisfied need produces a state of equilibrium and a resolution of tensions – we can advance the following sociological hypothesis (although it would be interesting and essential to articulate both desire and the social): if we acknowledge that a need is not a need for a particular object as much as it is a "need" for difference (the *desire for social meaning*), only then will we understand that satisfaction can never be *fulfilled*, and consequently that there can never be a *definition* of needs.

The fluidity of desire is supplemented by the fluidity of differential meanings (is there a metaphoric relation between the two?). Between them specific and finite needs only become meaningful as the focus of successive conversions. In their substitutions they signify, yet simultaneously veil, the true domain of signification – that of lack and difference – which overwhelms them from all sides.

### *The denial of pleasure*

The acquisition of objects is *without an object* ("objectless craving,"[27] for David Riesman). Consumer behavior, which appears to be focused and directed at the object and at pleasure, in fact, responds to quite different objectives: the metaphoric or displaced expression of desire, and the production of a code of social values through the use of differentiating signs. That which is determinant is not the function of individual interest within a corpus of objects, but rather the specifically social function of exchange, communication and distribution of values within a corpus of signs.

The truth about consumption is that it is *a function of production* and not a function of pleasure, and therefore, like material production, is not an individual function but one that is *directly and totally* collective. No theoretical analysis is possible without the reversal of the traditional givens: otherwise, no matter how we approach it, we revert to a phenomenology of pleasure.

Consumption is a system which assures the regulation of signs and the integration of the group: it is simultaneously a morality (a system of ideological values) and a system of communication, a structure of exchange. On this basis, and on the fact that this social function and this structural organization by far transcend individuals and are imposed on them according to an unconscious social constraint, we can formulate a theoretical hypothesis which is neither a recital of statistics nor a descriptive metaphysics.

According to this hypothesis, paradoxical though it may appear, consumption is defined as *exclusive of pleasure*. As a social logic, the system of consumption is established on the basis of the denial of pleasure. Pleasure no longer appears as an objective, as a rational end, but as the individual rationalization of a process whose objectives lie elsewhere. Pleasure would define consumption *for itself*, as autonomous and final. But consumption is never thus. Although we experience pleasure for ourselves, when we consume we never do it on our own (the isolated consumer is the carefully maintained illusion of the *ideological* discourse on consumption). Consumers are mutually implicated, despite themselves, in a general system of exchange and in the production of coded values.

In this sense, consumption is a system of meaning, like language, or like the kinship system in primitive societies.

### *A structural analysis?*

In the language of Lévi-Strauss we can say that the social aspect of consumption is not derived from what appears to be of the realm of nature (satisfaction or pleasure), but rather from the essential processes by which it separates itself from nature (what defines it as a code, an institution, or a system of organization). Consumption can be compared with the kinship system which is not determined in the final analysis by consanguinity and filiation, by a natural given, but rather by the arbitrary regulation of classification. In the final analysis, the system of consumption is based on a code of signs (object/signs) and differences, and not on need and pleasure.

Rules of marriage represent the multiple ways of assuring the circulation of women within the social group. It is the replacement of a consanguineous system of relations of biological origin by a sociological system of alliance. Thus, rules of marriage and kinship systems can be seen as a kind of language, that is a set of operations intended to assure, between individuals and groups, a certain kind of communication. The same is true for consumption: a sociological system of signs (the level characteristic of consumption) is substituted for a bio-functional and bio-economic system of commodities and products (the biological level of needs and subsistence). And the essential function of the regulated circulation of objects and commodities is the same as that of women and words. It is designed to assure a certain type of communication.

We will come back to the differences between these various types of "languages:" they are essentially related to the mode of production of the values exchanged and to the type of division of labor associated with it. Commodities obviously are produced, whereas women are not, and they are produced differently to words. Nevertheless, at the level of distribution, commodities and objects, like words and once like women, constitute a global, arbitrary, and coherent system of signs, a *cultural* system which substitutes a social order of values and classifications for a contingent world of needs and pleasures, the natural and biological order.

This is not to claim that there are no needs, or natural utilities, etc. The point is to see that consumption, as a concept specific to contemporary society, is not organized along these lines. For this is true of all societies. What is sociologically significant for us, and what marks our era under the sign of consumption, is precisely the generalized reorganization of this primary level in a system of signs which appears to be a particular mode of transition from nature to culture, perhaps *the* specific mode of our era.

Marketing, purchasing, sales, the acquisition of differentiated commodities and object/signs – all of these presently constitute our language, a code with which our entire society *communicates* and speaks of and to itself. Such is the present day structure of communication: a language (*langue*) in opposition to which individual needs and pleasures are but the *effects of speech* (*parole*).

### *The fun-system, or the constraint of pleasure*[28]

The best evidence that pleasure is not the basis or the objective of consumption is that nowadays pleasure is constrained and institutionalized, not as a right or enjoyment, but as the citizen's *duty*.

The puritans considered themselves, considered their actual being, to be an enterprise to make profit for the greater glory of God. Their "personal" qualities, and their "character," which they spent their lives producing, were capital to be invested wisely, and managed without speculation or waste. Conversely, yet in the same way, man-as-consumer considers the *experience of pleasure an obligation*, like an *enterprise of pleasure and satisfaction*; one is obliged to be happy, to be in love, to be adulating/adulated, seducing/seduced, participating, euphoric, and dynamic. This is the principle of the maximization of existence by the multiplication of contacts and relations, by the intensive use of signs and objects, and by the systematic exploitation of all the possibilities of pleasure.

The consumer, the modern citizen, cannot evade the constraint of happiness and pleasure, which in the new ethics is equivalent to the traditional constraint of labor and production. Modern man spends less and less of life in production, and more and more in the continuous production and creation of personal needs and of personal well-being. He must constantly be ready to actualize all of his potential, all of his capacity for consumption. If he forgets, he will be gently and instantly reminded that he has no right not to be happy. He is therefore not passive: he is engaged, and must be engaged, in continuous activity. Otherwise he runs the risk of being satisfied with what he has and of becoming asocial.

A *universal curiosity* (a concept to be exploited) has as a consequence been reawakened in the areas of cuisine, culture, science, religion, sexuality, etc. "Try Jesus!" says an American slogan. *Everything* must be tried: since man as consumer is haunted by the fear of "missing" something, any kind of pleasure. One never knows if such and such a contact, or experience (Christmas in the Canaries, eel in whisky, the Prado, LSD, love Japanese style) will not elicit a "sensation." It is no longer desire, nor even "taste" nor a specific preference which are at issue, but a generalized curiosity driven by a diffuse obsession, a *fun morality*,[29] whose imperative is enjoyment and the complete exploitation of all the possibilities of being thrilled, experiencing pleasure, and being gratified.

### *Consumption as the rise and control of new productive forces*

Consumption is a sector that only *appears* anomic, since, following the Durkheimian definition, it is not governed by formal rules. It appears to surrender to the individualistic immoderation and contingency of needs. Consumption is not, as one might generally imagine (which is why economic "science" is fundamentally averse to discussing it), an indeterminate marginal sector where an individual, elsewhere constrained by social rules, would finally recover, in the "private" sphere, a margin of freedom and personal play when left on his own. Consumption is a collective and active behavior, a constraint, a morality, and an institution. It is a complete system of values, with all that the term implies concerning group integration and social control.

Consumer society is also the society for the apprenticeship of consumption, for the social indoctrination of consumption. In other words, this is a new and specific mode of *socialization* related to the rise of new productive forces and the monopolistic restructuration of a high output economic system.

Credit here plays a determining role, even though it only has a marginal impact on the spending budget. The idea is exemplary. Presented under the guise of gratification, of a facilitated access to affluence, of a hedonistic mentality, and of "freedom from the old taboos of thrift, etc.," credit is in fact the systematic socioeconomic indoctrination of forced economizing and an economic calculus for generations of consumers who, in a life of subsistence, would have otherwise escaped the manipulation of demands and would have been unexploitable as a force of consumption. Credit is a disciplinary process which extorts savings and regulates demand – just as wage labor was a rational process in the extortion of labor power and in the increase of productivity. The case cited by Galbraith, of the Puerto Ricans who, having been passive and carefree, were transformed into a modern labor force by being motivated to consume, is striking evidence of the tactical value of a regulated, forced, instructed, and stimulated consumption within the modern socioeconomic order. As Marc Alexandre demonstrates, this is achieved through credit (and the discipline and budget constraints it imposes), by the mental indoctrination of the masses to a planned calculus and to "basic" capitalist investment and behavior.[30] The rational and disciplinary ethics, which according to Weber was at the origin of modern capitalist productivism, in a way, has come to inhabit a whole domain which previously escaped it.

We don't realize how much the current indoctrination into systematic and organized consumption is *the equivalent and the extension, in the twentieth century, of the great indoctrination of rural populations into industrial labor, which occurred throughout the nineteenth century*. The same process of rationalization of productive forces, which took place in the nineteenth century in the sector of *production* is accomplished, in the twentieth century, in the sector of *consumption*. Having socialized the masses into a labor force, the industrial system had to go further in order to fulfill itself and to socialize the masses (that is, to control them) into a force of consumption. The small investors or the sporadic consumers of the pre-war era, who were free to consume or not, no longer had a place in the system.

The ideology of consumption would have us believe that we have entered a new era, and that a decisive "human revolution" separates the grievous and heroic Age of Production from the euphoric Age of Consumption, where justice has finally been restored to Man and to his desires. But there is no truth in this. Production and Consumption are *one and the same grand logical process in the expanded reproduction of the productive forces and of their control*. This imperative, which belongs to the system, enters in an inverted form into the mentality, ethics, and everyday ideology, and that is its ultimate cunning: in the form of the liberation of needs, of individual fulfillment, of pleasure, and of affluence, etc. The themes of expenditure, pleasure, and non-calculation ("Buy now, pay later") have replaced the "puritan" themes of thrift, work, and patrimony. But this is only the appearance of a human revolution. In fact , this is the substitution of a new system of values for one that has become (relatively) ineffective: an internal substitution in a system essentially unchanged; a substitution within the guidelines of a more general process. What could have been a new finality, has become, stripped of any real content, an imposed mediation of the system's reproduction.

Consumer needs and satisfactions are productive forces which are now constrained and rationalized like all the others (labor power, etc.) From whichever perspective we chose (briefly) to examine it, consumption appeared quite opposite to the way we experience it as ideology, that is, as a dimension of constraint:

1 Governed by the *constraint of signification*, at the level of the structural analysis.
2 Governed by the *constraint of production* and the cycle of production in the analysis of strategies (socio-economico-political).

Thus, affluence and consumption are not the realization of Utopia, but a new objective state, governed by the same fundamental processes, yet overdetermined by a new morality. This corresponds to a *new* sphere of productive forces in the process of directed reintegration within the *same* expanded system. In this sense there is no objective "progress" (nor *a fortiori* "revolution"): it is simply the same thing and something else. What in fact results from the total *ambiguity* of affluence and consumption, which can be observed at the level of daily events, is that these are always lived as *myth* (the assumption of happiness, beyond history and morality), while they are simultaneously *endured as an objective process of adaptation* to a new type of collective behavior.

On the issue of consumption as a civic restraint, Eisenhower stated in 1958: "In a free society, government best encourages economic growth when it encourages the *efforts* of individuals and private groups. The government will never spend money as profitably as an individual tax-payer would have were he freed from the burden of taxation." He implies that consumption, not being directly imposed, could effectively replace taxation as a social levy. "With nine billion dollars of fiscal deductions," adds *Time* magazine, "the consumer went to two million retail stores in search of prosperity ... They realized that they could increase economic growth by replacing their fans with air conditioners. They *ensured the boom* of 1954 by purchasing five million miniaturized television sets, a million and a half electric knives, etc." In short, they performed their civic duty. "Thrift is un-American," said William H. Whyte.[31]

Regarding needs as productive forces, the equivalent in the heroic epoch to "manual labor as natural resource," an advertisement for movie advertising claims:

> The cinema allows you, thanks to its large screen, to present your product on site: colors, forms, conditioning. Each week 3,500,000 spectators frequent the 2,500 cinemas in our advertising network; 67 per cent of them are between the ages of fifteen and thirty-five. These

are consumers *in the fullness of their needs*, who want and are able to purchase . . .

Exactly, they are individuals in full (labor) force.

### *The logistic function of the individual*

> The individual serves the industrial system not by supplying it with savings and the resulting capital; he serves it by consuming its products. On no other matter, religious, political, or moral, is he so elaborately and skillfully and expensively instructed.[32]

The system needs people as workers (wage labor), and as economizers (taxes, loans, etc.), but increasingly they are needed *as consumers*. Labor productivity is increasingly replaced by the productivity obtained through technological and organizational improvements and increasingly investments are being redirected to the level of the corporation.[33] *But as consumer, the individual has become necessary and practically irreplaceable*. In the process of the extension of the techno-bureaucratic structures we can predict a bright future and the eventual realization of the individualist system of values, whose center of gravity will be displaced from the entrepreneur and the individual investor, figurehead of competitive capitalism, to the individual consumer, subsequently encompassing all individuals.

At the competitive stage, capitalism still sustained itself, for better or for worse, with an individualist system of values bastardized with altruism. The fiction of a social, altruistic morality (inherited from traditional spiritualism) "softened" the antagonisms of social relations. The "moral law" resulted from individual antagonisms, just as "the law of the market" resulted from competitive processes; they preserved the fiction of stability. For a long time we have believed in individual salvation for the community of all Christians, and in individual rights limited only by the rights of others. But this is impossible today. In the same way that "free enterprise" has virtually disappeared giving way to monopolistic, state and bureaucratic control, so the altruist ideology is no longer sufficient to reestablish a minimum of social integration. No other collective ideology has come to replace these values. Only the collective constraint of the state has thwarted the exacerbations of multiple individualisms. From this arises the profound contradiction of civil and political society as "consumer society:" the system is forced to produce more and more consumer individualism, which at the same time it is forced to repress more and more severely. This can only be resolved by an increase in altruistic ideology (which is itself bureaucratized, a "social lubrication" through concern, social reform, the gift, the handout, welfare propaganda and humane relations). But this incorporation of altruism in the system of consumption will not be sufficient to stabilize it.

Consumption is therefore a powerful element in social control (by atomizing individual consumers); yet at the same time it requires the intensification of *bureaucratic control* over the processes of consumption, which is subsequently heralded, with increased intensity, as the *reign of freedom.* We will never escape it.

Traffic and the automobile provide the classic example of this contradiction, where there is the unlimited promotion of individual consumption; the desperate call to collective responsibility and social morality; and increasingly severe restraints. The paradox is the following: one can not simultaneously remind the individual that "the level of consumption is the just measure of social merit" and expect of him or her a different type of social responsibility, since in the act of personal consumption the individual already fully assumes a social responsibility. Once again, consumption is *social labor*. The consumer is conscripted and mobilized as a laborer at this level *as well* (today perhaps just as much as at the level of "production"). All the same, one should not ask the "laborer of consumption" to sacrifice his income (his individual satisfactions) for the collective good. Somewhere in their social subconsciousness, these millions of consumers have a sort of practical intuition of their new status as alienated laborer. The call for public solidarity is immediately perceived as a mystification. Their tenacious resistance here is simply a reflex of *political* defense. The consumer's "fixated egoism" is also the gross subconscious re-cognition of being the new exploited subject of modern times, despite all the non-sense about affluence and well-being. The fact that resistance and "egoism" drives the system to insoluble contradictions, to which it responds by reinforcing constraints, only confirms that consumption is a gigantic *political* field, whose analysis, as well as that of production, is still to be achieved.

The entire discourse on consumption aims to transform the consumer into the Universal Being, the general, ideal, and final incarnation of the human species. It attempts also to make of consumption the premise for "human liberation", to be attained in lieu of, and despite the failures of, social and political liberation. The consumer is in no way a universal being, but rather a social and political being, and a productive force. As such, the consumer revives fundamental *historical* problems: those concerning the ownership of the means of consumption (and no longer the means of production), those regarding economic responsibility (responsibility towards the *content* of production), etc. There is here the potential for a deep crisis and for new contradictions.

## *Ego consumans*

Nowhere, up to the present day, have these contradictions been consciously manifested, except perhaps in a few strikes among American housewives and in the sporadic destruction of commodities (May 1968, the *No Bra Day*[34] when American women publicly burned their bras). "What does the consumer represent in the modern world? Nothing. What could he be? Everything, or almost everything. Because he stands alone next to millions of solitary individuals, he is at the mercy of all other interests."[35] One must add that the individualist ideology is an important element here (even though, as we saw, its contradictions are latent): since it affects the collective domain of social labor, exploitation by *dispossession* (of labor power), it produces (at a certain point) an effective solidarity. And this leads to a (relative) class consciousness. Whereas the directed *acquisition* of objects and commodities is individualizing, atomizing, and dehistoricizing. As a producer, and as a consequence of the division of labor, each laborer presupposes all others: exploitation is for everyone. As a consumer, humans become again solitary, cellular, and at best *gregarious* (for example in a family viewing TV, the crowd at a stadium or in a movie house, etc.) The structures of consumption are simultaneously fluid and enclosed. Can we imagine a coalition of drivers against car registration? Or a collective opposition to television? Even if every one of the million viewers is opposed to television advertising, advertisements will nevertheless be shown. That is because consumption is primarily organized as a discourse to oneself, and has a tendency to play itself out, with its gratifications and deceptions, in this minimal exchange. The object of consumption isolates. The private sphere lacks concrete negativity because it is collapsed on objects which themselves lack negativity. It is structured from outside by the system of production whose strategy is no longer ideological at this level, but still political; whose strategy of desire invests the materiality of our existence with its monotony and distractions. Or, as we saw, the object of consumption creates distinctions as a stratification of statuses: if it no longer isolates, it differentiates; it *collectively assigns* the consumers a place in relation to a code, without so much as giving rise to any *collective solidarity* (but quite the opposite).

In general then consumers, as such, are unconscious and unorganized, just as workers may have been at the beginning of the nineteenth century. As such consumers have been glorified, flattered, and eulogized as "public opinion," that mystical, providential, and *sovereign* reality. Just as The People is glorified by democracy provided they remain as such (that is provided they do not interfere on the political or social scene), the sovereignty of consumers is also recognized ("powerful consumers," according to Katona),[36] provided they do not try to act in this way on the social scene. The People – these are the laborers, provided they are unorganized; the Public, or public opinion – these are the consumers, provided they are content to consume.

## Notes

1 Karl Marx, *Contribution to a Critique of Political Economy* (NY: International Publishers, 1970) p. 87. [Trans.]
2 Baudrillard appears to be quoting from an advertising brochure here, and elsewhere in the text. But at times they sound contrived, and can easily be read as fictional. [Trans.]
3 Parly 2: a planned community (etymologically and geographically) between Paris and Orly (the airport in the southern suburb of Paris). Baudrillard offers his own description in the next section. [Trans.]
4 "Idleness-on-the-Wasteful" would be one anglo-saxon version of "Flaine-la-Prodigue," Baudrillard's parody of suburban communities around Paris. "Flaine": perhaps the conjunction of "flemme" (laziness) and "flâneur" (idle/loafer); "Prodigue" (extravagant/wasteful). [Trans.]
5 See Chapter 2, note 24. [Trans.]
6 Printemps, B. H. V., Dior, Prisunic, Lanvin, Frank et Fils are department stores. [Trans.]
7 Originally in English. [Trans.]
8 Knight: unable to identify the source of this quotation. [Trans.]
9 A French sociologist, author of *Pour une sociologie des aspirations* (Paris: Denoël, 1969). [Trans.]
10 Originally in English. [Trans.]
11 Ibid.
12 Ibid.
13 The translator is unable to identify the source of this quotation.
14 The translator is unable to identify the source of this quotation from Talcott Parsons.
15 Originally in English. [Trans.]
16 A study in *Sélection du Reader's Digest* (A. Piatier: *Structure et*

*perspectives de la consommation européenne*), found that consumption in Europe is the activity of a minority, in contrast to the large middle class in the USA, a consuming elite (the *A*s) which serves as a model for a majority that does not yet have access to this display of luxury (sports car, stereo system, summer home), without which there are no Europeans worthy of the name.

17 For these references see chapter 2, nn. 9 and 11. [Trans.]

18 John Kenneth Galbraith, *The New Industrial State* (New York: Signet, 1967) p. 215. [Trans.]

19 Ibid., p. 222.

20 The translator and editor are unable to locate this wonderful reference from Galbraith.

21 This is the "anticoagulant" effect of advertising (Elgozy).

22 Galbraith, *The New Industrial State*, p. 281. [Trans.]

23 Ibid., p. 279. [Trans.]

24 Ibid., p. 280. [Trans.]

25 'Happy end' was originally in English. [Trans.]

26 "The ideological genesis of needs," in *For a Critique of the Political Economy of the Sign*, trans. Charles Levin (St Louis: Telos Press, 1981).

27 Originally in English. [Trans.]

28 'Fun-system' was originally in English. [Trans.]

29 Originally in English. [Trans.]

30 Marc Alexandre, "Sur la société de consommation," *La Nef*, 37.

31 Originally in English. The translator is unable to identify the source of this quotation.

32 *The New Industrial State*, p. 49. [Trans.]

33 Cf. Paul Fabra's article in *Le Monde*, June 26, 1969, "Les superbenefices et la monopolization de l'epargne par les grandes entreprises."

34 Originally in English. [Trans.]

35 *Le Cooperateur*, 1965.

36 Originally in English from George Katona, *The Mass Consumption Society* (New York: McGraw-Hill, 1964). The translator is unable to identify the page of this citation.

OSGOODE HALL LAW JOURNAL

Vol. 13 No. 3 December 1975

# WINNERS AND LOSERS IN THE MODERN REGULATORY SYSTEM MUST THE CONSUMER ALWAYS LOSE?

By MICHAEL J. TREBILCOCK*

## A. THE POLITICS OF CONSUMERISM

Is modern consumerism simply a fad — just another passing protest movement of the sixties — or is it a serious social movement here to stay? A Canadian senator once claimed that consumerism is simply an outlet for the energies of frustrated women unable to keep their husbands under control.[1] An American ad man recently diagnosed it as "a contagious inflammation of the consumer interest portion of the brain often resulting from political ambition or desire to derive favor from groups of consumers through personal publicity. Symptoms include a strong tendency to invent issues where no real issues exist. If not treated severe cases may lead to demagoguery."[2] These views do not portend a healthy future for the consumer movement; once the dilettantes and demagogues have found new diversions, the cause will presumably wither unattended on the vine.

A somewhat more positive definition of consumerism might be that it is a movement which, in an age of bigness and bewildering technological

* Professor, University of Toronto, Faculty of Law; National Vice-President of the Consumers Association of Canada, 1974-75; Chairman of C.A.C.'s Advocacy Committee, 1973-75. This article was presented as a paper to the annual meeting of the Canadian Institute of Public Administration in Ottawa in September, 1975.

[1] Quoted in J. Ziegel, *The Future of Canadian Consumerism* (1973), 51 Can. B. R. 191 at 192.

[2] Quoted in J. Bishop and H. Hubbard, *Let the Seller Beware* (Washington: National Press, 1969) at 10, 11.

complexity and change, demands for consumers the right to influence significantly economic behaviour in the consumer marketplace — the right of consumers to be sovereign in a marketplace that exists, so classical free-market theory teaches us, only to serve their needs. So defined, consumerism means a share of political power and it implies the emergence of a political movement. For no movement that seeks to change the way things are done can succeed unless ultimately it can bring effective influence to bear on the political process.

Unfortunately for most politicians in this pluralistic age of interest group liberalism, decision-making means little more than harmonizing as far as possible the conflicting claims of competing interest groups. As Charles Reich puts it, in the context of regulatory agencies:

> As the agencies have sought a meaning for the public interest they have come to this: the public interest is served by agency policies which harmonize as many as possible of the competing interests present in a given situation . . . . Thus the agencies have evolved a meaning for their charters which makes them both philosopher-kings searching for the good and practical politicians trying to please a multi-voiced rabble.[3]

In a heavily regulated society, the doctrine of pluralism envisages competition amongst groups as a self-corrective mechanism analogous to Adam Smith's "invisible hand" in an unregulated marketplace.[4] Unless consumers as an interest group can find mechanisms for counting themselves in on this process of political decision-making by competition amongst groups,[5] they are likely to have minimal impact on the political process or its regulatory arms. However, some formidable obstacles stand in the way of consumerism sustaining itself as, or developing itself into, a major political force.

### 1. *Diffusion of the Consumer Interest*

Consumer concerns are diffused across the 50,000 or so products and services that each of us typically consumes in our life-time. An individual consumer's interest in any one product or service will usually be so small that it will not be worth his while registering his dissatisfaction with the item to business, government, or a government's regulatory agencies. At the same time, business interests concerned with the manufacturing or merchandising of that product have a sufficiently concentrated stake in any prospective regulation of it to make their views known very forcefully to government.

Professor Milton Friedman, a leading free-market economist, gives a homely but pointed example of the way the regulatory process acquires a pro-industry bias. He takes the case of the ever-escalating occupational licensing standards set by U.S. barber licensing bodies. The effect of the increasing rigour of entrance standards, as well as the frequent direct setting of minimum

---

[3] *The Law of the Planned Society* (1966), 75 Yale L. J. 1227 at 1234; cf. R. V. Presthus, *Elite Accommodation in Canadian Politics* (London: Cambridge Univ. Press, 1973) at 348-49.

[4] See T. Lowi, *The End of Liberalism* (New York: Norton, 1969) at 71.

[5] The important question of whether this is a defensible form of planning, with or without additional interest group inputs, will be considered later in this article.

charges, is, of course, to increase the costs to all consumers. Friedman explains:

> The declaration by a large number of different state legislatures that barbers must be approved by a committee of other barbers is hardly persuasive evidence that there is in fact a public interest in having such legislation. Surely the explanation is different; it is that a producer group tends to be more concentrated politically than a consumer group. This is an obvious point often made and yet one whose importance cannot be overstressed. Each of us is a producer and also a consumer. However, we are much more specialized and devote a much larger fraction of our attention to our activity as a producer than as a consumer. We consume literally thousands if not millions of items. The result is that people in the same trade, like barbers or physicians, all have an intense interest in the specific problems of this trade and are willing to devote considerable energy to doing something about them. On the other hand, those of us who use barbers at all, get barbered infrequently and spend only a minor fraction of our income in barber shops. Our interest is casual. Hardly any of us are [*sic*] willing to devote much time going to the legislature in order to testify against the iniquity of restricting the practice of barbering. The same point holds for tariffs. The groups that think they have a special interest in particular tariffs are concentrated groups to whom the issue makes a great deal of difference. The public interest is widely dispersed. In consequence, in the absence of any general arrangements to offset the pressure of special interests, producer groups will invariably have a much stronger influence on legislative action and the powers that be than will the diverse, widely spread consumer interest.[6]

Professor Anthony Downs, in his well-known book *An Economic Theory of Democracy*,[7] provides a powerful analytic rationale for the widely-held "capture" theory of regulatory agencies, and indeed the political process at large, by relating the concept of information costs to the intensity of the interest that a group has in a particular legislative or regulatory issue. It is worth quoting him at some length:

> Clearly, the cost of acquiring information and communicating opinions to government determines the structure of political influence. Only those who can afford to bear this cost are in a position to be influential.
>
> A striking example of this fact is the failure of consumers-at-large to exercise any cogent influence over government decisions affecting them. For instance, legislators are notorious for writing tariff laws which favor a few producers in each field at the expense of thousands of consumers. On the basis of votes alone, this practice is hardly compatible with our central hypothesis about government behaviour. But once we introduce the cost of information, the explanation springs full-armed from our theory. Each producer can afford to bring great influence to bear upon that section of the tariff law affecting his product. Conversely, few consumers can bring any influence to bear upon any parts of the law, since each consumer's interests are spread over so many products. In fact, most consumers cannot even afford to find out whether tariffs are raising the price they pay for any given product. Yet without such knowledge they cannot have policy preferences for the government to pay attention to.
>
> Under these conditions, government is bound to be more attentive to producers than consumers when it creates policy. This is true even though (1) government formulates policy so as to maximize votes and (2) more voting consumers are affected by any given policy than voting producers. As a result, such devices as tripartite industrial control boards with representatives from labor, management and consumers are doomed to failure. The consumer representative never has effective forces behind him comparable to those of labor and management. Hence

[6] *Capitalism and Freedom* (Chicago: Univ. of Chic. Press, 1962) at 143.

[7] (New York: Harper and Row, 1957).

these boards practically always seize any opportunities for labor and management jointly to exploit consumers. Even giant labor unions acting for their members' interests as consumers have to spread their influence across too many products to be truly effective as counterweights to producers in each field. Economically speaking, government policy in a democracy almost always exhibits an anti-consumer, pro-producer bias. And this bias in our model exists not because the various agents concerned are irrational, but because they behave rationally. This fact has tremendous implications for economic predictions in almost every field . . .[8]

Illustrations of Downs' analysis are readily found in Canada. On simple, relatively unimportant, issues such as abnormal bacteria counts in hamburger — "hockey helmet law" as a colleague calls it — the media are easily able to disseminate the facts, generate public concern, "widen the scope of the conflict",[9] and provoke a governmental response. But on more complex, and infinitely more important, issues, such as tax reform, competition, food, energy or housing policy, the information and re-communication costs for low-intensity groups, like consumers, are too high for them to engage in the interest group "bargaining" that surrounds each issue.[10]

A particularly striking feature of the views of those who hold that legislative and regulatory decision-making processes are, *in the nature of things,* skewed to reflect a pro-producer, anti-consumer bias, is that they come from all points on the political spectrum from Milton Friedman to Charles Reich, although the prescriptions for the disease vary radically, from massive deregulation[11] to much greater central planning.[12]

### 2. *The Fragmentation of the Consumer Interest*

Unlike the position generally with highly concentrated producer interests, the consumer interest is not homogeneous. Most consumers are also producers, and as producers we will often see things differently from the way we see them

---

[8] *Id.* at 255, 256.

[9] For a discussion of the importance of this element in the process of legislative change, see M. Nadel, *The Politics of Consumer Protection* (Indianapolis: Bobbs-Merrill, 1971), Chap. 5, and at 243 *et seq.*

[10] The systematic dismemberment of the Carter Commission's proposal for tax reform in Canada is instructive. Prime Minister Trudeau has been unusually frank in acknowledging the pressures that overwhelmed the proposals: "... I concede ... that it's likely we heard more from the vested interests than we did from the little taxpayer who didn't have . . . the high-paid lawyers to speak for him . . . I suppose in a participatory democracy there will always be some whose voice is louder than others . . .". (CTV, Dec. 28, 1971; cited in David Lewis, *Louder Voices: The Corporate Welfare Bums* (Toronto: Lewis & Samuel, 1972) at iv.) For recent general studies of interest groups in Canada, see Presthus, *supra*, note 3, and *Elites in the Policy Process* (London: Cambridge Univ. Press, 1974); A. P. Pross, ed., *Pressure Group Behaviour in Canadian Politics* (Scarborough: McGraw-Hill Ryerson, 1975).

[11] Apart from the citations already given, see also *e.g.* G. Stigler, *The Theory of Economic Regulation* (1971), 2 Bell J. Econ. and Mgmt. Sci. 3; R. Winter, in the M. Green, R. Nader, R. Winter debates on *Economic Regulation v. Competition* (1973), 82 Yale L. J. 871-919; R. Posner, *Economic Analysis of Law* (Boston: Little, Brown, 1972) at 329 *et seq.*; Engman, Chairman, U.S. Federal Trade Commission, Speech to the Fall Conference of the Financial Analysists Federation, Detroit, Oct. 7, 1974.

[12] See *e.g.* H. Kariel, *The Decline of American Pluralism* (Stanford: Stanford Univ. Press, 1961); Lowi, *supra*, note 4.

as consumers. If we come from an oil-producing province, we see things differently from consumers from an oil-importing province. If we work on an automobile production line, we may see questions of public transit, pollution and safety standards, and lower tariffs on imported cars differently from other consumers.[13] As environmentalists, we may favour underground wires but as consumers we may not be prepared to pay the cost. A higher-income consumer may be prepared to pay $500 for a safer, cleaner car but a lower-income consumer may not be able to afford the "luxury" of more safety and less pollution. Even in the case of inflation, role confusion causes problems for consumers. Whatever the relative contributions of "cost-push" or "demand pull" to the fact of inflation, consumers in demanding action against inflation in the first case are fighting their own expectations as wage-earners and in the second case their own expectations as consumers.

There is also a range of ideological issues pertaining ultimately to questions of life-style, such as the role and regulation of advertising, rules governing the availability of credit and product proliferation, and the relationship between expenditures in the private and public sectors about which wide consensus is unlikely to be forthcoming. The non-materialist ethic upon which the writings of many critics of the modern consumer marketplace, such as Galbraith and Packard, are premised is reflected in Packard's dedication to his book, *The Waste-Makers*:[14] "To my mother and father who have never confused the possession of goods with the good life", and his idolizing, in the same book, of the life-style of an old woman in a lonely New England coastal cottage, without worldly possessions, who spends her time making greeting cards out of sea-weed.[15] It is not clear that most consumers share these life-style ambitions, or that if they do they would be prepared to see them imposed on everyone by state fiat, which of course, would call into question the very nature of our existing social and economic order.

On yet another level, controversies over appropriate government policies toward the exploitation and allocation of finite resources carry the potential for deep divisions within consumer ranks over issues of distributive justice. Proponents of the "limits to growth" philosophy[16] take the view that the expansion of the present level of industrial activity, particularly to sustain burgeoning populations in under-developed nations, will soon exhaust our depletable resources. Only a modern-day *potlatch,* a new social ascetism, can stave off disaster. As Heilbroner points out,[17] in a "steady-state" economy, the only way one social class can improve its material position is at the expense of another social class, in contrast to the pattern of the recent past where all

---

[13] As evidenced by the recent request by the leadership of the United Auto Workers Union for a moratorium on cost-increasing pollution and safety standards for automobiles until the automobile market returns to buoyancy.

[14] (New York: Pocket Books, 1963).

[15] See generally, M. Trebilcock, *Consumer Protection in the Affluent Society* (1970), 16 McGill L. J. 263.

[16] See *e.g.* D. Meadows *et. al., The Limits to Growth* (New York: Signet, 1972); R. Heilbroner, *An Inquiry into the Human Prospect* (New York: Norton, 1974).

[17] *Id.*

social classes have tended to become more affluent by continued economic growth, while largely retaining their positions relative to one another. If increased affluence for all classes ceases to be a realistic social goal, Heilbroner predicts greatly exacerbated class divisions and tensions as the focus of public debate shifts from economic efficiency to economic equity.

The critics of the "limits to growth" thesis[18] rightly point out that these forecasts of doom largely over-look the function of price as a rationer of scarce resources. As resources become more scarce and thus more valuable in the future, their future value is discounted back to appropriately higher present values which will be sufficiently high to ensure that resources are not prematurely utilized. Higher present prices will also provide increased incentives to develop alternative technology and resources. This analysis, however, at best ensures that we may never run out of scarce resources or appropriate substitutes. But it leaves unresolved the question of economic equity, both as regards economically disadvantaged social classes domestically, and economically disadvantaged nations internationally, who simply will be squeezed out of a rationing game governed by price. While ends of economic efficiency may be served by allowing resources to be bid away to their highest-value use, consumers or consuming nations who cannot bid at all are unlikely to find efficiency an acceptable surrogate for equity. Thus, if it is in fact the case that the era in North America of ever-increasing affluence for everybody is over, consumers may find it increasingly difficult to cohere as a single interest group, marching to a single drum beat, when the question of non-market distribution of economic output is required to be urgently addressed.

All of these considerations bear on the fragmentation of the consumer interest and increase the difficulty of achieving a substantial, on-going coalition of consumer support around basic consumer issues. As organized consumer lobbies seek, on the one hand, to agree on a set of collective goals, and, on the other hand, to maximize numerical membership, like major political parties they will tend to drift to some fuzzy, middle-of-the-road position on the spectrum of consumers' value preferences, which will tend to confine them to taking relatively non-controversial positions on issues on an *ad hoc* basis, and eschewing any radical, and potentially divisive, critique of fundamental dysfunctions in the system.[19]

### 3. *The "Free Rider" Problem*

Even if a group of concerned consumers concert their efforts in order to promote their collective interests, the movement will never be as strong as the number of its potential beneficiaries would imply it should, because a number of potential contributors of money, time and expertise either need, or are able, to take a "free ride" at the expense of existing members.

---

[18] See *e.g.* Solow, *Notes on 'Doomsday Models'* (1972), 69 Proc. Nat. Acad. Sci. at 3832-33; M. Roberts, "The Limits of the Limits to Growth", in E. W. Erickson and L. Woverman, eds., *The Energy Question* (Toronto: Univ. of Toronto Press, 1972) at 351 *et seq.*

[19] For an analysis of the analogous behaviour of major political parties, see Downs, *supra*, note 7.

In a penetrating economic analysis of the nature of different kinds of interest groups, Olson draws an analogy between a member of a "latent" interest group and a seller in a perfectly competitive market:

> Some critics may argue that the rational person will, indeed, support a large organization, like a lobbying organization, that works in his interest, because he knows that if he does not, others will not do so either, and then the organization will fail, and he will be without the benefit that the organization could have provided. This argument shows the need for the analogy with the perfectly competitive market. For it would be quite as reasonable to argue that prices will never fall below the levels a monopoly would have charged in a perfectly competitive market, because if one firm increased its output, other firms would also, and the price would fall; but each firm could foresee this, so it would not start a chain of price-destroying increases in output. In fact, it does not work out this way in a competitive market; nor in a large organization. When the number of firms involved is large, no one will notice the effect on price if one firm increases its output, and so no one will change his plans because of it. Similarly, in a large organization the loss of one dues payer will not noticeably increase the burden for any other one dues payer, and so a rational person would not believe that if he were to withdraw from an organization he would drive others to do so.[20]

Olson points out that the nation state, as the extreme example of a large, latent group, cannot survive on voluntary dues or payments but must resort to coercive taxes.[21] His central thesis is that unless the number of individuals in a group is quite small, or unless there is some other special device or incentive to make individuals act in their common interest, rational, self-interested individuals will not act to achieve their common or group interests. Olson suggests that, in the absence of coercion, the explanation for membership in existing large pressure group organizations lies not primarily in the collective goods these organizations provide to their members but rather in the non-collective goods they provide to members. The pursuit of collective goods, *i.e.* common or group interests, is merely a by-product of the provision of non-collective goods.

Applying this analysis to consumer organizations in North America, it is clear as a matter of both theory and observation that the reason most people have become members of the Consumers Union in the United States or the Consumers Association of Canada (C.A.C.) in Canada is the provision of non-collective rather than collective goods. The associations' magazines, containing product tests etc., are of sufficient value, presumably, to individual members in each case to justify the expenditure of a membership fee. To the extent that some of the revenues from memberships are diverted to the pursuit of collective goods, this is strictly a by-product function. That these by-products exist at all, applying Olson's central thesis rigorously, seems inconsistent with rational self-interested behaviour by members, and would seem to imply "sleight-of-hand" cross-subsidization of collective goods at the expense of non-collective goods from membership revenues, which if revealed as such to members might rationally be repudiated.

These considerations largely explain the difference in the size of the membership of consumer groups, such as C.A.C., which offer to members

---

[20] *The Logic of Collective Action* (Cambridge: Harvard Univ. Press, 1971) at 12.

[21] *Id.* at 13, 14.

both non-collective goods and collective goods, and groups such as the Canadian Civil Liberties Association which offer almost exclusively collective goods.[22] The difference in membership in no way provides evidence that Canadians value consumerism as a collective good any more highly than civil libertarianism as a collective good.[23]

Assuming that most members join an organization out of self-interest, each member will have to countenance the fact that collective benefits generated by his and other members' fees will flow to all consumers, whether members or not. He will be making an indirect wealth transfer to non-members with whom he will have to share the returns on his investment in a membership. The returns will be spread so thinly across all consumers that the return to the individual member on his membership dues will not rationally justify his investment.[24] The only possible response to this impasse is to do what, for example, professional associations have done, and legislatively coerce all beneficiaries from association activities to become members so that the cost of the collective benefits will be spread as thinly as the benefits. In the case of consumer organizations the only practical instrument of coercion is the tax system: by the government paying grants to these organizations by subventions out of revenue, all taxpayers in the country are, in effect, compelled to become members of the organization so that all beneficiaries of the collective goods produced by the organization bear a share of the cost of obtaining them. In Canada, C.A.C. receives about $250,000 (about 40% of its budget) each year by way of grant from the federal government. This form of coercion raises important implications for theories of pluralism to which we will return shortly.

Dr. George Stigler concludes, from a recognition of these various political disabilities of consumerism, that *"we can't construct — and I know of no historical example of — a viable continuing broad based consumer political lobby"*.[25] The existing disabilities are impossible to gainsay; is there

---

22 The difference in membership is presently something in the order of 100,000 to 3,000.

23 Certain small groups, with highly concentrated memberships and the prospects of obtaining collective goods of very great value (*e.g.* the imposition of a protective tariff) will find it rational to pursue collective goals (see Olson, *supra*, note 20, chap. 1). Also, the transaction costs of organizing large groups, relative to the collective benefits achievable, are much greater than in the case of certain small groups (see Posner, *supra*, note 11 at 330).

24 However, Stigler has recently pointed out that a free rider's ride is never entirely free, merely cheap, because by not participating in the pursuit of collective goods from which he will benefit, he increases the risk that the collective action will not be undertaken or at least undertaken as effectively, thus reducing the possibility of obtaining the expected "free" gain: *Free Riders and Collective Action* (1974), 5 Bell J. of Econ. and Mgmt. Science 359. Stigler, in the same article, suggests that a partial explanation, at least, of some large, latent interest group organizations may lie in considerations of "asymmetry" of interests. For example, if a group of farmers with special interests were to abstain from membership in a general Farmers Association, there may be a serious risk that their interests would be abandoned altogether by the Association.

25 In G. Stigler and M. Cohen, *Can Regulatory Agencies Protect Consumers?* (Washington: American Enterprise Institute, 1971) at 49 (my italics).

anythng in the contemporary political experience to provide a justification for a more optimistic prognosis? By way of exploring whether Stigler's prognosis can be confounded, it is now proposed to examine the treatment accorded to the consumer interest in a specific class of public decisions, those made by state regulatory agencies. In the final part of this article, we will abstract ourselves from this particular body of experience and venture to generalize from it to some observations about the future role of the consumer interest in public decision-making at large.

## B. THE CONSUMER INTEREST IN THE REGULATORY PROCESS: RECENT POLICY RESPONSES

Three myths surrounding the present nature of public regulation widely persist. The first is that our economy is largely unregulated and is disciplined mainly by competitive forces. In fact, in Canada, there are over one hundred Federal regulatory agencies and in most provinces more than fifty regulatory agencies.[26] This does not include, of course, government Departments directly administering regulatory statutes or subsidy programmes. Agencies and Departments regulate everything from telephone, rail and air-line rates, foreign investment, capital markets, broadcasting licences, product tariffs, agricultural produce prices, food, drug and safety standards to the licensing of various classes of merchants, from insurance agents to door-to-door salesmen. Few areas of our lives are untouched by public regulation.

The second myth is that most regulation involves technical questions of little interest or relevance to the average citizen. Nothing could be further from the truth. While many regulatory decisions may involve initially an analysis of technically complex facts, once these facts have been ascertained, the ultimate decision to be made will often be of an immensely important political and social character, for example, highways versus public transport, energy resources versus the environment, foreign investment versus economic sovereignty.[27]

The third myth is that most major forms of regulation are forced on unwilling producers by hostile non-producer groups. In fact, the contrary is the truth. Most of the extensively regulated industries, at least, prefer being regulated to competing and actively seek and sustain accommodating regulatory regimes. As Stigler remarks,[28] "as a rule, regulation is acquired by the industry and is designed and operated primarily for its benefit."[29] The sheltered life of a regulated protectorate is likely to be more comfortable than life in a vigorously competitive market-place. As Stigler elsewhere remarks:

> Competition, like other therapeutic forms of hardship, is by wide and age-long consent, highly beneficial to society when imposed upon — other people. Every

---

[26] See Inventory of Provincial and Federal Regulatory Agencies prepared by the Canadian Consumer Council, 1971.

[27] Cf. Reich, *supra*, note 3.

[28] *Supra*, note 11.

[29] For a critique of Stigler's thesis, in terms of its ability to explain the emergence of regulation in all its contexts, see R. Posner, *Theories of Economic Regulation* (1974), 5 Bell J. of Econ. and Mgmt. Science 335.

industry that can afford a spokesman has emphasized both its devotion to the general principle, and the over-riding need for reducing competition within its own markets because this is the one area in which competition works poorly.[30]

Regulatory issues have massive impacts on many more interests than those of the regulatees, and the case for these other interests being represented in this form of regulatory decision-making is, on the face of it, undeniable. The consequences of a failure to be represented and heard are stated as follows by a former Canadian Minister of Consumer and Corporate Affairs, the Hon. John Turner (former Minister of Finance):

> I've looked at a lot of regulatory agencies, and the longer I'm around here, the more I believe that every one of these tends, in a period of time, to reflect the interests of the industry it is supposed to be regulating.[31]

The failure of government in the past to recognize that merely setting up regulatory agencies to protect the public interest is not in itself enough is vividly described by Rod Sykes, Mayor of Calgary, in Winnipeg, October 12, 1973:

> In those cases where protest has been organized within the neighbourhood, there is no funding to enable the residents to oppose the experts, the high-priced engineers, and the real estate dealers. The government, in effect, has all the power on its side. It sets up a public hearing format and says, now look, here you are, a fair deal, a public hearing. We're going to hear from both sides and deliver our verdict on the merits. That is exactly what Roman Emperors used to say to Christians when they invited them into the lion's den. One lion, one Christian, and may the best lion win.[32]

The same phenomenon has been the subject of longer and more intense concern in the U.S. As Roger C. Cramton, formerly Chairman of the U.S. Administrative Conference recently stated:

> The cardinal fact . . . is that governmental agencies rarely respond to interests that are not represented in their proceedings. And they are exposed, with rare and somewhat insignificant exceptions, only to the view of those who have a sufficient economic stake in a proceeding or succession of proceedings to warrant the substantial expense of having lawyers and expert witnesses to make a case for them. Non-economic interests or those economic interests that are diffuse in character tend to be inadequately represented . . . .[33]

---

[30] Stigler & Cohen, *supra*, note 25 at 9.

[31] Cited by Sack & Sack, *Citizen's Advocates and Poverty Lawyers*, Canadian Forum, May, 1972 at 37. See also the comments of the Hon. Robert Andras, now Minister of Manpower and Immigration, (formerly Minister of Consumer and Corporate Affairs):

> It is commonly observed phenomenon that sooner or later a regulating body tends to identify with the interests of those it is regulating, unless there is strong pressure either internally or externally to resist this tendency.
> (Address to 25th Annual Meeting of C.A.C. 1972.)

[32] Canadian Council on Urban & Regional Research, (1973) 5 Urban Research Bulletin, no. 3 at 3.

[33] *The Why, Where & How of Broadened Public Participation in the Administrative Process* (1972), 60 Georgetown L. J. 525 at 529; see also William O. Douglas, *Go East, Young Man* (New York: Random House, 1974) at 216, 217; see generally M. Bernstein, *Regulating Business By Independent Commission* (Princeton: Princeton Univ. Press, 1955).

The problem of the "empty consumer's chair"[34] in regulatory proceedings has now begun to elicit a variety of government responses, as governments have come to recognize that, as the creators of these agencies, they carry the primary responsibility for ensuring that their functions are effectively discharged.

### 1. *The U.S. Response: An Office of the Consumer Advocate*[35]

Early experiments, particularly during the New Deal of the Thirties when the regulatory ideal was central to programmes for economic reconstruction, tended to involve appointing consumer advisory committees to certain major agencies. Most of these quite quickly melted away as lack of independence, lack of resources, and lack of definition of role reduced them to little more than window-dressing.[36]

However, beginning in 1959 with the introduction of a bill by Senator Estes Kefauver, a new adversarial model for representing the consumer interest in regulatory proceedings began to emerge. Following Senator Kefauver's death in 1963, Congressman Benjamin Rosenthal began refining this model in a series of bills. Today a bi-partisan proposal with wide support has emerged in the form of a statutory, government-funded Consumer Protection Agency to represent the consumer interest before regulatory agencies and government departments exercising regulatory powers. In early debates on this proposal, the central idea itself attracted enormous controversy. Ralph Nader described the Consumer Advocate bills as "the most important consumer legislation ever considered by the U.S. Congress".[37] On the other hand, already entrenched interest groups were less enthusiastic. In a circular to its members in 1971, the Chamber of Commerce said that Rosenthal's bill (H.R. 16) would help "destroy the free enterprise system"[38] (although in earlier Congressional hearings they had described it as a "thoughtful bill"). The Grocery Manufacturers of America described the same bill to its members as "one of the most blatant anti-business bills ever introduced".[39] The National Small Business Association became even more excited. In a Congressional Committee brief, the Association said:

> Programs set forth by the international consumer movement in seeking to substitute a 'co-operative' society for our 'free enterprise' society are easily recognized

---

[34] See Congressman Benjamin S. Rosenthal in *Hearings on S. 1177 and H.R. 10835 Before the Subcommittee on Executive Reorganization and Government Research* of the U.S. Senate Committee on Government Operations, 92d Cong., 1st Sess. (1971).

[35] The details that follow pertaining to the U.S. response are drawn from a paper by the writer, *The Case for an Office of the Consumer Advocate,* prepared for the Canadian Consumer Council in 1972, and reproduced as Exhibit 36 of the *Joint Hearings on S. 707 and S. 160 of the Senate Committee on Government Operations and Committee on Commerce,* 93d Cong. 1st Sess. (March, April, June, 1973), to which all subsequent citations relate.

[36] See P. Campbell, *Consumer Representation in the New Deal* (New York: A.M.S. Press, 1968).

[37] See Trebilcock, *supra,* note 35 at 883.

[38] *Id.* at 871.

[39] *Id.*

> by the legislation pending before this subcommittee today. A campaign to make the business community look as though it operates only in order to steal from the poor has been successful. . . . Much that is being proposed today is based upon experience in countries dominated by the co-operative consumers movement. The blueprint for taking over private enterprise has been prepared. It is now being followed.[40]

As the central idea has won a measure of political acceptance, the focus of recent debates has shifted to the powers that should attach to the new Advocacy Office: for example, which agencies the Consumer Advocate should be entitled to appear before; whether he should be entitled to intervene as a full party in all agency proceedings, or whether his role should be that of *amicus curiae* only; whether he should be entitled to intervene in agency proceedings of a penal nature; what rights of access the Consumer Advocate should have to information held by other agencies and by the businesses regulated by those agencies; whether the Consumer Advocate should be able to participate in, or be able to monitor, informal agency activity, for example, hitherto *ex parte* informal communications, or decisions between regulators and regulatees; and whether the Consumer Advocate should have the usual rights to appeal to the Courts from agency decisions if he did not participate in the initial proceedings. Disputes between the executive and legislative branches on issues of independence, such as mechanisms for hiring and firing the Consumer Advocate, and for insulating him from budgetary pressures have also produced controversy. Finally, the issue of the extent of government funding to be committed to the Office has produced divergent views, with different sponsors' bills making provision for sums ranging from $7 million to $25 million a year.

However, by the time this article appears, it seems almost certain that a *Consumer Protection Agency Act* will have been passed by Congress, subject to a Presidential veto, and an Office of the Consumer Advocate created.[41]

### 2. *The United Kingdom Response: A Departmental National Consumers' Agency*

In September, 1974, the U.K. Secretary of State for Prices and Consumer Protection tabled in the House of Commons a document called *National Consumers' Agency* indicating the intention of the government to set up a government-funded, non-statutory agency, with members appointed by the

---

[40] *Id.*

[41] For the bill passed by the House, see H. R. 1316, 93d Cong. 2d. Sess. (April 4, 1974). For the bill before the Senate, see S. 707, 93d Cong. 2d. Sess. (February 1, 1973). For recent House Hearings, see *Hearings on H.R. 14, H.R. 21 and H.R. Before the House Committee on Government Operations*, 93d Cong. 1st Sess. (September & October, 1973). For recent Senate hearings, see *Joint Hearings on S. 707 and S. 1160 Before the Senate Committee on Government Operations and Committee on Commerce,* 93d Cong. 1st Sess. (March, April, and June, 1973). See also the House Committee on Government Operations Rep. No. 93-962 on H.R. 13163, 93d Cong. 2d Sess. (March 29, 1974); the Senate Committee on Government Operations Rep. No. 93-883 on S. 707, 93d Cong. 2d Sess. (May 28, 1974); the Minority Report of the same Committee (May 29, 1974), and the Senate Committee on Commerce Rep. No. 93-792 on S. 707, 93d Cong. 2d Sess. (April 11, 1974).

Minister, to represent the consumer interest on all consumer issues before all levels and agencies of government. Few further details were provided in the government's announcement but clearly the principal functions of the agency will be of an advocacy character.

3. *The Canadian Response: C.A.C.'s Advocacy Programme*

During the tenure of the Hon. Ron Basford as Minister of Consumer and Corporate Affairs, the Canadian Consumer Council, a citizens' advisory agency to government, was asked in 1971 to commission independent research over a four year period into the status of the consumer interest in proceedings of independent regulatory agencies, decisions by agricultural marketing boards, the conduct of the self-governing professions, and the operations of Crown corporations. The first two stages of this research have been completed and the last two stages are now proceeding under the aegis of the new Consumer Research Council.

In June, 1973, the Hon. Herb Gray, then Minister of Consumer and Corporate Affairs, announced that as an interim experiment the Government was making a special unconditional grant of $100,000 to the Consumers Association of Canada to enable it to intensify and expand its advocacy activities. Of this sum, $35,000 was allocated by C.A.C. to formal advocacy activities before regulatory agencies. Early in 1974, the Federal Government announced that it was extending the experiment a further year with a grant of $116,000, all of this money to be used in regulatory proceedings, appeals therefrom and test cases in the courts. For 1975-76, the grant has been increased to $215,000 to permit more fundamental policy research on the regulated industries to be undertaken. With these grants, C.A.C. has set up an advocacy unit in its Ottawa office, staffed by three lawyers, three secretaries and assisted by outside technical experts and counsel on retainer paid for out of the balance of the grant. Most of the activities of the programme have been directed at the regulatory arena.

While it is not the purpose of this article to explore the finer intricacies of public utility regulation and related regulatory issues, it may be useful to survey quickly the principal initiatives of the programme since it was implemented in September, 1973.

The first regulatory initiative by C.A.C.'s advocacy programme was taken in late 1973 following an application by Ontario Hydro (a Crown corporation) to the National Energy Board (N.E.B.) for a licence to export hydro-electric power to the United States. The particular proposal envisaged the importation of coal from Appalachia in the U.S. for firing coal-burning generators located in Ontario near major metropolitan centres and the exportation of the power so produced back to the U.S. (the U.S. was to get the power, Ontario the pollution). Ontario Hydro estimated that the net gain to Hydro from this proposal was of the order $6 to $8 million annually. C.A.C. and Pollution Probe, an environmental group, jointly intervened in the hearing before the N.E.B., objecting that the estimated net economic worth of the proposal failed to take into account substantial social costs in the form of environmental degradation which witnesses for the intervenors estimated at

$8.5 million per annum, and which Ontario Hydro was, in effect, attempting to disregard by imposing on the public at large. Ontario Hydro submitted no serious evidence on this issue. The N.E.B., in the result, found that these estimates of environmental costs were too speculative and granted the licence application. The decision was later confirmed by the federal Cabinet. C.A.C. and Pollution Probe then sought leave to appeal to the Federal Court of Appeal, asserting that the N.E.B. had failed to follow its own regulations and previous decisions in not requiring Ontario Hydro to carry the burden of satisfying the Board on the environmental impact of its proposal, and asserting further that the Board's submission of its decision to the Cabinet for confirmation before making it public allowed persons to participate in its decision who had not heard the evidence and were not members of the Board. Leave to appeal was refused by the Court.

On the face of it, the outcome of the case represented an unqualified loss for C.A.C. However, in this kind of advocacy, wins and losses are not so easily calculated. For example, both Ontario Hydro and the N.E.B. have subsequently hired social cost analysts to assist in future applications, and in similar cases that have since come before the Board much more rigorous requirements as to environmental impact considerations have been imposed. Moreover, the considerable media publicity that attended the case may have contributed to a heightened public consciousness about social costs — a consciousness needed, for example, to prompt decisions like that of the federal government to set up the Berger Commission to assess the impact of the Mackenzie Valley pipe-line on the Northern environment and native peoples.[42]

Early in 1974, the Bell Canada "B" rate application hearings before the Canadian Transport Commission commenced. The telephone rate increase sought would have given Bell an additional $51.8 million during 1974, had it been granted on January 1 of that year. The hearing lasted 47 days. Bell spent nearly $1 million on its case (all tax deductible and included in its rates). The outcome of the case was disappointing for C.A.C., which devoted a great deal of its time and limited resources to it. All but $4 million of the requested increase was granted. The $4 million reduction did, on the other hand, occur in areas where C.A.C. had placed some emphasis — the proposed across-the-board increases in charges for pay telephones, which were denied in institutions with a predominance of low-income consumers. Other issues which were argued with less success focussed on whether cross-subsidization of business subscribers by residential subscribers was involved; definition of the quality of service to be received for a given tariff; whether the company's huge construction programme really was needed (or might involve an element of rate base padding) and really would benefit consumers (as opposed to other classes of service user); whether Bell could be intelligently regulated when many of its most profitable activities had been spun off to unregulated subsidiaries, such as Northern Electric, enabling Bell to argue, in relation to its regulated activities, perpetual pending financial doom;

---

[42] Order-in-Council, 1974-641, March 21, 1974, pursuant to s. 19(h) of the *Territorial Lands Act,* R.S.C. 1970, c. T-6.

and whether some part of Bell's monopoly could be deregulated and exposed to market forces, for example, the provision of terminal equipment.

Again, however, it is difficult to make a long-term assessment of this kind of intervention by C.A.C. The hearings attracted considerable media publicity. Bell rate cases have long been matters of major public contention in Canada, and perhaps partly in response to a continuing climate of public concern at ever more frequent rate increases and partly, no doubt, as an attempt at rationalization, the federal government, shortly after this case, announced its intention to transfer all telecommunications regulation to the Canadian Radio and Television Commission, one of the most socially responsive federal regulatory agencies.[43]

On June 21, 1974, Air Canada (a Crown corporation), Canadian Pacific Airlines, and five regional air carriers filed simultaneously before the Canadian Transport Commission (C.T.C.) for a 9.5% average across-the-board air passenger fare increase. This followed only five months after a 10% increase in February, compounding to a 20% increase within that period. By simply filing a piece of paper containing the proposed rate increases and waiting thirty days the airlines automatically receive the increases unless the Commission decides to stop the increase. The C.T.C. has never exercised this power. At very short notice, C.A.C. decided to intervene before the C.T.C., asking the Commission for an injunction to hold up the rate increases long enough to allow a full hearing of the case. The C.T.C., after a preliminary hearing on the question of an injunction, decided on Friday, July 12 to grant a full hearing to commence on the following Tuesday. A request for a two-week adjournment by C.A.C. and the Government of Saskatchewan to consider the evidence of the airlines and to brief appropriate expert witnesses was refused, as was a request that the airlines be required to furnish relevant cost information to the intervenors.

On Tuesday, July 16, the Commission, in a preliminary ruling, held that the case would be heard under s. 10 of the *Aeronautics Act*,[44] rather than s. 23 of the *National Transportation Act*,[45] which had the effect of placing on C.A.C. the burden of proving that the proposed rates were not reasonable, rather than the airlines having to prove the converse. With no substantial evidence ready at that point, for C.A.C. the result was a foregone conclusion. The hearing concluded on Friday of the same week (47 days to analyze Bell, 4 days to master the airlines). The Commission intimated that it would reach its decision quickly so that the airlines would not have to wait for their increases (the 30 days had not run out), and the following Monday granted the rate increases in full, at the same time heavily criticizing C.A.C. for what it apparently regarded as a close-to-frivolous intervention.

However, demonstrating the importance of Nadel's "widening the scope of the conflict" theory of consumer effectiveness,[46] C.A.C. was able very

[43] See Bill C-5, October 2, 1974.

[44] R.S.C. 1970, c. A-3.

[45] R.S.C. 1970, c. N-17.

[46] *Supra*, note 9.

effectively to utilize the media during these proceedings, and in reportage and editorials, both the airlines and the Commission received heavy criticism — the airlines for the cumulative magnitude of their fare increases, for the apparent complicity that had occurred before the new rates were filed, and for their arrogance in charging the new rates before the Commission had confirmed them; the Commission because of its passivity toward the airlines, when in an era of runaway inflation each rate increase ought to be meticulously scrutinized and exactingly proved, and because of its patronizing attitude to consumers impertinent enough to disturb the tranquil regulatory waters by asking some pertinent questions. A more concrete result of the case and the publicity attending it is that while the airlines announced at the time of the hearing that they would need to file for further rate increases in the late fall of 1974, they did not deem it expedient to return to the regulatory bar for further public replenishment until May, 1975 — at a saving to consumers of perhaps $10 million a month.

The treatment of C.A.C. by the Commission in a passenger rail rate application further demonstrates the Commission's pro-industry passivity. C.A.C., in a preliminary hearing in April, 1974, asked for a full hearing on the merits on proposed new railway tariffs for Canadian National and Canadian Pacific. Five months later the Commission had still not decided whether to grant such a hearing on the merits. Because of the thirty day rule, the new rates had been in effect during most of the period and even if the Commission had decided that they were not justified, there was no practicable way of reimbursing consumers who, in the meantime, paid the higher tariff. Moreover, by the time of a hearing on the merits, the rate increases might well have been justified, if they had not been five months before, and, as well, the next rate application would be shortly pending. In protest at the Commission's handling of the case, C.A.C. in September withdrew its intervention, thus terminating proceedings, and in an open letter to the Minister of Transportation[47] drew attention to the "shocking" disparity in the way the Commission had handled the airline and rail rate cases.

In January, 1975, leave to appeal new rate increases by the railways was granted to C.A.C. and other consumer groups by the C.T.C. and a full, month's long inquiry ordered into all aspects of the passenger rail mode in Canada. An interim order to hold up the rate increases until the outcome of this inquiry is known was refused, but nevertheless the decision of the C.T.C. to institute, for the first time, a full-scale inquiry represents a substantial potential advance of the consumer interest in this area. A further application by the airlines for another 10% rate increase came before the C.T.C. in May, 1975, which, after an eight day hearing on the merits was granted in full, despite unrefuted evidence that economy-class passengers are massively subsidizing first-class passengers, passengers on western air-routes are subsidizing those on eastern air-routes, and expert evidence that Air Canada is substantially less efficient than Canadian Pacific. The C.T.C. took a week-end to arrive at a verbal decision. C.A.C. and several provincial governments have appealed the decision to the Federal Cabinet.

---

[47] The Hon. Jean Marchand, reported in the *Ottawa Journal*, Sept. 9, 1974.

The Federal Minister of Transport recently declared transportation policy in Canada to be "a mess"[48] and on June 16, 1975 tabled in Parliament a Green Paper proposing major changes to existing policy which would give much more direct authority to the Minister in inter-modal co-ordination and rationalization of transportation resources.

Several other regulatory initiatives should be briefly mentioned. Early in 1974, C.A.C. presented a brief at the National Energy Board hearings on oil export quotas, arguing that industry data on which the N.E.B. had previously relied vastly over-stated realistic oil reserves and asking for a rapid phasing-out of U.S. oil exports with a view to developing long-term self-sufficiency in Canada. C.A.C. presented similar arguments at recent hearings before the N.E.B. on natural gas export quotas. Gratifyingly, perhaps in part as a result of the intervention of C.A.C. and other similar organizations, the N.E.B. and the federal government have now dramatically revised their estimates of oil reserves and the federal government has announced a programme to scale down oil exports.

Several major non-regulatory initiatives by C.A.C.'s advocacy programme provincial regulatory arenas. Interventions have taken place before the Alberta Public Utilities Board in a Calgary Power hydro-electric rate hearing; before the Nova Scotia Public Utilities Commission in a Maritime Telegraph and Telephone rate hearing; before the New Brunswick Public Utilities Commission in a New Brunswick telephone rate hearing; before the British Columbia Energy Commission in a Pacific Northern Gas rate hearing; and in an Ontario Hydro rate hearing before the Ontario Energy Board. In both the latter two cases, substantial concessions were won for the consumer on the issue of cross-subsidization of high-volume industrial users (who had previously been given large volume discounts) by low-income residential users. On the regional advocacy front, several provincial governments are now actively considering funding consumer advocacy programmes.

Several major non-regulatory initiatives by C.A.C.'s advocacy programme have been taken. Late in 1973, in response to the Ontario Government's Green Paper on Consumer Warranties, C.A.C. presented a very detailed brief to the provincial Minister of Consumer and Commercial Relations pointing out that all the new substantive rights in the world would be of no value to the consumer without the introduction of realistic enforcement mechanisms. The brief developed an integrated set of proposals for utilizing arbitration mechanisms, reformed Small Claims Courts, superior courts, and class action procedures, relating these procedural instruments to defined categories of consumer complaints. At the same time C.A.C. commissioned a substantial, independent research paper from Professor Neil Williams of Osgoode Hall Law School on the law relating to consumer class actions in Canada, together with proposals for reform and a Model Consumer Class Actions Act. Now completed, the report has received wide currency within federal and provincial governments across Canada and is under active consideration by several who have reform of their class action rules under review.[49]

[48] *Financial Post*, November 2, 1974, p. T-1.

[49] See N. Williams, *Consumer Class Actions in Canada: Some Proposals for Reform* (1975), 13 O.H.L.J. 1.

In the civil test case area, C.A.C.'s major initiative has been to support with money, staff and outside expertise a $5 million class action commenced by a private law firm on behalf of 5,000 Firenza owners against General Motors claiming loss of resale value resulting from the bad reputation acquired by the cars as a model because of the abnormally high incidence of defects exhibited by an allegedly large number of units. This action will test a number of important substantive points of warranty and products liability law as well as important procedural points pertaining to consumer class actions. Even if the case is ultimately lost, it may well serve to dramatize the shortcomings of the present law and precipitate legislative action. Importantly, the economic case for collective consumer representation mechanisms in a civil context is similar to that for collective representation of the consumer interest in regulatory and legislative contexts: a single supplier may stand to make substantial gains from violation of consumers' civil rights but the damage to individual consumers will often be so thinly spread that collective, not individual, suit is the only rational avenue of redress.

How should we evaluate the aggregate impact of this flurry of specialized advocacy on behalf of the consumer? Have consumerism's political disabilities been effectively denied?

## C. AN INTERIM STOCK-TAKING

### 1. *Short Run Lessons*

(i) In the immediate context, the need for sustained, systematic consumer advocacy before regulatory agencies is unanswerable. Sensitizing regulators to interests other than those of the regulatees is not a short-term exercise and is not a matter that can be allowed to depend on fortuitous, sporadic interventions by the odd concerned citizen or group of citizens. Appropriate institutional forms need to be devised to ensure a consistent consumer presence.

(ii) The essentially political nature of the regulatory process must be recognized by both regulators and legislators. The argument that regulatory agencies should be "independent" of the political process misconceives their function. Because of the immensely important economic and social decisions that agencies make, strong emphasis must be placed by governments in searching out high calibre personnel for appointment to the boards and staff of these agencies. The tendency to retread retired political warriors and reward party bagmen by appointing them to positions on agencies, and the added tendency to appoint personnel with back-grounds, directly or indirectly, related to the regulated industries, on the grounds that they alone possess the requisite expertise, discounts the need to find appointees of high intellectual calibre with a wide range of social sensitivities.

A substantial increase in the quantity and quality of research as opposed to administrative resources available to an agency is needed if agencies are to become less dependent on industry data and analyses. Regulators also have to be educated to understand the fundamental difference between highly concentrated and thinly spread interest groups. In connection with the previous political anlysis of interest groups, regulators must be made to realize that to take the view that consumers should not be concerned about a $52 million telephone rate increase because it only costs them 20 or 30 cents more each a month (although, obviously, it costs them in aggregate \$52m) is subversive of the need ever to take the consumer interest into account in public decision-making. Without that recognition, consumers will systematically be "nickelled" and "dimed" into economic oblivion, dying the death of a thousand near-invisible cuts.

(iii) Low-intensity groups embarking on this form of advocacy need to recognize the importance of advocating their cause not only in relevant regulatory forums but also before the public, by proper utilization of the relatively costless media. By "widening the scope of the conflict", an appropriate climate of public concern in the regulatory outcome can be created which forces the regulators to address the matters about which the public is concerned. This involves advocacy skills which traditional professional training does not provide for public interest advocates. These have to be consciously learned. Also, new strategic criteria for assessing "wins" and "losses" have to be learned as alternatives to the way the traditional practising lawyer makes such an assessment in a case-to-case setting.

(iv) There is a powerful case for establishing a set of minimum procedural standards for guiding the conduct of regulatory proceedings. For example, there should be consistent rules applying to most agencies governing the amount and nature of notice to other parties; the right to a hearing on the merits; who carries the onus of proof; the right to issue interrogatories to, and cross-examine, parties and obtain relevant information from them; the right to standing both before an agency and before the courts on an appeal from an agency's decision; and the right of non-business intervenors to a free transcript. Also, agencies should be given a discretion at the outset of a hearing to award the costs of an intervention, out of the projected rate increase, or public funds in non-rate cases, to serious low-intensity, non-subsidized intervenors. This will help keep the process as open as possible. Either an omnibus Act, similar in concept to the Ontario *Statutory Powers Procedures Act*[50] or the U.S. *Administrative Procedure Act*[51] but emphasizing ease of access as much as due process, or at least amendment of individual regulatory statutes with a view to the same end, is badly needed.[52]

In addition, the much larger question of the right of public access to government information, whether within regulatory agencies or elsewhere within government urgently calls for a response. The continuing refusal of the Foreign Investment Review Agency, under the *Foreign Investment Review Act*,[53] to give more than derisory reasons for its decisions is a contemporary example of this need.

With government expenditures now comprising 40% of Canada's G.N.P., increasingly consumers are consuming, and paying for, public rather than private goods. Government has been very willing to impose packaging, label-

[50] S.O. 1971, c. 47.

[51] 5 U.S.C. Para. 551.

[52] See generally, Cramton, *supra*, note 33; S. Lazarus and J. Olek *The Regulators and the People* (1971), 57 Virginia L. Rev. 1069; G. Gellhorn, *Public Participation in Administrative Proceedings* (1971), 81 Yale L.J. 359.

[53] S.C. 1973-74, c. 46.

ling and other informational requirements on the private sector but has been much more reticent in imposing similar requirements on itself so that the public can more efficiently evaluate the worth of government programmes. Legislation similar to the U.S. *Freedom of Information Act*[54] should be developed and enacted in each legislative jurisdiction as a matter of the highest priority.[55] If these matters are attended to, the attaching of sweeping special powers to a Consumer Advocacy programme, as envisaged in the U.S. proposals, becomes less necessary and smacks of a special status for one interest group, which is hard to justify. Consistent with the previous political analysis, most of the foregoing suggestions involve ways of reducing information and participation costs (*i.e.* opportunity costs) to the public.

The teaching of Administrative Law in the law schools also needs to adjust to the real dynamics, and problems, of the regulatory process. Judicial review and the prerogative writs — favourite pre-occupations of administrative lawyers — are mostly irrelevant to the issues raised by the activities of major regulatory agencies today.

(v) It is important from the point of view of political legitimacy that any consumer advocacy programme, even though state subsidized, be under citizen control so that broad priorities and positions reflect the views of those on whose behalf they are presented. Without this, such a programme is likely to degenerate into a highly paternalistic, elitist, personal power play, in which an oblivious constituency is illegitimately co-opted to provided the professional advocates with the appearance of a populist platform. The absence of this safeguard appears to be a major weakness in the U.S. proposals. The sentiments expressed by Peter Newman, in an editorial in *Macleans* magazine of April, 1974, need to be nurtured:

> Many of the really important decisions that will fundamentally affect and transform our future are being made not by parliament but by regulatory agencies . . . . If [they] are to take the public interest seriously into account, [they] must provide a mechanism for hearing directly from the people. That will require the funding of third party interventions which represent no vested interests. . . . .
> Politicians and particularly bureaucrats get feeling edgy and threatened whenever they're faced by real people with live opinions. They shouldn't be. They are being threatened only with enlightenment.

2. *Long-run Problems*

While we have been focussing our attention on C.A.C.'s experience in the regulatory arena, the long-run issues raised by it are not confined to the regulatory arena but relate to the political process at large, and are not restricted to the consumer movement but relate to the role of any large, latent, interest group in the political process. Some serious long-run problems are exemplified by C.A.C.'s experience in the regulatory arena:

(i) Being funded by the party in power by executive grant, C.A.C.'s

---

[54] 5 U.S.C. para. 552.

[55] For rudimentary discussions of the U.S. *Administrative Procedure Act* and *Freedom of Information Act*, see B. Schwartz and H. W. R. Wade, *Legal Control of Government* (Oxford: Clarendon Press, 1972) at 108ff, 77ff 329ff, and 339ff. For a more detailed discussion of these two Acts, see generally K. C. Davis, *Administrative Law Text* (3rd ed. St. Paul: West Pub. Co., 1972).

advocacy programme faces the danger of compromising its independence through concern over funding continuity. This has not proved to be a problem to date, but as the programme becomes more effective, as government departments find their regulatory policies called into public question, and as other, entrenched, interest groups begin to find life less comfortable than formerly, it is reasonable to assume that this danger will not always be hypothetical. This problem would not seem insuperable and would seem to require a legislative framework for the programme that carries insulating elements designed to ensure its independence from party politics in matters of priorities, policies, personnel and budget. At least, then, changes would be effected through parliamentary, and thus public, debate.

(ii) The question of the constituency for whom consumer advocates speak poses more fundamental problems. Just as disproportionately few citizens will find it worthwhile to join a consumer organization offering mostly collective goods, so also will most of those who do join find that it is unlikely to be worthwhile to participate extensively in collective goods decision-making. Thus, in C.A.C., only a handful of members find it worth the effort even to vote for membership of the association's small Board of Directors, let alone involve themselves further in the formulation of the association's policies. This might have been predicted from Olson's analysis and is confirmed by Kariel,[56] who stresses the essentially oligarchical character of large, latent, interest groups.

Compounding this factor, in the case of C.A.C.'s advocacy programme, is the fact that every taxpaying citizen in the country has, in effect, been coerced into membership of the association, with all the massive role conflicts that this entails. Was C.A.C. speaking for the President of Bell Telephone and the Presidents and shareholders of the airlines and railways (all contributors to its programme) in its recent interventions? Who was it in fact speaking for, and with what mandate? Where all members of all interest groups are coerced into becoming members of one oligarchically controlled interest group, theories of pluralism and interest group liberalism start to look a little shaky.[57]

---

[56] *Supra*, note 12, chap. 14.

[57] The problem is, in fact, much more pervasive than this. Business lobby groups may deduct their lobbying expenses from income for tax purposes and thus, in effect, transfer some of the cost of their lobbying activities to the general body of taxpayers, who are not voluntarily part of their constituency. The financial figures involved in this form of coercion dwarf the government's grant to C.A.C. but collectively call into question the rationality of the whole theory of interest group pluralism when groups can no longer be clearly identified or delineated. As a matter of interest, should not every citizen who expends time and money in pursuing any collective good be able to claim the expenses as a tax deduction, if business can? Alternatively, should nobody be able to claim them? (cf. D. Bond, "Consumerism and Consumer Protection," in L. Smith, ed., *Issues in Canadian Economics* (Toronto: McGraw-Hill Ryerson, 1974) at 98). On a similar point, should not every consumer with a justified individual complaint against business be able to recover "aggravation" damage (transaction and opportunity costs) in pursuing the complaint to equalize business's ability to treat such costs on its side as costs of doing business? (cf. *Jarvis* v. *Swan Tours,* [1973] 1 All E.R. 71 (C.A.).)

For an argument favouring coerced support of collective goods decision-making to solve the free-rider problem, see J. Rawls, *A Theory of Justice* (Cambridge: Belknap Press, 1971) at 267.

(iii) Even if the constituency issue can somehow be resolved, pluralist concepts of interest group liberalism themselves are coming under increasing question as operational philosophies for intelligent government of modern mixed economies. Critics of pluralist philosophies point out that the open-ended delegations of power by legislatures to regulatory agencies which have become typical are antithetical to rational planning of societal priorities and policies. Lowi asserts bluntly: "Interest group liberalism renders government impotent. Liberal governments cannot plan".[58] Substituted both for the allocative function of a competitive marketplace and that of central planning is interest group bargaining through an almost infinite number of largely autonomous regulatory agencies under no compulsion to act in concert in furtherance of more general collective policy goals. Thus, *participation, organization, structure* and *process* become ends in themselves. Let students, women, workers, the poor, ethnic groups, consumers, etc. *organize,* and all problems (if any are agreed upon) will go away. The rationality and over-all coherence of substantive outputs become subordinate to these new means-ends.

A further objection sometimes urged against a pluralist approach is that it is impossible to ensure participation by all affected interest groups, present and future, in public decision-making processes affecting them. As Charles Reich writes:

> The very concept of balancing is in one sense a contradiction of the concept of planning. Fashioning values and goals out of existing interests prevents any really long-range policy-making or planning from ever being done. It equates policy-making with satisfying the majority or the most powerful interest, although the country might benefit more from policies which favour weaker or minority interests, or interests not yet in existence. It tends to place emphasis on those interests which have a commercial or pecuniary value as against intangible interests such as scenery or recreation. The most fundamental infirmity of the present concept of the public interest as a guide for planning is that it defeats planning by responding only to immediate pressures.[59]

To bring all affected, extant groups into the political process would involve massive state support.[60] This might create in turn several new problems, albeit of a lesser kind, such as the emergence of groups looking only for new, paid occupations (a new kind of unemployment insurance), and the further paralysis of regulatory proceedings as participants multiply. In the case of future interest groups (for example, the interest of people as yet unborn in present decisions affecting their environment), it is difficult to see any solution.

In addition to these pragmatic problems, there is the more fundamental question of the ideological stake which supporters of the doctrine of pluralism (particularly those who gain substantially from it) have in perpetuating the

---

[58] *Supra,* note 4 at 288; see also Kariel, *supra,* note 12; Presthus, *supra,* note 3 at 348.

[59] *Supra,* note 3 at 1239.

[60] The conscious creation by the State of necessary new countervailing power groups is explicitly urged by a number of commentators: see *e.g.* J. K. Galbraith, *American Capitalism: The Concept of Countervailing Power* (Boston: Houghton, Mifflin, 1956), chap. X; Kariel, *supra,* note 12 at 272.

pluralist philosophy and not admitting or encouraging groups who will expose the philosophy to fundamental challenge. As Wolff writes:

> Pluralism is not explicitly a philosophy of privilege or injustice — it is a philosophy of equality and justice whose *concrete application* supports inequality by ignoring the existence of certain legitimate social groups. This ideological function of pluralism helps to explain one of the peculiarities of American politics. There is a very sharp distinction in the public domain between legitimate interests and those which are absolutely beyond the pale. If a group or interest is within the framework of acceptability, then it can be sure of winning some measure of what it seeks, for the process of national politics is distributive and compromising. On the other hand, if an interest falls *outside* the circle of the acceptable, it receives no attention whatsoever and its proponents are treated as crackpots, extremists, or foreign agents.[61]

In other words, "plural" has a tendency to become strictly limited. The implication of this restricted interpretation of pluralism for citizens' advocacy programmes is that apart from problems of internal group dynamics which tend in the same direction, continued state support of such programmes over the long-term appears likely to be contingent on broad acceptance by the groups concerned of the parameters of the regulatory *status quo*. Funding for established groups is also likely to be used as an excuse for not supporting other groups who wish to challenge political and regulatory policies in very fundamental or radical ways. Public participation in the regulatory process is likely to be seen as lending new legitimacy to, and thus re-inforcing and perpetuating, what may be inherently illegitimate or irrational processes. Strategically, in terms of an interest group's public posture, it may be very difficult simultaneously to opt in and opt out. The danger of co-optation by the *status quo* is a critically serious one. Its costs will be more fully explored below in the discussion of the rationale of regulation.

One final objection to subscribing to a doctrine of pluralism that is sometimes urged is that the doctrine implies a fundamentally uncivilized view of society. Collectivists such as Wolff see it as involving a form of government by guerilla warfare. Wolff writes:

> We must give up the image of society as a battleground of competing groups and formulate an ideal society more exalted than the mere acceptance of opposed interests and diverse customs. There is need for a new philosophy of community.[62]

The dilemma raised by this view is that even if we wish to move to a more collectivist approach to decisions about resource allocations, how does one interest group detach itself from the adversary ethic without making itself highly vulnerable to the depredations of other groups? How do we reach for "Consciousness III" without becoming Uncle Toms? On the other hand, if the solution lies in a spontaneous shift in community-wide values, does this leave us waiting, perhaps forlornly, for the Apocalypse?

(iv) The possibility, through participation in the regulatory process, of being co-opted into accepting and endorsing its essential forms carries serious

[61] *The Poverty of Liberalism* (Boston: Beacon Press, 1968) at 154; cf. Presthus, *supra*, note 3 at 349.

[62] *Id*. at 161.

potential costs. First, it involves the consumer movement acquiescing in the incoherence and decisional dysfunctions produced by the random outputs of the fragmented, proliferating regulatory regimes of the modern state.[63] A related cost is acquiescence in the increasing paralysis of the total apparatus, in terms of its ability to respond quickly, rationally, and decisively, to rapidly changing social challenges and crises.[64] The inability of government in Canada to evolve coherent national or even regional policies in such key sectors as energy, food, transportation and housing, exemplifies these costs of the modern regulatory state.

Another cost goes to conventional considerations of economic efficiency raised by the fact of regulation itself. A growing group of commentators from Ralph Nader,[65] on the one hand, to Lewis Engman, the Nixon-appointed Chairman of the Federal Trade Commission, on the other, are now urging massive de-regulation of the economy and an attempt to restore vigorously competitive markets, wherever possible. At least in such a market, a consumer has to decide that it is worth his while to incur the transaction costs entailed in participating in a transaction before his interests can be affected. In other words, he will have to be privy to most market decisions which affect his economic interests as a consumer, unlike most regulatory decisions which affect those interests. In Canada, prime sectors for substantial de-regulation and enforced competition might include transportation, communications, banking, agriculture, and the professions. As a society, we can no longer operate effectively the elaborate, intricately interwoven regulatory

---

[63] A current example of this kind of incoherence is that, despite the declared goal of the Federal Government of national self-sufficiency in oil, the unco-ordinated attempts of the Federal Government, Provincial Governments and assorted Energy Boards and Commissions to tax and otherwise regulate the oil industry may produce exactly the opposite result.

A further example of regulatory confusion is the history of the 45-foot height limit by-law regulating development in downtown Toronto passed two years ago by the Toronto City Council and evolved and implemented through endless Council Committees. In its application, random exceptions were increasingly made and in late 1974, it was overturned by the Ontario Municipal Board (O.M.B.) from whose decision the City appealed to the Provincial Cabinet — in the meantime total confusion as to who is running Toronto, how, and towards what goals. Another interesting insight from this case is that in two municipal elections, a substantial percentage of citizens had felt it worthwhile to incur the information and opportunity costs entailed in voting in a "control development" council. In the lengthy hearings on the by-law before the O.M.B., a non-elected body of technocrats (who described the Council's decision as "political" — what else should it have been?), only 36 developers and the City Council itself found it rational to incur the much higher costs of participating. No citizens seriously participated. The outcome was predictable.

[64] A current example of this paralysis is the housing sector. While the federal government has made large sums of money available in an attempt to alleviate the acute shortage of low-income housing, various municipalities have refused the funding on the ground that the restricted property tax base given them by senior levels of government does not enable them to raise the revenues to service lower priced housing. The federal government, provincial government and municipalities seem incapable of co-ordinating all the pieces of a compatible policy capable of decisively addressing the housing crisis.

[65] See Green, Nader, & Winter, *supra*, note 11.

infra-structure that we have developed. Daniel Patrick Moynihan made this point simply but poignantly in a speech to a NATO meeting in 1970:

> . . . modern government must learn to respond to technologically induced difficulties with something of the same economy of talent that technology has devised. We cannot go on devising government arrangements that only extraordinary men can make work. Most of the work of the world has to be done by men of average endowment, energy, and social vision.

Where competitive markets are not possible, increasingly we must accept the stark alternative of much more direct, explicit, unashamed, central planning. A major political advantage of greater use of central planning instruments is that interest group inter-action is more focussed, more circumscribed, and more visible, and outcomes are subject to more political accountability.[66] Effective central planning entails, at a minimum, much greater use than at present of central regulatory instruments, such as tax, tariff, and competition policies. However, as the experience with competition policy and tax reform in this country has shown, a bold range of additional steps must be contemplated if the ideal of a more coherent, widely responsive central planning process is to be seriously pursued. An agenda for future research might focus on issues such as the following: Where regulatory agencies are found indispensable, would much more detailed, frequent, legislated policy directions to the agencies be desirable and feasible?[67] Should the central government, or, where appropriate, regional government, have the power to over-rule the decisions of major agencies on the basis of published reasons open to parliamentary and public debate? Should all major agencies and Crown corporations be accountable, through a Cabinet Minister, to Parliament? Should much greater research support from general revenues be provided to opposition parties (also large, latent, interest groups), individual M.P.'s and Parliamentary Committees, in the hope that the central political process might then exercise a more effective, direct, oversight role in relation to the agencies, Crown Corporations, and government subsidy programmes? Should the heads of these agencies and programmes be personally and regularly accountable to Parliament in Parliamentary Committee debates on estimates? Should traditional Anglo-Canadian concepts of civil service tenure be preserved, or should there be a much greater ability in the central political authority to hire (from anywhere) and fire (at any time) regulators, Deputy Ministers, Assistant Deputy Ministers and other senior civil servants influential in policy formulation to prevent dissonance and foot-dragging in the command structure.[68] Another line of inquiry which bears exploration is whether regulatory officials (and thus, indirectly, government) should, in some contexts (for example, food, drug, product safety, securities regulation, and welfare entitle-

---

[66] See Lowi, *supra*, note 4; Kariel, *supra*, note 12; Heilbroner, *supra*, note 16; G. Myrdal, *Beyond tha Welfare State* (New Haven: Yale Univ. Press, 1960).

[67] Cf. Lowi, *id.*, Chap. 10; Bernstein, *supra*, note 33 at 284-86.

[68] As to arguments for the need for appropriate lines of political accountability for regulatory decision-makers, see Bernstein, *id.* Chap. 5; The President's Advisory Council on Executive Organization, (the Ash Council), *Report on Selected Independent Regulatory Agencies*, January 1971 at 14 *et seq*; Kariel, *supra*, note 12, Chap. 15; Lowi, *id.*, Chap. 10.

ments) be held civilly liable for negligence to aggrieved citizens, thus attaching private costs to those who make bad public decisions and creating additional incentives for a more responsive regulatory environment?[69] Effective central planning may also entail a much more effective over-sight function by the Courts in relation to legislative and regulatory activity. For example, within the interstices of the law left open to judicial interpretation (for example "inter-provincial trade and commerce") should the courts more consciously promote substantive rationality of economic outputs, and retreat less into legal formalism?[70] In the case of the Federal Court of Appeal and the Supreme Court of Canada, is there a case for appointing to the Court two or three luminous non-legal intellects, with a pervasive sense of the larger social and economic fabric in which particular issues arise, and not merely the limited technical considerations raised by those issues? Should litigants be more actively encouraged to address issues of policy rationality in their submissions? Should Brandeis briefs be invited from interest groups indirectly affected by the outcome of major judicial decisions? Should legislation limit or prescribe corporate campaign contributions and provide for the funding of election campaigns out of public funds, so that the participation rate of high-intensity and low-intensity groups in the political process is more equal?[71] What rights of access should the public be given to government information? What additional forms of assistance should be given to citizens to facilitate participation in legislative and regulatory decision-making? The potential impact of something as seemingly trivial as the broadcasting and televising of parts of the Parliamentary process, so that information costs to the public about public decision-making are reduced, also requires assessment.

The costs of over-regulation and under-government have been eloquently articulated in a recent speech by Lewis Engman:

> Though most government regulation was enacted under the guise of protecting the consumer from abuse, much of today's regulatory machinery does little more than shelter producers from the normal competitive consequences of lassitude and inefficiency . . . . The consumer for whatever presumed abuse he is being spared is paying plenty in the form of government sanctioned price fixing.[72]

Engman proceeds to give a number of examples from the regulated industries of state-sanctioned monopoly profits, and estimates that in the transportation field alone hidden regulatory subsidies may cost consumers in excess of $16

---

[69] Cf. G. Tullock, *Public Decisions as Public Goods* (1971), 70 J. Pol. Ec. 913.

[70] As to the difficulties faced by courts making rational decisions in this area without the relevant economic data before them, see the observations of Laskin, J. in *A. G. for Manitoba* v. *Manitoba Egg & Poultry Association* (1971), 19 D.L.R. (3rd) 169 at 181, 182.

[71] Cf. *Election Expenses Act*, S.C. 1973-74, c. 51; *Election Finances Reform Act*, S.O. 1975, c. 12. Both Acts require disclosure of contributions and limit permissible expenses to a proportionate amount based on the number of registered electors in a constituency. Only the Ontario legislation (s.19(1)), actually limits *contributions* by any person or corporation to a cumulative maximum of $6,500.

[72] Speech to Fall Conference of the Financial Analysts Federation, Detroit, October 7, 1974.

billion a year ($80 per annum per man, woman and child in the U.S.).[73] He continues:

> To me, the most distressing development is the pervasive and well-accepted dishonesty that pervades the government's approach to regulation. The existing crazy quilt of anti-consumer subsidies embodied in the intricately woven fabric of federal and state statutes and regulations is pernicious because: (1) the subsidies are deliberately hidden from public view; (2) the government had irresponsibly lost track of the actual cost of these subsidies;[74] (3) in most, if not all cases, we have adopted the least efficient form of subsidy with the purpose of hiding the subsidy from the public and obfuscating its true cost . . . .[75]
>
> From time to time, proposals have been made to provide direct cash subsidies in lieu of the patchwork of regulatory subsidies that now pervade our economy. Opponents rise indignantly to object that hardworking individuals and businesses do not want handouts. Well, a rose by any other name . . . . Our airlines, our truckers, our railroads, our electronics media and countless others are on the dole. We get irate about welfare fraud. But, our complex systems of hidden regulatory subsidies make welfare fraud look like petty larceny . . . . The fact of the matter is that most regulated industries have become federal protectorates, living in the cozy world of cost-plus, safely protected from the ugly spectres of competition, efficiency and innovation.

Engman concludes that unless the whole regulatory apparatus can be radically rationalised, "our regulators will continue to stumble around in an increasingly expensive game of blind man's bluff".

His remarks are equally applicable to the Canadian regulatory scene. Apart from the regulated industries, which in many cases are effectively administering their own markets with the complicity of the State, other occupations have won the right from the State explicitly to administer their

73 Canadians are estimated to spend one dollar in five on transportation costs, how much on subsidies nobody knows.

74 A typical Canadian example of this kind of "dysfunction" is the current prosecution (the second in recent years) of sugar refiners for price-fixing by the Department of Consumer and Corporate Affairs, while the Department of Finance insists on maintaining a customs tariff on imported, refined sugar.

75 Recent notable examples of this last point in Canada are the egg marketing boards, where, in the alleged interest of the marginal farmer, a producer-determined subsidy is levied on all consumers of eggs indiscriminately, whether they can afford it or not (i.e. a regressive tax) and distributed to all producers indiscriminately, whether they need it or not. This produces bizarre wealth redistribution effects, and is also inconsistent with the Federal Government's declared intention of bringing down food prices by increasing supply rather than through controls, as witness the destruction in the summer of 1974 of 28 million eggs by the central egg marketing agency (CEMA). If an income transfer to marginal family farmers is thought socially desirable, why not a direct selective, transfer through the progressive income tax system? If the problem is also fluctuating farm incomes, why not better tax averaging provisions?

Another example concerns airlines regulation whereby in order to receive a profitable route, an airline has to agree to fly some unprofitable routes. This creates irrational cross-subsidy effects between passengers on high-traffic routes and those on low-traffic routes. Why not let all regional, national and international carriers compete on all routes as they please and if some are abandoned as uneconomic, let the government let out to competitive tender the right to fly these routes in return for a direct cash subsidy paid out of general revenues? We would have more competition, and in the case of subsidized routes, we would know, and decide, who is to pay what to whom (cf. address by J. W. Pickersgill to the Air Transport Association of Canada, Vancouver, Oct. 30, 1974).

own markets. For example, in Schedule I to the Quebec *Professional Code*,[76] 38 professions are listed, including social workers, agronomists, denturologists, industrial relations counsellors, vocational guidance counsellors, and town planners, all of whom are given some degree of monopoly power by the State. The medical profession has, of course, been given a State-sanctioned right to administer its own market with the helpful adjunct of being able to make its own subventions out of public revenues. Proving that State-sanctioned monopolies are contagiously attractive, most parts of the agricultural sector, drawing expressly on the precedent of "professional" marketing boards, have either received or are demanding the right to create producer-controlled agricultural marketing boards with comprehensive supply management powers. Add to this the emergence of international supply and price management cartels in oil, sugar, coffee and other staples, beyond the reach, of course, of domestic anti-trust laws, and the economic order in the world seems bent on a retreat from nineteenth century *laissez-faire* capitalism to thirteenth century feudalism, back from contract to status. Business (with the aid of government) has now emerged as the chief subverter of the competitive economy which it claims to remember so fondly.

It is submitted that the general form of the antidote to be urged by consumerism that emerges from the foregoing analysis is this: *As a first priority,* we should preserve or re-activate vigorously competitive markets wherever possible and not succumb to producer pleas to substitute accommodating regulatory regimes.[77] *As a second best solution,* in the event of demonstrated and significant market failure, or in the event of undesirable social outputs from admittedly competitive markets, we should invoke central planning instruments such as competition, tariff and tax policies or legislated direct subsidies, through a more publicly accountable central political process. On the level of more specific and limited legislative programmes that significant market imperfections might elicit, a substantial consumer consensus might be found for stronger laws sanctioning misleading advertising and sales practices so as to reduce the amount of misinformation given to consumers, disclosure requirements (for example, true interest rates, informative labelling, unit pricing), public product and service grading, public price comparisons, and business complaints rating services, whenever the potential benefits to consumers from possessing this information exceed the costs of providing it. Expanded consumer education programmes, and, very importantly, vastly improved access to effective civil grievance-solving mechanisms might also attract similar consumer support. These programmes would focus on the complementary concepts of feeding better information into the market-place and elevating the importance of civil enforcement mechanisms over criminal and administrative enforcement mechanisms thus seeking to squeeze as much non-competitive slack as possible out of the market. These twin approaches would try to ensure that consumers have instruments placed at their disposal which make them the principal agents in their own protection, and reduce

76 Bill 250, July 6, 1973, S.Q.

77 Cf. A. Phillips, ed., *Promoting Competition in Regulated Markets* (Washington, Brookings Institution, 1975).

their dependence on public regulatory responses. *Only as a third best solution,* where delegation of regulatory authority is unavoidable, should delegated regulatory agencies be utilized, provided, however, that they are much more publicly accessible and politically accountable than at present. In some situations, of course, a mix of all three approaches may be dictated but even here we should not lose sight of where, presumptively, the relative policy emphases should lie.

## D. CONCLUSION

This article has sought to identify some of the larger issues in the modern regulatory state that consumerism must constantly confront, if in Heilbroner's words, it is to claim a role as one of "the sentries of society"[78] For consumerism, in the last analysis, is about the fundamentals of our economic system. To eschew this role can only mean that consumerism will become part of the flotsam and jetsam of the modern regulatory state, adrift in a fathomless sea of regulatory dross, carried wherever the dictates of the tides and winds of the moment decree.

To come full circle to the opening political analysis of this article, two specific challenges now face modern consumerism. First, recognizing the diffusion of the consumer interest and the free rider problem, can the consumer movement overcome the organizational, and thus political, disabilities that afflict large, latent interest groups? Secondly, as the consumer movement seeks to mobilize substantial political support, is it at the same time possible for it to play the role of a fearless and far-sighted social critic by forging a broad-based coalition of citizens around a set of collective goals that embrace new and relevant concepts of economic justice? Or will the consumer interest always be too fragmented to allow of such a coalition? Does Dr. Stigler's prognosis express an eternal verity? As the analysis in this article has sought to show, these are daunting challenges, but to leave them unanswered may be also to have abdicated on many other seemingly more pressing questions about the future of our existing economic order.

---

[78] *Supra,* note 16.

# Part II
# Regulation of Unfair Trade Practices

# [5]

The
American
University
Law Review

VOLUME 19 | MARCH, 1970 | NUMBER 2

## CONTRACT AS THING

*Arthur Allen Leff**

In a large proportion of consumer transactions, paper passes between the parties.[1] The content and coverage of this paper varies widely, from a mere identification of goods and price all the way to the highly detailed retail installment sales contract. Many of these pieces of paper say extremely important things, especially about goods quality, and the parties' duties and remedies.[2] It is that paper which will be the subject of this paper.

My aim, however, while hardly unpretentious, is quite constricted. Granted that the present legal response to these papers is a mess, I do not aim to suggest any solutions. I intend instead to try to show how that current mess is rooted in our current *way* of thinking about these "contracts," and to propose a new way of thinking, a new metaphoric framework *for* thinking, about consumer-transaction "contracts."

---

* Associate Professor Law, Yale Law School. B.A. 1956, Amherst College. LL.B. 1959, Harvard University.

1. Though certainly not in all. By at least one criterion, gross number of individual transactions, the most prevalent consumer deal in the paperless over-the-counter or off-the-shelf cash sale. But paper-accompanied transactions are certainly a material part of the consumer-purchasing market, especially if one includes sales-slip transactions.

2. Actual surveys of the "typical" content of these forms, with analysis of what kinds of clauses are to be found, are rare. I have in my possession a study completed in May, 1969, of the fifty responses received to 200 form solicitations made more or less randomly to 200 merchants in three cities. This paper, prepared by John Sibley, of the Yale Law School class of 1969, includes such an analysis and tabulation, and I would be glad to send a copy to anyone who wants it.

### *Classification and Metaphor*

To get to that new mind set (and explain the critical significance of those quotation marks in the last sentence) it will be necessary to describe how we got to where we now are. And to get that far along, we will first have to make an excursion into the arid country of legal classification, a trip which may turn out, like a fourteen-day tour of Europe, simultaneously superficial and tedious. The point of embarkation is a question: why would one (even within the ramparts of quotation marks) characterize those pieces of paper which pass between those parties as "contracts"?

To call a thing a contract is to make a legal classification. It is to carry out that most basic step in what is sometimes called legal reasoning (and what is confused, often, with legal logic).[3] It is to make a move in the mind game which, to coarsen a lot of distinctions, goes something like this: given that I cannot efficiently treat this thing as *sui generis*, with what other thing or group of things can I best associate it for less-than-individual treatment.

As the crudity and non-specificity of that statement should certainly signal, classification, legal or not, is a sticky business. As G.E. Moore once put it, "Everything is what it is, and not another thing."[4] In other words, you cannot make classes the easy way, by putting together identical things. There are no identical things. Identity (that darling of logicians) is solely an intellectual construct: an identical thing is a thing which would be another thing except that it isn't. All that is perfectly clear. All that, in fact, is pretty trivial.

What is not always as clear, or as practically trivial, is the effect that this unreality of identity has on the classes the process creates. What it means, in effect, is that there is no such thing as a thoroughly homogenous class. To say that X is a member of the species Y is just to say that there is a way of looking at and talking about X which emphasizes its Y-ishness. There is, to use a currently modish phrase, a "family resemblance" between X and the items already "in" Y.[5] It does *not* mean that X is identical with any particular member of this class Y, because $Y_1$ is not identical with $Y_2$ or $Y_3$ or any of the individual members of the class Y either. All classification decisions

3. *See* O.C. JENSEN, THE NATURE OF LEGAL ARGUMENT 9-16 (1957) for a notable discussion of these processes, much more illuminating than my truncated version.

4. G.E. MOORE, PRINCIPIA ETHICA (1st paperback ed. 1960). The remark appears on the page facing the title page, and is attributed to Bishop Butler.

5. *See* L. WITTGENSTEIN, PHILOSOPHICAL INVESTIGATIONS, §§ 65-67 (G. Anscombe trans. 1967).

are, as far as the total class is concerned, choices among metaphors. X is *like* $Y_1$, $Y_2$, $Y_3$ . . . $Y_n$ the way $Y_1$ is like $Y_2$, $Y_3$, $Y_4$ . . . $Y_n$.[6] Even if, therefore, there is a common element of likeness, a discernible family resemblance upon which a classification decision may usefully be made, not even these happy families are all alike. The minute you shift your attention from the common element upon which your classification is based to some other, previously ignored, your classification explodes. Or at least it ought to.

It is, of course, exceedingly rare, especially in legal classification, most especially when the classification is at the level of generality that the "contract"—"not contract" decision represents, to classify by only one resemblance. But there is a very sharp limitation upon the number of classificatory criteria one can formally use. Let us say you are classifying bugs. Your criterion for classifying is to count legs; more than six legs to one pile, six or fewer to another. At that point you will have just two classes. If you add to the process another criterion, say blackness versus color, you will produce four classes, (1) black—6 or less; (2) black—more than 6; (3) not-black—6 or less; (4) not-black—more than 6. Choosing three criteria will create eight sub-classes,[7] four will make 16, five will produce 32 and ten will get you 1024.[8] To put things briefly, things can pretty quickly get out of hand when great refinement of classification is attempted. Thus in practical reason it would be common to classify phenomena into relatively crude categories, that is, group them on the basis of relatively few family resemblances.[9]

What follows from this is that most classificatory families have very many features that vary from member to member. One may get the nose and ears right, and maybe eye shape and brow height too, but cheekbones will point every which way, and teeth will snaggle randomly. Much of the time this makes no difference. Very crude discriminations are quite sufficient for equally crude purposes; if you have a spider collection and an insect collection, and you want to separate the day's catch temporarily, just counting legs will do nicely.[10]

---

6. But not *necessarily* in any other way. One who has said of his mistress "Red as a rose is she," need not be on the lookout for thorns, or remember to mulch and water her frequently (except, perhaps, pursuant to another set of metaphors).

7. ABC, AB*C*, A*B*C, A*BC*, *A*BC, *A*B*C*, *AB*C, *ABC*.

8. The formula is a pretty simple one: classifying subjects with respect to n criteria in mutually exclusive and exhaustive pairs will yield $2^n$ classes.

9. I must add here, without getting into any hassle about how the mind "actually works," that people regularly assign subjects to classes much faster than I or they can describe how they do it.

10. And if you're looking to pick up Fanny Schwartz' unmet son Morris at the airport, eyes,

But do for what? Why all this bother? Why classify at all? To promote intellectual and operational efficiency.[11] Picture a pile of lumps brought up from a coal mine. How does one separate them into piles? Well, if you're interested in heat, you separate the coal (i.e., that which will burn) from the rocks (which won't). If you're interested in fitness for different types of furnaces, you screen the lumps for size. If the combustion end-product is critical for your purposes, you might grade the coal lumps by sulphur content. If you were planning a fancy photograph, you might arrange piles by color and shape. And if you were just getting together some ship ballast, you most likely would treat all the lumps as "the same". Assuming that no two things are identical, some things *are* (by some particular set of criteria) *like* other things. On the further assumption that like things should be treated in like manner,[12] identifying likeness makes possible the generation of rules, i.e., statements about behavior (intellectual or practical) with respect to more-than-one-member sets. Once there is—stated, perceived or felt—a purposive aim and a classificatory criterion (or more) associatable with it (empirical causation being one of the most common associations used), classification becomes "useful" *to that end*.

Now this process, while seemingly simple (especially when grossly simplified examples are used to illustrate it), is frequently so complex as to be, finally, almost a mystery. Neither purposes nor raw material are so often so simple; think of all the people or even all the women, you have known. But the great power of the classificatory process lies in the fact that identification criteria for class membership are frequently different from, and easier to use than, the purposive aim which the classification was formed to serve. In the coal example, for instance, the purposive criterion might be burnability, but the recognition criteria would initially (and sufficiently for most purposes) be grossly sensory. Briefly, one knows what coal *looks* like and also that coal burns; hence to find out if that lump will burn one has only to look at it, not to light it.

ears, nose and hair style will most likely be plenty. In fact, nose alone might be enough, depending on the nose and the airport. *Cf.* L. WITTGENSTEIN, *supra* note 5, at * 71.

11. Actually, this utilitarian answer is at most only part of the story. I suspect that people classify for the same reason that tigers hunt and most animals copulate, which is *not* solely to have food and children, respectively. It is a terrible mistake, in assessing the powers of ends, to overlook the aesthetics of getting there.

12. On the operational level, that assumption may be empirically tested: if like treatment is given to A and to B, and such treatment eventuates in result X for both A and B, then A *is* (in that sense) like B. In other words, *a* "correct" classification has been made. But the "should" in the text should not be taken as an ethical "ought." As such it is just an assumption, and an unsupportable one at that.

Moreover, there is often an additional bonus paid by grouping individuals into classes. This segregation (physical or conceptual) frequently results in the perception for the first time of similarities, the classifying efficiency of which is greater even than the original recognition criteria upon which the class initially was based. Go back to the lumps of coal. Let us say that the aim of their classification was to separate high-sulphur from low-sulphur coal. Let us assume further that there is a chemical reagent which, when rubbed on the surface of any lump, will fizz in the presence of sulphur. The test is expensive, but the results are accurate. So you rub, listen, separate, and end up with two piles. Having done so, you notice that the high-sulphur pile is much lighter in color than the low-sulphur one. Now after sufficiently testing to eliminate accident, you may well find you have come up with a new, previously unsuspected association for future classifications, this time between coal *color* and sulphur oxide pollutants which, moreover, lends itself to more efficient classification technique (*e.g.*, by automated colorimeter scanning) than the reagent-fizz criterion. The classification itself has generated another (and "better") classifying criterion. And it has eliminated any need to use the original (reagent-fizz) criterion. In other words, it is frequently the case that one will discover, without necessarily knowing or understanding the associative mechanism involved, that objects with one thing in common have other things in common too, and that these other things are more practically useful identifying criteria than the ones first used.[13]

Thus, classification is a powerful intellectual device for efficiently identifying nonidentical things and concepts which may *for certain purposes* be treated identically. And like most such intellectual devices, it is powerfully dangerous too. First, the connection between identification criteria and the desired end of the classification may just be wrong. After all, that connection is ordinarily just an empirical one which means (with respect to classes) a statistical one, and empirical observations and statistical generalizations do frequently turn out to be wrong. This applies, of course, both to the initially chosen identification criteria and to the new internal correlations which become apparent among members of a class after classification.

Second, even if one's empirical observations are *more or less* correct, the correlation between identification criterion and end may be less

13. A model of the mechanism which generates this statistical correlation helps, of course, to validate its accuracy. Knowing what moves around what and from which direction does enhance one's certainty of where the sun tomorrow will "rise".

precise than others which have been or could be used. In our coal example, color may indeed identify threshold sulphur content with 90% accuracy; the reagent-fizz technique may have a 99% rate.

Third, and closely allied to the correlation slippage, is the problem of artificial class homogenization. Now note that this homogenization is one of the principal purposes of classification as an intellectual device. One is trying to ignore differences. Nonetheless, there does seem to be a tendency, once the identification is made, to ignore differences even after they become relevant to one's purposes. This is indeed "just" a sloppy classifying job, but a very tempting slip. Once one identifies and, more important, *names* a class member by that membership, it is easy to treat the individual member not as *a* member which *belongs to* a class, but as a sort of composite average of all the members of that class, *i.e.*, as a non-individual for *all* purposes. If, for instance, one exempts "automobiles" from execution (on the ground that it is good policy to allow debtors to retain transportation), one *might* also exempt a rare antique non-functional automobile. Having used a structural and visual identification criterion roughly to identify a kinetic purpose, it is easy to lose sight of the purpose.[14]

Last is the discernible fact that some identification criteria, even though not sole criteria for that particular classification, tend to overwhelm others in determining inclusion or exclusion. In other words, the purposes to be served by particular classification A may correlate very well with the confluence of identification criteria x, y and z. And indeed there may be some correlation between x, y and z too, that is, if x, or y or z is present, the other two are more likely than not also to be present. But the correlation between the purpose of class A and x *or* y *or* z singly may be much lower, perhaps approaching randomness, and certainly lower than the correlation between the purpose of class A and x, y *and* z together. This situation is pregnant with the threat of intellectual abortion. For it seems to me that when purposive classification is based on the confluence of many identification criteria, there is a tendency to rely on less than all of them to make classification decisions, even though one's feeling of safety (i.e., sense of correlation exactness) is based only on all of them together. Moreover, a single identifying criterion relied upon when less than all are is not necessarily that which *singly* correlates most highly with the aim of the classification.

14. Of course, that might still be an administratively rational decision, like letting a few lumps of high sulphur coal slip by if the alternative and more accurate test would double coal prices. The point here is not that all slippages like this are errors, but only that some are.

I will not, of course, be able to prove these tendencies; they are, after all, just empirical generalizations (this time about thinking patterns) and demand empirical evidence which I frankly do not have. But I will offer at least one rough-hewn pile of evidence for them: a history of the classification of the paper passing between the parties to a consumer transaction, the consumer-deal "contract".

### *Contract as Contract*

What belongs to the class "contract"? The "official" definition gives some clue of the difficulty of that question by answering it with breathtaking circularity . A contract is "a promise or set of promises for the breach of which the law gives a remedy . . . ."[15] In fact, asked generally that way, the question defies less begging answers. A lot of things are contracts, or at least a lot of them have from time to time and presently ended up being somewhat subject to contract principles. But like all classifications, "contract" has a purposive element. It is, as always, extremely doubtful that one can come up with *a* purpose, but a tight cluster is not too much to hope for. To follow Professor Kessler's lead in this (and to implode his admirable and already admirably tight summary) the common law's category "contract" was developed as a method of segregating, for a particular and predictable treatment, contemplated trading transactions between free-willed persons in an assumedly free enterprise, free market economic system.[16] Given this relatively shadowy "aim," there arose a few class-identifying criteria which, when present in sufficient confluence, made things look more contracty than not.

These identifying criteria are, of course, in the form of gross distinctions between alternative possibilities.[17] First of all, contracts seem to be some species of interpersonal behavior (as opposed to person-thing interactions).[18] Second, the interpersonal behavior

---

15. RESTATEMENT OF CONTRACTS § 1 (1932); RESTATEMENT (SECOND) OF CONTRACTS § 1 (Tent. Draft No.1, 1964).

16. *See* Kessler, *Contracts of Adhesion—Some Thoughts About Freedom of Contract*, 43 COLUM. L. REV. 629-31 (1943).

17. These may be set up as A-*A* distinctions, but in fact each of them is a softer-edged subtraction than that, much closer, in fact, to $A_1$, $A_2$, $A_3$ . . . $\mathit{A}_3$, $\mathit{A}_2$, $\mathit{A}_1$ than to A-*A* in almost any real-world instance.

18. But note the possibility of *implying* an actual promise out of certain activities toward non-persons, for instance, by accepting goods knowing they are not gifts. *See* the exemplary cases Day v. Caton, 119 Mass. 513 (1876), Austin v. Burge, 156 Mo. App. 286, 137 S.W. 618 (1911), and Louisville Tin & Stove Co. v. Lay, 251 Ky. 584, 65 S.W.2d 1002 (1933) collected in L. FULLER & R. BRAUCHER, BASIC CONTRACT LAW 365-68 (1964).

demanded for a contract seems to be more or less communicative[19] (rather than directly effective, like a punch in the mouth).[20] Moreover, the communication, to look contracty, ought to have a lot of future tense in it, and bear somewhat on the speakers' expected role in that future.[21] Next, bargain and trade seems to smell more of contract than beneficence; there is the continual pressure to separate deals from gifts.[22] Next is the limitedness of contract. There seems to be something significant to contract in the bordered relationship, "the deal," as opposed to more long-term, non-limit-bound interpersonal relationship like husband-wife and father-son.[23] Last (and keep a close and critical eye on this move, for it will become very important to the argument anon), closely allied to the trade-bargain idea, is the process aura of contract. Contract seems to presuppose not only a deal, but dealing. It is the product of a joint creative effort. At least classically, the idea seems to have been that the parties combine their impulses and desires into a resulting product which is a harmonization of their initial positions.[24] What results is neither's will; it is somehow a combination of their desires, the product of an ad hoc vector diagram the resulting arrow of which is "the contract".[25]

And, naturally, there is one more identifying criterion of "contract" which cannot safely be overlooked. The criteria heretofore mentioned had to do with contract as a process. But that process frequently results in a refined product, *a* contract, a piece of paper with words on it. Everyone knows that not every "contract" is a writing, but some are, and for classification purposes seeing a writing is certainly one factor in pushing the decision to rather than fro.

Now notice, I have picked out only a few identification criteria for the category "contract." I would certainly defend the proposition that the written product of a process of communication between persons about future activities of at least one of them in exchange for

19. But consider the whole objective-subjective contract controversy. *See* 1 A. CORBIN, CONTRACTS § 9 (1963).

20. Which, of course, like all "action," is at least partly communicative too. One can picture innumerable situations in which that would mean, among other things, "I reject your offer".

21. That is perhaps the only clear message from the Restatements. *See* note 15, *supra*.

22. See 1 A. CORBIN, CONTRACTS § 4 (1963). *See also* § 131 for the indifferent results of attempting this separation by consideration doctrine.

23. I am trying, of course, to keep from falling off the brink into the status-contract swamp, but that I am in fact hanging over it by my fingernails ought to be mentioned.

24. For this aspect blown up to the very limit of pretentious expression, *see* G. HEGEL, PHILOSOPHY OF RIGHT 57-58 (¶¶ 72-75) (T. Knox trans. 1942).

25. Trading (I'll give . . . if you'll give . . . . ; I'll give up . . . if you'll give up . . . .) is *one* of these harmonizing methods.

something from the other would be more likely to be classified as "contract" than the result of negating *all* those factors. I would also defend the proposition that while none of these factors is necessary to such a classification, all of them, as shadowy as they are, are important.[26] I would not for a moment contend, however, that I have isolated all of the relevant classifying criteria (that is, that even all my criteria together are necessarily sufficient), or that I have most effectively described the ones I have sensed and stated. Nonetheless, it seems to me that one could predict the legal classification of certain transactions quite precisely with reference to these relatively few criteria and not nearly so well by ignoring any of them.

It would be a mistake, however, to think that the classification "contract" has stayed forever static, with one set of identification criteria, or that transactions bearing the then relevant hallmarks have never escaped. Whatever the purpose of the particular classification "contract", the purpose of classification itself is to promote intellectual and practical efficiency. It has frequently happened that certain kinds of happenings have begun to resemble each other so much more than they resembled the "average" contract that they have split off for special treatment much more suited to the solution of their own, narrower group of recurrent problems.[27] Certainly that happened to labor contracts[28] and insurance contracts,[29] and, most pertinently, to sales transactions.[30] What seems to have happened again and again is that some transaction type[31] moved too far over the end of the scale[32]

---

26. I find it particularly striking that it is with respect to these particular $A_1$, $A_2$, $A_3$ . . . . $A_3$, $A_2$, $A_1$ distinctions, between past and future, gift and trade, creating and created, status and deal, for instance, that so many contractdlaw problems fall. Most of the grand conflicts in the field, mutual assent, past consideration, variation of ongoing transaction, consideration, and so on turn out to be voyages into those *maria incognita* charted only by the above dots. *See also* note 17, *supra*.

27. *See* L. *Friedman, Contract Law in America* 15-26 (1965).

28. *See* Summers, *Collective Agreements and the'Law of Contracts*, 78 YALE L.J. 525 (1969). The major burden of this article, in fact, is to question whether this "emanicipation" of "labor contract" from "contract" has not been overdone.

29. *See* N.Y. INS. L., especially §§ 140-74.

30. *See* UNIFORM COMMERCIAL CODE (1962 Official Text) [hereinafter "U.C.C."] art. 2; UNIFORM SALES ACT (1906), 1 & 1A UNIFORM LAWS ANNOTATED (1958). And note that even that most enthusiastic of generalists, Samuel Williston of Harvard, found it necessary to write two treatises, one on contracts and the other on sales.

31. On the significance of transaction types, that is, repetitive dramatic situations at a factual level more precise than "contract" or even "deal," see Llewellyn, *The First Struggle to Unhorse Sales*, 52 HARV. L. REV. 873 (1939); Llewellyn, *Through Title to Contract and a Bit Beyond*, 15 N.Y.U.L. REV. 159, 160 n.2 (1938).

32. *See* notes 17 and 26, *supra*.

on one or more identification criteria and developed one or more additional high frequency internal correlations, so that it was recognized that a new something had come into existence.[33] At any rate, what is most interesting for present purposes is that many long years ago precisely such a reclassification movement took place with respect to consumer transactions.

### *Contract as Contract of Adhesion*

The movement of thought about consumer transactions seems to have come about because of empirical pressure upon one particular criterion for contractness—joint creative process. The following factual situation was increasingly presented: A and B met to enter into a transaction. They talked about the price and identity of the goods, and maybe about a few other things. These terms they might indeed create between themselves. But then one of the parties would submit to the other a piece of paper covering several, perhaps many, other actually or potentially important terms of the deal. The dickered and discussed terms were added to that paper, and that paper then became "the terms of the transaction."

Now notice that this type of transaction did *not* differ from the previous horse-trade model in that once all terms were argued over, while later on only a few were. In *both* kinds of deals, only some of the terms were discussed. But in the horse-trade deal what was left out was covered by statute, custom or legal implication; in the new pattern, what was not discussed was covered by the proffered document. That does not mean that under the pre-modern deal all the terms were necessarily less onerous to the buyer. Some, indeeed, were beastly.[34] But the process of filling in and filling out a deal not by one party's will, but by the legal and political process, tended to lessen the possibility of monolithic one-sidedness; buyers were occasionally also powerful classes (*e.g.*, buyers of farm commodities), and what they won for themselves tended to slip over into other trades too, to protect the farmers, for instance, when they bought at retail. What the institution of the retail-form-pad sale created was the possibility of special

33. Consider also, for instance, quasi-contract, at least in part a device for dealing with non-donative, non-coercive but non-agreement transactions, that is, a mechanism for correcting enrichment stemming from neither gift, force, fraud, or bargain.

34. *See*, for instance, the common-law rule putting risk of "innocent" destruction of the goods on the holder of the title, 2 S. WILLISTON, SALES § 301 (1948), despite the immense burden that puts upon a buyer out of possession with respect to losses the causes of which are unclear. UCC § 2-509 is more realistic and particularistic, though results rarely differ.

governing rules for each transaction-type. The rules became custom-made rather than customary.

Thus in any sector of commerce where, in the circumstances, one party could impose most of its own terms, could unilaterally create *most* of the rules of *that* game, there was nothing to prevent highly disproportionate "contracts" from being created. These circumstances were, of course, those which decreased single-transaction market power more or less permanently and radically for one of the classes of usual parties. What the specific circumstances creating that power to impose terms, whether sanctioned monopoly, lawful or unlawful oligopoly, lack of mobility and information, lack of interest (because each deal was too trivial to think about, or the imposed terms covered contingencies too hypothetical to engage attention) or what all else will not concern us here. I will just take as a premise that there grew during this century an increasing number of transaction types in which most of the terms of the transaction were imposed by one of the parties on the other, rather than created between them or left to customary coverage.[35]

Naturally, there were a number of responses to this state of affairs. It would be an egregious error to suppose that those one-sided contracting processes and the one-sided contracts which resulted, were allowed to pass unnoticed and unmitigated by the law. The tight textual regulation of insurance policies combined with enthusiastic *contra proferentem* interpretation, for instance, was (and is) such a response still in the course of development.[36] Fraud and duress were stretched, consideration doctrine was mangled.[37] But there was (and is) an

35. Actually I have no empirical evidence that the frequency of this type of transaction has increased over, say, the last fifty years or so. But most people seem to assume so, *see, e.g.*, L. VOLD, SALES 447 (2d ed. 1959), and it seems certainly reasonable (given the increase in marketer concentration) to believe that it did. More important, there is no evidence that this move toward standardized contracts has in the net decreased social welfare, at least in any reasonably materialistic sense of the term. First, it is often the case that the form pad, as one-sided as it may be, does not present a deal as awful as one the free-willed but weak-minded can get for himself by dickering. In addition, it can unashamedly be argued that mass production has increased everyone's welfare (as defined here) and that mass production needs mass distribution. *See* Llewellyn, Book Review, 52 HARV. L. REV. 700, 701-02 (1939). But even assuming that all that is true, and that this new marketing pattern is, finally, "better" than dicker-distribution, it is so only "in the net" and "finally". Individual unpleasantness might (and does) still flow from this statistical good, and if it could be mitigated without any doomed attempt to return to an unrecoverable (and partially imaginary) past, and at bearable cost, that would be (and is) a respectable legal job.

36. *See, e.g.*, Lachs v. Fidelity and Casualty Co. of New York, 306 N.Y. 357, 118 N.E. 2d 555 (1954) on what you don't "know" even if the words are "there". *See* Wyatt v. Northwestern Mut. Ins. Co. of Seattle, 304 F. Supp. 781 (D. Minn. 1969) for a very recent garden-variety example.

37. *See* UCC § 2-302, Comment 1.

enormous conceptual difficulty in dealing thoroughly and systematically with the problem: since *all* contracts *to some extent* involve terms created by only one party, how do you meddle with one-sided contracts without destroying the basic rule that one is bound to the terms of "his" contracts?[38]

The conceptual move was to create a new category, once again by exploiting linkable differences within a necessarily non-homogenous class. The scholars, in a really dazzling series of discussions,[39] created from the residuary category "contracts," the new subcategory "contracts of adhesion." Their basic insight was a simple and elegant one: there is a critical difference between a bargaining process and an on-off light switch. In the typical consumer-goods deal, for instance, the consumer must take the whole deal (or most of it) as a deal, or leave it, all of it. Assuming that the seller is not a true or effective monopolist and the goods or services are not vital to life, the consumer does, in theory, have an option: he *can* flip the switch either way. But he is not presented with any rheostatic alternative which would permit him to vary the quality of the deal between the on-off poles. Surely, argued the commentators, there is a difference important enough between the dickered deal and the adhesion deal to justify a new category—contracts of adhesion—to be treated by the courts differently than plain old residuary-category contracts.

As an analytic device this new category was a brilliant coup. As a practical matter it has been, I think, a disaster. Fifty years after the first extended development of the adhesion doctrine,[40] and twenty-five years after its most elegant and powerful discussion,[41] the consumer-purchase transaction is still stumbling about, a diagnosed disease seeking a nostrum. Various patent remedies are still being applied like mustard plasters—public policy,[42] fundamental breach,[43]

38. RESTATEMENT OF CONTRACTS § 70 (1932).

39. *See* Isaacs, *The Standardization of Contracts*, 27 YALE L.J. 34 (1917); L. PRAUSNITZ, THE STANDARDIZATION OF COMMERCIAL CONTRACTS IN ENGLISH AND CONTINENTAL LAW (1937), reviewed by Llewellyn, 52 HARV. L. REV. 700 (1939); Kessler, *supra* note 16; Ehrenzweig, *Adhesion Contracts in the Conflict of Laws*, 53 COLUM. L. REV. 1072 (1953); Sales, *Standard Form Contracts*, 16 MODERN L. REV. 318 (1953); Lenhoff, *Contracts of Adhesion and the Freedom of Contract: A Comparative Study in the Light of American and Foreign Law*, 36 TUL. L. REV. 481 (1962); Meyer, *Contracts of Adhesion and the Doctrine of Fundamental Breach*, 50 VA. L. REV. 1178 (1964); Wilson, *Freedom of Contract and Adhesion Contracts*, 14 INT'L & COMP. L.Q. 172 (1965).

40. Isaacs, *supra* note 39.

41. Kessler, *supra* note 16.

42. Henningsen v. Bloomfield Motors, Inc., 32 N.J. 358, 161 A.2d 69 (1960).

43. *See* Meyer, *supra* note 39.

unconscionability[44]—and like such plasters, they seem to irritate more than they cure. There is presently no powerful legal theory successfully grappling with one-sided consumer deals.[45]

Why? Because, among other things, the phrase "contract of adhesion" fails to rivet the reformers' (and judges') attention on what is really at issue. In fact, "adhesion contract" turns out upon examination to be one of those magical language-game products like "darkness visible" or "incorporeal body," by the use of which one "describes" non-states of affairs (the principal historical use of which has been, interestingly enough, for descriptions of the theologically ineffable).

The intellectual process which led to "contract of adhesion" is, at least with hindsight, and in terms of my earlier classification discussion, relatively easy to describe. Prior to creation of the adhesion-contract category, "the law" had been guilty of a common misclassification technique. Seeing that consumer transactions were communicative (rather than, say, physically coercive), mercantile (rather than charitable or donative), and bounded (rather than status-relational), and so on,[46] "the law" continued to class them as contractual. This overlooked the fact that *these* "contracts" were not the product of a cooperative process, but the creation (essentially) of only one of the parties. In other words, "the law" was classing consumer transactions as contracts on the basis of less than all the criteria which actually shaped that particular class. The adhesion contract theorists corrected that particular error. They detected the non-process nature of some "contracts" (including consumer transactions) and thus created, so they thought, a new category, roughly speaking "that which would be a contract except that no bargaining process really shapes it." For describing such a beast the phrase "contract of adhesion" is not half bad. Its picture, such as it is, is one not of haggle or cooperative process but rather of a fly and flypaper.[47] Thus the phrase focussed on the fact that whatever

44. *See* Williams v. Walker-Thomas Furniture Company, 350 F.2d 445 (D.C. Cir. 1965).

45. There are those who argue that the unconscionability doctrine, UCC § 2-302, is just such a theory. *See, e.g.*, Spanogle, *Analyzing Unconscionability Problems*, 117 U. PA. L. REV. 931 (1969); Ellinghaus, *In Defense of Unconscionability*, 78 YALE L.J. 757 (1969). See Murray, *Unconscionability: Unconscionability*, 31 U. PITT. L. REV. ___ (1970) for a particularly evangelistic argument. (As of the writing of this, this last article had not been published, but Professor Murray was kind enough to permit a final manuscript copy to be shown to me.)

46. *See* "Contract as Contract," TAN 15-33,*supra*.

47. *See* Leff, *Unconscionability and the Code—The Emperor's New Clause*, 115 U. PA. L. REV. 485, 504 n.67 (1967) for the probable etiology of the term "contract of adhesion."

protection against overreaching and unfairness a process of cooperative creation might be supposed to give, an adhered-to document gave no such protection. Assuming that contract law is in some complex way tied up with belief in the good-maximizing powers of the market, itself based on the assumption that people know better what is of value to them than any state or other guardian, unbargainable deals were critically different from dickered deals.

But that insight got the commentators only half way. Once they had isolated the fact that there was no contracting-process protection in adhesion deals, their metaphor was exhausted. For if their new legal griffin was not an ordinary barnyard type of animal, it was still *some* kind of "contract," that is, an undertaken obligation which the law would ordinarily enforce. It might be an exotic animal indeed, but it was still an animal—to be fed, watered, and treated more or less like a cow. But *when* enforce these adhesion contracts? Certainly the phrase "*contract* of adhesion" doesn't push the answer "never" briskly forward. And the economics of the mass distribution of goods make that a commercially absurd answer anyway.[48] Certainly not "always;" the whole purpose of the addition of "of adhesion" was to negative that possibility (and in effect reserve it for plain old unmodified "contract"). But if clearly not "never" or "always", then when? The new metaphor gave (and gives) not the slightest color of any answer to that question. The new metaphoric category, since carved from the older category of "contract," and left with all the smell of freedom-of-contract enforceability clinging to it, was naked of any substantive criteria for evaluating the central problem: what is a "bad" contract?

### *Contract As Thing*

There was (and is) however, a ready-made new category for adhesion deals (including consumer-goods deals) which stayed overlooked, despite the fact that it fits better than "adhesion contract", the identification criteria of this new class of deals. Consider this phony historical paradigm.[49] Let us say that once upon a time all goods were custom made in the presence, and sometimes with the assistance, of the intended purchaser, who oversaw every detail. When the goods were not satisfactory, and the buyer complained to the authorities, he was

48. *See* note 35, *supra*.

49. Freud's primal-horde myth, Freud, *Totem and Taboo* in 13 THE STANDARD EDITION OF THE COMPLETE PSYCHOLOGICAL WORKS OF SIGMUND FREUD 1, 141-46 (J. Strachy tr. 1955), is my stylistic source for expression via non-historical historical parables.

regularly met with the answer that if he didn't like the way the thing was being done he should have said something then. Occasionally, when the craftsman was granted a royal patent of monopoly, or even when he achieved it "naturally," the rule would be relaxed. But in general the buyer was held to what he had helped to create or acceded to knowingly. Then a new method of production grew up. Men made things in closed factories and brought them to market. Their innards and construction were completed when the buyer came upon them. The goods proliferated and no man could be expert as to all of them. In such a situation the old "rule" would begin to look silly, and one could foresee (after some fencing over disclosure levels and the varieties of fraud and quasi-fraud) the creation of two legal categories, plain old goods (maybe now called "custom made goods") and "goods of adhesion." The focus of legal attention would nonetheless remain upon the nature and quality of the goods and certain rules would become natural candidates for adoption: "no junk," or "fair average quality," or "no hidden defects." The criteria of "goodness" could not possibly be rigid, but quality and access to knowledge about it would be the subject of the inquiry.[50]

Now consider one particular modern consumer transaction, the purchase of that most ubiquitous consumer good (or consumer "better" or consumer "best" perhaps, considering the advertising framework), the automobile.[51] Start with the scenario; we'll look more closely at the props in a moment.

*The curtain rises on a typical new automobile showroom, this one for products of Tyrannosaurus Motors. There are the usual tacky little salesmen's tables ranged against the rear wall, the usual banners on the walls ("Tyrannosaurus is Rex;" "Put a carnivore in your garden"), the ubiquitous colored brochures on every flat surface. Downstage left is a rumpled middle-aged man (call him "Mark") devotedly circling a huge car, occasionally giving it a cautious pat or gentle rub, emanating the taut glow of a man uncertain at what point courting might be treated as indecent liberties. Downstage center is a neatly dressed man of roughly the same age with a carefully trimmed mustache. He is trying, though not very hard, to appear as if he is staring out into space, but he knows, and Mark knows, and we know, that he is*

50. *See* B. NICHOLAS, AN INTRODUCTION TO ROMAN LAW 181-82 (1962) for an early actually historical instance of such a focus.

51. Insofar as the automobile purchase is atypical, involving as it does an expensive chattel over which consumers do take *some* care, it cuts against the points I am trying to make. That is why I chose it.

*following the scene with the eyes of a father with seven daughters and a shotgun watching the parlor couch from the upstairs landing. Mark opens and slams the car door once more, kicks the left front tire fondly but firmly, and sighs piteously. The other man immediately approaches:*

Salesman: May I help you?

Mark: Nice car.

S: A Beauty.

M: Powerful.

S: 385 HP. *Big* horses.

M: Expensive.

S: Not for what you're getting. (*There follows at this point, as a cadenza, a more or less detailed description, mostly in terminology that would make an analyst blush, of the delights of possession and use. This culminates with . . . .*)

M: How much?

S: *(clipped)* $4,782.37.) *At this point, the tone of both takes on a kind of chanting, ceremonial air, the performance of a ritual investiture between coreligionists.*)

M: From happy Harry I can get it for $4,600, plus $300 for my '62 Pteradactyl.

S: $4,300 net? You're talking cash?

M: Twenty-four months I'm talking.

S: *(Suppressing what is either a smile, or the yawn of a predator, and pointing toward one of the "desks" upstage)* Come, let's talk. *(They sit down together and one can hear only a low confused murmur, with occasional single words and phrases standing out, like* "dual exhausts," "superchargers", "whitewalls", "genuine leatherette" *and* "roof frescoes." *At last:*)

S: OK, that'll come to $4,782.37 plus financing. You want it? (*Or in Latin, spondesne.*)

M: OK. When can I pick it up? (*I.e., spondeo.*)

S: For midnight puce, you'll have to wait till next Friday. Now, if you'll just sign these papers . . . .

M: *(Signs)*

Now notice, there has been a lot of bargaining, usually much, much more than my truncated script indicates. But it has been over two things, price and standard variations in the product. In fact, there is only one element of the deal that has not been the subject of any contracting process: the contract. And what does that look like? It looks like a contract. But when one stands far enough back from the whole deal, from the whole process of goods buying, what one sees is a unitary, purchased bundle, of which the product, say a car, is just the most tangible (and, oddly enough, the *most* mutable) thing. One goes out and acquires the whole "set" which is a "deal on a car," and of the interchangeable subsets (object, extras, contract), it is in fact arguable that the contract is *more* of a "thing" than the goods which are sold pursuant to it.

Why then do people continue to call a certain thing a contract instead of a thing? What impels one to classify an X among the preexisting category "contracts," especially since so many of the family resemblances among contracts center on the physiogomy of bargain, agreement, dicker, process, mutability, becoming.[52] If that is so, why would people, very well aware of the non-bargained genesis of a consumer contract call it a contract? After all, the *key* insight about "contracts of adhesion" was that they were products of non-bargaining, unilaterally manufactured commodities.[53] Because as a thing, an object, it looks like the referent of the *noun* form of the word "contract;" it looks the way the *product* of the process of bargaining so often looks. What happened, it seems to me, is that of all the indicia which determine whether a thing is a contract or not, the most irrelevant—the physical appearance of the thing as a thing—turned out to be the most powerful. This thing, the consumer contract, just happens to look like the result of what in the consumer-contract context is a nonhappening,[54] the consumer contracting process.[55]

## *Practicalities*

What, if anything, might be the practical consequence of shifting the metaphoric framework within which consumer-transaction law develops from "contract" (of adhesion) to "thing" ("product")? Assuming for the moment the accuracy of my critical distinction between the classes "contract" and "thing", that a thing presents itself

52. *See* "Contract as Contract," TAN 15-33, *supra*.

53. Or, to be more accurate perhaps, contracting is to adhering what J. Press' custom suits are to its rack suits. Neither are either perfectly fixed or perfectly alterable, but the distinction is plain—and the necessary price differential is even plainer.

54. It is even more ironic, perhaps, that even to the extent that there *is* a happening leading to the consumer contract, it is in any event to a large extent shielded from effective judicial scrutiny by the vestigial parol evidence rule.

55. *See* [text after note 14], *supra*. In short, while everyone knows that not all contracts are writings, it was not fully appreicated how important it was in this context to recognize that not all writings were contracts either, even if commercial, bounded, future-regulating, etc. Or still another way to put it is that not every pair of identification criteria are, in fact, necessarily related to each other with any overwhelming correlation, even though each one singly may correlate highly with the classification itself.

as what it is, to take or leave, while contract implies the final phase of a process, it should not be a real jaw-dropper to suggest that regulatory and remedial strategies might vary depending upon whether one thought one was regulating process or product. There are, it seems to me, only three general strategies for regulating consumer transactions: you can focus your attention on the parties, the dealing, or the product. For current purposes,[56] the critical strategic decision seems to be between deal control and goods control. (Let me interject here, lest you all think me mad, that I am aware that it is not writ large in the heavens that one cannot mix techniques.) Now, keeping in mind the nature, factual and legal, of the usual consumer-goods (or services) transaction, deal control is ordinarily a stupid option: it is silly to seek to shape and control the contours of a process that does not take place. That does not mean that fraud, duress (both classical and "business duress[57]) or even "procedural unconscionability"[58] are totally irrelevant to the consumer-goods field. It's just that such approaches are beside the point most of the time; it's like bandaging a cut on a broken leg. The normal, non-pathological consumer sale,[59] is one in which a form is proferred by a non-monopolist selling non-life-essential goods pursuant to no huge quantum of lying, and in which that form is signed because no one is particularly interested in the sub-set of the whole package which is the contract. In such a context, how does one go about regulating the contract as a process. By facilitating more bargaining? But that is absurd (1) because, as Llewellyn saw as early as anybody,[60] the mass produced contract is complementary to, and has the same economic utility of, the mass-produced product; (2) most "objectionable" clauses of a consumer contract have only contingent, often highly contingent, importance, and no buyer not represented by a lawyer (whose job it is almost wholly to think about things which are not going to happen) is going to think much about them;[61] and (3)

56. It is conceivable that one could regulate consumer transactions by "regulating" the parties, for instance putting consumers under some kind of tutelary disenablement, or licensing merchants for honesty and competence. But for a host of reasons which I will not enlarge upon here, I do not consider person regulation a viable approach to consumer-contract regulation.

57. *See* Dawson, *Economic Duress—An Essay in Perspective*, 45 MICH. L. REV. 253 (1947).

58. *See* Leff, *supra* note 47, at 489-508.

59. There is certainly enough law to deal with lying and coercing. But unless one expands lying to include "inculcating desire by appealing to man's worst instincts through advertising," and subsumes form-padding under duress, most transactions are not, in *that* sense, pathological.

60. Llewellyn, *supra* note 35, at 701-02.

61. Contrast the law's treatment of penalties with its avowed policy not to take account of adequacy of consideration. Part of the source of that disparate treatment is that consideration is what *will* happen; penalty is treated by the parties much more lightly, as what most likely (or at least hopefully) will not. *See* 5 CORBIN, CONTRACTS § 1057 (1964).

even if the unrepresented consumer were interested, it is unlikely that he would have the necessary sophistication for such consideration. (One should not forget that even when a contract is hammered out *mit sturm und drang* by large law firms on behalf of industrial and financial giants, both principals "adhere" to most of the resulting document.) I would argue that so long as one is bemused by the word "contract," even when it is intelligently modified by the cognomen "adhesion," it is likely that one will sometimes seek to impress his controls on a process which does not exist. This type of misfocus is already patent. It may be seen, for instance, in § 2-302 of the UCC[62] and its issue § 5.107 of the UCCC,[63] both dealing with unconscionability; in UCC § 2-207[64] (on the battle of the forms); and in the continuing line of feeling that a large or conspicuous piece of writing (as contrasted with meaning) is sufficient, within a bargaining universe, to be the subject of that bargaining.[65]

What would happen, however, if one pushed the straddle that "contract of adhesion" represents off the wall in the other direction and made a quantum leap to the other regulatory focus, product control? What would happen, that is, if one did actually think about consumer contracts as things?

First of all, that would open up the law's long tradition, accelerating of late, of direct, explicit governmental control of the quality and safety of products. Autos now have mandatory seatbelts,[66] milk is bereft of its tubercles,[67] and outright poisonous substances are barred from the marketplace.[68] Even less reified "things", *when seen as products*, have been regulated as to quality for quite a long time. Life insurance contracts,[69] for instance, have been in effect written by deputy insurance

62. UCC § 2-302.

63. UNIFORM CONSUMER CREDIT CODE § 5.108 (1969 Revised Final Draft) [hereinafter cited as UCCC].

64. *See* Macaulay, *Contract Law and Contract Research (Part II)*, 20 J. LEG. ED. 460, 465 (1968).

65. *See, e.g.*, how the UNIFORM COMMERCIAL CODE defines "conspicuous" as "so written that a reasonable person . . . ought to have *noticed* it. . . . Language . . . is 'conspicuous' if it is in larger or other contrasting type or color." UCC § 1-201 (10) (emphasis added).

66. *See* 15 U.S.C. §§ 1381-1425 for automobile and tire safety standards.

67. *See* STATE OF NEW YORK, OFFICIAL COMPILATION OF CODES, RULES AND REGULATIONS, tit. 10, ch. I, part 3 (N.Y.S. Dep't. of Health, Sanitary Code, Milk and Milk Products).

68. In fact, it is even possible to ban a drug which, while it won't kill you, is unlikely to help you much either. *See* 21 U.S.C. § 355.

69. I do not wish to press this point too hard, but it seems to me very likely that along with the economic and social forces which have shaped the techniques for controlling iinsurance agreements, there has also functioned the fact that an insurance contract is a "policy," that is, that the most common label does *not* bring one up against the magically misleading word "contract" at all.

commissioners for years.[70] Nor has this quality-control device always required legislative action. The initial peculiar treatment of injurious foods in sealed packages[71] has almost ripened into the general "dangerous instrumentality" rule of the Restatement (Second) of Torts.[72] And even contract law, even traditional contract lore, is not wholly crippled as a mechanism for reific thinking. There is the frame-of-reference of "illegality" and its cousin, "against public policy," as a basis for decisions that some contract terms, no matter how they got into the contract, are too lousy to enforce.[73] When the static of *Henningsen*[74] subsides, for instance, one can hear the clear whinney of the unruly horse.[75] But "public policy" is so powerful a cure that wise physicians shun it. And illegality is a pretty slender reed, mostly because of the historical restrictions built into it. Generally, though with exceptions, the "harm" of the provision must be more substantial than getting a lousy deal, and it must be visited upon either some discernible person other than the parties, and maybe on the public generally.[76] In any event, the baggage that one totes along with "illegality" is presently too heavy for modern travel, and it is a deal-killing, not a deal-shaping technique anyway.

Not that I am suggesting for a moment that one *must* view a contract as a thing in order to regulate its content. In a few places that is openly done in the UCC,[77] and it is done much more frequently in the UCCC, which has two whole parts devoted to "illegal" provisions,[78] and even a few sections devoted to stipulating precise and mandatory language.[79] But I am willing to argue that viewing a contract as a product facilitates such a strategy, and, much more important, makes it necessary for the draftsman actually to think about what he is trying to do.[80]

70. *See* N.Y. INS. L. § 154 (approval of life, accident, health and annuity contracts); see also § 155 with its five pages of standard provisions.

71. *See* 1 S. WILLISTON, SALES §§ 241-42 (1948).

72. RESTATEMENT (SECOND) OF TORTS § 402A (1965).

73. *See* 6A A. CORBIN, CONTRACTS § 1375 (1962).

74. Henningsen v. Bloomfield Motors, Inc., 32 N.J.358, 161 A.2d 69 (1960).

75. *See* 32 N.J. at 403-08, 161 A.2d at 94-97.

76. 6A A. CORBIN, CONTRACTS (1962) is wholly devoted to the ins and outs of this powerful, arcane and peculiarly limited concept.

77. *See* UCC §§ 2-318, 2-725(1), 9-318(4).

78. UCCC art. 2, pt. 4, and art. 3, pt. 4 (§§ 2.401-2.416, and 3.401-3.409, respectively).

79. *See, e.g.*, UCCC § 2.503(2).

80. Unlike the situation with respect to § 2-302 of the UCC, as I have previously and stridently argued. *See* Leff, *supra* note 47, especially at 557-59.

*See* "Conclusion," TAN 103-04 *infra* for limitations upon this direct quality-control technique.

But talking about contracts as things, as "part of" the goods being sold, opens up another regulatory road. The pervasive weapon of the common law for controlling the quality of goods, at least to the extent of giving redress when the goods were abnormally shoddy or dangerous, has not been statutory or regulatory specification, but warranty. If nothing is said at the sale, said the law, the goods must be of fair average quality (which, I assume, turned out, most of the time, to be "minimum bearable quality") within the trade. Notice the delicious involutions of that development. Warranty law is at least initially *contract* law; much of its seamier history, for instance privity and disclaimer doctrine, comes out of that particular displacement of metaphor.[81] But out of that naissance came the word (and the field) "warranty". If something was said about the quality of the goods, that "contract" governed. But if nothing was said, what *was* said? That there were no huge surprises in store for anyone who bought this particular member of that general class of goods. In other words, that the goods were more or less what they purported to be.[82]

It is with respect to this mysterious "purporting" which *things* can apparently manage that there arises, it seems to me, a critical change in how one views a consumer-sale document *qua* thing rather than *qua* contract. The transformation is quite subtle, so subtle in fact that it may not exist. But this is what I have in mind: there is a fantasy deeply imbedded in the rites of linguistic use (of which contract interpretation is a branch) that words convey the information which they "mean".[83] If you can see and read a sentence, you have possession of the message. That does not mean that the law has made no provision for communication breakdown. At every stage of the communication process—sending set, medium, receiving set—critical malfunctions have been recognized. There are fine-print cases,[84] back-of-the-form cases,[85] foreign language cases,[86] illiteracy cases,[87] mental incompetence

---

81. Of course, it depends on how one places one's "initially". If one picks a very early "initially," it was first tort, then contract, and now, maybe, tort again. *See* 1 S. WILLISTON, SALES §§ 195-96 (1948).

82. The current statutory embodiment of warranty comprises UCC §§ 2-312-2-318. The statutory story told there is more complicated than, but not at odds with, my shorthand summary.

83. I say this in the face of the powerful, well known, and extensive efforts to correct this simplistic notion. *See, e.g.*, 3 A. CORBIN, CONTRACTS §§ 532-60 (1960); Farnsworth, *"Meaning" in the Law of Contracts*, 76 YALE L.J. 939 (1967).

84. *See* Vogel & Berstein, *Fine Print*, 21 BUS. LAW 544 (1966); Note, 63 HARV. L. REV. 494 (1950).

85. *See, e.g.*, Siegelman v. Cunard White Star Ltd., 221 F.2d 189 (2d Cir. 1955).

86. *See, e.g.*, Fricke v. Isbrandtson Co., 151 F. Supp. 465 (S.D.N.Y. 1957). See also Frostifresh Corp. v. Reynoso, 52 Misc. 2d 26, 274 N.Y.S. 2d 757 (Dist. Ct., Nassau County, 1966), *rev'd on other grounds*, 54 Misc. 2d 119, 281 N.Y.S. 2d 964 (Sup. Ct. 1967) (Spanish-speaking consumer and salesman, English contract).

87. *See, e.g.*, Dysarz v. Janczarek, 238 Mich. 529, 213 N.W. 694 (1927); Caton v. Wellershouse, 77 Pa. Super. 331 (1921).

cases,[88] drunkenness cases[89] and so on. But these cases are all seen and felt as somehow exceptional, to be understood against the background rule: if *words* become available to a consciousness capable of receiving them *as words*, then the *meaning* of those words is deemed also to have been conveyed. And "meaning", in such a formulation, refers to what they eventually unambiguously say.[90] This, of course, is quite a natural way to regard words; it is, in fact, hard to think about them any other way.

When things "purport" however, the communication process is "seen" quite differently. Things are not usually regarded as bearers of messages (the way hemoglobin "carries" oxygen compounds), but rather as messages themselves. They are, are amenable to the senses, and what they convey to the senses is *what* they are. Thus, for instance, judges thinking warranty did not always assume that just because a product was "there" it disclosed everything about itself that one would like to know.[91] Not only are parts of things inaccessible to all the senses, but not even everything *about* things "in the open" is disclosed to sight—or to the touch, smell, hearing and taste. There are, in fact, things about things which are opaque to the senses under all circumstances. There are other things which are opaque except under special sense-increasing circumstances.[92] But critically, what the judges realized was that the actual circumstances of the examination, including the situation, expeerience and knowledge of the buyer, determined what in fact the object, the product, "said" about itself. When the subject was a thing, rather than a contract, the question became what a reasonable (this?) purchaser knew or ought to have

88. *See* RESTATEMENT (SECOND) OF CONTRACTS § 18C (Tent. Draft No.1, 1964) and cases cited in Comments b-f.

89. *See id.*, § 18D and cases cited in Comments b & c.

*See also*, for a somewhat broader view, UCC § 6.111(3)(e), which describes as one of the factors to be taken into account by the administrator in determining whether to seek an injunction against a pattern of seller activity as "unconscionable," whether the "respondent has knowingly taken advantage of the inability of the debtor reasonably to protect his interests by reason of physical or mental infirmities, ignorance, illiteracy or inability to understand the language of the agreement, or similar factors."

90. *But see* note 83, *supra*.

91. *See, e.g.*, Rinaldi v. Mohican Co., 225 N.Y. 70, 121 N.E. 471 (1918) (cited in 2 F. HARPER & F. JAMES, Torts § 28.20 at 1581 n.13 (1956)) for a clear statement of how even looking, if not correctly motivated, will not "disclose" certain important facts about a thing.

92. For instance, metal fatigue, needing X-ray examination for discovery.

known under the actual circumstances. There was no pretence that objects were, just by being "seeable," omnidisclosive. This concept, often warily circled by the latent-patent defect terminology,[93] seems to have made it possible for the judges to focus somewhat more precisely on the actual position of the particular "receiving set" for the message, rather than merely lopping out crude chunks of competence like "insane," "illiterate" and "drunk".[94]

The differing impulse of the courts when approaching "contract", however, seems to have led to a different implicit "rule": subject to (a) gross defects in transmission of the words *as words* (small type, back of form, foreign language); and (b) the gross defects in the "receiving set" set out above (insanity, minority, sometimes illiteracy), a contract means that which it finally unambiguously means upon examination. But that view of meaning conveyance, of words as affective happenings, makes sense, *if at all*, only when the words are viewed as either the result of, or at least the basis for, a process of coming about. If, however, a particular contract is a mass-produced inalterable thing, then the words that make it up are just elements of the thing, like wheels and carburetors. They do not have, at least not common to the parties, any history or any future.

Perhaps another way to put this groping distinction is to say that a proposal for or product of a discussion is different from a label. If a label doesn't actually convey its message on the spot, in the actual conditions where it is to function, then it does no good at all. Certainly if a rule of law demanded a warning on a product it would give pause to a judge if the bottle said "Respiratory Depressant" rather than "Poison,"[95] or bore the Christian Omega of death rather than the Skull-and-Cross-Bones. And this unease would be hardly alleviated by the prominence or size of the type face. Certainly also, in a warranty case, if the manufacturer's defense against an electrocuted buyer's claim was that there was a wiring diagram on the front of the product which "clearly" showed the uninsulated power input snuggling against the metal door frame, the bookmaker's book would be heavy against the manufacturer.[96] And the odds would seem almost equally good if

93. *See* 77 C.J.S. *Sales* § 315 at pp. 1158-59 (1952).

94. *See* RESTATEMENT (SECOND) OF CONTRACTS §§ 18-18D (Tent. Draft No.1, 1964). *See also* note 56, *supra*.

95. For a very recent negligence case in which a warning label which in fact *did* verbally warn of possible death from use of the product was nevertheless (quite rightly) held to be insufficiently scarifying under the circumstances, *see* Griffin v. Planters Chemical Corp., 302 F. Supp. 937 (D.S.C. 1969).

96. *Cf.* Holmes, *The Path of the Law*, 10 HARV. L. REV. 457, 461 (1897): "The prophecies of what the courts will do in fact, and nothing more pretentious, are what I mean by the law."

pasted to the front of the door were the label "Voltage through door: 220." Only when the label said something like "DANGER—Wiring Fault—Do Not Plug In Until Corrected By Electrician" would one start betting on the defendant.

If indeed there is some such distinction in legal approach to "contract" messages and "thing" messages,[97] that would tend to explain, at least in part, certain otherwise extraordinary regulatory decisions to allow words which do "say" a warning to be a warning without regard to commercial realities, so long as the *word* delivery is sufficient. There leaps to mind the warranty-disclaimer section of the UCC,[98] pursuant to which "there are no warranties which extend beyond the description on the face hereof" will exclude all warranties of fitness, and pursuant to which, presumably, "There is no warranty of merchantability" will exclude that one—so long as the words are in writing and conspicuous (which means "in larger or other contrasting type or color").[99] Or look at the effect of the subliminal smell of contracting process in the most recent piece of consumer-protection drafting, the UCCC. One section provides[100] in its material part as follows:

> (1) In addition to *contracting* for a security interest in the goods sold, a seller of goods in a consumer credit sale may secure the debt arising from the sale by (a) *contracting* for a security interest in goods previously sold to the buyer by the seller if there is an existing security interest in the goods held by the seller; . . . . (emphasis supplied)

Now, this is the provision that is apparently designed to deal with the *Williams v. Walker-Thomas*[101] type of problem. How does it deal with it? Well, it seems to contemplate a little negotiating session between openminded dealers like the Walker-Thomas folks, and young sophisticates like Mrs. Williams, and, Heaven help us, over a contract provision in the permissible, and therefore presumable, form:

> From and after the date hereof, Seller shall have a security interest in all goods heretofore sold to buyer to secure payment for said goods and for the goods sold to the buyer hereunder.

97. Even to approach *proving* such a distinction one would have to have examined and described with fantastic insight and precision a vast body of decided cases—latent-patent cases, contract interpretation cases, fine print cases, and so on. I have not done so.

98. UCC § 2-316.

99. UCC § 1-201(10).

100. UCC § 2.408.

101. Williams v. Walker-Thomas Furniture Co., 350 F.2d 445 (D.C. Cir. 1965).

Fantasyville.[102]

If, on the other hand, one is not thinking "contract" or "agreement" at all, it seems more likely that one will demand something on the order of a warning label. If cross-collateral clauses are to be permitted at all, they should be treated as a latent danger and labelled as such. With one's mind tuned that way, while one might continue to demand "conspicuousness" for the words, one would also require conspicious meaning, *e.g.*,

> *Caution. If you don't pay on time for what you just bought, we may be able to take back everything we ever sold you.*

## *Conclusion*

The approach I have been touting is to think about the paper-with-words which accompanies the sale of a product as part of that product. This classifactory shift may perhaps have two effects. First, it would provide a better conceptual framework for direct governmental quality controls. When things are too dangerous or too worthless the government *does* directly intervene. There is no reason why that intervention should not take place as directly with respect to contracty things.

But the limitations of any quality-control approach must be considered, however briefly. Even if one does approach a contract as a thing, it is not so terribly easy to tell when even things should be regulated. One does not solve the evil-defining problem merely by approaching it as a species of goods-quality control. Bluntly, what kinds of clauses ought to be illegal? Certainly the answer is not "harsh ones". Almost all deal breakdowns are going to have harsh effects on one of the parties, and it is certainly not clear that ball harshness should be absorbed by the party able to spread the impact over all purchasers. It is not irrefutably clear that stable contract makers ought *necessarily* pick up the tab for those whose contracts break up. For among other things, this quality-control technique has important economic (and, therefore, social) costs. If carried forward with any vigor, no lawful contract could descend in "fairness" or "safety" below a certain qualitative minimum. In certain situations that would have the same effect as some building codes: the cheapest one can get is more expensive than one can afford.[103] One is less able to trade off

102. In fairness to the draftsmen of the UCC, it must be pointed out that they have eliminated, in § 2.409, the most vicious aspects of cross-collateral clauses. But note that they have done so by direct quality-control of the contract, not by playing with the "contracting" process.

103. Consider also, as another instance, the proposals that wage-garnishment be totally

quality or risk for price even if one wants to and is aware of what one is doing. In brief, the government-quality-control technique is a replacement for market-set quality and price levels and mixes. Whether the fundamental market-economy postulate, that individuals most often know what they want better than a government does, is empirically sound or not, there is certainly evidence that governments tend frequently to make an unacknowledged conflation of the two wildly different concepts "what they want" and "what is good for them," with numerous repressive effects.[104] Strict quality control is, after all, a regulatory approach the basis of which is "I don't care if you want it; you can't have it." This is highly justified when what you want is a poison, when a slip in making your own decision as to what is "good for you" is fatal. It may be justified for lesser risks when the market is, in fact, highly imperfect. As the price of an error becomes more and more merely economic (rather than organic), and the market becomes more subject to normal competitive correctives, this intrusion becomes more and more noxious. While this new metaphor may thus suggest a newly applicable frame of reference—governmental goods-quality control—it does not without more make any of the hard decisions about when and how to use it.[105]

Hence attempts *not* directly to regulate quality, but instead to increase the availability and quality of the information upon which buying (market) decisions are based, have good sense behind them. I have tried to indicate that the metaphoric shift here proposed has a subtle but important effect upon the workings of *that* regulatory device

forbidden, *e.g.*, Kerr, *Wage Garnishment Should Be Prohibited*, 2 PROSPECTUS 371 (1969), *i.e.*, to turn all wages into spendthrift trusts.

104. *See, e.g.*, 26 U.S.C. §§ 4742(a) and 7238 on marihuana.

105. Even after identifying the "unfair," in other words, there still remains the difficulty of describing and producing the fair, and this general problem is certainly not limited to the consumer-protection field. *See* H. WELLINGTON, LABOR AND THE LEGAL PROCESS 27-35 (Paperback ed. 1968) for a discussion in the context of labor policy.

Some experience with true goods-quality control is, however, suggestive. When the government mandates the quality of goods, the practice seems most effective and least objectionable when the threat is of a harm both serious and irreversible, like death or crippling from an ill-conceived drug. *See* notes 66-68, *supra*. In the consumer-contract area, the harms are never quite that dramatic, generally being limited to no more than the value of the bargain, but it may be intelligent to focus one's regulatory efforts in this context on losses beyond the value of the bargain (for instance, disclaimers of warranty affecting personal-injury claims, or contractual collection devices which cost the debtor much more than the debt). It is indeed possible that the courts, attempting to give content to UCC § 2-302, have adopted such an approach without being aware of any general principle informing their thus far *ad hoc* approach. *See* Murray, *supra* note 45, for a burgeoning but not quite expressed awareness of the significance of beyond-the-bargain clauses when adhesion contracts run against the unconscionability clause. I hope to expand a little on the idea in an article scheduled to appear in 31 U. PITT. L. REV., number 3.

too. Briefly, I have argued that viewing a consumer contract as a thing might in time lead to a perception of disclosure not in the old contract-interpretation terminology but in a more realistic context, more attuned to what happens at retail, to the ultimate production of more *actual* information disclosure. Certainly such a shift would not solve all the problems either. Many people don't read contracts at all; even a clear one won't help them. And some people would sign a contract even if "THIS IS A SWINDLE" were embossed across its top in electric pink. But assuming that the new metaphor would produce fuller *message* disclosure, at relatively small information cost, it might well increase the power of the market itself to control the price-quality mix.

And there is one last limitation upon the utility of this suggested metaphoric transformation which must finally be mentioned. While my suggestion has been wholly serious, I am quite aware of the fragility of this kind of effort. Language has never been much of a match for sense perceptions except as an analytic, and analytics have a way of being quickly swallowed up in the resurgant real world of synthetics. One of Hohfeld's great contributions to legal analysis, for instance, was the suggestion that some things, like "property," were not really, at law, "things" at all, but force fields. Intelligent discourse, he argued, should not be directed towards deciding to whom a thing belonged, because there was no thing to belong; there was only a bundle of forces demanding, for sensible talk, a sort of vector analysis with time coordinates.[106] With some historical distance, one can see that the partial but undeniable failure of that powerful suggestion to take hold was not primarily a product of Hohfeld's untimely death, or of some basic vice in his analysis, but more of the fact that a farm, for instance, bundle of powers, privileges, rights, etc. or not, persists in the consciousness as "dirt with boundaries". In like manner, a consumer contract of adhesion *looks* like a classic bargained contract. A consumer contract is *not* a thing, at least not the way cars, cows and couches are things, and no rhetoric is going to convince anyone for long that it is. Thus the real hope of an exercise like this is necessarily more modest than any total sensory transformation. It can aspire at most temporarily to smash the semantic box in which our current thinking is locked. The next step, and the harder one, is crafting a better cabinet out of materials really available in a real world.

106. *See, e.g.*, Hohfeld, *Faulty Analysis in Easement and License Cases*, 27 YALE L.J. 66 (1917), applying Hohfeld, *Some Fundamental Legal Conceptions As Applied in Judicial Reasoning* I & II, 23 YALE L.J. 16 (1913) and 26 YALE L.J. 710 (1917).

[6]

# The Dilemma of Consumer Fraud: Prosecute or Mediate

**by Eric H. Steele**

**Consumer fraud agencies often mediate disputes between consumers and businesses instead of using their resources only for prosecution. This results in part from a displacement of agency goals, but mediation is also a necessary part of any effective program for the prosecution of consumer fraud. A better means must be developed to interpret and use the information that comes in the form of consumer complaints.**

MISREPRESENTATION, chain referrals, pyramid and bait-and-switch schemes, high pressure salesmanship, false and misleading advertising, and other imaginative fraudulent and deceptive business practices have become the target of federal, state, and local laws. There is a growing awareness of the millions of dollars lost annually by the victims of these fraudulent schemes. Consumer groups are raising the political voice of the dissatisfied and the victimized consumer to an audible pitch. Consumer fraud even has taken a place in the encyclopedic list of factors contributing to social unrest, riots, and crime. Laws have been enacted, new enforcement agencies created, and the funding and staff of existing agencies dramatically increased.

One result of this increase in awareness and activity is a widespread disappointment with consumer agencies. In addition to the usual frustration that the war was not won in the first skirmish, there appears to be a sense that the enforcement agencies are not doing the right thing. Activist consumer groups see the law enforcement agencies as selling out by protecting the status quo rather than aggressively prosecuting predatory businesses. Much of the business community shares this sense that the agencies do not take aggressive action against the fly-by-night operators who give legitimate business a bad name.

The legal community seems to agree that law enforcement agencies dealing with consumer fraud somehow have not lived up to expectations and have not made much of an impact on the problem of consumer fraud. Much of this disappointment is articulated in the assertion that law enforcement agencies do not enforce the law but misallocate their resources on tasks that rarely deal with the real law violators.

What do consumer agencies do? Generally they spend a great deal of time and energy mediating consumer complaints that involve large and respectable businesses rather than aggressively ferreting out fraudulent merchants. They spend large portions of their energies and budgets counseling disgruntled consumers and trying to settle relatively minor consumer grievances. The goal of law enforcement has been largely displaced by the goal of settling individual consumer disputes. To find out why this displacement occurs and to evaluate its relationship to stated law enforcement goals, I examined in detail the operation of one consumer agency.

The first modern state consumer fraud bureau was created in New York in 1957. Since then, most of the states have created agencies to enforce burgeoning consumer fraud and deceptive practices laws. State legislation defines fraudulent business practices, prescribes penalties, and mandates consumer fraud agencies to enforce the prohibitions. The consumer fraud agency I examined is a division of the attorney general's office in a large industrial state. Its structure and operation are representative of many state consumer fraud agencies. The principal statute it enforces was described by the attorney general soon after its enactment:

> The law is designed to rid the state of merchants who habitually employ fraud, deception, and misrepresentation in connection with the sale of merchandise, real estate, and services.
>
> Under this act it is the duty of the attorney general to investigate unlawful practices, and he has the power to require written statements and reports, to examine witnesses under oath, to examine merchandise and records and to impound and retain merchandise and records pursuant to order of court. To carry out his duties, the attorney general is authorized to issue subpoenas, administer oaths, conduct hearings, prescribe forms, promulgate rules and regulations, and to institute legal proceedings including actions to obtain injunctions and the appointment of receivers.

After several years of operation this agency now receives annually about ten thousand complaints from consumers, sues about thirty businesses to enjoin unlawful practices, and obtains about ten agreements to cease and desist. The main activity of the agency, however, is settling complaints received from consumers. Screening and mediating the complaints occupy the bulk of the agency's lawyers and nonprofessional staff. The agency intervenes in and attempts to settle 75 per cent of the complaints it receives that concern businesses within the state not regulated by another state agency. The agency intervenes when it appears that the complainant has been treated unfairly or that a transaction has not been satisfactorily completed.

### Informal Hearings Settle Complaints

No determination that fraud may have occurred is necessary for this administrative intervention — and no such determination is made. The agency holds informal private hearings to mediate more than 20 per cent of the complaints — those not settled by correspondence. Forty-five per cent of the complaints on which the agency acts informally are settled with some tangible benefit to the complaining consumer — refund, repair, replacement, contract or debt cancellation, or completion of performance. Complaint files acted on generally are closed when a settlement is reached or when the bureau concludes that the complainant-consumer is not entitled to relief. If no relief can be obtained at the informal hearing, the file typically is closed on the theory that the agency has made a reasonable effort and no more resources ought to be used on a single complaint. The initial processing of complaints is oriented toward settling consumer disputes rather than investigating possible fraudulent practices.

The agency intervenes in a consumer complaint if the complainant states a good case that he is equitably entitled to relief from the seller. No judgment is made before or during the initial intervention process as to whether fraud is likely to have occurred. Only a small fraction of the complaints initially processed appeared to the agency's lawyers, to the complaining consumer, or to me as likely to involve fraud, misrepresentation, or deceptive practices.

Cases considered for substantive litigation were selected and investigated independently of the initial complaint-intervention process. A variety of events can trigger an investigation for possible litigation. The receipt by the bureau of a large number of similar complaints against a particular merchant may lead to an investigation. This chain of events, however, is relatively rare. Since the complaints are not systematically monitored for patterns of conduct or for industry-wide practices, few cases come to the attention of the bureau this way.

### Lawsuits Are Not Often Filed

This may result from several factors: the isolation of the litigation attorneys from the flow of complaints, the pervasive attitude that most of the consumers who complain are seeking private redress rather than blowing the whistle on fraudulent merchants, and the inherent difficulty of analyzing a large number of complaints for evidence of unlawful practices. As a practical matter, investigation for possible litigation is triggered more often by the investigative work of others — consumer groups, public agencies, the press, trade and professional groups, or by pressure from other influential sources, politicians, or community and business leaders. Only 8 per cent of the businesses complained against were investigated even perfunctorily by the litigation attorneys for possible law enforcement action. Even among those few cases in which substantive lawsuits were filed, 20 per cent were dropped on the sole basis of restitution.

What I have described is a law enforcement agency which was created to enforce consumer fraud statutes but which in practice spends most of its resources settling consumer disputes. Established to "rid the state of merchants who habitually employ fraud," the bureau was recently described (after several years of operation) by the state attorney general in these words:

> The attorney general's division of consumer protection battles fraudulent, deceptive, and unfair business practices throughout [the state]. To supplement our principal offices in downtown . . . branch offices have now been established the length of the state . . . in the low income sector [of the major city] . . . as well as in the suburbs. . . . Thus, any citizen who feels that he has been duped or wronged in a consumer transaction can file a complaint with the attorney general, who then becomes the face-to-face legal representative of the citizen in righting the wrong and recovering the individual's money whenever possible.

As this consumer fraud agency illustrates, there are two ways of perceiving and responding to conduct that is brought into question, in this case by consumer complaints. When it is suggested that certain conduct violates the norms of society, one may define the situation as one of crime or one of dispute. How situations are defined by those whose task it is to respond to them and how society defines entire classes of situations have important consequences for the nature of the response made to the situations.

By defining certain situations as involving criminal conduct, a society not only indicates that the particular

Eric H. Steele, after having practiced law in Chicago, is a research attorney in the American Bar Foundation. He received his A.B. from Yale in 1963 and his J.D. at Harvard in 1967.

norm violated is an important one but also that its violation requires a collective response. The state deals with conduct defined as criminal on its own initiative and with its own resources. The substantive criminal law attempts to define the moral boundaries of society. Its method of defining these boundaries is positive in that it takes as its starting point that certain conduct beyond the normative boundary has occurred. It focuses its attention on the normative quality of acts, locates responsibility for acts in the fault or guilt of individuals, selects individuals who have performed the acts defined, labels and stigmatizes these individuals as criminals, and metes out punishment. It is oriented to the past insofar as it concentrates on past acts and intentions and ignores the present interests of the people involved. There is, for instance, little emphasis on restitution to victims or otherwise ameliorating the damages, strains, and hostilities created by a criminal act.

Conduct is defined as dispute when the acts complained of are not so heinous as to threaten the moral order of society and demand the collective response of punishment. Rather, a more passive posture is adopted.

### Dispute Participants Must Engage the Law

When the conduct is perceived as not encroaching on moral boundaries, the matter is seen as a dispute. Attention is not focused entirely on the normative quality of the conduct but encompasses the concrete situation in which the conduct took place and the interests of the individuals involved. The dispute perspective focuses on distributive justice and the rearrangement of unsatisfactory relationships rather than on the individualization of fault or guilt. In short, collective society takes the more passive position that if the individuals involved in the dispute situation do not demand intervention, then the society has no overriding interest in how the dispute is eventually terminated. Thus it is left to the disputing individuals to mobilize the resources of the law.

The legal institutions that embody the dispute response are quite different from those that comprise the criminal justice system. The institutions of criminal justice are relatively centralized and systematized in hierarchical organizations. They are designed to take initiative and act aggressively. The institutions of dispute intervention form a decentralized, nonsystematic market of competing resources. Dispute intervention may be seen as a service available to individuals who are aggrieved about situations in which they find themselves. The mobilization of these reactive institutions is a matter of self-help. There is an array of competing resources offering various types of dispute settlement services.

The consumer fraud bureau has come to be used by consumers as one of this array of institutions providing dispute intervention services. Half of the complaints, for example, made to the agency had previously been taken to other dispute-settling institutions — newspaper and television action lines, better business bureaus, consumer trade groups, and public officials.

The bureau responds to complaints by intervening to provide dispute settlement services. By responding to complaints as disputes, the consumer fraud bureau reinforces its definition as a dispute-settling agency and encourages additional dispute complaints. The bureau is not simply diverting cases from prosecution, as the current concept of diversion contemplates; it has radically redefined its task. The consumer fraud bureau does not conceive of itself primarily as a law enforcement institution. Some cases are prosecuted in court, but these are not considered the main business of the agency. The settlement rather than prosecution of cases is not viewed as a diversion: it is the main purpose of the consumer fraud bureau.

Why have the goals of prosecution and law enforcement been displaced by consumer complaint handling and dispute resolution? Several reasons may be suggested:

**1. Empathy and the Nature of the Offense and Offender.** The absolute normative categories of a criminal definition of the situation seem out of scale with typical consumer complaints received by consumer agencies. The conduct complained about is seldom as morally unambiguous as a crime of violence; neither is the merchant involved easily labeled as a deviant outsider, as is a violent criminal. Most of the businesses complained about are relatively large and well-known corporations, which are not susceptible of any stereotyped labeling as members of a criminal class of predatory merchants. As with other types of so-called white collar crime, the definition of the acts as crimes and the actors as criminals is fragile and unstable. The actors are not much unlike those judging them, and the judges realize that they might have done likewise in the situation. Thus, it seems inappropriate to think in terms of crime and punishment. Single complaints rarely seem heinous enough to label the business as criminal and the complaining consumer as victim. In short, one's empathies are typically drawn toward both parties at once, preventing the adoption of a highly polarized definition of the parties and the situation. Once the situation presented by the consumer's complaint is defined firmly as a nonpolarized dispute, the sympathies of the agency are captured by the consumers who continually seek its aid and often appear entitled to redress. The bureau's motivation and objectives are thus realigned to the settlement of disputes and the redress of legitimate consumer complaints, and the goal of prosecuting crime is greatly subordinated.

**2. Practical Difficulties of Prosecuting Fraud.** Fraud is extraordinarily difficult to prove. The facts are usually ambiguous and difficult to discover. The consumers who have been victimized are often the only people who know of the unlawful conduct, and often they do not know they have been defrauded. Since direct investigation or surveillance of business practices is usually impossible, consumer complaints are the main source of information. Consumer complaints, however, are often highly emotional and partisan and contain no direct evidence of the business's intent or its patterns of conduct outside the single transaction involving the complainant. Consumer complaints are difficult to interpret. It is even more difficult to locate patterns of complaints arising from similar practices. Numerous consumer complaints may be required to disclose and prove a pattern of conduct clear enough to establish that fraudulent practices have been used or to prove the element of intent. Those businesses that intentionally employ unlawful fraudulent practices are notoriously mobile and transitory. Often they have no established place of business, few assets, and multiple names and corporate shells. They are difficult to locate, investigate, and serve with process. Typically the damage is done and the operation has moved on to another state (with a new name, product, and tactics) before a pattern of complaints becomes evident, often before the complaints are even received.

**3. Organizational Imperatives.** In addition to the difficulties of investigating and prosecuting fraud, the political influence of many large businesses and trade groups makes it difficult to take action against widespread practices of large or well-connected businesses. The ordinary pressures of politics also impel public consumer agencies to concentrate on activities that will have an immediate and visible payoff. A complex fraud litigation that requires a large portion of staff and budget and shows no results for several years, if ever, is not congruent with the political necessity to show quick results for money spent and to demonstrate progress against fraud — all before the next election. Helping individual consumers yields immediate, concrete, and visible results, serves an existing need, and communicates in a tangible way the efficiency of the agency to numerous consumers who will be eligible to vote for the attorney general in the next election. The consumer fraud agency serves a *de facto* coalition of the interests of individual aggrieved consumers, politicians, and the business community by functioning primarily as a dispute-settling institution and de-emphasizing its prosecutorial activities and objectives.

How is this extreme goal displacement to be evaluated on a policy level? One's first reaction may be simply that consumer fraud agencies should get back to doing what they were created to do — investigate and prosecute fraud — and leave dispute resolution to the courts and other institutions designed for that purpose. Others will argue that the dispute settlement activities of consumer agencies provide a needed service that is not being adequately provided elsewhere and that resources therefore are being properly allocated.

## Many Complaints May Reveal a Fraud

On further analysis, however, it appears that the two responses — prosecution and dispute settlement — may be complementary in function, although they arise from divergent definitions of the situation. The reason for this is the necessary reliance on consumer complaints to discover fraudulent practices. Defrauded consumers must be encouraged to bring their complaints to consumer agencies if the agencies are to find out about the fraud that is being perpetrated. While consumer complaints are an inefficient source of information on fraud (each of us sometimes sees fraud and dishonesty in his frustration about the most innocent mistakes), they are the only available source of intelligence about business practices in individual consumer transactions. A further inefficiency is that a single complaint may not reveal the existence of fraud even when it has occurred. The determination may require the interpretation of numerous similar complaints indicating an unlawful business practice rather than isolated instances of mistake, misunderstanding, or negligence. Thus, many complaints must be collected and reviewed to reveal the fraud. Most complaints will not involve fraud — objectively viewed — and when fraud is involved it may not be discernible from any single complaint but only from a series of similar complaints.

How can consumer agencies obtain the vast flow of complaints that must be reviewed to discern frauds requiring prosecution? Whether or not it is their duty — legally or as good citizens — to report illegal acts to the proper authorities, most people, as the economists tell us, will not make the effort to file a complaint unless it is justified in cost-benefit terms — that is, unless there is something in it for them. Some victims are motivated sufficiently by indignation to blow the whistle on a merchant in the hope that he will be punished and other consumers protected. Most consumers, however, are aware of the factual ambiguities in their situation and simply want to get it straightened out without undue time or expense. The complaints received by the consumer fraud bureau that I examined almost always requested repair, replacement, or delivery of merchandise, completion of performance of services, refund of money, correction of billings or accounts, cancellation of contracts, or other private remedies. Few expressed any desire that the merchant be punished or investigated or

• This article summaries the author's investigations and conclusions. The full report of his study appears in the May, 1975, issue of the *University of Pennsylvania Law Review*, page 1107.

Consumer Fraud

any awareness that this was the reason for the bureau.

To obtain the consumer complaints that can provide the information necessary to fulfill their investigatory and prosecutorial functions, consumer fraud agencies must compete with the array of other institutions providing dispute settlement services. To compete successfully, they must provide dispute intervention and settlement services. The official status of consumer fraud agencies, their *expertise* in dealing with consumer grievances, and the inherent threat of prosecution, including investigation and negative publicity, give them great leverage in dealing with businesses against which complaints are received. On being contacted by the bureau, businesses often will look into complaints they hitherto had ignored, give weight to complaints they had labeled as unreasonable or dishonest, and accede to consumers in close cases.

In short, the bureau can get action for consumers. Consumers have long felt helpless against large corporate business organizations. Altering the balance of power in consumer transactions is surely one legitimate policy position. Some businesses object that they are pressured unduly to take action that they are not obligated legally to take. It appears to an outside observer, however, that the fraud bureau frequently accepts the business's position.

### Settlement and Prosecution Go Together

There is a functional interdependence between the dispute settlement and criminal prosecution responses to consumer complaints: consumer complaints are indispensable sources of information for effective prosecution of consumer fraud; consumer agencies must provide dispute settlement services in order to encourage consumers to bring their complaints to them; consumer disputes can be effectively settled with the leverage of the implicit threat of prosecution; the effectiveness of the threat of prosecution requires that the bureau aggressively and visibly prosecute some cases; and aggressive and visible prosecution requires information about business practices in the community, which can be supplied best by a heavy flow of consumer complaints. Thus, dispute settlement and prosecution ultimately succeed or fail together.

The weakest aspect of the operation of the bureau and other consumer protection agencies is the interpretation and use of the information that is available. It is a herculean task to analyze thousands of consumer complaints, locate in them patterns of unlawful practices, and identify the businesses engaged in them. The immensity of this task is an additional reason for the displacement of energies away from the goal of prosecution toward the goal of dispute settlement. The problem is not that so many resources are devoted to dispute settlement, but that the data potentially available from consumer complaints are not more effectively used as a basis for investigation and prosecution. Both goals must be pursued to meet prosecutorial goals effectively. ▲

## Fellowships in Legal History

IF APPLICATIONS of sufficient merit are received, a number of legal history research fellowships for periods of three to nine months, with a maximum stipend of $4,500, are available in 1976 from the Program in Legal History of the American Bar Foundation. The purpose of the program is to encourage and assist scholars to begin or bring to fruition and publication original research in Anglo-American legal history, with principal concern for the period 1500-1815 in English legal history and the period prior to 1900 in American legal history. Constitutional history, as such, is seldom favored.

Fellowship recipients are expected to work substantially full time on the research during the period of the fellowship and not to fulfill teaching or other employment or professional duties, except on terms approved in advance by the American Bar Foundation.

The program director is Thomas G. Barnes of the Department of History at the University of California at Berkeley. The foundation advisory committee is John P. Frank of Phoenix, Morton J. Horwitz of the Harvard Law School, William J. Jones of the Department of History of the University of Alberta, Stanley N. Katz of the University of Chicago Law School, and Joseph H. Smith of Columbia Law School.

Applications for fellowships in 1976 must be presented by January 1, 1976, and the awards will be announced not later than March 31, 1976. Further information and application forms may be obtained from the Program in Legal History, American Bar Foundation, 1155 East Sixtieth Street, Chicago, Illinois 60637.

## Medical Institute for Attorneys

THE eighth medical institute for attorneys, sponsored by the University of Miami Law Center in cooperation with the university's School of Medicine, will be held February 25–28, 1976, at the Americana Hotel in Bal Harbour, Florida. The institute will consider the diagnosis, treatment, and rehabilitation of injuries to the nervous system.

Further information may be obtained from Eighth Medical Institute for Attorneys, University of Miami Law Center, Box 248087, Coral Gables, Florida 33124 (305/284-4762).

## Symposium on International Financing

THE FORDHAM Corporate Law Institute will present a two-day symposium on international financing on November 18 and 19, 1975, at the Lincoln Center Campus of Fordham University in New York City. Further information may be obtained from the Fordham Law Alumni Association, 140 West Sixty-second Street, New York, New York 10023 (telephone 212/956-6603).

# Part III
# Information and Advertising

# [7]

VOLUME 90 FEBRUARY 1977 NUMBER 4

HARVARD LAW REVIEW

# BEYOND NADER: CONSUMER PROTECTION AND THE REGULATION OF ADVERTISING

*Robert Pitofsky* *

*In the last ten years, there have been several significant developments in federal regulation of advertising. In this Article, Professor Pitofsky examines the economic and legal justifications for ad regulation, suggests the contours of a consumer-oriented regulatory program, and assesses recent departures from traditional ad regulation by the Federal Trade Commission.*

IT is almost fifteen years since President Kennedy delivered the first presidential special message to Congress on protecting the consumer interest,[1] and over ten years since agents of General Motors investigated Ralph Nader and possibly tried to have him seduced in the aisles of a Washington drugstore.[2] While no event serves perfectly to mark the initiation of the modern consumer movement, these two resulted in heightened visibility and public awareness of that movement and its leading spokesman, which in turn contributed to the subsequent surge of legislative and judicial activity designed to modify the balance of rights and liabilities between sellers and consumers.

Since 1962, almost a score of major new legislative systems or amendments to prior regulatory schemes have been enacted at the federal level.[3] A review of the accumulated body of this legis-

* Professor of Law, Georgetown University Law School. B.A., New York University, 1951; LL.B., Columbia Law School, 1954. The author served as Director of the Bureau of Consumer Protection at the Federal Trade Commission from 1970 to 1973 — a period when many of the cases discussed in Part III of this Article were initiated.

[1] J.F. KENNEDY, *Special Message to the Congress on Protecting the Consumer Interest*, in PUB. PAPERS: John F. Kennedy 235–43 (1962).

[2] C. McCARRY, CITIZEN NADER 15–16 (1972); R. BUCKHORN, NADER, THE PEOPLE'S LAWYER 11–34 (1972).

[3] Among the more significant are the Fair Packaging and Labeling Act, Pub. L. No. 89–755, 80 Stat. 1296 (1966) (codified at 15 U.S.C. §§ 1451–1461 (1970)) (requiring label disclosure of contents, and empowering FTC and Secretary of HEW to promulgate rules regulating package size, statements concerning sale prices, and non-functional slack fill); Consumer Credit Protection Act (Truth in Lending), Pub. L. No. 90–321, 82 Stat. 146 (1968) (codified at 15 U.S.C. §§ 1601–1677 (1970)) (comprehensive scheme regulating disclosures with respect to consumer credit); Interstate Land Sales Full Disclosure Act, Pub. L. No. 90–

lation is impressive evidence of the responsiveness of the national legislature to claims of injustice advanced on behalf of consumers, and of the scope and intensity of attempted legislative solutions. Other consequences of this politically potent movement are developing case law and rulemaking expanding consumer rights, and a considerable literature of protest against the system of law now governing rights of sellers and consumers.[4]

This Article deals with new developments in the federal regulation of advertising, an area where new and more vigorous enforcement of existing statutes and rules has been most pronounced. The analysis in the Article will suggest that several departures from traditional advertising regulation are grounded in consumer-oriented concerns. Part I will therefore attempt to analyze, within the context of advertising, some of the economic and legal justifications for governmental intrusion into the marketplace in order to protect consumers more fully. Part II turns to an examination of the traditional principles governing ad regulation by the Federal Trade Commission, the primary agency at the federal level charged with regulation of advertising practices. Part III examines the consumer-orientation of more recent developments in regulation of advertising, focusing on whether these new developments are merely the consequences of a potent political movement

448, §§ 1401–1422, 82 Stat. 476, 590–599 (1968), *as amended by* Pub. L. No. 93-383, tit. VIII, § 812(a), (b), (c)(i), 88 Stat. 736 (1974) (codified at 15 U.S.C. §§ 1701–1720 (Supp. V 1975)) (prohibiting certain fraudulent practices and requiring disclosure of key information relating to sale of interests in land subdivisions); Public Health Cigarette Smoking Act of 1969, Pub. L. No. 91-222, 84 Stat. 87 (codified at 15 U.S.C. §§ 1331–1340 (1970)) (banning advertising of cigarettes on radio and T.V.); Fair Credit Reporting Act, Pub. L. No. 91-508, 84 Stat. 1114 (1970) (codified at 15 U.S.C. §§ 1681–1681t (1970)) (regulating permissible uses of consumer credit reports, requiring disclosure of information requested by consumers, and establishing procedures to correct credit data in cases of disputed accuracy); Consumer Product Safety Act, Pub. L. No. 92-573, 86 Stat. 1207 (1972) (codified at 15 U.S.C. §§ 2051–2081 (Supp. IV 1974)) (establishing Consumer Product Safety Commission and giving it comprehensive powers, including authority to ban hazardous products); Trans-Alaska Pipeline Authorization Act, Pub. L. No. 93-153, 87 Stat. 576 (1973), and Federal Trade Commission Improvement Act, Pub. L. No. 93-637, 88 Stat. 2183 (1974) (codified at 15 U.S.C. §§ 45, 57b (Supp. IV 1974)) (broadly expanding FTC authority to obtain preliminary injunctions against unfair competitive practices and to award restitution to deceived consumers); Fair Credit Billing Act, Pub. L. No. 93-495, 88 Stat. 1511 (1974) (codified at 15 U.S.C. §§ 1601–1666j (Supp. V. 1975)) (requiring creditors to correct billing errors promptly and prohibiting interest charges on monthly bill items already paid). *See also* Consumer Protection Act of 1975, S.200, 94th Cong., 1st Sess., which if enacted would establish an Agency for Consumer Advocacy, which would be authorized to intervene in federal or state agency proceedings in order to represent consumer interests.

[4] *See, e.g.*, D. CAPLOVITZ, THE POOR PAY MORE (1963); M. MINTZ & J. COHEN, AMERICA INC. (1971); R. NADER, UNSAFE AT ANY SPEED (1965).

or whether, beyond Nader and other consumer advocates, they represent a sensible and durable new form of ad regulation.

## I. The Case For Government Regulation of Advertising

It is occasionally argued that the government has no legitimate role to play in the regulation of advertising, or a very modest role at best, since usually there are adequate market incentives for sellers to provide relevant market information, and to challenge, through their own access to advertising channels, false claims by rivals.[5] In the rare situations where market incentives are inadequate, competitors or consumers may resort to the courts to remedy the effects of false advertising. Finally, industry self-regulation may be seen as an alternative to government regulation.

This Part explores the market and legal impediments to these alternative forms of consumer protection and the consequent need for some government intervention. Possible constitutional limitations on such regulation are considered. Drawing upon this examination, the last section outlines the contours of a consumer-oriented approach to government regulation of advertising.

### *A. Market Failure as a Cause of Consumer Abuse*

Advertising substitutes for search costs by consumers by providing in a convenient and usable form information necessary for consumers to make choices among available brands, and in the process facilitates the functioning of a market economy. Free market theorists often assume that where there is a plurality of sellers of products with unequal attributes, sellers of superior products will accurately inform consumers, through advertising, of the attributes of their products and will expose fraudulent claims by competitors. Of course, even in theory consumers will never have perfect information. There are too many sellers offering too many products with a wide variety of characteristics changing over time, and in any event the self-serving source of the data will inevitably render the information somewhat inaccurate. Nevertheless, many appear to assume that information necessary to make choices among products will be generated by sellers whose natural incentive is to influence consumer purchases.[6] Those optimistic about market performance argue that the principal circumstances in which accurate information will not be provided are those in which either the purchasing decisions of relatively few

[5] *See* R. Posner, Seperate Statement in Report of the ABA Commission to Study the FTC 92, 104–05 (1969).

[6] *See id.* at 104; Stigler, *The Economics of Information*, 69 J. Pol. Econ. 213 (1961).

consumers are affected or the costs of disclosure are relatively high. According to this view, absence of information is consistent with the proposition that the market is functioning properly, providing information only up to the point where resulting benefits to sellers outweigh the costs of provision.[7]

While there is no need to quarrel with the premise that information with respect to most product characteristics is available as a result of sellers responding to incentives generated in the marketplace, there nevertheless remain many areas where key information necessary for consumers to make a sensible choice between rival brands, or to decide whether to buy the product at all, is absent. Until the government intervened and required or induced disclosure, accurate information was not available in the market concerning the durability of light bulbs,[8] octane ratings for gasoline,[9] tar and nicotine content of cigarettes,[10] mileage per gallon for automobiles,[11] or care labeling of textile wearing apparel.[12] At present, there continues to be little accurate information available to determine the comparative prices of life insurance policies, funeral services, eyeglasses sold at retail, and legal services;[13] the relative efficiencies of air conditioners and other electric appliances; the performance characteristics of tires; and the nutritional content of foods.[14] Moreover, while in many of these product categories there is a record of particular sellers exaggerating the

[7] *See* R. POSNER, *supra* note 5, at 104; Whitford, *The Functions of Disclosure Regulation in Consumer Transactions*, 1973 WIS. L. REV. 400, 428; *cf. Excerpts of FTC Staff Memorandum Evaluating Bureaus of Competition and Consumer Protection*, ANTITRUST & TRADE REG. REP. (BNA) Special Supplement 11–12 (July 22, 1975) (in absence of system to measure nutritional claims, competitors in food and beverage industry lacked incentive to rebut false claims).

[8] 16 C.F.R. § 409.1 (1976).

[9] 16 C.F.R. § 422.1 (1976).

[10] *See* note 17 *infra*.

[11] 16 C.F.R. §§ 259.1, 259.2 (1976).

[12] 16 C.F.R. § 423.1 (1976).

[13] Absence of information in some of these areas may be due to state prohibition of such advertising; these prohibitions appear to be subject to constitutional challenge, *see* Virginia State Bd. of Pharmacy v. Virginia Citizens Consumer Council, Inc., 96 S. Ct. 1817 (1976) (total ban on prescription drug advertising is unconstitutional).

[14] Admittedly, information failures can be remedied by non-governmental intermediaries. Publications such as CONSUMER REPORTS are devoted to disclosure of relevant product information and have been highly successful in recent years. Department stores offer a wide variety of competing products and also may perform the function of screening out low quality products. Trade associations, by setting standards of quality and safety, in effect may establish minimum standards of product quality on which consumers can rely. *See* R. POSNER, ECONOMIC ANALYSIS OF LAW 51 (1972). It is clear, however, that none of these alternatives supplies all the information that consumers reasonably can use or for which they would be willing to pay. *Id.* at 51–52.

qualities of their own product or service, rarely is there an instance of rivals explicitly challenging those questionable claims.

The causes of such market failures are not particularly difficult to trace. If the seller is a monopolist or near monopolist, it may concentrate promotional efforts on public image advertising, on the theory that it has nothing to fear from competition by imperfect substitutes and therefore need not discuss product qualities (including price) to maintain its market position. In tight oligopolistic markets, sellers may shy away from disclosures concerning product characteristics for the same reasons they avoid price cutting and emphasis on price terms — fear of triggering mutually disadvantageous competition. By emphasizing undesirable attributes of rival products, an "octane war," a "tar and nicotine derby," or competitive safety claims for pesticides or flammable fabrics may be as destructive of mutual oligopolistic interests as a price war would be. Thus, when no one company has a decisive competitive advantage over others, all may reach the conclusion that avoidance of certain kinds of product claims is mutually advantageous.

In particular instances, large, entrenched sellers may avoid disclosure of accurate product information because it creates opportunities for entry or expansion of sales by new entrants or independents which would not otherwise exist. For example, only one major integrated oil company [15] based an advertising campaign on octane content until octane disclosure was required under federal law, even though octane content varied considerably from brand to brand. One reason for avoidance of octane disclosure was that it would have spotlighted the substantially equivalent octane ratings of high-priced advertised brands and low-priced unadvertised brands. Since the market survival of independents depended on their maintaining a cost advantage by saving on advertising and other marketing expenses, they could not easily have undertaken an expensive advertising campaign to educate consumers and offer comparative data about octane ratings.[16]

In other product areas, disclosure may rebound to the disadvantage of all sellers. For instance, an intensive advertising campaign stressing low tar and nicotine content as a way of diminishing the health hazards involved in smoking could result in underscoring the health problem and reducing total cigarette sales. Even after it had become clear to smokers that the weight of

[15] The exception was Sun Oil Co. *See* Statement of Basis and Purpose for TRR Requiring Posting of Minimum Octane Ratings 4, 9–10 (1971).

[16] It may also be significant that octane content was difficult to measure and varied from pump to pump, thus making comparative ad campaigns by individual advertisers very difficult.

scientific opinion opposed cigarette smoking, advertisers with both low tar and high tar brands (which describes the six major cigarette companies in this country) were inclined to play down adverse comparative claims in order to avoid inflicting undue injury on other brands in their product lines. Aggressive marketing of low tar, low nicotine brands in recent years only occurred after government-induced public disclosure of tar and nicotine content.[17]

Accumulation and disclosure of accurate product information also might not be undertaken because it would be inordinately expensive — either in absolute terms or because only a relatively small class of consumers would use it. Chemical formulae for over-the-counter drugs, for example, may be incomprehensible to the average consumer. Complexity of disclosed information may also explain the apparent failure of unit pricing data to influence consumers to switch to lower priced brands.[18]

Somewhat different considerations may account for the fact that sellers rarely take advantage of their own media access to challenge claims made by others. In markets with many sellers, counter-advertising may have no appreciable impact on the counter-advertiser's share of the market. In oligopolistic markets, fear of mutually disadvantageous counter-advertising may discourage any firm from initiating such a program. In addition, until recently, explicit counter-advertising on T.V. was impossible because of network rules preventing advertisers from naming competitive products.[19] Explicit print counter-advertising, if inaccurate, opened the challenger to the possibility of a disparagement suit by the named competitor as well as a prosecution by the FTC for deceptive advertising.[20] Moreover, advertisers apparently share the conventional wisdom that unseemly debates about product qualities tend to diminish in the eyes of consumers both the allegedly false advertiser and the overly aggressive rival who exposes its deceptions. Thus most companies prefer to allocate their marketing budget to the accentuation of the affirmative qualities of their own products.

The inability of the free market to generate sufficient incen-

[17] The cigarette manufacturers, responding to threatened government action, decided voluntarily in December 1970 to report in their advertisements the government test results of tar and nicotine content. *See* 1971 ANTITRUST & TRADE REG. REP. (BNA) No. 482 at A-22 and No. 487 at A-8. Aggressive advertising of low tar, low nicotine brands is a relatively recent development, *see* N.Y. Times, Oct. 30, 1976, at 8; Barron's, "Puff Piece," Nov. 8, 1976, at 11.

[18] *See* Monroe & LaPaca, *What Are the Benefits of Unit Pricing?*, J. MARKETING, July 1972, at 16.

[19] *See* 5 TRADE REG. REP. (CCH) ¶¶ 50,196, 50,205 (1974) (NBC and ABC guidelines for comparative advertising).

[20] *See generally* pp. 675–77 *infra*.

tives for sellers to expose deceptive claims by competitors is indicated by the fact that in the scores of proceedings in which the FTC successfully challenged the truth of major advertising themes, there was not a single instance in which rivals used their own access to channels of consumer information to expose deceptions.[21] Indeed, even where comparative demonstrations were successfully challenged by the FTC as false and misleading, the company whose product was explicitly portrayed in an adverse light did not use counter-advertising to challenge the validity of the deceptive comparison.[22]

### *B. Alternative Systems of Consumer Protection*

Where there are instances of consumer abuse or exploitation as a result of false, misleading or irrelevant advertising, it does not necessarily follow that these need be remedied by governmental intrusion into the marketplace. It is theoretically possible for consumers' interests to be protected through resort to the courts either by consumers themselves or by those sellers with superior products who see their market shares declining in the face of inroads based on inaccurate information or deceptive marketing practices. In addition, industry self-regulation might overcome problems in the information market more cheaply and promptly than governmental intervention. In practice, however, these alternative approaches have been largely inoperative. Their ineffectiveness is an understandable product of the existing legal system.

The infrequency of consumer suits against advertisers is part of a larger institutional pattern in which consumers often find themselves powerless to vindicate what they conceive to be their legitimate rights. Much of the pressure on government in recent years to increase the amount of consumer protection — by enactment of new legislative schemes, development of new regulatory agencies, and more vigorous enforcement by existing agencies of their legislative powers — derives from the fact that the characteristic consumer injury is too small to justify individual resort to the judicial process. Moreover, consumer class suits often are impossible to bring because of decisions in the federal system making it impossible to aggregate separate claims in order to sat-

---

[21] *See, e.g.*, J. B. Williams Co. v. FTC, 381 F.2d 884 (6th Cir. 1967) (Geritol and "tired blood"); General Motors Corp., [1973–1976 Transfer Binder] TRADE REG. REP. (CCH) ¶ 20,747 (FTC 1975) (consent order involving G.M. safety claims); ITT Continental Baking Co., 79 F.T.C. 248 (1971) (consent order with respect to "Profile" bread diet claims).

[22] *See, e.g.*, American Home Prods. Corp., 81 F.T.C. 579 (1972) (consent order with respect to allegedly deceptive comparative claims for four household products).

isfy the $10,000 minimum jurisdictional amount [23] and because of the impracticality in many states of maintaining a class action.[24] As a result, even when consumers know their rights have been violated by sellers or creditors who are subject to punishment or capable of making the consumer whole in legal proceedings, they often suffer the frustration of a known wrong for which there is no recourse.

This situation is characteristic of the typical advertising deception. In most instances, the fraudulently induced purchase will involve an article of such small cost that it makes no sense to consider hiring a lawyer and taking the question to the courts. Even where relatively big ticket items are involved, the deceived consumer will rarely have received a completely worthless product. The extent of the consumer injury resulting from a fraudulent advertising claim will therefore be difficult to prove, adding to the complications and expense of any trial, and in any event is likely to be modest for each consumer.

Legal challenges among business units based on fraudulent or deceptive advertising are rare.[25] Competitive suits grounded on theories of fraud are likely to be expensive and available remedies often inadequate. More important, it is ordinarily extremely difficult to satisfy the common law requirement of injury by demonstrating that deceptive or unfair practices resulted in the wrongful appropriation of a particular seller's market share, even where general adverse market effects are evident.[26]

[23] Snyder v. Harris, 394 U.S. 332 (1969). *See also* Eisen v. Carlisle & Jacquelin, 417 U.S. 156 (1974) (requiring that individual notice be sent to all class members that can be identified through reasonable effort, even if cost of such notice would render class action impractical, and that cost of such notice be borne by plaintiff); Zahn v. International Paper Co., 414 U.S. 291 (1973) (each alleged class member, rather than only the representative member, must satisfy $10,000 amount-in-controversy requirement).

[24] Opportunities for consumer class actions in state court vary from state to state, and a few jurisdictions, notably California, have rejected the federal approach and have made available generous opportunities for enforcement of aggravated consumer class claims. *See* Vasquez v. Superior Court, 4 Cal. 3d 800, 484 P.2d 964, 94 Cal. Rptr. 796 (1971). *But see* Hall v. Coburn Corp., 26 N.Y.2d 396, 259 N.E.2d 720, 311 N.Y.S.2d 281 (1970); Hamburger, *State Class Actions and the Federal Rule*, 71 COLUM. L. REV. 609, 621–25 (1971).

[25] *See* Grimes, *Control of Advertising in the United States and Germany: Volkswagen Has a Better Idea*, 84 HARV. L. REV. 1769, 1775–76 (1971).

[26] *See Developments in the Law — Deceptive Advertising*, 80 HARV. L. REV. 1005, 1017–18 (1967). There were some indications that the broad language of § 43(a) of the Lanham Trade-Mark Act, 15 U.S.C. §§ 1051–1127 (1970), would provide a more effective vehicle for competitor suits, *see* L'Aiglon Apparel, Inc. v. Lana Lobell, Inc., 214 F.2d 649 (3d Cir. 1954), but the vast majority of suits filed under § 43(a) have in fact been premised on narrow and traditional notions of deception by palming-off, *see* 1 G. ROSDEN & P. ROSDEN, THE LAW OF ADVERTISING § 11.02[3] [a] (Cum. Supp. 1976).

Companies occasionally band together to share the expenses of combating "unfair competition" (and incidentally preventing consumer abuse) — for example, by setting standards which would screen out unsafe products or by expert review of substantiation of questionable advertising claims. This approach occasionally has had some effect, but is of little general significance. First, industry self-regulation must be carefully designed if problems under the anti-trust laws are to be avoided. Where groups of self-regulators exclude new entrants or significantly deter competitive opportunities — by denying a seal of approval to allegedly unsafe products, for instance — they run the risk of government or private suits charging an illegal boycott.[27] Even where industry members are confident that they can demonstrate that their screening process was not designed to achieve anti-competitive effects, their lawyers will advise them that they must follow expensive procedures, such as fair hearing for companies subjected to a screening process, to avoid antitrust problems. As a result, industry self-regulation often has been on a voluntary compliance basis, and has tended to break down when a small number of firms in the industry find it in their interest to depart from joint standards. Second, industry self-regulation schemes can involve considerable expense, and many sellers, satisfied that their products are superior to the average, prefer to spend their resources on advertising that proclaims the virtues of those products.

### *C. Toward a Consumer-Oriented Program of Advertising Regulation*

Market failure in the dissemination of product information and the ineffectiveness of possible alternative systems for ensuring truthful and relevant advertising indicate that some form of government regulation of the advertising process is warranted. Indeed, greater governmental regulation of the advertising industry, now accounting annually for well over twenty billion dollars in expenditures,[28] has been a prime concern of the recent consumer protection movement. As a result, in the last ten years or so there have been a large number of proceedings challenging major advertising campaigns as false, misleading or unfair,[29] and un-

---

[27] *See, e.g.*, Radiant Burners, Inc. v. Peoples Gas Light & Coke Co., 364 U.S. 656 (1961). *But see* Structural Laminates, Inc. v. Douglas Fir Plywood Ass'n, 261 F. Supp. 154 (D. Ore. 1966) (upholding denial of seal of approval on grounds that quality standards were reasonably applied and were not adopted with intention unlawfully to restrain trade), *aff'd*, 399 F.2d 155 (9th Cir. 1968), *cert. denied*, 393 U.S. 1024 (1969).

[28] J. Howard & J. Hulbert, Advertising and the Public Interest 7 (1973).

[29] *See, e.g.*, ITT Continental Baking Co., 83 F.T.C. 865, *modified*, 83 F.T.C. 1105 (1973) (complaint and final order against ads of largest bread manufac-

precedented government efforts to require by adjudication and rulemaking the disclosure of relevant product information.[30] A secondary effect of this emphasis on advertising practices has been a major renewed attempt at industry self-regulation.[31]

During this period, little attention has been paid to the theoretical justification for ad regulation, or to whether particular government programs serve sensible and consistent goals. The argument of the following section is that an indication of the proper goals and nature of an ad regulation program can be derived by examining the role of advertising in a market economy.

*1. Objectives.* — In typical buyer-seller transactions, it will be rare that buyers will be able efficiently to collect relevant information about the large number of products they seek or to take effective precautions against injuries sustained as a result of misplaced reliance on erroneous information. Sellers can accumulate and substantiate descriptive data about each product line once and make it available to all consumers; each consumer, if society left the task to consumers, would have to do it separately for every purchase of each individual item. As a result, it is socially useful to permit advertisers to assume expenses that substitute for search costs of consumers, and even to require advertisers to assume those expenses where market incentives are not adequate to stimulate them to do it themselves. In a rare reference to these kinds of considerations, the Federal Trade Commission in its *Pfizer* decision[32] implied a statutory duty on the part of sellers to substantiate product claims — based on the broad language of section five of the Federal Trade Commission Act[33] — in part because the Commission viewed as economically irrational the alternative ar-

turer), *aff'd*, 532 F.2d 207 (2d Cir. 1976); Bristol-Myers Co., [1970-1973 Transfer Binder] TRADE REG. REP. (CCH) ¶ 20,263 (FTC 1973) (complaint against producers of analgesics); Lorillard, Inc., 80 F.T.C. 455 (1972) (consent order requiring health warning on all cigarette advertising); E.I. duPont de Nemours & Co., [1970-1973 Transfer Binder] TRADE REG. REP. (CCH) ¶ 19,849 (FTC 1971) (complaint); 81 F.T.C. 169 (1972) (final order) (concerning major advertising campaign for antifreeze product).

[30] *See* pp. 685-86 & notes 103-109 *infra*.

[31] This has been accomplished principally through the efforts of the National Advertising Review Board, a joint creation of elements of the advertising industry and the Council for Better Business Bureaus. Materials describing its procedures and summarizing its early operations are in D. RICE, CONSUMER TRANSACTIONS 831-35 (1975). It is difficult at this point to determine whether the impressive early efforts of the Board will have a continuing significant effect on advertising practices.

[32] Pfizer, Inc., 81 F.T.C. 23, 62-64 (1972).

[33] Unfair methods of competition in [or affecting] commerce, and unfair or deceptive acts or practices in [or affecting] commerce, are hereby declared unlawful.

15 U.S.C. § 45(a)(1)(Supp. IV 1974). The words in brackets were added in 1973.

rangements whereby consumers conduct necessary tests or investigations in order to determine whether product claims are true.

Beyond the objective of ensuring that consumers are provided with truthful data, advertising also should be regulated with the objective of increasing effective competition in the market.[34] Accurate advertising can facilitate price comparisons and stimulate product improvement, while false advertising can result in misallocation of economic resources either through useless product expenditures, such as cold remedies that do not reduce lost work time due to colds, or by diverting trade to high priced premium products that differ from cheaper substitutes only in the quality and volume of advertising. Deceptive advertising if not controlled can eventually undermine the whole competitive system by reducing the extent to which consumers will rely on product claims and descriptions. In markets where product claims are viewed with utter suspicion, high price is adopted as an indication of quality, and price competition and product improvement become economically irrational.

Viewed in light of these principles, protection of consumers against advertising fraud should not be a broad, theoretical effort to achieve Truth, but rather a practical enterprise to ensure the existence of reliable data which in turn will facilitate an efficient and reliable competitive market process. A corollary of this approach would be that where consumers are fully capable, through common sense or simple observation, of protecting their interests against advertising exaggerations or distortions, there would be no reason for the law to intervene. Similarly, where cheap, safe products subject to repeat purchase are sold as a result of false advertising, there still would be little reason for government intervention if use of the product would clearly disclose that the advertising inducements had been deceptive.

2. *Constitutionality.* — In two recent decisions, the Supreme Court has expanded the zone of protected commercial speech and has thereby added a constitutional dimension to government regulation of the advertising process. The traditional view had been

---

[34] This has been recognized by Congress in its statement of policy in connection with promulgation of the Fair Packaging and Labeling Act of 1966, 15 U.S.C. § 1451 (1970):

> Informed consumers are essential to the fair and efficient functioning of a free market economy. Packages and labels should enable consumers to obtain accurate information as to the quantity of the contents and should facilitate value comparisons. Therefore, it is hereby declared to be the policy of the Congress to assist the consumers and manufacturers in reaching these goals in the marketing of consumer goods.

While much has been written about the *anticompetitive* impact of ad regulation, particularly at the FTC, the case is nowhere better stated than in R. POSNER, *supra* note 5, at 103–14.

that ad regulation has no constitutional implications because commercial speech is afforded minimal protection by the first amendment.[35] In *Bigelow v. Virginia*,[36] the Court, in striking down a state statute making it a misdemeanor to advertise the availability of abortions, indicated revived concern for limitations on commercial advertising, but declined to rule on the constitutionality of such restraints.[37] Last Term, in *Virginia State Board of Pharmacy v. Virginia Citizens Consumer Council, Inc.*,[38] the Court relied on a broad view of constitutional protection for commercial speech in finding that a state ban on prescription drug advertising violated the first amendment guarantee of freedom of speech.

It is unlikely that either *Bigelow* or *Virginia State Board* will appreciably circumscribe FTC regulation of advertising. In overturning state-imposed limitations on the availability of commercial information, the Court focused on the "strong interest in the free flow of commercial information"; [39] because a market economy depends on the private decisionmaking of consumers to achieve efficient resource allocation, public policy requires "that those decisions, in the aggregate, be intelligent and well informed." [40] This rationale would equally support restrictions on commercial speech where the information being introduced into the marketplace is false, deceptive or unfair, and would support required disclosure of product information necessary for informed choices by buyers where the market fails to provide that information.

This view is supported by a dictum in *Virginia State Board* in which the Court declared that the protection of commercial speech was by no means absolute:

> We of course do not hold that [commercial speech] can never be regulated in any way. Some forms of commercial speech regulation are surely permissible.[41]

A distinction was drawn between truthful dissemination of prescription drug prices and "false," "misleading," or "deceptive" commercial speech. The Court noted that, as to the latter, "the First Amendment . . . does not prohibit the State from insuring

[35] *See* Valentine v. Chrestensen, 316 U.S. 52 (1952); Firestone Tire & Rubber Co., 81 F.T.C. 398, 471–73 (1972), *aff'd*, 481 F.2d 246 (6th Cir.), *cert. denied*, 414 U.S. 1112 (1973); Note, *Corrective Advertising: The FTC's New Formula for Effective Relief*, 50 TEX. L. REV. 312, 318–20 (1972).

[36] 421 U.S. 809 (1975).

[37] *Id.* at 825.

[38] 96 S. Ct. 1817 (1976).

[39] *Id.* at 1827. On the public interest in dissemination of product information, see generally Redish, *The First Amendment in the Marketplace: Commercial Speech and the Values of Free Expression*, 39 GEO. WASH. L. REV. 429, 472 (1971).

[40] 96 S. Ct. at 1827.

[41] *Id.* at 1830.

that the stream of commercial information flows cleanly as well as freely."[42] This proposition was supported by a footnote stating in relevant part:

> [A] different degree of protection is necessary to insure that the flow of truthful and legitimate commercial information is unimpaired. The truth of commercial speech, for example, may be more easily verifiable . . . than . . . news reporting or political commentary . . . . Also, commercial speech may be more durable than other kinds. Since advertising is the *sine qua non* of commercial profits, there is little likelihood of its being chilled by proper regulation . . . .
>
> [It may also be] appropriate to require that a commercial message appear in such a form, or include such additional information, warnings and disclaimers, as are necessary to prevent its being deceptive.[43]

The Court's putative endorsement of advertising regulation was accentuated by its citation to a number of cases which had previously been regarded as shielding regulation from the strictures of the first amendment.[44]

In sum, the standards that the Supreme Court is likely to apply in constitutional review of ad regulation are consistent with what was described earlier as a consumer-oriented ad regulation program; that is, a program that emphasizes ensuring the existence of reliable data in the marketplace which in turn will facilitate an efficient competitive market process. Hence, traditional FTC enforcement actions against deceptive advertising — at least where the false ad claims are material to consumer purchasing decisions — will not be subject to first amendment defenses.[45] The more recent FTC requirements of ad substantiation, mandated disclosure, corrective advertising, and enforcement against "unfair" advertising, discussed subsequently, also should be sustained if the FTC can show its regulations contribute to the flow of accurate commercial information.

*3. Implementation.* — With allowances made for the inaccuracy of generalizations, the succeeding sections suggest that much recent regulation of deception in ads is securely tied to the objectives of ensuring reliable product information and strengthening

[42] *Id.* at 1830–31.

[43] *Id.* at 1830 n.24.

[44] *Id.*, citing, inter alia, Banzhaf v. FCC, 405 F.2d 1082 (1968), *cert. denied*, 396 U.S. 842 (1969).

[45] In 1976, the Supreme Court denied certiorari in a case in which the FTC had obtained an injunction barring continuation of false and deceptive ads. The first amendment objection had been considered and rejected by the Court of Appeals, *see* FTC v. National Comm'n on Egg Nutrition, 517 F.2d 485 (7th Cir. 1975), *cert. denied*, 49 L. Ed.2d 372 (1976).

competition, at least by comparison with the excesses of earlier periods. When the government acted as a surrogate enforcement arm for competitors, as it often did in ad regulation in the 1950's and early 1960's,[46] it characteristically became entangled in nit-picking, literalistic disputes over the meaning of words in ads. During this period, many enforcement actions against advertisers grew directly out of competitor complaints and appear to have been primarily intended to protect sellers against competition from cheaper substitutes.[47] That is the explanation for the hundreds of cases requiring disclosure of foreign origin, decisions prohibiting true claims because they might cause confusion with products offered by entrenched rivals, the passing off cases, and charges of disparagement of competitors.[48] Moreover, many of these cases involved disputes over relatively inconsequential items of information — *e.g.*, the number of tubes in a radio,[49] whether a flour seller could properly represent itself to be a "grinder,"[50] the percentage content of fibers in a fabric (90% wool/10% nylon, when wool content actually varied between 89.9% and 94.9%),[51] or the definition of "free."[52] After an analysis of some 200 decisions and orders entered by the Commission during the period July 1, 1962 to June 30, 1963, Professor Posner persuasively concluded that the FTC achieved "precious little consumer protection."[53]

By contrast, in recent years the FTC has been responding more to consumer-generated pressures. The major innovations in ad regulation in the last ten years or so — ad substantiation, required disclosure of various categories of information, and corrective advertising — grew out of proposals contained in submissions by petitioning or intervening consumer advocates. Given the difference in the source of pressure for enforcement against claimed unfair or deceptive advertising, one might also expect that new programs would differ in content and approach from earlier enforcement efforts. In particular, since market incentives are sometimes inadequate to ensure the availability of important product information, and since it is virtually impossible to redress consumer injuries after the fact, a consumer-oriented program would emphasize required disclosure of accurate and important

[46] *See* R. Posner, *supra* note 5, at 108–09.

[47] *See id.* at 109.

[48] *Id.* at 109–11.

[49] *See* Zenith Radio Corp. v. FTC, 143 F.2d 29 (7th Cir. 1944).

[50] *See* FTC v. Royal Milling Co., 288 U.S. 212 (1933).

[51] *See* Marcus v. FTC, 354 F.2d 85 (2d Cir. 1965).

[52] *See* FTC v. Mary Carter Paint Co., 382 U.S. 46 (1965), *discussed at* pp. 688–89 *infra*.

[53] R. Posner, *supra* note 5, at 113.

product information that consumers could then use to protect their interests in advance of injury. By the same token, such a program would deemphasize enforcement which tends to diminish the availability of useful information in the marketplace or which involves disputes over information that might be relevant to a purchasing decision but is at some remove from the concerns of most consumers. With the usual glaring exceptions, this appears to be what has occurred.

## II. Traditional Principles of Advertising Regulation

Despite the increase in intensity of government regulation of advertising, the remarkably few legal principles that govern this field have changed little in the past ten or fifteen years. Moreover, the few changes which have occurred have been almost exclusively a matter of reinterpreting existing legislation and developing new modes of enforcement, rather than enacting new statutes.[54]

For the last sixty years, national advertising has been regulated for the most part under section five of the Federal Trade Commission Act, which declares "deceptive" or "unfair" acts or practices unlawful.[55] Violations of the section are actionable where the injury is to either consumers or competitors of the advertiser.[56]

### A. Deception

The standard for "deception" has been the "average" or "ordinary" person in the audience addressed by the ad, taking into account that many who may be misled are unsophisticated and unwary.[57] Aside from the "ignorant, the unthinking and the

[54] The only significant legislative developments bearing directly on regulation of the content of advertising have been those few legislative schemes, such as the Consumer Credit Protection Act and the Interstate Land Sales Full Disclosure Act, *see* note 3 *supra*, which have used the vehicle of advertising to achieve market effects through the required disclosure of product information.

[55] 15 U.S.C. § 45(a)(1)(1970). Federal regulation of advertising was initially authorized in 1914 when Congress enacted the Federal Trade Commission Act, declaring unlawful "unfair methods of competition." A narrowing court interpretation was overruled by statute in 1938 by adding that "unfair or deceptive acts or practice in commerce" were also unlawful, 52 Stat. 111, 111 (1938).

[56] Pfizer, Inc., 81 F.T.C. 23, 60 (1972).

[57] *See* Feil v. FTC, 285 F.2d 879, 887 (9th Cir. 1960) (representations about efficacy of bedwetting "cure" made to "laity," who may be incapable of understanding their misleading character); Ford Motor Co. v. FTC, 120 F.2d 175, 182 (6th Cir.), *cert. denied*, 314 U.S. 668 (1941) (noting that average individual is unlikely to analyze carefully complicated deferred credit plans); Benrus Watch Co., 64 F.T.C. 1018, 1032 (1964), *aff'd*, 352 F.2d 313 (8th Cir. 1965), *cert. denied*, 384 U.S. 939 (1966) (violation found where evidence showed 14% of audience

credulous,"[58] an ad may have a greater or lesser capacity to deceive because of the special susceptibility of the target audience. For example, the Commission measured the capacity for deception of an ad for a drug claimed to relieve delayed menstruation, but seeming to suggest use to induce abortion, against the state of mind of women whose menstruation had been delayed.[59] Similarly, the Commission has taken the position that advertising that might be regarded as nondeceptive to an adult audience would be differently measured when the audience is comprised predominantly of children.[60]

Until recently,[61] the "unfairness" aspect of section five has seldom been asserted or viewed as an independent standard against which claims might be measured. In measuring either deception or unfairness, the traditional Commission practice has been to look at the total impression generated by the ad and to reject literal truth as a defense if that impression was false.[62] Vague claims or even silence can be "deceptive" if reasonably capable of being understood by a substantial number of the audience in a way that is false. It is this general principle that supports the rule that if an ad is capable of being interpreted in more than one way, and one of those interpretations is false and likely to mislead a substantial portion of the audience, the ad is unlawful under section five.[63]

Assuming that evidence shows that an ad is misleading, issues of materiality and causality relating to whether consumers were

---

was deceived). *But cf.* Heinz W. Kirchner, 63 F.T.C. 1282, 1290 (1963) ("An advertiser cannot be charged with . . . every conceivable misconception, however outlandish, to which his representations might be subject among the foolish or feebleminded."), *aff'd*, 337 F.2d 751 (9th Cir. 1964). *See generally* FTC v. R. F. Keppel & Bros., 291 U.S. 304 (1934); Thain, *Advertising Regulation: The Contemporary FTC Approach*, 1 FORDHAM URB. L.J. 349, 381–84 (1973).

[58] Aronberg v. FTC, 132 F.2d 165, 167 (7th Cir. 1942). Past Commissions occasionally have carried to astonishing lengths their mandate to protect the credulous against deception. In Gelb v. FTC, 144 F.2d 580, 582 (2d Cir. 1944), an advertiser had claimed that a hair application could "color hair permanently," and the Commission ruled the claim illegal because some people might believe it would color hair that had not yet grown out of the scalp. Other cases reaching similarly farfetched conclusions are collected in Millstein, *The Federal Trade Commission and False Advertising*, 64 COLUM. L. REV. 439, 458–62 (1964).

[59] Doris Savitch, 50 F.T.C. 828, 834 (1954), *aff'd per curiam*, 218 F.2d 817 (2d Cir. 1955).

[60] *See* Stupell Originals, Inc., 67 F.T.C. 173 (1965).

[61] *See* pp. 680–87 *infra*.

[62] *See, e.g.*, Rhodes Pharmacal Co. v. FTC, 208 F.2d 382, 387 (7th Cir. 1953), *rev'd in part on other grounds*, 348 U.S. 940 (1955) (per curiam); P. Lorillard Co. v. FTC, 186 F.2d 52, 58 (4th Cir. 1950); Colgate-Palmolive Co., 58 F.T.C. 422, 428 (1961).

[63] Giant Food, Inc. v. FTC, 322 F.2d 977, 981 (D.C. Cir. 1963), *cert. dismissed*, 376 U.S. 967 (1964).

influenced in purchasing decisions by the false claim are largely avoided by the Commission rules that it need show only capacity to deceive rather than actual deception, and capacity to affect purchasing decisions rather than actual effects.[64]

### B. The "Puffing" Defense

It has been traditional in advertising regulation to permit a "puffing" defense, which applies to claims not capable of measurement ("Bayer Works Wonders"; Coca Cola is the "Real Thing") or not intended by the advertiser to be taken seriously (Esso puts a "Tiger in Your Tank"; "When You're Out of Schlitz, You're Out of Beer"). It is hard to imagine that a significant number of sensible consumers would be deceived by such claims, and the governmental intrusion (including suppression of creativity and wit) necessary to protect the few who are deceived has been regarded as unjustified. Perhaps more to the point, it is unlikly that it could be established that many consumers believe that the examples of "puffing" listed above contain any product claim at all. If consumers have any common notion, it would be a product claim so vague that it would be impossible for the advertiser to know what characteristic it must be prepared to substantiate, and therefore it would be unfair to require substantiation.

Inevitably, the definition of permissible puffing will be a difficult matter. Thus a cigarette manufacturer claiming its product was "less irritating" was held to have made a claim capable of objective measurement,[65] while claims that a toothpaste will "beautify the smile" have been found to be within the scope of the puffing defense.[66]

### C. Meaning of the Ad — Interpretative Authority of the Commission

The meaning of an ad is a matter committed to the discretion of the Federal Trade Commission.[67] Since this modest sounding rule is a principal reason that the Commission has managed to prevail in the appellate courts in the overwhelming majority of its

[64] Charles of the Ritz Distribs. Co. v. FTC, 143 F.2d 676, 680 (2d Cir. 1944). *See also* FTC v. Colgate-Palmolive Co., 380 U.S. 374, 391–92 (1965).

[65] Liggett & Myers Tobacco Co., 55 F.T.C. 354, 375 (1958). *See also* FTC v. Sewell, 353 U.S. 969 (1957) (claim that shoe insert improved "poise and balance" and improved "foot action" found actionable) (per curiam), *rev'g* 240 F.2d 228 (9th Cir. 1956).

[66] Bristol-Myers Co., 46 F.T.C. 162, 175–76 (1949), *aff'd*, 185 F.2d 58 (4th Cir. 1950). *See also* Carlay Co. v. FTC, 153 F.2d 493, 496 (7th Cir. 1946); Kidder Oil Co. v. FTC, 117 F.2d 892, 901 (7th Cir. 1941).

[67] *See* Gellhorn, *Proof of Consumer Deception Before the Federal Trade Commission,* 17 U. KAN. L. REV. 559, 563–67 (1969).

decisions that have been appealed, it deserves some extended consideration.

The leading case is *Zenith Radio Corp. v. FTC*,[68] where the Commission challenged two sets of claims in a series of advertisements for Zenith radios. First, Zenith asserted in an ad that " 'Europe is talking to you every night in English. . . . You can hear all the leaders . . . all the daily news broadcasts.' "[69] In fact, atmospheric conditions made it impossible to obtain satisfactory reception of foreign broadcasts every day. The Commission concluded that the effect of the claims was to lead people to believe that radio reception difficulties would be completely overcome, particularly because public knowledge of difficulties of radio reception was limited. The second series of claims designated the number of tubes in the radio (for example: "Eleven-Tuber superheterodyne with Rotor Wavemagnet Aerial").[70] The Commission defined tubes as devices that perform " 'the primary function of detecting, amplifying, or receiving radio signals.' "[71] Several of the "tubes" Zenith relied on to arrive at a total number of eleven had to do with tuning or converting alternating current into direct current, and therefore did not qualify under the Commission's definition. The Commission held against Zenith after finding that a substantial portion of purchasers believed that a radio is better and more powerful if it has a larger number of tubes. In affirming the Commission's decisions on both sets of ad claims, the Court of Appeals concluded that the Commission may "decide for itself" whether advertisements are deceptive and is "not required to sample public opinion" to determine the meaning of the ad.[72]

Why questions of meaning should be submitted to the virtually unreviewable discretion of five commissioners of the FTC has never been articulated. Unlike other instances of deference to regulators as part of the administrative process, there is no reason to believe that commissioners of the FTC have unusual capacity or experience in coping with questions of meaning, nor any indication that successful regulation of advertising requires a balance of related regulatory considerations that commissioners are in a special position to handle. Significantly, if fact issues relating to the meaning of an ad arise when the FTC is seeking penalties for violation of a cease-and-desist order, "meaning" issues are submit-

---

[68] 143 F.2d 29 (7th Cir. 1944). *See also* Bantam Books, Inc. v. FTC, 275 F.2d 680 (2d. Cir.), *cert. denied*, 364 U.S. 819 (1960).

[69] 143 F.2d at 30.

[70] *Id.* at 31.

[71] *Id.*

[72] *Id.*

ted to a jury because on those questions jurors are likely to have "more experience than most judges." [73]

In large part, the grant of authority to the Commission in this area may be due to the administrative inconvenience of alternative approaches. If consumer perception were a litigable issue, survey evidence or testimony by experts on consumer perception would be required. The science of measuring consumer perception is so imprecise [74] that it is understandable that the Commission would want to avoid hosting such controversies. In addition, consumer survey evidence raises many separate evidentiary issues, including, for example, the adequacy of survey samples and rights of contesting parties to have discovery or cross-examination against not only the people conducting the survey but the consumers themselves. A full exploration of these issues would complicate and delay enforcement proceedings.

Perhaps because of its uncertain view of the validity of the rule committing determination of the meaning of an ad to its own discretion, the Commission has not consistently excluded consumer survey evidence or testimony of expert witnesses on the issue of meaning.[75] If such evidence failed to persuade the Commission, however, its presence in the record would be of little significance on appeal; discretion to weigh the validity of conflicting evidence is committed to the Commission, and will not be overturned as long as there is some evidence in the record to support the Commission's conclusion.[76]

## III. New Developments in Ad Regulation

Many advertising cases brought since 1969 have challenged major national advertising compaigns,[77] a sharp break from the roster of cases in earlier years which included a large number of challenges against claims made by small companies selling hemorroid cures, patent medicines or re-refined oil.[78] The traditional

---

[73] United States v. J.B. Williams Co., 498 F.2d 414, 429–30 (2d Cir. 1974).

[74] *See* J. Howard & H. Hulbert, *supra* note 28, at 34–35 for an indication of the complexities involved in understanding how consumers perceive, interpret and act upon advertising messages.

[75] *See, e.g.*, Korber Hats, Inc. v. FTC, 311 F.2d 358 (1st Cir. 1962); Exposition Press, Inc. v. FTC, 295 F.2d 869 (2d Cir. 1961), *cert. denied*, 370 U.S. 917 (1962).

[76] *See, e.g.*, Bakers Franchise Corp. v. FTC, 302 F.2d 258, 261 (3d Cir. 1962); Charles of the Ritz Distribs. Corp. v. FTC, 143 F.2d 676 (2d Cir. 1944) (by implication).

[77] *See* note 29 *supra*.

[78] Two instances of Commission action in the prior period which could not be characterized as trivial involved efforts by rule to require health warning disclosure in cigarette advertising, *see* Proposed Rule on Cigarettes in Relation to Health Hazards of Smoking, 34 Fed. Reg. 7911 (1969) (to have been codified in 16 C.F.R.

rules relating to deception, the puffing defense,[79] and Commission authority to determine the meaning of ads [80] have continued to govern disposition of most advertising cases in this recent period. The FTC has taken major steps, however, to augment the protection afforded by these principles.

First, the Commission has developed a separate category of "unfairness" violations, including the failure to undertake prior substantiation of ads. Second, the Commission has shifted its efforts away from protecting competitors and toward encouraging competition by virtually abandoning its extensive prior efforts to regulate comparative price claims and mock-up demonstrations; oddly, the Commission's broad authority in these areas had derived from its victories in the two major advertising cases decided by the Supreme Court in the period prior to 1965. Finally, there have been significant innovations in the imposition of remedies — most notably, the use of corrective advertising.

### *A. Evolution of a Separate Category of "Unfairness" Violations*

The challenging of ad claims that are "unfair" rather than deceptive was encouraged by the Supreme Court in its 1972 decision in *FTC v. Sperry & Hutchinson Co.*[81] S&H had attempted to suppress operations of trading stamp exchanges, small companies in the business of selling or swapping for a fee stamps necessary to fill a book for redemption of merchandise. S&H successfully defended against a Commission suit challenging its practice as "unfair" by arguing that section five applied only to prac-

§ 408), and the continuing efforts to regulate ads for Geritol, *see* J.B. Williams Co. v. F.T.C., 381 F.2d 884 (6th Cir. 1967).

[79] Although the puffing defense has been criticized, *see* I.L. PRESTON, THE GREAT AMERICAN BLOW-UPS: PUFFERY IN ADVERTISING AND SELLING (1975), it remains solidly a part of section 5 law, *see* Pfizer, Inc., 81 F.T.C. 23, 64–65 (1972).

[80] Recently, the Commission has allowed introduction into administrative proceedings of extensive survey evidence and expert testimony on the meaning of ads. *See, e.g.*, Firestone Tire & Rubber Co., 81 F.T.C. 398, 454 (1972), *aff'd*, 481 F.2d 246 (6th Cir.), *cert. denied*, 414 U.S. 1112 (1973); ITT Continental Baking Co., 83 F.T.C. 865, 954–56, *modified on unrelated matters*, 83 F.T.C. 1105 (1973), *aff'd*, 532 F.2d 207 (2d Cir. 1976) (market surveys on consumer attitudes admissible for purpose of showing representations made in ads). However, the Commission has not retreated from its position that it is authorized to determine the meaning of ads. *See, e.g.*, Bristol-Myers Co., [1973–1976 Transfer Binder] TRADE REG. REP. (CCH) ¶ 20,900 (FTC 1975), where five TV commericals for "Dry Ban" anti-perspirant spray were alleged to claim falsely that the product was not "wet." The Commission concluded, despite the contrary findings of its administrative law judge and of several consumer surveys in the record, that the commercials only represented Dry Ban as *comparatively* superior to leading competitors, rather than dry measured against some absolute standard. *Id.* at 20,749.

[81] 405 U.S. 233 (1972).

tices which violate the letter or spirit of the antitrust laws or are repugnant to public morals. In reversing, the Supreme Court authorized the Commission to enforce section five "like a court of equity," taking into account such factors as whether a practice (1) "without necessarily having been previously considered unlawful, offends public policy" as established "by statutes, the common law, or otherwise"; (2) is "immoral, unethical, oppressive, or unscrupulous"; or (3) causes "substantial injury to consumers (or competitors or other businessmen)." [82]

The Supreme Court's broad grant of authority to the FTC to develop new rules in the consumer protection field is too vague to provide any meaningful enforcement guidelines. There are three types of nondeceptive advertisements that plausibly might be regarded as "unfair": first, claims published without reasonable prior substantiation; second, claims which tend to overreach or exploit particularly vulnerable groups; [83] and third, instances in which sellers fail to provide consumers with information necessary to make choices among competing products.

*1. Ad Substantiation.* — In 1963, the Commission required that advertisers have substantiation for claims relating to health and safety prior to the dissemination of the advertisements in which the claims are made.[84] But it was not until the *Pfizer* decision [85] ten years later that the prior substantiation requirement was extended to other types of claims. In *Pfizer*, the Commission challenged claims that the lotion "Unburn" contained a special ingredient that anesthetized nerves in sunburned skin, and held unanimously that it is "unfair" under section five to make an affirmative product claim — "puffs" excepted — without reasonable prior substantiation. It was, of course, already the law that claims must be truthful and nondeceptive when made; [86] this decision

[82] *Id.* at 244–45 & n.5 (by implication); *see* All-State Indus., Inc., 75 F.T.C. 465, 491 (1969), *aff'd,* 423 F.2d 423 (4th Cir.), *cert. denied,* 400 U.S. 828 (1970).

[83] In state court proceedings, inequitable contracts have been declared unenforceable against uneducated, inexperienced or poor buyers; this notion of "unconscionability" would appear to respond to some of the factors listed in the *S&H* opinion. *See, e.g.,* Kugler v. Romain, 58 N.J. 522, 279 A.2d 640 (1971); Jones v. Star Credit Corp., 59 Misc. 2d 189, 298 N.Y.S.2d 264 (Sup. Ct. 1969).

[84] Heinz W. Kirchner, 63 F.T.C. 1282 (1963), *aff'd,* 337 F.2d 751 (9th Cir. 1964). *See* 63 F.T.C. at 1295 ("One who affirmatively advertises a product to be safe, in a context in which the prospective user's health or safety may be adversely affected if the claim is false, implicitly represents that he has a reasonable and substantial foundation in fact for making the claim.").

[85] Pfizer, Inc., 81 F.T.C. 23 (1972).

[86] Further, prior ad substantiation has been required in cease and desist orders for "deception" violations when the deception consists of the implication that there was a reasonable basis for claims but the claims were not substantiated in advance. *See, e.g.,* National Dynamics Corp., 82 F.T.C. 488, 568–69 (1973), *modified,* 492 F.2d 1333 (2d Cir.), *cert. denied,* 419 U.S. 993 (1974).

went further and concluded that even a nondeceptive claim not relating to health or safety would violate the law if it were not backed by adequate prior substantiation.[87]

One major impact of the *Pfizer* rule and its implementing program [88] is likely to be the development of a process of prior review and clearance which could be of long-term benefit both to consumers and to competitors. Lawyers and other experts traditionally have played a significant role in the development and evaluation of ad claims.[89] The substantiation requirement could strengthen their hands in demanding adequate substantiation or accurate qualification of claims before ads are run.

Unfortunately, the *Pfizer* opinion never mentions this prior review process and generally is vague in explaining the justification for ad substantiation. It notes that it is impractical to expect individual consumers to run tests on the thousands of products they purchase, and that it is more efficient for a seller to run tests once for each product claim.[90] Beyond this, the opinion simply asserts that consumers are "entitled" to the substantiation information and "should not be compelled to enter into an economic gamble to determine whether a product will or will not perform as represented." [91] The opinion failed to consider the costs generated by a substantiation program, the magnitude of which will depend on the standard adopted by the courts to define reasonable substantiation. The opinion also did not explicitly consider whether these costs should be incurred by sellers as opposed to not being incurred at all.

Justification for required prior substantiation of claims relating to significant health and safety concerns is obvious. The seller should know prior to marketing that a product is safe and that advertising does not conceal substantial latent hazards.

[87] 81 F.T.C. at 64. Prior to *Pfizer*, it appears that advertisers frequently published claims for which they had little prior substantiating data. *See* CONSUMER SUBCOMM. OF SENATE COMMERCE COMM., 92D CONG., 2D SESS., STAFF REPORT TO THE FEDERAL TRADE COMMISSION ON THE AD SUBSTANTIATION PROGRAM (Comm. Print 1972) 3, 4–5, 11 (independent public interest group found that over half of all reviewed claims for T.V. sets were inadequately substantiated).

[88] The Commission followed its *Pfizer* rule with a substantiation program pursuant to which demands for information are issued, usually on an industry-wide basis, requiring sellers to produce for the public record data substantiating recently circulated advertising claims. *See* CONSUMER SUBCOMM. OF SENATE COMMERCE COMM., 92D CONG., 2D SESS., STAFF REPORT TO THE FEDERAL TRADE COMMISSION ON THE AD SUBSTANTIATION PROGRAM (Comm. Print 1972). For additional analysis of this program, *see* Thain, *supra* note 57, at 386–89; Note, *The FTC Ad Substantiation Program*, 61 GEO. L.J. 1427 (1973). Unsubstantiated claims may be challenged in subsequent traditional enforcement actions.

[89] *See* J. HOWARD & J. HULBERT, *supra* note 28, at 18–19.

[90] 81 F.T.C. at 62.

[91] *Id.*

Since it would rarely occur that the expense in such cases of determining safety before marketing or accurately qualifying safety-related claims would outweigh the harm to consumers injured because of inadequate warnings, an across-the-board substantiation requirement seems justified.

When the focus shifts to minor economic injury, justification of required prior substantiation is not as clear. If all or most claims are true, the substantiation process adds little to consumer welfare. Even if a few claims are untrue and the substantiation process helps to disclose them to the seller or to the government, the costs of substantiation may outweigh the combined benefits of disclosure resulting from the avoidance of economic injury and from the greater certainty in the market of dissemination of accurate product information. Moreover, vigorous enforcement of the *Pfizer* doctrine might have less of a preclusive effect on false and deceptive advertising, which is already prohibited, than on truthful claims that are too expensive to substantiate. The greater the suppression of such claims, or suppression of informational advertising in favor of "puffs" not subject to the substantiation requirement, the more likely it is that the net effect of the requirement will be injurious to consumers.

It is understandable that the Commission would announce and implement a substantiation program without prior quantification and balancing of the costs and benefits associated with it. The exact extent of suppression of truthful information and the effects of more stringent clearance procedures instituted by advertisers would be virtually impossible to determine prior to inauguration of the program. But there is no reason that studies of effects could not be completed and published now that the program has been operational for several years. Until some follow-up analysis of the costs and benefits of the program is conducted, ad substantiation remains an appealing idea of uncertain value. Without a determination of competitive effects, the ad substantiation effort is not only questionable in terms of costs and benefits, but may also be vulnerable to constitutional challenge under recent Supreme Court interpretations of the first amendment, on grounds that by suppressing some truthful information in the market place without commensurate improvement in the accuracy of information that is disseminated, the program is an undue burden on the free flow of commercial information.[92]

2. *Claims Directed Toward Vulnerable Groups.* — With respect to exploitation of vulnerable audiences, the unfairness concept could be relied on to: (1) declare certain ads illegal even if true because they offend some other standard of acceptability

[92] *See* pp. 671–37 *supra*.

(at least to the extent that such action would not violate the first amendment),[93] (2) define truth differently when ads are directed to special audiences (*e.g.*, children, illiterates), or (3) duplicate the concept of deception already in the law.[94]

To date, Commission decisions have not pushed beyond the third position. In its only decision since *S&H* dealing with a charge of unfairness — *ITT Continental Baking Co.*[95] — the Commission dealt with the charge that Wonder Bread advertising was deceptive and unfair because, in stressing special nutritional features of the product by broadcasting dramatic growth sequences of children, it "exploit[ed] the aspirations of children [and] parental concerns for rapid and healthy growth and development . . . ."[96] After holding that the ad was deceptive, the Commission stated that although the same practice could conceivably give rise to both an unfairness and a deception violation, the record in *ITT* failed to provide evidence of a separate unfairness violation.[97] Other Commission complaints charging "unfairness" going beyond simple fraud and deception have not been contested by respondents.[98]

Reliance on "unfairness" in the regulation of stylistic excess in advertising is likely to be minimal. First, standards for what constitutes "exploitation" of "vulnerable" groups will be exceptionally elusive. Moreover, charges that an ad, though not deceptive, tends to take advantage of a vulnerable group will usually raise controversial questions of excessive government paternalism. Perhaps for these reasons, recent consumer pressure for the reform of advertising has been less a matter of concern about stylistic excess — although this concern has been expressed with respect to advertising addressed to children — and more a matter of ensuring the availability of accurate, relevant data for con-

[93] The extent to which advertising is protected by the first amendment is discussed at pp. 671–73 *supra*.

[94] *See* pp. 675–77 *supra*.

[95] 83 F.T.C. 865, *modified*, 83 F.T.C. 1105 (1973), *aff'd*, 532 F.2d 207 (2d Cir. 1976).

[96] 83 F.T.C. at 872.

[97] *Id.* at 964.

[98] *See* J.B. Williams Co., 81 F.T.C. 238 (1972) (complaint alleged exploitation of anxieties of married women by suggesting that marital problems could be alleviated if the woman took the stimulant Vivarin a few hours before her husband arrived home in the evening); Topper Corp., 79 F.T.C. 681 (1971), and Mattel, Inc., 79 F.T.C. 667 (1971) (complaints alleged exploitation of children through "special effects" achieved by lens use and sound techniques exaggerating speed and maneuverability of toy cars and mobility of dolls).

As noted, special restrictions on advertising directed toward children have been traditional in FTC enforcement, *see* p. 676 *supra*; and the complaint against the Vivarin ad is little different than earlier cases charging "deception" because the ad was directed at an audience that the Commission considered especially vulnerable.

sumers to use in their purchasing decisions. Thus, despite the blank-check authorization provided to the Commission in *S&H*, new limitations on ad "exploitation" grounded on unfairness concepts have not been developed.

*3. Unfairness Through Failure to Disclose.* — By contrast, the Commission has relied on "unfairness" authority to expand required disclosure in advertising of essential product information. Deception by silence has been a traditional theory of advertising regulation,[99] but the older cases often depended upon a finding by the Commission that, in light of express claims in the ad or the nature of the product, failure to disclose pertinent information would be misleading. Thus, in *Alberty v. FTC*,[100] where the Commission failed to make any such findings of deception or of other special circumstances,[101] the Court of Appeals reversed, noting that the Commission lacked the power simply to require advertisers to be more informative.[102]

It would be difficult to reconcile recent complaints and rules proposed by the Commission under the "unfairness" concept with the more cautious disclosure efforts of the earlier era. A dozen or so recent cases have challenged vocational school advertising on ground that it is "unfair" not to disclose the percentage of enrollees who do not complete the course, the percentage of graduates who do not obtain employment, and the salaries and employers of graduates who do obtain jobs.[103] Similarly, in complaints challenging allegedly fraudulent land sales schemes, separate violations have been charged for failure to disclose specifics about future land development programs and for failure to state that the purchase price of lots is not all-inclusive.[104]

---

[99] *See, e.g.*, J. B. Williams Co. v. FTC, 381 F.2d 884 (6th Cir. 1967) (failure to disclose in connection with advertisements of the iron tonic "Geritol" that most fatigue has nothing to do with iron deficiency anemia); Keele Hair & Scalp Specialists, Inc. v. FTC, 275 F.2d 18 (5th Cir. 1960) (failure to disclose that most baldness cures will not work because baldness is usually hereditary).

[100] 182 F.2d 36 (D.C. Cir.), *cert. denied*, 340 U.S. 818 (1950). A broader but tenuous interpretation of *Alberty* which would have denied the Commission the authority to require disclosure of any data adverse to the interest of the advertiser was rejected in Feil v. FTC, 285 F.2d 879, 900–01 (9th Cir. 1960).

[101] 182 F.2d at 39. The *Alberty* court also rejected the Commission's health and safety rationale for disclosure, finding only economic injury to consumers in this case, *see id.* at 38–39. Interestingly, prior substantiation requirements, *discussed at* pp. 681–83 *infra*, were also originally limited to health and safety claims.

[102] *Id.* at 39–40.

[103] *See, e.g.*, Lafayette United Corp., [1973–1976 Transfer Binder] TRADE REG. REP. (CCH) ¶ 20,499 (FTC 1974); Control Data Corp., [1970–1973 Transfer Binder] TRADE REG. REP. (CCH) ¶ 19,980 (FTC 1972).

[104] *See, e.g.*, AMREP Corp., [1973–1976 Transfer Binder] TRADE REG. REP. (CCH) ¶ 20,846 (FTC 1975); Horizon Corp., [1973–1976 Transfer Binder] TRADE REG. REP. (CCH) ¶ 20,845 (FTC 1975). In these cases, the purchase price

The Commission has been even more innovative in the promulgation of rules requiring disclosure of product information. Listed earlier [105] were a few of the many categories of information that will be required to be disclosed under rules promulgated in the last few years:[106] octane ratings on gasoline, mileage per gallon for cars, care labeling instructions on wearing apparel, and average durability of light bulbs. The Commission has also proposed disclosure of information with respect to the nutritional quality of food,[107] the effectiveness of hearing aids,[108] and the potential side effects of over-the-counter antacids.[109]

Several of these requirements of disclosure of information relate to situations where there is a history of extensive deceptive and unfair advertising, and extensive adjudication challenging that advertising. In some instances, the Commission has bottomed its disclosure requirements on its traditional policing authority with respect to false advertising.[110] Other rules, however, are grounded wholly or in part on the Commission's perception of a need on the part of consumers for strategic product information.

As previously noted, market failure occasionally leads to the absence of key product information. Moreover, consumers deceived or exploited through ignorance of key data — for example, when they purchase unreasonably costly funeral services or insurance because comparative price data is not available — have no practical recourse to relief in the courts. Therefore, as a general matter, the Commission's decision to devote its resources to disclosure programs responds to consumer needs and reflects a sound conception of the role of advertising in a market economy.

The advisability of any particular disclosure program will depend on the extent to which the data bear directly on important

did not include paved roads, sewer systems, or phone services. Electricity and water were available only at unreasonable prices.

[105] *See* notes 8–12 *supra.*

[106] *See also* Lorillard, Inc., 80 F.T.C. 455 (1972) (order requiring disclosure of the Surgeon General's warning in all cigarette ads).

[107] Proposed Trade Regulation Rule Concerning Food Advertising, 39 Fed. Reg. 39,842 (1974) (to be codified in 16 C.F.R. § 437).

[108] Proposed Trade Regulation Rule Concerning Hearing Aid Industry, 40 Fed. Reg. 59,746 (1975) (to be codified in 16 C.F.R. § 440).

[109] Initiation of Proceedings for Proposed Trade Regulation Rule Concerning Advertising for Over-the-Counter Antacids, 41 Fed. Reg. 14,534 (1976) (to be codified in 16 C.F.R. § 415). *See also* Proposed Disclosure Regulations Concerning Retail Prices for Prescription Drugs, 40 Fed. Reg. 24,031 (1975). After Virginia State Bd. of Pharmacy v. Virginia Citizens Consumer Council, Inc., 96 S. Ct. 1917 (1976), discussed at pp. 672–73 *supra*, the FTC decided to postpone indefinitely further proceedings on the proposed rule. *See* 41 Fed. Reg. 27,391 (1976).

[110] *See* pp. 675–79 *supra.*

features of the product, the cost to advertisers of accumulation of the disclosed data (compared to costs to consumers of gathering it for themselves), the extent to which it is comprehensible and useful to consumers, and the likelihood that sellers eventually would provide the data without government encouragement. Expensive disclosure systems could raise barriers to entry or favor large over small firms; despite the Commission's increased sensitivity to consumer concerns, any adverse competitive effect on industry structure still must be taken into account. Subject to these various caveats, however, information disclosure appears to be a sound general response to the pressures of the consumer movement.

### *B. Deemphasis of Two Areas of Traditional Enforcement Activity*

*1. Deceptive Comparative Price Advertising.* — In the late 1950's and early 1960's, the heyday of enforcement of the Commission's 1958 Guides Against Deceptive Pricing,[111] as many as thirty percent of all the cease-and-desist orders sought by the Commission related to deceptive (*i.e.*, "fictitious") price claims, such as that a product will be sold at "10% off list" or at an "all time low price." During the last eight years, enforcement of the fictitious pricing guides has been negligible.[112] On the other hand, product quality claims — for instance, that a car gets ten percent better gas mileage than any other car in its class or that a product is "high" in vitamins — have been more likely to be challenged. The question is whether this considerable reallocation of resources from price claims to product quality claims is justifiable in the context of a more consumer-oriented program of ad regulation.

When a seller deceptively asserts that it is selling at "20% off list" or "free," competitive or consumer injuries can result. Purchasers may be diverted from the more efficient low-price seller, and purchases may be executed that might not otherwise occur or at a time they would not otherwise occur. On the other hand, much alleged fictitious pricing is innocuous, either because consumers are in a position to check the validity of exaggerated claims (for example, where comparison shopping is relatively simple) or because the claims are so unlikely ("lowest price ever")

[111] 23 Fed. Reg. 7965 (1958).

[112] The fictitious price complaints that have been filed appear to involve instances in which deceptive price claims were a part of a broad pattern of fraudulent operations, *see, e.g.*, Tashof v. FTC, 437 F.2d 707 (D.C. Cir. 1970), or where comparative price claims did not simply exaggerate bargains being offered but rather claimed short duration sales by companies that in fact never departed from usual and customary offering prices, *see, e.g.*, Stevens Bedding Warehouse, Inc., [1973–1976 Transfer Binder] TRADE REG. REP. (CCH) ¶ 20,968 (FTC 1975).

or ambiguous ("10% off") that they will be ignored by almost all customers. Fictitious price claims that exaggerate the price against which the discount is compared may deny consumers the benefits of the bargain they thought they were receiving, but as long as consumers are accurately informed of the offering price, they can make sensible decisions, and the transactions may still be at prices lower than could be obtained at most other outlets in the marketing area.

Furthermore, much fictitious pricing enforcement entails considerable social and economic costs. A natural target for such enforcement has been discount houses, and the usual complainants have been nondiscounters who emphasize service and reliability rather than price. Aggressive enforcement against discounters that forces them to hew close to the line of accurate information may tend to dampen competitive activity. Often, "cents-off," free goods, couponing and other discount promotions are devices that assist new entrants in penetrating concentrated markets and that tend to unsettle stable and rigid pricing patterns. Couponing and free goods may be the *only* legal way that a seller can effectuate a price cut to consumers when intermediate distributors refuse to pass along a list price reduction. While the same pro-competitive effects can be achieved by accurate price claims in connection with these promotions, the cost to sellers of ascertaining whether particular discount claims are accurate may deter them from making such claims at all.[113]

An unusually clear example of enforcement against fictitious pricing which impaired competition while generating little or no consumer benefits is *FTC v. Mary Carter Paint Co.*,[114] where the Commission challenged the respondent's claim that with every purchase of a can of paint (price: $6.98), it would give a second can of paint away "free." An FTC Guide required that where the advertiser had not previously sold the product, the word "free" could not be used unless the sales price for two of the product was the usual and customary price in the relevant trade area for one. Where the advertiser had previously sold the product in the relevant trade area, the Guide required that the sales price for both products be the advertiser's usual and customary retail price for one. Since Mary Carter had sold paint in the relevant trade area but had never sold single cans of paint, its use of the word "free" did not meet either Guide requirement. In finding a violation of

[113] For example, if a seller must survey area prices to make the claim "no lower price in town" or any other area price claims, the claim probably will not be made at all. Of course, certain claims, such as "10% off list," can be easily verified at little cost to the seller.

[114] 60 F.T.C. 1827 (1962), *rev'd*, 333 F.2d 654 (5th Cir. 1964), *rev'd*, 382 U.S. 46 (1965).

its Guide, the Commission rejected an offer of proof by Mary Carter that each can of its paint matched in quality those paints usually and customarily sold in the $6.98 price range. The Supreme Court upheld the Commission's decision.[115]

As in so many fictitious price cases, the problem is to determine what possible consumer or competitive injury occurred. If the offer of proof was valid, Mary Carter was indeed offering two cans of paint at the price of one can sold by competitors, and competitors could hardly complain because consumers were receiving the equivalent of a second can of paint free. The only plausible deception is that consumers may have been misled into thinking that Mary Carter had a single can price, but it is hard to imagine how that misconception could have led to any injury.[116]

Assuming that Mary Carter was a more efficient producer of a quality product, there was an alternative marketing approach that would not have resulted in any consumer deception. Mary Carter could have sold single cans of paint at $3.49 each, a price which presumably would attract many purchasers. But this alternative would have deprived the company of an opportunity to make use of a distinctive ad campaign that might overcome sales resistance of consumers who associate low price in paint with low quality.

While few cases present the case against fictitious pricing enforcement as clearly as does *Mary Carter*, the FTC policy decision to downplay enforcement against alleged fictitious pricing, thereby permitting some exaggeration and ambiguity in price claims, is consistent with the principle of minimum enforcement where consumers, as opposed to competitors, are unlikely to be seriously injured and where rigid substantiation requirements might suppress a useful form of competition. Extreme examples of deceptive price claims might still be challenged, and fictitious price counts incorporated in omnibus complaints against clearly unethical sellers, but discontinuance of the effort to clear the market of ambiguous or exaggerated price claims seems justified.

2. *Phony Mock-Ups.* — Another major area of Commission enforcement in the late 1950's and early 1960's concerned phony mock-ups in television advertising[117] to simulate the real object or device being advertised. In classic deceptive demonstration cases, the advertiser falsely distorts qualities of its own or com-

[115] 382 U.S. 46 (1965).

[116] Justice Harlan in his dissent in *Mary Carter* pointed out that the record did not indicate any consumer complaints about the 2-for-1 sales method. *Id.* at 52 (dissenting opinion).

[117] For a collection of cases during that period, *see* Note, *Illusion or Deception: The Use of "Props" and "Mock-Ups" in Television Advertising*, 72 YALE L.J. 145, 151–54 n.34 (1962).

petitive products in order to create in the consumer's mind a perception of product qualities that the product does not possess — for example, lens angles that distort the size or speed of a toy racing car.[118] In "mock-up" cases, the characteristics perceived by the viewer on the T.V. screen are actually possessed by the product, though the means used in the studio to transmit the image is different than that perceived on the home screen — for example, mashed potatoes in place of ice cream, because ice cream would quickly melt under T.V. lights. The Commission's drive against mock-ups culminated in 1965 in the Supreme Court's decision in *FTC v. Colgate-Palmolive Co.*[119] Nevertheless, in the last six years, the Commission has not filed a single mock-up complaint.[120]

In *Colgate*, the advertiser sought to demonstrate that "Rapid-Shave" had super-moisturizing properties which permitted the shaving of sandpaper, and thus that it would be effective in shaving the toughest beards. Since sandpaper appears in television transmission as plain colored paper, the cream was applied instead to plexiglass covered with sand, which was then swept clean by a razor. The record showed that sandpaper could not be shaved unless it had been soaked for some eighty minutes, and therefore the demonstration was a clear deception without reference to the mock-up. The Supreme Court went on to find, however, that even if sandpaper could be shaved exactly as demonstrated in the commercial, it was a separate violation to use an undisclosed mock-up, since the advertiser was found to have represented to the public that it was presenting an actual demonstration of its product's qualities.[121] The Court limited its rule to situations in which a demonstration is offered as proof of an asserted claim. Thus, the rule would not extend to use of scenery as a backdrop, or actors playing roles in "slice of life" commercials, or even the use of mashed potatoes to simulate ice cream, where no product claim is made relating to the simulated demonstration.

It is not at all clear, however, how consumers could be injured by phony mock-ups. As Justice Harlan argued in dissent in *Colgate*, the image which the consumer perceives on the screen actually represents the qualities of the product.[122] The majority's

[118] *See, e.g.*, Mattel, Inc., 79 F.T.C. 667 (1971).

[119] 380 U.S. 374 (1965).

[120] It is always possible in a traditional deceptive demonstration case for the respondent to raise a mock-up defense. For example, Standard Oil of California, distributor of Chevron gasoline, was charged with falsely picturing the Palm Springs County Court House as its research lab, and offered, among other defenses, that it substituted buildings because of adverse weather conditions in the part of California where its research lab was located. *See* Standard Oil of California, 84 F.T.C. 1401, 1449–50 (1974).

[121] 380 U.S. at 390–91.

[122] 380 U.S. at 397–98 (dissenting opinion).

explanation was that even if experiments had been conducted verifying the claim that sandpaper could be shaved with Rapid-Shave, there was fraud in that viewers were not seeing that experiment for themselves. The majority supported its decision by citing several lines of precedent dealing with what it described as irrational preferences — situations in which fraud had been found on no evidence other than that ads had falsely claimed that the seller was a member of a particular class of dealers (for example, a wholesaler),[123] or failed to disclose that re-refined oil (crankcase drainings purified and processed to the point at which they equal the original product in chemical composition and effectiveness) was not virgin oil.[124] In these situations, there had been findings that consumers were getting something less than they had bargained for and that the missing element was something they preferred, whether or not the sought-after quality was universally viewed as desirable.[125] In the mock-up situation, however, consumers are receiving exactly the product for which they bargained (rational and irrational preferences included), with the alleged fraud relating exclusively to a technique designed to make allowances for distortions in the transmission of the demonstration. Viewed from this perspective, the Commission's conclusion that the fraud was *material* — *i.e.*, that a significant number of people would regard as important an adjustment designed to permit them to see accurately the results of a relevant test or demonstration — is an excellent example of ad regulation in the name of Truth for its own sake. In terms of market considerations — the role of advertising in providing relevant, accurate information to guide purchasing decisions — frauds inherent in phony mock-ups are obviously inconsequential.

It is possible to defend the *Colgate* decision, however, on separate, entirely practical grounds. If a mock-up defense is permissible, the issues it generates may tend to complicate and lengthen otherwise simple fraudulent demonstration cases. A classic example is the automobile windshield commercial which demonstrated the distortion-free properties of the product by filming

[123] FTC v. Royal Milling Co., 288 U.S. 212 (1933) (respondent represented his company as a miller when, in fact, it purchased and resold already milled flour).

[124] Kerran v. FTC, 265 F.2d 246, 248 (10th Cir.) ("the public is entitled to know the facts . . . and then make its own choice . . . even though the choice is predicated at least in part on ill-founded sentiment, belief, or caprice."), *cert. denied*, 361 U.S. 818 (1959).

[125] With respect to this issue, one might question whether the preferences were entirely irrational. Consumers might wisely conclude that quality control problems on re-refined oil would inevitably be somewhat greater than with the original product, or that buying direct from "wholesalers" would yield lower prices than buying through retail outlets.

passing scenery with the auto windows rolled down.[126] The advertiser justified the practice on the ground that technical difficulties necessitated a "mock-up" and, of course, offered to prove that its product was superior to rivals' products. An absolute rule against mock-ups eliminates such issues. Moreover, nothing is lost in terms of informational advertising, because simulated demonstrations made necessary by technical aspects of television broadcasting can still be performed as long as the simulation is disclosed. Given the presence of this simple alternative which eliminates, at little or no cost, the very slight fraud that may be present with mock-ups, *Colgate* was probably rightly decided. Since *Colgate*, advertisers have disclosed simulation in most mock-up situations. Even where not disclosed, mock-ups have not been challenged because the Commission has in effect abandoned enforcement in this area.

### C. *Remedy — Corrective Advertising*

The most significant recent developments in federal regulation of advertising involve efforts to devise a set of effective sanctions for deceptive or unfair claims. Previously, the standard remedy in deceptive advertising cases was a "cease and desist order" which defined, usually in fairly broad terms, those categories of claims which had been found to be illegal. Subsequent false advertising of the same type with respect to the same category of products could lead to penalties of $5,000 (recently raised by statute to $10,000) per day per violation.[127] The only significant alternative for these "go and sin no more" orders was to require affirmative disclosure of particular product facts — for example, health hazards in connection with cigarette smoking — where silence or implications from other express advertising would be reasonably certain to lead to misconceptions about the product in the minds of average consumers.[128]

---

[126] Libby-Owens-Ford Glass Co. v. FTC, 352 F.2d 415 (6th Cir. 1965).

[127] 15 U.S.C. § 45(m)(1)(B) (Supp. IV 1974).

[128] *See, e.g.*, J. B. Williams Co. v. FTC, 381 F.2d 884 (6th Cir. 1967) (upholding required disclosure in advertising of the iron tonic "Geritol" that the product will be of no benefit for the great majority of people exhibiting symptoms of tiredness); All-State Indus., Inc., 75 F.T.C. 465 (1969), *aff'd*, 423 F.2d 423 (4th Cir.), *cert. denied*, 400 U.S. 828 (1970) (requiring disclosure by creditors that instruments of indebtedness might be assigned to a third party, thereby resulting in a substantial alteration of the buyer's rights and liabilities).

Preliminary injunctions or restitution might have developed as remedies to deprive fraudulent advertisers of the advantages of other illegal behavior. The Commission has long had preliminary injunction powers with respect to advertising of foods, drugs, cosmetics or medical devices under 15 U.S.C. §§ 52–53 (1970), and this power was extended in 1973 to all advertising, *see* 15 U.S.C. § 53 (Supp. III 1973). The power to seek preliminary injunctions has rarely been exercised, how-

Faced with these pathetically inadequate remedies, many advertisers and advertising agencies violated the law with impunity. Rational advertisers could calculate that their chances of being detected and prosecuted were extremely slim, given the limited resources of the Federal Trade Commission and the vast amount of advertising it was required to review.[129] Moreover, since most advertising themes are designed to run for a year or less, and since the average time for investigation and trial of a deceptive advertising case extended well over two years,[130] the challenged advertising campaign usually had disappeared or was about to disappear prior to the time an order could be entered. This absence of effective government remedies was compounded by the virtual unavailability of private remedies against false advertising and the dearth of counter-advertising by competitors designed to expose exaggerated or unsubstantiated advertising claims.

---

ever, primarily because of court rulings that the Commission must demonstrate inadequacy of legal remedies and likelihood of irreparable injury stemming from the advertising if the preliminary injunction is not granted, *see* FTC v. National Health Aids, Inc., 108 F. Supp. 340, 346 (D. Md. 1952); Note, *"Corrective Advertising" Orders of the Federal Trade Commission*, 85 HARV. L. REV. 477, 485–87 & n.54 (1971). *But see* FTC v. Rhodes Pharmacal Co., 191 F.2d 744 (7th Cir. 1951) (preliminary injunction will issue where FTC shows reason to believe that the advertising of a drug is false and that the public interest is affected). *Rhodes'* continuing validity was questioned in FTC v. National Health Aids, Inc., 108 F. Supp. 340, 346 (D. Md. 1952).

A 1973 statutory expansion of the Commission's preliminary injunction authority relieved the Commission of the requirement of proving "irreparable injury." 15 U.S.C. § 57b (Supp. IV 1974). However, this statute may not lead to new remedial initiatives, because, except for blatant frauds, deceptive advertising cases involve complicated evidentiary issues relating to the meaning of the ad and adequacy of substantiation. By the time the Commission becomes aware of the ad and prepares its case for preliminary injunction, even 26 to 52 week ad campaigns are likely to have run their course.

Commission-directed restitution on behalf of defrauded consumers, now explicitly authorized under the Federal Trade Commission Improvement Act, Pub. L. No. 93–637, 88 Stat. 2183 (1974) (codified at 15 U.S.C. §§ 45, 57b (Supp. IV 1974)), might be another way of achieving stiffer penalties for deceptive advertising. However, the Commission has rarely sought to impose that remedy in false advertising cases. Attempts to do so encounter serious problems of proof of causality, actual injury, and the absence of windfall profits to the consumer.

[129] An average of fewer than 500 investigations of deceptive practices were initiated in each year during the period 1965–1969, with an average of fewer than 70 complaints issued each year. REPORT OF THE ABA COMMISSION TO STUDY THE FEDERAL TRADE COMMISSION 19–20 (1969). Many of these investigations and complaints involved relatively insignificant advertising themes.

[130] *See id.* at 28–31 (statistics concerning administrative delay at the FTC); Note, *supra* note 128, at 483 (delays of three to five years between complaint and order are common; in Carter Prods., Inc. v. FTC, 268 F.2d 461 (9th Cir.), *cert. denied*, 361 U.S. 884 (1959), it took the Commission 16 years to compel respondent to drop reference to liver in "Carter's Little Liver Pills").

Remedial innovation at the FTC has concentrated on efforts to eliminate this vacuum in law enforcement. The most significant development in this connection has been corrective advertising orders directing an advertiser found guilty of disseminating a false and misleading claim to inform consumers, usually through the same advertising media selected to disseminate the false claim in the first place, of the facts with respect to the claim. About a score of complaints filed since 1970 have proposed corrective advertising orders,[131] and in several the Commission has accepted consent orders incorporating a corrective message.[132]

*1. FTC Authority to Order Corrective Advertising.* — The Commission had asserted several times its view that it has the authority to impose corrective advertising,[133] but it was only in 1975, in a proceeding against Warner-Lambert involving advertising of the mouthwash Listerine,[134] that the Commission finally

[131] *See, e.g.*, American Home Prods. Corp., 77 F.T.C. 726 (1970) (complaint suggested order requiring firm to run ads showing how demonstration of products in prior ads would have worked without the fakery in the original ads); ITT Continental Baking Co., [1970–1973 Transfer Binder] TRADE REG. REP. (CCH) ¶ 19, 539 (FTC 1971) (would require ads for one year to carry message that FTC has alleged that certain products have been falsely advertised). The part of the proposed *ITT* order relating to corrective advertising was rejected by the Commission, 83 F.T.C. 865, 930–33, *modified on unrelated matters*, 83 F.T.C. 1105 (1973), *aff'd*, 532 F.2d 207 (2d Cir. 1976).

Corrective advertising had first been formally submitted in an FTC proceeding by SOUP, a group of students who attempted to intervene in a § 5 advertising proceeding against Campbell Soup Co., 77 F.T.C. 664 (1970).

[132] *E.g.*, Ocean Spray Cranberries, Inc., 80 F.T.C. 975 (1971) (25% of ad budget for one year must be devoted to informing public of past deception); ITT Continental Baking Co., 79 F.T.C. 248 (1971) (25% of ad budget for one year to be expended as ads that state Profile bread will not engender weight loss). *See also* Lens Craft Research & Devel. Co., [1973–1976 Transfer Binder] TRADE REG. REP. (CCH) ¶ 20,629 (FTC 1974) (ads for contact lenses); Wasem's, Inc., [1973–1976 Transfer Binder] TRADE REG. REP. (CCH) ¶ 20,536 (FTC 1974) (ads for vitamins); Amstar Corp., 83 F.T.C. 659 (1973) (ads for sugar).

[133] *See* Campbell Soup Co., 77 F.T.C. 664, 668 (1970) ("We have no doubt as to the Commission's power to require such affirmative disclosures when such disclosures are reasonably related to the deception found and are required in order to dissipate the effects of that deception."); Firestone Tire & Rubber Co., 81 F.T.C. 398, 471 (1972) ("[A]n order requiring corrective advertising is well within the arsenal of relief provisions which the Commission may draw upon. . . . "), *aff'd*, 481 F.2d 246 (6th Cir.), *cert. denied*, 414 U.S. 1112 (1973). In *Firestone*, the Commission also considered and rejected the claim that corrective orders might have an impermissible chilling effect on the first amendment rights of advertisers. Although the Commission originally declined to order corrective advertising in *Firestone*, mandatory corrective advertising was included in the recent negotiated settlement reached in the FTC's suit to enforce the original cease and desist order, United States v. Firestone, 1976–1 Trade Cas. ¶ 60, 729 (N.D. Ohio 1976).

[134] Warner-Lambert Co., [1973–1976 Transfer Binder] TRADE REG. REP. (CCH) ¶ 21,066 (FTC 1975), *appeal docketed*, No. 76–1138 (D.C. Cir., filed Feb. 13, 1976).

imposed the remedy in a litigated case. No federal court to date has considered whether the Commission has authority to impose corrective advertising and, if so, under what circumstances it should do so.

All Commission remedial authority traces to the broad delegation of discretion under section five (b) of the Federal Trade Commission Act, which empowers the Commission to order parties to "cease and desist" unfair or deceptive acts or practices in commerce. Traditionally the courts have accorded the Commission wide latitude, particularly in antitrust enforcement, to develop remedial approaches.[135] Thus the courts have ratified Commission orders of simple divestiture,[136] divestiture which required the previously acquired company to be re-established as an effective competitor,[137] compulsory licensing of patents on a reasonable royalty basis,[138] and affirmative disclosure of derogatory product characteristics.[139]

Resistance to corrective advertising has focused on the established rules that all Commission orders must be "prospective" and — a related point — that its orders must not be punitive.[140] Arguably, corrective advertising is not prospective and remedial — as would be an affirmative disclosure warning future purchasers of adverse information about product performance — because corrective advertising has the additional consequence of advising consumers that purchases may have been influenced by past deceptive product claims, which may loosen brand allegiance or reduce market share for the illegal advertiser. The process of rectifying past wrongs arguably places the remedy beyond Commission authority.

The problem with this argument is the assumption that Commission remedies must be *exclusively* prospective — an interpretation of Commission power that the agency has never accepted and that the courts have not imposed.[141] The only requirement imposed on FTC remedial orders is that they prevent some significant future illegal effect, and corrective advertising meets that

[135] *See* Jacob Siegel Co. v. FTC, 327 U.S. 608, 611 (1946) (judicial review of FTC remedies is limited because the "Commission has wide discretion in its choice of a remedy deemed adequate to cope with the unlawful practices in this area of trade").

[136] *See, e.g.*, L. G. Balfour Co. v. FTC, 442 F.2d 1, 23 (7th Cir. 1971).

[137] Ekco Prod. Co. v. FTC, 347 F.2d 745, 753–54 (7th Cir. 1965).

[138] American Cyanamid Co. v. FTC, 363 F.2d 757, 771–72 (6th Cir. 1966).

[139] *See* notes 8–12 *supra*.

[140] *Cf.* FTC v. Ruberoid Co., 343 U.S. 470, 473 (1952) ("Orders of the Federal Trade Commission are not intended to impose criminal punishment or exact compensatory damages for past acts, but to prevent illegal practices in the future.").

[141] *See* Curtis Publishing Co., 78 F.T.C. 1472, 1512–18 (1971) (real question is not whether remedy is prospective but whether it is punitive).

requirement if the effects of the prior deceptive ad campaign continue to influence market behavior for a substantial period of time after the campaign has been discontinued. Once consumers are persuaded by deceptive product information, something more than a simple cease and desist order is necessary to dissipate the future harmful effects of the prior fraud and to prevent future fraudulent transactions from occurring. The "prospective" aspect of a corrective advertising remedy is even more obvious when deceptive advertising is viewed in competitive terms. Assuming that an illegal advertising campaign resulted in the appropriation of some market share, the false advertiser will retain that market share until consumers are informed of the misinformation on which their decisions to purchase are based. Only a corrective order will dissipate the lingering effects of the false advertising. In that sense, corrective advertising is analogous to divestiture remedies, which the Commission has traditionally applied in merger cases because an order simply enjoining further future mergers obviously would be inadequate to prevent continuing violations. While divestiture has some retrospective effects in that it nullifies the effect of a past, illegal transaction, this has never been deemed sufficient to convert the remedy into one that is punitive and retroactive rather than remedial and prospective. In short, the Commission must have the authority to deprive illegal advertisers of the unlawful fruits of their violations in order to reestablish the market situation as it existed prior to the wrongdoing.[142]

Viewed against this background of analogous remedies and comparable circumstances, and the general latitude accorded the Commission in the development of novel remedial approaches, the surprise is not so much that the Commission will be held to have authority to impose corrective advertising, but rather that there has been such prolonged uncertainty and heated debate over the issue.

2. *Circumstances in Which Corrective Advertising May Be Imposed.* — In *Warner-Lambert*, the Commission offered only general guidelines as to the circumstances in which corrective advertising could be imposed:

> [I]f a deceptive advertisement has played a substantial role in creating or reinforcing in the public's mind a false and material belief which lives on after the false advertising ceases, there is clear and continuing injury to competition and to the consuming public as consumers continue to make purchasing decisions based on the false belief. Since this injury cannot be averted by merely requiring respondent to cease disseminating the advertisement,

[142] *Cf.* United States v. Paramount Pictures, Inc., 334 U.S. 131, 170–72 (1948) (where this rationale was cited as justification for divestiture remedies).

> we may appropriately order respondent to take affirmative action designed to terminate the otherwise continuing ill effects of the advertisement.[143]

Under the formulation put forth by the Commission, corrective advertising arguably could only be ordered once the Commission demonstrated that:

> (1) an advertisement was false, misleading or deceptive in a material respect;
>
> (2) a substantial number of purchasers were exposed to the advertisement and their subsequent purchases were influenced by the fraud;
>
> (3) the consumer's misguided belief was not attributable to other causal factors (such as word-of-mouth comments by satisfied users);
>
> (4) the effect of the deception was not dissipated in the course of use of the product; and
>
> (5) the fraudulent message was remembered by a significant number of purchasers, continued to influence purchasing decisions up to the date of entry of a final Commission order, and was likely to continue to be influential for a substantial segment of potential purchasers even if the false claims were no longer disseminated by the seller.

In traditional section five litigation, the Commission largely avoids the causal connection issues underlying prerequisites two through five by its rule that an ad violates the statute if it has a capacity to mislead, as determined by the Commissioners on the basis of their reading of the ad.[144] If these issues are made relevant in the corrective advertising context and the burden of proof for each is placed on the Commission staff, the remedy would be imposed rarely. In *Warner-Lambert*, the record did support each of those findings, but the Listerine ad campaign was unusual. In major ad campaigns disseminated for fifty-five years and broadcast to the date of the suit, the manufacturer had claimed that the mouthwash was effective in ameliorating, preventing and curing colds and sore throats.[145] Because the theme was uniquely as-

[143] Warner-Lambert Co., [1973–1976 Transfer Binder] TRADE REG. REP. (CCH) ¶ 21,066 at 20,934–35 (FTC 1975), *appeal docketed*, No. 76–1138 (D.C. Cir., filed Feb. 13, 1976).

[144] *See* pp. 677–79 *supra*.

[145] *See* Warner-Lambert Co., [1973–1976 Transfer Binder] TRADE REG. REP. (CCH) ¶ 21,066 at 20,936 (FTC 1975), *appeal docketed*, No. 76–1138 (D.C. Cir., filed Feb. 13, 1976).

serted on behalf of Listerine, there was little consumer confusion as to which mouthwash claimed a health feature. Further, there was persuasive evidence that the claim was believed by purchasers at least up to the time of suit.[146] Comparable proof of deception-perception-memory influence would be virtually impossible in most advertising cases.[147]

If the Commission is to do an effective job in regulating deceptive advertising, corrective advertising must apply to more than the one-in-a-million type of ad campaign present in *Warner-Lambert*. Specifically, it must apply to short run (twenty-six to fifty-two week) blatant advertising frauds, and should not impose on the Commission the virtually impossible burdens of demonstrating causal connection between advertising and the purchasing decision, and case-by-case residual recollections of the ad campaign by consumers up to the time of eventual appellate review of the Commission decision. On the other hand, the remedy should not be imposed against every commonplace advertising fraud. The purchase of advertising space or time for the corrective message is expensive, and the remedy is unusually embarrassing to the false advertiser. Further, a corrective message for an insignificant fraud (for example, that a car gets only twenty-four miles-per-gallon rather than the claimed twenty-five) or for a false claim of marginal significance in most consumers' purchasing decisions (*e.g.*, domestic origin claims or testimonials by celebrities who do not use the product) would impair rather than assist a consumer's ability to make purchasing decisions. Similarly, a corrective message disseminated after all but a few consumers have forgotten the original fraud will be useless and perhaps confusing from the point of view of ensuring accurate information in the marketplace. And when the original fraud is no longer influential to any significant degree at the time of suit, the remedy is no longer "remedial" in even an expanded conception of that term and is therefore beyond the authority of the Commission.

The following rule is designed to take these competing considerations into account and should decide most of the hard cases. To justify corrective advertising, the Commission should prove:

(1) the existence of a *material* fraud or deception with respect to a *major* advertising theme;

[146] An average of 53.8% of all persons surveyed during the period from 1963 through 1971 rated Listerine as "one of the best" in the category "effective for colds and sore throats." Many other responders rated Listerine "very good," "good" or "fair" in the cold-related categories. *Id.* at 20,935.

[147] This would be true in part because of the difficulty the Commission would encounter in financing the kind of surveys that appeared in the record in *Warner-Lambert*. The company had conducted its own surveys, which were introduced into evidence against it, at a cost of over $100,000. *Id.*

(2) that this fraud created in a substantial number of consumers a misconception about the product *consistent with the fraud*; and

(3) that this misconception significantly influenced the purchasing decisions of these consumers at the *time suit was brought*.

The principal impact of the proposed formulation would be to limit corrective advertising to "major" ad themes,[148] and to place on respondents the burden of proof of lack of causality and of de minimis residual effect subsequent to the time of suit. Burdening the advertiser with proof of lack of causality is consistent with Commission practice on proof of a substantive violation. Common sense also indicates that if an advertiser spends vast amounts of money to disseminate a deceptive product claim and large numbers of people exposed to the ads have views consistent with that claim, it is fair to assume that the advertisements have achieved their intended result. The advertiser would be allowed to demonstrate the exceedingly rare situations in which identity between the false claim and the false belief is a coincidence.

The placement of the burden of proving post-complaint dissipation of the effects of deceptive advertising is a more difficult question. The issues of perception, belief and memory are so elusive — and thus so difficult and expensive to measure — that the party enjoying the benefits of a presumption is likely to prevail in most cases. Several considerations suggest that the respondents should have the burden of proving post-complaint dissipation. First, virtually all advertisers treat advertising expenses as an investment and assume that they will enjoy returns from that investment over time.[149] Moreover, a rule focusing on advertising effects at the time of suit would take away from defendants any incentive to delay administrative proceedings and subsequent appeal to avoid the imposition of an onerous remedy. Since discontinuance of the ad campaign and delay of suit are within the control of the advertiser, such matters should not be permitted to deflect what would otherwise be an appropriate remedy. Of course, where the advertiser can meet the difficult burden of showing that the lag effect of its advertising has dissipated by the time a remedy is to be imposed, corrective advertising should not be

[148] Eventually, the Commission might publish a policy planning guide indicating the circumstances in which corrective advertising would be imposed, indicating the weight to be assigned such factors as the blatancy of the fraud, how widely it was disseminated, whether the audience would understand and benefit from a corrective message, and the subject-matter of the deception.

[149] *But cf.* Brozen, *Entry Barriers: Advertising and Product Differentiation*, in INDUSTRIAL CONCENTRATION: THE NEW LEARNING (Goldschmid, Mann & Weston, eds. 1974) 115, 124 (businesses do not usually capitalize advertising expenses).

ordered, because the only purpose it could serve would be punishment.

Under this proposed formulation, corrective advertising would not apply to a blatant advertising deception that is disseminated for such a brief period of time that even at the time of suit substantial consumer recall of the ad campaign cannot be proven. To avoid charges that remedies applied to such violations are punitive, the Commission would have to resort to such strained theories as that (1) the deception, though no longer recalled, was the cause of an original purchase, and thereafter brand loyalty and consumer inertia took over to generate repeat purchases, or (2) even though there is no present recall of the ad campaign, similar campaigns in the future will predictably trigger recall of the deception which will then influence market behavior. The likelihood that such effects will occur seems too slight to justify any kind of presumption, although in rare cases, it will of course be open to the Commission to demonstrate these effects.

*3. Content of Corrective Advertising Orders.* — Standard proposed corrective advertising orders to date have required that a company found to have violated section five either discontinue advertising for one year or disseminate a corrective message that accounts for twenty-five percent of the respondent's advertising budget for a period of one year.[150] These were arbitrary guidelines selected for a novel remedial program, and in a number of instances, the Commission has departed from this format, either by calling for mandatory corrective advertising [151] or by varying the nature of the disclosure or the time period in which it would take place.[152] In *Warner-Lambert*, the Commission, operating with the benefit of a full record on questions of lingering deception, required respondent to include a corrective message in all product advertising until it had expended an amount equal to its average annual advertising budget for the ten-year period from 1962 through 1972. This seems a thoughtful approach since it relates the corrective order to the investment qualities of advertising expenditures.

The content and coverage of corrective advertising orders are bound to be matters of some experimentation during early efforts to impose the remedy, and it is difficult, without much experience with the effect of such orders, to propose guidelines. As long as the central aim in imposing the remedy — to eliminate lingering

[150] *See* note 132 *supra*.

[151] Sugar Info., Inc., 81 F.T.C. 711, 723 (1972) (consent order requiring corrective advertising in certain magazines).

[152] *See, e.g.*, Bristol Myers Co., [1970–1973 Transfer Binder] TRADE REG. REP. (CCH) ¶ 20,262 (FTC 1973) (complaints against analgesic producers calling for corrective advertising for a period of two years).

consumer misimpressions or illegally achieved market share as a result of prior fraud — is served, the courts are likely to defer to Commission efforts to develop reasonable corrective advertising policies.

## IV. Conclusions

This Article has argued that developments in ad regulation over the last decade reflect the deemphasis of the role of such regulation as substitute enforcer of competitive rights and protector of the integrity of language. Increased efforts by case and rule to facilitate the availability of key product information and diminished enforcement efforts against comparative price claims and mock-ups are clear evidence of this reorientation. The ad substantiation program also appears consistent with a consumer-oriented enforcement program, though it is not yet clear that the cost of this program is justified. Corrective advertising is consistent with every approach to ad regulation — except perhaps the notion that advertising fraud is harmless and that impotent enforcement therefore serves social interests — since it makes all enforcement efforts credible and effective.

These new programs represent a change in emphasis rather than a complete break with prior practice. Many ad regulation efforts in the earlier period were completely consumer oriented — the health warning in cigarette advertising is the most obvious example — and, as discussed, even the most questionable regulatory efforts such as challenges to mock-ups and comparative price claims, had some impact on consumer welfare. But in broad outline, the more recent programs represent a notable departure.

It has not been a part of the argument of this Article to attempt to justify all of the cases, proposed rules, theories, and remedies devised during this recent active period. Wrongheaded case and rule selection will diminish useful information in the marketplace and generate unjustifiable costs regardless of whether undertaken under the banner of "consumer protection." The conclusions that are submitted are much more limited: first, that there is a legitimate role for government regulation of fairness and truth in advertising as a supplement to market incentives, and, second, that the major recent programs designed to discharge that role are based on a revised and more sensible view of the function of advertising in the market and should result in higher levels of consumer welfare.

# [8]

## THE FUNCTIONS OF DISCLOSURE REGULATION IN CONSUMER TRANSACTIONS†

WILLIAM C. WHITFORD*

One of the oldest and most prevalent methods of regulating consumer transactions has been to require the seller[1] to disclose to his consumer buyer various types of information about their contractual transaction.[2] The contract law doctrine ascribing voidability to a contract if its terms are too vague (whatever *too* vague is) can be viewed as an indirect form of such regulation.[3] The common law of misrepresentation and public law concerning deceptive advertising, although usually concerned with preventing the dissemination of misleading information, at times have been interpreted to re-

---

† Financial support in the preparation of this article has been provided by the Institute for Research on Poverty, University of Wisconsin, from funds made available by the Office of Economic Opportunity, pursuant to the Economic Opportunity Act of 1964. I have received valuable research assistance from Mr. Scott Herrick, third-year student at the University of Wisconsin Law School, and Mr. Robert Heidt, J.D., 1972, University of Wisconsin. I am grateful for helpful comments on earlier drafts of this article from Professors Paul Brest, Richard Danzig, Richard Markovits, and William Warren. all of Stanford Law School. The sole responsibility for views expressed and any errors is mine.

* Professor of Law, University of Wisconsin. Visiting Professor of Law, Stanford University, 1972-1973. LL.B., 1964, Yale University.

1. The term "seller" is used in this article to denote the professional party to a consumer transaction. It includes, therefore, not only the seller of goods and services but also the lender or provider of credit.

2. In this article I shall use the term "disclosure regulation" to describe this type of regulation. By disclosure regulation, I mean only regulation which *requires* the disclosure of information about a prospective transaction. The term does not include regulation prohibiting the dissemination of false or misleading information about a proposed transaction. *Cf.* note 191 *infra* and accompanying text.

This article discusses only disclosure regulation of consumer transactions. The term "'consumer transaction" has no accepted definition, of course. Regulation of the sale of securities can certainly be viewed as consumer protection regulation, and an excellent example of the use of disclosure as a regulatory technique. And the mushrooming regulation of franchising, where disclosure is also heavily relied upon, is often viewed as consumer protection legislation. *See, e.g.*, CAL. CORP. CODE § 31000 *et seq.* (West Supp. 1972). In this article, however, I have in mind principally transactions in which goods, services, or credit are purchased "primarily for personal, family or household purposes," to borrow from the definition of "consumer goods" in UNIFORM COMMERCIAL CODE § 9-109(1).

3. *See, e.g.*, Klimek v. Perisich, 231 Ore. 71, 371 P.2d 956 (1962). Another excellent example of a common law effort to induce disclosure is the so-called "ticket" cases, in which the courts have consistently held that a limitation-of-liability clause does not become part of the contract unless the seller provides notice of the term, in a manner that ought to bring it to the attention of the consumer. *E.g.*, Jones v. Great Northern Ry., 68 Mont. 231, 217 P. 673 (1923).

quire the disclosure of contractual information.[4] With the growth of consumer protection as an important regulatory concern in the last decade or two, there has been an increasing incidence of disclosure regulation. The retail installment sales acts enacted in numerous states emphasize disclosure of information deemed relevant to many or most consumer buyers.[5] The Uniform Commercial Code, in what few efforts it makes to regulate consumer transactions, generally stresses disclosure regulation.[6] In the 1960's the pace at which disclosure regulation was enacted increased, with the best known enactments being the truth-in-lending[7] and truth-in-packaging legislation.[8] And proposals abound for various new types of disclosure regulation—for disclosure of information pertaining to product safety,[9] for more complete labeling of products,[10] and so forth.

A recent state enactment and a bill which was nearly enacted by the recently adjourned Ninety-second Congress illustrate the important position disclosure regulation still occupies in the regulation of consumer transactions. The Wisconsin Consumer Act[11] was enacted in the spring of 1972 and became effective on March 1, 1973. A comprehensive regulation of consumer credit transactions, the Act is basically a compromise between the Uniform Consumer

4. *See, e.g.*, J.B. Williams Co. v. FTC, 381 F.2d 884 (6th Cir. 1967); Obde v. Schlemeyer, 56 Wash. 2d 449, 353 P.2d 672 (1960).

5. *See* B. CURRAN, TRENDS IN CONSUMER CREDIT LEGISLATION 95-100 (1965).

6. *E.g.*, UNIFORM COMMERCIAL CODE § 2-316(2). *See also id.* § 2-302, Comment 1; Leff, *Unconscionability and the Code—The Emperor's New Clause*, 115 U. PA. L. REV. 485 (1967).

7. Consumer Credit Protection Act, 15 U.S.C. §§ 1601 *et seq.* (1970). Only the first subchapter of this Act, sections 1601-65, concerns consumer credit cost disclosure and is known as the Truth in Lending Act. Henceforth this subchapter will be referred to as "truth-in-lending."

8. Fair Packaging and Labeling Act, 15 U.S.C. §§ 1451-61 (1970). *Cf.* Hart, *Can Federal Legislation Affecting Consumers' Economic Interests Be Enacted?*, 64 MICH. L. REV. 1255 (1966). Some of the history of the application of this legislation can be found in P. KEETON & M. SHAPO, PRODUCTS AND THE CONSUMER: DECEPTIVE PRACTICES 295-97 (1972) and sources cited therein.

9. Probably the most recent enactment of disclosure regulation was the Motor Vehicle Information and Cost Savings Act, Pub. L. No. 92-513 (U.S. CODE CONG. & AD. NEWS, 92D CONG., 2D SESS., at 1110 [1972]). Title II of the Act requires the Secretary of Transportation to compile information about damage suceptibility, repair costs, and insurance premiums for the various automobile makes and models and then to supply it to consumers in various ways.

10. *See* notes 132-34 *infra* and accompanying text.

11. Ch. 239, § 38, [1971] Wis. Laws 688 (codified at WIS. STAT. chs. 421-27 [1971]). The Act and its legislative history are discussed in considerable detail elsewhere in this issue. Crandall, *The Wisconsin Consumer Act: Wisconsin Consumer Credit Laws Before and After*, 1973 WIS. L. REV. 334. For further discussion see Eisenberg & Howard, *Warning From Wisconsin: New Regulatory Laws For Collection of Consumer Debts*, 77 COM. L.J. 246 (1972).

Credit Code[12] and the National Consumer Act.[13] Many of the Act's provisions substantively regulate contractual terms—that is, certain contractual arrangements in consumer credit transactions are prohibited, no matter how conspicuously the seller informs the prospective buyer of the arrangement.[14] In a number of important instances, however, the Wisconsin Consumer Act relies, sometimes rather innovatively, on required disclosure as a technique for regulating consumer credit transactions. Examples of the Act's disclosure requirements will be given later in this article.

The proposed federal legislation would have regulated warranties accompanying the sale of consumer products affecting interstate commerce.[15] The bill was nearly enacted in the past Congress[16] and similar legislation stands a good chance of passage in the present Congress. Compulsory disclosure was the principal regulatory technique proposed in the bill.[17] The bill would have

12. The Uniform Consumer Credit Code was first promulgated by the National Conference of Commissioners on Uniform State Laws in 1968. By the end of 1972, it had been enacted in six states. 1 CCH CONSUMER CREDIT GUIDE ¶ 4770 (1973). It has been introduced in most other states but has failed to be enacted. *Id.* at ¶ 4771. Although the National Conference has not officially withdrawn the Act, it is known that a committee of the Conference is preparing substantial revisions to the original Act. A revised version of the Act may be promulgated within a year or two.

13. NATIONAL CONSUMER ACT (First Final Draft). This proposed statute was drafted by the National Consumer Law Center, then associated with Boston College Law School. Yet to be enacted in any state, it was drafted primarily as an alternative to the Uniform Consumer Credit Code, which many consumer spokesmen have criticized as too protective of merchant and lender interests. *See, e.g.*, CONSUMER RESEARCH FOUNDATION, CONSUMER VIEWPOINTS: A CRITIQUE OF THE UNIFORM CONSUMER CREDIT CODE (R. Elbrecht ed. 1969).

14. For example, in many consumer credit transactions the seller or lender may take an enforceable security interest only in certain property —primarily the property the purchase of which is being financed. WIS. STAT. § 422.417 (1971).

15. S. 986, 96th Cong., 1st Sess. (1971). As enacted by the Senate, sales under $5 were excluded from the bill's most important provisions. *Id.* § 101(2). The bill also contained unrelated provisions expanding the Federal Trade Commission's powers.

16. The bill passed the Senate on November 8, 1971. It was never reported by the House Interstate and Foreign Commerce Committee. *See* 30 CONG. Q. WEEKLY REP. 2711 (Oct. 21, 1972). Most of the opposition to the bill stemmed from its provisions concerning the Federal Trade Commission's powers and not from the provisions pertaining directly to product warranties. *See, e.g.*, S. REP. No. 92-269, 92d Cong., 1st Sess. 56-63 (1971) (separate views of Mr. Cook).

17. This bill is an excellent example of the continued vitality of disclosure regulation. Bills regulating product warranties have been regularly introduced in the past several Congresses. The earlier bills relied quite substantially on direct substantive regulation of terms. S. 2726, 90th Cong., 1st Sess. (1967); S. 2727, 90th Cong., 1st Sess. (1967). For a discussion of these bills see Whitford, *Law and the Consumer Transaction: A Case Study of the Automobile Warranty*, 1968 WIS. L. REV. 1006,

established substantive standards for a comprehensive warranty, or in the bill's terms a "full warranty."[18] Only warranties complying with these federal standards could have been described to consumers as "full warranties."[19] Other warranties would have had to be "designated in such manner so as to indicate clearly and conspicuously the limited scope of the coverage afforded."[20] Further examples of the bill's use of disclosure as a regulatory technique will be given throughout this article.

The continued reliance on disclosure as an important technique for regulating consumer transactions is contrary to the advice of many commentators, who have argued that although not positively harmful, such regulation is typically almost useless.[21] The concern of these critics has not been principally with the difficulty in obtaining seller compliance with disclosure regulation, but rather with the alleged lack of effect either on consumer behavior or on the substance of transactions. They correctly point out that the proponents of disclosure regulation typically presume that conspicuous and comprehensible disclosure will cause many consumers to change their buying behavior so as either to refrain from buying particular products or services that they otherwise would have bought, or to shop more carefully among competing products or services. Once this effect takes hold, many proponents of disclosure regulation seem to presume, sellers will be forced to compete with regard to the disclosed aspects of the transactions they offer, with the result that all or nearly all consumer transactions will become "fairer," or more "proconsumer."[22] Critics argue this scenario

1072-75 (1968). By the 91st Congress, however, those provisions had been mostly deleted and reliance placed almost entirely on disclosure regulation. S. 3074, 91st Cong., 1st Sess. (1969). That bill, which was essentially identical to the bill introduced in the 92d Congress, also passed the Senate, only to die in the House without coming to a floor vote.

18. To qualify for a "full warranty," the seller or manufacturer must undertake *inter alia*: "(1) to repair or replace any malfunctioning or defective . . . consumer product; (2) within a reasonable time; and (3) without charge." S. 986, 92d Cong., 1st Sess. § 104(a)(1)-(3) (1971).

19. *Id.* § 104.

20. *Id.* § 103(2). *Id.* § 109 would have authorized the Federal Trade Commission to establish rules for the standardized designation of limited warranties.

In addition to providing for this technique of standardizing warranty designations, the bill would have required each written warranty itself to contain a "simple and readily understandable" explanation of the various terms of the warranty. *Id.* § 102.

21. Jordan & Warren, *Disclosure of Finance Charges: A Rationale*, 64 MICH. L. REV. 1285, 1320-22 (1966); Kripke, *Gesture and Reality in Consumer Credit Reform*, 44 N.Y.U.L. REV. 1, 1-11 (1969); Note, *Consumer Legislation and the Poor*, 76 YALE L.J. 745 (1967); *cf.* Travers, *Forward*, 17 KAN. L. REV. 551 (1969); Leff, *Unconscionability and the Crowd—Consumers and the Common Law Tradition*, 31 U. PITT. L. REV. 349 (1970).

22. It is, of course, impossible to prove that the legislative purpose of all disclosure regulation is consistent with the statements in the text. See text preceding note 24 *infra*. I believe the statements to be correct never-

rarely if ever takes place because the disclosed information either is not learned by consumers, or if it is, it is not used by them in reaching purchase decisions. The critics uniformly contend that this description of the effects of disclosure applies particularly to the response of low income consumers to disclosure regulation. But many critics also argue or assume that middle and upper class consumers react in a substantially similar way.[23]

In one sense this article is an attempted evaluation of the criticism of disclosure regulation made by the aforementioned commentators. More specifically, I will identify possible purposes of disclosure regulation, including the goal of inducing consumers to become more careful shoppers. Using both theory and existing data on impact, I will evaluate to what extent disclosure does or may be able to achieve these purposes at acceptable costs. And I will discuss ways in which disclosure regulation might be formulated so as to fulfill its potentially achievable purposes better than it generally has in the past.

It is necessary to make two preliminary points about the purposes of disclosure regulation. The commentators who criticize disclosure regulation as essentially useless assume that such regulation is intended to have impact on consumer behavior. Disclosure regulation might be justified even if it were primarily intended only to induce sellers to actually disclose the required information. Perhaps we would have a more just society if relations between consumer and merchant appeared more honest, even if there is no change in consumer behavior or the content of transactions. However, because my principle concern in this article is whether disclosure regulation can be a regulatory tool for adjusting the balance of power or advantage between merchant and consumer, I will share the assumption of the commentators that disclosure regulation is intended to have impact on consumer behavior.

Even given this assumption, it is useful to distinguish between two different types of impacts on consumer behavior that disclosure regulation might be intended to have. I have indicated that commentators usually assume that an important purpose in requiring disclosure is to affect the purchasing decisions of consumers. Much disclosure regulation does in fact purport to have this purpose. Where it does, since such regulation must necessarily require disclosure before the transaction is concluded, it will be called precon-

theless. That they are correct for truth-in-lending is quite evident. *See* Truth in Lending Act § 102, 15 U.S.C. § 1601 (1970); Note, *Truth in Lending: The Impossible Dream*, 22 W. RES. L. REV. 89 (1970). The proposed federal warranties legislation indicated that disclosure was to be required "[i]n order to . . . improve competition in the marketing of consumer products . . . ." S. 986, 92d Cong., 1st Sess. § 102(a) (1971).

23. *E.g.*, Note, *Consumer Legislation and the Poor, supra* note 21, at 767. In an earlier article, I also advanced this argument with regard to some types of disclosure regulation. Whitford, *supra* note 17, at 1097.

tract disclosure regulation. Disclosure regulation can be designed to affect a very different kind of consumer behavior—the many ways in which the consumer adjusts to a transaction after it is concluded. For example, product warranties are usually conditioned on the prompt return of a malfunctioning product to the seller and frequently on maintaining the product in a reasonable or specified manner. Providing a consumer with information about these requirements can assist him in planning his postcontract activities so as to protect these rights.[24] Where disclosure regulation is intended to affect behavior occurring subsequent to the conclusion of the contract, it will be called postcontract disclosure regulation.[25]

The distinction between precontract and postcontract disclosure regulation is crucial to much of the analysis in this article, particularly to determining how the manner and timing of required disclosure might be formulated so as to better fulfill the purpose of these different types of disclosure regulation. Subsequent discussion will therefore be organized on the basis of this conceptual distinction.

## I. PRECONTRACT DISCLOSURE REGULATION

### A. *Empirical Evaluation—Impact of Truth in Lending*

Before discussing the potential purposes of precontract disclosure regulation, it is useful first to summarize the information available about the impact of truth-in-lending, the outstanding recent example of precontract disclosure regulation. There are several reasons why truth-in-lending provides a good subject for studying the potential impact of precontract disclosure regulation on consumer buying behavior. First, the proponents of truth-in-lending clearly stated that they intended the legislation to affect credit purchasing decisions.[26] The two most important figures that must be disclosed

24. Of course, such information might also affect some consumers' purchasing decisions and regulation requiring disclosure of this information could be intended to affect both purchasing decisions and decisions pertaining to postcontract activities. I would consider legislation having this dual purpose to be both precontract and postcontract disclosure regulation.

25. I have borrowed this term, as well as "precontract disclosure regulation" from Curran, *Legislative Controls As a Response to Consumer Credit Problems*, 8 B.C. IND. & COM. L. REV. 409 (1967).

26. It has been suggested that perhaps truth-in-lending is intended only to have primary effects—that is, to induce compliance—without any intent to affect consumer behavior at all. *See* R. Pullen, The Impact of Truth in Lending Legislation: The Massachusetts Experience 5-6 (Research Rep. No. 43 to Federal Reserve Bank of Boston, Oct. 1968). The congressional declaration of purpose quite clearly negates this suggestion, however. Truth in Lending Act § 102, 15 U.S.C. § 1601 (1970). So do the many statements of Senator Paul Douglas, the principal proponent of truth-in-lending during the long battle to secure its enactment. *E.g., Hearings on S, 750 Before a Subcomm. of the Senate Comm. on Banking and Currency*, 88th Cong., 1st Sess., pt. 1, at 2 (1963) (statement of Sen. Douglas).

as a result of truth-in-lending are the "finance charge" and the "annual percentage rate."[27] The finance charge is supposed to enable consumers to consider more intelligently the economic advantage of paying cash rather than borrowing to make a purchase. Requiring disclosure of the annual percentage rate means that all sellers must disclose an interest rate calculated according to the same arithmetic formula, thereby enabling consumers to compare more easily the interest rates offered by different lending institutions. Second, the formula for determining the annual percentage rate yields a figure that is considerably higher both than was indicated by the formulas previously used by most lenders in stating interest rates and than was commonly assumed by consumers to be the level of interest rates before truth-in-lending.[28] Truth-in-lending, therefore, provides consumers with price information that previously was unknown to most of them. Since consumers are generally assumed to be more sensitive in their shopping behavior to price terms than to most other terms, it appears this legislation should affect consumer purchasing behavior if precontract disclosure regulation can ever have such impact. Third, a number of empirical studies—more than concern any other recent example of disclosure regulation—have attempted to assess the impact on consumers of the disclosures required by truth-in-lending.[29] Finally, there is reliable evidence that the vast majority of lenders had substantially complied with truth-in-lending disclosure requirements within several months after the legislation first became effective on July 1, 1969.[30] Thus any failure of truth-in-lending to affect

27. These terms are defined in Truth in Lending Act §§ 106-07, 15 U.S.C. §§ 1605-06 (1970). When disclosure is required, these terms must be printed more conspicuously than surrounding terminology. Federal Reserve Bd. (FRB) Reg. Z, 12 C.F.R. § 226.6 (1972). For other information that must be disclosed in consumer credit transactions see Truth in Lending Act §§ 127-29, 15 U.S.C. §§ 1637-39 (1970).

28. G. KATONA ET AL., 1969 SURVEY OF CONSUMER FINANCES 18-20 (1970) [hereinafter cited as KATONA]; W. MORS, CONSUMER CREDIT FINANCE CHARGES: RATE INFORMATION AND QUOTATION (1965). The congressional hearings on truth-in-lending that extended over the 10 years preceding its enactment also contain voluminous support for these statements. *See, e.g., Hearings on S. 2755 Before a Subcomm. of the Senate Comm. on Banking and Currency*, 86th Cong., 2d Sess. 583 (1960) (statement of Richard L.D. Morse); *Hearings on S. 750 Before a Subcomm. of the Senate Comm. on Banking and Currency*, 88th Cong., 1st Sess., pt. 1, at 1485 (1963).

29. The report of the National Commission on Consumer Finance did not become available until after I completed this article. NAT'L COMM'N ON CONSUMER FIN., CONSUMER CREDIT IN THE UNITED STATES, in CCH INSTAL. CREDIT GUIDE, Issue No. 215, Jan. 15, 1973 [hereinafter cited as COMMISSION REPORT]. Chapter 10 of the report, *id.* at 169-91, contains an evaluation of the impact of truth-in-lending. Publishing deadlines have prevented me from discussing that evaluation in the text. The Commission's evaluation is based, however, on the same studies that I discuss subsequently in the text. Wherever the Commission's assessment of these studies differs significantly from mine, I have tried so to indicate in the footnotes.

30. The most important evidence of substantial lender compliance with truth-in-lending are two Federal Trade Commission surveys measur-

consumer buying behavior cannot readily be explained on the ground that disclosure is simply not being made.

For truth-in-lending to have direct impact on individual consumer purchase decisions, the required disclosures must first cause more consumers to be aware of the annual percentage rates and/or finance charges proposed. This awareness must then cause these consumers either to shop comparatively for lower annual percentage rates and/or finance charges when purchasing credit, or to weigh more carefully the alternative of paying cash rather than buying on credit.

### 1. INTEREST RATE AWARENESS

There have been several efforts to determine the impact of truth-in-lending on consumer knowledge of interest rates, but very few

---

ing compliance by a sample of retail merchants operating in urban areas. Federal Trade Comm'n, Report on Surveys of Creditor Compliance With the Truth in Lending Act (April 1971) [hereinafter cited as Compliance Survey]. The surveys essentially measured compliance as of March and April 1970, approximately 9 months after truth-in-lending became effective. In all categories of merchants surveyed, over 80% were in full or substantial compliance with truth-in-lending. Moreover, because merchants with high sales volume were the most likely to be in compliance, an even higher percentage of credit transactions were accompanied by full or substantial disclosure of the information required by truth-in-lending. The survey considered a merchant to be in substantial compliance if he disclosed the most important information required by truth-in-lending: the annual percentage rate and the total finance charge. The methodology of the surveys permitted only compliance with disclosure terminology to be measured reliably, so use of these terms with some reasonable figure, whether or not accurate, was considered substantial compliance.

There are sufficient methodological problems with the compliance surveys to prevent interpretation of their results as a precise measure of the level of compliance. For example, the surveys measured compliance only among retail merchants. Federal Trade Commission officials have stated in private interviews with me, however, that they believe compliance is even more substantial among other types of lending institutions subject to Commission enforcement of truth-in-lending, such as loan companies. The survey also measured compliance only by merchants in urban areas. Little information is available on the level of compliance in rural areas and small towns. And there is no concrete information available on compliance by lending institutions not subject to Commission enforcement. *See* Truth in Lending Act § 108, 15 U.S.C. § 1607 (1970).

One can argue whether the compliance surveys should produce concern about the extent of noncompliance with truth-in-lending or satisfaction with the remarkable degree of compliance achieved in a very short time. It seems clear, however, that in a very short period of time a sufficiently high level of compliance was achieved to permit observation of possible behavior modification by consumers. Moreover, although no survey of compliance has been made since 1970, responsible officials uniformly believe that since then the level of compliance has, if anything, increased. *See* Board of Governors of the Federal Reserve System, Annual Report to Congress for the Year 1971, at 1 (1972) [hereinafter cited as 1971 Annual Report].

to determine the effect of the legislation on finance charge awareness.[31] The best known of the efforts to determine the degree of annual prcentage rate awareness are two surveys commissioned by the Federal Reserve Board, one conducted just before the Truth in Lending Act became effective, and the other 15 months after its

31. It is sensible, of course, to concentrate on determining awareness of annual percentage rates, since it is this information that best facilitates comparative shopping. Finance charges can feasibly be compared only if the amount financed (price less downpayment) and period of repayment are the same. On the other hand, information about the finance charge can importantly aid the decision whether to pay cash or credit, since it provides the consumer with easily understood information about the cost of credit. *See* Jordan & Warren, *supra* note 21.

In one survey, conducted 15 months after the effective date of truth-in-lending, respondents were asked to estimate the finance charge on a hypothetical purchase of a consumer durable. The purpose was to determine knowledge of prevailing charges. The results indicated a consistent tendency to overestimate finance charges. Because no similar survey was taken before truth-in-lending, it cannot be determined certainly to what extent truth-in-lending contributed to this tendency. However, a striking number of respondents who accurately estimated the annual percentage rate for the hypothetical credit purchase predicted a finance charge of roughly twice that indicated by their annual percentage rate estimate. The obvious inference is that many respondents were estimating the finance charge by simply multiplying the amount financed by the annual percentage rate. This would be an appropriate calculation if interest rates were quoted on an "add-on" basis, as they commonly were before truth-in-lending, but the calculation yields a finance charge roughly twice the proper amount if the annual percentage rate is used and the loan is repaid in periodic installments. G. Day & W. Brandt, A Study of Consumer Credit Decisions: Implications for Present and Prospective Legislation, pt. IV, at 21-27 (Stanford University 1972). [This monograph is expected to be published soon as a supplementary study accompanying the final report of the National Commission on Consumer Finance. Citations in this article are to a prepublication manuscript]. Many of the findings of the study are discussed in COMMISSION REPORT, *supra* note 29, at 175-83. *See* T. Deutscher, Credit Legislation Two Years Out: Awareness Changes and Behavioral Effects of Differential Awareness Levels, pt. III, at 14-18. [This monograph is expected to be published soon as a supplementary study accompanying the final report of the National Commission on Consumer Finance. Citations in this article are to a prepublication manuscript.] Some of the findings of this study are discussed in COMMISSION REPORT, *supra* note 29, at 180.

The conclusion suggested by this survey is that, at least in the short run, truth-in-lending causes many consumers to overestimate finance charges. It should be noted, however, that the survey was based on a hypothetical purchase. In real life, consumers would receive disclosures of both the annual percentage rate and the finance charge, and this disclosure, if seen and understood before a purchase is concluded, may prevent some consumers from making an overestimate of finance charges. Indeed, in the same survey, respondents were asked to estimate the finance charge on past purchases and apparently they could do so with about the same frequency as they could recall accurately the annual percentage rate. The validity of this data is doubtful, however, since the report on the survey indicated that most respondents would estimate finance charges only after the interviewer probed or asked them to consult their records. G. Day & W. Brandt, *supra*, pt. IV, at 29-32.

effective date.[32] In each survey the respondents were asked if they had entered into certain types of credit transactions within a specified time period preceding the interview, and, if so, what annual percentage rate they had agreed to pay.[33] Both surveys consisted primarily of two independent probability samples, one taken from poverty areas in metropolitan centers and the other from the universe of telephone subscribers outside defined poverty areas.[34]

The Federal Reserve Board's analysis of the results of these surveys compared the number of respondents to each survey who indicated they did not know what annual percentage rate they were paying. That comparison indicated that the percentage of "don't know" responses declined in the second survey for each transaction type.[35] This trend occurred for nearly all income and education levels, although there was a sharper reduction in "don't know" responses at higher income levels than at lower ones.[36] In both

32. For a description of the surveys see Board of Governors of the Federal Reserve System, Annual Report to Congress on Truth in Lending for the Year 1969, appendix B (1970) [hereinafter cited as 1969 Annual Report]; Board of Governors of the Federal Reserve System, Annual port to Congress on Truth in Lending for the Year 1970, appendix B (1971) [hereinafter the 1970 Annual Report]. The surveys are also described in Shay & Schober, Consumer Awareness of Annual Percentage Rates of Charge in Consumer Installment Credit: Before and After Truth in Lending Became Effective, at 10-19 (1971). [This monograph will be published soon as a supplementary study accompanying the final report of the National Commission on Consumer Finance. Citations in this article are to a prepublication manuscript.] Some of the findings of this study are discussed in COMMISSION REPORT, *supra* note 29, at 175-83.

33. In both surveys respondents holding open end retail charge accounts or bank credit cards were asked what interest would be charged if they did not pay within the "free ride" period, whether or not such an interest charge had in fact been imposed in any preceding period. Under truth-in-lending, disclosure in open end transactions is required at the time the overriding credit agreement is first consummated. Truth in Lending Act § 127(a), 15 U.S.C. § 1637(a) (1970).

34. *See* authorities cited note 32 *supra*. In the second survey there was in addition a third sample of 5,000 household heads from both poverty and nonpoverty areas. This sample was used solely to obtain more respondents who had entered home mortgage and home improvement credit transactions. Shay & Schober, *supra* note 32, at 15.

35. The following table was constructed from data presented in 1970 Annual Report, *supra* note 32, at appendix B.

PERCENTAGE OF "DON'T KNOW" RESPONSES

| TYPE OF TRANSACTION | BEFORE TRUTH IN LENDING (1969 SURVEY) | FIFTEEN MONTHS LATER (1970 SURVEY) |
|---|---|---|
| First Mortgage Loans | 26.7 | 12.7 |
| Home Improvement Loans | 35.0 | 27.3 |
| New Automobile Loans | 26.6 | 21.4 |
| Used Automobile Loans | 40.4 | 33.8 |
| Appliance and Furniture Loans | 57.7 | 41.6 |
| Personal Loans | 42.6 | 27.8 |
| Open End Retail Charge Accounts | 48.1 | 32.2 |

36. The following table was constructed from data presented in the 1970 Annual Report, *supra* note 32, at appendix B. First mortgage and

surveys the percentage of "don't know" responses was inversely related to both income and educational level.[37] The Federal Reserve Board analysis of the surveys also noted that in both surveys many respondents stated unrealistically low annual percentage rates. Since no effort was made to determine what rates the respondents were in fact paying, it was not possible to determine how many respondents accurately reported their rates. In the second survey there was a general increase in the size of rates reported, however, and the Federal Reserve Board considered this increase further evidence that truth-in-lending had induced a greater awareness of annual percentage rates by credit buyers.[38]

A study commissioned by the National Commission on Consumer Finance has analyzed the Federal Reserve Board data in a different way in an effort to take better account of the very low rates frequently reported by respondents to the surveys.[39] The study estimated a range within which annual percentage rates in each transaction type would most likely fall.[40] On the basis of these estimates, the study classified most of the responses to each survey as clearly indicating "unawareness," either because the re-

---

home improvement loans are excluded because the data is not available in the same income groupings, respondents in higher income groupings appeared to have higher awareness levels for these transaction types as well.

PERCENTAGE OF REDUCTION IN "DON'T KNOW" RESPONSES FROM 1969 TO 1970 FRB SURVEY

| TYPE OF TRANSACTION | HOUSEHOLD INCOME | | | |
|---|---|---|---|---|
| | LESS THAN $5,000 | $5,000-$8,000 | $8,000-$10,000 | MORE THAN $10,000 |
| New Automobile Loans | -3.4* | 24.5 | 21 | 15.5 |
| Used Automobile Loans | 10.2 | 5.8 | -1.5* | 32.5 |
| Appliance and Furniture Loans | 12.6 | 12 | 17.1 | 54 |
| Personal Loans | 22 | 15.9 | 21 | 46.6 |
| Retail Charge Accounts | 11.6 | 24 | 32 | 34.3 |

* There was actually an increase in "don't know" responses in these categories

The table suggests a very clear association between income and rate of reduction in "don't know" responses, at least at the highest and lowest income levels. The number of responses in some categories is quite small and may account for aberrations in the overall trend that can be observed in the middle-income categories.

37. This conclusion is evident from the tables presented in 1970 Annual Report, *supra* note 32, at appendix B.

38. *Id.* at 8-13.

39. Shay & Schober, *supra* note 32.

40. For a description of how these estimates were made see *id.* at 22-25. Estimates were based on data collected in the Federal Trade Commission's survey of creditor compliance with truth-in-lending. *See* note 31 *supra*. First mortgage transactions were excluded from the analysis made in this study. In making the estimates the authors were generous in their setting of ranges of awareness. Thus, purchasers of new automobiles were considered aware if they indicated they were paying 8% interest or above; purchasers of furniture and appliances were considered aware if they responded 12% or above.

spondent indicated he did not know what annual percentage rate he paid or because he gave a percentage that was improbably low. The remaining responses were classified as indicating awareness, although all that truly could be said about these responses is that probably they approximate the annual percentage rate paid.

Analyzed in this manner, the level of rate awareness for installment credit transactions rose from 14.5 percent in the first survey to 38.3 percent in the second survey.[41] The results for retail revolving credit indicated a similar degree of improvement in awareness, although the general level of awareness was much higher in each survey (35.2 percent and 55.5 percent).[42] Consistent with the findings of the Federal Reserve Board, both the absolute level of annual percentage rate awareness and the degree of improvement correlated directly with education and income.[43] The most dramatic differences of this nature occurred when respondents involved in installment credit transactions were classified according to those who lived in poverty areas and elsewhere—a classification not appearing in the Federal Reserve Board's analysis. The level of awareness of respondents in poverty areas was only 9.7 percent and 16.1 percent in the two surveys.[44] Thus, both the level of awareness and the rate of increase in awareness was substantially lower for residents of poverty areas than for those living elsewhere.[45]

---

41. Shay & Schober, *supra* note 32, at 28. Installment credit transactions are ones in which the debtor agrees to pay a predetermined number of payments of a predetermined amount in order to discharge the debt.

42. *Id.* The increase in awareness for holders of bank credit cards—like retail revolving credit, an open end credit plan—was even more substantial: 26.6% to 63.4%. *Id.*

43. *Id.* at 33-36. The percentage decrease in unawareness from the 1969 to the 1970 survey for all closed end (installment) transactions combined was as follows:

PERCENTAGE DECREASE IN UNAWARENESS

| HOUSEHOLD INCOME | PERCENTAGE DECREASE |
|---|---|
| Less than $5,000 | 18.6 |
| $5,000-$8,000 | 17.1 |
| $8,000-$10,000 | 24.9 |
| More than $10,000 | 37.2 |

*Id.* at 35. *Compare* the above table *with* table, *supra* note 36.

44. Shay & Schober, *supra* note 32, at 38. The rate of increase for poverty areas was also less, as awareness increased in nonpoverty areas from 14.7% to 41.3%. *Id.* However, if account is taken of a number of other variables which appear to explain much of the differential in level of interest rate awareness, residence in a poverty area or elsewhere disappears as an important explanation for the differential in awareness among subgroups in the population. These other variables are income, education, race, and knowledge of the existence of the truth-in-lending law. *Id.* at 59-76.

The data for poverty areas is based on the special survey of urban poverty centers. *See id.* at 36-37; text accompanying note 34 *supra.*

45. The awareness data for installment credit transactions was also classified by transaction type. Except for used car transactions, where the rate of increase was low, there was not substantial variance in the

Although there have been several other attempts to measure the level of annual percentage rate awareness,[46] I am aware of only one other study which compared levels of awareness both before and after the effective date of truth-in-lending. This study, conducted at the University of Michigan, also cured one of the major difficulties with the Federal Reserve Board surveys by determining awareness through a comparison of the actual rate paid by the respondent with the rate reported in the interview.[47] The results showed that, although the percentage of respondents who reported their rates with complete accuracy remained very low, reported rates tended to be closer to actual rates after truth-in-lending than before the law.[48]

A possible interpretation of the Michigan results is that truth-in-lending has been effective in improving consumer awareness of the general level of prevailing annual percentage rates, but that the legislation has done little to improve consumers' knowledge of the specific rates they are paying. This interpretation would be consistent with the findings of the Federal Reserve Board surveys. Even the analysis made by the National Commission on Consumer Finance classified a respondent as "aware" whenever the reported rate was in the general range of probable rates, and consequently all that can certainly be concluded from their analysis is that there has been improvement in consumer knowledge of prevailing rates. So interpreted, the degree of improvement in awareness of prevailing annual percentage rates indicated by the Michigan surveys was generally less than that suggested by the Federal Reserve Board surveys.[49] This result is somewhat remarkable because the Michigan surveys interviewed only persons who borrowed at least $500 to finance purchase of an automobile.[50] Because of the size of the transaction and the open competition between banks and fi-

rate of increase in awareness for different transaction types. Shay and Schober, *supra* note 32, at 31-32.

46. *See* G. Day & W. Brandt, *supra* note 31, at pt. IV; Comment, *The Impact of Truth in Lending on Automobile Financing—An Empirical Study*, 4 U. CAL. DAVIS L. REV. 179 (1971).

47. Mandell, *Consumer Perception of Incurred Interest Rates: An Empirical Test of the Efficacy of the Truth-in-Lending Law*, 26 J. FINANCE 1143 (1971). The actual rate paid by the respondent was calculated from information provided by the respondent about number and amount of payments, amount loaned, and so forth. Some effort was made to insure against response error in obtaining this data. *Id.* at 1145-46. The data was obtained from the annual surveys of consumer finances conducted by the Institute for Social Research at the University of Michigan. *See, e.g.*, KATONA, *supra* note 28. It is not indicated when the surveys were made, but the report of the study seems to be written on the assumption that the purchases about which the data pertains were made continuously over periods of several months before and after the effective date of truth-in-lending.

48. Mandell, *supra* note 47, at 1147-48.

49. *Id.*

50. *Id.* at 1145.

nance companies for automobile installment credit business, it was commonly assumed even before truth-in-lending that automobile purchasers were more likely to engage in comparative shopping for credit than were other credit purchasers of goods and services.[51] A second interesting finding of the Michigan surveys was that neither before nor after truth-in-lending did the level of rate awareness depend on income. The size of the amount borrowed proved to be a much more important predictor of awareness.[52] The number of respondents in low income levels was so small in the Michigan surveys, however, that it is doubtful any conclusions about the relationship between low income and rate awareness should be drawn.[53]

There are a number of reasons why the results of these surveys are not fully reliable measures of the effect of truth-in-lending on consumer awareness of annual percentage rates at the time they enter into credit transactions. In addition to the methodological problems already mentioned,[54] none of the surveys test whether the source of heightened rate awareness was solely due to truth-in-lending. It is quite possible, for example, that as a result of the increased visibility of consumer issues in newspapers and legislatures some or all of the increase in annual percentage rate awareness would have occurred even if truth-in-lending regulation had not existed. Most importantly, however, the surveys did not measure rate awareness at the time the transaction was concluded—the important time if truth-in-lending is to have direct impact on buying behavior. Rather, the surveys measured recall of the annual percentage rate that the respondents agreed to pay some time prior to the interview. It is impossible to know whether measuring recall rather than knowledge at the time the transaction was concluded yielded a higher or lower estimate of rate awareness.[55] It is

51. *See, e.g.*, Kripke, *Consumer Credit Regulation: A Creditor-Oriented Viewpoint*, 68 COLUM. L. REV. 445 (1968).

52. Mandell, *supra* note 47, at 1148-53.

53. In the below $5,000 income bracket, there were 18 respondents who had concluded contracts before truth-in-lending and 14 who had done so after the Act. *Id.* at 1149.

54. None of the surveys discussed in the text attempted to measure the effect of truth-in-lending on the rate awareness of persons who had not made credit purchases since the Act. It is possible that truth-in-lending had its most substantial impact by impressing many consumers with the high cost of consumer credit and accordingly inducing a greater percentage of cash purchases. *See* note 58 *infra* and accompanying text. If this effect occurred, one would expect to find the greatest increase in interest rate awareness among a group of consumers who did not make credit purchases. Other studies have shown, however, that even after truth-in-lending the level of rate awareness has not been a significant determinant of the decision to use credit rather than to pay cash. *See* note 76 *infra* and accompanying text.

55. On the one hand, it is probable that many consumers who were unaware of the annual percentage rate at the time they entered into the transaction later became aware while paying a bill or looking over papers

possible that during the time between the two surveys the size of the difference, if any, between the number of consumers who could recall rates accurately and the number who had accurate knowledge when the transaction was concluded remained unchanged. On this assumption, measuring the increase in recall would be an appropriate surrogate for measuring increase in knowledge at the time a transaction was concluded. However, comparability of the two surveys is compromised by the fact that the period of recall was not the same. In the first survey, for most transaction types, inquiry about annual percentage rate awareness was made only if the respondent had concluded a transaction within the previous year. For home improvement and home mortgage credit transactions inquiry was made if the respondent had entered into a transaction within 3 and 5 years of the survey respectively. In the second survey the same questions were asked in all cases as to credit transactions consummated since the effective date of truth-in-lending—that is, over a period of about 15 months preceding the interview.[56]

Despite the difficulties in interpreting their significance, the surveys pretty clearly suggest that in the first year or so of truth-in-lending there was only modest improvement in consumer awareness of prevailing annual percentage rates. It is more difficult to measure improvement in consumer knowledge of specific annual percentage rates at the time a transaction is concluded, but the available evidence implies that any improvement has also been at best modest. Moreover, any improvement in awareness has been concentrated in upper income groups.

A question that remains is whether further improvement in rate awareness has occurred or can be expected. Since lender compliance with the disclosure requirements was already quite substantial, only a small increase in awareness can be expected due to increased compliance.[57] Furthermore, it was in the first year that truth-in-lending could be expected to have had its greatest "shock"

connected with the transaction. On the other hand, it is also reasonable to assume that some persons who were aware of the rate at the time they entered a credit transaction forgot it by the time they responded to the surveys.

56. Shay & Schober, *supra* note 32, at 14, 18.

57. *See* note 30 *supra*. It is interesting to note that the compliance survey found compliance by used car dealers to be "very poor." Compliance Survey, *supra* note 30, at 13. The Federal Reserve Board surveys also indicated that the rate of increase in awareness for used car buyers was less than for other transaction types. *See* note 45 *supra*. Perhaps, therefore, increased compliance can yield substantial increases in awareness by used car buyers. On the other hand, the compliance survey found compliance by new car dealers to be "almost flawless," Compliance Survey, *supra* note 30, at 13, yet the level of unawareness for new car buyers in the 1970 Federal Reserve Board survey was still 57%. Shay & Schober, *supra* note 32, at 32.

effect, since it was then that consumers were first provided information suggesting that interest rates were sharply higher than most consumers previously assumed.[58] For several reasons significant improvement in future consumer awareness is nevertheless possible, and perhaps should be expected.

First, at least until recently, one of the loopholes in truth-in-lending has been that the annual percentage rate needed to be disclosed only in the written contract. Many creditors quickly learned they could legally quote orally interest rates calculated according to some other formula—for example, discount or add-on—yielding a lower figure than does the annual percentage rate formula.[59] Probably, these oral quotations were often what consumers remembered when responding to the various surveys. The Federal Trade Commission has now indicated that it will consider it a violation of section 5 of the Federal Trade Commission Act[60] to quote orally interest rates calculated according to any formula other than one required by truth-in-lending.[61] It is also possible that legislation to similar effect will be introduced.[61a] If either of these avenues is successful in halting the oral quotation of interest rates not determined according to the annual percentage rate formula, further improvement in consumer awareness could result.

Second, it seems to be a common assumption that there will be continuing increases in rate awareness as more consumers experience several credit transactions in which truth-in-lending disclosures are made.[62] Consumers, of course, were experiencing credit transactions before the advent of truth-in-lending. The disclosures

58. Many creditors apparently feared that truth-in-lending would have this "shock" effect and in the short run induce a much lower level of credit buying. Indeed, one of the principal arguments against enactment of truth-in-lending was that such an effect would cause a reduction in the level of consumer durable purchases, thereby triggering a recession. *Hearings on S. 2755 Before a Subcomm. of the Senate Comm. on Banking and Currency*, 86th Cong., 1st Sess. 803, 809 (1960) (statement of George Katona). *See also* note 28 *supra* and accompanying text.

59. G. Day & W. Brandt, *supra* note 31, pt. IV, at 3; Comment, *The Impact of Truth in Lending on Automobile Financing—An Empirical Study*, *supra* note 46, at 199-202.

60. 15 U.S.C. § 45 (1970).

61. FTC Consumer Credit Policy Statement No. 5, Nov. 22, 1971, 4 CCH CONSUMER CREDIT GUIDE ¶ 30,750. I am aware of no Federal Trade Commission enforcement proceeding initiated to implement this policy statement. The policy statement is in sharp contrast to the Federal Reserve Board's interpretation of the current requirements of the Truth in Lending Act. FRB Letter No. 137, Oct. 10, 1969, 4 CCH CONSUMER CREDIT GUIDE ¶ 30,482; FRB Letter No. 407, Sept. 22, 1970, 4 CCH CONSUMER CREDIT GUIDE ¶ 30,590.

61a. The National Commission on Consumer Finance so recommends. COMMISSION REPORT, *supra* note 29, at 189.

62. *Id.* at 180; Comment, *The Impact of Truth in Lending on Automobile Financing—An Empirical Study*, *supra* note 46, at 193; Note, *Truth in Lending: The Impossible Dream*, *supra* note 22, at 107-08.

required by truth-in-lending are sufficiently complicated, however, that intuitively it seems possible that practice in reading the disclosures will enhance future understanding of them by at least some consumers.

The plausibility of assuming that for this reason rate awareness will increase over time has been significantly diminished by a recent study. It compared levels of awareness of the same group of consumers at two points in time, both substantially after the effective date of truth-in-lending.[63] The study found very little improvement in the ability of consumers to recall the annual percentage rates they paid on credit purchases concluded within comparable periods before the interview.[64] There was a significant increase in awareness of prevailing rates, as measured by responses to a question asking what rates the respondents would expect to pay in a hypothetical credit purchase.[65] There were also, however, a number of respondents who indicated awareness of prevailing rates at the time of the first interview but who had lost that awareness by the time of the second interview.[66] This "forgetting" factor suggests at some point an equilibrium awareness point will be reached—when the number of new "learners" are balanced by "forgetters"—and the study estimated that at equilibrium there would still be a very sizeable percentage of unaware consumers.[67] Perhaps even more importantly, the "learners" about prevailing rates between the first and second interviews were no more likely than nonlearners to have had an experience in credit buying since the first interview.[68] Demographic variables, particularly high in-

63. T. Deutscher, *supra* note 31. The first survey is the same one reported in G. Day & W. Brandt, *supra* note 31. Deutscher reinterviewed a portion of the Day and Brandt sample approximately 9 months later.

64. T. Deutscher, *supra* note 31, pt. III, at 2. Actually, in the second survey the period over which respondents were asked to recall purchases was only about 9 months, whereas for the first survey the recall period was about 12 months. *Id.* pt. III, at 4-5. If it is assumed that recall would tend to be more accurate the closer the interview was to the actual purchase, for this reason alone greater awareness should have been expected in the second survey. The fact that it was not found, therefore, substantially undercuts the hypothesis that experience will enhance understanding. It may suggest a contrary hypothesis that as disclosures under truth-in-lending come to be accepted as a normal part of credit transaction, and as truth-in-lending receives less publicity from the news media, there will be a reduction in rate awareness.

65. *Id.* pt. III, at 3, 7-8.

66. *Id.* pt. III, at 14-16.

67. *Id.* pt. III, at 20-26. Based on the data collected in the surveys, the study estimated the equilibrium point for awareness of prevailing rates (as measured by what annual percentage rate respondents would expect to pay in a hypothetical credit purchase) was 50%, a point the study estimated was reached in June 1971.

68. *Id.* pt. IV, at 4-12. G. Day & W. Brandt, *supra* note 31, who surveyed annual percentage rate awareness at a single point in time, found credit experience over a long term to be an important determinant both of ability to recall the rate paid on an actual transaction and of knowledge

come and education, were the only variables tested that were significantly associated with "learning."[69] Although this study cannot be considered conclusive due to a number of methodological considerations,[70] it strongly suggests that time and experience in credit buying will not themselves yield a significant increase in consumer awareness of annual percentage rates, particularly among those groups of consumers which presently are most substantially unaware.

Finally, rate awareness may increase over time because some factor other than disclosure, such as the increased visibility of consumer issues or drastically expanded consumer education programs, causes consumers to become more interested in the terms of their transactions. Alternatively, truth-in-lending might be amended to provide for new techniques of disseminating rate information and these new techniques may cause greater awareness.

### 2. COMPARATIVE INTEREST RATE SHOPPING

The ultimate goal of truth-in-lending is not simply to increase the level of annual percentage rate awareness, but rather to produce a greater degree of cost-effective comparative shopping for interest rates, and perhaps as well to affect decisions whether to enter credit transactions at all.[71] Yet there has been much less effort to determine empirically the impact of truth-in-lending on credit shopping behavior. The most substantial effort is a study conducted at Stanford based on a survey taken at about the same time as the second Federal Reserve Board survey.[72] The respondents to the survey were asked not only about their awareness of annual percentage rates but also to report on their shopping activity preceding a significant purchase of an automobile or major appliance made within a year of the interview. Probably the most important finding of the study was that, although a significant number of major purchases are made on credit, there is little credit shopping behavior of any kind. Most consumers apparently prefer to

---

of prevailing rates as measured by what rates would be anticipated in a hypothetical transaction. *Id.* pt. IV, at 15-17, 18-21. A possible conclusion suggested by these studies, therefore, is that credit experience enhances rate awareness but that experience with credit transactions in which there were truth-in-lending disclosures enhances awareness no more than credit experience in any other circumstance.

It should be noted that T. Deutscher, *supra* note 31, found that "forgetting" was negatively correlated with credit experience—that is, of the group of respondents who indicated awareness of prevailing rates in the first survey, those who had made a credit purchase between the interviews were less likely to have lost that awareness at the time of the second interview. *Id.* pt. IV, at 4-8, 12-14.

69. T. Deutscher, *supra* note 31, pt. IV, at 8-12.

70. Methodological problems with the study are discussed in *id.* pt. II.

71. *See* note 26 *supra*.

72. G. Day & W. Brandt, *supra* note 31.

spend whatever time they devote to comparison shopping to searching for the product rather than for credit.[73] The study was unable to determine conclusively whether truth-in-lending helped stimulate whatever credit shopping behavior was found or aided credit shoppers in reaching more intelligent and cost-effective credit decisions. Because of a low degree of correlation between awareness of prevailing rates and credit shopping behavior, however, the study suggested that truth-in-lending had an "at best modest" effect on stimulating credit shopping behavior.[74]

Among its other interesting findings, the Stanford study found that in the purchase of durables significant credit shopping among different types of credit sources, to the extent it exists at all, is apparently concentrated among upper and middle income groups. Lower income consumers appear much more likely to finance through the retailer and not even consider independent financing from a bank or other lending institution that generally offers lower rates.[75] The Stanford study was also able to conclude, with considerable certainty, that annual percentage rate awareness had almost no impact on the decision to use credit. Situational variables, such as availability of cash resources and need for the item purchased, almost completely accounted for variations in behavior with regard to paying cash.[76]

The Stanford study is partly corraborated by a study of the effect of state-enacted rate disclosure regulation that became effective in Massachusetts more than two years before federal truth-in-

73. *Id.* pt. III, at 31-35, pt. V, at 7-8.

74. *Id.* pt. V, at 18. Awareness of prevailing rates was measured by a question asking what rates respondents would expect to pay in a hypothetical credit purchase.

Deutscher was able to confirm this finding in his study, described in part at notes 63-70 *supra* and accompanying text. Respondents who had made a significant credit purchase between the first and second interviews were asked about the shopping behavior preceding the purchase. Respondents who demonstrated awareness of prevailing rates in the first interview tended to engage in somewhat greater credit shopping activity than those who exhibited unawareness, but the differences were not substantial. T. Deutscher, *supra* note 31, at pt. V.

75. G. Day & W. Brandt, *supra* note 31, pt. VI, at 15-17. This result is consistent with the findings of Juster and Shay. They tested the reactions of a group of consumers to a series of hypothetical credit purchase situations and concluded that the only ones who would use interest rate information in making credit purchasing decisions are those whose credit rating permitted them to borrow from low-rate lenders, such as banks. Consumers who can only borrow from more expensive lenders, they concluded, want and use information about the size of the downpayment and of the monthly payment. F. Juster & R. Shay, Consumer Sensitivity to Finance Rates: An Empirical and Analytical Investigation (Nat'l Bur. of Econ. Research, Occasional Paper No. 88 [1968]), *discussed* in W. Mors, *supra* note 28, at 46-52.

76. G. Day & W. Brandt, *supra* note 31, pt. V, at 18-22. Deutscher's study reconfirmed this conclusion. T. Deutscher, *supra* note 31, pt. V, at 18-21.

lending became effective. The study was based on over 60 interviews with businessmen, conducted 6 to 8 months after the effective date of the Massachusetts legislation. The very clear conclusion from the interviews was that, in the opinion of businessmen, the Massachusetts regulation had almost no immediate impact on the level of comparison credit shopping by consumers of any economic class.[77]

Neither the Stanford nor Massachusetts studies can conclusively prove that in the long run truth-in-lending will have only minor impact on credit shopping behavior. In addition to other difficulties,[78] both studies were made shortly after disclosure legislation became effective. Even though it seems likely consumers will remain largely ignorant of the particular rates they are charged, it is possible that rate disclosure will substantially increase consumer awareness of prevailing annual percentage rates. If it does, consumers may become more sensitive to aberrational rates, particularly high ones, and react accordingly in their credit buying, even though they do not undertake comparative shopping on a regular basis.

Nevertheless, it is the opinion of nearly all businessmen with whom I have discussed the matter that even though there has been effective compliance with truth-in-lending for over 3 years, there has been little effect on credit shopping behavior. And this conclusion is consistent with the implications of a number of earlier studies on consumers' sensitivity, in their shopping behavior, to interest rate information. These studies suggest that before truth-in-lending a large percentage of consumers of all income classes were aware in a general way of which lending insitutions offered the lowest interest rates. Some consumers were influenced by this knowledge in making credit buying decisions, particularly where a large amount was to be borrowed. But large numbers of consumers obtained credit at high rates even though they knew that they might be able to obtain a lower rate from another lending institution.[79] Given this general knowledge of interest rate

77. R. Pullen, *supra* note 26. The same conclusion about the effect of the Massachusetts legislation was reached by a separate survey, limited to large department stores offering revolving charge plans. Note, *A Survey of Experience Under the Massachusetts Retail Installment Sales Act*, 9 B.C. IND. & COMM. L. REV. 1020 (1968).

78. In the Stanford study the response rate was only 46%. Furthermore, only California consumers, who are known to be more active credit users than Americans generally, were interviewed. Although there is some reason to believe these factors did not distort the representativeness of the sample, that possibility cannot be completely discounted. *See* G. Day & W. Brandt, *supra* note 31, at pt. II.

79. *E.g.*, White & Munger, *Consumer Sensitivity to Interest Rates: An Empirical Study of New-Car Buyers and Auto Loans*, 69 MICH. L. REV. 1207 (1971); *Hearings on S. 750 Before a Subcomm. of the Senate Comm. on Banking and Currency*, 88th Cong., 2d Sess., pt. 1, at 1485, 1489 (1963)

differentials, it is difficult to see how the more specific rate information provided by truth-in-lending, even if learned, could affect credit shopping behavior.

There are obviously too few studies to permit any final conclusions to be drawn about the impact of truth-in-lending. Nevertheless, the evidence presently available suggests that any success truth-in-lending will have inducing credit shopping for lower interest rates will be modest and concentrated among higher income groups. In other words, our experience with truth-in-lending appears largely, although not completely, to be consistent with the criticisms of disclosure regulation discussed in the introduction. And, as indicated earlier, if truth-in-lending has only modest impact on consumer buying behavior, then one would expect most other disclosure regulation to have at best modest impact as well. What evidence exists about the impact of other disclosure regulation generally supports this expectation. Thus, a survey of new car buyers I conducted several years ago suggested that few buyers were aware or understood the disclaimer of implied warranties contained in all new automobile warranties,[80] yet these disclaimers uniformly contained bold print as required by section 2-316(2) of the Uniform Commercial Code.

### B. *Theoretical Evaluation*

#### 1. EXPLANATIONS FOR THE TRUTH-IN-LENDING EXPERIENCE

A variety of possible explanations have been offered for the limited impact of truth-in-lending on consumer buying behavior. Some of the explanations relate directly to the lack of impact on the lower economic classes. It has been suggested, for example, that many poor have few outlets for credit available to them. Even if these poor comparatively shopped for credit, in many instances the only choice that would be available to them would be either to obtain credit from whoever offered it or to do without the often necessary goods or services the credit would purchase. Un-

(statement of George Katona); *see* Kripke, *Consumer Credit Regulation: A Creditor-Oriented Viewpoint*, *supra* note 51, at 460-66.

Federal Trade Commission enforcement officials have indicated to me in interviews that they receive very few complaints from businessmen that a competitor is not in compliance. If credit shopping behavior were widespread, there would presumably be a competitive advantage in understating the annual percentage rate, and in other areas of Federal Trade Commission authority it is not uncommon for a businessman to complain of a competitor's unlawful practices. Moreover, the compliance survey does indicate that there is still some degree of noncompliance. *See* note 30 *supra*. Thus, the lack of complaints from businessmen may constitute independent evidence that truth-in-lending has little impact on credit shopping behavior.

80. Whitford, *Strict Products Liability and the Automobile Industry: Much Ado About Nothing*, 1968 WIS. L. REV. 83, 143-50.

less the latter is perceived as a realistic alternative, there is little incentive for these persons even to become aware of interest rates or total finance charges.[81]

81. *E.g.*, Kripke, *Gesture and Reality in Consumer Credit Reform*, 44 N.Y.U.L. REV. 1, 1-13 (1969); Note, *Consumer Legislation and the Poor*, 76 YALE L.J. 745, 745-54 (1967); *see* F. Juster & R. Shay, *supra* note 75.

Another explanation directed especially at truth-in-lending's lack of impact on the poor relies on the lack of mobility of many low-income persons. The poor apparently are much more likely than consumers generally to restrict their shopping to the immediate neighborhood, and consequently they may not consider credit sources elsewhere which potentially would be available to them. *See* D. CAPLOVITZ, THE POOR PAY MORE (2d ed. 1967); FEDERAL TRADE COMM'N, ECONOMIC REPORT ON FOOD CHAIN SELLING PRACTICES IN THE DISTRICT OF COLUMBIA AND SAN FRANCISCO (1969).

Still a further explanation offered for the lack of impact of truth-in-lending on the poor is based on the practice of many merchants of "burying" finance charges in the cash price. "Burying" finance charges occurs when the merchant represents that he has no or very low finance charges, yet his cash price is far above the relevant market price. Such a merchant, of course, makes nearly all his sales on credit and is essentially uninterested in competing for the cash customer. Consequently, merchants burying finance charges tend to be ones catering to low income consumers. Moreover, since available evidence indicates that on the whole consumers are more likely to shop for the product than for credit—*see* note 73 *supra* and accompanying text—such a merchant has probably decided to concentrate on consumers who do not shop at all and on that small group of low income consumers who do shop for low cost credit terms. In connection with this latter group it is interesting to recall the suggestion that truth-in-lending is causing those consumers who are acquiring awareness of prevailing annual percentage rates to overestimate finance charges. *See* note 31 *supra*. Thus, truth-in-lending may be having the unintended effect of making the burying of finance charges a more effective pricing policy competitively.

The Federal Reserve Board, which issues regulations under truth-in-lending, has made the Act applicable to any extension of credit "which, pursuant to an agreement, is or may be payable in more than four installments," thereby extending the Act to any creditor who buries his finance charges. FRB Reg. Z, 12 C.F.R. § 226.2(k) (1971). This more-than-four-installments regulation does not require such a creditor to disclose a finance charge or an annual percentage rate other than zero, but does subject him to other provisions of the Act, and in particular to its provisions concerning credit advertising. *See* Warren & Larmore, *Truth in Lending: Problems of Coverage*, 24 STAN. L. REV. 793, 816-21 (1972). The validity of the more-than-four-installments regulation was recently upheld. Mourning v. Family Publications Serv., Inc., 93 S. Ct. 1652 (1973).

Probably the only effective way under current law to eliminate the practice of burying credit charges is to consider the practice "unfair or deceptive" under section 5 of the Federal Trade Commission Act, 15 U.S.C. § 45(a)(1) (1970). In one case a few years ago, the FTC staff made just such a contention. The merchant involved did business in an urban ghetto and buried his credit charges in cash prices that were about 500% above his cost. Moreover, he had a very rigid credit enforcement policy, generally suing his credit customers as soon as their payments fell behind. Finally, he advertised his credit as being available on "easy" terms—apparently a reference to the lack of a finance charge as such. The Commission refused to hold that burying credit charges in the cash price was in itself deceptive, but it did clearly hold that it was misleading to ad-

Another suggested explanation for the limited impact of truth-in-lending, and one that is most interesting for purposes of evaluating disclosure regulation generally, is that most consumers are not motivated to shop comparatively for the lowest interest rate, at least with regard to all but their largest credit transactions.[82] A variety of possible reasons have been advanced for this lack of motivation. If the amount borrowed is not large, often the amount to be saved by obtaining the lowest available interest rate is not sufficient to justify the inconvenience and costs of comparative shopping.[83] Many consumers apparently prefer to use an established or other source of credit known to be available, perhaps in order to avoid the anxieties of asking for credit from an unfamiliar institution—for example, a bank, which frequently will offer the lowest available interest rate.[84] Even when some comparative shopping for credit occurs, consumers—particularly low income consumers—are apparently more concerned with the size of the required downpayment and monthly payments than with interest rates.[85] No doubt there are also many other reasons for a lack of

---

vertise that terms were "easy," or perhaps to advertise anything about them except that they were harsh, if the cash price was very high and obviously included credit charges. Leon A. Tashof, [1967-70 Transfer Binder] TRADE REG. REP. ¶ 18,606, at 20,941 (FTC 1968). If the Commission decision had stood, it might have constituted a fairly significant deterrent to the practice of burying credit charges in cash prices, for once such a practice was engaged in, the merchant would be foreclosed from saying almost anything good about his credit terms. Unfortunately, on appeal the Commission order was affirmed by the court of appeals on a narrower ground—that it was misleading to argue that credit terms were "easy" when the merchant maintained a very rigorous debt enforcement policy. The court expressed no opinion on the Commission's rationale concerning the excessiveness of the cash price. Tashof v. FTC, 437 F.2d 707 (D.C. Cir. 1970). The Federal Trade Commission has made little effort to follow up the *Tashof* decision.

82. This explanation is frequently offered not only for the apparent failure of truth-in-lending to stimulate comparative credit shopping, but also as an explanation of earlier studies indicating that before truth-in-lending consumers frequently did not comparatively shop even though aware of differentials in available interest rates. *See, e.g.*, White & Munger, *supra* note 79; *Hearings on S. 2755 Before a Subcomm. of the Senate Comm. on Banking and Currency*, 86th Cong., 1st Sess. 806-08 (1960).

83. This will particularly be the case if the amount of time the consumer can devote to comparative shopping is relatively fixed because of other claims on his time. In such circumstances many consumers apparently decide, no doubt quite reasonably, that greater savings will probably be realized by devoting all available shopping time to the product selection decision rather than the credit selection decision. *See* note 73 *supra* and accompanying text.

84. White & Munger, *supra* note 79; *see* D. CAPLOVITZ, *supra* note 81.

85. Thus, one of the studies discussed previously found that although there was a substantial degree of unawareness of annual percentage rates, there was near perfect awareness of the size of monthly payments. G. Day & W. Brandt, *supra* note 31, pt. IV, at 32. This conclusion is also clearly indicated by the study by Juster and Shay. *See* note 75 *supra*.

motivation to shop comparatively for low interest rates.

### 2. GENERALIZING FROM THE TRUTH-IN-LENDING EXPERIENCE

For the purpose of evaluating disclosure regulation, the important lesson from truth-in-lending is not so much the reasons as the fact that consumers often base credit purchase decisions on factors other than the annual interest rate. If precontract disclosure regulation is intended to affect consumer purchase decisions, it must be drafted on the basis of some model of factors considered by consumers in making purchase decisions (or at least that would be considered if the needed information were available). Obviously it would be impossible to require conspicuous disclosure of all information that is in some way connected with the transaction. By presuming some model or models of the mixture of wants that consumers maximize through their purchasing decisions, it is possible to determine what information is most needed to reach purchasing decisions consistent with those models. Disclosure regulation can then be employed to provide consumers with that information when it is not otherwise available.

#### a. *Models of consumer decisionmaking and disclosure*

The models of consumer decisionmaking on which precontract disclosure regulation may be based could be either predictive or normative models. A predictive model is one which attempts to describe actual behavior. Precontract disclosure regulation based on such a model would have as its purpose providing information, not otherwise easily available, that is needed by a substantial proportion of consumers if they are to fulfill existing buying motivations and which therefore they would put to immediate use in making buying decisions. A normative model makes no pretentions of describing reality but rather describes the manner in which somebody—usually the formulator of the model—believes people should behave. Precontract disclosure regulation based on this type of model would have purposes other than providing consumers with information they need to fulfill existing motivations. Most likely, a major purpose would be to help persuade consumers to base purchasing decisions on the normative model, whatever their existing inclinations might be.

There are conflicting indications as to whether precontract disclosure regulation is typically based on predictive or normative models. If decisions about what information should be subject to compulsory disclosure are based on predictive models, efforts should be made to determine empirically the actual buying motivations or actions of at least a plurality of consumers. Surveys measuring such motivations are often undertaken by business in order to plan marketing strategies.[86] Rarely, however, do they play an

86. *See* E. DICHTER, HANDBOOK OF CONSUMER MOTIVATIONS (1964); V. PACKARD, THE HIDDEN PERSUADERS (1958).

important role in the formulation of disclosure regulation. Indeed, truth-in-lending was enacted despite the existence at the time of a considerable amount of evidence indicating that, with the possible exception of automobile loans and home mortgages, information about annual percentage rates was unlikely to affect the credit shopping behavior of the vast majority of consumers, particularly low-income consumers.[87]

Yet, with remarkable consistency precontract disclosure information almost inevitably concerns price, quantity, warranty, or similar terms. It is very difficult to describe a single concept or model of buying behavior which points solely to this cluster of considerations as useful in making purchasing decisions. Almost any model based on maximization of economic gain would provide for weighing considerations of shopping convenience in making purchase decisions, yet information about shopping convenience is rarely, if ever, subject to compulsory precontract disclosure.[88] In a rough layman's sense, it might be said that disclosure regulation typically pertains to a cluster of considerations that need to be weighed in determining the "best buy" for one's money. Henceforth, for convenience, this cluster of considerations will be called the "best buy

87. *See, e.g.*, Jordan & Warren, *supra* note 21, at 1299-1304; Kripke, *supra* note 81, at 1-13. It should be noted that it was not even clear that annual percentage rate disclosure would have impact on shopping for automobile and home mortgage credit. Although it was assumed consumers were more disposed to shop for this type of credit than other types, even prior to truth-in-lending there was evidence of substantial consumer awareness about what credit sources offered the lowest rates. This information alone should have been sufficient to induce considerable credit shopping behavior to the extent consumers were motivated to shop. *See, e.g.*, Kripke, *supra* note 81. Of course, there was also considerable evidence prior to truth-in-lending of consumer unawareness of the actual level of annual percentage rates. Perhaps Congress believed that, where there were pre-existing motivations to shop for credit, truth-in-lending would facilitate more careful and intelligent credit shopping by standardizing the basis of interest rate quotations. *See* note 100 *infra*.

88. The usual maximization models provide, of course, for a consumer to weigh any consideration which in fact is consistent with his own value set. *Cf.* Leff, *The Cultural and Social Impact of Society on American Advertising*, 1970 LAW & SOCIAL ORDER 397, 400-01. In the text I am referring to an imprecise version of a maximization model which would provide only for purchasing decisions that enhance the consumer's economic net worth. But even such a model fails to explain why the type of information subjected to compulsory precontract disclosure is so limited.

It is arguable that precontract disclosure regulation is based on a traditional maximization model, with the information subjected to compulsory disclosure limited to attributes, such as price and quality, that are easily measured and stated in a standardized manner so as to permit comparative shopping. Although there may be some merit to this explanation, I doubt that it is sufficient explanation for the uniformity in the type of information subject to compulsory disclosure. For further discussion see note 123 *infra*.

model" of buying motivations, even though the lack of a precise concept of buying behavior pointing solely to these considerations makes the use of the term "model" somewhat inappropriate.

The points just discussed suggest that precontract disclosure regulation is based on a normative model. There are also indications, however, that it typically is based on a predictive model. Certainly, the rhetoric accompanying the enactment of most precontract disclosure regulation, particularly truth-in-lending, and the manner in which such regulation is evaluated by commentators,[89] so suggest. The most persuasive indication, however, is the manner in which most precontract disclosure regulation provides for dissemination of the information to be disclosed. The manner of disclosure is typically such as to negate any possible objective of persuading consumers to use the information. Rather the information is typically disclosed in such a manner that it is likely to be noticed only by consumers who have a strong desire for the information and practically conduct a search for it sometime before becoming legally committed to the transaction.[90] Frequently, for example, the language used in the disclosure is comprehensible to most consumers, if ever, only after considerable study. Thus, the Uniform Commercial Code requires a disclaimer of the implied warranty of merchantability to use the word "merchantability."[91] Empirical research has demonstrated that even if their attention is drawn to it, many consumers cannot understand a warranty disclaimer provision written in a manner almost compelled by this Code provision.[92]

The best evidence that the usual manner of disclosure implies use of a predictive model, however, is that precontract disclosure is most often required only in the written document called the contract.[93] Sellers have long known that it is precisely in the con-

89. I refer, of course, to the fact that commentators deem it irrelevant to ask if consumers want the information disclosed. *See* notes 21-23 *supra* and accompanying text.

90. *See* notes 91-96 *infra* and accompanying text.

91. UNIFORM COMMERCIAL CODE § 2-316(2). If a seller wishes to disclaim all implied warranties, he can use a common phrase such as "with all faults." *Id.* § 2-316(3).

92. Whitford, *supra* note 80, at 146-47. Requiring the use of technical language may also be one of the difficulties of truth-in-lending, since the Act forces disclosure of a complicated set of arithmetical calculations.

93. There are several possible explanations for the tendency to fix the place of disclosure as the contract. Providing a valid contract must be in writing, which is typically the case under the various state retail installment sales acts, *see* B. CURRAN, *supra* note 5, at 95, disclosure in the contract guarantees that the disclosure is available to the consumer *before* he legally commits himself. The tendency to require disclosure in the contract itself may also stem from the basic contract law principle, underlying the parol evidence rule, that where there is a writing, the terms of the party's relationship are more or less those stated in the contract. *Cf.* UNIFORM COMMERCIAL CODE § 2-202. As a result of this principle, a seller

tract, and only in the contract, that information consumers are *not* supposed to notice is to be put. Admittedly, sellers have often buried unfavorable information in small type. But the use of large, bold type, commonly required by disclosure regulations, will rarely communicate information prior to the signing of the contract unless the consumer is searching for the information and has reason to expect it to be in the contract. In nearly all consumer transactions—and to a very great extent in all contractual transactions—the effective agreement, an oral one, is made before the buyer ever sees the written contract. To the parties, the signing of the written contract is usually only a ritual, roughly equivalent to a handshake. The written contract is likely to be read carefully enough to be understood at some time subsequent to its signing, if at all.[94] Even in the rare case in which a consumer actually reads the contract before signing, it must be remembered that he usually views himself as already morally committed. If he comes across information in the written contract which ordinarily would persuade him not to sign, it puts him in a conflict situation and one which, in accordance with the theory of cognitive dissonance, he may resolve by discounting the disclosed information.[95] Certainly in this situation, unless the information pertains to a buying desire valued very highly by the consumer, he is likely to be receptive to a conflict-resolving suggestion by a salesman that the disclosed information is not really significant and is only included because the law so requires.[96]

Given the conflicting indications about the essential purpose of most precontract disclosure regulation, probably the most reasonable resolution, and the one in my judgment most commentators implicitly make, is to presume that the regulation is intended to be based on a predictive model—that the intent is to provide consumers with information that they will use without further urging—and that the usual decision to base such regulation on what I have denominated the best buy model reflects a "seat of

desiring to impose a particular obligation on a consumer must ordinarily include the provision in the contract in some way. Thus, for example, the obligation to pay interest must be stated in some way, even if not as an annual percentage rate. It does not necessarily follow that the required clear and conspicuous disclosure of that provision also must be made in the contract. Nevertheless, this contract law notion may be partly responsible for the tendency to require disclosure in the contract itself.

94. *See* Curran, *supra* note 25, at 424; Jordan & Warren, *supra* note 21, at 1320.

95. The dissonance can arise not only because the consumer sees himself as morally committed, but also because the information disclosed may tend to convince him that his decision to enter into the transaction was an unwise one, a conclusion he may be reluctant to reach. *See also* Friedman, *Using Simulation Techniques to Predict the Behavioral Effects of New Laws: The Case of Truth-in-Lending Legislation and the Consumer*, 54 J. APPLIED PSYCHOLOGY 297 (1970).

96. *See* R. Pullen, *supra* note 26, at 7-8.

the pants" judgment about the actual buying motivations of large numbers of consumers. Given this assumption about purpose, there are several evident explanations for why precontract disclosure regulation so rarely has had the intended effects on shopping behavior. The most obvious explanation is that the best buy model is a complete description of the buying motivations of few, if any, consumers. For example, considerations of convenience in shopping obviously affect purchasing decisions very substantially. The existence of so much advertising encouraging the purchase of various products or services in order to satisfy assorted psychological needs (such as status and sexual attractiveness) is also strong evidence that at least advertisers believe consumers make purchases for reasons that are essentially inconsistent with the best buy model. A considerable body of social science research about consumer buying motivations suggests that the use of such advertising themes is very effective.[97] Moreover, before precontract disclosure regulation based on a best buy model can actually have impact on purchasing behavior, it is necessary either that a decision not to buy a good or service be practical (*e.g.*, to pay cash rather than arrange for credit), or that the market offer significant choices to which information disclosed pertains (*e.g.*, that choices as to interest rate level are available). In the case of truth-in-lending, it has already been suggested that even after the legislation became effective, neither of these choices was effectively available to many consumers, particularly low-income consumers.[98]

It is, of course, true that with respect to much precontract disclosure regulation practical choices are available to which the disclosed information relates. Moreover, the buying behavior of a consumer in any particular purchase is the product of a mix of several different motivations. Most consumers undoubtedly weigh to some extent the considerations indicated by the best buy model in most purchasing situations, and some consumers probably often weigh them heavily. For these reasons, one might expect most precontract disclosure regulation to have measurable impact on shopping behavior, and in a few instances, when by happenstance the information disclosed is weighed heavily by large numbers of consumers, it might be expected to have substantial impact. Before reaching that conclusion, however, it is necessary to consider the theoretical implications of the fact that disclosure regulation will have impact only when the information disclosed was not readily available prior to regulation.

*b. Implications of the lack of voluntary disclosure*

According to economic theory, excluding collusion, choices in a

97. *E.g.*, CONSUMER BEHAVIOR (J. Engel ed. 1968); T. ROBERTSON, CONSUMER BEHAVIOR (1970).

98. *See* note 81 *supra* and accompanying text.

fully competitive market can usually be expected to develop with regard to any factors on which significant numbers of consumers will base their purchase decisions. The principal situation in which choices will not develop is where the costs of developing the choices exceed the competitive benefits the developers are likely to gain. Thus, the fewer the number of consumers whose purchasing behavior will be affected substantially by the development of the choices, the less likely it is that the choices will be developed. Assuming the existence of relevant choices, voluntary disclosure of information about them can also usually be expected, since it will be to the advantage of various sellers to point out that their product or service has attributes that make it appear more advantageous to many consumers than the product or service of their competitiors. The principal situation in which voluntary disclosure of such information would not occur is where the number of consumers whose purchasing decisions will be affected by the information is sufficiently small as not to justify the costs of disclosure.[99] Since the costs of voluntary disclosure are relatively small, the fact that disclosure of choices is required indicates that the disclosed information will affect few purchasing decisions.[100]

---

99. *See* Stigler, *The Economics of Information,* 69 J. POL. ECON. 213 (1961). It is interesting to note in this connection that before truth-in-lending there was considerable advertising of downpayment and monthly payment terms. The available evidence indicates that large numbers of consumers were and still are basing credit purchasing decisions on this information. *See* note 85 *supra* and accompanying text.

100. There are some exceptions to this analysis concerning the implications of the lack of voluntary disclosure information in competitive markets, two of which are important enough to be mentioned. First, disclosure regulation can compel revelation of information that would tend to cause many consumers not to buy a product at all. No seller of the product will have an incentive to disclose that kind of information. However, if technologically feasible, some sellers can usually be expected to develop product innovations which tend to make the product less undesirable to consumers. If these sellers then urge purchase of their product because it is less undesirable, they will likely disclose much of the information that would be subject to compulsory disclosure. Thus, even before health warnings were required on packages and in advertising, some cigarette sellers voluntarily advertised the relatively low nicotine and tar content of their product. Moreover, often in this situation there will be some elasticity in the demand for the product in question and for a potential substitute product that does not possess the negative attribute. Consequently, depending in part on the extent of the elasticity in demand, sellers of the substitute product will have an incentive to disclose voluntarily the negative information. Nevertheless, in competitive markets there may be some situations in which compulsory disclosure of information, not otherwise readily available, may tend to discourage any purchase of a product.

The second exception concerns the fact that in some situations in which there is a good deal of voluntary disclosure, the information is not stated in a standardized manner and therefore does not facilitate comparative shopping. Before truth-in-lending, for example, interest rate information was generally available before purchase, but interest rates

It is commonplace that many markets in consumer products or services in this country are quite oligopolistic, and that in these markets the competitive processes just described will not always occur. Rather the major sellers will sometimes reach parallel, although perhaps independent, decisions not to compete with regard to various factors, including at times those indicated by the best buy model. When there are only a few major sellers in a market, often each can be expected to keep informed as to the others' activities, and thereby, to the extent each seller can feasibly do so, adjust his affairs so that no one seller obtains a competitive advantage with regard to a factor valued highly by large numbers of consumers. Consequently, all sellers will be reluctant to introduce product innovations or price reductions, since they have reason to believe that if detected, their competitors will simply match the innovation or reduction, yielding little or no competitive advantage to the initiating seller.[101] Where sellers reach such parallel decisions not to compete, for similar reasons, they very likely will also reach parallel decisions to withhold information that is needed if a purchasing decision is to be based on the best buy model. Such information, if truthful, would not indicate that any single seller offers a superior (according to the best buy model) or cheaper product or service, and it may convince some consumers not to purchase the product or service at all. In such situations, therefore,

---

were calculated in so many different ways they were not comparable. Even in this situation, if a seller would benefit substantially from increased comparative shopping, he would have an incentive to compile and disclose comparable information about the terms offered by all or a large number of sellers in the industry. Since the compilation and disclosure of such information can be more expensive than ordinary disclosure, however, greater expected impact on buying behavior would be needed to induce voluntary disclosure than if no standardization problem existed.

There can be other situations, of course, in which it is costly for the sellers to compile or disclose information, and in these situations also compulsory disclosure may have greater effect. In this connection it is interesting to note that in the recently enacted Motor Vehicle Information and Cost Savings Act, Pub. L. No. 92-513 (U.S. CODE CONG. & AD. NEWS, 92D CONG., 2D SESS., at 1110 [1972]), the burden of compiling information to be disclosed was placed on the Secretary of Transportation in part because it was considered unfair to impose those costs on automobile manufacturers and dealers. *See* note 9 *supra*.

101. Moreover, detection of product innovation or price reduction should generally be easier in consumer markets than in markets where buyers regularly purchase large quantities. In the former markets, information about the innovation or reduction can be communicated efficiently to buyers only in manners, such as media advertising, that make difficult or impossible concealment of the information from competing sellers. In the latter markets, communication techniques which facilitate concealment, such as personal contact, are more feasible. Consequently, in consumer product industries with oligopolistic structures, one should expect to find more readily the parallel decisions not to develop choices or to withhold information that are discussed in the text.

precontract disclosure regulation can often be expected to have significant effects.[102] Thus, I would not be surprised if regulation requiring disclosure of known medical facts about the effectiveness of different analgesics would induce many consumers not to buy these products at all.[103] By stimulating such effects, it might cause the manufacturers of analgesics to begin to compete as to many of the factors indicated by the best buy model, in an effort to keep as many customers as possible.

Although all markets are to some extent oligopolistic, it would be unrealistic to assume therefore, that uniformly basing disclosure regulation on a best buy model will inevitably produce substantial impact. As markets become less oligopolistic, the pressures that cause noncompetitive behavior become less effective, since it becomes more difficult for each seller to keep informed about and to respond to the actions of competitors. Consequently, it is more likely both that choices will develop in the market place and that there will be voluntary disclosure of information if it would be used by sufficiently large numbers of consumers. In the relatively competitive consumer credit market,[104] for example, even before truth-in-lending there were choices available as to level of interest rates. One might have expected many credit sellers voluntarily to disclose interest rates on a standardized basis if large numbers of consumers would have used the information. When these competitive considerations are combined with the fact that disclosure regulation based on the best buy model will often provide only some of the considerations consumers weigh in making purchase decisions, and frequently the less important ones, it seems clear that for theoretical reasons disclosure regulation making available information previously difficult to obtain can be expected very often to have limited impact on buying behavior.

### *C. Some Conclusions About the Desirability of Traditional Precontract Disclosure*

In essence, what I have suggested so far is that, if it is assumed

102. I am not aware of any empirical studies about the effects of disclosure regulation in oligopolistic markets that would test this hypothesis. One possible reason for the lack of empirical evidence about the effects of disclosure regulation in oligopolistic markets could be that such regulation is rarely enacted precisely because it can be expected to have substantial effects on buying behavior. *See* notes 121-22 *infra* and accompanying text.

103. The Federal Trade Commission's complaints against the makers of a number of leading brand name analgesics are particularly interesting in this regard. American Home Prod. Corp., 3 TRADE REG. REP. ¶¶ 19,962 (FTC April 19, 1972) (proposed complaints); 20,263 (FTC Feb. 23, 1973) (complaints issued). *See also* Motor Vehicle Information and Cost Savings Act, Pub. L. No. 92-513 (U.S. CODE CONG. & AD. NEWS, 92D CONG., 2D SESS., at 1110 [1972]), discussed in note 9 *supra*.

104. *See* Kripke, *supra* note 81, at 3-5.

that the purpose of precontract disclosure regulation is to provide consumers with information that without further prompting they will use in making purchase decisions, then both empirical observations of the effects of such regulation—as illustrated by the earlier discussion of truth-in-lending—and theoretical considerations indicate precontract disclosure regulation, based on the best buy model, in most instances will have little impact on consumer buying behavior. It must be emphasized that this conclusion is only a tentative one. Most of the empirical evidence concerns only one example of precontract disclosure regulation—truth-in-lending—and not even that evidence is conclusive. Moreover, my theoretical analysis has suggested several situations in which substantial impact is at least possible. Nevertheless, on the available evidence, the criticisms of disclosure regulation discussed in the introduction appear sound, both empirically and theoretically.

It does not follow from this conclusion, however, that traditional precontract disclosure should be abandoned as a regulatory technique, if the alternative is no disclosure regulation at all. My previous analysis has suggested such regulation may sometimes have very useful impact in highly oligopolistic markets. Even in relatively competitive markets, the benefits to society of compulsory disclosure can exceed its costs even though there is no voluntary disclosure because the private benefits of such disclosure to an individual seller are less than his costs. The societal benefits of compulsory disclosure may not always be limited to savings realized by consumers who use the information. Changing the shopping behavior of only a very small number of consumers can sometimes have impact on the substantive content of a much larger number of transactions. If one assumes a competitive market and a product or contractual term that is highly standardized and not susceptible to differentiation to meet the desires of different sets of consumers, then changing the behavior of only a marginal group of consumers may set off a competition for that group and in the process produce changes in the content of the transactions of a very large number of consumers.[105] Thus, because "interest rate" is a term which is difficult for a seller to differentiate according to the buying motivations of his customers, some expected this "marginal buyer" effect to take hold under truth-in-lending and lead to a competitive re-

105. It does not necessarily follow from the goals heretofore ascribed to disclosure regulation that this "marginal buyer" effect on the content of consumer transactions is desirable public policy; these goals prescribe only that in making purchase decisions consumers be enabled to act on whatever motivations they hold. But I am confident that many, probably most, proponents of disclosure regulation would welcome a change in the terms of large numbers of consumer transactions that make those terms more favorable, in terms of the factors indicated by the best buy model, to consumers, whether or not most consumers place sufficient value on that change to affect their shopping behavior when choices are available. *Cf.* notes 123-25 *infra* and accompanying text.

duction in interest rates. However, no such effect is yet observable.[106]

Not only may the benefits of compulsory disclosure exceed those of voluntary disclosure,[107] but it is at least possible for the costs of compulsory disclosure to be less than the costs of voluntary disclosure. If only one or a few sellers are trying to disclose previously unavailable information, they may be forced to use relatively expensive communication techniques, such as media advertising, in order to reach consumers with whom they do not ordinarily come into contact. Traditional disclosure regulation, however, by providing for disclosure only in the contract, rarely requires sellers to expend more than is necessary to hire a lawyer to draft a few additional forms.[108] And since all sellers must disclose, inclusion in the contract will make the information available to most consumers who might use it.[109]

If disclosure is compulsory, there must be added to the cost side of the cost-benefit equation the expenditures for enforcement. Experience with truth-in-lending has demonstrated, however, that it is feasible to achieve a high degree of compliance with traditional disclosure regulation without significant expenditures for enforcement. The basic strategy for achieving compliance at low cost is as follows. Since disclosure is made by standardized form, public enforcement officials can effectively determine compliance in a large number of transactions by checking the forms used in a single transaction. Of course, there are often so many different sellers subject to the disclosure regulation that checking even one form for each seller can be a tremendous task. This problem is eased

106. The National Commission on Consumer Finance seems to argue that truth-in-lending has had such an effect in other than low-income markets, but offers no data at all to support such a conclusion. COMMISSION REPORT, *supra* note 29, at 176-79.

107. I have discussed only the effects of disclosure regulation on consumer buying behavior, and through such effects on the content of consumer transactions. Precontract disclosure regulation can also have possibly desirable effects other than on shopping behavior. For example, compelling sellers to disclose certain information can often aid in the enforcement of other laws regulating the substantive content of consumer transactions. Thus, truth-in-lending probably made it easier for consumers to detect violations of the usury laws and by so doing may have made private remedies a more efficient tool for enforcing those laws.

108. *See* notes 91-96 *supra* and accompanying text. Of course, there are exceptions. It may, for example be difficult for the seller to compile the information that must be disclosed. In the recently enacted Motor Vehicle Information and Cost Savings Act the burden of compiling information to be disclosed was placed on the Secretary of Transportation in part because it was considered unfair to impose those costs on automobile manufacturers and dealers. *See* note 9 *supra*.

109. There may be some consumers who do not purchase the product at all but who would if the disclosed information were available to them. Disclosure in the contract will not necessarily convey the information to them, of course.

substantially, however, by providing legislatively that any consumer party to a transaction in which a required disclosure has not been made is entitled to a minimum amount of damages, irrespective of proof of actual loss. Because disclosure is inevitably made by standard form, once damages are standardized in this manner, violation of a disclosure regulation presents a situation in which a class action is frequently appropriate. All issues, even the damages issues, are often standardized for the entire class. Since the potential liability of the nondisclosing seller in a class action is often enormous, the threat of a class action can provide an effective deterrent to intentional or careless violation of disclosure regulation.

As I indicated, truth-in-lending demonstrates the efficacy of this low-cost enforcement strategy. A high level of compliance with truth-in-lending was apparently achieved in less than one year.[110] Yet this degree of compliance was achieved with the expenditure of relatively few government resources for enforcement. The Federal Trade Commission has principal enforcement responsibility and has never assigned many personnel to monitoring compliance. The few Commission personnel who have worked on truth-in-lending enforcement[111] have devoted their energies mostly to helping businesses who wished to comply to understand the requirements of truth-in-lending.[112]

The Federal Trade Commission did bring a few highly visible actions shortly after the legislation became effective, apparently in the hope of misleading merchants into believing that noncompliance would be routinely prosecuted.[113] And it still does bring enough actions to insure that the trade journals note the Commission's enforcement efforts relatively consistently.[114] It seems highly doubtful, however, that the level of compliance should be attributed to these occasional threats of prosecution by the Commission. The outcome of a Commission proceeding is only a cease-and-desist order,[115] and in any event it is obvious to all but the most casual

110. *See* note 30 *supra*.

111. For the Federal Trade Commission's enforcement powers see Truth in Lending Act § 108(c), 15 U.S.C. § 1607(c) (1970).

112. For a discussion of the Commission's enforcement activities see Federal Trade Comm'n, Report to the Board of Governors of the Federal Reserve System on Enforcement of the Truth in Lending Act (Oct. 1970).

113. *E.g.*, Chrysler Corp., 4 CCH CONSUMER CREDIT GUIDE ¶ 99,857 (FTC Nov. 7, 1969) (proposed complaint).

114. Local Fin. Corp., 1 CCH CONSUMER CREDIT GUIDE 908 (FTC June 20, 1972) (proposed complaint); Derby Constr., Inc., 1 CCH CONSUMER CREDIT GUIDE 882 (FTC Nov. 13, 1972) (consent order). Both proceedings are noted in BNA ANTITRUST & TRADE REG. REP., Oct. 3, 1972, at A-19.

115. *See* Truth in Lending Act § 108(c), 15 U.S.C. § 1607(c) (1970). Section 112 of the Act, 15 U.S.C. § 1611 (1970), also provides for criminal penalties for wilfull violation of its disclosure requirements, but very few criminal prosecutions have been initiated. *See Report of the Attorney General to the Congress of the United States on the Enforcement of Title*

observer that the Commission is not going to expand its staff sufficiently to initiate many enforcement actions.

It seems much more probable that the crucial factor in the high level of compliance with truth-in-lending has been the private remedies (minimum recovery is $100) afforded a consumer entering a transaction in which the required disclosure is not made.[116] A large number of class actions have been filed against noncompliant merchants for recovery of these private damages.[117] Because of the large damages involved, these suits have prompted a great deal of concern by the credit industry.[118] Indeed, the Federal Trade

---

*I of the Consumer Credit Protection Act of 1968 for the Calendar Year 1971,* Jan. 10, 1972, in 4 CCH CONSUMER CREDIT GUIDE ¶ 99,248. Of course, many merchants have undoubtedly complied because of a commitment to obey the law or because they perceive no reason to take *any* risk of prosecution, given the low direct costs of compliance and the evident lack of impact of truth-in-lending on buying behavior.

116. Truth in Lending Act § 130(a)(1), 15 U.S.C. § 1640(a)(1) (1970). A victorious consumer litigant is also entitled to court costs and reasonable attorney fees. Truth in Lending Act § 130(a)(2), 15 U.S.C. § 1640(a)(2) (1970).

117. These actions can be brought in federal court, irrespective of the amount in controversy. Truth in Lending Act § 130(e), 15 U.S.C. § 1640(e) (1970). *See generally* Snyder v. Harris, 394 U.S. 332 (1969). For an excellent discussion of the requirements for a valid class action under the Federal Rules of Civil Procedure see Travers & Landers, *The Consumer Class Action,* 18 KAN. L. REV. 811 (1970). The Board of Governors of the Federal Reserve System has been able to locate at least 49 class actions alleging violation of truth-in-lending. 1971 ANNUAL REPORT, *supra* note 30, at 9.

118. *See, e.g.,* BNA ANTITRUST & TRADE REG. REP., March 14, 1972, at B-1.

I do not mean to suggest that providing for enforcement through this deterrence technique is entirely costless. The magnitude of the deterrence may cause sellers to expend resources to avoid mistakes in disclosure that far exceed the harm that would result from the mistakes that are avoided. *Cf.* Posner, *A Theory of Negligence,* 1 J. LEGAL STUDIES 29 (1972). And when the inevitable mistake occurs, the cost to the seller, and in the long run through him to consumers generally, will far exceed the harm caused. Section 130(c) of the Truth in Lending Act, 15 U.S.C. § 1640(c) (1970), tries to ameliorate this difficulty by providing that a creditor whose noncompliance is due to bona fide error is exempted from the private remedies provisions. Recently, it was held that this exemption applied to just clerical errors, such as miscalculations of the annual percentage rate, and not to "errors of law" of the type that are likely to be made systematically on a large number of forms. Ratner v. Chemical Bank New York Trust Co., 329 F. Supp. 270 (S.D.N.Y. 1971).

Apparently because the exemption for the bona fide error was not considered adequate to avoid the resource misallocation effects that can result from the availability of high punitive recoveries, legislation was passed in the Senate during the last session of Congress that would have restricted recovery in a truth-in-lending class action to $100,000 for the entire class. S. 652, 92d Cong., 2d Sess. § 208 (1972). As passed in the Senate, the bill is printed in 118 CONG. REC. 6926 (daily ed. April 27, 1972). The bill was not reported for floor action in the House. 30 CONG. Q. WEEKLY REV. 2711 (Oct. 21, 1972).

Probably for similar reasons, a number of recent decisions have held

Commission itself has assigned an increasing enforcement role to private actions, particularly the class action.[119] Thus, one FTC enforcement official reported to me that currently he has considerable success in obtaining voluntary compliance by indicating to the merchant that he viewed his function as helping the merchant avoid the potential liability of a class action.

### D. *Discovering New Purposes for Disclosure Regulation*

Continued use of precontract disclosure regulation as it is now typically formulated can be justified, even if applied to relatively competitive industries, on the ground that its benefits may marginally exceed its costs. However, such regulation would be a more useful tool of consumer protection if it could be formulated in different ways, or perhaps assigned different purposes, that would provide it greater potential impact. There are essentially two basic approaches in this regard. Disclosure of information about factors other than those indicated by the best buy model could be required, or regulation based on the best buy model could be assigned purposes, at least theoretically capable of significant fulfillment, other than those indicated by the assumption that it is based on a predictive model.

Of these two possibilities, the first seems less promising. If large numbers of consumers would use the information required to be disclosed, in most instances there should be no need for the regulation. Sellers most capable of satisfying the desires of consumers with regard to the aspect to be disclosed could be expected voluntarily to provide the information. Nor would basing disclosure regulation on models of consumer behavior other than the best buy model appear consistent with an intuitive sense about what are proper subjects for compulsory disclosure. Thus, assuming the information is readily available and easily described, I doubt that

that under the Federal Rules of Civil Procedure class actions may not be maintained for alleged truth-in-lending violations. These decisions do not point to any lack of commonality in the questions of law and fact, and indeed there is none. Rather they seem to reason from the inequity of a judgment for millions of dollars for a highly technical violation of truth-in-lending to the conclusion that a truth-in-lending class action fails to satisfy the requirement of FED. R. CIV. P. 23(b) (3) that, in order to be maintainable, a class action must be "superior to other available methods for fair and efficient adjudication of the controversy." *E.g.*, Ratner v. Chemical Bank New York Trust Co., BNA ANTITRUST & TRADE REG. REP., Feb. 22, 1972, at E-1 (S.D.N.Y. 1972); Rogers v. Coburn Fin. Corp., BNA ANTITRUST & TRADE REG. REP., Feb. 22, 1972, at A-14 (N.D. Ga. 1972). *Contra, e.g.*, La Mar v. H&B Novelty & Loan Co., BNA ANTITRUST & TRADE REG. REP., Feb. 1, 1972, at A-2 (D. Ore. 1972); Joseph v. Norman's Health Club, Inc., 336 F. Supp. 307 (E.D. Mo. 1971). Since there is a conflict in the decisions, a merchant violating truth-in-lending still faces a substantial threat of a valid class action.

119. *See, e.g.*, BNA ANTITRUST & TRADE REG. REP., May 16, 1972, at A-12 (statement of Commissioner Jones).

many persons would seriously consider enacting a law requiring disclosure of general attitudes in the population towards owners of expensive, prestige automobiles, even if there is reliable evidence that many consumers are acting on mistaken assumptions about such attitudes when making automobile purchase decisions.[120]

It is more fruitful, I believe, to inquire whether precontract disclosure regulation based on the best buy model can have purposes other than those indicated by an assumption that it is based on a predictive model. For one thing, it seems highly likely that many of the participants in the drafting of such regulation know or sense how unrealistic it is in most instances to assume regulation based on the best buy model provides information large numbers of consumers will use without further prompting. Since precontract disclosure regulation nevertheless is almost inevitably based on the best buy model, it is reasonable to assume that, implicitly at least, many of the drafters of disclosure regulation have other than the usually assumed purposes in mind.

One possible alternative explanation of purpose is that, despite appearances to the contrary, precontract disclosure regulation is enacted precisely because it is expected to have little impact on consumer purchasing decisions. According to this explanation, the enactment of precontract disclosure regulation is intended primarily to satisfy a strong, but transitory, political demand for legislation benefiting consumers. Because the political demand is transitory, if consumers are to gain anything, their spokesmen may be forced to seek legislation which will have little impact and therefore does not produce strong opposition. The result is frequently disclosure regulation based on the best buy model, which satisfies the political demand for consumer legislation because it appears and is represented to be proconsumer and because the ordinary citizen simply has neither the sophistication nor the information needed to realize that the legislation will have little impact.[121]

Undoubtedly political considerations such as these have played an important role in determining the content and obtaining the

120. In buying expensive, prestige automobiles, some consumers no doubt are more interested subjectively in acquiring a personal belief that others have certain attitudes towards them than in actually stimulating those attitudes in others. *See* Leff, *supra* note 88. These consumers can satisfy their buying motivations without any factual information about attitudes, although concrete information about attitudes could affect their beliefs about prevailing attitudes and thereby affect shopping behavior. I assume, however, that many purchasers of prestige automobiles are principally interested in stimulating attitudes in others as a means of achieving still other external goals, and these buyers have a legitimate "need" for factual information about attitudes if they are to maximize satisfaction of their buying motivations.

121. For a fuller explanation of this theory of political action see J. EDELMAN, POLITICS AS SYMBOLIC ACTION (1971); J. EDELMAN, THE SYMBOLIC USES OF POLITICS (1964). *Cf.* Kripke, *supra* note 81.

enactment of much precontract disclosure regulation. However, I think there is reason to believe that the explanation is not sufficient to explain the existence and content of all such regulation.[122] In any event this article is not concerned so much with what purposes precontract disclosure regulation has in fact as with determining whether such regulation can be formulated in ways that will have substantial impact on consumer transactions.

The most plausible remaining alternative explanation for use of the best buy model in formulating precontract disclosure regulation[123] is to assume that the drafters are using a normative rather

---

122. Thus, proposals for disclosure regulation have often generated fierce opposition from seller interests. *See* Hart, *supra* note 8.

123. There are, of course, a number of other possible explanations, none of them very plausible to me. For example, it might be argued that the drafters intend not so much to induce change in consumer buying motivations as to favor those already motivated to follow the best buy model by providing them the information they need. This explanation is also essentially a normative one; it necessitates a judgment to use the apparatus of the state to favor certain buying motivations over others. And the ultimate result sought remains increased comparative shopping according to factors indicated by the best buy model. It differs from the normative explanation in the text, however, in that there is no desire to change existing purchasing motivations.

A second possible explanation for the consistent decision to disclose factors indicated by the best buy model is that other attributes of a product or service about which consumers may want to know are often hard to measure (*e.g.*, the degree to which use of different toothpastes will enhance sexual attractiveness). Such information simply may not be available, perhaps because the product quality is essentially not measurable. Alternatively, the information may be sufficiently complex that it is difficult to convey meaningfully through disclosure. This latter explanation may be especially applicable to the failure to compel disclosure of information pertaining to shopping convenience. Although there may be some merit in this type of explanation, I doubt that it fully accounts for the consistency in the type of information made subject to compulsory disclosure. It fails, for example, to take account of the intuitive sense about what are proper subjects for disclosure that I discussed earlier. *See* note 120 *supra* and accompanying text.

My analysis of the inadequacies of predictive models as a basis for disclosure regulation mostly assumes that any such regulation necessarily provides for disclosure in the written contract, or in some similarly inadequate but inexpensive manner. It is possible, of course, that such disclosure regulation has little impact on shopping behavior not because many consumers do not in some sense "want" the information disclosed but because the costs to them of discovering the information—in terms, for example, of shopping time, since it is necessary to visit each place of business to obtain the information about each seller—exceed whatever value they place on use of the information. On this assumption it follows that if disclosure regulation provided for disclosure in manners that permitted many consumers to obtain and use the information at little cost to themselves, the regulation would have substantial impact because in some sense it would make available information consumers "want." Such regulation could be said to be based on a predictive model.

The principal operational implication of this mode of analysis—that the main reform needed in most present-day disclosure regulation is in the

than a predictive model; that such regulation reflects a belief that consumers should make purchasing decisions in accordance with the best buy model, whether or not they are naturally inclined to do so. Thus, in the case of truth-in-lending, the decision to place primary emphasis on the annual interest rate and total finance charge reflected not so much a prediction that consumers *would* make substantial use of this information in making buying decisions as a belief that they *should* make use of this information.

The view that disclosure regulation is based on normative models has a number of substantial implications. Most importantly, it means that disclosure regulation, perhaps in conjunction with some other regulation, is intended somehow to encourage or persuade more consumers than otherwise would be inclined to do so to make purchasing decisions on the favored bases. No longer is it assumed, as it would be if predictive models were being used, that large numbers of consumers will use, without further prompting, the information disclosed in making their shopping decisions. Secondly, while disclosure regulation has generally been characterized as a regulating approach that is consistent with freedom of contract values,[124] use of normative models for the purposes I have described requires a governmental judgment as to what kinds of considerations should be weighed by a consumer when deciding whether to enter into a transaction. There is a perpetual debate about the wisdom of the government making such judgments, and any effort to resolve that debate is beyond both the scope of this article and the competence of its author. It should be noted, however, that attributing the purposes I have described to disclosure regulation would not make such regulation unique. Substantive

manner in which disclosure is required—is strikingly similar to the operational implications I shall develop subsequently of my contention that disclosure regulation is more reasonably viewed as based on normative models. I prefer my view of the basis of disclosure regulation for several reasons. For me, it "rings truer" in an intuitive sense. It makes easier the justification of disclosure regulation on a cost-benefit basis even though the market does not induce voluntary disclosure of the information. *Compare* notes 105-19 *supra* and accompanying text *with* note 129 *infra* and accompanying text. And it avoids the necessity of explaining how disclosure regulation could be based on predictive models when few, if any, empirical studies on what information consumers "want" typically precede enactment of the regulation. *See* notes 86-88 *supra* and accompanying text. On the other hand, to the extent the type of disclosure regulation I discuss subsequently could be based on predictive models, it would avoid the need to meet the arguments about the appropriateness of government making the decisions that are required by normatively based disclosure regulation. These arguments are noted in the next paragraph of the text.

124. The argument, of course, is that disclosure regulation in no way controls the substantive content of contracts. Rather it is designed to insure only that the assumption underlying freedom-of-contract values —that the parties have consented to the substantive terms—is a practical reality. *See generally* Murray, *Unconscionability: Unconscionability,* 31 U. PITT. L. REV. 1 (1969).

regulation of the terms of consumer transactions (*e.g.*, regulation of the terms of insurance policies) is usually designed to insure that transactions are, in terms of the best buy model, more in the interests of the consumer than predictably they otherwise would be. And government-sponsored consumer education programs typically try to persuade consumers to act more consistently with the best buy model. Moreover, disclosure regulation based on the best buy model is still more consistent with freedom-of-contract values than most alternative forms of consumer protection regulation; disclosure regulation seeks only to persuade rather than to compel purchases according to a predetermined model.[125]

It is, of course, impossible to prove that disclosure regulation is typically based on a normative view of how consumers should behave, although I believe such is often the case. For purposes of this article, however, the important point is that it is the most plausible explanation for use of the best buy model that also indicates precontract disclosure regulation, at least implicitly, is intended to have more than marginal impact on consumer buying behavior. Consequently, for the balance of this discussion of precontract disclosure regulation, it will be assumed that such regulation in effect, although rarely explicitly, is intended to induce or persuade consumers to weigh the information disclosed more heavily in their purchasing decisions than they otherwise are inclined to do.

### *E. Formulating Precontract Disclosure Regulation to Have Persuasive Impact*

In this section I make the assumption that it is possible to persuade consumers to act in ways other than they would absent the persuasion. Given this assumption, normatively oriented disclosure regulation, unlike much regulation based on predictive models, has theoretical potential for significant impact on consumer buying behavior.[126] Before disclosure regulation can have this persuasive impact, however, in most instances the manner and timing of disclosure must be revised to reflect the goal of persuasion rather

125. Furthermore, since disclosure regulation leaves the ultimate determination of the terms of a transaction to the parties, it permits adaptation of those terms to the special circumstances facing one or both parties. Special circumstances can indicate that the terms of a contract should not follow the usual pattern for such contracts, even if it is to adhere to the best buy model. The provision of flexibility to adjust to special circumstances is often considered one of the principal benefits of freedom of contract.

126. *See generally* notes 99-104 *supra* and accompanying text. I assume, of course, that choices exist in the market with regard to the factors the normative disclosure regulation indicates should be weighed heavily in purchasing decisions, or at least will become available if the disclosure regulation successfully persuades large numbers of consumers. Except in highly oligopolistic markets concerning products for which the choice not to buy is impractical, this can be expected.

than the assumption that consumers will search for and then use without further urging the disclosed information.[127] I will discuss a range of disclosure techniques that might have persuasive impact and some of the considerations, both legal and practical, that must be taken into account before deciding to use any of them. Each of the techniques discussed will be based on an existing or proposed program for communicating information to consumers. Although rarely drawn upon in formulating disclosure regulation, there is, of course, considerable literature on the problems of mass persuasion. This section is not intended to be a comprehensive analysis of this literature. My main purpose is only to demonstrate that there are disclosure techniques which have not often been tried but which have the potential for substantial impact on buying behavior.

#### 1. SOME GENERAL CONSIDERATIONS

In my discussion of possible persuasive disclosure techniques, it will often be assumed that the effectiveness of the technique can be evaluated without regard to the subject matter of the disclosure. This may be an oversimplification. One disclosure technique may be most effective in persuading consumers to use certain types of information in making purchase decisions, yet another technique may be most effective with respect to other types of information. Similarly, it is unlikely that the same disclosure technique will be most effective in bringing the information to the attention of all groups of consumers. In particular, it seems probable that communication techniques which most effectively persuade low-income urban consumers to use the information disclosed will often be different from communication techniques which best reach other economic classes, since considerable evidence suggests that the shopping behavior of the poor, and most importantly their procedures for obtaining information about buying choices, tend to be distinctive.[128] As a result, most disclosure regulation, if it is to serve the interests of all economic classes, should probably attempt persuasion through several different communication methods simultaneously.

Each proposed disclosure technique will raise cost-benefit effectiveness issues. At the present time it is not possible to resolve these issues with regard to any of the proposed disclosure techniques I will discuss.[129] Even assuming that the costs of disclosure

127. *See* notes 90-96 *supra* and accompanying text.

128. D. CAPLOVITZ, *supra* note 81; G. Day & W. Brandt, *supra* note 31, at pts. III, VI.

129. Sellers who offer goods or services on terms more advantageous with respect to the factors subject to compulsory disclosure than other sellers will have an incentive to persuade consumers to base purchasing decisions on those factors even in the absence of regulation. It does not follow, however, from the absence or limited nature of such voluntary persuasive efforts that the costs of substantial persuasive efforts through disclosure regulation necessarily exceed the benefits to be gained.

could be determined, calculation of the benefits is not possible until there is further empirical evidence about the persuasive impact of each disclosure technique. Moreover, even if it were possible to calculate the dollars saved by consumers persuaded to make the "best buy" as a result of disclosure, these savings would not necessarily be the sole measure of the benefits derived from the disclosure regulation. I have not articulated the reasons why government might decide consumers should make purchasing decisions on favored bases, but at least one reason might be a belief that somehow the "quality of life" will increase if consumers can be persuaded to behave more consistently with the best buy model. Such intangible benefits are, of course, almost impossible to quantify. Nevertheless, some of the disclosure techniques discussed will involve particularly large costs and consequently raise serious doubts about their cost-benefit effectiveness. I will note these more costly techniques as I go along.

There are three basic approaches to persuading consumers to make purchases on favored bases. Traditionally, disclosure regulation has relied on the seller to provide information to consumers, and heretofore in this article I have assumed disclosure regulation relies on this technique of communication. At the same time, however, other devices have been, and obviously could be, used to persuade or encourage consumers to make purchasing decisions on favored bases. Government could itself disclose the information and attempt to persuade consumers to use it, or alternatively arrange to subsidize some nonseller to do the same. Rather than providing consumers with information, government might attempt to structure the environment in which consumers make purchasing decisions so that any existing inclinations to act in accordance with the best buy model are more likely to be reflected in behavior. For example, formal consumer education classes could attempt to train consumers to act in accordance with the best buy model without providing information about any specific product. In the subsequent discussion I will first discuss possible techniques that

All the reasons why the social benefits of disclosure regulation based on predictive models can exceed its costs even though there is no voluntary disclosure are potentially applicable here as well. *See* notes 105-19 *supra* and accompanying text. In addition, as noted subsequently in the text, one of the anticipated benefits of normatively oriented disclosure regulation may be improvement in the "quality of life," yet this type of intangible benefit would not ordinarily be taken into account by an individual seller considering voluntary persuasive disclosure. Moreover, sellers voluntarily undertaking to persuade consumers to base purchasing decisions on factors other than those to which they are accustomed may not reap all the benefits that sellers as a class stand to gain from his endeavor. Many consumers who are persuaded may decide to buy from other sellers who also offer advantageous bargains, or who alter their bargains to be as advantageous once the persuasive endeavors approach success. This is sometimes called the "free rider" problem in economics.

rely on seller disclosure, then techniques that rely on communication of information by nonsellers, and finally techniques which focus principally on structuring the purchase decision environment.

### 2. SELLER DISCLOSURE

The basic strategy I propose for enhancing the persuasive impact of seller disclosure is to manipulate the manner and timing of disclosure so that it is as unlikely as possible that consumers will reach purchase decisions without first having the disclosed information brought to their attention. My strategy is based on the assumptions that nearly all consumers in making purchase decisions give some weight to the considerations indicated by the best buy model and that many consumers perceive behavior in accordance with the best buy model as generally regarded by others as the most desirable type of purchasing behavior. Consequently, if disclosure regulation can be formulated so as to bring the disclosed information to the conscious attention of most consumers before they make purchase decisions, rather than merely making it available in a manner in which it is almost certain to be ignored, I believe it is likely that the regulation will succeed in inducing a significant number of consumers to make the type of purchase decision that the regulation is intended to encourage.

Whatever methods are devised for disclosing information in a manner likely to bring it to the attention of consumers, sellers could be required to include also a statement to the effect that the government, or some agency of it, recommends that consumers consider this type of information before making a purchase decision.[130] Such a statement might help draw the attention of consumers to the information. And when a seller perceives a competitive advantage accruing to him if consumers base purchase decisions on the information disclosed, he may be able to use the government statement as a selling tool. When sellers consider the making of a required disclosure contrary to their interest, however, one can anticpate that they will endeavor to discount the importance of the disclosure and accompanying statement of government recommendation as much as possible. In these situations a statement about government recommendation may have little persuasive effect other than whatever utility it has in drawing consumers' attention to the disclosed information.

130. What I am suggesting here is considerably different from government endorsement of a particular brand. The latter has been consistently rejected in the past, partly on the ground that the needs of consumers are so diverse that it is impossible for anybody to recommend any particular brand as best suited for everybody. *Cf.* Consumers Union of United States, Inc. v. Veterans Administration, 301 F. Supp. 796, 807 (S.D.N.Y. 1969), *appeal dismissed as moot*, 436 F.2d 1363 (2d Cir. 1971). I am proposing only that government urge consumers to consider some particular factor, such as interest rates, before making a purchase decision.

*a. Separate statement requirement*

Both the Wisconsin Consumer Act and the proposed federal warranties legislation contain provisions illustrating techniques of potentially more effective prepurchase communication. One technique is to require the seller to state important information in an instrument which is separate from the basic contract and which must be separately signed. Thus, the Wisconsin Consumer Act provides that before a cosigner becomes personally liable for the debt of another arising out of a consumer credit transaction, he must sign a separate statement in large type which states clearly and simply the obligations of a cosigner.[131] The apparent theory behind a separate statement requirement is that the signer's attention is more likely to be drawn to information in the separate statement than to information included in a written contract, since the contract contains so much information that many persons will be disinclined to read any of it. It is a theory, of course, that could be applied to any disclosure regulation. Even if this theory should prove empirically sound, however, the separate statement technique would still suffer from the infirmity that the statement will typically be presented to the consumer (or cosigner) only after the effective agreement—the oral agreement—is concluded. Thus, this technique represents, at best, a very modest effort at more effective prepurchase communication.

*b. Product labeling*

Somewhat related to providing disclosure in a document executed simultaneously with the contract is providing disclosure in product labeling or other point-of-sale material. This disclosure is potentially more effective in communicating information before the consumer has made his effective decision to purchase. At least as regards products sold in self-service stores, it permits the consumer to see the information while browsing. There is, of course, a great deal of compulsory labeling in this country now, some of which[132] is clearly designed to affect purchase decisions, such as the unit-cost or code-dating labeling of food products. Experience with health warnings on cigarette packages seems to suggest that labeling has much less impact on consumer buying behavior than media advertising.[133] Moreover, if too much information is put on the

131. WIS. STAT. § 422.305 (1971).

132. Much compulsory labeling is designed primarily to promote safe use of hazardous products after purchase. *E.g.*, 15 U.S.C. §§ 1261-74 (1970). Such regulation I would call postcontract disclosure regulation.

133. Changes in the rate of per capita cigarette consumption after the emergence and then disappearance of antismoking spot announcements on television are discussed in Capital Broadcasting Co. v. Mitchell, 333 F. Supp. 582, 587-90 (D.D.C. 1971) (Wright, J., dissenting), *aff'd mem.*, 405 U.S. 1000 (1972). Briefly, although compulsory health hazard labeling apparently had little effect on cigarette consumption, the antismoking television announcements seem to have had significant effect.

label, it will look like the fine print in a contract and undoubtedly be ignored by most consumers. On the whole, however, there is not now enough information to assess the impact of this type of disclosure.[134]

c. *Compulsory advertising*

Media advertising is the most obvious means of communicating effectively with consumers before they make their effective purchase decisions. Judging by the amount of resources they devote to it, sellers find advertising to be a very effective means for persuading consumers to act in desired ways. Traditionally, regulation of advertising in this country has not required the disclosure of specified information but rather has forbidden the disclosure of information considered false and misleading. Infrequently, the nondisclosure of a material fact in the course of an advertisement about a particular aspect of a product or service has been considered a violation of the false-and-misleading standard. On these occasions the advertiser has been required affirmatively to disclose the material fact if he continues advertising that particular aspect of his product or service.[135]

Some recent legislation has adopted an expanded but essentially similar approach to affirmative disclosure in advertising. For example, although the principal thrust of the proposed federal warranties legislation was to require disclosure of the warranty details in the written contract itself, the bill would have also authorized the Federal Trade Commission to establish rules determining "the manner and form in which information with respect to any written warranty shall be clearly and conspicuously presented or displayed when such information is contained in advertising, labeling, point-of-sale material, or other representations in writing."[136] Similarly, truth-in-lending requires a lender or credit seller to include, among other things, the annual percentage rate in almost any advertising in which he states other terms of the credit arrangements he offers.[137]

One risk in using this technique for compelling disclosure in advertising is that the advertiser can avoid the duty to disclose simply by refraining from stating anything in its advertising about the aspect of the product or service to which the disclosure relates. Thus, it is widely conceded that at least the shortrun effect of the

134. It should be noted that several Western European countries have adopted rather extensive labeling programs (in England called a "teltag") and consequently comparative research might provide useful information about potential impact of labeling regulation. *See* Trade Descriptions Act 1968, c. 29, § 8; P. KEETON & R. SHAPO, PRODUCTS AND THE CONSUMER: DECEPTIVE PRACTICES 622-28 (1972).

135. *E.g.*, J.B. Williams Co. v. FTC, 381 F.2d 884 (6th Cir. 1967).

136. S. 986, 92d Cong., 1st Sess. § 102(b) (1971).

137. Truth in Lending Act §§ 141-45, 15 U.S.C. §§ 1661-65 (1970).

truth-in-lending provisions concerning advertising has been to discourage the advertising of credit terms altogether, and thus to deprive most consumers of almost any pretransaction information about credit.[138]

The reasons that truth-in-lending's advertising provisions have had this effect are not clear. Some have suggested that advertisers fear consumers would be shocked by the size of the annual percentage rate, since, prior to truth-in-lending, interest rates tended to be quoted in manners which suggested a lower rate. Consequently, advertisers refrain from stating the annual percentage rate (and therefore from stating other credit terms as well) in order not to scare off potential customers.[139] Others have suggested that advertisers believe that advertising which contains a great amount of detail, as required by truth-in-lending, is not effective because the consumer essentially remembers nothing about the advertisement.[140] To the extent this latter possibility accounts for the lack of credit advertising, it could be overcome, of course, by structuring the advertising regulation so as not to require disclosure of so much detail. On the other hand, simplifying the information to be disclosed limits the amount of information that can be communicated and in that way can limit the ability of disclosure regulation to have the desired impact.

The possible explanation mentioned first for the reaction to truth-in-lending's credit advertising provisions suggests a more serious limitation on this technique of disclosure regulation, for disclosure regulation inevitably compels disclosure of information that at least many sellers consider unfavorable. Since all disclosure regulation relates just to certain aspects of a product or service, advertisers will usually find it feasible to redirect their advertising to aspects of their product or service other than those to which the disclosure regulation relates. Thus, I expect that much of the proposed regulation of warranty advertising would have been avoided by advertisers choosing not to discuss warranties in their advertising.

One way to overcome the risk that disclosure regulation pertaining to advertising will be avoided is to compel sellers to advertise

138. *E.g.*, 1970 Annual Report, *supra* note 32, at 23-24. This reduction in credit advertising has been a mixed blessing. While informative credit advertising has been sharply reduced, so has advertising, such as "no downpayment," which may tend to mislead consumers by implying that credit is inexpensive. *See* R. Pullen, *supra* note 26, at 21-24. For a discussion of the competitive impact of the reduction in credit advertising see *id.* at 24-29. Recently the Board of Governors of the Federal Reserve System indicated that "there are informal indications that the use of more specific [credit] advertising is increasing," although it did not identify what those indications are. 1971 Annual Report, *supra* note 30, at 17.

139. R. Pullen, *supra* note 26, at 23.

140. *Cf.* 1970 Annual Report, *supra* note 32, at 23-24.

certain information about their products. Compulsory media advertising of consumer products or services is largely unknown in this country. The proposed federal legislation on warranties took a step in this direction by providing that sellers issuing a "full" warranty "attempt in good faith to cause the disclosure of the duration of the warranty period . . . to the purchaser prior to the time of purchase through advertising, by providing point-of-sale materials, or by other reasonable means."[141] The provision, qualified as it was by the "attempt in good faith" and "other reasonable means" language, may not have actually required a seller to advertise very much, and in any event it applied only to sellers who offered comprehensive—in the terms of the bill, "full"—warranties.[142] Sellers offering partial or no warranties did not need to disclose that fact except in the written contract.

The Federal Trade Commission's current development of the "corrective advertising" remedy represents another, and perhaps more significant, step in the direction of compelling disclosure through advertising. The corrective advertising remedy has yet to be upheld in court. If it is sustained, it would permit the Commission to require advertisers found to have engaged in false and misleading advertising to include in future advertising a statement indicating that particular past advertising has been found to be false, or at least a statement contradicting earlier assertions that the Commission has found to be false and misleading. Perhaps both statements will be required.[143]

141. S. 986, 92d Cong., 1st Sess. § 103(a)(1) (1971).

142. *See id.* §§ 101(10)(a), 104(a). The National Commission on Consumer Finance considered and explicitly rejected a suggestion that creditors include their annual percentage rate in any advertising, whether or not it contained any other mention of credit terms. COMMISSION REPORT, *supra* note 29, at 188. Since nearly all creditors advertise to some extent, the suggestion in effect was for compulsory advertising.

143. For a discussion of the Commission's use of the corrective advertising remedy see Note, *"Corrective Advertising" Orders of the Federal Trade Commission*, 85 HARV. L. REV. 477 (1971). The Commission clearly asserted its power to use the remedy, although holding it inapplicable on the facts of the case, in Firestone Tire & Rubber Co., 3 TRADE REG. REP. ¶ 20,112 (FTC Sept. 22, 1972). The Commission has yet to apply the remedy in a contested case. Several consent orders have been entered, however, in which the advertiser agreed to place "corrective" advertisements. The text of these advertisements has often been stipulated in the order and uniformly they have provided for a much milder "confession of error" than was indicated by the proposed order contained in the complaint. *Compare, e.g.*, Ocean Spray Cranberries, Inc., 3 TRADE REG. REP. ¶ 19,981 (FTC March 2, 1972) (provisional consent order), *with* Ocean Spray Cranberries, Inc., 3 TRADE REG. REP. ¶ 19,477 (FTC Feb. 11, 1971) (proposed complaint).

Actually, as the proposed remedy has usually been formulated in complaints, it has not beeen technically a compulsory advertising requirement, since the advertiser has been given the option to stop advertising altogether. The Commission has made it very clear, however, that it considers the option illusory. To exercise the option, the advertiser must

Even if the Federal Trade Commission's authority to direct corrective advertsing is sustained, it will not provide a legal basis for directing compulsory advertising of all types. The Commission's primary rationale for corrective advertising is that it is needed to counteract the lingering effect of earlier deceptive advertising.[144] Under existing legislation, it seems inevitable that the courts, if they sustain the Commission at all, will restrict the Commission's power to compel advertising to situations indicated by the latter's rationale—that is, to where there has initially been deceptive advertising. Nevertheless, experience with the corrective advertising remedy may provide useful information on the ability of compulsory advertising to affect consumers' purchasing decisions.

It should be noted that even if compulsory advertising is found to be an effective way to "market" information to consumers, there are other problems that can hinder use. Probably the most important is cost. Unless, as generally with corrective advertising, compulsory advertising can be made part of advertising the seller would undertake in any event, it will significantly increase the seller's direct costs of compliance with disclosure regulation. In this connection it should be noted that disclosure regulation through media advertising is a costly communication technique in part because the disclosure will be addressed to many people who in no event would have purchased the good or service to which the disclosure relates.[145] Moreover, there is no assurance, absent truly massive advertising, that the disclosure will reach all consumers who are contemplating a purchase. Individual sellers typically use media advertising despite this inefficiency because it is the only practical way to communicate with prospective purchasers who will not otherwise frequent their place of business. By requiring point-of-sale disclosure by all sellers, however, disclosure regulation may be able to insure at much less cost that the information will reach

stop all advertising; he cannot avoid the confession of past deception simply by switching his advertising to other aspects of his product. The Commission clearly believes that today no major seller of goods or services can afford to cease advertising entirely. In the one case in which the Commission believed that the option not to advertise was a viable one, since the advertiser was a trade association promoting the general use of sugar, the Commission's proposed order did not allow the option. Sugar Association, Inc., 3 TRADE REG. REP. ¶ 19,857 (FTC Dec. 2, 1971) (proposed complaint).

144. *See* Firestone Tire & Rubber Co., 3 TRADE REG. REP. ¶ 20,112, at 22,083-85 (FTC Sept. 22, 1972). Other rationales offered include: (1) corrective advertising redresses any competitive imbalance caused by the illegal conduct of one company in the market-place to the detriment of companies which did not engage in similar illegal conduct; and (2) corrective advertising represents an attempt to deprive malefactors of the illegal fruit gained by their unlawful conduct. *See* Note, *"Corrective Advertising" Orders of the Federal Trade Commission, supra* note 143, at 493-95.

145. *See* Travers, *supra* note 21, at 556.

all or most consumers who should receive it. On the other hand, compulsory media advertising may be much more effective than point-of-sale disclosure in encouraging comparative shopping, because it reduces the search time needed by a consumer to acquire comparable information about a large number of competing products or services. The conclusions suggested that when disclosure regulation seeks primarily to induce comparative shopping, compulsory media advertising should be considered. But when the primary goal of the regulation is to discourage any consumption of the product or service, point-of-sale materials may generally be a more efficient technique of disclosure. This is providing—and this is a very important caveat—that techniques of disclosure regulation through point-of-sale materials can be developed that communicate information in fact and before most consumers make an effective decision to purchase.

### d. *Disclosure during preagreement negotiations*

Everyday experience teaches us that effective agreement in the vast majority of consumer transactions is reached orally. It would seem logical, therefore, to require disclosure during these negotiations if at all possible. It may also be that such disclosure would be most effective if it were in an oral form. Sellers often seem to choose that form for the messages they believe are most likely to influence consumer decisionmaking.

There are problems with any requirement of disclosure during preagreement negotiations. Enforcement is likely to be difficult, since it may often require an assessment of the credibility of a seller's and a consumer's conflicting versions of their negotiations. Perhaps some technique for eavesdropping randomly on negotiations while in progress would effectively induce compliance, but there are many obvious objections to use of this enforcement technique.

Furthermore, a seller probably could lessen the impact of preagreement disclosures, particularly oral disclosures, by his tone of voice or by explaining away the significance of the disclosure. It would appear to be very difficult to devise standards for controlling these devices for evading the spirit of the disclosure regulation. Finally, it may prove difficult to define the time period during oral negotiations at which the disclosure should occur in order to insure that it occurs before effective agreement.

Although there are difficulties in enforcement, the potential advantages of requiring disclosure, perhaps orally, at the time of oral negotiations suggest the need for experimentation. Probably the most evident advantage is the timing of the disclosure. Such disclosure, coming before the effective agreement, avoids the difficulty of overcoming the consumer's prior commitment to the transaction, yet it comes not so early, as may be the case with much media advertising, that the consumer has forgotten the disclosed information by the time of the purchase decision. Research may also show that such disclosure is more likely than other forms to induce understanding and appreciation of the disclosed information, partly because there is an opportunity to ask questions about parts of the disclosure not understood, and partly because there may be a greater likelihood that the consumer's attention will be focused on the disclosure than it would be if the disclosure was made by media advertising.

Oral disclosure during preagreement negotiations may be a particularly effective technique for communicating information to low-income consumers. Many low-income persons in this country have substandard reading abilities. Moreover, there is some evidence that low-income consumers are more likely than other consumers to rely on personal relationships with sellers, instead of media advertising and other sources of information, in making purchase decisions.[146]

These latter considerations apparently have played an important role in the Federal Trade Commission's decision on a few occasions to require preagreement oral disclosures by merchants selling primarily to low-income consumers.[147] These decisions by the Federal Trade Commission are among the apparently very few instances in which disclosure during preagreement negotiations has been required.[148] Unfortunately, no effort has been made to determine the efficacy of these few examples, either in terms of ease of enforcement or of effect on consumer decisionmaking.

A survey of new car buyers that I conducted several years ago yielded some data relevant to determining whether consumers are

146. *See* D. CAPLOVITZ, *supra* note 81.

147. *E.g.*, Tashof v. FTC, 437 F.2d 707 (D.C. Cir. 1970). In its report on its pilot consumer protection program in the District of Columbia, out of which the *Tashof* case arose, the Federal Trade Commission explained that it began requiring oral as well as written disclosures "on the theory that most consumers, and especially low income consumers, will not be really aware of . . . written disclosure in a conditional sale contract, regardless of its conspicuousness." FEDERAL TRADE COMM'N REPORT ON THE DISTRICT OF COLUMBIA CONSUMER PROTECTION PROGRAM 10 (1967). The report makes no mention of the problem in enforcing oral disclosure requirements.

148. One area in which a preagreement disclosure requirement is becoming increasingly common is in the regulation of door-to-door sales. A number of states now require such sellers to identify their purpose upon initial contact with a prospective customer. *E.g.*, WIS. AD. CODE § AG 127.02 (1972).

Although not an example of disclosure during preagreement negotiations, the Federal Trade Commission's proposed trade regulation rule on door-to-door sales would require a seller to inform the buyer orally of his right to cancel the contract without liability within 3 days of signing the contract. 37 Fed. Reg. 22,934 (1972). The FTC has postponed the effective date of this rule pending the outcome of current litigation about whether the Commission possesses rulemaking power. *Id.* at 22,961.

more likely to learn through oral rather than written disclosure.[149] When a consumer buys a car, it is fairly common for the selling dealer to explain orally many of the conditions and limitations on the coverage of the express warranty to repair or replace defective parts. The explanation is typically made at the time the car is delivered to the consumer, which is after the consumer has signed a contract and committed himself to the purchase.[150] Consequently, my survey could not test the effectiveness of disclosure during preagreement negotiations on purchasing behavior.

On the basis of responses to questions testing understanding of the warranty 4 to 6 months after purchase, I was able to categorize most of the survey respondents as at that time understanding the warranty quite well, about average, or poorly.[151] The table below illustrates the warranty knowledge level for both respondents who had received an oral explanation and for those who had not. In constructing this table, I have eliminated those repondents who prior to the interview had experienced difficulty in obtaining a warranty repair to which, at least initially, they thought they were entitled, since that experience must often be an educational one in itself.[152]

149. The survey is described in Whitford, *supra* note 17, at 1010-13. The survey was conducted by the Wisconsin Survey Research Laboratory with funds provided by Consumers Union, Walter H. Meyer Institute of Law, and the University of Wisconsin Graduate School. Mr. Peter Wolfe has helped me with the data analysis that is discussed subsequently in the text.

150. The oral explanation is given in hopes that better understanding of the warranty will reduce the number of subsequent disputes about warranty coverage arising because of owner misunderstanding of the warranty provisions. *Id.* at 1049-51.

151. The results for the individual questions testing knowledge of specific warranty provisions are published in *id.* at 1055. In constructing an overall knowledge score for each respondent, I weighted the answers to the individual questions according to my own judgment as to the importance of the warranty provision. Answers to the question concerning clutch repairs were not weighted at all, since this question was not asked of all respondents. In some instances partial credit was given for an answer that revealed knowledge about a warranty provision that I considered important, even though the answer was incorrect in some particulars. Consequently, the overall knowledge score is essentially an arbitrary construct.

152. Primarily because the number of respondents to the survey was low, more refined controls, such as by income and educational achievement, proved infeasible. *See* note 154 *infra*. It should be noted that, although I have eliminated those respondents who experience difficulty in obtaining a warranty repair, many of the respondents included in the table had occasion to request a warranty repair and received it without difficulty. That experience as well may often have been an educational one. If those respondents are eliminated, although the remaining size of the sample becomes quite small, the distribution of knowledge levels among those who received and did not receive oral explanations remains about the same, as is illustrated by the following table:

WARRANTY KNOWLEDGE ACCORDING TO WHETHER RESPONDENT RECEIVED ORAL EXPLANATION—IN PERCENTAGE

| | RECEIVED ORAL EXPLANATION | | | |
|---|---|---|---|---|
| | YES | | NO | |
| KNOWLEDGE LEVEL | | | | |
| Low | 25.0 | | 31.9 | |
| Medium | 52.3 | | 52.1 | |
| High | 22.7 | | 16.0 | |
| | 100.0 | (n = 128) | 100.0 | (n = 94) |

The differences in knowledge level illustrated in the table are not great, and certainly not great enough to be statistically significant.[153] Indeed, they tend to suggest that oral explanations have only a marginal affect on awareness. Moreover, basically because of the low number of respondents, it has not been possible to make meaningful determination whether oral explanation has a differential effect on consumers of differing levels of income and education.[154] Nevertheless, the results are consistent with a hypothesis that an oral explanation of warranty terms helps some con-

| KNOWLEDGE LEVEL—IN PERCENTAGE | RECEIVED ORAL EXPLANATION | | | |
|---|---|---|---|---|
| | YES | | NO | |
| Low | 23.9 | | 30.8 | |
| Medium | 53.5 | | 57.7 | |
| High | 22.5 | | 11.5 | |
| | 99.9 | (n = 71) | 100.0 | (n = 52) |

153. $X^2$ (Chi-Square) (2 d.f.) = 2.16, $p < .5$. For a discussion of the Chi-Square test of statistical significance see Whitford, *supra* note 17, at 1056 n.121.

154. Knowledge score did correlate significantly with level of educational achievement ($X^2$ [4 d.f.] = 26.23, $p < .005$), although not with size of personal income. Efforts were made to control for level of income and educational achievement to see if some income or education groups were benefited more by oral explanations than others, and one finding of statistical significance was discovered. High school graduates who received oral explanations were found to have significantly higher knowledge scores than those who did not. $X^2$ (2 d.f.) = 6.17, $p < .05$. No similar significant or near significant relationships between knowledge score and oral explanation were found for respondents with different levels of educational achievement, however, nor did controlling for level of income yield significant correlations between knowledge score and oral explanation. Consequently, it would be a mistake to attach too much importance to the isolated finding for high school graduates. Neither, of course, can the possibility that oral explanation has differing impact on knowledge score for different income and educational levels be discounted.

It should be noted the knowledge score correlated significantly with a number of factors besides education—for example, with self-evaluation of knowledge of the mechanical workings of an automobile. These other groups who performed well on the knowledge test received oral explanations with almost precisely the same frequency as the total sample population, however.

sumers learn and suggests the need for further research on the effectiveness of oral disclosure, particularly during preagreement negotiations.

In summary, there have been few attempts to require disclosure during oral negotiations preceding a sale, although commonsense assumptions about the processes by which many consumers reach purchase decisions suggest this could be an effective time for disclosure. Further research and experimentation with both oral and written disclosure at this time seems advisable.

### 3. NONSELLER DISCLOSURE

#### a. *Consumer education*

Nonseller disclosure regulation can either directly provide consumers with product information and encourage them to use it or focus principally on persuading consumers to use information that is provided through seller disclosure. Consumer education is a technique that usually concentrates on the latter approach. Although consumer education seems to be everybody's ultimate solution to consumer problems, and programs of various types have existed for years, it is obvious that many more resources could be devoted to this effort. Moreover, disclosure regulation providing for seller disclosure can importantly aid in the success of consumer education programs by standardizing methods of reporting information (such as interest rates). This will make it easier for consumers to understand and to shop comparatively on the basis of that information.[155]

Furthermore, consumer education need not be limited to formal classes. Government and other nonseller agencies can prepare pamphlets, or public service announcements for use on the broadcast media, that encourage consumers to use particular purchase information. Newspapers and magazines frequently print articles of similar import. And, it should be noted, in connection with truth-in-lending the government has used all these avenues in seeking to promote use of information disclosed by sellers as a result of that legislation.[156]

#### b. *Advertising substantiation*

One of the most recent examples of a nonseller disclosure program that directly provides consumers with product information is the Federal Trade Commission's advertising substantiation pro-

155. *See* note 100 *supra*. The proposed federal warranties legislation would perform a similar function. *See* notes 18-20 *supra* and accompanying text.

156. *See* 1970 Annual Report, *supra* note 32, at 14-16. Of course, much more extensive use of these communication techniques is possible, and probably desirable.

gram.[157] Under this program, the Commission has required leading manufacturers in various industries to submit whatever technical documentation they have for various advertising claims selected by the Commission.[158] Many of the product claims for which documentation has been requested are claims that would be relevant to a consumer acting in accordance with the best buy model. The Commission has then made the submitted documentation available for public inspection at its regional offices.[159] Although the Commission regularly states it may initiate a proceeding for deceptive advertising in any instance in which the documentation fails to substantiate the advertising claim,[160] it is evident the program has other important purposes, one of which is to provide consumers with more product information.[161]

A major difficulty with this program has been that the information provided is usually technical and difficult to understand.[162] Furthermore, at the time of this writing, the Commission

157. For the Commission's formal announcement of this program, including a brief statement of purposes, see 36 Fed. Reg. 12,058 (1971). For a full report on the program, including an analysis of submissions by advertisers pursuant to the program, see STAFF OF THE BUREAU OF CONSUMER PROTECTION, FEDERAL TRADE COMM'N, REPORT TO THE FEDERAL TRADE COMM'N ON THE AD SUBSTANTIATION PROGRAM (printed by the Senate Comm. on Commerce, 92d Cong., 2d Sess., 1972) [hereinafter cited as STAFF REPORT].

158. The automobile industry was the first one asked to substantiate its advertising. 3 TRADE REG. REP. ¶ 19,698 (FTC July 13, 1971). Since then various manufacturers in several other industries have been asked to submit documentation for selected advertising claims. *E.g.*, 3 TRADE REG. REP. ¶¶ 19,828 (FTC Oct. 14, 1971) (televisions and air conditioners); 19,879 (FTC Dec. 22, 1971) (dentifrices); 20,040 (FTC June 28, 1972) (soaps and other detergent products).

159. The Commission, of course, will refrain from publicizing trade secrets, but it reserves the right to make its own judgment whether substantiating material submitted contains trade secrets. *See* STAFF REPORT, *supra* note 157, at 15.

160. The first proposed complaints to arise out of the advertising substantiation program were announced October 12, 1972. Fedders Corp., 3 TRADE REG. REP. ¶ 20,120 (FTC Oct. 12, 1972) (proposed complaints). The proposed complaints are premised in part on the theory that whether or not the advertising claims were "deceptive," it was an "unfair" trade practice to make claims without having available adequate substantiating data prior to the making of the claims. *See* Pfizer, Inc., 3 TRADE REG. REP. ¶ 20,056 at 22,031-33 (FTC July 11, 1972). The Supreme Court recently upheld the authority of the Commission to prohibit "unfair" trade practices even though they are not "deceptive" in the traditional sense. FTC v. Sperry & Hutchinson Co., 405 U.S. 233, 239-44 (1972).

161. *See* STAFF REPORT, *supra* note 157 *passim*. Chairman Kirkpatrick of the Commission consistently opposed a proposed Truth in Advertising Act, S. 1461, 92d Cong., 1st Sess. (1971), that would have required advertisers to provide substantiation for advertising claims to any individual who requested it. Kirkpatrick attributed similar purposes to the Commission's program and to the proposed act and felt that more time was needed to evaluate the Commission's own program. BNA ANTITRUST & TRADE REG. REP., May 16, 1972, at A-19.

162. The FTC staff mailed a questionnaire to 45 persons, mostly consumers or members of consumer-oriented groups, who sought access to the

has not devised ways to make the information easily available to consumers.[163] Even if these difficulties were overcome, however, information is provided only about product characteristics which the manufacturer chooses to advertise. Since manufacturers frequently choose to say nothing in their advertising about many product characteristics, there is no way this program can be designed to insure that consumers receive the same kind of information about all products of the same type. It is the latter type of information, of course, that best facilitates comparison shopping.

c. *Product information systems*

To promote better comparison shopping, there has been some discussion in recent years of establishing systems which would provide consumers, at their request, with easily understood comparative product information of various kinds. One of the many organizations associated with Ralph Nader reportedly has drafted plans for such a system. The product information would be stored on computers and provided to consumers, for a small fee to cover operational expenses, through computer outlets scattered throughout the country.[164] Systems such as these would extend the idea underlying *Consumer Reports* magazine by making product information more widely available than does that magazine. In a few places, private companies are now providing similar information, for a fee, to prospective new car purchasers.[165] There is no information available on the actual or potential impact of these programs on consumer buying behavior. I would hypothesize that these programs will have only modest impact until accompanied by

materials submitted by the automobile manufacturers. Only 13 responses were received and of this number, only one thought studying the submissions would be useful; the others agreed that the submissions were too technical to be understood by the layman. STAFF REPORT, *supra* note 157, at 11.

163. The Commission staff hopes that various groups will study the submissions and publish their conclusions in easily understood and widely distributed pamphlets. *Id.* at 12. Recently the Institute for Public Interest Representation at Georgetown University Law Center prepared a simplified analysis of the substantiating material concerning television sets, and the analysis was published by the Senate Committee on Commerce. SENATE COMM. ON COMMERCE, 92D CONG., 2D SESS., ADVERTISING FOR TELEVISION SETS: A PUBLIC INTEREST EVALUATION (Comm. Print 1972). It is not known how widely this report has been distributed.

164. I have never seen this information published but it has been reported to me in personal interviews with several reliable sources. A model for such a system is described in Baran, *Some Changes in Information Technology Affecting Marketing in the Year 2000*, in CHANGING MARKETING SYSTEMS: CONSUMER, CORPORATE AND GOVERNMENT INTERFACES 76 (R. Moyer ed. 1968).

165. The basic information provided is the cost of the new automobile to the dealer. This enables the prospective purchaser to estimate the lowest price he should be able to obtain. See OF CONSUMING INTEREST, April 5, 1972, at 5.

consumer education and other programs to encourage consumers to use the information.

*d. Counteradvertising*

Probably the best known proposal for nonseller disclosure is the effort by various "public interest" groups to use the Federal Communication Commission's "fairness" doctrine to require broadcasting stations to broadcast "counteradvertising" messages rebutting various claims made in broadcast product advertising. Recent efforts[166] to develop this technique of nonseller disclosure began with *Banzhaf v. FCC*,[167] in which the courts upheld a Federal Communications Commission determination that cigarette advertising raised a "controversial issue of public importance"—namely the desirability of cigarette smoking—and consequently that broadcasting stations carrying such advertising had a duty under the fairness doctrine to broadcast other views on the issue.

The result of *Banzhaf* was the appearance of many spot announcements ("counterads") pointing to the health hazards of smoking.[168]

166. The earliest application of the fairness doctrine to product advertising was in Sam Morris, 11 F.C.C. 197 (1946). Until Banzhaf v. FCC, 405 F.2d 1082 (D.C. Cir. 1968), *cert. denied*, 396 U.S. 842 (1969), however, there were few applications of the doctrine to commercial advertising. The fairness doctrine itself has no explicit statutory basis but has been developed by the FCC as a specification of the "public interest" standard. Editorializing by Broadcast Licensees, 13 F.C.C. 1246 (1949). The United States Supreme Court recently approved the fairness doctrine in a case not concerning product advertising. Red Lion Broadcasting Co. v. FCC, 395 U.S. 367 (1969). For further discussion of the doctrine see Jaffe, *The Editorial Responsibility of the Broadcaster: Reflections on Fairness and Access*, 85 HARV. L. REV. 768 (1971); Comment, *And Now a Word Against Our Sponsor: Extending the FCC's Fairness Doctrine to Advertising*, 60 CALIF. L. REV. 1416 (1972).

167. 405 F.2d 1082 (D.C. Cir. 1968), *cert. denied*, 396 U.S. 842 (1969).

168. The Commission never explicitly compelled the broadcasting of spot announcements concerning the dangers of smoking, but the result of a series of FCC rulings following *Banzhaf* clearly induced broadcasters to choose that route to satisfy their fairness obligation. The FCC's original decision in the *Banzhaf* litigation had suggested that stations might accept an offer of the American Cancer Society to provide spot announcements. Television Station WCBS-TV, 8 F.C.C.2d 381, 382 (1967). On rehearing, the Commission indicated that although antismoking views are not entitled to "equal time" with cigarette commercials, the frequency of the appearance of cigarette commercials required "some regularity in the presentation on the other side of the issue." Television Station WCBS-TV, 9 F.C.C.2d 921, 941 (1967). A subsequent FCC decision established that a reasonable proportion of the antismoking presentations must be during prime time. National Broadcasting Co., 16 F.C.C.2d 956 (1969); *see* Comment, *And Now a Word Against Our Sponsor: Extending the FCC's Fairness Doctrine to Advertising*, *supra* note 166, at 1439-40.

It is important, in terms of remedy, to distinguish the "fairness" concept from the "equal time" concept. Under the latter concept, which applies primarily to the political candidates, broadcasting stations are required to offer equal time to all candidates on the same basis (paid or

These counterads were apparently quite effective. Cigarette consumption declined, both absolutely and per capita, during the period the counterads were broadcast.[169] When Congress, with tobacco industry support, banned cigarette advertising effective January 1, 1971,[170] most counterads left the air, and cigarette consumption again began to increase.[171]

Since *Banzhaf*, there has been considerable litigation testing the limits of the fairness doctrine's applicability to product advertising.[172] In *Banzhaf* both the FCC and the courts indicated the fairness doctrine did not apply generally to product advertising but that cigarettes presented a unique case because of the overriding concern for public health. The lack of a substantial logical basis for that conclusion has stimulated a number of attempts to extend the doctrine to other products, some of them successful. Most significantly, in *Friends of the Earth v. FCC*,[173] a court of appeals extended the *Banzhaf* rationale to product commercials for high horsepower cars and high test gasolines. By so doing, the court established the possibility that nearly all product advertising on broadcast media will create counteradvertising responsibilities under the fairness doctrine. The only recognized test is whether the commercial takes a position on a "controversial issue of public importance"—whatever that means.[174]

Another important question for the future of counteradvertising is the issue of remedy. Although following *Banzhaf* the FCC in effect compelled the use of spot announcements as the medium for presenting contrasting views, more recently it has seemed to

---

free). Under the "fairness" concept, however, if one viewpoint is presented in a paid broadcast, the station is required to present the other viewpoint even though there are no paying sponsors for those viewpoints. Cullman Broadcasting Co., 40 F.C.C. 576 (1963). Traditionally, however, there has been no requirement that equal time be allotted to each viewpoint. *See* Applicability of the Fairness Doctrine in the Handling of Controversial Issues of Public Importance, 40 F.C.C. 598, 606-08 (1964).

169. Capital Broadcasting Co. v. Mitchell, 333 F. Supp. 582, 587-90 (D.D.C. 1971) (Wright, J., dissenting), *aff'd mem.*, 405 U.S. 1000 (1972).

170. Public Health Cigarette Smoking Act of 1969 § 6, 15 U.S.C. § 1335 (1970).

171. Capital Broadcasting Co. v. Mitchell, 333 F. Supp. 582, 589 & n.18 (D.D.C. 1971) (Wright, J., dissenting), *aff'd mem.*, 405 U.S. 1000 (1972).

172. *E.g.*, Retail Stores Employees Union, Local 880 v. FCC, 436 F.2d 248 (D.C. Cir. 1970). For the best account of litigation concerning this extension of the fairness doctrine see Comment, *And Now a Word Against Our Sponsor: Extending the FCC's Fairness Doctrine to Advertising*, *supra* note 166.

173. 449 F.2d 1164 (D.C. Cir. 1971).

174. The court recognized the "thorny nature" of this problem, but left it to the Federal Communications Commission to resolve. *Id.* at 1170, 1171. The Commission has initiated a formal inquiry into this as well as other issues related to the fairness doctrine. Handling of Public Issues Under the Fairness Standard, 36 Fed. Reg. 11,825 (1971).

back away from that position.[175] And in *Friends of the Earth* the court suggested that even though the original advertisement raising the controversial issue was a spot commercial, the counterad need not necessarily be a spot commercial. The court strongly hinted that a few minutes devoted to the issue in the course of a documentary program might suffice, although it remanded the proceeding to the FCC for final determination of the manner in which the broadcaster should fulfill its "fairness" responsibility.

The future of counteradvertising as a disclosure technique remains unclear today. The counteradvertising concept has stimulated tremendous opposition in the advertising and broadcasting industries, as well as by the White House.[176] The reasons for their opposition are not altogether clear, but realistically it probably will retard the development of counteradvertising in the near future. Even if the concept of counteradvertising were to be fully developed, it would not, of course, be the complete answer to problems of precontract disclosure regulation. Under the FCC's fairness doctrine, the duty to present all sides of a controversial issue arises only after a station has broadcast one viewpoint. Counteradvertising might be avoided, therefore, by diverting advertising to print media, which is not subject to the Federal Communications Act and hence to the fairness doctrine.[177] Alternatively, depending in part on what types of advertising are ultimately determined to raise controversial issues of public importance, avoidance could be accomplished by broadcasting only innocuous advertising—for example, a jingle.[178] Because of the avoidance potential, it would be

175. *See* note 168 *supra*; National Broadcasting Co., 30 F.C.C.2d 643 (1971).

176. *See, e.g.*, N.Y. Times, March 29, 1972, at 87, col. 1; *id.*, May 16, 1972, at 67, col. 3. Much of the opposition has been directed at a Federal Trade Commission statement submitted in the Federal Communications Commission's inquiry into the fairness doctrine. *See* note 174 *supra*. The Federal Trade Commission statement supported a counteradvertising requirement in certain circumstances. N.Y. Times, Jan. 7, 1972, at 6, col. 3. A major reason for the opposition, of course, is the potential financial impact of counteradvertising on broadcasters. For a discussion of this impact see Comment, *And Now a Word Against Our Sponsor: Extending the FCC's Fairness Doctrine to Advertising*, *supra* note 166, at 1444-49.

177. Counterads can be expected to focus often on information relevant to the decision whether to buy a type of product at all, as in the cigarette case. Consequently, if one seller sponsors advertisements raising controversial issues about use of that product, counterads could frequently address themselves to issues pertaining to the purchase of all products of that type. Thus, in order to avoid counteradvertising entirely, all sellers would need to refrain from advertising on the broadcast media. A concerted decision not to advertise in the broadcast media may violate the antitrust laws. It may have been this consideration which prompted the tobacco industry not to oppose legislation prohibiting cigarette commercials on the broadcast media. *See* Capital Broadcasting Co. v. Mitchell, 333 F. Supp. 582, 588-89 (D.D.C. 1971) (Wright, J., dissenting), *aff'd mem.*, 405 U.S. 1000 (1972).

178. In Television Station WCBS-TV, 9 F.C.C.2d 921, 938-40 (1967), *aff'd*

a mistake to rely solely on counteradvertising as a technique of disclosure regulation, although it might be part of a comprehensive program of disclosure.

Moreover, viewed as disclosure regulation, counteradvertising differs from most other types in that governmental control of the content of the disclosure is not precise. A broadcasting station is only required to air a range of contrasting views. There is not even any assurance that counteradvertising will seek to persuade consumers to act consistently with the best buy model. To be sure, the FCC can regulate the content of the disclosures to some extent by determining whether there has been an adequate presentation of contrasting views.[179] But the FCC is not a body primarily concerned with or experienced in regulating the marketing of goods and services. It cannot be known what bearing this fact will have on the ultimate efficacy of counteradvertising as a disclosure technique, but there are obvious dangers that counteradvertising regulation will not be well coordinated with other government disclosure regulation.

*e. Summary*

As indicated by this discussion, there has been relatively little effort extended to date towards establishing programs of nonseller disclosure regulation. There is a particular lack of programs having as their principal purpose the provision of specific purchase information for all brands of a product in order to facilitate and encourage comparative shopping. Obviously some existing nonseller disclosure programs could be expanded and adapted to serve this latter purpose, and new ones could be established to serve this and other appropriate disclosure purposes.

4. COMPARISON OF SELLER AND NONSELLER DISCLOSURE

There is reason to believe such nonseller disclosure could be more effective and provide for fairer cost allocation than most seller disclosure programs. A principal advantage of nonseller disclosure is that the context in which the disclosure is made is not

*sub nom.*, Banzhaf v. FCC, 405 F.2d 1082 (D.C. Cir. 1968), *cert. denied*, 396 U.S. 842 (1969), the FCC took the position that cigarette commercials inevitably raised controversial issues by suggesting that cigarette consumption was desirable and that it was not necessary to examine each cigarette commercial to determine if it gave rise to fairness obligations. If the Commission adheres to this approach, advertisers will not find it easy to avoid counteradvertising in the manner suggested in the text.

179. In practice, under the fairness doctrine the broadcaster has, and probably must, be given considerable discretion in determining which contrasting views to present. *See* Applicability of the Fairness Doctrine in the Handling of Controversial Issues of Public Importance, 40 F.C.C. 598 (1964); *cf.* Republican Nat'l Comm., 25 F.C.C.2d 283 (1970), *rev'd sub nom*, Columbia Broadcasting Sys., Inc. v. FCC, 454 F.2d 1018 (D.C. Cir. 1971).

subject to the discretion of the seller. In many instances, of course, a seller will consider the making of a required disclosure contrary to his interests and be motivated to make it in a context which detracts from its impact on the consumer. Although legislation can prescribe the form of disclosure and thereby limit the seller's ability to detract from its effectiveness, some degree of discretion almost inevitably remains with the seller.[180] And for similar reasons it is probably not terribly useful to require sellers to accompany disclosure with prescribed statements explicitly encouraging consumers to use the information.[181] By providing for disclosure by a nonseller who is motivated to communicate information effectively, these problems can be mostly eliminated. Indeed, it is precisely this factor that accounts for the great interest in the counteradvertising concept.

Cost is the most significant among a number of disadvantages of extensive programs of nonseller disclosure. Disclosure by sellers generally imposes few direct costs on anybody, for usually the seller can satisfy the disclosure requirements by including the information in the course of communications he would normally direct at the consumer. A nonseller, however, usually must establish a new communications channel, and that can be expensive.[182] Indeed, the few efforts of the government to provide information directly to consumers have had little effect in large part because of the failure of the government to establish effective communication channels,[183] a failure that no doubt reflects in part a reluctance, perhaps justifiable, to make the necessary investment.

While nonseller disclosure will usually necessitate greater overall expenditures, it can permit an allocation of those costs in a more equitable manner than the costs of seller disclosure are often allocated. When sellers must absorb the initial costs of disclosure, they can be expected to pass on the costs to their customers if competitive conditions permit.[184] Assuming the disclosure regulation is normatively based, consumers who are persuaded by the disclosure not to purchase that type of product or service at all

180. *See* note 96 *supra* and accompanying text.

181. *See* text accompanying note 130 *supra*.

182. For an analysis of the ultimate incidence of the costs of existing programs of nonseller disclosure see note 190 *infra*.

183. *See* note 163 *supra* and accompanying text.

184. Even though all sellers of a particular product or service will usually be required to bear disclosure costs, it will not be feasible to raise the price if overall demand is especially price elastic, perhaps due to competition from substitute products or services not subject to the disclosure regulation. In such circumstances the seller will be required to absorb all or part of the disclosure costs, with a consequent reduction in profits. As a result, less investment can be anticipated in the affected industry, which may be an appropriate effect if the normative purpose of the disclosure regulation is to discourage use and development of the product or service.

will not bear any of the cost even though they have benefited from it, perhaps more than any other group of consumers. Similarly, consumers who are persuaded by seller disclosure to shop comparatively for products or services that are more advantageous in terms of the characteristics subject to compulsory disclosure will pay no greater proportion of the disclosure cost than purchasers of products or services of that type who are not persuaded. This is so even though the former group might be considered to have benefited from the disclosure more than the latter.[185]

In one sense, allocating some of the costs of disclosure to those who are unpersuaded is consistent with the purposes of normative disclosure regulation. The costs paid by those who make undesired purchases can be considered a disincentive to purchase in addition to the information disclosed. On the other hand, frequently the most important reason for adopting disclosure regulation rather than direct substantive regulation (such as prohibition of the sale of a product or service) is a recognition that some consumers will have appropriate reasons to purchase a product or service that for the most consumers would be considered an undesirable purchase.[186] It may be difficult to justify imposition of the disclosure costs on these consumers, since they benefit less than other consumers, or not at all, from disclosure, yet make buying decisions that are not socially disapproved. Furthermore, it is probably reasonable to expect even persuasive disclosure regulation to benefit middle and upper income consumers more than lower income consumers. Consequently, permitting the costs of disclosure to be borne ultimately by purchasers of the product or service can be seen as a form of regressive taxation.[187]

It needs to be emphasized that the total cost of many forms of seller disclosure is low. In these circumstances questions about the allocation of those costs are not really very important. But if compulsory advertising or other forms of seller disclosure that require substantial overall expenditures are used, then some measure for altering the usual incidence of these costs might be considered. Sellers could be reimbursed for disclosure costs out of general tax revenues. Alternatively, if nonseller disclosure was equal to or more efficient than seller disclosure in persuasive effectiveness and overall costs, a form of tax-supported nonseller disclosure

185. If the disclosure regulation is based on a predictive model, similar cost misallocations can occur. Presumably not all buyers of the product or service will use the disclosed information and others would have access to the information even without the regulation. Yet all buyers will be required to bear the costs of disclosure.

186. *See* note 125 *supra* and accompanying text.

187. Imposing the costs of disclosure initially on the seller can also increase the cost of entry into that market. Consequently, seller disclosure regulation can have some anticompetitive effects which may offset the procompetitive effects resulting from an increase in comparison shopping.

might be considered. Use of tax revenues to support disclosure could be justified on the grounds that the regulation is designed to achieve a public benefit—perhaps an enhancement of the quality of life.[188] If the disclosure regulation is designed to encourage competititon in oligopolistic markets,[189] a fairly compelling case can be made for public financial support.[190]

### 5. RESTRUCTURING THE CONSUMER ENVIRONMENT

There are wide varieties of ways in which the environment in which the consumer acts could be structured in the hope of enhancing the possibility that any existing inclinations favorable to the best buy model will be reflected in purchasing behavior. Consumer education programs, by essentially emphasizing that socially approved buying behavior requires utilization of the best buy model, probably perform this function. Another obvious strategy is to deter or limit the impact of communications to the consumer that are designed to persuade him to make purchase decisions on disfavored bases. Traditional prohibition of factually false advertising can be viewed as an example of this strategy.

188. *See* text following note 129 *supra*.

189. *See* notes 101-03 *supra* and accompanying text.

190. It should be noted that the two principal forms of nonseller disclosure that have actually been developed do not necessarily possess these cost allocation advantages. The Federal Trade Commission's advertising substantiation program imposes on the advertiser the often significant costs of gathering substantiating data and these costs presumably will be allocated in the same manner as the costs of seller disclosure. Presently there is very little dissemination of the substantiating data. Tax revenues could be used to support dissemination by the Commission itself. Current indications are, however, that the Commission will rely on nongovernmental "public interest" groups to disseminate the information. *See* note 163 *supra*. Still a third possibility would be for the Commission to sell the substantiating data to interested consumers, as one commercial firm already does. *See* STAFF REPORT, *supra* note 157, at 4. Charging the users of the information for the cost of dissemination is consistent with the goals of disclosure regulation based on predictive models, but it is not likely to yield wide enough dissemination to fulfill at all significantly the objectives of normatively based disclosure regulation.

The incidence of costs associated with counteradvertising is more complicated. Under the fairness doctrine, once one viewpoint on a controversial issue of public importance is presented, a broadcaster is required to present other views even though there are no paying sponsors for those views. *See* note 168 *supra*. The broadcaster can probably be expected to pass on much or most of these costs to advertisers. Perhaps the broadcasters will devise means to allocate the costs just to advertisers whose commercials create a duty to counteradvertise. If so, then those advertisers will have an extra incentive to avoid application of the fairness doctrine by diverting their advertising to the print media or by broadcasting advertisements—for example, jingles—that probably will not be interpreted as addressing controversial issues of public importance. To the extent sellers do not avoid counteradvertising costs in this manner, they presumably will be allocated in the same manner as the costs of seller disclosure. *See* notes 184-85 *supra* and accompanying text.

In this connection it is interesting to note the current speculations that the Federal Trade Commission will seek to enjoin much advertising that encourages purchasing decisions on the basis of various psychological needs, even though such advertising is not deceptive in any traditional sense.[191] Such advertising, of course, is essentially counterproductive to the goals presumed here for most precontract disclosure regulation. The implications of such an approach to advertising regulation are tremendous and well beyond the scope of this article. Suffice it to say here that, although such advertising regulation would be consistent with normative disclosure regulation prevailing notions about freedom of speech and freedom of contract would make it quite logical for government to adopt a policy of encouraging buying decisions on one basis while allowing others to encourage buying decisions on other bases.

Another common approach to inhibiting the impact of communications encouraging consumers to act in undesired ways is to provide for "cooling-off" periods after the conclusion of a transaction, during which a consumer can change his mind and cancel the transaction without liability. Both the federal Consumer Credit Protection Act (of which truth-in-lending is a part)[192] and several state enactments[193] already provide for "cooling-off" periods in a number of different types of transactions, typically transactions concluded away from the seller's principal place of business. Uniformly, the proffered justification for such legislation is that it will enable the consumer to reach a more "informed" purchase decision by giving him or her a longer period to contemplate its wisdom, and in particular by giving him or her time to contemplate while not being subjected to the blandishments of a salesman.[194] If one assumes that these blandishments more often than not encourage purchase decisions on other than the bases desired by most

191. *See* Comment, *Psychological Advertising: A New Area of FTC Regulation,* 1972 WIS. L. REV. 1097. Gerald Thain, currently head of the Division of National Advertising, Bureau of Competition, of the Federal Trade Commission, has been quoted as considering "unlawful advertising techniques which give the consumer a sense of involvement which cannot be achieved, such as ones that suggest assurance of social acceptance or appeal to the opposite sex, or ones that sell products to children by exploiting strongly held aspirations." OF CONSUMING INTEREST, April 25, 1971, at 3.

192. 15 U.S.C. § 1635 (1970).

193. The Wisconsin Consumer Act provides for a "cooling-off" period. WIS. STAT. §§ 423.201-.205 (1971). The Uniform Consumer Credit Code, now in effect in several states—see note 12 *supra*—also provides for one. UNIFORM CONSUMER CREDIT CODE § 2.501-.505. The Federal Trade Commission's proposed trade regulation rule on door-to-door sales, 37 Fed. Reg. 22,934 (1972), when and if it becomes effective, will impose a nationwide "cooling-off" period for door-to-door sales. *See also* note 148 *supra.*

194. *See* Sher, *The "Cooling-Off" Period in Door-to-Door Sales,* 15 U.C.L.A.L. REV. 717 (1968).

disclosure regulation—and at least for door-to-door sales there is some evidence that it does[195]—a "cooling-off" period could be expected to have desirable effects. Nearly all consumers give some weight in their purchase decisions to considerations indicated by the best buy model, and many will undoubtedly discount these considerations more than they otherwise would if a salesman is constantly emphasizing other factors. Moreover, if any relevant disclosure regulation provides for disclosure only in the written contract, a "cooling-off" period provides the consumer an opportunity to peruse the contract and absorb the disclosed information before he is irrevocably bound. In this sense, a "cooling-off" period can be part of a program to encourage use of information provided by seller disclosure.

It is very difficult to assess the impact of environment-creating efforts to influence consumer purchasing behavior. About the only evidence of which I am aware is one empirical study of the actual impact of a "cooling-off" period, which suggested it had little effect—at least if effect is measured by the number of cancellations that occur within the "cooling-off" period.[196] One of the reasons may be that "cooling-off" periods create a new disclosure regulation problem—informing consumers that they have a right to cancel within the specified period. Although nearly all legislation providing for "cooling-off" periods also provides for disclosure of the cancellation right, the apparently limited impact of such legislation may be attributable in important part to the manner in which such disclosure is required.[197]

## II. POSTCONTRACT DISCLOSURE REGULATION

### A. *Purposes*

In commentaries on compulsory disclosure as a technique of consumer protection regulation, little is ever said about the utility of disclosure in aiding the consumer in his postcontract activities.[198] After the contract is concluded, there is little, of course, that the consumer can do to insure that he gets the "best buy." But often there are actions he needs to take if he is to maximize his economic gain from the contract he entered. For example, frequently the contract requires the consumer to take certain actions in order to

195. *Id.* at 721-22; D. CAPLOVITZ, *supra* note 81, at ch. 2.

196. Comment, *A Case Study of the Impact of Consumer Legislation: The Elimination of Negotiability and the Cooling-Off Period,* 78 YALE L.J. 618 (1969). It has been suggested that a "cooling-off" period could induce salesmen to recast their sales pitch to be less misleading so that prospective customers will not have so much reason to become quickly disillusioned with the transaction. If it does, then, of course, the number of cancellations would not be a good measure of impact. *See* Sher, *supra* note 194, at 734-35.

197. *See id.* at 760-63.

198. *But see* Curran, *supra* note 25, at 426.

preserve his contract rights—a product warranty may require the consumer to procure maintenance regularly for the product and keep receipts as evidence thereof.[199]

If the consumer is to structure his postcontract activities so as to maximize his gain from the contract, he will need information that is not always easily available. To take actions required by the contract to preserve contractual rights, for example, the consumer needs to be aware of the contents of the contract. Assuming it is determined that, as it is desirable to encourage consumers to consider the "best buy," so it is desirable to encourage consumers to consider maximizing their contractual gain, disclosure regulation is indicated as a means of providing the needed information and encouraging consumers to use or consider it. Both the Wisconsin Consumer Act and the proposed federal warranties legislation contain some innovative attempts to provide the consumer with useful information of this type. Rather than merely requiring the seller to provide the consumer with a copy of the contract,[200] they require disclosure which emphasizes provisions of the contract that are particularly important to consider if the consumer is to plan his postcontract actions to maximize his contractual benefits. Thus, the warranties legislation would have authorized the Federal Trade Commission to promulgate rules requiring the seller to provide the consumer with the following information:

> A statement of what the purchaser must do and expenses he must bear.
>
> Exceptions and exclusions from the terms of the warranty.
>
> The step-by-step procedure which the purchaser should take in order to obtain performance of any obligation under the warranty . . . .
>
> . . . .
>
> The period of time within which, after notice of malfunction or defect, the warrantor will under normal circumstances repair, replace, or otherwise perform any obligations under the warranty.[201]

A second purpose of postcontract disclosure regulation can be to provide information that can assist a consumer when a seller breaches a contract. A consumer usually needs to take a number of actions in this situation in order to maximize his contractual

199. *See, e.g.*, Whitford, *supra* note 17, at 1014-15.

200. This requirement was a common feature in state retail installment sales acts, and one of the purposes of the provision was precisely to aid postcontract decisions. *See* Curran, *supra* note 25, at 425. It should be noted that sellers are sometimes motivated to disclose information that can aid postcontract decisions even in the absence of a requirement that they do so. *See* note 150 *supra*.

201. S. 986, 92d Cong., 1st Sess. § 102(a)(5)-(7), (9) (1972). For a provision of the same type in the Wisconsin Consumer Act see WIS. STAT. §§ 425.104-.105 (1971).

gain. But unless he takes some initiative, he almost certainly will not receive his due under the contract. Studies have demonstrated that many consumers, and especially low-income consumers, will not undertake any effective action in such circumstances to protect their rights. The reasons for this lack of initiative vary, but in many instances an important contributor is lack of knowledge, either about effective courses of action or that a breach has occurred.[202]

Some consumers may believe that their only recourse upon breach is in court, but feel that without a lawyer, who cannot feasibly be retained in view of the amount in dispute, they would not stand a chance there. Today, however, consumers very commonly have effective avenues of redress other than a *pro se* appearance in court. There are now many statutes providing a victorious consumer litigant with punitive damages and attorney's fees, and if one of these statutes is applicable, it may be much more feasible for the consumer to retain an attorney.[203] Informal consumer complaint mediation services of various kinds may also be available.[204]

Commentators have rarely indicated that this type of information is an appropriate subject for disclosure regulation, yet it is the type of information that will not usually be provided by the seller absent compulsion.[205] The proposed federal warranties legislation, if enacted, would have become one of the rare examples of disclosure regulation of this type. It would have authorized the Federal Trade Commission to adopt rules requiring the inclusion in the written warranty of the following information:

---

202. D. CAPLOVITZ, *supra* note 81, at ch. 2.

203. *See* Rice, *Exemplary Damages in Private Consumer Actions,* 55 IOWA L. REV. 307 (1969).

204. A wide variety of state and local agencies now mediate consumer complaints. The offices of state attorneys general frequently provide this service. *See* NATIONAL ASS'N OF ATTORNEYS GENERAL, STUDY OF THE OFFICE OF ATTORNEY GENERAL § 6.6 (1971). Various specialized state agencies provide similar services. In Wisconsin, for example, the Office of the Commissioner of Insurance has long mediated complaints by insureds against insurance companies. *See, e.g.,* OFFICE OF THE COMM'R OF INSURANCE, 1971 WISCONSIN INSURANCE REPORT 80-82 (1971). For a discussion of consumer complaint mediation at the county and municipal level see CONSUMERS UNION, REPORT ON NEW CITY AND COUNTY CONSUMER PROTECTION AGENCIES (1972). Of course, various better business bureaus and industry trade associations have long provided consumer complaint mediation services. *See generally* Eovaldi & Gestrin, *Justice For Consumers: The Mechanisms of Redress,* 66 NW. U.L. REV. 281 (1971).

205. There are some exceptions, of course. Both Ford Motor Company and Chrysler Corporation are currently engaging in advertising campaigns which emphasize internal corporate procedures for resolving consumer complaints about automobile repairs, and in particular warranty repairs. Even these advertisements do not mention avenues of redress outside the corporate structure, however. For a description of the automobile manufacturers' procedures in 1967 for resolving consumer complaints see Whitford, *supra* note 17, at 1023-24.

> The availability of any informal dispute settlement procedure offered by the warrantor . . . .
>
> A recital that any purchaser who successfully pursues his legal remedies in court may recover the reasonable costs incurred, including reasonable attorneys' fees.[206]

A second reason many consumers do not take initiative upon breach may be that they are simply unaware that a breach has occurred, either out of sheer ignorance of their contractual rights or due to acceptance of the seller's convincing but wrongful explanation that there is a legal basis for his action or inaction. The indicated remedy, of course, is to provide the consumer with information about his contractual rights. For this purpose, however, rather than emphasizing contract provisions which require the consumer to take particular actions to preserve his contractual benefits, disclosure should emphasize those obligations which the seller is most likely to breach, which are the most difficult to understand, or which are most likely to seriously harm the consumer.

### B. *Attractive Features of Postcontract Disclosure*

Although it has received scant attention from the commentators, in a number of important ways compulsory postcontract disclosure is an attractive type of regulation. The attractive features are best illustrated by comparing postcontract and precontract disclosure regulation. First, although there is an absence of relevant empirical evidence, I would anticipate that postcontract disclosure regulation is more likely to cause behavior change in consumers than is precontract disclosure regulation. In reaching a purchase decision, a consumer frequently balances a large and varied number of conflicting considerations, including desires for status, reassurance, shopping convenience, and to get the "best buy." Precontract disclosure regulation, designed to induce consumers to place primary emphasis on only some of these considerations, faces a substantial task of persuasion. In determining actions subsequent to the contract, however, I would hypothesize that for most consumers there are fewer considerations that conflict with a desire to maximize contractual gain.

A second advantage of postcontract disclosure regulation is a corollary of the first. Most precontract disclosure regulation neces-

---

206. S. 986, 92d Cong., 1st Sess. § 102(a)(10)-(11) (1971). Although a useful innovation, even more information could be included. For example, mention might be made of the many informal consumer complaint mediation facilities now provided by state and local governments, see note 204 *supra*, or the availability in many localities of small claims courts with simplified procedures to facilitate *pro se* appearances. Of course, small claims courts do not always provide fully adequate avenues of redress for consumers. *See, e.g.*, Note, *The Persecution and Intimidation of the Low-Income Litigant as Performed by the Small Claims Court in California*, 21 STAN. L. REV. 1657 (1969).

sitates a policy determination to encourage consumers to behave according to particular norms. The making of such judgments runs counter to the deeply held beliefs of many that the government should not make such judgments. Postcontract disclosure regulation probably raises less severe ideological problems of this nature. As I have argued above, it seems plausible to assume that a model of maximizing one's economic gain after contract formation is a closer approximation of the goals of large numbers of consumers than is the best buy model of the goals of consumers in deciding what to purchase. Consequently, with postcontract disclosure regulation it is easier for the government to assume the posture of providing consumers information they want and will use. Moreover, postcontract disclosure regulation for the purposes I have previously discussed is supported not only by a norm of encouraging consumers to maximize their contractual gains but also by the norm of protecting expectations based on contract. The latter is a long-held value in this society, a commitment to which is not likely to produce controversy at an ideological level.

A third, and probably the most important, attractive feature of postcontract disclosure regulation is the ease with which the manner and timing of disclosure can be structured so as to be reasonably sure most consumers' attention will be drawn to the disclosed information before they make whatever decision the disclosure is supposed to affect. Precontract disclosure regulation must somehow draw the consumer's attention to the information before he makes his effective purchase decision, a task previous discussion has indicated is neither easy nor costless. But postcontract disclosure need not be made until after the contract is signed, when the consumer is less likely to be barraged by other distracting information. Indeed, postcontract disclosure made substantially after the contract is concluded may be the most effective, since it is likely to come closer in time to when the consumer actually needs the information.[207]

Moreover, if the disclosure is made after the transaction is concluded, it seems probable that nonseller disclosure will have fewer advantages over seller disclosure than it does when disclo-

207. Sometimes the formulators of disclosure regulation will want to disclose information for both precontract and postcontract purposes. For example, perhaps an effort should be made to inform consumers before purchase of the mileage and/or time limitations on product warranties so that they can better evaluate the warranty's worth. Certainly the consumer should have this information after purchase so that he can insure that all possible warranty claims are made within the applicable limits. In such situations it is tempting to devise one disclosure to serve both purposes. Since disclosure after the contract is generally a more efficient technique for achieving postcontract purposes, however, and can be provided at little cost, it ordinarily will be more desirable to provide for two disclosures.

sure is made before contract formation. Since the seller will not risk loss of a sale by revealing the information, he will be less motivated to minimize orally the importance of the information.[208] And, for reasons previously discussed, seller disclosure is generally less costly than nonseller disclosure.[209] Finally, if large numbers of consumers are receptive and interested in postcontract disclosure, as I have argued is likely, it may be possible to include substantial detail in postcontract disclosure without running as great a risk as with precontract disclosure of discouraging consumers from reading the information because it is too inconvenient or time consuming to do so.

The proposed federal warranties legislation provided an excellent illustration of the greater flexibility and efficiency in seller disclosure techniques that are available if the disclosures to be required are intended to affect postcontract activities. The many examples I have given of postcontract disclosure that would have been required by this legislation were to be contained in the "written warranty."[210] The legislation did not prescribe the time at which the written warranty was to be provided to the consumer, but presumably it would have been at or near the time of the signing of the underlying sales contract.[211] The making of the disclosure at this time, which typically will be after the effective oral agreement to purchase, probably would not have deprived the postcontract disclosure regulation of impact, however.[212] Most consumers can be expected to keep the sales contract and warranty, perhaps peruse it in their leisure time, and in any event have it available when and if the information is needed.

The Wisconsin Consumer Act also contains several illustrations of the flexibility in the time and manner of disclosure permitted by postcontract disclosure regulation. A good example is contained in the Act's provisions on third-party freedom from consumer defenses. The Act prohibits the taking of a negotiable instrument,

208. *See generally* notes 95-96, 180-81 *supra* and accompanying text.

209. *See* notes 182-83 *supra* and accompanying text.

210. S. 986, 92d Cong., 1st Sess. § 102(a) (1971).

211. The Federal Trade Commission would have been granted rulemaking authority to prescribe the precise manner and timing of disclosure. *Id.* §§ 102(a), 109. If the bill had been enacted, the Commission would have been well advised to require disclosure of the postcontract information not only in the written warranty but also in the "Owner's Manual," since these manuals are customarily kept and read by new car buyers.

212. The proposed warranties legislation did not eschew precontract disclosure regulation entirely, of course. For this purpose, the legislation permitted the Federal Trade Commission to establish rules requiring the disclosure of much less detailed and simplified information in any advertising, labeling, or other effort to communicate with a prospective purchaser. *Id.* §§ 103(a)(1), 109. The legislation thus recognized the greater difficulty of effectively communicating detailed information prior to purchase and the inadvisability of providing for a single disclosure of information designed to affect both precontract and postcontract activities. *See* note 207 *supra*.

other than a check, in a consumer credit transaction,[213] but it does afford a limited effectiveness to clauses waiving consumer defenses against an assignee. In particular, certain assignees of the creditor are permitted to enforce the debt free of most defenses of which they do not receive notice within a 12-month period.[214] The 12-month period does not begin running until after the consumer receives both a written notification of assignment and a "clear and conspicuous" statement of the consequences of not notifying the assignee of any defenses within 12 months.[215] By requiring disclosure at this time the Act insures that the consumer receives needed postcontract information at a time close to when it will be needed.

## III. CONCLUSIONS

The major purpose of this article has been to analyze the contention of several commentators that disclosure regulation is essentially useless, because it has little or no impact on consumer behavior, especially the behavior of low-income consumers. This contention needs analysis since much of the major new consumer legislation, such as the proposed federal warranties legislation and the Wisconsin Consumer Act, relies substantially on disclosure regulation. And there is indeed considerable evidence to support the contention of the critics of disclosure regulation; at least much existing precontract disclosure regulation, such as truth-in-lending, has had little impact on consumer purchasing behavior. When the purposes of precontract disclosure regulation are analyzed closely, however, this conclusion is hardly surprising. It seems evident that most precontract disclosure regulation is formulated not on the belief—or at least not on the reasonable belief—that a large number of consumers want the information that must be disclosed, but rather on the belief that most consumers should use the information in making purchase decisions. Precontract disclosure regulation, therefore, usually faces the task not only of providing consumers with information but also of persuading consumers to use that information. Yet the manner of disclosure typically required —inclusion of information in the written contract—obviously can have little if any persuasive impact, particularly since it is not likely to be brought to the attention of consumers until after they have effectively made the very purchase decision it is supposed to affect. There is a need, consequently, if precontract disclosure regulation is ever to achieve its purpose, to develop new techniques for communicating the disclosed information to consumers.

In developing new communication techniques it must be recognized that consumers vary in their receptivity to different modes of communication. Only rarely should disclosure regulation rely,

213. WIS. STAT. § 422.406 (1971).
214. *Id.* § 422.407.
215. *Id.* §§ 422.407(2), 422.409(2).

for persuasive impact, on a single communication technique. And since empirical evidence pretty clearly indicates that low-income consumers are less likely to learn from, or be persuaded by, traditional communication techniques, special attention should be given to the development of communication techniques that will have impact on their purchasing behavior.

A second major conclusion I have reached concerns postcontract disclosure regulation—regulation designed to affect decisions consumers make after they enter into a contract. Commentators have usually not discussed the utility of this type of disclosure regulation. I have hypothesized, however, that, although there is an absence of relevant empirical data, it seems probable that postcontract disclosure regulation has greater potential than precontract regulation for actually affecting consumer decisions. Furthermore, it appears that it will be less costly to devise effective methods of communicating information intended to affect postcontract decisions. I would urge, therefore, that in the future greater attention be given to the development of postcontract disclosure regulation.

I should not close before noting two important points. This article is not intended to be a comprehensive analysis of all problems or issues associated with disclosure regulation. Much more research and discussion is needed, especially with regard to the development of effective but practical techniques for communicating information subject to disclosure regulation. Moreover, many of the conclusions I have reached perhaps are more properly considered only suggestions or hypotheses, given the substantial lack of empirical information about the impact of different types of disclosure regulation. There is a particular lack of empirical information about the impact of postcontract disclosure regulation.

Second, the critics of disclosure regulation are certainly correct when they argue that many supporters of such regulation, and in particular the supporters (and even the opponents) of truth-in-lending,[216] have vastly exaggerated its potential impact. The critics may also be correct in contending that disclosure regulation alone is not sufficient to satisfy the demand or need for more extensive consumer protection. Yet it is evident I would be disappointed if disclosure regulation were abandoned, or not further developed, as a technique of consumer protection. The case has yet to be made that disclosure regulation can have no significant impact. And even if disclosure regulation is viewed as having normative objectives, as I have argued it should be, it does have significant advantages over the other principal approach of consumer protection legislation—regulation of the substantive terms of transactions. It necessitates a less complete interference with freedom of contract, with all that implies.

216. *See* Note, *Truth in Lending: The Impossible Dream, supra* note 22; note 58 *supra*.

# [9]



## THE PONTIAC PROSPECTUS

*Arthur Allen Leff**

I have just, for the first time in eight years, bought a car. It wasn't a particularly ugly experience. I used Consumer Reports, word-of-mouth, pre-bargaining pep talks from my wife, and a great deal of anxiety and time. Maybe I got the right brand and model for my present needs, for about as good a price as I could expect. But I really can't tell; despite my compulsive care I simply could not get enough information to make a fully-educated choice. What I do now know is that the whole process of retail distribution of automobiles in America, upon which a large chunk of this country's retail sales directly or indirectly depend, could be easily, vastly, and inexpensively improved. Carrying out the idea, however, would demand some governmental coercion, and I've spent enough time looking at, say, welfare and public housing, to think that by now such governmental intervention always demands *some* justification, which I will presently try to supply. But let me say first what I think ought to be done, before explaining why.

What I propose is this: Let the government require that there be available each year, no later than the time when the new year's automobiles may be bought by the public, a "Prospectus" setting forth a huge amount of data about every vehicle sold by a particular manufacturer. Whatever this data is (and I'm coming to that), *it should be in such form as to make it easily comparable* with data about other vehicles, both of the same manufacture and others. The Prospectus should be available free in showrooms, and by mail for at most the cost of postage from the manufacturers and an agency of government. They should be so designed that a car shopper can gather a Prospectus from each manufacturer, put them together on the same table, and find data about the same thing on the same page of each.

### I. WHAT THE PROSPECTUS SHOULD CONTAIN

#### A. Mechanical Specifications and Performance Data

What should this Prospectus contain? Some things are easy. First, it should contain the measurable physical and mechanical specifications of the car. That is so easy to do that it's already done by each

* Professor of Law, Yale University. B.A. 1956, Amherst College; LL.B. 1959, Harvard University.

1. An alternative scheme would have all the information gathered in *one* prospectus. But the bulk of information involved, often about alternatives of no real interest to the particular buyer, makes that move ostentatiously unattractive, at least on first shuddering contemplation.

manufacturer, though generally model by model and at levels of completeness varying from the usual back-page box on the "car-in-the-meadow" brochure to Ford's send-for-it-specially big fat book. *Consumer Reports* does it pretty nicely for some proportion of all cars. All that would be necessary to effect this proposed extension would be to pick and standardize the categories and vocabulary of comparison. If the Securities and Exchange Commission can try that for financial statements (a harder job, by the way),[2] our own little "Automotive Marketing Board" (God protect us, I'm pushing another agency) can do it for the physical specs. The information is essentially free; it's a "by-product" of the manufacturing process which is presently thrown away, at least so far as consumers are concerned.[3] But to what may be a large number of consumers more engine-smart than me and my friends, such information could be of critical interest.

Then, of course, there should be performance characteristics. That's harder. A car is what it is. But it is also what it does, and it does so many different things that you can't specify its dynamic reality over the whole spectrum of potential possibility. It stops (or doesn't) on dry pavement and wet, from 60 mph and from 10, with twenty miles on the brakes and with twenty thousand. It corners at various speeds, tucks in at some speeds and out at others, and at still others goes straight through the guard rails. With you in the car it zaps; with you, your kids, and your fat inlaws along, it may yaw and wiggle. All you can do is choose some probabilities out of the welter of infinite possibility and put tested numbers on those. "Fully loaded", "pulling a trailer", and "just the driver" hardly describe all the states of being and becoming, even of a car; and while extrapolating and interpolating may be hazardous, it can't be better to know nothing.[4] If getting this information and standardizing its presentation were difficult and expensive, one might justly howl. But it isn't, so one can't.[5]

---

2. Observe the bulk and complexity of Regulation S-X, governing financial accounting under the various securities acts, 4 CCH FED. SEC. L. REP. ¶ 68,501 *et. seq.*

3. *See* A. ALCHIAN & W. ALLEN, EXCHANGE AND PRODUCTION--THEORY IN USE 308-10 (1969) on joint products with common costs.

4. That is not quite true. There is always the "Theory of the Second Best" which in broadest form "...takes the position that if some of the conditions needed for optimal resource allocation are not being met, one cannot show that meeting the other conditions will be a good thing in terms of resource allocation." G. CALABRESI, THE COSTS OF ACCIDENTS 86 (1970).

That means that an action taken in the right direction is not *necessarily* the right action to take. For instance, one does not improve his wealth position in swimming from a barren riverbank toward a lush one unless one makes it all the way across. Thus, strictly speaking, it *could* be better to know nothing; it just doesn't seem very likely in this instance.

5. The manufacturers not only do a great deal of product-testing already, they are set up to do a great deal more. Competitors can therefore easily test each other's cars, as well as their own, just to keep each other honest. And if *Consumer Reports* can afford to spot-check cars, the United States government can manage it too. *See* text at note 15, *infra*.

B. The "Contract" as a Purchased "Product"

So now we've got some cheap and useful information on the car as a mechanical thing. But it isn't just a car you buy when you trade money and promises to a smiling dealer; it's (not surprisingly) a *deal* that you buy. That little old piece of paper that goes along with the chunk of steel and technology, the "contract" (as it's laughingly labelled), is another purchased *product*. In fact, if one defines a "product" as "an immutable already-made object" and a "contract" as "something created by both the parties", the piece of paper is more a "product" than the car itself, for at least the latter has options.[6] You can, within limits, negotiate the presented reality of the car ("ok, roof frescoes instead of disc brakes"), but if you try to modify any clause in the contract, you have your choice in seller response between giggling incredulity and icy hostility. Well, if it's a *product* you're buying when you "buy" the contract, why not have *those* "specifications" disclosed too -- again in understandable and comparable form.

A typical contract might say:

> It is expressly agreed that there are no warranties, express or implied, made by either the dealer or the manufacturer on the motor vehicle, chassis, or parts furnished hereunder except as follows.
> The manufacturer warrants each new motor vehicle (including original equipment placed thereon by the manufacturer except tires), chassis or parts manufactured by it to be free from defects in material or workmanship under normal use and service. Its obligation under this warranty being limited to making good at its factory any part or parts thereof which shall, within one (1) year after delivery of such vehicle to the original purchaser or before such vehicle has been driven 12,000 miles, whichever event shall first occur, be returned to it with transportation charges prepaid and which its examination shall disclose to its satisfaction to have been thus defective; this warranty being expressly in lieu of all other warranties expressed or implied, *including the implied warranties of merchantability and fitness for a particular purpose* and all other obligations or liabilities on its part.[7]

6. *See* Leff, *Contract As Thing*, 19 AM. U. L. REV. 131 (1970) for a more extended development of these ideas.

7. The quoted disclaimer is based on the famous one in Henningsen v. Bloomfield Motors, 32 N.J. 358,367, 161 A.2d 69, 74 (1960). It would, by the way, satisfy, at least in form, the requirements of UNIFORM COMMERCIAL CODE § 2-316 on disclaimers of warranty.

Would it be so awful if the booklet said:

> If you get problems with the car, for 12,000 miles or one year we'll supply new parts and corkscrew some grudging labor out of your dealer. But *we'll* decide if it's necessary. And if the car cracks up and you get maimed or killed, we're still only responsible for the parts and the labor; don't expect to recover from us for property damage or personal injuries. We suggest you insure yourself, because we sure aren't going to insure you.

Of course, put that way it does look a little nasty. But if that *is* the way it is,[8] and if actually writing down the actual nastiness is too horrifying for the vice-president in charge of sales, he can get the actuality changed rather than the language. He might, for instance, suggest *as a competitive device* changing things so that his company *does* insure you, if only for a year and for a special extra premium. And it would not hurt if the Prospectus demystified a few other "mechanical" aspects of this contract-product. For instance:

> You know that bit about "repossession" in the contract? Well, that means that if you miss a payment we can take back the car and resell it, and if we do the chances are that you'll end up without the car, without the money you already paid us, and maybe you'll actually still owe us some.

C. Pedigree and Track Record

Thus far, our proposed Prospectus has carried current information about the actual car-and-deal being bought. A trickier question involves the relevance of the past. To pick a problem hardly at random, what of defects in, and callbacks of, previous years' models? After all, *you're* buying the current Tyrannosaurus, not last year's. What if all of the earlier model had to be recalled to put the brake pedal into communication with the fluid and shoes? Does that have any bearing on this year's model, in the making of which that *particular* jolly oversight was not indulged?

The question is not, despite my tone, a simple one. It would seem that you could learn what *kind* of outfit a company is by seeing a longer-term pattern; if Company A for the past five years had had callbacks of many more cars with much more serious faults than Company B, it is a natural inference that Company A is a "sloppier company" than B. Certainly the Securities Exchange Commission (SEC) seems to

8. With respect to personal injuries, any such language would by now most likely be insufficient to preclude liability in the majority of jurisdictons. *See* W. PROSSER, THE LAW OF TORTS 656-658 (4th ed. 1971). When that is the case, of course, it too ought accurately to be described.

think that a company's last five years' earnings are of justified interest to a securities buyer.[9]

The trouble is, the idea that you can tell about this year by studying the past, no matter how logical it seems, may be twaddle. I have very intelligent colleagues who tell me that reading five-year financials to descry a "trend" is really concealed "chartism", the astrology of financial analysis.[10] Admittedly, a ballplayer who has hit .220 for five seasons is less likely in the sixth suddenly to learn about curve balls; and whatever that tells me about baseball and learning processess carries over, some, into business.

But there may even be an *inverse* relationship between a naughty past and a problematic present. The accumulation of prior failures may eventually stimulate remedial action. 220 hitters eventually get fired. The question is, even assuming that a company with a higher call-back total was less reliable during that period, is it still so today? My inclination would be to include prior call-back information insofar as that data would act as a sanction against loose quality control, but such a sanction may work by fostering irrational factual conclusions, and that makes me exceedingly nervous.

D. Sticker Price and Terms

What else should go into the Prospectus? Certainly the sticker price of every car and every option. That would help a lot to cope when faced with the common salesman pitch: "You think that's too high? You think you can't afford $4600? Tell you what I'm gonna do. I'm going to throw in laser-beam headlights and a spring-gun for your glove compartment (our 'aggression -- defense package') and take out the electrical ego booster, and all for the same price." With the sticker information one would at least have a prayer of figuring out if you were gaining or losing ground. (Of course, you'd know a lot more if you also got the *dealer's* cost for each item, but I see no present reason to give the sellers a corporate coronary by suggesting that.)

---

9. *See* Item 6 (Summary of Earnings) of Form S-1, the usual form governing the content of Prospectuses distributed pursuant to the Securities Act of 1933.

10. *Cf.* Fama, *Random Walks in Stock Market Prices*, 21(5) FINANCIAL ANALYSTS J. 55 (Sept.-Oct. 1965), *reprinted in* V. BRUDNEY & M. CHIRELSTEIN, CORPORATE FINANCE 1112 (1972).

E. Other Things

I suppose I could imagine other cheap and relevant information for this kind of Prospectus,[11] but it seems to me unnecessary to work out further details now. What does seem to me to be critically important to recognize from the beginning is that more information does not necessarily mean a better aggregate message. The danger in mandating a new communications medium is that at any given moment it looks as if *every* information addition to be carried on that channel has a nearly-nil marginal cost.[12] But, in fact, too much information on a wavelength causes static. The new messages not only fail to get through, but they garble the intelligible and relevant messages already there; and one of the normal results of sensory overload in a commercial context is impulse buying.[13]

Thus it would seem wise to be chary of too much. Specifically, one should stick to the car *as a car* and play down (by exclusion) things like emotional puffery (which by its nature is not set up for comparability anyway) and data about matters like the social, moral and political views of the manufacturers. Arguments in the form of "Don't buy those commie carrots" aren't particularly attractive anyway.[14]

## II. THE PROSPECTUS PRICE TAG; OR, WHAT PRICE KNOWLEDGE?

Much of the beauty of this proposed auto Prospectus requirement lies in its cheapness and cost-effectiveness. The expense of information is a function of the cost of getting it, the cost of rendering it communicable, the cost of disseminating it, and the cost of metering its accuracy. In this case, most of the information will already exist, and will usually already be in communicable and easily comparable form. As I said earlier, the "messages" are cheap because they have for the most part already arisen as "by-products" of the manufacturing and distribution process.

As for printing cost, given all the informationless color gravure car buyers already get, it's hard to weep over requiring a cheaper booklet to sell a large-ticket item like a car. But much more important, the media

---

11. One of my students has indeed explored the question of includable information in greater detail. G. Neigher, Automobile Merchandizing: Prospects For a Prospectus (1971). A copy of his unpublished paper is in my possession.

12. *See* text at note 15, *infra.*

13. *See* BEHAVIORAL SCIENCE FOUNDATIONS OF CONSUMER BEHAVIOR (J. Cohen ed. 1972); and PERSPECTIVES IN CONSUMER BEHAVIOR (H. Kassarjian & T. Robertson eds. 1968) for collections of recent essays devoted to the complexity of consumer choice, especially its tendency not to be improved as a sole function of information bulk. *Cf.* note 4, *supra.*

14. *See, e.g.,* Hampden-Turner, *A Proposal For Political Marketing,* 1 YALE REV. OF L. & SOC. ACTION 93 (1970) for a typical suggestion that product-purchase decisions take account of the morals of the makers.

channels have already been bought. Having established at great expense all those selling showrooms and already arranged to fill them with "literature", the per unit marginal cost of distributing additional or different information is close to nil. And since, by this distribution technique, the information goes only to those interested in it, it is even better as a cost-benefit matter: this is not like an abortion service advertised in *The Diocesan Weekly*, or even in *Reader's Digest*; this goes right into *Women's Freedom Now*. In brief, it's getting the right channel that costs the most, but once you've bought it, it is very efficient to fill the pipe.

The administration could also be very, very cheap. Our Automotive Marketing Board could be a little teeny agency, having only to set standards of comparability of language and breadth of subject inclusiveness. After all, it's not like the SEC prospectus people trying to cope with every "public" corporation. There are, after all, a maximum of what -- a score of major auto manufacturers worldwide? And, the accuracy of the data furnished is easy to monitor. The agency might do spot checks (the information is pretty objective and the tests replicatable) and so could independent consumers and consumer groups. And most important, *so could and would competitors.*

For once the selling is done on comparative information, everyone is going to try to make sure no one else is fibbing, and in this case *everyone* has the wherewithal to try. Just make the penalty for falsity big and economic -- say, $1,000,000 per error and the duty to put a corrective label on the prospectus -- and people will be careful. Well-heeled enemies are watching, and they watch hard.

## III. IS THIS TRIP NECESSARY?

Let us then say that this auto prospectus is a feasible proposition, mechanically easy and relatively cheap. Still, why do it? After all, we do have a lot of ugly experience on what happens when the government decides to coerce people to efficiency and/or virtue. Why should it be different in this case?[15]

---

15. At this point, it might as well be confessed that something similar to the Prospectus (and not really ugly at all) already exists for airplanes. By Federal Regulation, every private plane must come equipped with a little manual filled with details as to both the physical characteristics of the plane and proper operating procedures. *See* 14 C.F.R. § 23, pts. 18-23 (1972). The pilot is expected to familiarize him or herself with such information before flying the plane. 14 C.F.R. § 91.5(b)(1) (1972). While the obstensible purpose of requiring these manuals is to insure that airplanes, and their passengers, return to earth in substantially the same condition as when they took off, prospective purchasers of aircraft are well advised to consult the manuals for various makes before deciding which one to buy. Not only do the manuals contain information relevant to the buyer, they also demonstate the feasibility of their contents being regulated by a governmental agency.

As Nader knows (presumably God too), one of the critical pressure points for optimizing the distribution of goods is information. If information is defective, the "market" will be too, even if people can and do act freely and rationally in "buying", and this is true whether the "product" is a washing machine or a president. If the world were gracious enough to accord with even elegant theories about it, the idea of having the government coerce better information would be wholly gratuitous and sublimely insane.

For THE THEORY says that everyone should always be getting about what he wants (within the constraints of his wherewithal). THE MARKET (so the argument goes) will handle it, by facilitating not only the exchange of goods, but the exchange of information too. In this market, as in the political "market", everyone "votes": but the economic voting is with an almost infinitely divisible medium -- money -- that facilitates the expression not merely of preferences, but the intensity of those preferences. If one can make safe goods as cheaply as dangerous ones, one will capture the market by offering more utility for the same outlay. If people will pay extra for safety, they will be serviced. The mechanism is competition: if oaf-like X, a clumsy sort, won't respond to his potential customers' desires for safety and quality, then clever Y will make clear that he will, thereby taking X's customers away and putting X (justly) out of business.

But even if X doesn't go out of business, that's all right too. He may not, after all, be such a clod. His customers may prefer chrome to safety, sexual innuendo to durability. That's not just all right, as THE THEORY has it, that's superkeen. For at the wrist-bone of the whole invisible-hand conception is the ethical belief that a man is entitled to get from it whatever it is *he* wants, be it ("objectively") a pinch or a tickle. The idea is that if everyone's individual desires are satisfied, the result will be the highest valued use of all of the assets of the entire

---

The Federal Aviation Agency requires aircraft manufacturers to include in their "Airplane Flight Manuals", among other things, the following information; airspeed limitations (*i.e.*, how fast the plane can be flown before it will part company with its wings), takeoff weight limitations (including temperature and altitude factors) and the methods used by the manufacturer in obtaining such information, climb and landing configurations and performance figures, proper operating procedures, explanations of "significant or unusual flight or ground handling characteristics" (one might hesitate to think what *that* could involve), and the location of the plane's center of gravity (so that it can be properly balanced when loaded). Certain emergency procedures are also included in the manuals, such as how to restart turbine engines in flight, and, one might suppose, how to affix a spare propeller at 15,000 feet. Airplanes are even required to provide a space, accessible to the pilot, in which the manual can be stowed. 42 C.F.R. §§ 23 (pts. 18-23), 23.1581 - 89 (1972).

All of the required information can be neatly tucked into a surprisingly compact booklet (available from dealers and also from rental agencies, who prefer that renters bring their planes back as intact as possible). Aircraft manufacturers like to see people with copies of these booklets because they make for safer flying, and also because the manufacturers could conceivably be held civilly liable for failure to warn users of the airplane adequately as to its potential hazards. *See* L.S. KREINDLER, AVIATION ACCIDENT LAW, pt. 1, § 7.01, 7.02(3), and 7.02(4) (1972).

community. That's known as "Pareto optimality",[16] and for many economists that's a situation right up there with God and country, and considerably ahead of Yale.

But information, of course, is not a free good. Nothing is. Someone will have to pay to produce and distribute it, and no one is crazy enough to pay for perfection in that or any other product. That still does not mean the market mechanism could not, in theory, cope with information production problems. If you make a car that goes from 0-60 in eight seconds and back again in four (in both cases without killing the driver), lasts seventeen years, produces a pretty fair orgasm (whether you have a passenger or not), includes in its warranty total protection against all the small disappointments of life, keeps you safe in head-ons with cement trucks, and costs about as much as a steam iron, you are competitively impelled to get the word across. You are even impelled, if necessary, to bad-mouth your competitor's 8-cylinder feh.

But the fact that information can be seen as a market commodity also implies that it is subject, like any other, to market failure.[17] And indeed, there are reasons why the supply of information is not optimized, even in a market unconstrained by regulation. First of all, ones competitive product advantage is rarely as mouth-watering as the one described above. The discriminations you will have to make *and then convey* are likely to be demanding of far subtler selling speech. This is especially so because the nice things about a product tend to be contradictory: great heavy lunkers of sheet steel off of which large meteorites bounce do not go so easily from 0 to 60; and if they do, they get about two miles per gallon. Thus, to advertise an advantage is frequently to give screaming currency to a disadvantage.[18] And if your actual advantages (and disadvantages) are slight (and that is likely, for there are good technological reasons why the gap between competitive products tends to be undramatic), it is hard to get *any* impact for them. So it's 0 to 60 in 10 seconds rather than 12. So your warranty covers rubber

16. *See, e.g.*, Bator, *The Simple Analytics of Welfare Maximization*, 47 AMER. ECON. REV. 22 (1957).

17. *See, e.g.*, Bator, *The Anatomy of Market Failure*, 72 Q. J. ECON. 351 (1958), *reprinted in*, READINGS IN MICROECONOMICS 457 (W. Breit & H. Hochman eds. 1968).

18. This is particularly dramatic when there is one body of information about a good without close substitutes which is incandescently unpleasant to all producers thereof, *e.g.*, the cunning little extra costs of cigarette smoking. *See* R. WINTER, JR., THE CONSUMER ADVOCATE VERSUS THE CONSUMER 12-13 (1972).

The obverse situation involves information which benefits one's competitors as much as oneself. It is hard to get a property interest in information. Thus one is insufficiently motivated to create "public goods" at one's own expense if everyone gets the whole benefit of it along with you. *See* A. ALCHIAN & W. ALLEN, *op. cit. supra*. note 3, at 164-165, 251-53. It is arguable, for instance, that there would be more safe-driving information produced if there were only one liability insurer.

parts as well as power trains. So what? -- especially if the extra goodies cost extra.

Then there is the cost-of-learning problem.[19] If one buys an automobile whose steering wheel is given to casual driver-evisceration, one *will* learn. "I'm not going to buy *that* model again," say you, trying neatly to refold and repack the last 17 feet of disheveled intestine. "If those guys at Pterodactyl Motors aren't going to level with me, that's the last time they see any of *my* money." Well, I suppose so, but that's a pretty expensive bit of information to shove into your personal computer for future reference. And though there are mechanisms beside the market (warranty and tort law, for instance) which theoretically should change the ultimate nesting place of that little information cost, they have their own complexities, costs, and risks.[20]

In addition, there are the time-lag and "research" problems. As a long-run competitive device, lying is most likely a bad idea. But not all competition has as its most significant span any particularly long run. The word that Hymie spits in his pickles might do in Hymie in favor of Moe, even if Moe is actually the one who does the spitting and the lying. More than that, even if Moe spits but doesn't lie, how is Hymie to get at Moe's barrel to know? Moe has an interest in keeping Hymie from knowing that particular bacillus count. Fraud *doth* often prosper, and over a long enough time-span to justify the existence of fraud law.

But most important, Moe has a strong interest in preventing Hymie from coming up with a way to present his information *in comparable form*. When it comes to commerce, it is mostly the symbols we manipulate, not the things themselves. The things are eventually shipped out and variously transferred, but the *deals* are mostly over the labels. Those labels, however, aren't worth a damn unless one can *compare* their messages. A badly situated seller has no interest in making telling comparisons easy for his competitors; and it's not easy for his competitors (who are, after all, each other's competitors too, and who in addition have anti-trust laws to sweat about) to agree and combine on an informational matrix that they can impose on him. That is, what one needs is a stabilized comparable vocabulary, *and even a reasonably competitive market may not be able to supply it.* Even in the absence of "monopoly" it may be more efficient to allow the government, as grand lexiocographer, to supply the vocabulary of comparison and impose it on the market.[21] Indeed, the most unambiguously successful "consumer

19. *Cf.* R. WINTER, JR., *op cit. supra.* note 18, at 12.

20. *See* G. CALABRESI, *op. cit. supra.* note 4, *passim.*

21. Let me emphasize here that I am *not* justifying this proposed governmental incursion into information marketing on the ground that the auto companies form a "shared monopoly" or "oligopoly." It can be argued that since monopolists tend to restrict production of goods, and

protection" job ever done by government was its mandatory standardization, from a very early period, of labels for weights, measures and quantities; it is, after all, very tempting as a short-run competitive device to sell eleven-ounce "pounds".

## IV. PROSPECTUS PERSPECTIVE

Now, there are at least two things that should not be adduced from the above. The first is the fantasy (as bizarre as the perfect-market one) that the market doesn't work at all; either in general, or specifically with respect to information. Without my wanting to get into a screaming match with anyone, I suggest that it works pretty well, especially considering the alternatives. The second unwarranted belief is that since it works pretty well, it *has* to work worse if the government meddles with it. It frequently turns out this way, but sometimes it doesn't. After all, the market imperfecting mechanisms described above are so common in practical economic thought that they all even have pet names, like "externality", "free-rider", "public goods under-investment", and "hold-out".[22] What I'm asking is this: If, as I suspect the case is here, the costs of all shapes of government intervention -- direct, bureaucratic, political, and spiritual -- are less than the value of repairing the market mechanism, then why not make the necessary repairs?

For it might even work. -- Not to make cars, or the process of shopping for them, "perfect" (whatever that might mean), but at a very low cost (economic, psychic, and political) to make it very much *more* nearly perfect in getting people what they want. This will not stop them from wanting what you or I or Ralph Nader think they ought not to want, but that really isn't so terrible. For a government to try to design high-quality information is much cheaper than its trying to design high-quality goods,and much better than its trying to design high-quality people.

---

information is a good, oligopolists will also tend to restrict production of goods, including information, and that this suboptimal production requires governmental repair. The trouble with the argument is (a) monopolists don't always restrict production in order to maximize; (b) oligopolists are not monopolists. Thus we have really no idea what their information-production function is.

More important, however, I do not rely on any oligopoly theory to justify this lexicographic governmental role because I think it is as much needed in competitive industries as in concentrated ones. Indeed it can be argued that it is more needed the less concentrated the industry. A few firms would seem to have less trouble, *i.e.*, lower transaction costs, than many firms in reaching a standardized linguistic product, because of their greater ease of collusion, and of their greater probability of each guessing what each of the others would guess. *See* A. RAPOPORT, FIGHTS, GAMES, AND DEBATES 213-25 (1960). One might, in fact, fairly describe my proposal as a suggestion that the government create and coordinate a limited cartel in the production of certain standardized commercial language. But then again, isn't the creation and coordination of cartels what regulatory agencies are all and always about? *See, e.g.*, Coase, *The Federal Communications Commission*, 2 J. LAW & ECON. 1 (1959).

22. *See* Bator, *op. cit. supra.* note 14.

# Part IV
# Warranties and Product Quality

[10]

The Yale Law Journal

Volume 90, Number 6, May 1981

# A Theory of the Consumer Product Warranty

George L. Priest†

Consumer product warranties are our most common of written contracts, but little is known about what determines their content or how they relate to the reliability and the durability of goods. Since the first appearance of standardized warranties early in this century, two theories have been proposed to explain their role in sales transactions. The first emphasizes the absence of bargaining over warranty provisions. It views warranties as devices of manufacturers to exploit consumers by unilaterally limiting legal obligations. The second and more recent theory focuses on the difficulty consumers face at the time of purchase in estimating the risk of product defects. This theory regards express warranties as messages signaling the mechanical attributes of goods.

Both theories have influenced substantially judicial and legislative responses to product warranties. The view of the warranty as an exploitative device has provided crucial support to the policy of enterprise liability and the replacement of contract principles with tort principles in product defect cases.[1] In addition, the exploitation theory is the intellectual basis for the modern judicial treatment of consumer warranty issues, in particular for the expansive interpretation of warranties implied by law, for the elimination of the requirement of privity of contract, and for the restric-

† Professor of Law, Yale University. I wish to thank Lawrence Kanter and Jacqueline Schmitt of the Federal Trade Commission for providing copies of the warranties examined in this article and for helpful advice; Bruce A. Ackerman, Yoram Barzel, Alvin K. Klevorick, Anthony T. Kronman, William M. Landes, Alan Schwartz, Gary T. Schwartz, and the participants of many workshops for valuable comments on earlier drafts; and William Lundquist, Robert E. Priest, Carol S. Maue, Timothy Johnson, Jean Doerr, Daniel Meyer, and Kenneth Landau for research assistance. Support for the completion of the paper was provided by the Program in Civil Liability of the Yale Law School for which I am very grateful. I am responsible for errors.

1. *See* note 37 *infra* (discussing influence of exploitation theory on tort law). *See generally* Morris, *Enterprise Liability and the Actuarial Process—The Insignificance of Foresight*, 70 YALE L.J. 554 (1961) (history of theory of enterprise liability).

tion of the manufacturer's authority to limit available remedies or to disclaim general obligations.[2] More recently, the signal theory has informed the design of the federal Magnuson-Moss Warranty Act,[3] which directly regulates both the form and content of consumer product warranties.[4]

Neither the exploitation nor the signal theory, however, has contributed to the understanding of warranty practices. The exploitation theory derives from the presupposition of overwhelming manufacturer market power, but the connection remains vague between the extent of market power and the specific definition of warranty coverage. Similarly, the signal theory derives from the assumption of consumer misperception of product risks. However plausible this assumption as a general matter, consumer perceptions are very difficult to identify or to measure. As a consequence, hypotheses concerning the relationship between perceptions and specific warranty provisions are highly speculative and essentially nonfalsifiable.

This article proposes a new theory of the standardized warranty and of the determinants of the content of the warranties of individual products. The first Part reviews in more detail the exploitation and signal theories and their observable implications. Part II presents the theory itself. A warranty is viewed as a contract that optimizes the productive services of goods by allocating responsibility between a manufacturer and consumer for investments to prolong the useful life of a product and to insure against product losses. According to the theory, the terms of warranty contracts are determined solely by the relative costs to the parties of these investments. An insurance function of warranty coverage, of course, is well-known.[5] The novelty of the theory is its emphasis on the variety of allocative investments that consumers may make to extend productive capacity and its consideration of the difficulties of drafting warranty contracts to encourage such investments.

The third Part compares the investment theory of the article with the exploitation and signal theories in a review of the content of sixty-two consumer product warranties. Although more comprehensive and detailed data are needed for a confident judgment, the review demonstrates that the content of these various warranties is generally more consistent with the

2. *See* J. WHITE & R. SUMMERS, HANDBOOK OF THE LAW UNDER THE UNIFORM COMMERCIAL CODE §§ 9-1 to -13, 11-1 to 12-12 (2d ed. 1980) (reviewing these developments).

3. Magnuson-Moss Warranty—Federal Trade Commission Improvement Act, Pub. L. No. 93-637, §§ 101-112, 88 Stat. 2183 (1975) (codified at 15 U.S.C. §§ 2301-2312 (1976)).

4. *See* pp. 1306-07 *infra* (discussing Act).

5. *See e.g.*, Brown, *Product Liability: The Case of an Asset with Random Life*, 64 AM. ECON. REV. 149, 157-58 (1974). The description of a warranty as an insurance policy has not illuminated specific warranty practices and has had little influence on the treatment of warranties in courts or legislatures. *Cf. id.* at 159-60 (impossible to determine *a priori* optimal distribution of product defect risk between manufacturer and consumer).

implications of the investment theory than of the exploitation or signal theory. Finally, Part IV considers the implications of the investment theory for questions of liability for product defects, including defects causing personal injury. This Part shows that, if the investment theory explains warranty practices, developments in modern warranty law are likely to have increased, rather than diminished, the rate of product losses, including personal injury losses.

## I. The Implications of the Exploitation and Signal Theories for Warranty Practices

During the last four decades, most approaches to consumer warranty issues by courts and legislatures have accepted the presuppositions of either the exploitation or signal theory. This Part defines the two theories and their implications and reviews the empirical evidence that has led to their acceptance.

### A. *The Exploitation Theory*

Standardized product warranties were first introduced, apparently, in the last decades of the nineteenth century.[6] Initially, these warranties were treated as normal contracts. The principles of nineteenth-century contract law derived from a view of the contract as an arms-length exchange between informed and competent parties. Because of its standardized character, no bargaining between the parties or adjustment of the terms of warranty contracts occurred. As a consequence, throughout the early decades of the twentieth century, courts vacillated between enforcing warranties strictly as normal contracts and enforcing them selectively according to other conceptions of the exchange.[7]

Although common themes appear in early treatments,[8] a coherent and persuasive theory of the standardized warranty first developed in the extensive literature and case law that followed Friedrich Kessler's celebrated manifesto, *Contracts of Adhesion—Some Thoughts about Freedom of*

6. *See* Bogert & Fink, *Business Practice Regarding Warranties in the Sale of Goods*, 25 ILL. L. REV. 400, 410-11 (1930).

7. *Compare* MacPherson v. Buick Motor Co., 217 N.Y. 382, 389, 111 N.E. 1050, 1053 (1916) (irrespective of contract, automobile maufacturer liable for defects) *with* Cadillac Motor Car Co. v. Johnson, 221 F. 801, 802 (2d Cir. 1915) (automobile manufacturer liable only to parties with whom it has contractual relation). *See, e.g.*, Llewellyn, Book Review, 52 HARV. L. REV. 700, 704 (1939) (judges equipped to distinguish between freely bargained-for contracts, which they should enforce, and contracts imposed on one party by another, the provisions of which should be interpreted more flexibly) [hereinafter cited as Llewellyn, Book Review]. The nineteenth-century implication of product warranties (such as the warranty of merchantability or fitness), of course, represents a substitution of a legal for a consensual standard of obligation. *See generally* Llewellyn, *On Warranty of Quality, and Society* (pt. 1), 36 COLUM. L. REV. 699 (1936).

8. *E.g.*, Bogert & Fink, *supra* note 6, at 413-14; Llewellyn, Book Review, *supra* note 7, at 704.

*Contract.*[9] According to the theory, a standardized contract is unique principally because its terms are drafted unilaterally by the seller and only involuntarily "adhered to" by the consumer.[10] The seller possesses "unfettered discretion"[11] to incorporate terms that serve its interests because its bargaining position is superior to that of the consumer.[12] In some industries, the manufacturer's superior position stems from the forces of natural monopoly.[13] In others, firms gain power by unleashing corporate weapons such as patents[14] or tying arrangements.[15] Kessler, in fact, believed that standardized contracts themselves were "devices to build up and strengthen industrial empires," contributing to what he viewed as the "innate trend of competitive capitalism toward monopoly."[16]

Even in industries with multiple sellers, however, all warranties are alike or substantially similar so that the consumer "is not in a position to shop around for better terms."[17] Some manufacturers directly collude in establishing warranty terms.[18] Trade associations standardize warranty practices to achieve the same result.[19] Thus, whether there is one seller or many, the consumer possesses no meaningful choice.[20] In Kessler's words, the consumer's "contractual intention is but a subjection more or less vol-

9. Kessler, *Contracts of Adhesion—Some Thoughts about Freedom of Contract*, 43 COLUM. L. REV. 629, 629-31 (1943); *see* Leff, *Contract as Thing*, 19 AM. U.L. REV. 131, 140-44 (1970) (discussing history of contract-of-adhesion theory).

10. Kessler, *supra* note 9, at 632. *See also* Leff, *Unconscionability and the Code—The Emperor's New Clause*, 115 U. PA. L. REV. 485, 504-05 & n.67 (1967) (discussing origins of "adhesion" metaphor). Kessler's principal focus was upon standardized insurance contracts, but the analysis has been extended routinely to standardized product warranties. *See* Henningsen v. Bloomfield Motors, Inc., 32 N.J. 358, 389-91, 161 A.2d 69, 86-87 (1960); Bogert & Fink, *supra* note 6, at 413-14; Leff, *supra* note 9, at 140-44. Kessler himself, however, thought that the problems of standardized insurance contracts were substantially more serious than those of standardized product warranties. Kessler, *Forces Shaping the Insurance Contract*, 14 U. CHI. CONF. SER. 3, 9 (1954).

11. Kessler, *supra* note 9, at 640; Whitford, *Law and the Consumer Transaction: A Case Study of the Automobile Warranty*, 1968 WIS. L. REV. 1006, 1039.

12. Henningsen v. Bloomfield Motors, Inc., 32 N.J. 358, 386, 389, 161 A.2d 69, 86-87 (1960); Bogert & Fink, *supra* note 6, at 413-14; Hale, *Bargaining, Duress, and Economic Liberty*, 43 COLUM. L. REV. 603, 605 (1943); Kessler, *supra* note 9, at 632; Llewellyn, Book Review, *supra* note 7, at 704.

13. *See* Kessler, *supra* note 9, at 632; Leff, *supra* note 9, at 141.

14. Bogert & Fink, *supra* note 6, at 414.

15. Whitford, *supra* note 11, at 1068-70.

16. Kessler, *supra* note 9, at 632, 640.

17. *Id.* at 632. Leff has emphasized that even if the consumer has a choice between different warranties, the terms of either warranty cannot be varied, so no true assent is present. Leff, *supra* note 9, at 142.

18. Bogert & Fink, *supra* note 6, at 414; Kessler, *supra* note 9, at 632; Leff, *supra* note 9, at 141.

19. *See* Bogert & Fink, *supra* note 6, at 407-09, 413-14. The efforts of trade associations were emphasized in the judicial adoption of the exploitation theory. *See* Henningsen v. Bloomfield Motors, Inc., 32 N.J. 358, 375, 390-91, 161 A.2d 69, 78, 87 (1960).

20. Henningsen v. Bloomfield Motors, Inc., 32 N.J. 358, 404, 161 A.2d 69, 95 (1960); Bogert & Fink, *supra* note 6, at 413; Prosser, *The Fall of the Citadel (Strict Liability to the Consumer)*, 50 MINN. L. REV. 791, 832 (1966); Whitford, *Strict Products Liability and the Automobile Industry: Much Ado About Nothing*, 1968 WIS. L. REV. 83, 96-97.

Warranties

untary to terms dictated by the stronger party."[21]

The exploitation theory predicts, in general, that manufacturers will limit their legal obligations to consumers as much as possible.[22] If collusion is widespread, then warranties within individual industries are likely to be similar. It also would be consistent with the assumptions of the theory, however, for the terms of coverage to be correlated with the degree of manufacturer market power.[23] Kessler believed that sellers are especially likely to exclude coverage of risks that are difficult to calculate and of unforseeable contingencies such as "strikes, fires and transport difficulties."[24] He also predicted that manufacturers would attempt to incorporate terms that reduce the risk of a court or jury being influenced by " 'irrational forces' to decide against a powerful defendant."[25] Kessler thought this reason explained why manufacturers in the machinery industry, for example, exclude warranty recovery for consequential damages.[26]

The exploitation theory does not specify unambiguously the relationship between a manufacturer's warranty practices and its other production or marketing decisions. In an early article, Dean Prosser argued that, without judicial intervention to imply warranties of quality in sales transactions, many manufacturers would provide consumers with "worthless junk."[27] Such relationships, however, have not been addressed extensively. More recent statements of the theory emphasize the marketing power gained from coordinating advertising that makes extravagant promises to consumers with warranties that disclaim responsibility for the promises.[28] Professor Slawson, in fact, argues that all standardized contracts are instruments of this type of fraud.[29]

The exploitation theory found wide acceptance in part because it was the only coherent explanation of standardized warranties until the 1970s. The theory also seemed consistent with descriptions of warranty practices. In an early empirical study of warranty content, Bogert and Fink found widespread exclusions of coverage of component parts, transportation

21. Kessler, *supra* note 9, at 632.

22. *See* Henningsen v. Bloomfield Motors, Inc., 32 N.J. 358, 375-78, 161 A.2d 69, 78-80 (1960); Bogert & Fink, *supra* note 6, at 411-13; Whitford, *supra* note 11, at 1041.

23. *See* Kessler, *supra* note 9, at 642; Leff, *supra* note 9, at 141.

24. Kessler, *supra* note 9, at 631 (referring specifically to insurance contracts, although principle is general).

25. *Id.*

26. *Id.* at 632.

27. Prosser, *The Implied Warranty of Merchantable Quality*, 27 MINN. L. REV. 117, 158-65 (1943).

28. Henningsen v. Bloomfield Motors, Inc., 32 N.J. 358, 373, 384-85, 161 A.2d 69, 77, 83-84 (1960); Prosser, *The Assault upon the Citadel (Strict Liability to the Consumer)*, 69 YALE L.J. 1099, 1123 (1960).

29. Slawson, *Mass Contracts: Lawful Fraud in California*, 48 S. CAL. L. REV. 1, 12 (1974). Professor Posner also describes standardized contracts as serving fraudulent ends. R. POSNER, ECONOMIC ANALYSIS OF LAW 85-86 (2d ed. 1977).

costs, and consequential damages, as well as more general limitations of warranty remedies.[30] In addition, they claimed to identify a trend in warranty content over time from broad assurances of product fitness toward more narrow representations of strictly mechanical perfection of products.[31] Kessler's wide experience with standardized contracts in the insurance industry seemed to provide further support.[32] More recently, Professor Whitford, in an intensive study of warranty practices in the automobile industry, concluded that automobile manufacturers could draft warranties in any manner desired, that warranties had in fact been drafted to minimize manufacturer's costs, that many warranty provisions were not "commercially justified," and that consumers did not possess sufficient expertise to deal intelligently with the problems of product defects.[33]

The most convincing evidence to support the exploitation theory, however, arose from case histories of warranty practices. Courts were asked repeatedly to give effect to warranty provisions that they interpreted as exploitative. In the case of *Henningsen v. Bloomfield Motors, Inc.*,[34] involving serious personal injury from an allegedly defective automobile, the terms of the warranty at issue disclaimed the implied warranty of merchantability, excluded consequential damages, and limited warranty remedies to repair or replacement of the defective part as long as the victim had prepaid transport charges for the part. The New Jersey Supreme Court remarked, "It is difficult to imagine . . . a less satisfactory remedy . . . . An instinctively felt sense of justice cries out against such a sharp bargain."[35] In a decision that has been followed by virtually all other American jurisdictions,[36] the court embraced the exploitation theory and refused to enforce the terms of the standardized warranty.[37]

30. Bogert & Fink, *supra* note 6, at 405-06, 409, 412-13.

31. *Id.* at 410-11.

32. Kessler's essay, *Forces Shaping the Insurance Contract*, *supra* note 10, was particularly influential.

33. Whitford, *supra* note 11, at 1039, 1062. Whitford also mentioned, however, that manufacturers seemed to be concerned about maintaining consumer goodwill. *Id.* at 1016, 1040. *But see id.* at 1036 (dealer makes little effort to maintain goodwill of price shoppers). Whitford did not attempt to reconcile exploitative warranty practices with the concern for goodwill.

34. 32 N.J. 358, 161 A.2d 69 (1960).

35. *Id.* at 375, 388, 161 A.2d at 79, 85.

36. *See* Prosser, *supra* note 20, at 793-98.

37. Henningsen v. Bloomfield Motors, Inc., 32 N.J. 358, 408, 161 A.2d 69, 97 (1960). The adoption of the standard of strict liability for product defects is based upon the acceptance of the empirical presumption of the exploitation theory: consumers are powerless in relation to manufacturers. James, *General Products—Should Manufacturers be Liable without Negligence?* 24 TENN. L. REV. 923, 925 (1951) (victims of accidents are not culpable; strict liability preferred over fault system where accidents are inevitable); *see* Vandermark v. Ford Motor Co., 61 Cal. 2d 256, 261, 263, 391 P.2d 168, 170-72, 37 Cal. Rptr. 896, 898, 900 (1964) (manufacturer strictly liable to consumer, regardless of contractual provisions, because in business of selling automobiles that turn out to be defective); Greenman v. Yuba Power Prods., Inc., 59 Cal. 2d 57, 63, 377 P.2d 897, 901, 27 Cal. Rptr. 697, 701 (1963) (strict

Warranties

## B. *The Signal Theory*

The signal theory of the consumer product warranty maintains that warranty terms provide information to consumers about the mechanical reliability of the product.[38] The signal theory builds upon a growing economic literature that examines the "market" for information[39] and views the warranty as a tool consumers can use to "process" information about products. According to the theory, a consumer finds it excessively costly to determine precisely product reliability at the time of purchase by direct inspection of the product.[40] A consumer, however, may look to the warranty as a "signal" of product reliability because reliability is correlated negatively with the costs of warranty coverage;[41] that is, the more reliable the product, the lower the costs of warranty coverage for the manufacturer, and the more extensive the coverage for the consumer. Thus, although a consumer has neither experience with nor knowledge of a product, he may infer its mechanical reliability by inspecting the terms of the warranty alone.

Signals, however, only reduce information costs to consumers. Some consumer misperception of product risks is inevitable.[42] The extent of misperception is determined by the costs and benefits to consumers of obtaining product information by means of warranty signals, which is to say, by the utility of the warranty as an information-processing tool. The implications of the theory for specific warranty practices are derived by estimating the costs and benefits of processing information in the context

liability designed to protect "powerless" consumer). A strict liability regime presupposes the inappropriateness of allowing manufacturers to define liability by contract. Henningsen v. Bloomfield Motors, Inc., 32 N.J. 358, 404, 161 A.2d 69, 95 (1960) (contractual disclaimer of warranty of merchantability and limitation of remedies invalid because of manufacturer's "grossly disproportionate bargaining power").

38. An early statement of this theory was suggested in Akerlof, *The Market for "Lemons": Quality Uncertainty and the Market Mechanism*, 84 Q.J. ECON. 488 (1970).

39. *See* Stigler, *The Economics of Information*, 69 J. POL. ECON. 213 (1961), *reprinted in* G. STIGLER, THE ORGANIZATION OF INDUSTRY 171 (1968).

40. Some degree of consumer ignorance was an important, but not central, assumption of the case law, *see* Henningsen v. Bloomfield Motors, Inc., 32 N.J. 358, 365, 375, 379, 384, 161 A.2d 69, 74, 78, 80-81, 84 (1960), and of the writings of the exploitation theorists, *see, e.g.*, Kessler, *supra* note 9, at 632; Kessler, *The Protection of the Consumer under Modern Sales Law, Part I*, 74 YALE L.J. 262, 267-78 (1964); Leff, *supra* note 9, at 156; Prosser, *supra* note 28, at 1133. Professor Slawson, on the other hand, believes that making standard form contracts understandable would hurt rather than help consumers. Slawson, *supra* note 29, at 16-17 (consumers would not read or could not understand standard form contracts even if they were made "understandable," but courts would not hesitate to enforce such contracts).

41. A.M. SPENCE, MARKET SIGNALING 88-90 (1974).

42. *Cf.* Spence, *Consumer Misperceptions, Product Failure and Producer Liability*, 44 REV. ECON. STUD. 561, 561 (1977) (presuming that consumers will misperceive likelihood of losses from products). Spence recommends governmental fines to repair this form of market failure. *Id.* at 565-67. Of course, the problem of product warranties is more interesting where consumers systematically misperceive product risks—because the market mechanism requires correction—than where consumers make estimates that are highly variant, but on average accurate.

of specific consumer transactions.

The first implication of the signal theory is that warranties of different products are likely to contain similar, if not identical, provisions. This implication follows from the presumption that the more often a consumer expects to buy a product, the greater the value is to him of information about product characteristics. But since a consumer purchases any single appliance or durable only occasionally, the benefit of obtaining warranty information specific to a single appliance is small relative to the benefit of compiling information common to a wide set of consumer goods.[43] Thus, a manufacturer's warranty signal is more likely to be successful if it resembles the warranty signals of other products. For this reason, the warranty terms of different products should be similar, each taking advantage of the greater benefit to consumers of general rather than of product-specific information.

A second implication of the signal theory is that wherever warranty terms diverge from the near-uniform standards of most warranties, the divergent terms will offer coverage more generous—not more restrictive—than the uniform terms. According to the theory, upon the discovery of a defect, a consumer acts on the basis of perceptions formed from general information or experience regarding products. In particular, the consumer presumes that the warranty terms of the specific product equal the average terms of all other products.[44] Such perceptions, however, disadvantage manufacturers who offer less than average warranty coverage because their products are less reliable than the average.[45] For those defective products, consumers file warranty claims even though the warranties do not extend coverage, thus imposing administrative expenses on the manufacturers and costing them goodwill.[46] Indeed, it may be cheaper for those manufacturers to expand warranty coverage to the average level than to process "invalid" claims.[47] As a consequence, warranties that persist in offering coverage different from the average should offer more generous rather than more restrictive coverage.[48]

The third implication of the theory is that subordinate terms of a warranty, as opposed to central terms, are more likely to diverge from the norm and to offer relatively more restrictive coverage. The theory proposes that a consumer benefits more from information relating to the cen-

43. *See* A.M. SPENCE, *supra* note 41, at 89; Gerner & Bryant, *The Price of a Warranty: The Case for Refrigerators*, 12 J. CONSUMER AFF. 30, 32 (1978); Gerner & Bryant, *Appliance Warranties as a Market Signal?* 15 J. CONSUMER AFF. 75, 78-79 (1981) [hereinafter cited as *Market Signal*].

44. *See Market Signal*, *supra* note 43, at 78-79.

45. *Id.* at 79.

46. *Id.*

47. *Id.*

48. *Id.*

tral terms of a warranty than to subordinate terms.[49] As a consequence, the pressures leading toward uniform warranty provisions ought to have greater effect with respect to central provisions than to subordinate provisions.[50] In addition, since consumers are less aware of subordinate terms (because the value of information about them is less), warranties are likely to define subordinate terms more restrictively than average, because invalid claims based upon perceptions of those terms will be rare.[51]

Moreover, since consumers remain largely ignorant of the content of subordinate provisions, normal competitive pressures are absent. Manufacturers will define those provisions with reference only to costs of coverage and not to consumer benefits.[52] At this point, the exploitation and signal theories converge. Signal theorists expect competition to influence the content of central warranty provisions, subject to information processing costs.[53] But, like the exploitation theorists, they expect subordinate warranty provisions to be defined in a manner that disregards consumer interests.[54]

The implications of the signal theory have been examined recently by the economists Gerner and Bryant in an empirical study of the content of 108 warranties of washing machines, ranges, refrigerators, air conditioners, and televisions.[55] Their findings offer mild support for the theory. First, Gerner and Bryant report that most warranties provide coverage of parts and labor costs for one year,[56] a finding they interpret as confirmation of the advantage of general over product-specific information.[57] Exceptions to even this basic term of coverage exist, however. For example, only fifty percent of washing machine warranties provide one-year parts coverage, and seventy-one percent of television warranties offer one-year labor coverage.[58]

Gerner and Bryant find less uniformity within the set of warranties whose terms diverge from the basic one-year term. It is consistent with the signal theory that warranties offering a different duration of parts cover-

49. *See id.* at 78-79 (by inference).
50. *See id.* at 79, 84 (by inference).
51. *See id.* at 79-85 (by inference).
52. *See id.* at 84-85 (by inference).
53. *See id.* at 79-86 (by inference).
54. *See id.* at 84-85 (by inference).
55. Their sample incorporates 90% of the models sold during the 1975 model year. *Id.* at 80.
56. This "finding" appears to be accurate only when the terms of coverage are defined very generally. *See* note 174 *infra* (discussing prevalence of one-year parts and labor coverage).
57. *Market Signal, supra* note 43, at 81-82.
58. *Id.* at 82 (Table 1). There are exceptions to the one-year term with respect to the other appliances as well. Gerner and Bryant do not suggest that consumers of different products possess different levels of information. Such an assumption would conflict with the prediction of generalized warranty signals. As a consequence, however, the signal theory does not provide a basis for explaining differences in the terms of warranties of different products. *See* pp. 1328-46 *infra* (examining differences in warranties).

age provide only extended coverage; that is, coverage greater than the average.[59] The great majority of warranties that provide a different term of labor coverage, however, restrict coverage below the average one-year term.[60] Gerner and Bryant explain this difference by supposing that manufacturers find it cheaper to monitor invalid labor claims than parts claims and that manufacturers thus are more willing to suffer consumer dissatisfaction where expensive labor costs are at stake.[61]

Finally, as predicted by the theory, Gerner and Bryant find little uniformity in what they assume to be the warranties' subordinate terms: the exclusions and limitations of coverage.[62] There is some evidence, in addition, that these exclusions are defined solely with reference to manufacturers' costs. One example is the exclusion of consequential damages, which they observe most frequently in refrigerator warranties. According to Gerner and Bryant, refrigerators are more likely than other defective appliances to generate consequential damages in the form of food losses.[63]

The signal theory has exerted substantial influence on consumer product warranty policy. The objective of the 1974 Magnuson-Moss Warranty Act[64] is to make warranties more efficient signals.[65] The Act requires manufacturers to redraft warranties in "simple and readily understood language,"[66] to disclose all important provisions "conspicuously,"[67] and to display warranties prominently so that they are available for consumer inspection prior to purchase of the product.[68] The Act requires manufacturers to designate all express warranties as either "Full" (if they comply with certain minimum standards) or "Limited" (if they do not comply with those standards), in order to reduce the costs of comprehending warranty content.[69] The drafters hoped that the pressures toward greater than

59. *Market Signal*, *supra* note 43, at 79-80, 81-82 (Table 1).

60. *Id.* at 82-83.

61. *Id.*

62. *Id.* at 84-85 (Table 3).

63. *Id.* at 85.

64. Magnuson-Moss Warranty—Federal Trade Commission Improvement Act §§ 101-112, 88 Stat. 2183 (1975) (codified at 15 U.S.C. §§ 2301-2312 (1976)).

65. *See* H. REP. NO. 1107, 93d Cong., 2d Sess. 36, *reprinted in* [1974] U.S. CODE CONG. & AD. NEWS 7702, 7718 (conspicuous and clear disclosure required under § 102(a) of Act in order "to improve the adequacy of information available to consumers, prevent deception, and improve competition in the marketing of consumer products"); Priest, *The Structure and Operation of the Magnuson-Moss Warranty Act*, in ECONOMIC REGULATION AND CONSUMER WELFARE: THE FEDERAL TRADE COMMISSION IN THE 1970S at 246 (K. Clarkson & T. Muris eds. 1981) (discussing theory of Act).

66. Magnuson-Moss Warranty—Federal Trade Commission Improvement Act § 102(a), 15 U.S.C. § 2302(a) (1976).

67. *Id.* §§ 102(a), 103(a), 105, 106, 108(b), 15 U.S.C. §§ 2302(a), 2303(a), 2305, 2306, 2308(b) (1976).

68. *Id.* § 102(b)(1)(A), 15 U.S.C. § 2302(b)(1)(A) (1976). Kessler emphasized the advantage to manufacturers of warranties with obscure printing and language. Kessler, *supra* note 10, at 9.

69. Magnuson-Moss Warranty—Federal Trade Commission Improvement Act §§ 103-104, 15 U.S.C. §§ 2303-2304 (1976).

Warranties

average coverage would lead to universal compliance with Full warranty standards.[70]

The Act's disclosure, availability, and designation requirements, however, affect only the central provisions of warranties. Subordinate provisions, which, according to the theory, consumers are less likely to comprehend, are subjected to direct regulation. The Act prohibits disclaimers of the implied warranties for all warranties,[71] and expands consumer remedies and prohibits tying provisions for Full warranties.[72]

## II. The Investment Theory of the Warranty

In this Part I develop a theory of the consumer product warranty based solely upon the relative costs to the consumer and manufacturer of investments to prolong productive capacity and to insure for product losses. I then define how warranty contracts are likely to be drafted in cases in which contract standardization reduces costs.

### A. *The Basic Theory Defined*

Let us relax the empirical assumptions that are the foundations of the signal and exploitation theories in order to predict the contents of warranties where the costs of extending product life and of insuring product losses are the sole determinants of their contents. Imagine that consumers are perfectly informed about the likelihood of a product defect and about the losses that will be suffered should a product become defective. Imagine also that consumers somehow make their preferences regarding warranty terms known to manufacturers[73] and that manufacturers are responsive to those preferences. Imagine that warranty contracts are standardized *only* to reduce negotiation costs[74] and thus that the standardized form itself does not affect the substantive obligations of consumers relative to manufacturers.[75] Finally, imagine that all products are manufactured under conditions of perfect competition, so that each characteristic of a prod-

70. *See* S. REP. NO. 151, 93d Cong., lst Sess. 8 (1973); 120 CONG. REC. 40,712 (1974) (remarks of Sen. Magnuson).

71. Magnuson-Moss Warranty — Federal Trade Commission Improvement Act § 108, 15 U.S.C. § 2308 (1976). A manufacturer offering a Limited, rather than Full, warranty, however, may disclaim the implied warranties for the period after expiration of the warranty. *Id.*

72. *Id.* § 102(c), 15 U.S.C. § 2302(c) (1976). Other subordinate provisions have been regulated under the Act by Federal Trade Commission rule. *See* 16 C.F.R. §§ 700-703 (1980).

73. *See* pp. 1346-47 *infra* (discussing how consumer preferences may be registered).

74. Kessler acknowledged the cost savings from standardization. Kessler, *supra* note 10, at 12.

75. This assumption is not unrealistic and is accepted generally with respect to a wide range of product characteristics. Anyone, for example, could arrange to purchase appliances with characteristics designed to personal specifications. Most, however, seem willing to accept machines with standard characteristics, designed to be generally suitable for the large majority of consumers, in order to take advantage of the cost savings.

uct—including warranty terms—serves to optimize the welfare of some dominant class of consumers.[76] What would be the terms of product warranties?

In the common view, a warranty serves as both an insurance policy and a repair contract. As an insurance policy, a warranty provides that if, within a certain period, the product or some part of the product becomes defective, the manufacturer will compensate the buyer for the loss by repair, replacement, or refund of the purchase price.[77] As a repair contract, a warranty fixes an obligation upon the manufacturer for some period of time to provide, without charge, services necessary to repair a defect in order to prolong the useful capacity of the product.

A warranty operates as an insurance policy to the extent that the occurrence of a product defect is probabilistic. To insure for a loss is to redistribute wealth from periods in which no losses are suffered to the period in which the loss occurs. A manufacturer can redistribute wealth in this manner by collecting a premium in the sale price from a broad set of consumers for whom the prospects of loss during any single period are unrelated. The market insurance premium reflects both the expected loss for the period and some share of the costs to the insurer of aggregating these unrelated contingencies, called loading costs. A consumer may prefer, however, some personal form of temporal wealth redistribution in the face of a loss. A consumer self-insures for product losses by accumulating savings for the replacement of defective products, by reserving future time for product repair, or, more simply, by expecting to tolerate a defect once it occurs. These methods of self-insurance, of course, also involve costs of transaction. As a general proposition, therefore, we may expect to observe market insurance in a warranty only where the sum of the expected loss and loading costs of market insurance is less than the sum of the expected loss and transaction costs of self-insurance.

As a repair contract, a warranty reflects the respective costs to the consumer and the manufacturer of repair services. Repair by the consumer and manufacturer are substitutes, and the consumer can be expected to purchase repair services as part of the warranty wherever the manufacturer's price is less than the consumer's cost of providing the repair himself. Obviously, a consumer can (and frequently does) provide many repair services more cheaply than a manufacturer. It is plausible, for example, that where shelves fall in a refrigerator, repair by the consumer

76. Because of the standardized form, contracts are not specific to individuals but rather to classes of consumers.

77. I ignore, at this point, personal injury losses from defective products for which product warranties, partly because of acceptance of the exploitation theory, currently are irrelevant. *See* note 37 *supra*. The investment theory is extended to consider personal injury liability below. *See* pp. 1350-51 *infra*.

is cheaper. Of course, since the consumer and manufacturer are always free after the purchase of the good to negotiate for the provision of services of this kind, the warranty itself is valuable only if it reduces transaction costs for future agreements. Thus, a warranty may be expected to allocate responsibility to the manufacturer for those types of repairs that most frequently are difficult or burdensome for consumers to provide themselves.

Although the above example, as well as most uses of the word "repair," refers to investments designed to return a product to a condition it enjoyed at some previous period of time, it is worthwhile to consider "repair service" to a product more broadly as any investment designed to optimize the performance of the product over time. Viewed in this light, for example, restraining young children from swinging on a refrigerator door represents an investment in a form of "repair" that may well be less costly than hiring a serviceman at a later date to install new hinges. Similarly, a manufacturer may anticipate future repair services by technological investments in the design of the product that make its operation less susceptible to interruption—designing brackets to hold refrigerator shelves more securely, for example—or by investments to control a consistent quality of production.

With respect to repair investments of this nature, however, a warranty serves a role beyond that of reducing transaction costs. The warranty promise establishes and enforces the obligation of the manufacturer to make investments in the design of the good or in quality control. Such an agreement between the parties subsequent to the sale could not achieve the same result as easily,[78] so that there are advantages to "tying" the warranty to the sale of the product.[79] The warranty in this regard operates as a performance bond of the manufacturer.[80] The value of the bond is equal to the costs to the manufacturer of defective product claims.[81] As long as

78. The terms of subsequent repair agreements preferred by consumers might influence product design to the extent that they provide the basis for the consumers' repeat purchase decisions. *See* p. 1347 *infra*.

79. The advantage of tying the warranty to the product diminishes, however, to the extent that a manufacturer seeks to capture repeat purchase sales. *See* note 199 *infra*. The desire for future custom alone will provide an incentive for optimal manufacturer investments. *See generally* Klein & Leffler, *The Role of Price in Guaranteeing Quality*, 89 J. POL. ECON. (forthcoming 1981) (discussing repeat purchase mechanism).

80. *See* Barzel, *Some Fallacies in the Interpretation of Information Costs*, 20 J.L. & ECON. 291, 303 n.26 (1977). As an independent example of the warranty's role as a performance bond, the Wilbert burial vault warranty (not included in the sample analyzed below, *see* pp. 1319-46 *infra*) provides 50-year coverage against deterioration. Because of the extraordinary duration of coverage, the warranty informs the buyer that the manufacturer has established a trust fund in the amount not less than $25,000 for the payment of warranty claims, "in the event the Manufacturer is no longer in business." I am grateful to J.H. Schlegal for this observation.

81. The signal theory, similarly, presumes that a warranty signal is credible because the manufacturer will incur the costs of coverage. *See* p. 1303 *supra* (discussing negative correlation between warranty coverage and reliability). The signal theory, however, views consumer information as a more significant determinant of warranty content than costs.

the manufacturer makes appropriate investments, the bond will not be forfeited. The decision to allocate repair investments of this nature between the manufacturer and consumer, however, is identical to the decision of who should bear typical repair costs. As before, we would expect the parties to allocate between themselves, according to relative costs, all investments in "repair," whether in the form of direct reconditioning services, of product design, or of a consumer's care for or maintenance of the product so as to extend its useful life.

It is evident that the various activities described as repair are substitutes for insurance. Repair, like insurance, is a means of reducing the magnitude of a loss from an unexpected event such as a defect. It is important now, however, to depart from the common view of the warranty and to distinguish more clearly between repair as a redistribution of wealth over time, like insurance, and repair as an allocative investment which alters the productive capacity of the good.[82] The first example of repair—the reinstallation of the refrigerator shelves by the consumer—is a form of self-insurance for the loss. The owner bears the full cost of time and energy necessary to replace the shelves after the event occurs, which, in this case, appears to be cheaper than buying market insurance requiring the manufacturer to replace the shelves. But neither repair by the consumer nor by the manufacturer directly alters the probability of the loss occurring and, thus, is like insurance. The second example—restraining the child from swinging on the refrigerator door—is an allocative investment by a consumer that extends the useful life of the product by reducing the probability of a future loss. Certainly, the burdens of a parent increase as the discipline of children becomes more strict or specific. But, again, it may well be cheaper for a consumer to restrain his child than either to buy market insurance for repair of the door or to pay the manufacturer to design a refrigerator with hinges as sturdy as playground equipment.

Thus, in this terminology, a consumer's decision to accommodate himself to a scratch in the surface of an appliance is an example of self-insurance of the defect. The consumer's earlier efforts to reduce the likelihood of the scratch, for example, by increasing the level of his care or by ablating the appliance, is an allocative investment by the consumer. The manufacturer's promise in a warranty to repair the scratch after it occurs is market insurance. And the manufacturer's production decision to make the surface more resistant to abrasion is an example of an allocative investment by the manufacturer.

Self-insurance, market insurance, and allocative investments by con-

82. Ehrlich & Becker, *Market Insurance, Self-Insurance, and Self-Protection*, 80 J. POL. ECON. 623, 633-43 (1972).

sumers and manufacturers, therefore, are each substitute methods of reducing losses in order to optimize productive services. A consumer selects among these methods according to the relative prices and marginal productivities of each with respect to expected elements of product loss. As the price of market insurance rises, other things equal, the quantity of it demanded will decline, and the demand for self-insurance and for manufacturer or consumer allocative investments will increase. Similarly, as the cost of an allocative investment by the consumer rises—say, in our second example, by the addition of a child to the consumer's family, which makes it more difficult to reduce the probability of loss—the relative attractiveness of market insurance, self-insurance, or an allocative investment by the manufacturer is enhanced. These various ways of reducing product losses, however, may not be perfect substitutes. An individual is likely to select some combination of these four methods to optimize expected utility.[83] For example, as the value of a consumer product or of the consumer's life increases—and, as a result, the potential risk from a defect increases—the consumer may increase consumption of each of the four.[84]

Most discussions of product defects in the economics literature[85] and most legal decisions involving warranties[86] regard the probability of loss from a defect as inherent in the nature of the product and independent of actions of the consumer. According to this approach, allocative investments by a consumer which serve to reduce the probability of losses are nonexistent, and the only relevant consumer and public policy choice is between consumer self-insurance and manufacturer liability, whether leading to an allocative investment or insurance.[87] Often these analyses are qualified by a reference to consumer behavior, although seldom by more than an acknowledgement that in some cases a consumer may actively misuse a

83. Of course, a consumer may choose different methods to optimize the value of different characteristics of a product—that is, he may select market insurance for the motor, but self-insurance for scratches—so that some combination of the four methods in the purchase and use of any single consumer product is likely to be observed.

84. This proposition assumes that income effects are held constant.

85. *See, e.g.*, A.M. SPENCE, *supra* note 41, at 88; Brown, *supra* note 5, at 149; Heal, *Guarantees and Risk-Sharing*, 44 REV. ECON. STUD. 549, 550 (1977). *But see* J.P. Brown, The Perverse Effect of Guarantees on Maintenance by Buyers 14-17 (June 1976) (manuscript, Cornell University) (discussing disincentives to consumer maintenance created by product guarantees) (on file with *Yale Law Journal*) .

86. *See, e.g.*, Greenman v. Yuba Power Prods., Inc., 59 Cal. 2d 57, 63, 377 P.2d 897, 901, 27 Cal. Rptr. 697, 701 (1963) (consumers of defective products "powerless to protect themselves").

87. When the problem is characterized in this way, the appropriate legal standard is obviously strict liability of the manufacturer; that is, except where there is reason to believe that consumer self-insurance is optimal, a standard of strict liability leads the manufacturer to select between investments to prevent loss and insurance. *See, e.g.*, James & Dickinson, *Accident Proneness and Accident Law*, 63 HARV. L. REV. 769, 780 (1950) (government and large companies in position to reduce accidents; individual's conscious free choice has insignificant effect on occurrence of accidents); Morris, *supra* note 1, at 583-99 (arguing for enterprise liability because enterprises better able to spread risks).

product.[88] The implicit conclusion of each of these discussions is that allocative investments by a consumer are empirically unimportant to the optimization of the productive life of the good.[89]

Of course, there is no theoretical justification for disregarding allocative investments by consumers. A more important implication of the theory, however, is that there is no meaningful way to consider a product defect independently of a consumer's allocative investments.[90] Investments to reduce the probability of losses may take very subtle forms. I have alluded earlier to the control of children and the placement of an appliance—as it affects the number of times the appliance is scratched or jarred—as representing allocative investments. As a more general proposition, however, two forms of investment by consumers will affect the likelihood of defects in any consumer product. The first is the consumer's selection of a product suitable for his expected needs. Warranty claims are likely to be more frequent, for example, where a washing machine is undersized or a vacuum cleaner underpowered, or where there occurs some unexpected increase in the demands that the consumer makes on the product. If the consumer accurately anticipates his uses, and if he selects a product designed most appropriately for those uses, the productive capacity of the good is more likely to be preserved.[91] The second form of investment is the consumer's decision about the extent to which he will use the product. A consumer who operates an appliance infrequently may be said to be preserving the life of the product by choosing to store rather than to use it.

Initially, this conception may seem foreign because it is common to infer from personal experience some "normal" use of a product. Indeed, the law requires judges and juries to make inferences of "normal" use by implying in product sales a warranty of merchantability that a product is "of fair average quality" and is "fit for the ordinary purposes for which such goods are used."[92] If it were possible to infer some "normal" use of a good, then the decision of an individual consumer to use or not to use the good would be analytically irrelevant.

But preferences regarding the frequency of use of a product differ among consumers. The preferences of the particular set of consumers for whom the product has been designed in order to optimize sales cannot be determined by inference. Where the dominant set of purchasers operates the good infrequently and, thus, where the "normal" use of the good is

88. *See, e.g.*, Spence, *supra* note 42, at 566 & n.5.

89. Of course, this presumption is critical both to the exploitation theory and to the theory of enterprise liability. *See* notes 37 & 87 *supra*; James & Dickinson, *supra* note 87, at 780.

90. *See* Ehrlich & Becker, *supra* note 82, at 624, 637-43.

91. Thus a consumer can influence even the relationship between the rate of defects and product design.

92. U.C.C. § 2-314(2)(b), (c).

Warranties

storage, the level of the consumers' allocative investments in preservation of the product is high.[93] As a consequence, the level of the manufacturer's allocative investment in product design or in insurance that optimizes productive services may be very low. In such a case, the design or manner of production of the product may be optimal even though the product appears grossly defective when operated with greater frequency, which is to say, when operated with lower allocative investments in care by consumers.

A warranty in this view is the instrument that expresses consumer preferences for allocative or insurance investments. It is a contract that divides responsibility for allocative investments and insurance between the consumer and the manufacturer. The content of the contract is determined by the respective costs to the two parties of allocative investments or insurance. According to this approach, a manufacturer makes investments to prolong product life up to the point at which the marginal cost of such investments equals the marginal benefit. A manufacturer, then, offers market insurance for those losses or items of service for which market insurance is less costly than insurance or allocative investments by the consumer himself.

To the extent that a manufacturer disclaims liability or excludes or limits its warranty coverage, however, it shifts to the consumer the obligation to make allocative investments to preserve the product or to self-insure for its loss. A disclaimer or an exclusion of coverage is the functional equivalent of provisions, common in other contracts, that explicitly require one of the parties to take certain actions to prevent breach or to insure for losses from uncertain events. The theory predicts that disclaimers of liability and exclusions of coverage will be observed in consumer product warranties for those specific allocative or insurance investments that the consumer can provide more cheaply than the manufacturer. In this view, disclaimers and exclusions can be said to be demanded by consumers because of the relative cheapness of consumer allocative investments or of self-insurance.

## B. *A Note on Moral Hazard*

This discussion of the factors leading to an optimal division between the consumer and the manufacturer of allocative and insurance investments is identical conceptually to the problem of moral hazard which has been discussed extensively in insurance literature, in particular, in the context of medical insurance.[94] Following Arrow and Pauly, the usual approach to

93. Put another way, the reduced frequency of defects is attributable to the choice of consumers to forgo use of the machine.

94. *See, e.g.*, Feldstein, *The Welfare Loss of Excess Health Insurance*, 81 J. POL. ECON. 251 (1973); Marshall, *Moral Hazard*, 66 AM. ECON. REV. 880 (1976); Rosett & Huang, *The Effect of*

the problem is to regard the existence of insurance itself as encouraging the purchaser to use too much of the good or service that the insurance supplies.[95] Thus, an individual who would purchase a certain amount of medical care when charged the marginal cost of the care, demands a greater amount of care if fully insured. Full insurance reduces the price of future purchases to zero, and leads the individual to a socially "excessive" level of consumption, a result said to illustrate the "moral hazard" of insurance.[96]

Moral hazard in the context of health insurance has been shown to represent a shift from ex ante allocative investments in care toward ex post investments in medical services which, given insurance, cost less at the margin.[97] Thus, medical insurance diminishes the individual's marginal incentive to invest in the preservation of his health. In general, however, moral hazard will appear in every context in which the investments or actions of the insured affect the probability of loss. The moral hazard problem is resolved, as in the investment analysis of warranties, by an ex ante definition of the insurance contract according to the relative costs of preservation (allocative investments) and of insurance.[98]

### C. *Defining Standardized Contracts: Reducing Differences in Risks*

The task of defining optimal warranty provisions[99] resembles the task of defining optimal rate classes in insurance contracts. In all insurance contexts, it is advantageous for an insurer to segregate applicants according to the level of risks added to the insurance pool. If the risk of loss of an individual can be predicted, then the insurance premium can be tailored to reflect the likelihood of future payouts. In particular, insurance coverage can be offered at a lower premium to an individual for whom the risk of loss is relatively low.

For most types of insurance, of course, it is prohibitively costly either to

*Health Insurance on the Demand for Medical Care*, 81 J. POL. ECON. 281 (1973).

95. Arrow, *Uncertainty and the Welfare Economics of Medical Care*, 53 AM. ECON. REV. 941, 961-62 (1963); Pauly, *The Economics of Moral Hazard: Comment*, 58 AM. ECON. REV. 531, 532-35 (1968).

96. This formulation is taken from Pauly, *supra* note 95, at 535.

97. *See* Rosett & Huang, *supra* note 94, at 298.

98. *See* Ehrlich & Becker, *supra* note 82, at 641-43 (explaining reduction of moral hazard). The moral hazard literature raises the optimization question from the standpoint of the seller of insurance rather than the buyer. The content of product warranties might be analyzed in this manner by asking how a manufacturer selects the elements and level of coverage by observation of product sales. The analytical solution is identical: the manufacturer declines to extend coverage where the costs of coverage exceed the benefits to consumers because of the substitution by consumers away from less costly investments in prevention or self-insurance.

99. I assume in the following discussion that the standardization of warranties reduces the joint costs of contract formation of the manufacturer and consumer, an uncontroversial assumption. *See* note 74 *supra*.

predict exactly the risk that an individual brings to a pool or to charge individual premiums. As a consequence, an insurer is forced to lump individuals into separate classes or, sometimes, into a single class. The premium charged each member of the class must reflect the average level of risk of the class. Thus, the premium undercharges relatively high-risk individuals and overcharges relatively low-risk individuals. At the margin, some low-risk individuals are likely to find that the cost of market insurance exceeds the benefit, and will shift to allocative investments that reduce the likelihood of the loss or to self-insurance. In the context of consumer products, these individuals will shift their purchases to products sold without, or with less, warranty coverage. The more precisely the insurer is able to construct classes comprising individuals with relatively similar levels of risk, however, the smaller the discrepancy will be between the premium and the value of insurance to the lower risk members of the pool. Thus, the lower risk members become less inclined to substitute self-insurance for market insurance. As a general proposition, therefore, discrimination that reduces differences in risk between members of a given insurance class optimizes the sale of insurance.

It is common for life, medical, accident, and home insurers to obtain information about applicants prior to making contracts in order to place applicants in appropriate insurance classes. Insurers routinely solicit information about age, sex, property location and value, as well as medical records and driving histories in order to construct rate classes.[100] Some insurers make it possible for individuals with characteristics that tend to be correlated with low levels of risk, such as abstemious smoking and drinking habits, to identify themselves in order to qualify for lower premiums. Analogues to these methods of discrimination, however, are not immediately apparent in the context of consumer product insurance. Typically, insurance policies for consumer product losses are tied to the sale of the product itself, so that the insurance pool invariably consists of all consumers who have purchased the product.

Consumers may differ in two general ways with respect to risk under a product warranty. First, the amount of use of a product during the period of warranty coverage may vary considerably between consumers. Compare, for example, the expected service costs to a washing machine manufacturer from a family with many children and from a family with only a single child. The costs of service to the large family will almost certainly be greater. If the manufacturer could define warranty coverage in terms of number of washloads, however, as an automobile manufacturer defines

100. The information on which the medical or accident insurer relies, of course, is frequently a by-product of the activities of other industries, such as the rendering of medical diagnosis or the administration of the traffic laws.

coverage in terms of mileage, then the expected costs from the two families to the manufacturer might be similar. But for washing machines, as well as for most other consumer appliances, the least costly measure of use appears to be duration of ownership. As a consequence, no matter what the period of coverage, the amount of use of the machine by the two families is likely to differ greatly. The insurance premium must be set to cover all expected costs of service. Thus, smaller families at the margin may find warranty protection to be worth less than its cost.

Second, the risk of loss may differ between consumers with respect to what I will call the "intensity" of product use. Compare now for the large and small families, the expected service costs to a television manufacturer. The amount of use of the television—that is, the number of viewing hours—might be identical for the two families. Nonetheless, the probability of a warranty claim is likely to be higher for the larger family, because of the greater number of individuals operating the set, because of the greater frequency of channel changes, and because of the greater risk in a large family that the set will be jostled, that the antenna will be struck, or that the machine will otherwise be treated roughly.

I define "intensity" of use as inversely related to the marginal cost to the consumer of "care" for the machine,[101] that is, the cost of allocative investments to reduce the probability of a loss. The cost of monitoring the activities of children is likely to increase as the number of children increases. Thus, the family with many children is more likely than the family with a single child to substitute recovery under a warranty for allocative investments in care of the machine. As a consequence, the cost to the manufacturer of warranty coverage will be greater for the machine sold to the larger family. Again, at the margin, consumers with smaller families may find it advantageous to shift their purchases to machines sold without, or with less, warranty coverage.

Although product insurers do not directly acquire information about consumers prior to sale, a variety of subtle methods can enable them to segregate consumers. For example, a manufacturer can develop models of a product that differ with respect to characteristics related to differences in intensities or amounts of consumer use. A manufacturer of washing machines may produce models that differ in motor size or washbasket volume that are differentially convenient to families of different sizes. If these product characteristics segregate consumers according to the extent or intensity of use, then the manufacturer can offer, for each individual model,

101. The distinction between "intensity" and amount of use corresponds to the distinction in economics between movements along a cost (supply) curve and movements of the cost curve with respect to different scales of operation. *See* J. HIRSCHLEIFER, PRICE THEORY AND APPLICATIONS 115-18 (2d ed. 1980).

different allocative investments and levels of warranty coverage determined by the expected warranty claims for each model.

This technique, however, may achieve only partial success. The advantage to a manufacturer of culling out higher intensity or higher volume consumers from a particular insurance pool is to enable it to offer warranty coverage at a relatively lower premium, or greater coverage at the same premium, of models designed for lower volume or intensity uses. A lower premium or more extended coverage, however, makes those machines relatively more attractive to all consumers, including those who expect to use the machine with greater intensity or in higher volume. At the margin, some of these consumers can be expected to purchase machines undersized for their needs. Such purchases substitute the extended warranty coverage of the lower volume machine for the mechanical superiority of the higher volume machine. This adverse selection by higher volume or intensity consumers will force manufacturers to reduce the extended coverage of the lower volume machine or to charge a higher premium for it. Either reaction will reduce the attractiveness of the lower volume machine to the lower risk members of the pool.[102]

A separate but closely related method of segregating consumers is to offer warranty contracts with different terms at different premiums in conjunction with the sale of a given product. Recently, the domestic automobile manufacturers have introduced insurance policies for separate fees extending coverage for periods beyond the basic twelve-month warranty.[103] The optional service contract of many appliances is similar. These contracts segregate consumers according to the amount of insurance coverage they wish to buy.[104] The warranty provides a term of basic coverage demanded by the lowest risk members of the pool. Those consumers for whom the risk is greater, however, can purchase more extensive coverage. Because relatively high-risk consumers are more likely to select such contracts, their premiums are likely to be proportionally higher for a given duration of coverage than the premiums of the basic warranty included in the sale price.[105]

A more subtle method of differentiating consumers is the offer by many retailers of warranty coverage that is separate from and, typically, more

102. This discussion is similar to that of Akerlof, *supra* note 38, at 492-93. Akerlof, however, focuses in his principal illustration upon the technological characteristics of a product rather than upon differential product use by consumers.

103. Wall St. J., Oct. 11, 1979, at 1, col. 4.

104. *See* Pauly, *Overinsurance and Public Provision of Insurance: The Roles of Moral Hazard and Adverse Selection*, 88 Q.J. ECON. 44, 60 (1974); Rothschild & Stiglitz, *Equilibrium in Competitive Insurance Markets: An Essay on the Economics of Imperfect Information*, 90 Q.J. ECON. 629, 641-42 (1976).

105. *See* Pauly, *supra* note 104, at 60.

extensive than the coverage offered by the product manufacturers themselves.[106] This additional coverage need not be explicit. It may take the form only of a more liberal or courteous return or exchange policy. It is not uncommon, however, for retailers to announce and, thus, to make contractual a guarantee of consumer "satisfaction"[107] that far exceeds the typical manufacturer warranty. This practice enables consumers to segregate themselves according to the level of protection each desires. Those consumers who value their time highly and who avoid allocative investments in care and maintenance or insurance investments in self-repair of products, may seek out retailers with liberal policies, although the products can be purchased at lower retail prices elsewhere. Dealers who offer more extensive warranty coverage are undoubtedly fully compensated for doing so, but their customers are less likely to to be those for whom the costs of allocative investments or self-insurance are relatively low.

Finally, a manufacturer may segregate consumers by means of explicit contractual provisions in the warranty. A manufacturer, for example, may exclude warranty coverage for a particular use of a product or specific class of consumers for which the volume or intensity of use is relatively high. The common provision that excludes coverage of commercial use is an obvious example. This provision narrows the class of those insured to domestic users of the product and may be incorporated to enforce a manufacturer's segregation of domestic and commercial purchasers by model design.

Some elements of product loss, however, may be excluded from coverage in the warranties of all product models. A common example is the exclusion of liability for consequential damages. The unavailability of any coverage of some loss, nonetheless, may be related to the reduction of differences in risk between members of the insurance pool. Where consumers differ substantially in the incidence or magnitude of a loss, such as consequential damages, there may be no single premium attractive to a sufficient number to justify offering coverage. Put another way, the increase in the premium required for coverage of such losses may be greater than the benefit of coverage to large numbers of consumers. If so, the sale of product insurance may be optimized by excluding coverage altogether.

Warranty exclusions are a form of product standardization. An exclusion of some element of loss is indistinguishable analytically from the exclusion of, say, magenta and acquamarine as product colors. If the number of consumers willing to purchase machines of unusual colors is very small, it may not be worth the cost for the manufacturer to introduce the

106. *See* Ross & Littlefield, *Complaint as a Problem-Solving Mechanism*, 12 LAW & SOC'Y REV. 199, 207, 211 (1978) (retailer studied offered coverage far more extensive than any manufacturer).
107. *See id.* at 211-12 (discussing Sears, Roebuck guarantee).

colors into the product line. Similarly, if the incidence or magnitude of an element of loss differs greatly between consumers of a product, the market for insurance may not be sufficiently large to justify offering insurance. Such a warranty exclusion enables the manufacturer to offer, for losses not excluded, either more extensive or less costly warranty coverage than if no exclusion were made, just as the production of appliances in a limited range of colors lowers price by reducing the costs of production and distribution. In this respect, consumers of the product may be said to have demanded the exclusions.

The segregation of consumers by explicit contractual provisions, however, is effective only to the extent that the manufacturer can identify prior to sale those consumers, product uses, or elements of loss for which differences in risk across the set of potential consumers are great. All those not identified and segregated must be lumped into a common pool, high-risk and low-risk alike. The terms of the standard warranty, then, establish the minimum level of coverage that is demanded uniformly by each member of the large class of purchasers; that is, a base level that can be supplemented in the variety of ways suggested above by those consumers desiring more extensive protection. The standard level of coverage comprises the minimum performance bond necessary to encourage appropriate investments by manufacturers in the design or mechanical qualities of the product and the minimum insurance coverage demanded by the lowest risk members of the consumer pool.[108]

## III. An Empirical Examination of the Theories

This Part evaluates whether the exploitation, signal, or investment theory best explains the content of consumer product warranties by reviewing the provisions of warranties issued in 1974 of sixty-two consumer products comprising sixteen different product groups.[109] The sample warranties were taken from a wide range of consumer products, including household appliances such as refrigerators, ranges, washers, dryers, and

108. Yoram Barzel suggests, as part of a general theory of measurement costs, that the duration of warranty coverage will be that period sufficient to allow the consumer to discover latent defects where inspection is cheaper for the consumer than for the manufacturer. Y. Barzel, Measurement Cost and the Organization of Markets (July 1979) (manuscript, University of Washington) (on file with *Yale Law Journal*). Others have expressed a more limited version of this theory. *See* Bogert & Fink, *supra* note 6, at 403; Best & Andreasen, *Consumer Response to Unsatisfactory Purchases: A Survey of Perceiving Defects, Voicing Complaints, and Obtaining Redress*, 11 LAW & SOC'Y REV 701, 702 (1977). Because there are no readily available means of measuring consumers' inspection costs, this theory cannot account—except by definition—for differences in warranty duration.

109. The warranties were compiled by the Federal Trade Commission for a study of the effects of the Magnuson-Moss Warranty Act. *See* J. SCHMITT, L. KANTER, & R. MILLER, IMPACT REPORT ON THE MAGNUSON-MOSS WARRANTY ACT, BUREAU OF CONSUMER PROTECTION, FEDERAL TRADE COMMISSION (STAFF REPORT) 11 (1980). The warranties surveyed in this article were issued in 1974, prior to the enactment of the Warranty Act.

televisions, relatively inexpensive products such as cookware, and more significant durables such as automobiles, recreational vehicles,[110] and on-site mobile homes.[111]

For this study I have inspected only copies of the warranties; I have collected no information regarding the frequency or magnitude of warranty claims of individual products or of warranty practices of manufacturers. A comparison of warranty terms alone, however, cannot provide sufficient grounds to accept or reject any of the theories. The investment theory, in particular, implies a precise relationship among price, cost, and warranty coverage, which I cannot examine. The results of the survey nevertheless are highly suggestive and support, I believe, more detailed empirical work.

### A. *Direct Tests of the Exploitation and Signal Theories*

This subpart examines the exploitation theory by comparing warranty coverage to measures of manufacturer power, and the signal theory by comparing warranty duration to estimates of the service life of various products.

#### 1. *The Exploitation Theory: Warranty Coverage and Manufacturer Market Power*

According to the exploitation theory, manufacturers exercise their powerful market position by imposing one-sided warranty terms on weaker consumers. Although some discussions treat the bargaining position of all manufacturers as superior to that of consumers,[112] most consider the size of the manufacturer crucial, so that warranties less favorable to consumers are offered by the larger rather than the smaller firms within an industry.[113] Still other treatments describe manufacturer market power as a

110. There are four leisure vehicles represented in the warranty sample. "Travel trailers" are large units (often with kitchens and bedrooms) towed behind a principal vehicle. "Recreational vehicles" (Type A Motor Homes) are large, self-propelled motor homes (often with kitchens and side-beds). "Coaches" (Type C Motor Homes) consist of a normal auto van chassis and cab to which is attached a relatively small living area (with beds and kitchen). "Truck mounts" are camping units attached to the bed of a pick-up truck.

111. The sample was not randomly drawn, but includes warranties of both dominant and relatively insignificant firms within the various industries. *See* p. 1321 *infra* (Table 1). The warranties of this sample represent a broader set of products than those of the Gerner and Bryant sample, *see Market Signal, supra* note 43, at 80 (household appliances only), but are less inclusive. The Gerner and Bryant sample contained at least eighteen warranties of each of five products. The provisions of the warranties of my sample appear very similar to those of both the Gerner and Bryant sample and the sample in Bogert & Fink, *supra* note 6, at 403-09 (describing sample). *But see* p. 1337 *infra* (apparent differences between Gerner and Bryant sample and this sample with respect to original purchaser limitation).

112. *See, e.g.*, Slawson, *supra* note 29, at 2.

113. A recent study compared warranty content with manufacturer size as measured by annual

consequence of the absence of competition, whether because of monopolization or of express or tacit collusion.[114] Thus, although a firm is large, its warranty practices may be constrained by competition with a group of small firms.

A principal weakness of the exploitation theory is that it provides no theoretical link between market power and product warranty terms. Why would a firm with market power maximize its returns by offering one-sided warranty terms rather than by manufacturing shoddy goods or by charging a monopoly price? Generally, monopoly profits are maximized by selling a product identical in all respects (except price) to the product offered under competition.[115] Thus, in theory, a monopolist (or a group of conspiring firms) will gain the greatest return by offering the consumer an optimal warranty, but at a price that exceeds marginal costs.

Table 1 tests the exploitation hypothesis empirically. It compares individual firm power in appliance markets with the content of each firm's warranty. Columns (2) through (10) array individual manufacturers according to each firm's share of the sales of a single appliance. The rows describe the content of each firm's warranty for the appliance, including the duration of basic and extended parts and labor coverage and the major exclusions and limitations of liability. The exploitation theory implies that the larger a firm's market share, the more restrictive the terms of its warranty will be.

Table 1 offers little support for the exploitation theory. The basic parts coverage of the firms with larger market shares is similar to that of firms with smaller market shares, although two relatively small firms offer unusually long coverage—five years (columns (7) and (9)). Moreover, the extended parts coverage of the smaller firms appears less generous than

sales volume in dollars. Note, *An Empirical Study of the Magnuson-Moss Warranty Act*, 31 STAN. L. REV. 1117, 1141-44 (1979). As a measure of size, dollar sales volume alone fails to distinguish between firms producing differently priced products. Thus, for example, a dominant manufacturer of cookware may appear less significant than a relatively small manufacturer of on-site mobile homes. The study found that manufacturers with relatively larger sales volumes offered the more generous warranty terms. *Id.* at 1141-42.

114. This was Kessler's view. Kessler, *supra* note 9, at 632; *see* Henningsen v. Bloomfield Motors, Inc., 32 N.J. 358, 390-91, 161 A.2d 69, 87 (1960) (three auto manufacturers using identical warranties had 93.5% share of market).

115. Sales in any market are maximized by the offer of product characteristics that are most responsive to consumer demands. *See* Posner, *Natural Monopoly and its Regulation*, 21 STAN. L. REV. 548, 548-85 (1969); Swan, *Optimum Durability, Second-Hand Markets, and Planned Obsolescence*, 80 J. POL. ECON. 575, 577, 582 (1972). It is possible that warranty provisions could be employed to enable discrimination in prices to increase profits further. Product warranties, however, tend to exclude from coverage high- rather than low-intensity users. *See* pp. 1330-46 *infra*. High-intensity users are usually those for whom the costs of the substitutes for warranty coverage—the consumer's allocative or insurance investments—are relatively high. Consumers who face costly substitutes, however, are the principal targets of price discrimination. Thus, the profit-maximizing discriminatory tactic would seek to include high-intensity users in the warranty pool, and to charge them a price that exploits the relative difficulty of substitution, rather than to exclude them.

Table 1. Warranty Coverage and Firm Market Share by Number of Firms, for Selected Appliances,* 1974

| Warranty Provision[1] | (1) | (2) | (3) | (4) | (5) | (6) | (7) | (8) | (9) | (10) |
|---|---|---|---|---|---|---|---|---|---|---|
| | | Percent Market Share by Product[2] | | | | | | | | Insignif- |
| | | >20 | 18-19 | 12-13 | 10-11 | 8-9 | 6-7 | 4-5 | <3 | icant[3] |
| N | | 2 | 2 | 2 | 1 | 2 | 4 | 2 | 8 | 7 |
| Basic Parts Coverage (years) | 1 | 1 | 2 | 1 | 1 | 2 | 3 | 2 | 6 | 6 |
| | 2 | 1 | | 1 | | | | | 1 | 1 |
| | 5 | | | | | | 1 | | 1 | |
| Extended Parts Coverage (years) | 0 | | | 1 | | | 1 | 1 | 2 | 1 |
| | 2 | 1 | | | 1 | 1 | 1 | | | 1 |
| | 5 | 1 | 2‡ | 1 | | 1 | 2† | 1 | 6 | 5 |
| Basic Labor Coverage (years) | 0 | | | 1 | | 1 | | | 1 | 1 |
| | 1 | 1 | 1 | 1 | | | 3 | 2 | 6 | 6 |
| | 2 | 1 | | | 1 | 1 | | | 1 | |
| | 5 | | 1 | | | | 1 | | | |
| Extended Labor Coverage (years) | 0 | 1 | 1 | 2 | 1 | 1 | 2 | 2 | 4 | 3 |
| | 1 | 1 | | | | 1 | | | | |
| | 5 | | 1‡ | | | | 2 | | 4 | 4 |
| Original Purchaser Limitation | | 1 | | | | 1 | 3 | 1 | 4 | 3 |
| Exclude Consequential Damages | | | 1 | | | 1 | 1 | | 1 | |
| Dislaim Merchantability | | | 1 | | | 1 | 1 | | 1 | |

* Refrigerators, gas & electric ranges, washers, room air conditioners, color televisions. Both dryer warranties are issued by the same firm (different subdivisions); their terms are generally identical. Only their composite market share is available; thus, I treat them as one firm.

† Where all parts are covered for five years, I indicate extended as well as basic coverage.

‡ One manufacturer offers 10-year coverage of certain parts and labor expenses.

Sources:

1. Warranties provided by Federal Trade Commission, June 1978.
2. Derived from *Who's Who and What's What in the Appliance Industry*, 22 APPLIANCE MANUFACTURER 60, 65 (1974).
3. *Id.*

that of larger firms. Five of twenty-one relatively small firms (seven percent market share or less) offer no extended parts coverage, whereas only one of nine firms with a market share greater than seven percent offers no coverage. Basic labor coverage appears equivalent between large and small firms. Extended labor coverage provisions, however, provide greater support for the exploitation theory. A greater proportion of smaller than of larger firms offer five-year labor coverage, although one firm with a nineteen percent market share—General Electric, the largest manufacturer of air conditioners—offers ten-year extended coverage of selected parts and labor expenses. Finally, the distribution of the exclusions of liability tends to refute the exploitation theory. Limitations of coverage to the original purchaser, disclaimers of the implied warranties, and exclusions of consequential damages are relatively infrequent in the warranties of firms possessing more than nine percent of a product market, but appear more often in the warranties of smaller firms.

The results of Table 1 might fail to support the exploitation theory because the Table does not distinguish atomistic from concentrated industries. Perhaps market power is more accurately measured by considering the extent of competition between manufacturers in individual industries, rather than the absolute size of the manufacturer alone. Tables 2 and 3 compare industry concentration to warranty content. Table 2 compares concentration to the warranty duration and the service life expectancy of the appliances. Column (2) presents Herfindahl concentration index estimates[116] for these product groups, in descending order of concentration. Columns (3) and (4) show the duration of extended parts and labor coverage, respectively. The exploitation theory implies that as concentration is greater, duration of coverage will be shorter.

Table 2. Industry Concentration, Warranty and Service-Life Duration, by Product, 1974

| (1) Product | N | (2) Herfindahl Index[1] | (3) Extended Parts Coverage[2] (years) | (4) Extended Labor Coverage[2] (years) | (5) Service Life Expectancy[3] (years) |
|---|---|---|---|---|---|
| Freezers | 1 | .225 | 5* | 5* | 20.4 |
| Washers | 5 | .197 | 5 (4 manufacturers) | 0 | 10.8 |
| Electric Ranges | 4 | .193 | 3 (1 manufacturer) | 0 | 12.1 |
| Dryers | 2 | .191 | 2, 5 (1 manufacturer) | 0 | 13.7 |
| Refrigerators | 5 | .159 | 5 | 5* | 15.2 |
| Gas Ranges | 2 | .151 | 0 | 0 | 13.5 |
| Color Televisions | 3 | .125 | 2 | 0 | 12.0 |
| Room Air Conditioners | 10 | .099 | 5* (7 manufacturers) | 5 | |

* Where all parts are covered for five years, I indicate extended coverage.

Sources:

1. Derived from *Who's Who and What's What in the Appliance Industry*, 22 APPLIANCE MANUFACTURER 60, 65 (1974).
2. Warranties provided by Federal Trade Commission, June 1978.
3. Ruffin & Tippett, *Service-Life Expectancy of Household Appliances: New Estimates from the USDA*, 3 HOME ECON. RESEARCH J. 159, 169 (1975) (April 1973 sample).

Table 2 fails to support this implication. The least concentrated product group—air conditioners—offers a duration of warranty coverage identical to that of both a moderately concentrated product group—refrigerators—and a highly concentrated product group—freezers.[117] A

116. The Herfindahl index consists of the sum of the squares of the market shares (in percent of sales) of each firm. *See* G. STIGLER, *The Measurement of Concentration*, in THE ORGANIZATION OF INDUSTRY 29, 31 (1968). This measure is consistent with the exploitation theory because it gives relatively greater weight to the market shares of larger firms than does the standard four-firm concentration ratio.

117. These three products are similar in that each contains a sealed refrigeration unit. *Cf.* pp. 1330-31 *infra* (discussing implication of investment theory with respect to extended coverage of products that contain sealed refrigeration systems).

relatively unconcentrated product group—gas ranges—offers the least extensive duration of coverage.[118] Column (5) gives estimates of the first-owner service life expectancy of the various appliances: a measure of the average period of service of the product to the original purchaser.[119] Some exploitation theorists would suggest that the power to exploit consumers will be expressed in the technological durability of the product as well as in warranty terms.[120] Column (5), however, does not confirm that hypothesis. Indeed, the product of the most concentrated group—freezers—is also the most durable.

The evidence most persuasive to judicial acceptance of the exploitation theory, however, was the correspondence between the high level of concentration in the automobile industry and the restrictive content of automobile warranties, in particular, the prevalence of disclaimers and exclusions of liability.[121] The automobile industry, of course, is more highly concentrated than any of the appliance industries, and its warranties are more restrictive. Perhaps a view of concentration and warranty content that incorporates a broader range of products would confirm the implications of the exploitation theory?

Table 3 compares the major warranty exclusions with industry concentration for thirteen product groups: the automotive products (automobiles, recreational vehicles, coaches, and travel trailers), the appliances, and on-site mobile homes. Columns (2) and (3) present Herfindahl index and four-firm concentration measures for these products; columns (4), (5), and (6) indicate the proportion of sample warranties incorporating the major exclusions.

Table 3 confirms the extraordinary concentration of the automobile industry and the great frequency of exclusions in automobile warranties, at least in comparison to the appliance groups (except, notably, dryers). Table 3 shows, however, that the frequency of exclusions in recreational vehicles, coaches, and, in part, in travel trailers is as high as in warranties of automobiles. Recreational vehicles, coaches, and travel trailers, of course, are industries of low concentration. By either of the two measures, they are many times less concentrated than even the appliance groups and are among the most atomistic of all manufacturing industries.

118. Although this sample contains only one freezer and two gas range warranties, the Gerner and Bryant study showed similar durations of warranty coverage for these products. *Market Signal*, *supra* note 43, at 13 (Table 2).

119. The estimate was drawn from a nationwide sample, although the article does not indicate when the survey was conducted. *See* Roussos & Konopa, *Ownership Levels, Acquisition and Disposition Channels of Selected Consumer Durable Used-Goods*, 8 AKRON BUS. & ECON. REV. 30 (1977).

120. *See* Prosser, *supra* note 27, at 158-65 (unless courts regulate sales transactions, manufacturers will sell "worthless junk").

121. *See* p. 1302 *supra* (discussing Henningsen v. Bloomfield Motors, Inc., 32 N.J. 358, 161 A.2d 69 (1960)); note 114 *supra* (same).

## Warranties

Table 3. Industry Concentration and Warranty Exclusions, by Product, 1974

| Product | N | Herfindahl Index[1] | Four-firm Concentration[1] | Proportion Disclaiming Merchantability[2] | Proportion Excluding Consequential Damages[2] | Proportion Limiting Coverage to Original Purchaser[2] |
|---|---|---|---|---|---|---|
| Automobiles | 4 | .359 | 100 | 75 | 75 | 0 |
| Freezers | 1 | .225 | 71 | 0 | 0 | 0 |
| Washers | 5 | .197 | 73 | 0 | 0 | 40 |
| Electric Ranges | 4 | .193 | 73 | 0 | 0 | 25 |
| Dryers | 2 | .191 | 73 | 100 | 100 | 100 |
| Refrigerators | 5 | .159 | 72 | 20 | 20 | 20 |
| Gas Ranges | 2 | .151 | 75 | 0 | 0 | 50 |
| Color Televisions | 3 | .125 | 60 | 0 | 0 | 66 |
| Room Air Conditioners | 10 | .099 | 59 | 20 | 20 | 40 |
| Recreational Vehicles | 5 | .078[3] | 44[3] | 80 | 100 | 80 |
| Travel Trailers | 4 | .053 | 33 | 50 | 50 | 100 |
| Coaches | 5 | .034[3] | 28[3] | 80 | 80 | 60 |
| Mobile Homes | 4 | .027 | 29 | 50 | 25 | 25 |

Sources:

1. Derived from 1975 AUTOMOBILE FACTS & FIGURES 14 (automobiles); *Who's Who and What's What in the Appliance Industry*, 22 APPLIANCE MANUFACTURER 60, 65 (1974) (freezers, washers, electric ranges, dryers, refrigerators, gas ranges, color televisions, and room air conditioners); R.L. POLK & CO., NEW MOTOR HOME, TRAVEL TRAILER AND MOBILE HOME REGISTRATION SERVICE (1974) (includes all United States registrations, except Oklahoma; concentration measures include manufacturer rather than brand product share, which may overstate concentration; insignificant firms not accounted for individually comprise 10%, 14%, 8%, and 20% of recreational vehicle, coach, travel trailer, and mobile home figures, respectively; these firms were not included in concentration measures).
2. Warranties provided by Federal Trade Commission, June 1978.
3. For some firms, only joint recreational vehicle-coach registrations were available. I use the summary figure in both categories, and thus overstate actual concentration. Recreational vehicles and coaches are built upon chassis manufactured by the three largest automobile firms. Recreational vehicle and coach warranties, however, extend only to independently added equipment; chassis are warranted separately. *See* p. 1329 *infra* (Table 5).

These data suggest that the correlation between concentration and restrictive warranty content in automobile warranties is spurious. Indeed, Table 3 demonstrates that there is no clear relation between concentration levels and product warranty content. Table 3 does suggest that, with respect to exclusions of liability, there are great similarities, first, within the warranties of the automotive products and, second, within the warranties of appliances, regardless of concentration. I shall explain, below, that these similarities appear to derive from the different ways consumers use appliances and automotive products, an explanation which is consistent with the investment theory.[122]

122. *See* pp. 1333, 1334, 1338, 1345-46 *infra*.

The Yale Law Journal Vol. 90: 1297, 1981

### 2. *The Signal Theory: Warranty Duration and Service Life Expectancy*

The signal theory rests on the assumption that warranty terms reflect the mechanical durability of the product. According to the theory, the costs of comprehending warranty information require consumers to generalize information about a range of related products. Generalization may attenuate to some extent the correspondence between warranty duration and service life.[123] Thus, the duration of coverage may not equal product service life exactly. The signal theory's fundamental implication, however, is that the relationship between warranty duration and service life expectancy is direct and positive and is a relationship upon which consumers can, with confidence, base their purchasing decisions.[124]

Table 4 compares the duration of basic and extended parts coverage with measures of expected service life for various appliances and for automobiles. The products are listed in descending order of service life expectancy. Column (4) gives estimates of the duration of service life to original owners of these products. Column (5) gives estimates of the total service life of the product itself, regardless of the number of owners.[125]

Table 4 shows only a very crude relationship between warranty duration and life expectancy. The single warranty of the most durable product—freezers—offers the longest period of basic parts coverage. However, three of five warranties of the appliance with the least durability—washers—offer a period of basic parts coverage twice that of seventeen warranties of the more durable products—color televisions, electric and gas ranges, dryers—and four warranties of refrigerators. In addition, the warranties of two appliances that are most durable—freezers and refrigerators—offer the longest period of extended parts coverage, but so do the warranties of the least durable appliance—washers. Moreover, there is no ordinal relationship among the appliances of intermediate durability.

More curious is the relationship that Table 4 reveals between service life expectancy and the absolute level of warranty duration. The service life expectancies of the appliances range from eleven to twenty years. The signal theory assumes that it is economical for consumers to generalize information about the basic coverage terms of various products. The simplified categories of Table 4, in fact, seem to bear out the generalization hypothesis. Although there are some variations, seventeen of the twenty-

123. *Market Signal*, *supra* note 43, at 77-78.

124. *Id.* at 77-79.

125. The figures result from separate studies: the estimates of service life to first owners, column (4), derive from an extensive nationwide sample. *See* note 119 *supra*. The estimates of total product life (all owners), column (5), derive from a 1970 Whirlpool Corporation study of Whirlpool products, which may differ from the average.

Warranties

Table 4. Product Service-Life Expectancy and Duration of Parts Coverage, by Appliance, 1974

| Appliance | (1) N | (2) Duration Basic Coverage[1] (years) (by firm) | (3) Duration Extended Coverage[1] (years) (by firm) | (4) Service Life Expectancy for First Owner[2] (years) | (5) Total Service Life Expectancy[3] (years) |
|---|---|---|---|---|---|
| Freezers | 1 | 5 | 5* | 20.4 | 18 |
| Refrigerators | 5 | 1 (4), 5(1) | 5* | 15.2 | 15 |
| Dryers | 2 | 1 | 2, 5 | 13.7 | 15 |
| Gas Ranges | 2 | 1 | 0 | 13.5 | |
| Electric Ranges | 4 | 1 | 3 (1) | 12.1 | 14 |
| Color Televisions | 3 | 1 | 2 | 12.0 | |
| Washers | 5 | 1 (2)<br>2 (3) | 5 (4) | 10.8 | 12 |
| Appliance Average (nonweighted) | | | | 14.0 | 14.8 |
| Automobiles | 4 | 1 | 0 | | 9.4 |

Note: Numbers in parentheses within the table indicate manufacturers.

* Where all parts are covered for five years, I indicate extended as well as basic coverage.

Sources:

1. Warranties provided by Federal Trade Commission, June 1978.
2. Ruffin & Tippett, *Service-Life Expectancy of Household Appliances: New Estimates from the USDA*, 3 HOME ECON. RESEARCH J. 159, 169 (1975) (April 1973 sample).
3. Appliances: Whirlpool Corporation, Marketing Studies Department, 1970 Study (on file with *Yale Law Journal*). Automobiles: Teknekron, Inc., Factors Influencing Product Durability, *reprinted* in SEN. REP. No. 12, 93d Cong., 1st Sess., 139, 168 (1973) (study undertaken around 1970).

two appliance warranties, as well as the four automobile warranties, offer basic-parts coverage for one year.[126]

The peculiarity of this finding, however, is apparent. Why is basic-parts coverage of one year the generalized durability signal of these products? The average service life of all appliances is, according to one measure, 14.0 years and, according to the other, 14.8 years. The shortest service life expectancy of the appliances within the set is, by one measure, 10.8 years and, by the other, 12 years. If warranty duration is a signal of the purely mechanical characteristics of a product, without regard to a consumer's allocative investments in prolonging product life, what explains a durability signal of one year, rather than ten years or fourteen years? The signal theory does not answer this question and suggests no method for discovering an answer.[127]

126. A more careful inspection of the warranties, however, discloses that one-year parts coverage is only a residual term from which there are many variations. *See* note 174 *infra.*

127. Also inconsistent with the signal theory are the offer by retailers and manufacturers of different warranty coverage, *see* p. 1318 *supra*, and the distinctions with respect to coverage among types of purchasers and uses of the product, *see* pp. 1331-38 *infra*. In each case, the technological characteristics of the product—the subject matter of the signal—are identical, even though the signals are different.

B. *Differences in Specific Warranty Provisions*

This subpart examines the contents of the sample warranties more carefully. It reviews specific warranty provisions and considers whether differences with respect to these provisions in the warranties of different products are explained most persuasively by the exploitation, signal, or investment theory.

1. *The Duration of Parts Coverage*

The parts coverage provision of most product warranties has two elements: the first establishes coverage of most product parts for some basic term—commonly one year;[128] the second defines exceptions to this basic coverage.[129] The exceptions consist, for specific product parts, of exclusions from coverage altogether, limitations of coverage to periods less than the basic term, or extensions of coverage beyond the basic term.

The three theories interpret these parts provisions differently. Provisions excluding or limiting parts coverage are consistent with the exploitation theory. This theory, however, does not indicate which parts will be excluded from coverage nor, for that matter, why all parts are not excluded from coverage. In addition, it does not explain why some parts are given extended coverage. The implications of the signal theory are equally unclear. Gerner and Bryant predict a lack of uniformity across products in the parts excluded from coverage because consumers are unaware of the exclusions.[130] They also predict, at one point, that manufacturers will exclude those aspects of coverage most costly to them[131] but, at another, that the parts excluded will be those inexpensive and easily repaired by consumers.[132] Finally, according to the investment theory, the treatment of product parts will be related to differences in risk between consumers as a consequence of differences either in intensity or volume of use of the product.[133]

128. For a more precise evaluation of how common one-year parts and labor coverage is, see note 174 *infra*.

129. In my view, this structure itself influenced the formation of the exploitation theory. Some statements of the exploitation theory view the warranty as giving the appearance of coverage while in fact limiting and disclaiming coverage. The structure also influenced the formulation of the signal theory, which views a consumer as comprehending the basic terms of coverage but ignoring exceptions and exclusions of liability. Since the number of exclusions and disclaimers is quite small, the advantage in simplicity of this structure is apparent. It is difficult to imagine, for example, a warranty in which the manufacturer lists all the parts and characteristics of the product to which coverage is extended.

130. *Market Signal*, *supra* note 43, at 84.

131. *Id.* at 84-85.

132. *Id.* at 81 n.7.

133. Gerner and Bryant, in the sole empirical study of parts coverage, found warranties providing only extended rather than limited terms of parts coverage, a fact they interpret to be consistent with the signal theory's prediction of pressures toward greater-than-average coverage. *Id.* at 82-84 (Tables 1 & 2).

## Warranties

Table 5 lists product parts excluded from coverage in the warranties of my sample. There is little uniformity across products in parts excluded, which is consistent with the (weak) implication of the signal theory. The signal theory's more precise implication, however, is not confirmed. The parts excluded appear to be neither those most costly to manufacturers nor those most easily repaired by consumers. Certainly, the dollar value of light bulbs and gaskets in comparison to other product parts is small. But many excluded parts, such as plastic parts, the trim and finish, enamel, and porcelain and glass pieces, are likely to be specific to the particular product model. The consumer has no evident cost advantage in providing replacements for these parts.[134]

Table 5. Product Parts Totally Excluded from Warranty Coverage, 1974

| Product | (N) | |
|---|---|---|
| Cookware | 1 | None |
| Refrigerators | 5 | Light bulbs, plastic parts, gasket, porcelain, exterior finish, fuses |
| Freezers | 1 | Plastic parts, gasket |
| Gas and Electric Ranges | 6 | Light bulbs, finish or trim |
| Washers | 5 | Light bulbs, porcelain |
| Dryers | 2 | Light bulbs, glass pieces (one manufacturer excludes all nonworking parts) |
| Room Air Conditioners | 10 | Air filters |
| Color Televisions | 3 | Antenna system (two manufacturers) |
| Stereo Equipment | 2 | Plastic parts, needles, batteries, knobs, cabinets |
| Automobiles | 4 | Paint, appearance (one manufacturer); tires separately warranted |
| Recreational Vehicles | 5 | Chassis, tires, appliances, all separately warranted |
| Coaches | 5 | Fabrics, carpets, windows, windshield (one manufacturer); chassis, tires, appliances, all separately warranted |
| Truck Mounts | 4 | Interior surface (one manufacturer); chassis, tires, all separately warranted |
| Travel Trailers | 5 | Tires, batteries, appliances, all separately warranted |
| On-site Mobile Homes | 4 | Non-integral furniture, plumbing and appliances, all separately warranted |

Source: Warranties provided by Federal Trade Commission, June 1978.

134. Some warranties exclude only those components warranted separately by the component manufacturer. Prosser believed that exclusions of this nature were unfair to consumers because of the potential obstacles to recovery from the component manufacturer. *See* Prosser, *supra* note 28, at 1124. Several warrantors in the sample, however, offer to aid the consumer in pursuing component warranty claims.

The parts excluded from coverage in Table 5, however, can be interpreted as those product components most vulnerable to different intensities of use by consumers. The parts typically appear to be either easily breakable—glass and plastic parts, porcelain, phonograph needles—or exterior parts sensitive to scratching, abrasion, or rough use—paint, cabinets, the finish or trim. Differences between consumers in volume of use may affect some of the parts, such as batteries and fuses.[135]

Product parts given coverage less than the standard one-year term are similar.[136] One range warranty limits coverage of glass and other finishes on the range to a thirty-day period. A stereo warranty limits coverage for defects in cabinets, wood products, plastic protective covering, knobs, dress panels, and trim to a period of ten days. Several warranties offer coverage of porcelain parts and other parts of the finish only until the buyer has completed an initial inspection of the product. These warranties offer some insurance against defects in manufacture or delivery, but they require consumers to determine the existence of such defects within a very short period, before the risk of the consumer's participation in the damage increases substantially.

Many warranties also cover specific product parts for periods well beyond the basic one-year term. Refrigerator, freezer, and air conditioner warranties, for example, commonly offer five-year coverage of the sealed refrigeration system. Similarly, most warranties of washing machines in the sample offer five-year coverage of the machine's transmission. The Airstream travel trailer warranty covers the metal shell, frame, and axle assembly for life to the first owner. Each of the television manufacturers offers two-year coverage of the picture tube.[137]

Again, the selection of these parts for extended coverage cannot be explained convincingly as a form of exploitation or signaling. Yet the parts have two similar characteristics that lend support to the investment theory. First, they are the parts most critical to the continued productive capacity of the good.[138] The failure of a refrigerator's sealed cooling system, for example, imposes a much greater loss on a consumer than does dam-

135. The exclusion of coverage of the antenna system in the two television warranties is difficult to interpret. The third television warranty, which describes coverage more elaborately, excludes coverage of home antenna systems, rather than coverage of the system that accompanies the individual set. Perhaps the other two warranties are meant to be interpreted similarly.

136. Gerner and Bryant do not discuss such provisions. *See Market Signal, supra* note 43.

137. In addition, coverage is offered, in one recreational vehicle warranty, of defects in body lamination for the lifetime of the product; in one air conditioner warranty, of the "Lexan" protective cover for ten years; in one electric range warranty, of the heating unit and surface controls for three years; in one dryer warranty, of the drum assembly for five years; and in one stereo equipment warranty, of the turntable and receiver for two years and of the speakers for five years.

138. Gerner and Bryant make a similar observation, but do not attempt to reconcile it with the implications of the signal theory. *Market Signal, supra* note 43, at 82.

age to a tray or shelf. Where the magnitude of the potential loss is greater, consumer demand for a performance bond from the manufacturer—or for insurance[139]—is likely to be greater.

Second, these parts are housed deep within the product, protected by the product's outer shell and often by padding and internal bracing. They are thus likely to be less susceptible to damage from rough handling or careless treatment short of active misuse.[140] These parts, of course, remain subject to differences in the volume of use between consumers—which could explain why the duration of extended coverage is substantially less than most measures of the productive life of the machine.[141] But it is plausible that differences between consumers in prevention costs affect these parts less than they do the exterior cover and operating controls of which coverage is shorter.[142]

## 2. *The Commercial Use Exclusion*

Product warranties commonly deny coverage altogether if the product is put to commercial, rather than to domestic, use. Neither the exploitation nor the signal theory provides a plausible explanation of this exclusion. As a first approximation, the bargaining position of a commercial buyer is equivalent to that of a manufacturer, or at least is much less disparate than the bargaining position of a consumer. Yet it is the commercial buyer rather than the consumer who is excluded from coverage.

The exclusion of commercial use also seems inconsistent with the signal theory. If warranty terms signal the purely technological characteristics of a good at the time of purchase, then there is no reason to distinguish between domestic and commercial buyers. Furthermore, the signal theory suggests that exclusions appear in warranties where the costs of information about the likelihood of losses are relatively high. It stretches the imagination, however, to believe that information about the likelihood of

139. It is very difficult to segregate empirically demand for a performance bond from demand for insurance. The dollar value of many consumer products is sufficiently low to question whether the loading costs of manufacturer-insurance are worth bearing.

140. The manufacturers universally exclude coverage of "defects" caused by consumer misuse.

141. *See* p. 1327 *supra* (Table 4).

142. Some warranties incorporate provisions limiting coverage of repair parts to the original duration of the warranty. There is no reason why coverage of repair parts, but not of original parts, is an avenue of exploitation. Nor is there a coherent description of how differential consumer information would lead to a distinctive treatment of repair parts.

Two possible explanations of the provision are consistent with the investment theory. First, the interaction of a new part with the remaining used parts, like a new saddle on a horse, could increase the likelihood of product breakdown. Thus, the level of claims regarding even the new part could be differentially greater. Second, the repair itself may indicate a significantly higher intensity of consumer use of some specific product part. Thus, the provision might serve to segregate ex post, rather than ex ante, those consumers for whom the costs of repair are differentially higher. The provision might also serve to record for the manufacturer exactly when its obligation ends. The costs of accounting for the remaining coverage of repaired items, however, are probably not significant.

product losses is less available to a commercial buyer than to a consumer.

According to the investment theory, an exclusion from coverage reduces differences in risk between purchasers of a product. Commercial purchasers may subject a product both to a greater volume of use over a given period and to a greater intensity of use, especially where the product is rented to others, such as a washer or dryer at a laundromat. A person renting rather than owning a product is less likely to invest in "care" in order to optimize the productive life of the machine.[143] According to the investment theory, however, the express exclusion of commercial use from warranty coverage is related to other methods a manufacturer may have to segregate consumers by differences in risk, such as differences in model design or selective marketing techniques. Unfortunately, the warranty sample provides no information concerning such alternative methods available to manufacturers.

Within the sample, the warranties of washers, dryers, freezers, and gas ranges exclude commercial use universally; the warranties of some refrigerators (four of five), electric ranges (three of four), televisions (one of three), travel trailers (one of five), recreational vehicles (two of five), coaches (two of five), and truck mounts (two of four) exclude it; and the warranties of cookware, air conditioners, stereos, automobiles, and on-site mobile homes do not exclude commercial use.

The warranty data alone are insufficient to support fully an explanation of these different treatments of the commercial use exclusion consistent with the investment theory. Two limited observations, however, can be made. First, subtle differences in definitions of the commercial use exclusion in various warranties indicate attempts to reduce differences in risk. Several warranties, for example, define coverage in terms of the product's household function rather than of its actual use. Thus, the product is warranted to commercial users, but only to the extent normal for a household. In addition, one refrigerator warranty excludes commercial use only for the extended period of coverage (second through fifth years) of the sealed refrigeration system; commercial and domestic purchasers alike receive warranty coverage for the first year of use. The effect of the more precise definition of the exclusion in these provisions is to extend coverage more broadly for the residual set of consumers.

Second, manufacturers that are able to define the duration of warranty coverage according to the volume of use of the product—manufacturers of automobiles, coaches, and recreational vehicles who can measure warranty duration by mileage—exclude commercial use less frequently, an outcome

143. A renter will invest only to the extent that he can gain the return from the investment during the rental period.

consistent with the investment theory. Of the eight warranties measuring duration by mileage, only one excludes commercial use; in contrast, of the six measuring duration by time, three exclude commercial use. These relationships are not strong, and the distinction remains tentative. It is plausible, however, that a manufacturer reduces the difference in the risks introduced by commercial and domestic users by defining coverage in a way that equalizes differences in rates of use over time between these purchasers. Some difference in risk will persist, of course, because of differences in the intensity of commercial and domestic product use.

### 3. *Miscellaneous Use and Repair Exclusions*

Several of the sample warranties exclude coverage of miscellaneous uses or types of repairs peculiar to individual products. For example, the Chrysler automobile warranty excludes coverage of repairs resulting from "racing, sustained high speed use, . . . high speed acceleration or shifting transmission gears at high engine RPM." The Midas recreational vehicle warranty excludes coverage not only of all commercial uses but also of personal recreational uses by a club or group. Several of the automotive product warranties exclude repairs that result from carrying heavy loads or hauling trailers. The KLH warranty excludes coverage of the costs of demagnetizing stereo equipment.

None of these various exclusions can be easily explained as serving a signaling function or as reflecting some special exploitative opportunity.[144] The exclusions, however, seem related to uses of the product for which warranty costs are likely to be substantially greater than usual. A club or group, for example, can be expected to subject a recreational vehicle to more intensive use than any single purchaser.[145] Similarly, the strain on an engine or transmission is likely to be greater if an automobile is used for racing rather than for commuting or family driving.[146] This interpretation does not suggest that the products are not or could not be made suitable for uses excluded from coverage, but only that repair costs for these uses are likely to be substantially higher than for average use. A dominant group of consumers not expecting to use the products in these ways may prefer those products sold with the lower insurance premiums made possible by the exclusions.[147]

144. Neither the exploitation nor signal theorists have addressed these exclusions.

145. A gas range warrantor incorporates a similar distinction: the 1974 warranty limits coverage to "normal household use." The 1978 warranty for the same product limits coverage more precisely to "normal single family household use." Thus, multiple family household use was excluded in 1978.

146. *See* Whitford, *supra* note 11, at 1063.

147. The universal exclusion of damage due to consumer misuse is an obvious illustration of the same point.

Provisions that exclude coverage of defects that result from exposure of the product—usually a vehicle—to natural weather or use conditions illustrate the principle in a different way. The Superior coach warranty, for example, excludes coverage if "circumstances beyond the control of the manufacturer . . . cause the body or parts to become defective depending . . . on where and how the owner drives, weather, atmospheric conditions, varying road surfaces, individual driving habits and vehicle usage." The Swinger truck mount warranty excludes coverage of damage from "deterioration of paint, bright metal or soft trim from wear or exposure or any stains to any surface or fabric . . . regardless of cause." In addition, the Swinger warranty disclaims responsibility for "the re-caulking of the body periodically, the re-coating of the roof around the vents, . . . [and] the recoating of seams and roof edges."

The exploitation or signal theory might interpret these provisions as indications that the product is particularly vulnerable to expected weather conditions. The investment theory, on the other hand, suggests two reasons why warranties might exclude deterioration from weather conditions. First, consumers are likely to make different investments to prevent deterioration, such as in the extent to which they garage vehicles or in the frequency with which they clean and wax them. Second, in a national market, individual products are likely to be exposed to weather conditions that differ substantially in severity. For either reason, a dominant set of consumers could prefer the exclusion of coverage of losses to products subjected to deterioration from weather or use. The warranty sample alone, of course, is insufficient to confirm either interpretation. It is instructive to note, however, that the Swinger truck mount warranty does not exclude coverage generally of the repair of all leaks in the roof or body, but only excludes the obligation to repair leaks by the recaulking and recoating of the body and seams after some period of initial use. The need to recaulk a truck mount, as opposed to the need for initial caulking, is likely to differ among consumers according to the extent of exposure to rapid temperature changes or other severe conditions.[148]

Finally, the warranties of virtually all products terminate coverage if

148. Similarly, two automobile manufacturers offer basic coverage for 12 months, but restrict to 90 days the obligation to perform engine adjustments. A color television warranty limits coverage of labor costs in adjusting and repairing the set to 90 days. A stereo warranty excludes coverage of stylus wear, dial alignment calibration, and tape head cleaning. The vehicle warranties also commonly exclude coverage of parts frequently replaced in normal maintenance such as spark plugs, filters, and windshield wipers, although coverage is extended to original parts. These provisions illustrate the same principle. All consumers expect to demand *some* level or number of adjustments or maintenance parts, but the level or number may differ substantially according to the intensity of use or the particularity of the individual consumer. As a consequence, some dominant set of consumers who use the product less intensively may express a preference for the exclusion of adjustments and maintenance parts from coverage.

Warranties

the consumer modifies or alters the product. Again, such a restriction has no apparent exploitative or signaling function. It is not implausible, however, that the consumer's decision to substitute his own design expertise for that of the manufacturer might lead to higher levels of product failure.[149] The virtually universal provision terminating warranty coverage if repairs are made by an unauthorized service person or shop may be only a special case of the same point.[150]

### 4. *Limitation of Coverage to the Original Purchaser*

Many warranties cancel coverage if the original purchaser sells or otherwise transfers ownership of the product prior to the expiration of the period of basic or extended coverage. These provisions would be consistent with the exploitation theory only in the unlikely event that there exist differences between the bargaining power of purchasers who resell products and of purchasers who retain them for the relatively limited periods of warranty coverage.[151] The signal theory provides a more plausible hypothesis. If the buyer is uninformed at the time of the original purchase—either because he does not read the warranty or because he does not consider whether he will later want to resell the product—the original purchaser limitation will mean nothing to him and will not affect his purchase decision.[152] Thus the manufacturer may incorporate freely this limitation into the warranty.[153] The signal explanation, of course, does not distinguish among individual products; because coverage to subsequent purchasers always imposes some costs, the limitation should appear universally.[154]

The investment theory suggests a different explanation. To the extent that the intensity of the first purchaser's use cannot be detected by second-

149. Many warranties specify that the exclusion applies only if the modification contributes to the defect, although others are drafted to exclude coverage if any modification is made. If the modification is unrelated to the defect, the exclusion of coverage may appear exploitative. (But can it be shown to be profit-maximizing?) For a confident conclusion, information is needed about the invocation of the exclusion in practice.

150. The service center requirement may also provide a convenient means for the manufacturer to obtain information about the sources of product defects. The requirement may be particularly important to a manufacturer where the dealer has responsibility for preadjustment or assembly of the product, so that dealer and manufacturer obligations are correctly allocated. The Federal Trade Commission under the Magnuson-Moss Warranty Act, however, has prohibited the requirement in Full warranties because of the fear of tying arrangements. *See* Priest, *supra* note 65, at 251-52.

151. The service-life expectancy of products appears to be universally more extensive than the term of warranty coverage. *See* p. 1327 *supra* (Table 4).

152. It is not sufficient, according to this hypothesis, that the buyer at the time of purchase appreciate only some probability of future resale; rather, the buyer must systematically underestimate the likelihood of resale and thus the cost to him of the original purchaser limitation. Spence believes that consumers will systematically underestimate product risks. Spence, *supra* note 42, at 569-71.

153. *Market Signal*, *supra* note 43, at 78-79.

154. *See id.* (by inference).

hand purchasers, those first purchasers who expect to transfer products to others may invest relatively less in care and maintenance or may subject products to a relatively greater volume or intensity of use prior to resale.[155] If so, second-hand items are more likely to require servicing.[156] As a consequence, purchasers who expect to retain products will prefer warranties that limit coverage to the original purchaser in order to remove second-hand items from the warranty pool. This explanation implies that the appearance of the limitation will not be universal but will be correlated, first, with the duration of basic or extended coverage—because the longer the term, the greater the opportunity for the owner to use the good intensively prior to resale—and, second, with the product's susceptibility to reduction in service life from intensive use.

An extension of this theory explains why markets for second-hand goods exist at all for some products and not for others. It is well known that the size of second-hand markets differs dramatically for different goods.[157] The extent of the second-hand market in any product will be determined by the relationship between the difficulty of estimating the remaining productive life of the good and the product's susceptibility to deterioration from intensive use by earlier owners.[158] Theoretical treatments of markets for new and used durable goods have focused exclusively on manufacturers' technological investments in order to demonstrate, in general, that manufacturers in both competitive and monopolistic industries will invest equally in increasing product durability.[159] None of the studies,

155. In economic terms, purchasers expecting to resell resemble renters. *See* note 143 *supra*. Of course, consumers may decide to resell a product after they discover that they have subjected it to intense use.

156. A similar point is made in Akerlof, *supra* note 38, at 489-91, although his principal illustration assumes differentially inferior technological characteristics of certain items—"lemons"—rather than differential levels of consumer investments. Akerlof considers consumer investments in illustrations of health insurance, honesty, and credit but does not apply the point to products. *See id.* at 492-94, 495-99. Akerlof also remarks that warranties are a means of counteracting the adverse selection problem. *Id.* at 499.

157. A recent study, for example, shows that second-hand typewriters constitute 32.6% of the total typewriter inventory while second-hand clothes dryers constitute only 11.5% and second-hand blenders only 4.5% of the total dryer and blender inventories, respectively. *See* Roussos & Konopa, *supra* note 119, at 31 (Table 2).

158. The ability to estimate remaining service life and the technological susceptibility of the product to deterioration are related determinants of second-hand markets. As it becomes more difficult to estimate service life, first-owners can employ an item with greater intensity without affecting the resale price of the individual item. Such intense use, however, affects the price of the set of items because the expected service life to second-hand purchasers diminishes.

159. Of course, price is higher in monopolistic industries. *See, e.g.*, Benjamin & Kormendi, *The Interrelationship Between Markets for New and Used Durable Goods*, 17 J.L. & ECON. 381, 388-401 (1974) (competitive and monopolistic manufacturers have similar attitudes towards second-hand markets); Miller, *On Killing off the Market for Used Textbooks and the Relationship between Markets for New and Secondhand Goods*, 82 J. POL. ECON. 612, 613-16 (1974) (comparing prices paid for new and used books in competitive and monopolistic industries); Swan, *Alcoa: The Influence of Recycling on Monopoly Power*, 88 J. POL. ECON. 76, 90-92 (1980) (prices rise when monopoly is achieved in either primary or second-hand market); Swan, *supra* note 115, at 582 (monopolists ensure

Warranties

however, has considered the role of investments by consumers in influencing the size of the second-hand market[160] or the role of the warranty in influencing optimal investments by consumers.[161] The investment explanation suggests that the inclusion of the original purchaser limitation should be inversely correlated (roughly)[162] with the size of the second-hand market. The more susceptible a product is to intensive use, the smaller the second-hand market for the product will be, and the more likely it will be that warranty coverage is limited to the original purchaser.

Table 6 compares the original purchaser limitation in the sample warranties to estimates of the extent of a second-hand market for each appliance. Column (2) lists in declining order the proportion of warranties of each product that incorporates the original purchaser limitation. Column (2) shows that the limitation is far from universal, a result inconsistent with the implications of the signal theory.[163] Column (3) presents estimates from a study of the proportion of used products among the total market inventory of those products.[164] The two sets of figures appear to support the implication that an inverse relationship exists between the original purchaser limitation and the size of the used-goods market.[165] The limited number of warranties of each product in the sample, however, makes the result only suggestive. Column (4) lists the findings of the Gerner and Bryant study, which fail to support the relationship.[166] A further, more careful study is needed.

greater profits by raising price rather than by reducing quality).

160. The point, however, may be inferred from Akerlof, *supra* note 38, at 489-91, *discussed in* note 156 *supra*.

161. Most studies have considered goods that are relatively insensitive to consumer use, such as aluminum, *see* Swan, *supra* note 159, land, *see* Coase, *Durability and Monopoly*, 15 J.L. & ECON. 143 (1972), and (perhaps, *see* note 157 *supra*) typewriters, *see* Benjamin & Kormendi, *supra* note 159.

162. Of course, there are other determinants of the extent of second-hand markets, including changes over time in a particular consumer's demand for a product. For example, of the respective total inventories of their products, second-hand boats comprise 48.3%, pool and ping-pong tables, 38.3%, and cribs, 27.7%. Roussos & Konopa, *supra* note 119, at 31 (Table 2).

163. Of the 62 warranties of the sample, 31 limit coverage to the original purchaser. Of the 106 warranties of the Gerner and Bryant sample, 36 limit coverage to the original purchaser. *Market Signal*, *supra* note 43, at 85 (Table 3). Gerner and Bryant do not attempt to explain why the limitation is not incorporated universally.

164. Roussos & Konopa, *supra* note 119, at 31 (Table 2). The article does not indicate when the survey was conducted.

165. The inverse relationship is obvious, but the second-hand market estimates must be analyzed carefully. Although individual product figures were not given for the sample as a whole, 37% of second-hand products were obtained as gifts rather than by purchase. It is possible that products given to others—say, by parents to children—are used prior to transfer relatively less intensively than products resold. Furthermore, the Roussos and Konopa study was conducted in Cedar Rapids, Iowa, which may contain a population unusually homogenous in various respects including product use. If so, the figures may reflect a larger second-hand market than exists in other cities.

166. I have corrected what appear to be arithmetical errors in the Gerner and Bryant table, *Market Signal*, *supra* note 43, at 85 (Table 3).

Table 6. Original Purchaser Limitation (1974) and Used Product Inventory (1977), by Appliances

| Product | (1) N | (2) Original Purchaser Limitation[1] (percentage) | (3) Used Products in Total Inventory[2] (percentage) | (4) Gerner-Bryant Estimates Transferability Limitation[3] (percentage) |
|---|---|---|---|---|
| Dryers | 2 | 100 | 11.5 | |
| Televisions | 3 | 66 | 12.3 | 38 |
| Stereo Equipment | 2 | 50 | 12.5 | |
| Washers | 5 | 40 | 14.4 | 33 |
| Room Air Conditioners | 10 | 40 | 29.6 | 23 |
| Gas and Electric Ranges | 6 | 33 | 29.4 | 44 |
| Refrigerators | 5 | 20 | 27.4 | 30 |
| Freezers | 1 | 0 | 25.7 | |

Sources:

1. Warranties provided by Federal Trade Commission, June 1978.
2. Roussos & Konopa, *Ownership Levels, Acquisitions and Disposition Channels of Selected Consumer Durable Used-Goods*, 8 AKRON BUS. & ECON. REV. 30 (1977).
3. *Market Signal, supra* note 43, at 14 (Table 3 (corrected)).

The investment hypothesis may be tested differently by examining the original purchaser limitation in the warranties of automobiles, recreational vehicles, and coaches. The hypothesis implies that the original purchaser limitation is less likely to be incorporated where purchasers who use the product relatively extensively are removed from the warranty pool by defining duration in terms of volume of use (for these products, mileage).[167] Of the eight warranties that define coverage by mileage, two limit coverage to the original purchaser. Of the six warranties that define coverage by periods of time, however, five limit coverage to the original purchaser. This finding tends to support the investment theory.[168]

### 5. *The Allocation of Warranty Labor Charges*

The most basic form of warranty coverage is the promise to provide replacements for parts found to be defective during the warranty term. Most warranties also cover the labor costs necessary to complete the repair; that is, the direct costs of replacing the defective part. Other warranties, however, offer only partial coverage or no coverage of labor charges. Some warranties, for example, cover the costs of the repair itself, but require the consumer to pay the serviceman's travel charges. Many more

167. Mileage can be observed by a second-hand purchaser. Thus, except to the extent of fraudulent resetting of odometers, there is likely to be a less direct relationship between the size of the second-hand market for these products and the incorporation of the original purchaser limitation. Mileage, however, measures only volume and not intensity of use.

168. It is also consistent with the theory that one refrigerator warrantor limits coverage to the original purchaser only for the five-year period of extended parts and labor coverage. Both the original and subsequent purchasers of the refrigerator receive parts and labor coverage for the basic one-year term.

warranties require the consumer to pay the costs of transporting the defective product to a service center for repair.

Neither the exploitation nor signal theory suggests explanations of the allocation of these various service charges. The signal theory implies, in general, that the assignment will be similar across different products because of the need for uniform signals.[169] Gerner and Bryant find one-year parts and labor coverage in the warranties of at least seventy-one percent of four of the five appliances studied, which they claim confirms the signal theory.[170] They admit, however, that a large number of warranties provide coverage of both parts and labor for periods greater and less than one year. Many warranties offer parts coverage beyond one year, which they explain as the consequence of the lower frequency of invalid claims where coverage above rather than below the average is offered.[171] A much larger proportion of their sample warranties, however, restricts labor service coverage below the one-year term, a finding which is inconsistent both with the prediction of uniformity and with the special explanation of parts coverage. Gerner and Bryant explain the less extensive coverage of labor charges as related to the lower costs to the manufacturer of monitoring "warranty claims for invalid labor [as opposed to parts] charges."[172] They also assert that because of the greater dollar magnitude of labor costs than parts costs, "dealers and manufacturers may prefer incurring consumer dissatisfaction" by shifting labor costs to consumers.[173] There is no plausible explanation consistent with the exploitation theory for differential coverage of parts and labor charges.[174]

The warranties of my sample show substantial variations from the uniformity predicted by the signal theory.[175] Like the Gerner and Bryant

169. *Market Signal, supra* note 43, at 78-79.

170. In the fifth appliance, washing machines, one-year coverage appeared in 50% of the warranties. *Id.* at 82.

171. *See id.* at 79, 82-83.

172. *Id.* at 82.

173. *Id.* at 83.

174. Is it more exploitative to offer a longer period of labor than parts coverage, or the reverse? It is commonly thought that manufacturers exploit consumers by charging high prices for repair parts. Consumers seem especially vulnerable because of the difficulty of finding substitute parts designed specially to fit certain products. Substitutes for labor services to replace the parts, however, are available at any service shop. Thus, it is inconsistent with the exploitation theory that, to the extent parts and labor coverage differ, the warranties in the sample universally offer longer parts than labor coverage. In addition, some manufacturers guarantee that replacement parts will be kept in stock. The Roper range warranties, for example, promise to stock functional parts for ten years and nonfunctional parts for seven years.

175. My warranty sample confirms the uniformity hypothesis only by a superficial reading. If only the basic term of coverage is examined—that is, if one ignores provisions extending or restricting coverage of either parts or labor—then 41 of the 61 warranties provide coverage for one year. On the other hand, if the provisions extending or restricting parts and labor coverage are included, only 12 of the 61 warranties provide one-year parts and labor coverage. Most of these 12 warranties are of vehicular products. One-year coverage of all parts and labor expenses is offered by 9 of the 23 vehicu-

sample, most common are warranties that offer shorter periods of labor than of parts coverage. The investment theory implies that manufacturers will allocate labor charges in order to reduce differences between consumers in the expected magnitude of those charges.

Table 7 indicates warranties that distinguish coverage of labor and parts charges. Columns (2) and (4) indicate the number of warranties of which the period of labor coverage is less than the period of parts coverage—in column (2) for the basic term and in column (4) for the extended term of coverage. The warranties of washers, air conditioners, televisions, dryers, on-site mobile homes, and, occasionally, vehicular products most frequently offer more restricted labor than parts coverage. There are no immediately apparent similarities among these products, although some more limited observations suggest an investment theory explanation.

First, the allocation to the consumer of labor charges may be related to the availability of service contracts. Many warranties allude to optional service contracts that cover labor expenses for periods beyond those of warranty coverage.[176] The option of a separate service contract suggests an interpretation different from those of the exploitation or signal theories. Where a separate service contract is available, a consumer can determine independently whether the additional labor coverage is worth the price. The separate offer of labor coverage, for a separate price, reduces the warranty premium tied to the sale of the basic product and thus may optimize insurance sales. Only one of the sample warranties incorporates the terms of the optional service contract. The Emerson air conditioner service contract offers in-shop coverage of the sealed refrigeration system for four years beyond the one-year warranty term at a price of five dollars. Although I have no basis for evaluation, the price seems remarkably low for the coverage offered and illustrates that the Emerson company believes that most consumers prefer air conditioners with one year of labor coverage and a five dollar discount than five years of labor coverage at the higher price. Those consumers who prefer longer coverage, then, can transact for it separately.

Second, the exclusion of coverage of service call and transport charges may be consistent with the investment theory. These costs are likely to differ among consumers according to the distance between the consumer's

lar product warranties, but by only 1 of the 34 appliance warranties and by 2 of the 4 on-site mobile home warranties. A peculiar theory of consumer information must be fashioned to regard the similarity between these 12 warranties as a signaling phenomenon.

176. Service contracts, typically, are sold separately; they were not provided with the sample warranties.

Table 7. Parts & Labor Coverage, Transport Coverage, and Exclusion of Damages by Firm, 1974

| Product | (1) N | (2) Basic Labor< Parts | (3) Duration Extended Parts (years) | (4) Extended Labor< Parts | (5) Exclude Service Call | (6) Exclude Transport | (7) Foreign Exclusion | (8) Disclaim Merchant-ability | (9) Exclude Conse-quential Damages |
|---|---|---|---|---|---|---|---|---|---|
| Cookware | 1 | n.a.* | n.a.* | n.a.* | n.a.* | 1 | 0 | 0 | 0 |
| Refrigerators | 5 | 0 | 5 | 0 | 1 (total) | 3 | 4 | 1 | 1 |
| | | | | | 2 (after 1 year) | | | | |
| Freezers | 1 | 0 | 5† | 0 | 1 (total) | 1 | 1 | 0 | 0 |
| Gas Ranges | 2 | 0 | 0 | n.a. | 2 (after 1 year) | 0 | 1 | 0 | 0 |
| Electric Ranges | 4 | 1 | 3 | 1 | 1 (total) | 1 | 2 | 0 | 0 |
| | | | (1 manufacturer) | | 3 (after 1 year) | | | | |
| Washers | 5 | 3 | 5 | 4 | 1 (total) | 1 | 3 | 0 | 0 |
| | | | (4 manufacturers) | | 4 (after 1 year) | | | | |
| Dryers | 2 | 0 | 2 | 2 | 2 (after 1 year) | 1 | 2 | 2 | 2 |
| Room Air Conditioners | 10 | 3 | 5† | 3 | 4 (total) | 5 | 7 | 2 | 2 |
| | | | | | 1 (after 2 years) | | | | |
| Color Televisions | 3 | 1 | 2 | 3 | 2 (total) | 1 | 3 | 0 | 0 |
| | | | | | 1 (after 1 year) | | | | |
| Stereo | 2 | 0 | 5, 2 | 0 | 2 (total) | 2 | 0 | 1 | 0 |
| | | | (1 manufacturer) | | | | | | |
| Automobiles | 4 | 0 | 0 | n.a. | 3 (total) | 3 | 3 | 3 | 3 |
| | | | | | 1 (after 1 year) | | | | |
| Recreational Vehicles | 5 | 1 | 0 | n.a. | 5 (total) | 5 | 0 | 4 | 5 |
| Coaches | 5 | 1 | 0 | n.a. | 5 (total) | 5 | 0 | 4 | 4 |
| Truck Mounts | 4 | 1 | 0 | n.a. | 4 (total) | 4 | 0 | 2 | 3 |
| Travel Trailers | 5 | 1 | 0 | n.a. | 5 (total) | 5 | 0 | 3 | 2 |
| On-site Mobile Homes | 4 | 2 | 0 | n.a. | 2 (total) | 2 | 0 | 2 | 1 |
| | | | | | 2 (after 1 year) | | | | |

* The single cookware manufacturer promises to replace the entire product if it fails during the warranty period. As a consequence, labor charges are irrelevant.

† I include firms whose term of basic coverage is 5 years.

Source: Warranties provided by Federal Trade Commission, June 1978.

home and the manufacturer's service center.[177] For products sold nationwide, some consumers may live a sufficient distance from a service center to affect significantly total service call and transport costs. Consumers located more centrally may find it cheaper to bear service call and transport charges themselves than to purchase coverage for such charges in a warranty. In the sample, fifty-four of sixty-one warranties exclude service call charges for some period of warranty coverage, and thirty-six of sixty-one exclude service call charges completely (column (5)). Forty of sixty-two warranties exclude coverage of transport charges (column (6)).

Service call and transport charges also seem to influence provisions that limit warranty coverage on the basis of the location of the product at the time it becomes defective. Many warranties provide that coverage is available only if the product is located within the United States and Canada, within the United States alone, or within the contiguous United States (excluding coverage in Alaska and Hawaii). The exploitation and signal theories offer no ready explanation of these exclusions. All warranties in the sample were collected from sources within the contiguous states. The purchasers affected, thus, are not necessarily foreigners, who might be especially vulnerable or uninformed, but rather individuals who purchase the product within the United States for foreign transport. Furthermore, it is implausible that Canadians, Alaskans, or Hawaiians, as classes, are more easily exploited or less able to process product information.

These exclusions might possibly be related to substandard performance of electrical or water utilities in these locations, an explanation consistent with the investment theory. Many warranties, however, specifically exclude coverage of defects caused by abnormal electrical supply or mineral deposits. Nevertheless, I cannot reject this explanation.[178]

In my view the location exclusions are related to service call and transport charges. It is not implausible that charges are high relative to the mean for a serviceman to travel or for the good to be transported within foreign countries, across the expanses of Alaska or between the various Hawaiian islands, and are especially high for transport to the contiguous

177. The allocation to the consumer of various labor charges resembles coinsurance or deductible provisions in more typical insurance contracts. Coinsurance requires the insured to pay some share of the total expense of each claim. An insurance deductible, on the other hand, requires the insured to pay upon recovery some initial fixed amount, unrelated to the magnitude of the claim. The obligation to pay the labor costs of repairing a defect resembles coinsurance, because the payment that the consumer makes is likely to vary with the seriousness of the defect. The consumer's obligation to pay the serviceman's travel charges to the site of the product or the cost of transporting the product to a service center resembles an insurance deductible. The cost is incurred for each claim, but is fixed and, thus, unrelated to the seriousness of the defect. Coinsurance and deductibles, of course, are common methods of placing incentives on the insured to take precautions to avoid losses.

178. The foreign use exclusions are not incorporated universally in the warranties. Thus, it is not likely that they are related to differences in warranty law between jurisdictions.

Warranties

states. This explanation does not presume that these locations lack dealers or service centers, but only that the distance between service centers and consumers is relatively greater—perhaps only because there are fewer centers—in these locations than in the contiguous United States. Again, both manufacturers and the dominant set of consumers may gain by shifting these charges to foreign buyers who can differentially invest to prolong service life, rather than by increasing the insurance premium for all buyers to cover the additional costs peculiar to this relatively small set.

This hypothesis implies that manufacturers are more likely to exclude foreign coverage if the warranty allocates transport charges to the manufacturer than to the consumer. The evidence from the sample is generally consistent. Of twenty-two warranties allocating transport costs to the manufacturer, fourteen exclude foreign coverage (sixty-four percent). On the other hand, of forty warranties allocating transport charges to consumers, twelve exclude foreign coverage (thirty percent). Examined differently, of sixty-two warranties, twenty-six exclude foreign coverage and twenty-eight require consumers to pay transport charges. Only eight warranties in the sample provide foreign coverage of transport charges. Similarly, only thirteen of the sixty-two sample warranties provide coverage of transport charges from Canada. Finally, several warranties incorporate separate terms offering coverage in Alaska and Hawaii, but specifically excluding coverage of transport charges from these locations.

### 6. *The Disclaimer of the Implied Warranty of Merchantability and the Exclusion of Consequential Damages*

The Uniform Commercial Code implies a warranty of merchantability in all sales contracts.[179] The warranty requires that the item be of sufficient quality to "pass without objection in the trade" and that it be "fit for . . . ordinary purposes."[180] The Code allows a disclaimer of the warranty of merchantability provided that certain technical requirements are met.[181] At the time the warranties in the sample were issued, however, such a disclaimer was prohibited by statute in several states and was rendered ineffective by judicial decision in many others.[182] If the warranty of merchantability or any other general warranty is breached, the Code awards the buyer the costs of repairing or replacing the product as well as

179. U.C.C. § 2-314(1).
180. *Id.* § 2-314(2)(a), (c).
181. *Id.* § 2-316.
182. *See* Clark & Davis, *Beefing Up Product Warranties: A New Dimension in Consumer Protection*, 23 U. KAN. L. REV. 567, 577-97 (1975). Unfortunately, I have no information about the particular sales areas of the sample products.

consequential damages.[183] Consequential damages represent losses that result from the inability of the buyer to make use of the product for a purpose that could be anticipated by the seller.[184] In modern times, consequential damages of the greatest magnitude occur where product failure causes personal injury, and may include hospitalization costs, disability income, and the value of pain and suffering.

The disclaimer of the warranty of merchantability has always appeared suspect. It seems peculiar for a manufacturer to deny openly that its product can "pass without objection" or is ordinarily fit. Indeed, the attitude of manufacturers toward what appears to be an unexacting standard has provided substantial fuel for both the exploitation and signal theories. The disclaimer of a warranty of no greater than ordinary product quality appears quintessentially exploitative.[185] Similarly, such a disclaimer displayed conspicuously in a product warranty[186] seems to corroborate the signal theory's assumption that consumers are ignorant of warranty terms at the time of purchase.

The exploitation theory implies that all manufacturers will both disclaim the implied warranty of merchantability and exclude coverage of consequential damages. The implication of the signal theory is similar, except that the disclaimer and exclusion derive from consumer ignorance rather than more typical sources of monopoly power. The investment theory, however, suggests different interpretations of the two provisions. The effect of the legal implication of the warranty of merchantability is to delegate to a jury the judgment of what are the "ordinary" purposes to which a product may be put. A jury may appreciate the class of consumers and uses for which the product is designed. But if the jury errs, its verdict will charge a manufacturer for the failure of a product to satisfy a use not preferred by the dominant class of consumers, making both the class of consumers and the manufacturer worse off. Manufacturers whose

183. U.C.C. §§ 2-713(1), -714(3). In addition, the Code awards incidental damages, which include the costs of inspecting or storing a defective product, arranging for its repair, or buying a replacement. *Id.* § 2-715(1); *see* J. WHITE & R. SUMMERS, *supra* note 2, § 10-3 (surveying case law defining incidental damages).

184. *See* U.C.C. § 2-715(2); *see* J. WHITE & R. SUMMERS, *supra* note 2, § 10-4 (surveying case law defining consequential damages).

185. According to the New Jersey Supreme Court, Chrysler Motor's reliance on a disclaimer of implied warranties and on an exclusion of consequential damages to deny Mrs. Henningsen recovery for her injuries most clearly revealed the operative characteristics of modern warranties. Henningsen v. Bloomfield Motors, Inc., 32 N.J. 358, 388, 405, 161 A.2d 69, 85, 95 (1960); *see* p. 1302 *supra* (discussing *Henningsen*). Following *Henningsen*, most jurisdictions have routinely disregarded product warranty terms where a consumer suffers personal injury. *See* Whitford, *supra* note 20, at 127 (in automobile defect cases involving personal injury, courts have applied strict liability theory, and disclaimer of liability clauses have insignificant role). Thus, the consequential damages excluded by the sample warranties are only commonplace forms of property loss, lost time, or inconvenience. *See* pp. 1350-51 *infra* (discussing implications of investment theory for personal injury liability).

186. *See* U.C.C. § 2-316(2) (requiring conspicuous display).

products have a wide range of potential uses are exposed to greater risk from this delegation and will be more likely to disclaim the implied warranty of merchantability.[187] On the other hand, manufacturers will exclude consequential damages where the expected differences among consumers in consequential losses are high.

Columns (8) and (9) of Table 7[188] list the number of warranties that disclaim the implied warranty of merchantability and exclude consequential damages.[189] The disclaimers and exclusions are far from universal. Of sixty-two warranties, only twenty-four disclaim merchantability and only twenty-three exclude consequential damages. Furthermore, none of the manufacturers within six of the sixteen product groups disclaims merchantability and none within seven of the sixteen groups excludes consequential damages. These figures, of course, are inconsistent with both the exploitation and signal theories. Moreover, the data tend to refute the exploitation and signal hypotheses in other ways. We have seen that there is little apparent relation between firm market power and disclaimers or exclusions.[190] Furthermore, the distribution of disclaimers and exclusions does not seem to correspond to coherent estimates of the level of consumer information. Why should purchasers of dryers, automobiles, recreational vehicles, and coaches be systematically less informed about disclaimers and exclusions than purchasers of washers, televisions, ranges, and mobile homes?

Upon closer examination of the data, it is warranties of the vehicular products that most frequently disclaim the warranty of merchantability and exclude consequential damages. The warranty of merchantability is disclaimed in sixteen of twenty-three vehicular product warranties, as compared with only six of thirty-four appliance warranties and two of four mobile home warranties. Similarly, consequential damages are excluded in seventeen of twenty-three vehicular product warranties, but in only five of thirty-four appliance warranties and in one of four mobile home warranties.[191] With respect to the disclaimer, the range of potential uses may be greater for vehicular products than for appliances such as ranges, washers, and televisions.[192] Moreover, the vehicular product war-

187. Provisions naming the manufacturer as the sole judge of whether a product is defective serve the same function. *See* Marshall, *supra* note 94, at 883; Pauly, *supra* note 104, at 61.

188. *See* p. 1341 *supra* (Table 7).

189. Incidental damages are excluded by 11 of 62 firms. The exclusion may be related to the allocation of service costs since the costs of a repair are considered as incidental damage. Nine of 11 warranties that exclude incidental damages place liability for transportation costs on the consumer.

190. *See* p. 1325 *supra* (Table 3).

191. The disclaimer of merchantability is not always accompanied by an exclusion of consequential damages. Of 24 warranties that incorporate at least one of the provisions, however, 18 warranties both exclude consequential damages and disclaim merchantability.

192. I have no explanation, however, for the occasional appearance of the disclaimer in the war-

ranties are those which most frequently incorporate exclusions of specific uses, such as racing, towing, or hauling heavy loads.[193]

Similarly, differences among consumers in the potential magnitude of consequential damages may be greater for vehicular than for other products. Many vehicular warranties enumerate several elements of loss stemming from the incapacity of the vehicle—loss of time, meals, lodging, the cost of a rental car—that are specifically excluded from coverage. The magnitude of these losses, of course, varies with the driving patterns of each consumer. A more significant element of consequential loss is damage to property where a defect leads to a traffic accident. The exclusion of recovery for this loss, however, is likely to reflect only the relative superiority of consumer self-insurance—by means of an accident or collision policy more carefully designed to the individual's needs.[194] These explanations of the data, however, are only suppositions. They cannot be confirmed or refuted from the warranty sample.

### C. *How Consumers May Register Preferences*

It is a common belief that warranty content has little influence on consumer purchase decisions because a consumer only learns warranty terms after purchase or after discovery of a defect.[195] This belief has been closely connected with the exploitation theory;[196] it explains how a manufacturer is able to impose one-sided warranty terms. The signal theory also accepts the proposition in large part: although consumers may possess some general warranty information prior to purchase, they remain totally ignorant of large numbers of significant provisions.[197] Thus, according to both the exploitation and signal theories, there is little relationship between consumer preferences and warranty terms.

The actual influence of consumer preferences, of course, is an empirical question. Neither exploitation nor signal theorists have compiled direct empirical support for the absence of influence. The strongest direct evidence, perhaps, derives from introspection. Most of us can recall occasions as consumers in which we have been uninformed about warranty content at the time of purchase. If the large majority of consumers behave similarly, how is it possible, even in competitive product markets, for consumer preferences to influence the way manufacturers draft warranties?

ranties of refrigerators (1), dryers (2), room air conditioners (2), and stereo equipment (1).

193. *See* p. 1333 *supra*.

194. *See* pp. 1350-51 *infra* (discussing superiority of self-insurance).

195. *See, e.g.*, Staff Report on Consumer Product Warranties, House Interstate and Foreign Commerce Comm. 13 (Sept. 17, 1974) (on file with *Yale Law Journal*).

196. *See* pp. 1300-01 *supra*.

197. *See* pp. 1303, 1305 *supra*.

Warranties

Competition with respect to warranty content may take two forms. First, manufacturers compete, not over the entire set of consumers, but over the set of marginal consumers. If a small group of consumers reads warranties and selects among products according to warranty content, manufacturers may be forced to draft warranties responsive to the group's preferences, even though the large majority of consumers generally neglect warranty terms. Second, warranty content may affect the repeat purchase rather than the initial purchase decision. A consumer may select among competing brands according to his experience with a specific product and with its warranty.[198] If so, manufacturers may be forced to draft warranties responsive to consumer preferences in order to assure a continued custom.[199]

The warranty sample provides only indirect (but highly suggestive) evidence that consumer preferences for allocative investments and insurance influence warranty terms. Further empirical study is needed for a precise definition of the process of competition over warranty provisions.

## IV. Implications of the Investment Theory

The previous Part shows, I believe, that the investment theory explains warranty practices more comprehensively than either the exploitation or signal theory. The evidence tends to confirm that the allocation of responsibilities between manufacturers and different sets of consumers by standardized warranties is responsive to consumer preferences, and establishes coherent economic incentives for manufacturer and consumer investments to optimize productive services. Further research, of course, is required before a confident conclusion can be reached. If, however, the validity of the investment theory is presumed, that is, if manufacturers and consumers invest to optimize productive services, what have been the effects of modern judicial and legislative policies with respect to consumer product warranties?

### A. *Optimal Prevention and Insurance*

Courts have accepted the view that manufacturers employ standardized

198. A consumer, of course, may also rely on the advice of family members or friends with respect to their experience with product warranties.

199. To the extent that its content is influenced by repeat purchase decisions, the warranty operates as a guide to the service and insurance that a warrantor will provide rather than as a performance bond. *See* p. 1309 *supra*. A warranty is necessary as a performance bond only where the consumer fears that after purchase, the manufacturer will refuse service or insurance if the product is defective. A manufacturer seeking repeat purchasers, of course, could not consistently refuse such performance. The warranty may continue to serve as a performance bond, however, to first-purchasers.

warranties to exploit consumers,[200] and they have responded to exploitative behavior in two ways. Courts have interpreted sales transactions to provide more extensive warranty protection to consumers than the manufacturers themselves have offered voluntarily. The implication of warranties of merchantability and fitness—as well as the prohibition on disclaiming these warranties—and the expansion of the set of beneficiaries of warranties by the elimination of the privity of contract requirement are examples. In addition, courts have refused to give effect to manufacturer attempts to segregate consumers by the level of risk they bring to the warranty pool. Courts have refused to enforce warranty provisions that limit remedies and that exclude consequential damages, in particular, personal injury damages for which manufacturers are now strictly liable.

The implications of the investment theory with respect to these developments are clear: the warranty coverage required by courts is suboptimal and increases the likelihood of product defects. It is well-established that if, in a competitive market, consumers have different accident probabilities, sales of contracts to insure—or to invest to reduce the probability of loss—are optimized where the seller segregates consumers according to levels of risk and sells each class of consumers a separate contract at a separate premium reflecting the accident probability of the class.[201] If sellers are prevented from segregating consumers according to risk levels, however, both manufacturers and consumers are worse off. First, there may be no single insurance-allocative investment contract that satisfies the preferences of both low- and high-risk consumers.[202] Put another way, at a common premium, losses may be so disparate as to be uninsurable. Second, even if a manufacturer can devise some single insurance-allocative investment package that is attractive to some high- and low-risk consumers, such a contract is likely to satisfy the preferences of these consumers less fully than would separate contracts. Rothschild and Stiglitz have shown that a single contract of this nature is likely to make high-risk consumers no better off than would separate contracts, but will make low-risk consumers worse off.[203]

In limiting the segregation of consumers, courts and legislatures have focused primarily on the remedial provisions of warranties—for example, the exclusion of consequential damages, in particular, personal injury

200. *See* p. 1302 *supra*.

201. *See, e.g.*, Rothschild & Stiglitz, *supra* note 104, at 629.

202. Akerlof, *supra* note 38, at 492-94; Rothschild & Stiglitz, *supra* note 104, at 637. For ease of exposition, I discuss two risk levels, but the proposition holds for the grouping of any set of consumers for which the risk of loss differs.

203. Relatively low-risk consumers are worse off because the premium (and perhaps the amount of insurance available) are higher than if separate contracts were offered. Rothschild & Stiglitz, *supra* note 104, at 638.

damages. Subject to competitive pressures, manufacturers may be expected to respond to these legal constraints by canvassing the range of alternative techniques for identifying and segregating different risk classes. It is possible that some of the provisions discussed above[204] that serve to segregate different uses or consumers of products were introduced in response to the extension of general warranty liability and the suppression of other risk segregating methods. The term of basic coverage itself segregates consumers by risk levels if consumers with different accident probabilities demand different quantities of insurance.[205] The one-year basic warranty term may be especially common because it represents, given judicial and legislative restrictions on other forms of risk segregation, a common minimum point at which the insurance preferences of high- and low-risk consumers converge.

A third implication of the investment theory is more striking and suggests another method of testing the theory. The investment theory regards consumer investments to prolong the life of a product as a substitute for manufacturer investments to prolong product life.[206] The warranty allocates responsibilities between the parties according to the relative costs of these investments; that is, the warranty allocates responsibilities to (places liability on) consumers where the marginal cost of consumer investments is lower than the marginal cost of manufacturer investments. Judicial decisions expanding the manufacturer's warranty liability lead, however, to the substitution of manufacturer investments for consumer investments. It follows that judicial decisions lead to the substitution of more costly investments in place of less costly investments and, thus, increase the marginal cost of investments to prolong product life. As the price of prolonging product life (or any commodity) increases, the quantity of it demanded declines. Therefore, judicial decisions expanding the warranty liability of manufacturers will lead, at the margin, to fewer investments that serve to prolong product life and to prevent defects than before. As a consequence, product life will diminish and fewer defects will be prevented. Although seemingly ironic, the investment theory implies that the judicial expansion of manufacturer warranty liability diminishes product life and increases the rate of product defects.[207]

204. *See* pp. 1328-46 *supra.*

205. *See* p. 1319 *supra.*

206. *See* pp. 1309-11 *supra.*

207. Increased costs may lead to the sale of fewer products. As a consequence, the absolute number of defects may decline, although the rate of defects in those products sold will increase. The total social loss from and increase in the defect rate, of course, must also consider those losses to third parties previously disregarded by consumers in their purchase decisions.

The investment theory suggests that legal rules regarding warranties are inefficient, a finding inconsistent with Professor Posner's hypothesis of common-law rule efficiency. *See* R. POSNER, *supra* note 29, at 179-81. Many of these rules—the implication of warranties by law, restrictions on privity of

B. *The Investment Theory, Personal Injury Loss, and Strict Liability*

The most dramatic development in product warranty law in the last two decades is the abandonment of principles of warranty interpretation and the adoption of a strict liability standard in cases involving personal injury from a defective product. Crucial to the adoption of the strict liability standard is the empirical assumption that consumers can take no action to prevent personal injury loss.[208] Given the assumption, it is difficult to justify warranty provisions excluding recovery for personal injury damages.

Consumers, however, may prefer the exclusion of personal injury losses from warranty coverage for various reasons. If personal injury losses, like other forms of product loss, differ substantially among consumers of a product, those consumers for whom the risk is relatively low may be better off if no personal injury coverage whatsoever is offered. First, contrary to the empirical assumption of the policy of strict liability, consumers may differ with respect to the precautions that they take or the care with which they use the product. Again, actions "preventing" (reducing the probability of) personal injury loss may take subtle forms. Consumers who take care, say, not to use machine products in the presence of bystanders[209] or who use such products only infrequently may subject the warranty pool to a substantially lower level of risk than more intensive users. This class of consumers may demand the exclusion of personal injury losses from warranty coverage, and if the class is sufficiently large, manufacturers might find that competition requires incorporation of the exclusion.

The exclusion of personal injury losses can optimize investments to reduce the probability of product losses and to insure in a second way. Product insurers are seldom able to obtain information about individual consumers that health, home, and automobile insurers commonly employ to define optimal risk classes.[210] In general, product insurers must treat all consumers as equals and charge each a warranty premium reflecting the average risk level of the pool. The individual information collected in other insurance contexts, however, may be effective in segregating optimal classes for product insurance. If so, it would optimize insurance sales to

contract—derive from the nineteenth or early twentieth centuries, a period from which Posner draws much of the support for his hypothesis.

208. *See, e.g.*, James & Dickinson, *supra* note 87, at 780.

209. This situation suggests how the requirement of horizontal privity of contract may serve to reduce differences in risk. The requirement culls from the warranty pool family members, guests, and bystanders. The number of such individuals exposed to risk from a product defect may vary substantially among consumers. If the dominant class of consumers infrequently operates products in the presence of third parties, the privity rule may optimize product sales.

210. *See* p. 1315 *supra*.

Warranties

offer product liability coverage as an aspect of health, home, or automobile insurance, rather than as a separate policy tied to the sale of each product.[211] An insurer could charge a lower than average premium to a consumer for whom the risk of loss or the magnitude of expected damage is relatively low, such as a consumer who is employed as a manual laborer, earns a wage rather than a salary, makes lower than average earnings, or has a small family or relatively less valuable possessions. Again, it is the consumer who subjects the pool to relatively low levels of risk—whether the low level of risk derives from relative carefulness or from a lower expected dollar loss from a disabling accident—who is most harmed by lumping consumers into a single product insurance pool. Thus the adoption of a strict liability standard has a regressive redistributional effect. Consumers who are more careless or earn higher than average incomes are those for whom the warranty premium is less than the level of risk that they introduce into the pool and are therefore the beneficiaries of the strict liability standard.

The implications of involuntary manufacturer liability for personal injury losses are similar to the implications of the expansion of warranty liability generally.[212] Most significantly, at the margin, consumer investments and manufacturer investments are substitute means of reducing the probability of defects causing personal injury. As a consequence, the shift to manufacturer liability increases the cost of these investments. Fewer investments to prevent personal injury losses are likely to be made. Again, the adoption of the strict liability standard is likely to have increased the rate of personal injury losses from defective products.[213]

Conclusion

The superior predictive ability of the investment theory over the exploitation and signal theories could result from the greater empirical significance, at the margin, of the determinants of the investment theory. I do not believe, however, that sufficient evidence has been compiled to support such a conclusion. Rather, the superiority of the investment theory with respect to warranty content derives, in my view, from the nature of the determinants of the theories. The determinants of the investment theory are the costs of warranty coverage and differences in costs between consumers; the determinants of the exploitation theory, the relative bargain-

211. The standard homeowner insurance policy offers coverage of various losses from defective products, such as explosion or electric shock. INSURANCE INFORMATION INSTITUTE, SAMPLE INSURANCE POLICIES 14 (1975). I am indebted to Richard Epstein for this observation. Of course, most automobile policies provide coverage of various losses that result from a defective automobile.

212. *See* pp. 1348-49 *supra*.

213. *See* note 207 *supra*.

ing position of manufacturers and consumers; and the determinants of the signal theory, the level of consumer information.

The determinants of the investment theory differ from the others in two important respects. First, the costs of warranty coverage are more easily defined and measured than either relative bargaining position or the quantum of consumer information. As a result, the investment theory's implications are likely to be both more precise and more readily verified or refuted. Market share and concentration measures, for example, are too crude to demonstrate any relationship between bargaining power and warranty content.[214] Similarly, although it is admittedly costly for consumers to obtain information about product reliability, it is difficult to judge how costly it is and what alternative sources of information are available. The more specific implications of the signal theory thus have no verifiable basis. The implication that consumers generalize information from a range of products requires a belief that consumers cannot read individual product warranties to obtain current and specific information directly.[215] In addition, the distinction between basic warranty terms that serve a signaling function and exclusions that consumers ignore is arbitrary. Neither of these implications can be refuted within the terms of the theory itself. Gerner and Bryant justify several of the implications by comparing the relative benefits to consumers with the costs to manufacturers of provisions and exclusions.[216] But if the benefits and costs of a provision determine consumer perceptions of the provision, then the study of benefits and costs, rather than of perceptions, will provide the most accurate method of predicting warranty practices.[217]

The second important advantage of the determinants of the investment theory over those of the alternative theories is that aspects of design, manufacture, and use of a product are more likely to be determined by costs than by relative bargaining position or consumer information. As a consequence, a theory based upon costs allows the immediate comparison of warranty practices to other production decisions and, thus, is more comprehensive than competing theories. It is the generality of costs as the determinant of warranty content that generates the rich and diverse implications of the investment theory.

214. *See* pp. 1322-25 *supra* (Tables 1-3).

215. *See* note 58 *supra* (related criticism of signal theory).

216. *Market Signal*, *supra* note 43, at 78-79.

217. The signal theory, in addition, does not provide a comprehensive theory of consumer perception. For example, the theory offers no insight into the relationship between manufacturer investments in establishing a reputation or brand name and in offering warranty coverage as signals of product reliability.

# [11]

# Comments

## Comment on A Theory of the Consumer Product Warranty

**William C. Whitford†**

Professor George Priest's recent article, *A Theory of the Consumer Product Warranty*,[1] performs a valuable service by reminding us that consumers can sometimes reduce losses from defective products more cheaply than manufacturers. Where losses from product defects are essentially unavoidable, consumers may be the most efficient insurers of those losses. Professor Priest's comprehensive and technically proficient analysis of the implications of these points for the content of consumer product warranties is an important contribution to the literature.

Nonetheless, I believe that Professor Priest's article has serious analytic flaws.[2] In addition, its policy suggestions are premised on a mistaken assumption about the law on an important point.[3] Partly because of these mistakes, the article provides little support for its principal thesis, or for the implication derived from the thesis that complete judicial deference to the terms of consumer product warranties would reduce the losses from defective products. After briefly summarizing Professor Priest's article, I will detail and document these criticisms.

### I. A Synopsis of the Article

An important objective of the article is to develop a positive theory of the content of consumer product warranties, that is, a theory that predicts

† Professor of Law, University of Wisconsin Law School. I owe much thanks for helpful suggestions by my many colleagues who read earlier drafts of this comment; William Clune, Robert Gordon, Neil Komesar, Judith Lachman, Stewart Macaulay, Gerald Thain, and David Trubek. Of course, I bear sole responsibility for the views expressed and for any errors.

1. 90 YALE L.J. 1297 (1981) [hereinafter cited by page number only].
2. The most serious problem of this nature is Professor Priest's failure to consider a wide number of competing explanations for the content of warranties. *See infra* pp. 1380-84 & notes 32-44. Part of the analysis also seems premised on mistaken assumptions about the content of other relevant scholarship. *Infra* note 29.
3. *Infra* pp. 1384-85.

warranty content. Professor Priest's "investment theory" predicts that warranties will contain the same terms that they would contain in a nearly perfect market.[4] According to his investment theory, there are two principal determinants of warranty content in such a market.

First, if the losses from product defects are avoidable through appropriate actions, the warranty will allocate the loss to the party who can avoid it at least cost.[5] Sometimes losses are best avoided through preventive investments — by the manufacturer through investments in product design or quality control, or by the consumer through investments in a search for the product best adapted to the intended use and investments in proper care and maintenance of the product after purchase. In other instances, losses are best avoided through the repair of a malfunctioning product, and either the manufacturer or the consumer can be the least-cost repairer. Whatever the cheapest method of loss avoidance, the investment theory predicts that warranty terms will allocate losses to induce efficient loss avoidance by the efficient loss avoider.

If losses from product defects are not totally avoidable, then the second determinant of warranty content under the investment theory is the effectiveness of the manufacturer as an insurer against losses. For example, if the risk of loss from product defects varies greatly among consumers, due to important differences in the circumstances of each consumer, Priest believes that the manufacturer is a relatively poor insurer because it usually cannot segregate consumers into risk classes as cheaply and effectively as alternative insurers.[6] In these circumstances, the investment theory predicts that manufacturers will limit warranty coverage to those risks that virtually all consumers share, forcing consumers that face greater risks to self-insure or to obtain alternative insurance. Thus, low risk consumers will not pay for more insurance than their circumstances require. Warranties are likely to exclude consequential damages on this basis, for example, if the potential magnitude of consequential damages varies dramatically among consumers.[7]

Together with the investment theory, Professor Priest outlines two com-

4. Pp. 1307-13. Priest's hypothetical market exhibits perfect information and perfect competition, but deviates from the ideal of a completely perfect market by utilizing standardized contracts to minimize transaction costs.

5. Pp. 1308-09. For example, the investment theory suggests that refrigerator warranties exclude coverage for dislodged refrigerator shelves because consumers can repair dislodged shelves more cheaply than manufacturers, who would have to incur the cost of sending a repairperson to the consumer's home.

6. Pp. 1314-19. In considering economies of information acquisition, Professor Priest again deviates from the assumption of a perfect market and considers transaction costs. *See supra* note 4. Consumers can often arrange for alternative insurance against losses from product defects through homeowners, medical and automobile insurance policies.

7. Pp. 1318, 1346.

peting theories of warranty content. He attributes the "exploitation theory" to several scholars who have written on the problems posed by standard-form contracts, such as Friederich Kessler, Dean Prosser and Arthur Leff. According to Priest, the "exploitation theory predicts, in general, that manufacturers will limit their legal obligations to consumers as much as possible,"[8] and that manufacturers have the power to limit their obligations because of their superior bargaining power. In Priest's opinion, the exploitation theory has induced the courts to impose liability on some manufacturers irrespective of exclusionary warranty terms.[9]

The third theory of warranty content that the article identifies is the "signal theory". This theory postulates that consumers regard the extent of warranty coverage as a "signal" of a product's reliability. If a product has no warranty coverage, consumers will believe that the manufacturer has little confidence in the product's quality. As a result, successful marketing of a product requires that the major terms of warranty meet industry norms. The aberrant warranties, if any, are likely to offer better than normal coverage, as a few manufacturers try to convince consumers that their products are of better than average quality. With respect to the less prominent terms of a warranty, however, signal theorists do not expect market pressures to affect warranty coverage, and manufacturers are likely to draft the less prominent terms so as to limit warranty coverage. In Professor Priest's words, "(a)t this point, the exploitation and signal theories converge."[10]

After describing the three theories, Professor Priest tests them by examining the content of sixty-two product warranties issued in 1974. He states that according to exploitation theory warranty coverage should decline as the manufacturer's market power increases. Priest finds that his data are inconsistent with that hypothesis.[11] The data do indicate considerable uniformity within industries in some of the more prominent warranty terms, thus partly confirming the signal theory, but Professor Priest emphasizes that the signal theory is unable to explain other findings, such as the apparent lack of correlation between warranty duration and the service-life expectancy of warranted products.[12]

The longest section of the article specifically anlayzes six categories of warranty provisions.[13] Within each category, Professor Priest concludes

8. P. 1301.

9. His principal illustration is the famous case of Henningsen v. Bloomfield Motors, 32 N.J. 358, 161 A.2d 69 (1960).

10. P. 1305.

11. Pp. 1320-25.

12. Pp. 1326-27.

13. Pp. 1328-46.

that his investment theory "more comprehensively"[14] explains warranty content than the other two theories. This conclusion rests primarily on the considerable variation of warranty provisions within each category. The exploitation theory, in his view, can explain variation only in terms of the market power of manufacturers, but the data do not support that explanation. The signal theory predicts substantial uniformity in warranties, with variations limited to a few firms offering more extensive coverage than the norm. In each category, Professor Priest finds greater variation in warranty terms than the signal theory predicts. As to the investment theory, however, Professor Priest suggests possible differences among firms and products that affect whether the firm or its customers can most cheaply insure or avoid the risk of loss from product defects, and then illustrates how these differences might account for many of the observed variations in the six categories of warranty terms.

Professor Priest concludes that this analysis provides substantial evidence for his investment theory, although he liberally calls for further research.[15] He then proceeds to discuss the policy implications of the investment theory if established.[16] That discussion focuses on various court decisions that expand manufacturer liability beyond the warranty contract, and especially on decisions that adopt strict products liability. According to Priest, the investment theory implies that such decisions "diminish . . . product life and increase . . . the rate of product defects,"[17] and have "a regressive redistributional effect."[18] The clear implication of this discussion is that regulation of consumer product warranties is undesirable, and that courts should respect disclaimers and limitation of remedy clauses.

## II. Critique of the Article

Professor Priest presents his investment theory as what I will call a *complete* theory of warranty content. That is, Priest hypothesizes that if one knew who is the least-cost risk avoider or the most effective insurer with respect to a particular product, one could accurately predict all of the terms of the product's warranty.[19]

14. Pp. 1347.

15. At one point Professor Priest characterizes the results of his survey of warranty content as "highly suggestive," presumably of the validity of his investment theory. P. 1320. At another point he states "that the investment theory explains warranty practices more comprehensively than either the exploitation or signal theory." P. 1347. Denials that the theory has been conclusively proved, and calls for further research and study, are made repeatedly throughout the article. *See* p. 1347.

16. Pp. 1347-51.

17. P. 1349.

18. P. 1351.

19. That Professor Priest posits his investment theory as a complete theory is clear in the passage where he first introduces the theory. P. 1307.

Comment

Professor Priest might have advanced the investment theory as suggesting several but not all of the determinants of warranty content—what I will call a *partial* theory of warranty content. If he had done so, the theory would not be controversial. Few commentators would doubt that the considerations identified in Professor Priest's investment theory do and should influence warranty content.[20] It is the suggestion that the investment theory is a complete theory of warranty content that makes Priest's position noteworthy and provocative.

The importance of this distinction between a complete theory and a partial theory is clear in Professor Priest's discussion of the implications of his position. He suggests that if the investment theory is correct, judicial

Priest does not argue that the investment theory is an accurate predictor of warranty content because the consumer product market is a perfectly operating market, save only a few accommodations for transaction costs. Rather, he apparently concedes that many consumers lack important information at the time of contracting. *See* pp. 1346-47. Thus, it appears to be his hypothesis that product warranty content in a less-than-perfect world is the same as it would be if the market operated perfectly.

The distinction between a market that operates perfectly and one that performs as if it were perfect is not important to an understanding of Professor Priest's discussion of the evidence supporting his investment theory. In either instance, the case for the investment theory as a complete theory rests on its ability to refute alternative theories of warranty content. The distinction becomes quite important, however, in assessing the policy implications that Professor Priest attributes to the investment theory. *See infra* p. 1384.

20. Thirteen years ago, in an article cited many times by Professor Priest, I identified several factors similar to those identified by the investment theory as justifying various conditions and limitations in the standard automobile warranty. Whitford, *Law and the Consumer Transaction: A Case Study of the Automobile Warranty*, 1968 WIS. L. REV. 1006, 1063-65. That Professor Priest considers his theory novel nonetheless is further indication that he intends it as a complete theory of warranty content.

Professor Priest may disagree that most commentators consider the investment theory uncontroversial as a partial theory of warranty content. At one point, Professor Priest identifies as "critical" to exploitation theory the presumption that "allocative investments by a consumer are empirically unimportant to the optimization of the productive life of the good." P. 1312 n.89. The principal commentator cited in support of this statement is the late Professor James. James, *General Products—Should Manufacturers Be Liable Without Negligence*? 24 TENN. L. REV. 923 (1951); James & Dickinson, *Accident Proneness and Accident Law*, 63 HARV. L. REV. 769 (1950). In both of these articles, however, Professor James principally argues that the contributory negligence principle should not necessarily exculpate a defendant from tort liability because of the accident victim's moral fault. If the victim's accident is foreseeable and preventable by an appropriate investment by the defendant, James contends that the law should provide an incentive to make that investment even if the victim's blameworthy conduct is one cause of the accident. That Professor James was not oblivious to the need for investments by consumers is clear in the following passage:

> While liability . . . would be strict, in the sense that *negligence* would no longer be required, yet this does not mean that the maker [of the product] would be held for all injuries caused by his products. Any product may become the instrumentality of serious injury or death—consider for instance the lethal possibilities that lie in a book placed strategically at the top of a long dark flight of strairs. In [strict liability] as well as negligence a plaintiff must trace his injury to a quality or condition of the product which was unreasonably dangerous either for a use to which the product would ordinarily be put, or for some special use which was brought to the attention of the defendant.

James, *supra*, at 923, 926-27 (emphasis in original). Concededly, there are passages in Professor James's articles that tend to support the quotation from Professor Priest at the beginning of the paragraph. In my opinion, Professor Priest has read those passages out of context. And even if I am wrong, I doubt that Professor Priest could find other "exploitation theorists" who doubt the validity of the investment theory as a partial theory of warranty content.

decisions that expand a manufacturer's warranty liability beyond its contractual limits increase losses from product defects.[21] If the investment theory is just a partial theory of warranty content, however, Priest should concede that judicial decisions that expand warranty liability might improve the efficiency of loss allocation in some instances. That is, such decisions might counteract the effects of warranty determinants other than those suggested by the investment theory.[22] If Professor Priest's investment theory is correct as a complete theory of product warranty content, on the other hand, judicial review can only undermine the efficiency of the contractual scheme for minimizing product-defect losses because contractual terms are the same as they would be if negotiated under conditions of perfect information and competition. Thus, the question whether the investment theory is a complete or a partial theory is absolutely crucial to its policy implications.

Professor Priest's case for the investment theory as a complete theory of warranty content, or even as a predominant theory of warranty content,[23] rests on three principal points. First, he argues that consumer preferences influence warranty content, even in the absence of bargaining. Second, he examines the content of the product warranties in his sample and argues that the content, and particularly the variance in the content among different warranties, is consistent with his investment theory. Third, he argues that his data tend to refute alternative theories of warranty content. I will now examine each of these arguments. It is my contention that Professor Priest's case for his investment theory as a complete or predominant explanation of warranty content rests entirely on his third argument, and that this argument is seriously deficient because it fails to consider many alternative theories of warranty content.

*Consumer preferences and warranty content.* Professor Priest identifies

21. P. 1349.

22. This statement presumes that courts, in deciding whether to expand warranty liability, give some weight to the considerations that the investment theory identifies. Judicial decisions are commonly based on considerations such as reasonableness and conscionability, which are sufficiently general to permit courts to weigh such considerations.

The judiciary, like the market, is an imperfect institution. Despite market failures, judicial involvement may be counterproductive if judicial imperfections are of greater consequence than market imperfections. *See* Komesar, *In Search of a General Approach to Legal Analysis: A Comparative Institutional Alternative*, 79 MICH. L. REV. 1350 (1981).

23. Though Professor Priest presents his investment theory as a complete theory of warranty content, readers of the article may interpret the theory as one that more comprehensively explains the predominant influences on warranty content than do other theories. As a predominant theory of warranty content, the investment theory, even if validated, cannot establish that judicial decisions expanding warranty liability increase losses from product defects, but it may raise questions about the desirability of those decisions. The case for the investment theory as a predominant theory of warranty content, however, is essentially the same as the case for a complete theory—that is, it depends on refutation of plausible alternative explanations of warranty content—and hence can be critiqued in the same manner.

two ways in which consumer preferences can influence warranty content, while conceding that consumers usually lack knowledge of warranty content at the time of bargaining.[24] Sellers who are financially dependent on repeat sales to customers will not want consumers to learn of limited warranty coverage when a defect appears. Moreover, manufacturers may compete for the patronage of a small group of consumers who are knowledgeable about warranty content and whose purchase decisions are influenced by that content.[25] Although consumer preferences probably do influence warranty content to some extent for these reasons, this fact alone cannot establish the investment theory as a complete or predominant explanation of warranty content. It establishes only that consumer preferences are one factor, perhaps among many, that influence warranty content and that explain variations in warranty terms.

*The consistency of warranty content and the investment theory.* Professor Priest's illustrations of how various product warranty terms may reflect investment theory considerations are on the whole plausible. As Professor Priest sometimes recognizes,[26] however, this part of his argument is very much in the realm of armchair theorizing. His information about the technologies of the products that he discusses, the risks presented by their use, and the kinds of insurance policies readily available to consumers appears no greater than that possessed by any reasonably intelligent lay observer. Without greater information of this nature, this prong of the argument cannot possibly establish that warranty terms allocate losses to the least-cost risk avoider and the most effective insurer. Therefore, it cannot possibly refute the existence of determinants of product warranty content that cause warranties to vary from the predictions of the investment theory.

For example, Professor Priest observes that two-thirds of the warranties in his sample require the consumer to bear the cost of transporting a defective good, perhaps over a considerable distance, to a manufacturer's service center. This provision may be consistent with the investment theory, he observes, because "[c]onsumers located more centrally may find it cheaper to bear . . . transport charges themselves than to purchase coverage for such charges in a warranty."[27] Though plausible, it is also possible

24. Pp. 1346-47.

25. *See generally* Schwartz & Wilde, *Intervening in Markets on the Basis of Imperfect Information: A Legal and Economic Analysis*, 127 U. PA. L. REV. 630 (1979).

26. Professor Priest states: "These explanations of the data . . . are only suppositions." P. 1346. The statement is apparently limited to his discussion of disclaimers of merchantability and exclusions of consequential damages.

27. P. 1342. In Professor Priest's terminology, this means that many consumers find it less costly to self-insure against this risk of loss from a product defect, as compared with having the manufacturer provide insurance through the warranty.

Professor Priest's explanation for variations in the inclusion of the transport charge provision is that transportation clauses induce manufacturers to forego the expense of decentralizing service centers or otherwise minimizing transport charges. This increases the consumer's cost and inconvenience of making warranty claims, thereby presumably reducing the number of claims put forward. If transport charge clauses are among the warranty terms less likely to be noticed by consumers at the time of contracting, manufacturers may include them precisely to reduce warranty costs in these ways without suffering adverse sales consequences.[28] If so, some of the warranty claims deterred by the transport clauses probably concern product defects that manufacturers can repair more cheaply than consumers.

*Refutation of alternative theories.* It should now be clear that Professor Priest's case for his investment theory as a complete or predominant explanation of warranty content rests mainly on the third prong of his argument—refutation of alternative theories of warranty content. If Priest could refute all alternative theories that have intuitive plausibility, he would generate considerable evidence for the investment theory as a complete theory. But he considers only two alternatives—the exploitation theory and the signal theory.

What Professor Priest calls the exploitation theory predicts that warranty coverage will vary inversely with the market power of manufacturers. Professor Priest tests the theory by searching for a relationship between warranty coverage and the manufacturer's share of sales in the relevant market, or between warranty coverage and the degree of industry concentration in the market. The data he collects do not support the existence of either relationship.[29]

apparently that some products are sold nationwide, others more locally. For products sold nationwide there is likely to be greater variation among consumers in the cost of transporting a defective good to a service center, and consequently a substantial consumer preference for exclusion of average transport costs from the warranty. P. 1342. Professor Priest makes no effort to test this explanation empirically, perhaps because he lacks information as to which of the products in his sample are marketed nationwide.

28. This explanation for why transport clauses might vary from the investment theory is consistent with the signal theory. Variations among warranties in transport clauses may reflect in part a variation among manufacturers in the extent to which they rely on repeat sales. A manufacturer heavily dependent on repeat sales does not want to impress customers encountering product malfunctions with the impracticality of collecting on warranty coverage.

29. A disturbing aspect of Professor Priest's article is his attribution of exploitation theory in general, as well as at least one of the specific propositions he tests empirically, to a wide group of previous scholars. In fact, none of the legal scholars cited by him, nor any of which I am aware, have specifically suggested the propositions Professor Priest tests in refuting what he calls exploitation theory. By associating so many earlier scholars with exploitation theory, Professor Priest gives the impression, perhaps unintentionally, that in refuting alternatives to investment theory he has considered the main alternatives suggested in the literature. It is my principal contention in this comment, developed subsequently in the text, that he has not done so.

Professor Priest's first empirical test of the exploitation theory centers upon the proposition that "warranties less favorable to consumers are offered by the larger rather than the smaller firms within an industry." Professor Priest expressly attributes this view to "most" exploitation theorists, but without citation of any authority that propounds that view. P. 1320. In another place in the article,

Comment

Professor Priest next considers signal theory. His data, as well as other published data, offer significant support for the principal hypothesis of signal theory—that the prominent terms of product warranties tend to converge to an industry norm.[30] Professor Priest seems to discard signal theory nonetheless because it cannot explain other aspects of warranty content. In particular, he notes a considerable disparity between the duration of warranty coverage and the service-life expectancy of the products that he examines. If consumers regard warranty duration as a surrogate measure for product quality, as the signal theory presupposes, then such a disparity should not exist.[31] This analysis only refutes signal theory as a complete theory of warranty content, however, and Professor Priest's own

Professor Priest states: "[i]t . . . would be consistent with the assumptions of the [exploitation] theory . . . for the terms of coverage to be correlated with the degree of manufacturer market power." P. 1301. Here he cites two commentators, Friederich Kessler and Arthur Leff. *See* Kessler, *Contracts of Adhesion—Some Thoughts About Freedom of Contract*, 43 COLUM. L. REV. 629 (1943); Leff, *Contract as Thing*, 19 AM. U. L. REV. 131 (1970).

In one very limited sense, Professor Priest's specification of the exploitation theory is "consistent" with the work of earlier scholars that Priest cites. Those commentators have not developed explicit theories of warranty content. Instead, the thrust of their scholarship has been to demonstrate that standard form contracts involving consumers are not usually executed under perfect market conditions. They argue that because consumers often lack information about the content of contracts, one cannot be certain that the contracts are fair and efficient. Sometimes they assert that contracts are one-sided and unfair, without attention to the actual determinants of warranty content. Most any theory of warranty content, including one that associates warranty coverage with manufacturer market power, is potentially consistent with these propositions.

Certainly, however, in citing the work of Professors Kessler and Leff, Professor Priest can claim no *direct* support for the proposition that warranty coverage within an industry relates inversely to the size of the manufacturer. Professor Kessler comes closest to suggesting this proposition when he speaks of standard form contracts being "typically used" by enterprises with "strong bargaining power" and discusses the inability of the weaker party to shop for better terms "because the author of the standard contract has a monopoly . . . or because all competitors use the same clauses." Kessler, *supra*, at 632. But this language does not directly state that the content of standard contracts correlates with manufacturer size, and in my judgment, it suggests at least as clearly that warranty content is associated with market imperfections on the buyer side, rather than with the imperfections on the seller side that are the focus of Professor Priest's version of the exploitation hypothesis. *See also infra* p. 1380.

Nor can Professor Priest's first specification of the expolitation hypothesis be attributed to Professor Leff, as is clear from the following passage:

> What the specific circumstances creating . . . [manufacturer] power to impose terms [in an adhesion contract], whether sanctioned monopoly, lawful or unlawful oligopoly, lack of mobility and information, lack of interest [because each deal was too trivial to think about, or the imposed terms covered contingencies too hypothetical to engage attention] or what else *will not concern us here.*

Leff, *supra*, at 141 (emphasis added).

Professor Priest's other specification of the exploitation hypothesis is that warranty content is inversely related to the degree of concentration in the industry. P. 1323. Again he cites no commentator propounding this view, nor do I know of any. Later in this article, I suggest a reason why industry concentration may correlate directly with extensive warranty coverage. *See infra* p. 1383. Admittedly, however, some courts express views similar to this specification of the exploitation hypotheses. *See* Henningsen v. Bloomfield Motors, 32 N.J. 358, 391, 161 A.2d 69, 87 (1960).

30. Pp. 1320, 1339; *see also* Gerner & Bryant, *Appliance Warranties as a Market Signal*, 15 J. CONSUMER AFF. 75 (1981).

31. P. 1327. There are other aspects of warranty content that Professor Priest also finds signal theory inadequate to explain. *See* pp. 1329, 1339.

data offer impressive support for signal theory as a partial theory of warranty content. Moreover, because signal theory posits a determinant of warranty content that seems likely to cause warranty content to differ from the predictions of the investment theory, Priest's inability to refute the signal theory as a partial theory of warranty content undercuts his most persuasive argument for the investment theory as a complete theory.

*Theories of warranty content neglected by Priest.* Perhaps the most serious flaw in Professor Priest's article is its failure to consider other partial theories of warranty content. There are many such theories that seem to explain aspects of warranty content as plausibly as the investment theory. I will identify and briefly discuss four alternative partial theories of warranty content that Priest failed to consider. The existence of such theories rebuts the principal argument that Priest makes for the investment theory as a complete or predominant theory of warranty content.

The first alternative theory of warranty content—one frequently suggested in the literature—emphasizes market imperfections on the buyer side, such as consumer ignorance and lack of sophistication, in contrast to the market imperfections on the seller side that Professor Priest associates with exploitation theory.[32] The signal theory is one possible version of this position; its assumption that consumers associate warranty content with product quality presumes less than perfect information on the buyer side. Another version, not considered by Professor Priest, is the hypothesis that warranty coverage is less extensive for products that are sold primarily to consumers with little education, little experience in buying products of that type, and few practical choices available in the marketplace (most importantly, the poor). This hypothesis takes the much-discussed argument that the poor pay more than the middle class for similar products[33] and extends that principle to warranty coverage.

To test this hypothesis, one should examine the performance of war-

32. Indeed, many of the commentators that Professor Priest considers exploitation theorists emphasize consumer ignorance and lack of information as important determinants of warranty content. *See, e.g.*, Llewellyn, *Book Review*, 52 HARV. L. REV. 700 (1939); Kessler, *supra* note 29; Leff, *supra* note 29. In a footnote, Professor Priest acknowledges that many exploitation theorists presume some degree of consumer ignorance. P. 1303 n.40. For unexplained reasons, Professor Priest states that this assumption is "important, but not central" to these theorists. *Id.*

33. *See* D. CAPLOVITZ, THE POOR PAY MORE (1967). Much of the difference between the poor and the middle class in the prices that they pay can be attributed to the extra costs of supplying goods at retail, and often on credit, in poor neighborhoods. *See* FEDERAL TRADE COMMISSION, ECONOMIC REPORT ON INSTALLMENT CREDIT AND RETAIL SALES IN THE DISTRICT OF COLUMBIA (1969).

Professor Priest suggests reasons why the poor may prefer less warranty coverage than wealthier consumers. Because of their lower incomes and less valuable assets, poor consumers on the average incur smaller losses from product defects than other consumers. The cost of warranty coverage does not vary with the income class of the buyer, however, and hence poorer consumers may prefer products with less extensive warranty coverage. P. 1351. For this reason, a differential in warranty coverage for products marketed to different classes of consumers, if established, could be consistent with the investment theory.

Comment

ranty contracts as well as their content.[34] The same consumer characteristics that may result in lower warranty coverage may also result in lesser ability to secure performance of warranty promises once a product defect becomes apparent. Consequently, for products sold primarily to the poor, manufacturers may promise more than they intend to perform. Even if warranty content does not vary according to the class of buyers, therefore, the hypothesis that the poor receive less warranty coverage cannot be refuted without attention to both warranty-in-the-books and warranty-in-action.

A second partial theory of warranty content emphasizes the organizational structure of the manufacturer. At the time that the warranties examined by Professor Priest were drafted, it made little difference to a manufacturer's legal position whether the warranty excluded liability for personal injury from a product defect. As Professor Priest acknowledges, such a clause would have no effect on the manufacturer's liability in tort, and probably would not limit damages for personal injury on a warranty theory as well.[35] The question arises, therefore, why clauses excluding such liability were included in warranties, given that their presence might have had a negative impact on sales to consumers who were ignorant of the law. Though there are several possible explanations,[36] I suspect that the variation among firms in exclusions of personal injury liability are attributable in significant part to such factors as the role of the legal department in the firm, and the personal relationships between house counsel or other lawyers and the head of the sales department (which often has primary organizational responsibility for determining warranty content).[37]

34. Priest acknowledges the importance of information about warranty performance to the formulation of a theory of warranty content. P. 1320.

35. P. 1308 n.77. *See* U.C.C. § 2-719(3) (1978) .

36. Exclusion of liability for personal injury is often part of a more general warranty clause excluding all liability for "consequential damages." A general exclusion clause can have practical consequences. It may effectively foreclose a purchaser from seeking rescission of the sales contract and return of the purchase price as a remedy for breach of warranty. Under existing law, it is also potentially effective to exclude manufacturer liability for consequential property damage resulting from a product defect, such as the loss of property contained in a motor vehicle involved in a product-caused accident. The legal tradition of using a single contract clause to exclude these potential liabilities as well as liability for personal injury may account for many exclusions of the latter liability.

37. The investment theory accounts for variations in the exclusion of consequential damages on the ground that the range of injuries suffered by the users of some defective products (those sold with exclusion clauses) are greater than the range of injuries suffered by the users of other defective products (those without exclusion clauses). Professor Priest predicts that enough consumers of the first type of product will prefer self-insurance for injuries from product defects to insurance through the warranty to induce manufacturers to exclude consequential damages. Pp. 1343-46. There is some plausibility to this explanation, but the one in the text seems a priori equally plausible. Furthermore, Professor Priest's finding that all dryer warranties in his sample excluded consequential damages while none of the range warranties contained such an exclusion tends to refute the investment theory explanation. Although his sample included only two dryer warranties, and therefore may not be reliable, it seems implausible that there is a greater range in the extent of injuries suffered by users of defective dryers than in the extent of injuries suffered by users of defective ranges.

The exclusion of personal injury liability has the earmark of a lawyer's afterthought—it is unlikely to make much difference but it cannot hurt. The inclusion of such clauses, therefore, may be as much a function of how much a lawyer participated in the drafting of the warranty as anything else.[38] Many factors may account for the degree of lawyer participation in warranty drafting. Some may be consistent with the investment theory, but others seem at variance. For example, whether the chief executive officer or other high management official has legal training or is close socially to the firm's lawyer may have an important effect on lawyer participation.

A third partial theory suggests the fear of government regulation as a determinant of warranty content. It seems highly plausible that corporate managers decide not to restrict warranty coverage as extensively as marketplace conditions might permit, for fear that such behavior might stimulate legislative and judicial regulation of warranty content.[39] It is surprising that Professor Priest did not mention this possibility, because his warranty sample was drawn from 1974—the very year that Congress considered legislation that became the Magnuson-Moss Warranty Act.[40] Fear of government regulation as a determinant of warranty content can be consistent with the variations in warranty content that Priest observes if one supposes that corporate managers differ in the extent to which they fear government regulation. Government regulation is often thought most appropriate in concentrated industries and managers in those industries may be particularly fearful that their warranty practices will come under legislative scrutiny. Ironically, this argument suggests that warranties in concentrated industries will offer greater coverage than warranties in more competitive industries, precisely the opposite of one of Professor

38. A related factor may be the tendency in some industries for firms to copy the technical details of the warranties of another firm, perhaps because the latter firm is known to have cleared its warranty through a lawyer. Such a tendency may account for the uniformity that Professor Priest observes in the presence or absence of exclusion clauses within particular industries.

39. The effect of this fear, as well as other partial determinants of warranty content, could be to induce the drafting of warranty terms that are consistent with the investment theory. In the absence of direct evidence that warranty content is consistent with investment theory, however, the unrefuted possibility of these various partial determinants of warranty content is sufficient to rebut the principal evidence that Professor Priest has for the investment theory—refutation of alternative theories of warranty content. Moreover, even if the net effect of these different partial determinants on warranty content were consistent with the predictions of investment theory, the theory would not have the policy implications suggested by Professor Priest. Eliminating the possibility of warranty regulation might produce a substantial change in warranty content. *See infra* p. 1384.

40. 15 U.S.C. §§ 2301-2312 (1976). There has been little decline in the extent of warranty coverage since the Act. Note, *An Empirical Study of the Magnuson-Moss Warranty Act*, 31 STAN. L. REV. 1117, 1140 (1979). The Act largely eschews substantive regulation of warranty content, but manufacturers may fear that restriction of warranty coverage would induce Congress to reconsider its decision to refrain from substantive regulation. Indeed, for a period preceding the adoption of the Magnuson-Moss Warranty Act, Congress seriously considered a proposal to subject automobile warranties to special substantive regulation. *See* Whitford, *supra* note 20, at 1072-75.

Priest's versions of the exploitation hypothesis.[41]

A fourth alternative theory of warranty content arises from the admittedly controversial proposition that consumers tend to overdiscount long term risks (such as the consequences of product defects) in favor of short term gratification (such as a lower purchase price).[42] This propensity may result from psychological factors or from systematic lack of information, experience and sophistication. If this proposition is correct, it implies that consumers prefer less extensive warranty coverage than the investment theory predicts. If consumer preferences influence warranty content, as Priest argues, then the investment theory would be inadequate as a complete predictor of warranty content.

All of these alternative theories of warranty content are partial theories. They suggest a complete theory of warranty content that posits many determinants of content, including the least-cost risk avoider and most-effective insurer considerations described by Professor Priest. Each determinant would have a somewhat different degree of influence. Professor Priest might object to such a theory on the ground that it is so complicated and unspecified as to be empirically unverifiable.[43] I might answer that, with enough inclination, time and money, I could construct a more specific and verifiable complete theory of warranty content through the use of regression equations and similar social science techniques. A more fitting answer is that this complete theory is no less verifiable than Professor Priest's investment theory. The investment theory cannot be validated on the ground that consumer product warranty contracts are concluded in perfect markets, or on the ground that all alternative theories of warranty

41. Still another reason to anticipate more extensive warranties in concentrated industries stems from the theories of some economists about the nature of competition in such industries. Firms in concentrated industries may try to create barriers to entry that foreclose new entrants and protect the firms' ability to realize monopoly profits. *See generally* J. BAIN, BARRIERS TO COMPETITION (1956); J. BAIN, INDUSTRIAL ORGANIZATION (1959). A new entrant probably requires more capital when the new product must be sold with an extensive warranty. If the signal theory is correct in predicting that firms offering less warranty protection than the industry norm give consumers the impression that their goods are of lesser quality, then the firms in a concentrated industry could create barriers to entry by establishing extensive warranty protection as the norm. Professor Priest was unable to find any relation between industry concentration and warranty content on the basis of his data, but as he would readily concede that data was limited and the question cannot be regarded as settled.

42. I have discussed this point more extensively elsewhere. Whitford, *A Critique of the Consumer Credit Collection System*, 1979 WIS. L. REV. 1047, 1074. Professor Priest notes the hypothesis that consumers may systematically overdiscount long-term risk in a footnote to his article, but he does not take account of it in developing his thesis, perhaps because he does not agree with it. P. 1335 n.152.

I recognize the difficulty in stating that consumers "overly" discount long term risk, for it presupposes an ability to determine an "appropriate" discount rate. I discuss this problem elsewhere. Whitford, *supra*, at 1074 n.95. For purposes of this comment, however, it is sufficient to posit that consumers discount long-term risk more than the least-cost risk avoider and most-effective insurer concerns of the investment theory would contemplate.

43. At one point Professor Priest identifies a partial theory of warranty content suggested by others but dismisses it because the critical determinant of warranty content could not be accurately measured. Consequently, the theory was not verifiable. P. 1319 n.108.

can be refuted. The only remaining means of validation is to determine through detailed empirical inquiry whether existing warranty terms best implement the least-cost risk avoider and most effective insurer considerations underlying the investment theory. I have already adverted to the vast amounts of data necessary for this task.[44]

*Policy implications of the investment theory.* Although Professor Priest is not clear on this point, he does not appear to contend that the investment theory identifies all the determinants of warranty content—he seems to argue only that warranty terms are consistent with the investment theory, whatever the actual determinants of warranty terms. If this is his argument, then alteration of any of the social conditions that underlie warranty decisionmaking risks changing a key determinant of warranty content. For example, Professor Priest suggests that the adoption of strict products liability has increased the rate of product defects. Yet it may be precisely because of strict liability that manufacturers do not uniformly exclude liability for consequential losses, permitting Professor Priest to observe variations in the presence of exclusion clauses that, if enforced, might further least-cost risk avoider and most-effective insurer concerns. Consequently, the abandonment of strict products liability might have the unfortunate effect of moving warranty terms away from this optimal state.[45]

Aside from this concern, however, it is clear that Professor Priest's analysis of the implications of the investment theory is premised on a mistaken conception of the nature of strict products liability. He states that "[c]rucial to the adoption of the strict liability standard is the empirical assumption that consumers can take no action to prevent personal injury loss,"[46] a position quite at odds with the investment theory. The quoted statement clearly implies that strict products liability law imposes no duty of reasonable care on consumers. Yet strict products liability is not really absolute liability; it does not hold the manufacturer liable for all product-connected injuries. Instead, the plaintiff must show that the product was "defective," perhaps that as a result of the defects the product was "unreasonably dangerous,"[47] and that the defects "caused" the injury. It is

44. *See supra* p. 1377. I also disagree with Professor Priest's assertion that the determinants of warranty content under the investment theory are reasonably easy to measure. *See* p. 1352.

45. Strict products liability results in the non-enforcement of certain warranty terms—in particular, exclusion clauses—while the investment theory hypothesizes that all warranty terms should be enforced. Yet, because of imperfections in the market, repeal of strict products liability may lead to an excessive number of exclusion clauses in warranties. This conundrum is a consequence of the presumption that warranties generally promote an efficient loss allocation even in the absence of a perfect market.

46. P. 1350.

47. *See* RESTATEMENT (SECOND) OF TORTS § 402A (1965).

Comment

now accepted both in the case law[48] and in the literature[49] that these concepts incorporate many of the least-cost risk avoider and most-effective insurer concerns that underlie the investment theory. This point is an important one, for if Professor Priest's characterization of strict products liability were correct, strict liability would certainly be undesirable. In fact, however, under a legal regime of strict liability courts can accommodate the concerns that underlie the investment theory.[50]

Conclusion

The key points in Professor Priest's article are the apparent suggestion that the investment theory is a complete theory of warranty content and the claim that the evidence, though not conclusive, tends to support the investment theory. As a partial theory of warranty content, the investment theory is uncontroversial and lacks the implications that Professor Priest identifies. Analysis indicates that the case for the investment theory as a complete theory rests almost entirely on Professor Priest's ability to refute alternative theories of warranty content. But he considers only two such alternative theories. One of these alternatives, the exploitation theory, is really his own creation, although he attributes it to a large group of earlier commentators. The other alternative, the signal theory, is actually substantiated as a partial theory of warranty content. More importantly, there are many alternative theories that Professor Priest does not identify or discuss. As a result, the evidence in favor of the investment theory as a complete explanation of warranty content is weak indeed. Warranty content is almost surely the product of numerous forces, and by conventional theory, some of those forces most likely justify legal regulation of warranty content.

48. *See* Barker v. Lull Engineering Co., 143 Cal. Rptr. 335, 573 P.2d 443 (1978).

49. *See* Schwartz, *Foreword: Understanding Products Liability*, 67 CALIF. L. REV. 435 (1979); Whitford, *Strict Products Liability and the Automobile Industry: Much Ado About Nothing*, 1968 WIS. L. REV. 83.

50. Apart from his apparent misunderstanding of the state of the law, Professor Priest's focus on strict products liability in discussing the implications of his theory is also puzzling. The logic of his position suggests an objection to all liability that exceeds the scope of the warranty, whether based on negligence, *see* McPherson v. Buick Motor Co., 217 N.Y. 382, 111 N.E. 1050 (1916), or on modern strict products liability.

# Part V
# Consumer Safety

# [12]

## CHAPTER 7

# THE ADMINISTRATION OF THE *HAZARDOUS PRODUCTS ACT*

RONALD HIRSHHORN

## I. INTRODUCTION

In previous chapters it was argued that there may be a case for government intervention in product markets when there are major information problems, and this is likely to be particularly so when risks to health and safety are at issue. In Parts I and II of this volume the alternative instruments available for addressing market problems were described and considerations relating to the choice of instrument were examined. This chapter attempts to provide a further insight into these and related issues by looking at specific regulatory problems and the general regulatory process in the hazardous product area. The material comes in part from discussions with individuals involved in the administration of the *Hazardous Products Act*,[1] and from an examination of committee meeting minutes and other documentation pertaining to the development of specific product safety regulations. The main analysis upon which this chapter draws was completed in early 1981, and the discussion refers for the most part to the first decade of Canada's experience under hazardous products legislation.

Section II provides a description of the *Hazardous Products Act* and a general perspective on the Act's administration. The following sections look at specific components of the regulatory process—the identification of product hazards, the development of regulations, and the enforcement of the Act—in greater detail. Decisions taken at each of these stages are examined in relation to the general objective of obtaining the maximum degree of risk reduction from a given commitment of resources. In the course of this examination there is an attempt to understand how influences on the decision-making process affect the achievement of an efficient system of product safety regulation.

[1] R.S.C. 1970, c. H-3 as am.

## II. THE HAZARDOUS PRODUCTS ACT AND ITS ADMINISTRATION: AN OVERVIEW

The *Hazardous Products Act* was passed in 1969[2] in the wake of concerns about the appearance on the Canadian market of a number of hazardous substances which were outside the reach of existing federal legislation.[3] The provinces could be alerted to these problems and requested to exercise their power to prohibit sales within their boundaries, but this would be a slow and inadequate means by which to respond to these perceived emergencies. The federal government was already involved in regulating the safety of consumer products through the *Food and Drugs Act*[4] and the *Pest Control Products Act*[5] (covering disinfectants, pesticides and preservatives), and an obvious solution was to extend the scope and coverage of federal legislation in this area.

The legislation that was passed provides the government with extensive powers to regulate the sale of hazardous or potentially hazardous consumer goods. The Governor in Council may insert in the schedule to the *Hazardous Products Act* any consumer good that "he is satisfied is or is likely to be a danger to the health or safety of the public".[6] When a product is inserted into Part I or Part II of the schedule to the Act, it is by definition a "hazardous product". Products in Part I of the schedule cannot be advertised, sold, or imported into Canada, while products in Part II can only be sold if they conform to certain prescribed standards. While the Act is primarily concerned with consumer products, it extends to "*any* product or substance that is or contains a poisonous, toxic, inflammable, explosive or corrosive product or substance or other product or substance of a similar nature".[7]

The broad very general authority provided by the *Hazardous Products Act* can be contrasted with U.S. legislation in this area. The latter focuses not on risks *per se* but on "unreasonable" risks; and successive court decisions have made it clear that in developing new regulations the Consumer Product Safety Commission (CPSC) in the U.S. has the burden of demon-

---

[2] 1968-69 (Can.), c. 42.

[3] Immediate concern centered on the appearance in the Canadian market of necklaces made from poisonous jequirity beans and ice balls containing contaminated water. In 1967, in an appearance before the Senate Committee on Banking and Commerce, the Deputy Minister of National Health and Welfare, indicated how the Department had to respond to these emergencies:

> Well, we had to deal with the provincial departments on this. We telephoned and telegraphed and told them of the hazard which was in their shops and they dealt with it provincially. This is how we had to handle that situation. Of course it was a pretty time-consuming process.

See *Hansard*, February 20, 1969, p. 5887.

[4] R.S.C. 1970, c. F-27 as am.

[5] R.S.C. 1970, c. P-10 as am.

[6] *Supra* note 1, s. 8(1).

[7] *Supra* note 1, s. 8(1)(a); emphasis added.

strating both the presence of an unreasonable risk and the likelihood that a proposed regulation would significantly reduce that risk.[8] United States legislation does, however, provide much greater flexibility when it comes to dealing with suspected offenders. The *Hazardous Products Act* is criminal law and the relatively high standards of proof established for criminal cases must be met to gain a conviction under the Act. United States product safety legislation, by contrast, provides for both civil and criminal penalties, and as an alternative to prosecution it empowers the CPSC to order remedial actions, such as the replacement of a product or the refund of its purchase price.

The *Hazardous Products Act* is administered by the Product Safety Branch (PSB) within Consumer and Corporate Affairs Canada (CCA). Over the 1979/80 fiscal year administration and enforcement of the Act involved the efforts of 87 people and total budgetary expenditures (including salaries) of about $2.5 million dollars. Almost half the staff are involved in field inspection and enforcement activities with the remainder employed in the product safety laboratory, or associated with headquarters work either in the identification of hazards and the development of new regulations, or in the administration of compliance and enforcement activities.

The development of product safety regulations in Canada has proceeded in a relatively informal environment and one which stands very much in contrast to that in the U.S. Product regulation in Canada has involved a significant degree of consultation, but it has largely been what might be termed an internally open system, with the main participants in the process consisting of industry representatives and individuals who have a mutual professional interest in the technical problems related to product design and performance.[9] The federal guidelines recently introduced, which require that major new regulations be pre-published in the Canada Gazette, along with the results of the required socio-economic impact analysis, is designed to encourage somewhat greater public participation in the regulatory process. The Canadian approach can be contrasted with a more publicly open system such as in the U.S., which provides an extensive opportunity for public input into regulatory decisions, and offers considerable scope for legal recourse. But while the experience of CPSC in the U.S. illustrates the benefits of openness it also demonstrates how excessive procedural and legal requirements can burden the regulatory process. As a result of the elaborate administrative procedures designed to give affected parties a voice in determining both the need for a standard and its final form, it has frequently taken several years in the U.S. to move from an initial proposal to the issuance of a final regulation.

---

[8] See, for example, the court's decision in, *Aqua Slide'n Dive Corp. v. CPSC*, 569 Fed. 831 (C.A., 5th Cir. 1978).

[9] The distinction between an "internally" or "professionally open" process, and a "democratically open" process is made in Doern (1977, pp. 26-28).

The less legalistic and less adversarial climate in Canada has also influenced the character of product safety regulations issued under the *Hazardous Products Act*. For example, both Canada and the United States have developed similar regulations to address the hazard which arises from small parts which may become detached from toys and ingested by very young children. The regulations in both countries incorporate a "use and abuse" test to determine if toy components are likely to become detached, and a size test which involves determining whether the component or part can be enclosed within a volumetric container of specified dimensions. Both regulations are furthermore aimed specifically at products intended for children under three. The small parts regulation which became effective in Canada in 1974 leaves the determination of whether the product is likely to be used by a child under three entirely to the PSB and its enforcement staff. An early proposal to allow similar discretion in the U.S. regulation met severe criticism and so the regulation that ultimately came into effect January 1, 1980, attempts to be more precise about product coverage. The U.S. small parts regulation contains: a list of articles which the Commission believes are intended for children under three; a list of factors the staff will consider before determining whether products not specifically listed are covered; and a procedure by which firms may challenge the enforcement staffs' interpretation of their product's intended use. The willingness of manufacturers and retailers to rely on PSB's judgment with respect to these types of subjective issues has significantly simplified the making of product safety regulations in Canada.

### (a) General Results of Product Safety Regulation

Due in part to these types of environmental and institutional factors, the PSB has been able to respond efficiently to concerns about new product hazards. In a little over a decade a substantial number of regulations have been issued to cover many of the most basic product hazards. Among the 30 or so items which are covered in Part I of the schedule and prohibited from being sold in Canada are: highly flammable textiles, bed linens and children's sleepwear; children's toys with a lead coating or containing any one of a number of hazardous substances; asbestos clothing not specially designed for fire protection; bath tub and exterior household doors not made of safety glass; hockey helmets that do not meet Canadian Standards Association (CSA) standards; clothing containing tris; consumer products containing nitrobenzine and ethy/bromacetate; and candles that re-ignite spontaneously. Part II of the schedule covers some 35 items, and includes: labelling requirements for a range of hazardous substances; standards designed to reduce the likelihood of cuts, burns, electrical shock, asphyxiation and other accidents from toy products; standards for rattles, cribs and playpens; minimum performance requiremens for children's car seats; flammability test requirements for carpets; and minimum performance standards for smoke detectors and fire alarms. As a complement to, or substitute for, its regulations, the PSB at times attempts to encourage industry to voluntarily upgrade its standards and increase the safety of its products. Where voluntary standards and a program of certification are administered by an accredited standards body, such as the CSA, the department of Consumer and Corporate Affairs may have little involvement. In other cases the PSB may in fact establish very explicit requirements for the "voluntary" program, and it may become involved in monitoring the degree of industry compliance to determine if further measures are required. The vast majority of the PSB's resources, however, are directed towards the establishment and enforcement of regulations specified in the schedule to the *Hazardous Products Act*, and these regulations provide a reliable basis on which to measure and assess product safety activity.

The absence of a reporting system in Canada which provides information on product-related injuries treated in hospital emergency departments, is a major impediment to the analysis of product accidents in Canada. One recent study, however, which looked at the hospitalizations due to home accidents in the province of British Columbia found some evidence of the Act's effect (Hirshhorn, 1981). Various formulations were tested but the regressions that yielded the most significant results were those that focussed on the home accident rate of children ages one to four. In this case the results were consistent with the hypothesis that product safety regulation has reduced the severity of home accidents and/or the number of severe accidents among young children. The regulations in the Act give a strong emphasis to risks to children and infants: about half of the items in Part I and Part II relate specifically to products used by children; in addition, other more general regulations, such as the important hazardous substance regulations in Part II, are concerned primarily with the hazards confronted by children. These findings therefore suggest that the *Hazardous Products Act* has succeeded in lowering product risks among the population group where it has been primarily targeted.

An examination of some specific regulations provides a further perspective on the gains that are available from product safety regulation. The original hazardous substance regulations were introduced in March 1970, being among the earliest regulations issued under the Act. The approach in this area involved a combination of selective product bans, the imposition of broad labelling requirements, and the establishment of specific requirements for both labelling and the use of child-resistant containers. The PSB has made an effort to inform and educate the consumer about hazardous substances generally and about the prescribed hazardous product labels in particular. This area is particularly well-suited to an informational approach and, based on consumer awareness and comprehension of the hazardous product symbols, the PSB's efforts have been highly successful.[10] The evidence suggests, moreover, that the hazardous substance regulations have effectively reduced poisonings among young children; the rate of hospitalization due to the particular forms of poisoning covered in the Act was found to be significantly lower in the post-regulation period than one would expect based on previous trends (Hirshhorn, 1981). At the same time, the costs of the hazardous substance regulations have generally been minimal due to the heavy emphasis on informing the consumer, and the very sparing use of CCA's power to ban hazardous products. The prohibitions introduced apply for the most part to a narrow group of highly toxic or highly flammable products for which reasonable substitutes are available.

A similarly favourable impression emerges from an examination of the regulations pertaining to rattles, pacifiers, and cribs. All three of these infant products involved hazards which most consumers would not know or even suspect existed, and in all cases there was a basic problem of a medical or anthropometrical nature which producers themselves were ill-equipped to address. In the case of rattles the problem was to come up with some minimal size specifications which would ensure that a rattle could not project into an infants throat to a depth that could cause choking. The risk from pacifiers arose from the attached cord which had caused strangulation in a number of instances, from the inadequate size of the guard or shield, which could cause choking, and from the softness of the material used, which created a tendency for parts of the pacifier to break off after repeated use. The main requirement in the case of cribs was to determine the appropriate spacing of the vertical slats to avoid the possibility of small infants slipping through the sides of the crib with potentially fatal consequences. The PSB responded to these problems on the basis of well-researched technical studies that provided an understanding of the defects in product design.[11] In all three cases the basic problems were found to be amenable to a solution involving fairly minor design changes. It has been estimated that if costs associated with the required mold changes and retooling were passed on to the consumer, the price increases for rattles and pacifiers would be in the order of five cents.[12] While the crib standard was much more costly, the risk associated with cribs and the magnitude of the potential gain from effective standards were commensurately higher. Subsequent evidence sug-

[10] A study for the department found an exceptionally high rate of awareness and comprehension of the hazardous substance symbols. The proportion of those surveyed who were aware of the symbols for poison and flammable substances were 91% and 83% respectively. See Contemporary Research Centre Ltd. (1977).

[11] In the case of cribs, the department could rely on the extensive research that had already been undertaken in the U.S. For a description of events leading to the development of the U.S. crib standard see Kelman (1974).

[12] Based on estimates made by the Bureau of Economic Analysis with respect to similar U.S. standards. See Consumer Product Safety Commission Bureau of Economic Analysis, (1977 and 1978).

gests that Canadian along with similar U.S. crib regulations have indeed been effective, and that crib related deaths have significantly declined in both countries since the issuance of these regulations (Consumer Product Safety Commission. Office of Strategic Planning, 1979; Hirshhorn, 1981). Given the nature of the costs and benefits, it is reasonable to believe that CCA was reliably reflecting the wishes of consumers in the case of all three infant products.

This same conclusion could not be applied to a number of other product safety regulations. These particular examples in fact portray only part of Canada's quite varied experience with product safety regulation. Some regulations under the *Hazardous Products Act* (such as the child car seat standard and the 1.5 litre pop bottle ban, which are later discussed) have been heavily criticised. Questions have been raised about whether government intervention was justified at all in the case of some product hazards, and about whether the appropriate form of intervention was chosen in the case of others. Even where product regulation would seem to be producing beneficial results, it is not always clear that the level of safety approaches the optimal level. And concerns arise in connection with the coverage of the Act; there is reason to suspect that there may be important opportunities for the reduction of product safety risks that may have been missed.

The general impression that emerges is that the *Hazardous Products Act* is fulfilling an important role and yielding significant benefits, but that opportunities for the efficient production of safety have not been nearly realized. When the Act was passed in 1969 it filled a major gap in the legislative framework that had been established to address failings of the market with potentially serious social and economic consequences. A number of product safety regulations respond to very major problems with which other mechanisms such as the product liability system are ill-suited to cope. At the same time the regulations reflect a number of shortcomings in the administration of the Act. A better understanding of these general results can be gained by looking at some important aspects of the decision-making process in the product safety area.

## III. THE IDENTIFICATION OF PRODUCT HAZARDS

The success of a system of product regulation depends very much on the ability of the authorities to identify areas where there are information and other market imperfections which may have potentially serious consequences. The extent to which this is achieved depends in turn on the information and data on product risks to which regulatory officials have access, and the sensitivity of these officials to the conditions under which government intervention is justified. In evaluating the process for identifying hazards, it should be kept in mind that we are interested not only in those risks which have been addressed, but also those which may have been overlooked or ignored. One of the important questions to be considered is whether there are likely to be major opportunities for the reduction of health and safety risks that have not been identified.

### (a) The Process for Identifying Hazards

As we noted previously, there has been no systematic attempt in Canada to compile information on product-related injuries treated in doctor's offices or hospital emergency departments. The information that has been available to the PSB comes from a variety of sources including consumer complaints, coroners' reports, studies of provincial governments or other federal departments, and media reports. Consumer and Corporate Affairs Canada keeps abreast of the product safety activities undertaken in other countries, and it has access to the published tabulations from the injury surveillance system which is maintained by the CPSC in the U.S. While some Canadian accident data are available—such as fire statistics published by provincial governments, the data on poisonings collected by Health and Welfare Canada, and the data on emergency treatments compiled by the Sick Children's Hospital in Toronto—these have been of limited use, and they have not significantly diminished CCA's reliance on individual case information. In contrast to an identification process which is linked to a data collection system, the existing approach is very dependent on the willingness of individuals, firms and institutions to report product hazards to the department. And, unlike the situation in the U.S., there is no legal requirement in Canada compelling producers and retailers to notify the authorities of hazards or suspected hazards. There is a clear danger that the selective information flowing into the department will provide a biased and misleading indication of the extent and nature of the hazards associated with the use of consumer products.

There is a recognition by officials of the need to focus on "involuntary" or hidden risks. The director of the PSB (Black, 1973) has made the point, as follows:

> The common thread throughout all [the] regulations is the concern with hidden dangers. The consumer can cope with the obvious such as the sharp knife which has been part of his environmental experience but he has no basis for reaction where he is unaware that an earthenware jug is releasing toxic quantities of lead into his orange juice everyday. . . .There is then the basic concern that regulated products should be designed free of hidden dangers in the first instance.

The items included in the schedule to the Act for the most part fit comfortably under the label of hidden or involuntary risk. There are basic problems of consumer knowledge and awareness relating, for example, to the risks from hazardous substances, flammable products, cribs and rattles.

While some of the specified toy hazards are not hidden in the same sense, special problems arise because of the vulnerability of young children and the fact that the purchasers of child products are not directly involved in their use. The concept of "hidden risk", however, applies much less easily to a few of the regulations. One of these is the regulation introduced in 1973, requiring that all bath tub enclosures, shower doors, and exterior doors for household use be made of safety glass. Consumers are clearly aware that glass is an inherently risky product and that if appropriate caution is not exercised, the probability of injury is substantial. The changes to the *Hazardous Products Act*, and similar changes to the National Building Code, were prompted by estimates that 10,000 injuries occur annually involving architectural glass products. This is not in itself, however, an indication that consumers were badly informed and thereby assuming greater risks than they were in fact desiring to accept. Fully informed consumers would continue to buy ordinary glasss products if they could do so at a price discount which, in their view, more than adequately compensated for its inferior quality relative to the safety-glazed alternative. There may be other types of market problems and the safety glass market may not be particularly responsive to consumer preferences, as a recent study (O'Riordan and McCabe, 1980) speculates, but judging simply by the nature of the hazard this would seem to be a highly questionable area for government intervention.

While the PSB has generally been conscious of the need to direct its efforts to problems characterized by information failures, it has not attempted to establish a ranking of priorities for its activities based on the extent and the consequences of the information problem. There has been no systematic attempt, that is, to order the branch's activities and to concentrate on problems where potential benefits are likely to be greatest relative to costs. A systematic attempt to evaluate the net benefits of intervention in each product area would be a formidable undertaking, given the branch's existing resources and information sources. Notwithstanding existing limitations, however, one might expect that there would at least be some emphasis given to problem areas where information deficiencies are likely to be particularly pronounced. In the case of health hazards, where the consequences often only become apparent long after exposure and where cause and effect relationships are very difficult to establish, the protections afforded both by the market system and the legal system are highly deficient. This would appear to be a particularly important area for government attention. Some of the consumer products that raise possible concerns of this nature, such as microwave ovens and pesticides, are outside the CCA's mandate, but many products which are potential health risks are under the scope of the *Hazardous Products Act*. In these areas, however, the PSB has largely been dependent on the advice provided by Health and Welfare Canada and it has been unable to pursue potentially important initiatives such as, for example, the large-scale investigation recently launched by the CPSC into asbestos hazards in consumer products.[13]

In the absence of any systematic process for priority-setting, the direction of the PSB activities has been very much influenced by the winds of public attention and concern, and by the department's own sense of where the requirement for protective regulation is most urgent. We mentioned the heavy emphasis in the regulations to product risks confronted by young children. This emphasis could emerge from benefit-cost calculations as a result of the high probability of accidents to this population segment and the amenability of the relevant risks to regulatory solutions. In the present context, however, the attention given to child and infant risks is very much a reflection of the particular concerns of the director and other officials within the PSB. Young children are an especially vulnerable group, and certainly potential product hazards affecting this segment deserve careful examination. It is not clear, however, that the government can effectively respond to all the concerns that have been singled out in this area. Some of the toy regulations, for example, raise major problems of enforcement (as we later describe) and there are serious questions about the payoff from the resources the department is devoting to this specific type of product hazard.

Similarly, the pressure emanating from public and media attention may provide a much needed sense of urgency in dealing with some particularly serious product risks. But again, it is not necessarily the case that the perceptions which are behind this impetus for intervention will bear a close relationship to the magnitude of the risk and the gains which are likely to be forthcoming from product regulation. The media will tend to highlight certain types of accidents which are especially likely to elicit public sympathy; more mundane incidents and risks which are fairly subtle and complex will tend to receive less coverage, though in fact these may represent areas in which government intervention would be highly desirable. There is indeed a danger that public concern and the resulting pressure to take some action could lead to intervention where the evidence on cause and effect relationships is highly imprecise and unreliable; or alternatively that it could lead to more restrictive and costly regulation than is justified by the nature and extent of the risk involved.

### (b) Media Influence and the Regulation Banning 1.5 Litre Bottles

The interim regulation banning commercial sales of carbonated

[13] A preliminary study for the CPSC found more than 100 consumer products that might contain asbestos, including such everyday products as toothbrushes and car mufflers. The information from that study, which came largely from a search of published sources and patent reports, is being expanded and amended on the basis of manufacturers' reports. It should be noted that the focus of the *Hazardous Products Act* is much broader than U.S. legislation in this area, and would also cover the risk posed by asbestos in industrial use and construction.

beverages in 1.5 litre glass containers provides an illustration of the influential role that the media can play. The ban, which was issued in August 1979, was lifted a little over a year later and replaced with a regulation permitting the use of 1.5 litre containers that could meet the requirements set out in a "drop and drill" test. Plastic coated bottles conforming to the standard began to appear on the market in 1982.

The 1979 ban raises some interesting issues. For one thing, the 1979 regulation had some quite distinctive features. Most of the items prohibited under the Act relate to relatively small industries and affect quite narrow specialized industry segments. The Canadian soft drink bottling industry, by contrast, generates about $1 billion a year in revenue, and the 1.5 litre bottle had accounted for more than ten percent of total sales revenue. Another striking feature was the abruptness with which this regulation was introduced; it was only about three months from the time a Toronto engineer initially became alerted to the problem until the date the regulation became effective. While the department has moved swiftly in the past to clear the market of highly dangerous products, it is generally the case that manufacturers have been forewarned for some time that regulatory action was likely. A third notable aspect of the regulation was its temporary or interim nature. Again the regulation was not unique in this respect, but it does take exceptional circumstance to prompt the department to act prior to undertaking the necessary regulatory development work.

While the ban on 1.5 litre bottles was exceptionally costly in comparison to most regulatory activities in the product safety area, in part because of these characteristics, these costs were seen to be more than justified by the urgency of eliminating the particular hazard from the market. Subsequent analysis, however, casts serious doubt on this conclusion. One study estimated that the cost of the ban over one year worked out to in excess of $20,000 per accident prevented (Hirshhorn, 1981). Since the vast majority of injuries involving soft drink bottles are very minor cuts, these costs seem clearly excessive. The resources that went into complying with this regulation could undoubtedly have prevented many more accidents, and much more severe accidents if they had been more effectively employed.

To understand how the hazard associated with the 1.5 litre container came to be perceived as an emergency justifying the rather stringent measures that were adopted, one has to look at the very intense media coverage which this product risk received. Over the summer of 1979, television and newspaper reporters highlighted the dangers arising from "torpedo-shaped" bottles which could "explode", and graphically portrayed the details of a few particularly frightening incidents. The Minister was repeatedly queried in the House of Commons on the issue, and within a very short span of time, a danger of which most people had previously been unaware was raised to the status of a major concern. Eisner and Strotz (1961) have suggested that people continue to buy air accident insurance, in part because the extensive publicity air accidents receive leads them to believe such cases are relatively frequent. Similarly, individuals who looked at Canadian newspapers or television over the summer of 1979, could not help but have an inflated view of the probability and severity of accidents associated with soft drink bottles. As a result, they were willing to pay what was in fact an inordinate price, to obtain the required regulatory insurance.

### (c) The Establishment of Regulatory Priorities

Even if the PSB had established a priority system based on an analysis of the relative gains from addressing alternative hazards, it is very unlikely that the department could have resisted the pressure for an immediate response to the dangers of 1.5 litre containers. But the ban on 1.5 litre bottles is not a typical regulation. In the case of most product hazards there is much less publicity and a much greter opportunity for a more considered response. While the Department could not be expected to adhere strictly to the dictates of a planning system, the latter could have substantial influence. There is considerable scope for the application of a more systematic approach which would help the department appraise the many complaints it receives and determine the most desirable allocation of its resources in terms of product safety.

In the U.S., data on product injuries is collected through the National Electronic Injury Surveillance System (NEISS), a central computerized data bank that is fed data on product-related injuries from 72 statistically selected hospital emergency rooms. This is supplemented by more in-depth studies of a sample of reported accidents. In ordering priorities, the CPSC has relied in part on a hazard index that is derived by combining the accident data from NEISS with weights intended to reflect the relative severity of various injuries. Less importance has been attached to the hazard index in recent years due to its recognized deficiencies as a guide to where resources should be targeted.[14] The main problems stem from: the arbitrary nature of the weights; the failure of the index to adjust for product usage (so that products which have a low accident rate but are infrequently used would have an unrealistically high value on the index); the total reliance on emergency room data which understates deaths, ignores health problems and gives no consideration to property damage; and the inability of the data to indicate those hazards which are most amenable to a regulatory solution. In addition, many of the product risks which rank high on the hazard index are well understood and voluntarily assumed by consumers.

The criticisms of the hazard index are based on the general view that regulatory activity should concentrate on those areas where potential benefits are greatest relative to costs. An accident reporting system cannot,

[14] See, for example, Cornell, Noll, and Weingast (1976, pp. 457-504).

of course, make this determination. But an information system which includes reference to factors such as the frequency with which a product is used, and which distinguishes between known and hidden risks, can help signal the product risks which may warrant action and which therefore deserve further analysis.

The resources which have been devoted to analysis and planning in the Canadian system have been, and undoubtedly in the near future will continue to be, extremely limited. This gives added importance to the establishment of an information system which could help screen the reports on product risk so as to produce a manageable list of candidates for further research and analysis. The United States' experience illustrates that even a very sophisticated data collection system cannot substitute for economic analysis as a means of targeting product safety activities. It also indicates that an information system which is to fulfill a successful "screening" or "signalling" role must indicate more than the number and severity of product accidents associated with various products. In particular, it must indicate which risks are likely to be involuntary, it must provide data on product usage and thereby the exposure to various risks, and it must be broadened to cover important risks which are unlikely to be treated in hospital emergency rooms. There has long been discussion about the possibilities of establishing a limited accident reporting system in Canada, and some experimentation in this regard is presently underway. The alternative would seem to involve placing a greater reliance on NEISS data, suitably adjusted to allow for differences in sales of various products and various makes and models of products in the Canadian and U.S. markets.[15] Whichever approach is adopted, it would be necessary to supplement the resulting data and to integrate it with other sources of information on product risks to develop an information system which could contribute to a more rational process for the establishment of product safety priorities.

## IV. THE DEVELOPMENT OF PRODUCT SAFETY REGULATIONS

Once a product risk has been targeted and the decision to intervene has been made, a number of important questions arise: What form should intervention take? If a standard is to be established, how rigorous should this standard be? And how soon should the regulation take effect? The department's choices can be set out along a continuum ranging from the least ex-

[15] In assessing those product hazards for which no Canadian data is available, analysts have traditionally relied on U.S. accident data adjusted to take into account differences in market size and, perhaps, differences in the relative importance of various product brands. In some cases this approach could produce seriously misleading results. The question, from an administrative perspective, is whether the value of the marginal improvement in analytical capability from the development of a Canadian accident reporting system would more than offset the expenditure involved.

pensive set of options, consisting of an information program or a very minor design change which is phased in over a long period, and extending right up to a product ban which is to become effective immediately. Parliament's expectation, as set out in the original legislation was that the department would take whatever action was necessary to effectively respond to perceived risks to the public's health or safety. While the department has not been insensitive to the broader effects of product regulations and to the increasing costs associated with efforts to achieve higher levels of safety, this view of the intent of legislation has clearly had a major influence on the way in which these questions have been resolved.

### (a) The Standard-Setting Process

When there is a decision to begin work on a standard, an advisory committee is established which typically has representatives from the relevant industry association, major manufacturing and retail firms, a standards organization, an importers association and other government departments with related interests. Consumers have a relatively minor input and are represented only where there is a product hazard which is of particular concern to the Consumers Association of Canada or to a related group, such as the Canadian Toy Testing Council. An individual from the PSB chairs the committee and co-ordinates the discussions and the development work that goes on within the product safety laboratory. The developmental process is usually characterized by a heavy emphasis on the engineering and design problems which contribute to product hazards. One of the most challenging problems involves the design of test procedures in those cases where standards have not already been implemented in the U.S. or elsewhere and foreign experience cannot therefore be relied upon. The advice of the advisory committee is particularly useful in these circumstances in helping to determine whether the test methodology developed is appropriate and properly specified. In later stages of the development process, the information provided by manufacturers and retailers on the size of existing inventories and the length of the lead time required to implement a change in product design, contributes to the determination of when new regulations are to become effective.

The process of relatively informal consultation through advisory committees along with the favourable relations the PSB has established with most industry associations has produced a congenial climate for the interchange of information and the frank discussion of technical problems. It has furthermore allowed the very limited resources of the PSB to be concentrated on substantive questions with respect to product safety rather than on procedural and legal requirements of the regulatory process itself. But while the PSB has been able to respond promptly to concerns about new product hazards, the quality of that response has at times left much to be desired.

The solutions developed in particular for some of the more complex regulatory problems reveal the weaknesses of a decision-making process in which there is limited consultation and no attempt to systematically analyse the impact of proposed initiatives. The discussions of the product safety advisory committee tend to highlight some, but only some, of the issues which are relevant to a determination of regulatory costs and impacts. The minutes of various advisory committee meetings suggest that officials generally understand the nature of product risks and the factors contributing to product accidents, but that they seldom have a reasonable notion of the number of accidents likely to be prevented by a specific change in product design. Accident data are cited in some discussions, but these generally do not indicate the number of accidents that are attributable to a specific product feature. And there is seldom any consideration given to the possibility that a proposed regulation might be less than 100 percent effective due to human and other factors which tend to make "real world" effects quite different from those observed in the laboratory. Costs involved in implementing a proposed standard sometimes enter explicitly into the committee discussions, but often they do not. On the other hand, product changes that are likely to significantly affect the utility and appeal of a product tend to be subject to critical analysis and review.

The factors that are highlighted in committee discussions to a considerable degree reflect the particular interests and concerns of the main participants in the regulatory development process. The PSB, which is the dominant participant in the process, is primarily concerned with ensuring that the letter and intent of the *Hazardous Products Act* is seen to be effectively fulfilled. The everpresent danger that the Minister of Consumer and Corporate Affairs could be implicated in a major tragedy because of the department's failure to respond, and to respond adequately, to information on the hazards of particular products, clearly weighs heavily in the minds of those charged with the day-to-day administration of the Act. The Minister's responsibility is seen to require that the department not just react to product accidents, but that it anticipate these dangers and take appropriate preventative action. The PSB attaches importance to the goodwilll it has established with most industry associations. There is an appreciation that both the development and enforcement of product safety regulations would become more onerous without the co-operation of manufacturers and retailers. But while the branch will often go some distance towards accommodating industry concerns with respect, for example, to the restrictiveness of a standard, the particulars of a test procedure, or the implementation date for a regulation, there are some matters where firm and immediate action is seen to be necessary and there is little room for compromise.

The knowledge and information of manufacturers and retailers and the desire of the PSB to maintain reasonably favourable working relations with industry has allowed these groups to influence the development of product safety regulations. Industry members of the advisory committee seem to appreciate, however, that there are some areas where the considerable weight the department has attached to safety considerations leaves them relatively little scope to influence the form and timing of proposed regulations. For the most part, industry representatives have used what leverage they had to press for less restrictive standards and for a sufficient lead time to allow for the disposal of existing stocks. New product standards can entail significant capital and operating expenditures and in most cases, it is difficult for a manufacturer to pass the full amount of these cost increases on to the consumer. But industry groups may not always act as a restraining influence. In some circumstances, regulation can yield significant benefits to Canadian manufacturers and at times industry has itself prompted government intervention. The industry association may see regulation as a way of eliminating low-cost domestic and imported products from the market. Product safety regulation may thereby serve both to eliminate a troubling source of competition and to improve the image of the industry's product among consumers. Toy manufacturers in particular have recognized the importance of consumer confidence in the safety of their products, and prior to the issuance of the toy regulations, the Canadian Toy Manufacturers Association had attempted to fill this need by developing a system of voluntary standards. Manufacturers may also be concerned about their liability in the case of accidents involving their products, and see the advantages of a set of regulatory standards which help to define their responsibilities in this respect.

In discussing product safety regulation in the U.S., Grabowski and Vernon (1978) have contended that the decision-making process of the CPSC embodies a strong "safety imperative". While the CPSC calculates economic impact analyses of its decisions, Grabowski and Vernon claim that these generally take on an "after the fact" character, and that the Commission's decisions are heavily influenced by potential benefits, and much less so, if at all, by estimated costs. There is similar evidence of a "safety imperative" in the decisions of Canadian officials, but the resulting bias is not a consistent and systematic element underlying the decision-making calculus. In dealing, for example, with hazards which entail potentially serious consequences and which affect young children, officials have been loathe to even admit that costs are a relevant consideration. While it is possible to sympathize with the reluctance to enter into the valuation of human lives, the failure to even compare the costs of reducing comparable risks through various alternatives could conceivably lead to some exceedingly costly regulations. Choices must inevitably be made and priorities established, but the result is that the department must make these decisions in the absence of data on the cost-effectiveness of alternative regulations.

When dealing with other hazards, however, where the risk may appear less direct and/or the consequences of a mishap less serious, the PSB has been sensitive to the cost implications of its decisions and amenable to suggestions which could reduce these costs. While compliance costs may not be directly addressed in the committee discussion they are often an implicit consideration related to concerns about the magnitude of the design change and the degree of dislocation a particular regulatory decision would entail.

The heightened sensitivity of officials to costs which are likely to impact visibly on consumers has also led the PSB to make decisions at odds with the concept of a "safety imperative". While standards which may result in slightly higher prices are likely to receive little or no attention by consumers, the PSB is well aware that a regulation which would eliminate or significantly reduce the quality and appeal of a widely used product is likely to elicit a very strong reaction. By eliminating from the market only a very narrow group of particularly hazardous toys, infant products and hazardous substances, and employing less restrictive policies for most risks in these areas, the PSB has implicitly recognized the need to balance the benefits of increased safety against the cost of significant reductions in consumers' freedom of choice. This implicit balancing of costs and benefits is not an appropriate substitute for economic analysis, but it does lead to very different results from situations in which costs are totally ignored.

It can be seen, then, that a range of influences underlie decisions taken in the product safety area, and that these may be quite different depending on the nature of the product risk, and, perhaps, the competitive structure of the industry concerned. While these influences have not led the department to concentrate exclusively on risk reduction and to dismiss the cost implications of its decisions, neither have they resulted in a process in which there is a careful balancing of the costs and the beneficial effects of various alternative courses of action. In some cases the need for an effective and immediate response to a product hazard has been the dominant consideration. At other times the PSB has been more responsive to the concerns raised by industry groups about the problems and costs of compliance. Industry representatives may not always provide the required countervailing influence, however; rigorous standards may serve the purposes of major producers by providing an effective barrier to imports and eliminating the competition from lower quality sources of supply. In virtually all cases, regardless of the motivations of the participants, the development of product safety regulations has suffered from a lack of information on costs and impacts, and the absence of any framework for evaluating the effects of proposed decisions and comparing them with the results of alternative actions.

### (b) Biases in the Choice of Regulatory Instrument

The interaction of these various elements has created some discernible biases in the development of product safety regulations. One result has been that in selecting the form by which it should intervene, the PSB has shown a strong preference for standards over an informational-type of approach.

The hazardous substance regulations, which place considerable reliance on labelling requirements and on an accompanying information program, constitute a notable exception. For the most part, the branch has viewed enforced labelling and the provision of information by the department as complements to, rather than substitutes for, the use of other more restrictive instruments. The department's budget for informational activities in the hazardous product area has been extremely meager, ranging from $50,000 to $175,000 in the years to 1979/80. Moreover, the assignment of much of the responsibility for Consumer and Corporate Affairs's advertising and publicity to a central information branch has reinforced the tendency to regard the provision of information as a distinctive activity rather than something to be considered at the planning stage where possible responses to a product hazard are initially considered.

Academic economists have been partial to the use of informational-type remedies because these respond directly to the problem, which is the cause of the market failure. As we noted in Chapter 3, information dissemination will not always constitute an appropriate and sufficient response: in some cases consumers may not be very receptive to information explaining the nature of the product risk; and in some cases risks may be so serious that consumers would be virtually unaminous in their desire for a product ban or the establishment of a particular set of standards. There is a strong view among academic economists, however, that government departments and agencies generally are too ready to impose their own judgment on markets and give far too little attention to the possibilities for using information programs to strengthen and support the workings of these markets.

The reluctance of the PSB to place greater reliance on information dissemination can perhaps be understood in the context of the branch's role and responsibilities under the Act, as these are likely to be perceived. What is of prime importance from the PSB's perspective is that the Minister is *seen* to be responding effectively to significant consumer hazards. As compared to a product ban or the establishment of standards, an information approach is a less clear and less certain means of addressing the immediate problem. Even if it was reasonable to expect that consumers would take account of the information provided, there can be no certainty that the market will react so as to result in a gradual reduction in the market share of the more hazardous brand; informed consumers could continue to buy the particular brands, voluntarily choosing to accept the risk. While the government program may have successfully filled the information gap in the market, the persistence of product accidents is most likely to be perceived as a failure of the government to deal effectively with the problem. Even where an information program does produce the anticipated result, the connection between cause and effect is much less apparent than in the case of standards or a product ban. An information approach may therefore provide a low cost, relatively effective response, but one for which the department and the Minister will receive little recognition and little appreciation.

In the case of hazardous substances, the PSB considered the possibilities for conveying the essential information to consumers through a labelling program, centered on a set of captivating symbols. The fact that the basic information can be conveyed in such a way as to be easily comprehended by consumers and even most children, is an important feature of hazardous substances. What was perhaps most significant from the perspective of the PSB, however, was that the usual solution involving the establishment of a set of product standards was simply not available in the case of hazardous substances. Chemical products cannot be "redesigned" like cribs to reduce the degree of risk they present. Certain particular hazardous chemical substances can be prohibited from use in consumer products, but this essentially involves eliminating from the market all consumer products with the specified chemicals and with a particular set of characteristics. As we noted in discussing product bans generally, this type of instrument has highly visible costs and accordingly, the department's tendency has been to try and confine its use to a narrow and selective group of products. In the case of hazardous substances, a ban has been extended to chemicals such as tetrachlorethane and hydrocyanic acid, which are extremely toxic. But for a large number of hazardous chemical substances, many of which had only very imperfect substitutes, the costs of employing a product ban were understandably judged to be unacceptable. In such circumstances, a labelling program is a particularly appealing alternative.

A very different and in many ways more typical, example is the regulation applying to hockey helmets. The department's involvement with this product originated with the concern of the Canadian Amateur Hockey Association (CAHA) for the frequency of head injuries to amateur hockey players wearing helmets. Through the facilities of the Canadian Standards Association and the joint efforts of several groups including CAHA and the sports equipment industry, a voluntary hockey helmet standard was developed by 1973. The PSB mandated this standard shortly afterwards, making it a requirement for any helmet advertised, sold or imported into Canada as of January 1, 1974. There were of course other alternatives open to the department: it need not have taken any action, trusting that the market would react to the information provided through CSA certification; or it could have initiated a more elaborate labelling program which would indicate to consumers the protective capacity of different models of hockey helmets. It would appear that these information-type solutions were, in fact, given virtually no consideration.

The department's approach is open to criticism because this is an area which is particularly well-suited to a solution involving the provision of information. As we noted in Part II, the problem with many types of product hazard is that consumers are likely to ignore or greatly underestimate the risks. If consumers are not aware of, or concerned about a risk, they are unlikely to invest even the minimum time and effort necessary to absorb the contents of a labelling or information program. In the case of hockey helmets, as in the case of hazardous substances, this problem does not arise: people know of the tragic consequences that might result from inattention to the dangers of toxic substances; and consumers of hockey helmets are aware of, and concerned about, the risks of head injury. It is reasonable to expect, therefore, that consumers of hockey helmets would be receptive to a program which provided them with the information they required on the protective quality of helmets in a clear and easily understandable form.

The case for an information approach is strengthened by concerns that arise in connection with the restructive approach that was actually adopted. A particularly important consideration relates to the fact that a hockey helmet is a "life-saving" product and that expanded use would generally seem to be in the public interest. The danger in this regard is that a regulation which raises the price of the product and narrows the choice available on the market will cause some consumers to reject the use of helmets altogether. When this occurs, the reduction in risk from the use of higher quality helmets is at least partly eroded by the decline in the overall use of protective headgear.

Another concern stems from the widely differing needs of consumers in terms of protective helmets. Hockey helmets are used in a great variety of circumstances. The needs of the professional hockey player for head protection are quite different from those of the young child learning how to skate or riding on the back carrier of an adult's bicycle. A standard which is appropriate for one type of use is likely to be inappropriate for another. This point is illustrated by an examination of the extensive injury data compiled by the B.C. Amateur Hockey Association (Hirshhorn, 1981). Benefits were evaluated by assigning a value to the various types of head injuries that were likely to be reduced by using the higher quality helmets required by the standard; these were compared with estimates of the increase in manufacturing costs. What the analysis shows quite clearly is the difference in requirements of different types of players; while the standard was found to yield substantial net benefits for players at the Junior B level, benefits were less than costs under most assumptions for players in the Bantam division. Taking all potential consumers of this product, the disparity in net benefits would be even more marked.

What was required in the case of hockey helmets was an approach that responded to the very differing needs and preferences of users as well as potential users, and that took account of the ability of consumers to make the "correct" market decisions when the essential information is made appropriately available. Due to the inclination of the department to turn to standards, such an approach was not adopted.

## (c) Problems in the Establishment of Regulatory Standards

Where a regulatory standard is employed, there is a need to determine how stringent that standard should be, or to decide in other words what level of safety should be sought. Here as well, the influences on the decision-making process have not always provided for a careful consideration of the issues involved. We have noted that in some cases, as when there are products which pose a serious risk to young children, the department will focus, almost entirely, on safety considerations and will, if necessary, establish very stringent standards. Such an approach is not necessarily inconsistent with the development of cost-beneficial regulations. The costs of even very restrictive standards will often bear a reasonable relationship to the benefits arising from the elimination or reduction of serious product risks. The preoccupation with the benefit side of the equation and the narrow focus on the technical aspects of standard-setting can, however, lead to some undesirable and even perverse results. It is generally the case that as a product is redesigned to reduce the level of risk it poses, improvements become gradually more difficult and more costly to secure. A failure to take account of the diminishing returns to risk reduction can lead to efforts to increase safety well beyond the point at which such efforts are likely to yield a reasonable payoff. Problems may also arise as a result of the emphasis of the PSB on the technical and engineering aspects of product safety, and the little attention given to the broader effects of product regulations. In the case of hockey helmets for example, regulations can affect product use, which in turn can have some implications for safety that merit consideration. The issues that arise in standard-setting are well illustrated by one of the most important as well as one of the most controversial set of regulations issued under the Act—that pertaining to children's car seats.

In reaction to public concern over the poor quality of car seats on the market, a subcommittee of the Canadian Standards Association was formed in early 1971 to consider the development of a standard for child restraints. The subcommittee decided that dynamic testing in which automobile impacts are simulated was preferable to static testing as a measure of safety performance. Since there was no precedent to be relied upon in applying crash simulation tests to child car seats and considerable development work was necessary, it was decided that an interim standard should be established based on static testing and modelled on the U.S. child restraint standard issued in 1970 (FMVSS 213). The resulting regulation which was issued in April 1972 eliminated many of the poorly designed "hook-over seats" which provided no real protection. About two years later, in March 1974, the Minister of Consumer and Corporate Affairs announced proposals to strengthen the regulations in two stages. The second, which did not become effective until November 1975, contained the long-awaited requirements based on dynamic testing of forward-facing restraints. These were based on the proposals of the CSA subcommittee, but they included more restrictive limitations on the allowable movement of the head of the test dummy in crash simulation tests. With a view to reducing the likelihood that a child's head could come in contact with the dashboard or the front seat, a limit of 18 inches was imposed on frontal head movement. Additional limits were established with respect to lateral (15 inches), vertical (27 inches) and rear (8 inches) head movement. In his press announcement, the Minister acknowledged that parts of the proposed regulations were "somewhat ahead of the current state of technology", but the 18 month lead time before the regulation was to come into effect was viewed as sufficient to allow companies to develop a car seat that would comply with the new requirements.

The present regulation and the head excursion limits established for dynamic testing in particular, have been the subject of substantial criticism.[16] To meet Canadian test requirements, a forward-facing car seat must have tether straps which can be bolted into the rear parcel shelf. This involves an additional element of cost and inconvenience and it is a requirement which is particularly susceptible to misuse by consumers. The Canadian requirements, which are considerably more rigid than U.S. standards, have also reduced the variety of car seats that can be imported and sold in Canada. Product Safety Branch officials have claimed that these aspects are more than offset by the value of having a restraint system which takes account of interior vehicle dimensions and reduces the probability of head injuries to children using car seats. Some critics, however, have challenged Consumer and Corporate Affairs' interpretation of the available data on "vehicle survival space". They have also expressed concern that deceleration of the infant over the distances imposed by the regulation could in itself lead to significant injury, including possible spinal cord damage. Questions have been raised as well about test procedures and enforcement practices.[17] The Consumer's Association of Canada has charged that the approved seat which dominated the market with over 80 percent of sales from 1975 to 1978 is unacceptable and has collapsed in a number of independent laboratory tests.

While the technical information required to evaluate the car seat regulation is exceedingly complex, the basic problem is not unlike that in other product areas where the appropriate level for a standard is to be determined. The general guideline in all cases is that a standard should be established with a view to minimizing the sum of accident costs and accident

[16] Most of these criticisms are contained in the Task Force submission of the Consumer's Association of Canada (1979). The criticisms are discussed in Consumer and Corporate Affairs Canada. Product Safety Branch (1979a and 1979b).

[17] These criticisms are raised in various submissions to the Minister's Task Force on Crash Protection for Infant and Child Passengers in Motor Vehicles, 1979.

prevention costs; and this requires the level of the standard to be increased as long as the value of the resources going towards the production of safety is less than the value of the reduction in risk which results. The merits of adopting the rigid head excursion requirements, therefore depends on the marginal costs and benefits as opposed to a somewhat less restrictive alternative which does not require the use of tether straps. There are gaps in our understanding of some of the factors that bear on this calculus. For example, there is disagreement among experts over the risk of spinal or abdominal injury resulting from the more restrictive head excursion limit. It is unclear whether and to what extent children can tolerate some impact with the interior of the vehicle. And it is not certain what the effect will be where approved seats are used without being correctly anchored. However, notwithstanding the legitimate disputes in areas where further technical research is necessary, it would appear that some of the important factors relating to the determination of marginal costs and benefits were given less careful consideration than was warranted.

One of the most important questions that arises is whether the adoption of a more rigid standard is likely to affect the use of child restraint systems. There is general agreement that the use of any adequate restraint system can substantially reduce the probability of death and serious injury in automobile accidents. It would be of considerable concern, therefore, if there was any decline in use arising from the effect of the standard on price, availability, and the inconvenience of employing child restraints. Even a modest and temporary decline in use could more than offset the incremental benefits arising from the use of a more rigid standard.

These concerns were dismissed by the PSB on the basis of a survey undertaken for the department which indicated that a very high proportion of parents use child car restraints—much higher than in the U.S. where a less restrictive standard has been adopted—and that only a small percentage were concerned about the inconvenience and difficulty of anchoring the seats. However, it is clear from studies of seat belt use that surveys in which individuals are asked to report on their usage tend to be highly unreliable. Given the large number of factors influencing car seat usage, it is also very difficult to draw any conclusions from the apparent differences reported to exist between Canada and the U.S.

In estimating the marginal benefits of the more restrictive requirements, it is necessary to take account of the fact that tether strap systems which require anchoring are particularly susceptible to misuse. A recent report of the Task Force on child restraints estimated misuse to be in the area of 50 percent (*Task Force*, 1980). This suggests that only a portion of the potential benefits from a higher standard are likely to be realized; it indicates as well that there could be additional costs to consider if the restraints with tether straps perform less adequately than alternative seats when these straps are not properly anchored. The latter problem could be addressed by requiring that child restraints meet additional performance criteria when the tether strap is not secured. The PSB has been opposed to misuse testing, but where there is an obvious and potentially important form of misuse, a standard which takes this into account can offer substantially greater protection.

The expected benefits of the car seat regulation have been eroded by problems connected with the implementation of dynamic test procedures. A great deal of uncertainty and confusion arose because independent laboratories using the test procedures outlined in the regulations were producing different results. One test result showed all car seats on the market to be unacceptable by current standards. This sort of ambiguity can discourage the development and marketing of products for the Canadian market, and undermine public confidence in the reliability of those products that are available. The basic problem was the failure of the regulations to define dynamic test procedures with sufficient precision and detail. At a more general level, however, one might suggest that the problem here as in other areas, related to the determination of the department to establish a regulation consistent with the highest technical standards, without adequately considering the practical complexities involved.[18]

### (d) The Need for Increased Analysis and Broader Consultation

The car seat and the hockey helmet regulations illustrate the deficiencies of the existing standard-setting process and the need for reforms which will contribute to a broader perspective and a more thorough consideration of proposed standards. An important requirement is a set of management controls to ensure that proposed regulations are thoroughly analyzed, that direct and indirect regulatory impacts are examined, and that alternative possibilities for achieving the desired objectives are considered. For economic analysis to be an important component of the planning process it is necessary that impact studies be prepared for all proposed regulations, and not strictly major regulations, as is the requirement under the recently introduced federal review program.[19] Even, where as in the case of infant restraints, the information required to fully understand the effects of regulation may be lacking, economic analysis can fulfill an important function by ensuring that the right questions are asked and that there is some consistency in the approach towards different product hazards.

The standard-setting process could also be improved by reforms to provide for greater openness and more extensive consultation. While the pro-

[18] Responsibility for the design of car seat standards has now been assigned to the Department of Transport. It is expected that new regulations pertaining to both forward-facing restraints and infant restraints will come into effect in 1983.

[19] Treasury Board Secretariat. *Administrative Policy Manual*, chapter 490 (revised June 1982).

cess for developing standards in Canada allows the authorities to respond promptly to concerns about hazardous products, this advantage has been achieved at some cost in terms of the limited range of inputs into the regulatory process. There are, of course, dangers of moving too far in the other direction, and the delays and frustrations which characterize the standard-setting process in the U.S. are a warning of the problems that may arise with excessively elaborate procedures to allow representations and appeals. The PSB is now required to give notification of major proposed regulations and to make its analysis (or socio-economic impact analysis) available to interested parties. (Regulations that are addressed at what are perceived as "emergency" situations are exempt from the requirements for advance analysis and publication.) The regulatory process would not be unduly burdened if this same procedure was followed for all product safety regulations—major and minor. Access to the information and analysis used by the branch would help to encourage broader participation in the standard-setting process. And the mere fact that the analyses underlying proposed regulations are to be made publicly available should have a beneficial influence on the quality and comprehensiveness of these studies.

## V. THE ENFORCEMENT OF PRODUCT SAFETY REGULATIONS

Inspectors designated under the *Hazardous Products Act* are given the power to enter any place where a hazardous product is believed to be manufactured and stored for sale; to take samples of the product and to examine any records or documents thought to be relevant to the enforcement of the Act; and to seize any products believed to be in contravention of the Act. Where an individual is convicted of a violation of the Act, the offence is punishable on summary conviction by a fine of $1,000, imprisonment of up to six months or both. A conviction for an indictable offence can lead to imprisonment of up to two years. The department has in fact exercised its powers under the Act very sparingly. Where violations are discovered, officials have preferred to proceed by gaining the co-operation of retailers and manufacturers in removing the product from the market. Products will be seized if necessary, however, and manufacturers and retailers are aware that this alternative is available if they refuse to co-operate. There have been very few attempts to prosecute suspected violators; since its inception there have only been nine convictions under the Act. Part of the problem in this area stems from the nature of the legislation the department is administering and the limited options it provides for penalizing violators. If the department wants to take action against an individual who is disregarding the legislation, it must be prepared to prosecute the suspected offender and to meet the rigid standards of proof required to gain a conviction under criminal law.

While the very low probability that violations will result in prosecution combined with the low penalties upon conviction reduce the deterrent effect of the Act, manufacturers are very sensitive to the negative publicity which could result from product recalls or seizures. They may also be concerned that by breaking a safety standard they will be vulnerable to civil suit under product liability law. Therefore, notwithstanding the minimal sanctions provided by the Act, many, and perhaps most, manufacturers have a strong incentive to abide by the product safety regulations. Enforcement problems have been most acute for imported products. There also tends to be a significant difference in the compliance rate of large and small domestic producers. This has been highlighted in the U.S. by compliance surveys conducted by the CPSC which indicated the much greater responsiveness of large producers to a change in the U.S. standard on mattress flammability. Compared to the major domestic manufacturers of a product, importers and small producers are likely to face both more substantial problems in adjusting to a standard and a lower probability that violations will be detected. The negative publicity that may result from product seizure or recall would also be of less concern in the case of lower quality domestic and imported products where there is little consumer awareness of the brand or of the manufacturer.

While the emphasis of the department on performance, as opposed to design, standards has been beneficial in terms of allowing for new and innovative approaches to meeting safety objectives, it has increased the magnitude and costs of the enforcement function. Whereas compliance with design standards can generally be determined by simple observation, it is often impossible to determine if performance standards are being met without appropriate laboratory testing. This makes it less likely that violations of the Act will be noticed by retailers or consumers and reported to the department. In some cases enforcement problems have been further exacerbated by a failure to adequately define the hazard and/or the required test procedure. The phase II child car seat regulations issued in 1974 are the most notable example of the latter problem.

Violations of the Act tend to be most common in the period immediately after a regulation is introduced. Many of the initial difficulties will come to be resolved as producers and retailers become conversant with the regulations, as small manufacturers complete the alterations in their production process, and as the inventory of products manufactured and imported prior to the issuance of the regulation works its way through the system. Problems that are associated with the introduction of product safety regulations in Canada prior to their adoption in other countries are also likely to diminish over time. Where regulations among Canada's trading partners are reasonably similar to, or more stringent than, those in the *Hazardous Products Act*, the enforcement activities of these governments will support the activities of Canada's product safety inspectors. In these circumstances, there is much less reason for concern about the degree of compliance by importers, and by domestic manufacturers who are also producing for the export market.

The department has attempted to respond to enforcement problems by devoting increased inspection resources to those areas which have a particularly poor record of compliance. At the beginning of each fiscal year, the PSB develops a work plan which contains priorities for inspection activity based on officials' perceptions as to which sectors have the poorest record of compliance and their sense as to the urgency of ridding the market of various types of hazardous products. Special emphasis is thereby given both to problem sectors, and to products such as cribs and rattles where the hazard is such that even a small degree of non-compliance is viewed as unacceptable. The overall work plan which is established by the PSB is converted to an implementation plan by the managers responsible for product safety field operations in each of the regions.

The inspection priorities established by the department would often be inconsistent with a strategy designed to maximize the gain from enforcement activities. The latter would require that inspection resources be distributed in relation to both the net benefits from compliance in various areas and the expected increase in compliance from a given commitment of resources. Given the lack of information on the relative benefits and costs of various regulations, however, the current emphasis on problem areas is a reasonable one. Since significant improvements are most likely to be secured in areas where compliance is now relatively poor, the existing approach does at least offer the prospect of improved levels of compliance. The relatively limited resources the department has devoted to inspection activities has, however, greatly restricted the range of enforcement activities that can be undertaken. It is important generally that inspection activities incorporate an element of random checking so that producers and importers cannot predict these activities and adapt to them. With limited field staff devoted to product safety activities it is difficult to make an onslaught on problems areas and still maintain a significant capacity for randomized inspection.

### (a) Problems of Enforcement and the Hazardous Toy Regulations

One of the most difficult areas from an enforcement perspective has been the regulations pertaining to hazardous toys. In 1977, for example, approximately 700 toys were tested by the PSB and 46 percent of these products were found to be in contravention of the Act.[20] This is a strongly biased sample since only those toys which were suspected of being hazardous were submitted for testing; nonetheless this very high rate of non-compliance

[20] Information contained in the files of the Product Safety Branch.

suggests that the regulations are probably relatively ineffective in some areas. The reasons for this can be traced to both the nature of the regulations and the characteristics of the toy market.

When Canada originally issued its toy regulations in 1970, it was one of the first countries to attempt to respond to concerns over child injuries by establishing a comprehensive system of standards for toy safety. The fact that Canadian regulations preceded by several years those issued in the U.S. and most other countries, combined with the fact that imports account for about 45 percent of annual toy sales in Canada, was almost bound to lead to major enforcement difficulties. An important feature of the toy regulations is that they do not prohibit specific toys, but rather certain design features which involve a significant element of risk. While this is desirable in that it covers new as well as existing toys, it requires those enforcing the Act to inspect an exceedingly large number of products. Further complications arise from the fact that the design or construction feature causing concern does not always lend itself to the application of objective criteria. There is an important element of judgment involved in determining whether the metal and wooden edges on toys are sufficiently smooth.[21] It is probably impossible to come up with a near satisfactory definition or inventory of toys that "are or are likely to be used by a child of less than three years of age".[22]

Enforcement of product safety regulations tends to be most successful in markets with few or no imports, a small number of domestic manufacturers, and a relatively small and stable selection of products. The toy market is the opposite in all aspects. The Canadian Toy Manufacturer's Association has over 80 members, approximately half of which are relatively small companies subject to very high rates of turnover. Imports are extremely important in this industry. Moreover, there are approximately 10,000-15,000 different kinds of toys on the market, and about one-third of the total consists of new toys which come on the market on an annual basis. The vast range of products and the rapid changes that occur in product lines, in particular, make the job of the product safety inspectors exceedingly difficult.

Notwithstanding the problems involved in enforcing the regulations, there is general agreement that standards of toy safety have improved considerably in recent years. This can be attributed to a number of factors including, particularly, the recognition by producers that individually, and as a group, they have a considerable stake in reducing the risks associated with children's toys. With increasing consumer awareness and concern about toy hazards producers have a strong incentive to promote public confidence in the quality and safety of their products. Changes in product liability law in Canada and the U.S. have also undoubtedly contributed to the removal of many poorly designed toys from the market. While in earlier chapters we

[21] *Hazardous Products Act, supra* note 1, Sched. Part II, items 12d, g.
[22] *Ibid.*, Sched. Part II, items 12c, r.

expressed some reservations about the contribution of liability law, it is clear that this can constitute an important deterrent to the production of unsafe products for an industry in which even the threat of civil suit could irreparably harm a firm's reputation. The higher toy standards in other countries have also probably made an important contribution to the change. Higher standards of toy safety have been achieved less because of the threat posed by sanctions in the *Hazardous Products Act*, than because it was in the best interests of manufacturers to improve the quality of their products. As one might expect in the areas where the dictates of the Act did not coincide with the interests of producers and importers, the toy regulations have been substantially less effective.

## VI. CONCLUSION

In the period of slightly over decade in which the *Hazardous Products Act* has been in existence, a number of extremely serious product hazards have been effectively addressed. When viewed in terms of the general goal of maximizing the degree of risk reduction from a limited commitment of resources, however, the administration of the Act has been wanting in several important respects. The lack of an information system which could signal potentially important hazards and the failure to use economic-impact analysis as a planning tool has made it impossible for the branch to target resources to areas offering the greatest net benefits. The process adopted by the PSB for the identification of product hazards raises the possibility that the department may be responding to some relatively minor hazards while ignoring some highly significant risks which are amenable to correction. In the choice of how the department is to intervene, there has been too much emphasis on standards; although the possibilities for a less restrictive approach involving the dissemination of information are limited, available opportunities have not been fully pursued. The standards established have at times been highly restrictive, reflecting a heavy emphasis on safety and a lack of sensitivity to costs including particularly the indirect costs which may arise as a result of the reaction of consumers to regulation. And enforcement of the Act has suffered from the minimal commitment of resources to inspection activities, and from the inability to direct enforcement efforts to areas with greatest potential payoff.

It is not surprising that the administration of the Act has a number of deficiencies from the perspective of this discussion, since the government has not, until perhaps very recently, suggested that it attaches importance to the efficient production of safety. When the *Hazardous Products Act* was passed, the objective was simply to create a capacity to respond to significant consumer hazards. Accordingly the branch has been manned almost exclusively with individuals who could deal with the technical issues related to specific problems of product design and performance. There has been no group within the PSB to address the broader issues related to the overall allocation of resources to product safety. While the PSB has not been insensitive to the costs of product regulation, it has been keenly aware of the expectations which arise from the Act and of the strong pressures for an immediate and effective solution to hazards of significant public concern.

Quite clearly, there are a number of product safety issues where the extent and nature of media and public involvement would make it almost impossible to develop a measured response based on an objective analysis of all the relevant variables. However, while there are very real constraints arising from the political pressures in this area, there is nonetheless substantial scope for a more systematic approach to regulation. As we noted, the federal government now requires that economic impact analyses be prepared for all major new proposed social regulations, and the department has recently initiated such studies for some of its recent proposals. The new requirements for economic analysis and for broad consultation represent potentially important reforms, although it is particularly necessary in the product safety area that these procedures be extended to the preponderent number of minor regulations. The danger is that these measures will be undertaken largely after the fact and that the analysis will be geared to justifying a proposed course of action, rather than being an aspect of the planning and priority-setting process. In the product safety area, rational planning requires not only a capacity for economic analysis but also the existence of a supporting information system which can screen the data on product hazards and help to pinpoint those risks warranting further examination. It is important as well that specific hazards are analysed with a view to the range of possible solutions, besides regulation, that may be available. More generally what is required is an increased sensitivity to the fact that the resources society chooses to divert from the production of consumer goods and services to the production of safety are limited. Under the condition of limited resources, poor planning and ill-conceived regulation will have a cost in terms of the government's overall capacity to reduce the degree of risk to which individuals are exposed.

## REFERENCES

Black, J. "Product Safety—A Federal Presence." Paper presented at the Product Design Conference, Humber College of Applied Arts and Technology, Toronto, May 1973.

Consumer and Corporate Affairs Canada. Product Safety Branch. Submismion to the Task Force on Crash Protection for Infant and Child Passengers in Motor Vehicles, 1979a.

Consumer and Corporate Affairs Canada. Product Safety Branch. Comments on Submissions to the Task Force on Crash Protection for Infant and Child Passengers in Motor Vehicles, 1979b.

Consumer Product Safety Commission. Bureau of Economic Analysis. See reports by Dale Ray and Ellen F. Kandell.

Consumer Product Safety Commission. Office of Strategic Planning. "Impact of Crib Safety Activities on Injuries and Deaths Associated with Cribs." Washington, D.C., February 1979. (Mimeographed).

Consumer's Association of Canada. Submission to the Task Force on Crash Protection for Infant and Child Passengers in Motor Vehicles, 1979.

Contemporary Research Centre Ltd. *A Study of Awareness and Identification of Hazardous Product Symbols.* Prepared for Department of Consumer and Corporate Affairs Canada. Toronto: CRC Ltd., January 1977.

Cornell, Nina; Noll, Roger G.; and Weingast, Barry. "Safety Regulation." In *Setting National Priorities: The Next Ten Years*, pp. 457-504. Edited by Henry Owen and Charles Schultze. Washington, D.C.: The Brookings Institution, 1976.

Doern, G. Bruce. *Regulatory Processes and Jurisdictional Issues in the Regulation of Hazardous Products in Canada.* Background Study, no. 41. Ottawa: Science Council of Canada, October 1977.

Eisner, Robert, and Strotz, Robert. "Flight Insurance and the Theory of Choice." *Journal of Political Economy* 69 (1961): 355-368.

Grabowski, Henry G., and Vernon, John M. "Consumer Product Safety Regulation." *American Economic Review* (May 1978): 284-289.

Hirshhorn, Ronald. *Product Safety Regulation and the Hazardous Products Act.* Regultion Reference Technical Report, no. 10. Ottawa: Economic Council of Canada, 1981.

Kandell, Ellen F. "Probable Economic Effects of the Rattle Regulation." Prepared for Consumer Product Safety Commission, Bureau of Economic Analysis, March 8, 1978. (Mimeographed.)

Kelman, Steven. "Regulation by the Numbers—A Report on the Consumer Product Safety Commission." *The Public Interest* 36 (Summer 1974): 82-102.

O'Riordan, Fred, and McCabe, Lee. *A Case Study: Safety Glass Regulations Under the Hazardous Products Act*. Ottawa: Treasury Board and Department of Consumer and Corporate Affairs Canada, 1980.

Ray, Dale. "Potential Economic Effects of the Pacifier Regulation." Prepared for Consumer Product Safety Commission, Bureau of Economic Analysis, April 5, 1977. (Mimeographed.)

*Task Force Report to the Minister of Consumer and Corporate Affairs Canada on Crash Protection for Infant and Child Passengers in Motor Vehicles*. C. B. Williams, Chairman. Ottawa: Minister of Supply and Services Canada, January 1980.

# Part VI
# Consumer Redress

# [13]

Iain D.C. Ramsay*

# CONSUMER REDRESS MECHANISMS FOR POOR-QUALITY AND DEFECTIVE PRODUCTS†

## *Introduction*

Black's Law Dictionary defines redress as 'receiving satisfaction for injury sustained.' This article investigates some of the formal and informal methods which consumers might attempt to use to receive satisfaction when they are faced with defective and poor quality products.[1] One important technique for achieving this objective has been reform of the existing private law rights of consumers. A recent example of this approach is the comprehensive Saskatchewan Consumer Products Warranties Act,[2] which provides a consumer with a complex battery of individual rights and remedies including the possibility of punitive damages. Commentators have, however, been troubled by the difficulties which consumers might encounter in attempting to enforce these rights.[3] This has led to calls for greater access to small claims courts and also to proposals for more informal procedures of mediation and arbitration which might deal 'quickly, inexpensively, simply and justly with consumer

* Institute of Law Research and Reform, University of Alberta

† I gratefully acknowledge the assistance of J. Enzle, now of the Alberta Bar, who collected and analysed the data referred to at pages 000–0 and who drew up the appendices outlining the methodology, sampling procedure, and questionnaire used in the study.

1 The phrase *formal and informal* is intended to include a spectrum which stretches from informal two-party negotiation between retailer and consumer to formal adjudication.

2 R.S.S. 1978 c C-30. An analysis of the act may be found in (1979) 43 *Sask. L.R.* 81 and (1980) 44 *Sask. L.R.* 261. See also the Consumer Product Warranty and Liability Act S.N.B. 1977 C-18.1. Private law remedies are a primary method of enforcing the trade practices acts which have been enacted in several Canadian provinces. The author of the most comprehensive article on these statutes argues that '[a] broader recognition of the desirability of private action by individual consumers is required' and that '[t]he desirability of a broader emphasis in trade practices legislation upon private action is in essence a reflection of the growing realization that 'private attorneys general' may well be the best vindicators of the public interest.' See Belobaba, Unfair trade practices legislation: Symbolism and substance in consumer protection (1977) 15 *Osgoode Hall L.J.* 327. See also Trebilcock et al. *A Study on Consumer Misleading and Unfair Trade Practices* (1976), at 275 and 280. A useful analysis of private law remedies in relation to misleading advertising is provided in Trebilcock, Private law remedies for misleading advertising (1972) 22 U.T.L.J. 1.

3 For an excellent survey of the difficulties in providing consumer 'access to justice' see Cappelletti and Garth, Access to justice: The newest wave in the worldwide movement to make rights effective (1978) 27 *Buffalo L.R.* 181.

(1981), 31 UNIVERSITY OF TORONTO LAW JOURNAL 117
0042-0220/81/0400/0117/$1.25/0 

problems.'[4] For example, the Saskatchewan act contains provisions for governmental mediation.[5]

The purpose of this article is to offer an exploratory critique of these directions in consumer protection. I shall suggest that there may be significant deficiencies in informal processes of consumer dispute resolution which are attributable both to the power relationship of the parties involved and to the general nature of such processes. In relation to the legal system my argument will be not simply that private law remedies are an inadequate protection for consumers,[6] an argument made by a number of writers, but that reforms still have the unfortunate tendency to conceptualize consumer problems in the context of individual case-by-case adjudication.[7] A general problem which will appear throughout the essay and which constitutes a central theme is that of upgrading consumer competence. My conclusion is that a primary objective of consumer protection must be to 're-conceptualize little injustices as collective harms.'[8] Only if this objective is achieved will individual consumer redress mechanisms operate effectively.

I stated that this article is exploratory, and this statement contains an implied criticism of the mainstream of legal scholarship in this area. In a concern to provide access to the court system or mediation, reformers and scholars have often assumed that this is what consumers want or need,[9]

4 Sigurdson and Roine *Consumer Redress Mechanisms* (1977), at 3

5 R.S.S. 1978 c C-30, ss 31(a) and (b)

6 This is one of the main themes of Cranston *Consumers and the Law* (1978). See in particular ch 3: 'The aim of this part of the book is to demonstrate that the private law is an inadequate tool of consumer protection' (at 67). Cranston argues that public law would provide better protection for consumers than private law.

7 This is also one of the arguments of Ison *Credit Marketing and Consumer Protection* (1978) (see p 18). For other developments of this particular argument see Leff, Unconscionability and the crowd – Consumers and the common law tradition (1970) 31 *U. Pitt. L.R.* 349, at 354; Belobaba, supra note 2.

8 Nader, Disputing without the force of law (1979) 88 *Yale L.J.* 998, at 1021

9 There are a number of difficult empirical and philosophical issues embedded in the idea of 'giving consumers what they want.'

Although this is not the forum to discuss these issues fully, three points ought to be made. Firstly, much of consumer protection literature has stressed what seems to me a misleading dichotomy in arguing that 'either we give people what they want or the state prescribes what they will want.' See, eg, Trebilcock, Consumer protection in the affluent society (1969) 16 *McGill L.J.* 263. Bernard Williams has pointed out the falseness in that dichotomy, arguing that 'there is no such thing as giving people what they want': 'There is no such thing as just following. To engage in those processes which utilitarianism regards as just "following" is – by a style of argument which, ironically, utilitarianism is particularly fond of – itself doing something: it is choosing to endorse those preferences, or some set of them, which lie on the surface, as determined by such things as what people at a given moment regard as possible – something which in its turn is affected by the activities of government' (Smart and Williams *Utilitarianism, For and Against* (1973), at 147–8).

Second, when writers on consumer protection discuss the inroads on individual liberty made by consumer protection statutes (eg, see Director, The parity of the

and research has rarely gone beyond the doors of the court house to explore the possibly complex relationships between formal and informal consumer redress mechanisms.[10] We are only beginning to understand the behaviour and problems of differing groups of consumers and sellers in the marketplace and the relationship between this private behaviour and activity within the official legal system.[11] An underlying argument of this article is that without further understanding of this relationship, policy making in this area may be at best incomplete and at worst an exercise in legitimation of the status quo.

These issues are of more than academic importance. The climate of public opinion is much cooler towards consumer-protection efforts than it was ten years ago.[12] Its assumptions are no longer self-evident, and

economic marketplace, in Manne (ed) *The Economics of Legal Relationships: Readings in the Theory of Property Rights* (1975) at 98), they use liberty in a manner which suggests that all government intervention is wrong because it diminishes a citizen's liberty. But if we accept the argument that citizens have a right to this conception of liberty as licence then *all* government intervention, whether to protect against murder or against buying adulterated food, is suspect. The consequences of this position are that it 'creates a false sense of necessary conflict between liberty and other values when social regulation ... is proposed ... and ... it provides too easy an answer to the question why we regard certain kinds of restraint as especially unjust.' (Dworkin, What rights do we have? in Dworkin *Taking Rights Seriously* (1977), at 271. This essay is an excellent example of the potential practical application of a philosophical essay.

Finally, a number of writers, eg, F.A. Hayek, seem to misunderstand the philosophy of liberalism as propounded by John Stuart Mill. Mill saw no necessary connection between the issue of individual liberty and free trade (*On Liberty*, 164). His famous principle of non-interference with the individual concerned only those acts which are self-regarding, of which trade is not one. Unfortunately, this distinction has often been neglected. See, eg, Trebilcock, supra, at 273, n 20.

10 M. Galanter's comments are appropriate here: 'The mainstream of legal scholarship has tended to look out from within the official legal order, abetting the pretensions of the official law to stand in a relationship of hierarchic control to other normative orderings in society. Social research on law has been characterized by a repeated rediscovery of this other hemisphere of the legal world. This has entailed recurrent rediscovery that law in modern society is plural rather than monolithic, that it is private as well as public in character and that the national (public, official) legal system is often a secondary rather than a primary locus of regulation' Galanter *Justice in Many Rooms*, working paper 1979-4, Disputes Processing Research Program, University of Wisconsin Law School).

11 It now appears that this defect is being remedied by a number of major research projects. In the USA the Disputes Processing Research Program at the University of Wisconsin is conducting a study of consumer disputing and has published a number of working papers. I found the following to be of particular value in writing this article: Macaulay *Lawyers and Consumer Protection Laws: An Empirical Study* (working paper 1979-1); Ladinsky et al *The Milwaukee Dispute Mapping Project: A Preliminary Report* (working paper 1979-3); Galanter, supra note 10; Tomasic, *Mediation as an Alternative to Adjudication: Rhetoric and Reality in the Neighbourhood Justice Project* (working paper 1980-2). Co-ordinated empirical research is also being carried out in Europe into law and dispute treatment. Consumer problems are one area of the research.

12 This diagnosis is the starting point of a recent essay on strategies for consumer protection, Reich, Towards a new consumer protection (1979) 128 *U.Pa.L.R.* 1, in which the author suggests the following reasons for the consumer protection retreat:

writers have questioned whether we may have gone too far in giving rights to consumers.[13] Consumer protection has become for a number of commentators a synonym for bureaucracy and the inefficiencies of government regulation.[14] It is desirable, therefore, that consumer protection effort be channelled into the least costly and most effective mechanisms and institutions.

The article is divided into three parts. Part 1 describes the findings of existing empirical studies on consumer complaints and problem solving in the marketplace and discusses the advantages and disadvantages of informal extra-legal complaint mechanisms. Part 2 focuses on the legal system. A legal system is made up of several parts: a body of norms, a system of specialized institutions, a tradition of legal doctrine, a legal profession, and persons or groups with claims which they might take to the legal system (parties).[15] This section of the paper will describe the effects of lawyers and the organization of parties on the effectiveness of consumer reforms. Finally, in part 3 a critique of the recently enacted Saskatchewan Consumer Products Warranties Act is made in the light of

unfavourable economic conditions, greater sophistication in the business community about lobbying and grass-roots politicking, and distrust of big government. The author argues that the latter is the critical factor: 'Ask the average consumer whether he wants unsafe cars, carcinogenic drugs, adulterated foods, dangerous toys, or advertising intended to exploit the gullibility of his four-year-old and he will answer with a resounding "no". But ask him whether government regulators should intervene to remedy these problems and his response is likely to be ambivalent. Increasingly, the public debate about consumer protection has centered less upon the question of which marketplace evils should be cured than upon the propriety of having the government administer the remedy. In its crudest form the question has become: whom do you trust less – big business or big government?' (ibid, at 3).

13 Sutton, Let the seller beware (1978) 10 *Ottawa L. R.* 35

14 Reich, supra note 12, at 3. This distrust of government intervention also appears in the writings of those who might be described as consumer activists. See Ziegel, The future of Canadian consumerism (1973) 51 *Can. Bar Rev.* 191, at 198; Belobaba, supra note 2. However, these critics attribute the defects in governmental intervention primarily to problems of understaffing and poor funding. They do not, therefore, view the problem as structural but rather contingent on certain defects being eradicated in the existing system.

An excellent comparative analysis of the inherent structural deficiencies in governmental protection of various social and group interests is provided by Cappelletti and Jolowicz in *Public Interest Parties and the Active Role of the Judge in Civil Litigation* (1975). They identify, among other factors, the bureaucratic nature of agencies, the career pressures within the organization, the well-documented problem of 'capture' by the interests under regulation, and the tendency to follow traditional approaches and not to seek out new problems or avenues of approach (reactive rather than proactive). See also Cappelletti and Garth, supra note 3.

Similar points were documented in the Canadian Consumer Council's study *On the Question of Consumer Advocacy – A Working Paper* (1972), at 2–12.

15 Galanter, Why the 'haves' come out ahead: Speculations on the limits of legal change (1974) 9 *Law and Soc. R.* 95, at 96.

insights drawn from parts 1 and 2. Some general conclusions will then be drawn on directions for reform.

*Defective products and consumer grievances: The submerged part of the iceberg*

The most significant Canadian document in this area is the report of the Ontario Law Reform Commission on consumer warranties and guarantees in the sale of goods.[16] Published in 1972, it represents a thorough and perceptive analysis of the problems faced by those who purchase defective and poor-quality products. Although its substantive proposals have not yet been adopted in Ontario, it has provided the basis for the recently enacted Saskatchewan Consumer Products Warranties Act and has been referred to extensively by reformers in other jurisdictions.[17] It is unfortunate, however, that subsequent reforms have paid insufficient attention to one of the central themes of the report.

This theme concerned the difficulties and frustrations which consumers experienced in attempting to obtain redress for their grievances. As a preliminary to reform the research team of the commission had collected consumer complaint statistics compiled by government agencies. These figures, in the commission's opinion, 'did not convey even remotely an impression of the frustrations and anxieties suffered by individual

16 *Report on Consumer Warranties and Guarantees in the Sale of Goods* (1972). See also the *Third Report of the Consumer Protection Project, Province of New Brunswick* (1976). For a commentary on the Ontario report see Ziegel (1973) 22 *I.C.L.Q.* 363. The Ontario Commission proposed a balanced scheme of public and private law measures, with a significant role for government to complement the individual remedies of the consumer. Indeed, if the commission had accepted all the recommendations of the research team, in particular those relating to class actions, then Ontario consumers would have obtained a significant degree of protection.

However, the Ontario government has shown little serious inclination to implement the package of recommendations proposed by the commission. It introduced Bill 110, which deals with consumer warranties and would depend on individual enforcement. It therefore failed to note the necessity of recognizing the interlocking nature of the public and private aspects of the commission's recommendations. By restricting the legislation in this way the Ontario government delivered a severely deficient response to the commission's recommendations. The Ontario government is not alone in this 'salami slicing' approach to comprehensive proposals for reform. The UK government reacted in a similar way to the recommendations of the Payne Committee on the Enforcement of Judgments, prompting one commentator to note that it was 'a weak and half-hearted attempt to deal with an important social and economic problem.' See Glasser, Administration of Justice Act 1970: Enforcement of debt provisions (1971) 34 *Mod. L.R.* 61.

17 The commission in its recent report on products liability (1979) noted at p 39 that the Saskatchewan act was based on the Ontario Law Reform Commission report on consumer warranties. It also noted at p 49 that the Ontario report 'appears to have had considerable influence in Australia.'

purchasers as they seek to obtain redress for a defective product.'[18] In addition, the commission found that in reviewing complaint files they had discovered that all parties (consumers, retailers, and industry representatives) attached minor importance to the conventional sales law.[19] Indeed few appeared to know the relevant law. Industry representatives did not know that disclaimer clauses had been largely nullified as a result of legislative amendments, and consumer complaint letters rarely referred to the law or threatened legal action.

On the basis of these findings, the commission concluded that if consumers were to have an effective redress for their grievances then reform must not be limited to substantive rule changes or private law remedies. Thus it concluded: '[O]ur sales law is private law and it has failed to provide any meaningful machinery for the redress of consumer grievances. This last weakness is perhaps the most serious of all weaknesses, for as has been frequently observed, a right is only as strong as the remedy available to enforce it.'[20]

The commission argued that solutions for this problem must be sought outside the traditional court structure. It proposed government-sponsored mediation and arbitration administered by the Consumer Protection Bureau. The objective of the dispute settlement provisions was 'the expeditious and inexpensive resolution of many of those genuine grievances of consumers that now fall outside the practical ambit of the ordinary courts.'[21] The proposed Consumer Protection Bureau would also have an important administrative role as watchdog of the consumer interest and would be empowered to enjoin violations of the act, and to act as a prosecutor of violations.

The Consumers' Association of Canada criticized these proposals on the basis that they were too vague. It proposed three different classes of procedure for consumer claims, each tailored to the amount in dispute. In framing their proposals, the Consumers' Association made the assumption that most consumers do not want to go to court and 'would not go to court very often even if the legal impediments are removed.'[22]

Both the Consumers' Association and the Ontario Law Reform Commission were, however, agreed on one fundamental issue. Effective reform ought to go beyond the traditional formal legal process, which in their joint opinion dealt only with 'the tip of the iceberg'[23] of consumer

18 Supra note 16, at 22
19 Ibid
20 Ibid, at 23
21 Ibid, at 117
22 Cited in Roine and Sigurdson, supra note 4, at 195
23 Best and Andreasen, Consumer response to unsatisfactory purchases: A survey of perceiving defects, voicing complaints and obtaining redress (1976–7) 11 *Law and Soc. R.* 701.

disputes and problems. Moreover the commission had pointed out that the law appeared to have at best a marginal impact on consumer complaint handling.

The commission's research provided a glimpse of the submerged seven-eighths of the iceberg of consumer problem solving. The next section describes those studies which have sought a more systematic analysis of this phenomenon.

## EXPLORING THE ICEBERG: EMPIRICAL EVIDENCE OF CONSUMER RESPONSES TO UNSATISFACTORY PURCHASES AND COMPLAINT AS A PROBLEM-SOLVING MECHANISM

The most comprehensive exploration of consumer problems and responses to unsatisfactory purchases is that of Best and Andreasen.[24] Based on 2419 telephone interviews with consumers in 34 US cities, this study gathered valuable information on consumer perceptions of and action taken concerning problems with 34 typical consumer products and services. The findings of this study provide valuable information on the characteristics of individuals who perceive problems and complain; the nature of the defects which are complained about; the individuals and institutions to whom consumers channel their complaints; and the extent to which complaints resulted in a satisfactory outcome for the consumer.

The study indicated that approximately one in five purchases led to the perception of a non-price problem.[25] Consumer perception of a problem was hindered by a number of factors. These were low socio-economic status, lack of interest in consumer issues, and the complexity of the problem. For example, a complex judgmental topic such as product design was unlikely to be perceived as problem.

Only 39.7% of consumers who perceived a problem took any kind of action. The most common response was to voice a complaint to the seller and ask for a refund, replacement, or repair. The other significant

24 Ibid

25 Ibid, at 727–8. A similar percentage has appeared in other studies in Europe and North America. See, eg, Ison, supra note 7, at 138 (25%); Blegvad, 'Indigenous' law and consumer protection (unpublished paper delivered at 1980 Annual Meeting of the Law and Society Association Madison, Wisconsin 1980); Ross and Littlefield, Complaint as a problem solving mechanism (1977–8) 12 *Law and Soc. R.* 199.

Cranston, supra note 6, at 106–7, notes that 'a comprehensive survey of domestic consumer durables in E.E.C. countries showed that an average of 16 per cent of consumers bought products which were faulty on delivery and an average of 30 per cent had to have products repaired while under guarantee.' The study referred to is titled *After Sales Services in the E.E.C.* (Bureau Européen des Unions de Consommateurs 1976).

Certain products in the Best and Andreasen study had a higher percentage of problems. Automobiles, mail order purchases, toys, and automobile repairs had problem rates of 30%; vacuum cleaners, clothing, grocery store items, and appliance repairs exceeded 25%.

response was exit – making a conscious decision to change the seller patronized or brand purchased. Only 1.2% of consumers perceiving problems voiced a complaint to a third party (for example, a Better Business Bureau, Consumer Affairs Department, media ombudsman). Important factors in affecting the rate of voicing complaints were the cost of purchase, the complexity of the problem, and the cost of repairing the defect. Manifest problems – for example, breakage or the wrong product – were voiced more frequently than judgmental problems such as durability or product design.[26] After a complaint was voiced satisfactory[27] solutions were reached in 56.5% of cases (manifest problems 61%, judgmental 50%). When complaints were presented to a third party, one third of all resolutions were satisfactory to the buyer.[28]

The general conclusions of the study were that 'voiced complaints overrepresent problems that are simple, that involve high cost, and that are experienced by high socio-economic status households'[29] and that 'third parties deal only with a small segment of the problems people perceive and the complaints people voice.'[30] They also noted a general disinclination among consumers in general either to be identified as a victim of a consumer problem or as a person who complained.

Other studies have confirmed these findings, in relation to both the demographic characteristics of consumers who voice complaints and the forms of actions taken by consumers faced with an unsatisfactory

26 Best and Andreasen indicated that judgmental problems might often involve factual differences, eg. where buyer and seller agree on some facts but differ on whether they indicate poor design or workmanship, or situations where the problem was attributed by the buyer to the inherent nature of the product and by the seller to the buyer's misuse. An example of the latter was reported by a household that had voiced a clothing complaint – 'You wear it once or twice and it falls apart' – and was told in reply by the clothing store, 'The kids could have ripped them up themselves' (supra note 23, at 717). The basic point about judgmental problems is that 'a disappointed buyer might reasonably anticipate that mere presentation of the facts may not establish the right to redress' (ibid).

Ison's study also indicated a distinction in voicing rates for manifest as opposed to judgmental problems. He noted two particular distinctions. Firstly there was a perceptible difference between cases in which the item was not working properly and those in which the buyer could point to a more readily identifiable defect, for example, a broken part. Second, defects in the condition of goods are more likely to result in complaints to the seller than abuses in the selling methods (supra note 7, at 139 and 143).

27 The authors note that they employed a 'generous definition of satisfactory resolutions' (Best and Andreasen, supra note 23, at 720 and see 725.

28 Purchase categories with relatively high use of third parties included home repairs, cars, appliance repairs, furniture, floor covering, legal services, and mail order items (ibid, at 714).

29 Ibid, at 729

30 Ibid

purchase.[31] They indicate that those who complained to third parties were better educated, had higher incomes, and were managerial or professional men or women.

A central finding of Best and Andreasen's study for those interested in consumer redress mechanisms was the almost perfect monopoly that sellers had on complaint handling. Few consumers made use of third-party mechanisms even if they were dissatisfied with the seller's response. Two-party negotiation was therefore the most important institution for the solution of a consumer's problems with poor quality and defective products. How useful is this institution to the consumer, what are its dynamics, and what sort of norms are applied at this level of complaint handling? A number of studies have attempted to provide partial answers to these important questions and also to document in greater detail the nature of two-party negotiation between consumer and retailer.

Ross and Littlefield[32] conducted a study of the complaint-handling practices of a major appliance store in Denver, Colorado. The most significant finding of their study was that complaint to a retailer was both a cheap and an effective form of redress for consumers. Consumer satisfaction was achieved most commonly by repair, but if a consumer insisted on replacement or refund then this was granted. Indeed, a consumer often obtained more than the law required under the sales provisions (Article 2) of the Uniform Commercial Code.[33] For example, retailers accepted back goods notwithstanding that the consumer's decision to return them was arbitrary. This policy was also followed by other large firms operating in the home appliance field in Denver.

The study also indicated that middle-class individuals who complained (the bulk of retailers' customers were described as middle class) seemed to be well served by retail enterprises but that 'the factors producing

31 Studies in Canada include Liefeld, Edgecombe, and Wolfe (1975) 9 *Journal of Consumer Affairs* 73. Also relevant is Hannigan, The newspaper ombudsman and consumer complaints: An empirical assessment (1976–7) 11 *Law and Soc. R.* 679. See also Cranston *Regulating Business* (1979), at 5, where he states in relation to the UK consumer market: 'The most striking feature of national surveys is that many consumers who think that they have experienced consumer problems fail to complain, lack a rudimentary knowledge of their legal rights, and are ignorant of official bodies, such as consumer agencies, which may be able to assist them.' Later, discussing interviews with complaining consumers he notes: 'There is an underrepresentation of those in the lowest income groups, which seems to arise because socio-economic position is associated with social attributes such as confidence. Complaining involves more than knowledge, for even consumers who know that consumer agencies exist must find the local agency and feel that it is worthwhile approaching it' (ibid, at 6). But cf McNeil et al, Market discrimination against the poor and the impact of consumer disclosure laws: The used car industry (1979) 13 *Law and Soc. R.* 695.

32 Ross and Littlefield, supra note 25

33 Ibid, at 211

generous responses to their complaints may be absent for economically disadvantaged consumers and other special groups.'[34] These factors included willingness and ability to complain, and the important fact that customers for appliances in the mass market are likely to be repeat players.[35] Moreover, a liberal complaint policy may be related to its relatively low cost in comparison with the size and capitalization of the retailer. The cost to Sears Roebuck in replacing a washing machine is significantly less than the cost to Jones Motors in replacing a Chevrolet.[36]

The authors concluded by questioning the conventional wisdom of consumer reform which placed emphasis on providing consumers with greater access to legal remedies. While recognizing that this policy was of some importance, they nevertheless argued that the energies of consumer activists ought to be channelled into fostering conditions under which complaint is likely to be effective. They concluded: 'Two-party negotiation is generally simpler, quicker, and less costly than any third-party institution even when the latter is modified to handle small claims. Similarly, changing the substantive law of sales is unlikely to produce outcomes as favorable to consumers as those they can obtain through the complaint mechanisms.'[37]

A further exploration of consumer complaint handling from the perspective of the retailer was carried out by myself in collaboration with J. Enzle.[38] The next section sets out the results of that study.

## SATISFACTION GUARANTEED OR MONEY REFUNDED?[39]

### THE EMPIRICAL EVIDENCE

Our study was an exploratory investigation of the return policies of retailers in Edmonton, Alberta, for unsatisfactory consumer purchases. Our purpose was to ascertain the extent to which the retail consumer marketplace had adopted the so-called 'Eaton's rule' of satisfaction guaranteed or money refunded. The study was limited to retail products and excluded services. In addition, the policies of automobile and mobile home dealers were deliberately excluded. The sampling method and a description of the categories of stores sampled and the questionnaire are included as appendix A.

34 Ibid, at 212
35 Ibid, at 213
36 Ibid, at 213
37 Ibid, at 214–15
38 Of the Alberta bar
39 The idea of legislating 'satisfaction guaranteed or money refunded' as a norm for consumer sales is suggested in an unpublished essay by M.G. Baer of Queen's University. This paper was prepared as a background paper for the Institute of Law Research and Reform. The idea is also noted (and rejected) by Best and Andreasen, supra note 23.

TABLE 1
Return policies

| | absolute frequency | percentage |
|---|---|---|
| a / cash refund | | |
| yes | 93 | 88 |
| no | 12 | 11 |
| no answer | 1 | 1 |
| TOTAL | 106 | 100 |
| b / store credit | | |
| yes | 66 | 62 |
| no | 39 | 37 |
| no answer | 1 | 1 |
| TOTAL | 106 | 100 |
| c / exchange | | |
| yes | 86 | 81 |
| no | 19 | 18 |
| no answer | 1 | 1 |
| TOTAL | 106 | 100 |

The findings of the study partially confirmed the argument that consumer complaint and two-party negotiations between buyer and seller might play an important role in protecting the consumer against defective and poor-quality products. Thus the overwhelming majority of retailers responding had a policy of accepting returned merchandise. Table 1 indicates that cash refunds were given by 88% of retailers, store credits by 62%, and exchanges by 81%.

Only 1 of the 106 respondents indicated that they would accept no returns at all. Significantly over 75% of stores would refund or exchange goods where the customer was returning the goods simply because of the wrong size or colour or for some other reason of personal taste. All department stores followed this policy. The consumer might therefore expect to receive more generous treatment than he is entitled to under the provisions of the Sale of Goods Act.

However, although almost all stores accepted returned goods, they placed a variety of limitations on their return policies. Table 2 indicates the nature of these limitations.

Two factors were of importance in affecting return policies. These were the retailer's perception of the customer as a repeat player and the market advantages gained by satisfied customers communicating their

TABLE 2
Limitations on return

| | absolute frequency | percentage |
|---|---|---|
| a / time limit? | | |
| yes | 50 | 47 |
| no | 50 | 47 |
| no answer | 6 | 6 |
| TOTAL | 106 | 100 |
| b / limitations on type of goods? | | |
| yes | 38 | 36 |
| no | 62 | 58 |
| no answer | 6 | 6 |
| TOTAL | 106 | 100 |
| c / proof of sale required? | | |
| yes | 68 | 64 |
| no | 31 | 29 |
| no answer | 7 | 7 |
| TOTAL | 106 | 100 |
| d / who determines acceptability of goods? | | |
| retailer | 24 | 23 |
| customer | 30 | 28 |
| both | 30 | 28 |
| no answer | 22 | 21 |
| TOTAL | 106 | 100 |

satisfaction to potential customers.[40] Thus one clothing store owner stated: 'If he [the retailer] takes the long-range view he feels that the customer will make it up in some other purchase and things even out,' and a lumber store responded: 'I consider the overall cost [of returns] to be minimal as a customer will usually tell his friends where [he's] satisfied or dissatisfied. I feel a large percentage of our sales come from having satisfied ones.'

It was clear that legal rules were of no apparent significance in a decision to grant an exchange or a refund.[41] No retailers mentioned the

40 See also Cranston, supra note 31, at 159–67; Diener and Greyser, Consumer views of redress needs (1978) 42 *Journal of Marketing* 21.

41 Recent studies have talked about 'bargaining in the shadow of the law.' See Mnookin, Bargaining in the shadow of the law: The case of divorce (1979) 88 Yale *L.J.* 950. Two-party consumer-retailer negotiation appears to be an area where legal rules do

relevance of legal rights or duties to the issue of consumer returns or complaints.

Many retailers perceived themselves as exercising a discretionary power, applying reasonable business standards of the marketplace for the privilege of reasonable customers as interpreted by store personnel. Evidence of this discretion may be found in their answer to the question: 'Who determines the acceptability of goods?' The responses to this question were approximately equally divided between retailer, customer, and both. In the case of department stores it was simply a matter of store policy rather than the discretion of the individual assistant. A useful example of retailers' perception of a justified return is the following comment: 'In four out of five cases, the return is justified either because of wrong size or colour.'

I obtained the impression that it might be easier for a consumer to obtain a refund or replacement where he was returning goods on arbitrary grounds for which there is no legal justification than if goods were being returned for judgmental problems (for example, faulty design) for which there might be legal justification.

Many retailers stated that if, for example, the goods were damaged, they would check for customer abuse. The problem that may arise is that the retailer exercises a discretion in determining whether a defect is or is not caused by the fault of the customer. If a consumer is for some reason not competent (for example, because of lack of technical expertise) or effective in pressing his complaint, then he may obtain no redress. This may be especially true if the consumer is complaining about judgmental problems such as durability or misrepresentation or if a defect could be attributed partly to customer use and partly to the defect. He or she may not be perceived as a 'reasonable' customer.

Consumers' 'rights' at this level of two-party negotiation are therefore dependent on norms generated by sellers partly in response to market forces rather than in response to legal rules. The parties do not appear to 'bargain in the shadow of the law.' The norms applied may be more generous than the legal rules and may be a potentially useful tool for consumer protection. However, as I have noted, in many of these cases

not provide a framework for bargaining. This conclusion suggests that perhaps we ought to turn upside down the metaphor of bargaining in the shadow of the law and suggest rather that the law is in the shadow of the norms applied at this level of negotiation. See Galanter, supra note 10. Similar conclusions have been drawn concerning the regulatory activity of businessmen in settling disputes: Macaulay, Non-contractual relations in business: A preliminary study (1963) 28 *American Sociological Review* 55; Macaulay, Elegant models, empirical pictures and the complexities of contract (1976-7) 11 *Law and Soc. R.* 507. See also *Report of the Ontario Law Reform Commission on Sale of Goods* (1979) vol 1, at 25. Ison and Cranston also note the insignificance of law at this level of consumer disputing (supra note 7, at 251, and supra note 31, at 168).

where retailers accept returned goods, there is no 'dispute' between the consumer and retailer. The goods are not defective, the consumer need not convince the store that there is a defect for which it ought to be responsible, and the goods may often be resold. The consumer is unlikely to know his legal rights, which might constitute an important bargaining lever.

Our study indicated that the return policies did not appear to be costly to retailers. Goods are often resold or returned to the manufacturer or wholesaler. Only 7% of respondents discarded returned goods. In the opinion of retailers, few sales result in returns. Almost two-thirds of those responding stated that 1% or less of their sales are returned. This figure should be compared with Best and Andreasen's data on problem perception and action taken by consumers. If their data are relevant to Edmonton, the low percentage of returns may be attributable to consumer inaction or exit. The respondents were reluctant to estimate the cost of providing services to dissatisfied customers, but the great majority of those who responded stated that the cost was 1% or less of their gross sales. Since the long-term market value of goodwill and repeat customers may offset any immediate costs, it would appear that return policies are a negligible cost to retailers.

We received some interesting comments on the relationship between retailers and suppliers which suggest that this might be a fertile field for further research. A majority of retailers (58%) claimed not to be influenced by their suppliers in arriving at their return policies, but a significant portion stated that their policies were, at least to some extent, determined by the policies of their suppliers. Ross and Littlefield indicated that by using the complaint mechanism consumers could play a significant role in quality control. The retailer is an important conduit in communicating issues of quality control to a supplier or manufacturer. However, we clearly need further study of their role in this process.

At this point it may be useful to summarize some conclusions and suggest some hypotheses on the basis of these empirical studies of informal complaint mechanisms.

### CONCLUSIONS ON MARKET MECHANISMS AND INFORMAL REDRESS MECHANISMS

Although consumers do perceive deficiencies in many of the products which they purchase, they make no complaints regarding a substantial number of these problems. The two most important ways in which consumers currently do express dissatisfaction with poor-quality products are through voice to a retailer or exit. The latter is the classic economic response. It is also simple, impersonal, and definite, requiring no particular competence. Yet other studies[42] suggest that unless carried out on an extensive scale it may not have an optimal effect on a firm's performance or quality control. Moreover, it is an inadequate alternative for consumers of expensive defective products or where the exit option is unavailable. It is hardly surprising that Best and Andreasen noted higher rates of complaints for automobiles, appliances, and house repairs.

If voice to a retailer has potential as an informal consumer redress mechanism then what measures ought to be taken to reinforce its effectiveness? Hirschman in his work titled *Exit, Voice and Loyalty* notes that 'voice is costly, and [is] conditioned on the influence and bargaining power customers ... can bring to bear within the firm from which they buy.'[43] Reforms ought therefore to concentrate on reinforcing that influence and bargaining power.

As a first step in reform, policy makers ought to identify those markets where voice needs to be either reinforced or particularly encouraged. Examples of the first category might be markets where sellers are not dependent on repeat purchases or where the item is an infrequently purchased product. Consumer information on complaint handling could give sellers a greater stake in creating and maintaining goodwill.[44]

Information must be collected on the complaint-handling practices of retailers. Stores might be required to keep a record of their complaint handling. In this way, consumers will be able to avoid (that is, exit before purchase) those firms with poor complaint records. Voice and exit might therefore complement each other.

Voicing complaints is an art. The empirical studies suggest that the competence of parties is an important factor both in making a decision to complain and in a successful resolution of the complaint. An important method of improving competence is by organizing. I have already mentioned government organizations, but other 'information brokers' (for example, media ombudsmen) may also play a part. Michael Trebilcock's proposal for a consumer advocate would include the important function of monitoring and disseminating information to consumers on complaint handling. The consumer advocate might also play an important role in facilitating communication between the consumer and the 'right' person in the business organization. He might also attempt to aid a consumer in those areas where complaint is particularly difficult, for example, providing access to expert reliable information on a judgmental

42 See generally Stone *Where the Law Ends* (1975).
43 (1971), at 40
44 See Katz *Protecting the Consumer Interest* (1976) at 81. A number of similar suggestions are made in Best and Andreasen, supra note 23, at 730–4.

issue such as product design.[45] This was one of the roles which the Ontario Law Reform Commission foresaw for the Consumer Protection Bureau. The drawbacks of these proposals are that they involve third parties, even though the third party may be only providing information for two-party negotiation. We have already noted the reluctance of consumers to use third parties.

A further method of upgrading competence might be to legislate as a norm for the majority of consumer sales the practice of satisfaction guaranteed or money refunded. This would give the consumer a limited time to return goods for whatever reason.[46] It would have the advantage of providing a clear and straightforward remedy to a consumer. Existing precedents for this policy can be found in the various provincial Direct Sales Cancellation Acts which regulate door-to-door sales. The legislative endorsement of this norm of the marketplace could act as a symbol or model of the public endorsement of the best commercial standards. Consumer activists have underestimated the symbolic importance of law.[47] The legislative norm would support the private bargaining of the consumer with the retailer, could have a socializing and educative effect, and would be self-enforcing by simply recognizing what many businesses already do. Retailers who did not wish to endorse this practice could contract out by displaying prominent notices so that a consumer was aware of market choices. It would be a norm that would be expected to increase competence over a period of time as it penetrated through the informal brokerage system of 'family members, friends, neighbors ... bartenders' which recent studies have indicated plays a crucial role in decisions to take action.[48]

It might also be argued on the basis of these studies that a refund, replacement, or repair is 'what consumers want' as a solution to their consumer problems rather than damages or other legal remedies. However, what the consumer wants may be based on expectations of what

45 A number of writers suggest that one of the attractive features of the Public Complaints Board in Sweden is its use of technical expertise, which it also makes available to small claims courts. See Cappelletti and Garth, supra note 3, at 266–8; Roine, Mediation and arbitration of consumer disputes in Sigurdson and Roine, supra note 4, at 152.

46 One would have to decide whether to include all consumer products or to exclude certain goods, eg, automobiles or mobile homes.

47 By concentrating on the instrumental effects of law, consumer reformers may have underestimated the important educative and socializing effect which law reforms might have. They may be quite right, however, in drawing attention to the fact that 'unorganized and diffused publics tend to receive symbolic rewards, while organized professional ones reap tangible rewards' (Galanter, supra note 15, at 137, citing Edelman *Politics as Symbolic Action* ch 2). A useful introduction to the symbolic role of law is Gusfield *Moral Crusade* (1963).

48 See Ladinsky et al, supra note 11, at 10; Zander *Legal Services for the Community* (1978), at 292.

is possible or available, and Best and Andreasen indicate that 'the decision to take any voicing actions concerning a perceived problem is made against the background of widespread knowledge that complaining can be difficult and costly'[49] and perhaps is not a socially praiseworthy activity.

A further suggestion made in the articles concerns the role which consumer complaints might play in quality control. This can only happen, however, if the information which is received by the retailer is transmitted to the manufacturer and the manufacturer is induced to change its production behaviour. The bargaining power of large department stores and retailers in relation to suppliers and manufacturers may make them important agents of quality control.[50] If, however, consumers do not complain or the retailer either absorbs the costs of quality control or does not communicate information to the manufacturer, then complaint may be a defective method of communicating issues of quality control. A recent work on corporate organizations[51] argues that attempting to use the market mechanism to change corporate production practices in response to poor quality control may be like attempting to turn round a giant oil tanker. Hirschman also argues that management, in order to preserve its autonomy, will invariably attempt to preserve its freedom of movement by converting a feedback mechanism such as complaint into a safety valve. Voice then becomes mere '"blowing off steam" as it is being emasculated by the institutionalisation and domestication of dissent.'[52] An individual consumer may or may not have his complaint satisfied, but there is little effect on the production organization.

This argument returns us to a reflection on the two types of consumer problems in the marketplace, the individual misunderstanding or dispute and the more generalized problem such as faulty product design.[53] The

49 Supra note 23, at 715

50 For example, Reich, supra note 12, notes at 34 that Montgomery Ward complained to Firestone about the poor quality of its radial tires as early as 1976, two years before the National Highway Transportation Safety Administration ordered a recall. The Ontario Law Reform Commission, in its background study for the warranties report, also indicated the important power of the department store in relation to suppliers (supra note 16, at 73).

51 See Stone, supra note 42.

52 Hirschman, supra note 43, at 124. Stone also notes that 'all large organizations seek to seal off or "buffer" their technical core from disruptive environmental influences (like the market – or the law) (supra note 42, at 92). Stone indicates (ibid 89) four assumptions in relation to market pressure: (1) that the persons who are going to withdraw patronage know the fact that they are being "injured"; (2) that they know where to apply pressure of some sort; (3) that they are in a position to apply pressure of some sort; and (4) that their pressure will be translated into changes in the institution's behavior.' He continues: 'None of these assumptions is particularly well founded.'

53 See Rice, Remedies, enforcement procedures and the duality of consumer transaction problems (1968) 48 *Bos. U.L.R.* 559.

studies on complaint note its potential usefulness as a solution for individual problems, but we ought not to overestimate its possibilities as a method of systematically policing business behaviour. In addition, the fact that many consumers do not complain and the deficiencies in the complaint mechanism as a solution to judgmental problems point to the necessity for some form of continuing group activity on behalf of consumers to buttress individual conduct. It also illustrates the extent to which group activity (either through government or independent organizations) and private activity must feed on each other. For example, only if a consumer agency takes an active role in seeking out problems and providing consumers with expert and reliable information will the consumer be able to voice an effective complaint. In turn, if this information is collected by the agency, it provides more data on consumer problem solving and a basis for a systematic surveillance of the marketplace. Existing statistics compiled by government agencies on third-party complaint handling must be regarded as an inadequate basis for policy making since these statistics only represent 'the tip of the iceberg' of consumer problems.[54]

I shall return to this theme of the balance between public and private activity. I want now, however, to turn to one of the oldest methods of consumer redress, individual litigation through the legal system.

### *Repeat players, lawyers, and the legal system*

Recent literature provides depressing reading for those consumers interested in mobilizing the legal system.[55] The reactive nature of legal institutions[56] means that consumers must expend significant transaction costs if they wish to use the court system. It is not surprising to find either that few consumers are willing or able to take their disputes to court or that the great majority of product-quality cases involve automobiles or mobile homes.[57]

54 See also Ison, supra note 7, at 137.

55 See, eg, Belobaba, supra note 2, and see also Belobaba, The resolution of common law contract doctrinal problems through legislative and administrative intervention, in Swan and Reiter (eds) *Studies in Contract Law* (1980), at 443.

56 See Black, The mobilization of law (1973) 2 *J. of Legal Studies* 125. Black indicates two ways in which a case might enter a legal system: 'A citizen may set the legal process in motion by bringing a complaint; or the state may initiate a complaint upon its own authority, with no participation of a citizen complainant.' He refers to the former process as reactive, the latter as proactive. He notes in relation to a reactive system that 'the reluctance of citizens to mobilize the law is so widespread, indeed, that it may be appropriate to view legal inaction as the dominant pattern in empirical legal life' (ibid, at 128 and 133).

57 My conclusion appears to be substantiated by a brief perusal of the index to the Western Weekly Law Reports over approximately the past ten years.

Law reformers have concentrated much of their effort on changes within the structure of the existing court system. Greater access to small claims courts and more extensive and effective private law remedies have been advocated and in some cases legislated. The focus has been primarily on dispute resolution and case-by-case adjudication of individual claims. Yet reformers have not adequately solved the fundamental problem of the difference between the competence of one-shotters and repeat-player organizations in effectively using the legal system.

The majority of civil litigation in Canada and the United States involves organizations suing individuals, primarily for default on debts.[58] These cases are part of the bureaucratic process of debt collection, and the judgment (usually by default) of the court provides formal validity to a creditor's claims. Few of these cases could be classified as disputes about legal rules. Many of these organizations use the court system on a continuing basis. They are repeat players and thus have many strategic advantages over the one shotter. An individual consumer, unless he is a lawyer[59] or a self-appointed consumer advocate, is a one shotter. Individuals suing organizations account for only 5% of civil litigation in Canada.[60] Among the advantages of the repeat player are the ability to use 'advance intelligence' and 'structure transactions in advance' (the form contract), to develop 'expertise and access to specialists' such as lawyers, and to 'develop continuing relations with institutional incumbents' such as court personnel. They have 'the ability to play for rules as well as for immediate gain. It pays a recurrent litigant to expend resources in influencing the making of the relevant rules and avoiding unfavourable litigation outcomes through settlements.'[61]

58 See *Civil Justice in Canada: A Statistical Study* Research Study no. 8, Justice Statistics Division, Statistics Canada (1979). See Also Wanner, The public ordering of private relations (1974) 8 *Law and Soc. R.* 421. The authors of the Canadian study comment (at 34) that 'Wanner in 1976 reported that the hard-core of civil actions in the American courts he studied was comprised of cases in which an organisation sued an individual for the balance of a debt. In the present survey this pattern is confirmed to an even greater degree.'

59 As in the recent case of *General Motors Products of Canada Ltd.* v *Kravitz* (1979) 93 D.L.R. (3d.) 481. Arthur Leff, in Injury, ignorance and spite (1970) 80 *Yale L.J.* 1, suggests at 21 that a consumer who wishes to vindicate a claim for a small amount would normally require 'superspite ... that is infliction by the consumer of greater harm on himself than he can inflict on his enemy. It may still be done; the history of law is filled with cranks (lawyers or clients, it's often hard to tell) who spend large and unrecoverable sums to assuage feelings of outrage, moral or economic. But it is not bloody likely.'

60 *Civil Justice in Canada*, supra note 58, at 35

61 Galanter, supra note 15 at 97–102. *Civil Justice in Canada*, supra note 58, indicated that cases in which an individual sues an organization tend to take much longer than those where an organization sues an individual. The authors of the report suggest, at 30, that 'this offers the intriguing possibility that there is purposeful delay in some kinds of cases, particularly since, as we shall subsequently show, organizations tend to make

There is also a clear dichotomy between legal services provided to organizations and to individuals.[62] This is reflected in the division within the legal profession between those who provide a limited range of services to individuals on an occasional basis and those who provide a far wider range of preventive and counselling services to organizations on a continuing basis.

It is becoming clear, therefore, that the disparity in the use of legal services and recourse to litigation is not simply a question of individual social status or income or of rich and poor individuals but is rather a disparity between organizations and individuals.[63] For example, statistics indicate that organizations as plaintiffs tend to be represented more often by counsel than are individual defendants.

One conclusion from these studies, therefore, is the importance of organization as a strategy for reform if consumers are to become 'effective players of the law game.' Changing the rules either at the legislative or the judicial level may have little effect if there are not competent parties capable of fully taking advantage of the benefit of the rules. Thus Galanter notes: 'Like everything else, favourable rules are resources and those who enjoy disproportionate shares of other resources tend also to reap the benefit of rules. The basic question is how to supply the resources that enable parties to secure the benefit of favorable rules.'[64]

We note again the important theme of competence as a key to consumer success. Galanter suggests a number of methods of upgrading competence. I shall return to these later, but I wish now to examine the role of lawyers in the 'delivery' of consumer protection.

The ability to have continuing access to expert legal services is an obvious strategic advantage for any group or individual. A recent study of lawyers and consumer protection laws raises a number of serious questions concerning the potential role of lawyers as advocates for consumers.[65] The study suggests that on the rare occasions when lawyers face consumer issues, they do not play the role of advocate on behalf of a consumer. They act rather as mediators or conciliators between a business and a consumer client, playing 'counsel for the situation.' They may 'cool

heavy use of the legal profession's services. Perhaps corporations succeed in gaining momentum in case proceedings when they are plaintiffs, but as defendants are successful in retarding the momentum of persistent individual plaintiffs.'

62 See Heinz and Laumann, The legal profession: Client interests, professional roles, and social hierarchies (1978) 76 *Mich. L.R.* 1111, at 1114.

63 Although many individuals even at the lower end of the income scale may use a lawyer on an episodic basis – eg, for defence of a criminal action or a debt action – only organizations have the ability to resort to legal services on a continuing basis.

64 Galanter, Delivering legality: Some proposals for the direction of research (1976) 11 *Law and Soc. R.* 225, at 229

65 Macaulay, Lawyers and consumer protection laws (1979) 14 *Law and Soc. R.* 115

the client out,' act as therapist, or help the consumer to communicate with the right person in the organization.

The study argues also that it is not only the economic realities of practice or the fact that lawyers are usually retained by business creditors which deter them from pursuing consumer claims. The interests and values of the lawyers themselves affect the way they handle disputes. They are engaged in small business, are unlikely personally to face serious consumer problems, and probably understand the consumer contracts which they sign. They are also prone to feel that there are 'legitimate' and 'not so legitimate' ways of resolving problems, and the study noted that lawyers who are agressive in asserting consumer rights are often regarded by other membes of the bar as 'members of "rag tag bar" who have no rating in Martindale Hubbell and who ignore the economic realities of practice.'[66] Lawyers also appeared to distrust consumers who complain, viewing them at times as 'flaky' or 'freaks.' In addition, judges and their clerks apparently disliked consumer cases because they were unfamiliar with much of the new law.

The discretion which lawyers exercise in dealing with consumer claims raises important issues beyond those of consumer protection. Thus, Macaulay states:

> What qualifies these lawyers as experts in problem solving? ... In short, there is a problem of legitimacy. As is true in the case of so many empirical studies related to law, once again we have stumbled on the problem of discretion and the expert whose skill rests on experience rather than on training and science (see Macaulay and Macaulay, 1978). And a counsel for the situation has little accountability to much beyond his or her own conscience (cf. Brown and Brown, 1976).[67]

Reformers ought also to be sensitive to the legal ideology[68] which several writers have associated with the legal profession. The characteristics of this ideology include a tendency to view law as an autonomous set of rules separate from politics and political considerations. This ideal of legality which can become deformed into legalism[69] stresses the formal

66 Ibid, at 140. It is instructive to note that Estey J, in an interview commenting on class actions, stated that unless there is liability for costs, in ten years the courts would be 'glutted by nuts' bringing class actions. The class actions mentioned in the interview included consumer cases. See *Toronto Star*, 30 April 1977.

67 Supra note 65, at 159

68 See generally Galanter supra note 15, at 118–19.

69 The severest indictment of legalism as a structure of thought is found in Shklar *Legalism* (1964). The ideal of legality is championed in Rawls *A Theory of Justice* (1971), at 239–40. A useful discussion of legality and legalism can be found in Nonet and Selznick *Towards Responsive Law* (1978), at 67. See also Unger *Law in Modern Society* (1976) and Weber *On Law in Economy and Society* (ed Rheinstein), at 812. I have not attempted a Marxist analysis of the role of lawyers, nor have I developed the Marxist concept of

equality of the law where rules are applied uniformly and impartially, ignoring all differences in power and influence between litigants, except those recognized by the law. The problem with this ideal which emphasises due process and procedural fairness is that it may lose touch with the social reality of the difference in power and influence between litigants outside the courtroom. It is trite to note that formal justice has the vice of 'being consistent with serving existing systems of power.'[70] Yet lawyers and judges are generally uneasy with reform measures which undermine the image of law as an autonomous process.[71] It is this particular structure of thought which might retard the development of class actions which expose the political nature of the judicial process, since they are an obvious attempt to redistribute power.[72]

Moreover, the lawyer's preference for 'complex and finely tuned bodies of rules, for adversary proceedings, for individualized case-by-case decision-making and the tendency to render recovery problematic where lawyers are involved in reforming statutes'[73] may have unfortunate consequences for the structure of consumer-protection legislation.

In addition, if lawyers are to have a significant role in delivering legal services to consumers, serious thought must be given to whether traditional models of legal practice are appropriate. Wexler, for example, has argued that practising law for poor people ought not to be the same as practising law for rich people with less money.[74] He suggests that the poverty lawyer must play the role of organizer, helping the poor to help themselves and acting as a resource person and lobbyist for poverty organizations. He therefore rejects what he calls the 'law school model' of the individual client with the individual legal problem, primarily because, in his words, 'If all the lawyers in the country worked full time, they could not deal with even the articulated legal problems of the poor. And even if somehow lawyers could deal with those articulated problems, they would not change very much the tangle of unarticulated legal problems in which poor people live.'[75] While the analogy of poverty law may only be suggestive, the general sentiments expressed might clearly have applica-

legitimation, of which consumer protection laws may be a useful example. That is the subject of a separate essay which I am preparing. For a somewhat flawed Marxist analysis of class justice in Canada, see Olsen *The State Elite* (1979), esp ch 3.

70 Nonet and Selznick, supra note 69, at 67

71 Galanter, supra note 15, at 119

72 For example, the Ontario Law Reform Commission refused to recommend the introduction of consumer class actions in the White Paper on consumer guarantees and warranties, despite the fact that the research team had presented strong arguments in favour of their introduction.

73 Galanter, supra note 15, at 119

74 Wexler, Practicing law for poor people (1970) 79 *Yale L.J.* 1049

75 Ibid, at 1052

tion to the consumer context. Only if lawyers adopt this role will they be able to offset the advantages of the repeat players who have the capacity to structure the transaction, play the odds, and influence rule-development and enforcement policy.[76]

### *The Saskatchewan Consumer Products Warranties Act: Symbolic legitimation?*

Described as a 'comprehensive and systematic response to the problems faced by consumers of defective products,'[77] this act regulates warranties in the sale of consumer products and indicates the substantive rights and remedies arising from these warranties.

The central concepts of the act are statutory warranties of 'acceptable quality' and 'durability' in sales of consumer products. These warranties are deemed to be given by the manufacturer in addition to the retailer. They may not be contracted out of by a retail seller, although there are exceptions for second-hand consumer products if the disclaimer is brought to the notice of the consumer and its effect made clear to him.

The concepts of acceptable quality and durability are drawn in very general terms. The former, for example, is defined as 'the characteristics and the quality of a consumer product that consumers can reasonably expect the product to have, having regard to all the relevant circumstances of the sale of the product, including the description of the product, its purchase price and the express warranties of the retail seller or manufacturer of the product, and includes merchantable quality within the meaning of the Sale of Goods Act.'[78]

The drafters of the act appear to envisage that primary enforcement of it will be through the private individual remedies of rejection and damages. These are documented in detail, and their exercise turns on issues such as whether there has been a 'breach of a substantial character,'[79] thus rejecting the a priori classification under the Sale of Goods Act. There are provisions for exemplary damages, and some encouragement to a consumer is provided by section 29, which allows no costs to be awarded against a consumer even if he is unsuccessful in his action.

A preliminary issue in evaluating the statute is to indicate criteria to judge its effect. A classification might distinguish two general classes of criteria: instrumental and symbolic. The former would include the

76 Galanter, supra note 15
77 Romero, The Consumer Products Warranties Act (1979) 43 *Sask. L.R.* 81, at 83
78 R.S.S. 1978, c C-30, s 2(a)
79 Ibid, s 2(c)

adequate provision of remedies to consumers and the deterrence of shoddy and poor-quality products.

The symbolic effects of the legislation might be further divided into three headings: participation, publicity, and attitude.[80] Firstly, the private damage action provides a method for the individual to participate in the government process. Second, the publicity that may surround a lawsuit can draw attention to issues raised by the action and act as a potential catalyst for change in other parts in the system. Third, the development of a jurisprudence of consumer product quality cases has a potential socializing effect in the development of new norms of liability which will filter through to affect business standards and attitudes. How does the Saskatchewan act measure against these criteria?

The act is an excellent example of the imposition of a structure of legal thought on a social problem.[81] Substantively, the problem of defective consumer products is conceptualized within the pre-existing historical framework of private sales legislation and contract and tort doctrine. The intellectual traditions of legal learning and the expertise of lawyers are brought to bear on the issue. The result is a complex interlocking body of rules designed for adversary adjudication on a case-by-case basis. Courts play a central role in reform. Recovery under the statute is problematic, preserving the complexity and mystique of the law. Success in litigation would undoubtedly require the services of a lawyer and the expense of expert testimony. The Ontario Law Reform Commission, for example, noted that 'legal disputes involving warranty claims are ... rarely simple and the consumer generally lacks knowledge of the substantive and evidentiary rules essential for the successful prosecution of his action. The need for professional assistance therefore still exists.'[82] The act is not a self-contained code, and only a person acquainted with pre-existing legal doctrine and theories of recovery could adequately develop an argument to elucidate the meaning of, for example, 'a breach of a substantial character.' The preoccupation with courts and litigation seems to have led the reformers to overlook the continuing advantages of parties outside the courtroom, and there is no provision to redress this imbalance, for example, through class actions.

Moreover, the nebulous concept of 'acceptability' will be of little use to a

80 See Tribe *Channelling Technology Through Law* (1971), at 98–9.

81 In a related context the comments of Philip Lewis seem particularly appropriate: 'If certain problems are spoken of as legal ones, and official support is given to legal methods of solving them, that is to take a particular attitude to problems of that kind, problems which may be capable of solution in some other way, and which may be seen by those most closely concerned as best solved in that other way' (Unmet legal needs, in Morris et al *Social Needs and Legal Action* (1973), at 75).

82 *Report on Consumer Warranties and Guarantees*, supra note 16, at 107

non-expert court in deciding issues of minimum product quality. It is as slippery as the concept of merchantability which it replaces.[83] A consumer attempting to negotiate with a seller would find little clear bargaining leverage in the concept. The rules in the act are unlikely to alter the pattern of product quality litigation. Since most private law product-quality litigation concerns automobiles, trucks, and trailers, a cynic might argue that the reformers would have done better if they had set more detailed standards of quality for these particular products. It is possible that this is contemplated by those provisions of the act which confer on the Lieutenant Governor in Council the power to make regulations prescribing standards, which if breached would constitute prima facie evidence that the consumer product is not of acceptable quality.[84]

There is also a section entitling consumers to refer disputes to the Department of Consumer Affairs for mediation or, with the written consent of all parties, to submit disputes to arbitration. It might be expected that this process will play a significant part in enforcement and dispute settlement under the act. But what standards will be used in the mediation process since the act provides such vague guidelines? To the extent that mediation or arbitration draws on expert standards in the particular industry involved, it is then questionable whether the general standard adds anything to the specific standard.

I have suggested, therefore, that the act may be deficient if judged by the instrumental standard of effectively providing greater redress to consumers than exists under present legislation. Moreover, the inefficient nature of the private law system suggests that the act is unlikely to have an effect on quality control.[85] But what of its symbolic significance? The role of mediation under the act provides an introduction to this issue.

Introducing a government agency as a mediator might be regarded as a way of improving consumer competence and making dispute resolution more accessible to the consumer. However, there are a number of issues which raise doubts concerning the enforcement of consumer legislation

83 P.S. Atiyah comments: 'It does not seem to be going too far to say that, in effect, the concept merely requires the goods to be of the sort of quality reasonably to be expected having regard to all the circumstances of the case. The new definition, far from being, as definitions frequently are, a straightjacket, turns out to be largely a non-definition; it delegates to the court the task of deciding what is reasonable in the circumstances of each particular case, guided no doubt by general acceptance of what reasonableness requires in various classes of cases' (*The Sale of Goods* (5th ed 1975), at 91). The issue, of course, is whether such a flexible concept, which takes its meaning from a background of commercial practice where there may be bargaining equality, is appropriate for consumer transactions.

84 R.S.S. 1978, c C-30, ss 37 and 34(1)

85 'One cannot think of a more expensive and frustrating course than to seek to regulate goods or contract quality through repeated lawsuits' (Leff, supra note 7, at 356).

by this process. A mediator exercises significant discretion in handling complaints. He 'inevitably brings with him certain ideas, knowledge and assumptions, as well as certain interests and concerns, his own and those of people whom he represents ... He is not and cannot be neutral.'[86] If government consumer agencies perceive their role as reactive and as satisfactorily negotiating the problems of the individual consumer without recourse to litigation, what does this imply for the consumer interest?[87] Mediation is generally a compromise which may or may not get what the consumer wants – usually restitution or a refund. It is a private process of negotiation, with government officials acting as 'information brokers' and playing a negotiating role. Like the informal complaint mechanism it may provide the individual consumer with a remedy while doing little to affect business practice or quality control *systematically*. Moreover, the fact that many agencies are understaffed and their concentration on individual complaints may cause them to lose sight of the larger purposes of consumer legislation.

There is no opportunity, given the private nature of the mediation process, either for the generation of the publicity which surrounds a court action or for the development of public norms which might act as a catalyst to changes in other parts of the system.[88] Notwithstanding the limitations of full-scale private litigation, it does at least have the potential to help inform and raise the consciousness of the public and other interest groups in the political process.[89] Mediation might indeed be regarded as a process which defuses consumer problems by fragmenting them and

86 Gulliver, On mediators, in Hamnett (ed) *Social Anthropology and Law* (1977), at 34

87 Belobaba, supra note 2, at 54, suggests that British Columbia was the only province which took a proactive stand towards business practices. The approach in Alberta, as communicated informally to me by the director of trade practices, was that the approach is definitely reactive. It is also of interest to note that in an unpublished paper on consumer protection offered by the Legal Education Society of Alberta, the director states among other things: 'The Director's policy in the past and I believe in the future will be to rely heavily on undertakings, informal assurances, policy statements and guidelines and leave actions in the court as a last resort. I am sure that most clients would generally prefer to have others make their mark in the law reports.' This is rather odd, since two lines above there is the statement 'Certainly the judicial interpretation stage remains an important element in the maturation of this piece of legislation' (*Consumer Protection*: *Both Sides of the Fence* Legal Education Society of Alberta (1980), at 17).

88 This point and the following comments are drawn from a fascinating paper entitled Mediation: A means of cooperating with business, an unpublished paper by S. Silbey delivered at the 1980 Law and Society Association meeting in Madison, Wisconsin. A useful discussion of this role of litigation is also provided in ch 3 of Handler *Social Movements and the Legal System: A Theory of Law Reform and Social Change* (1978). See also Weisbrod and Trubek *Public Interest Law* (1978).

89 For example, it might be interesting to trace the cumulative effects, if any, of cases such as *General Motors Products of Canada Ltd.* v *Kravitz*, supra note 59, or the class action of *Naken* v *General Motors* (1978) 79 D.L.R. (3d.) 718.

keeping them out of public view. It has been described as 'a communicating and learning process leading to some degree of coordination.'[90] But one wonders what a consumer learns – that it would be better to accept the business offer, that the pursuit of private remedies is not the right way to solve the problem? There is, in addition, a clear danger that the norms which are developed through mediation will, given the continuing relationship of business to government, reflect business interests or at best 'reasonable business standards.'[91]

These comments have profound implications, since, as Silbey argues, it extends the influence of business interests beyond the public policy process[92] into the law-enforcement process. It is of fundamental importance to underscore the fact that government agencies may have almost abdicated their crucial role as a general supervisor of the marketplace without at the same time necessarily dealing effectively with individual complaints. They thus fail to carry out either task. It might be argued that a more cost-effective strategy would be for government to subsidize public-interest lawyers or consumer organizations who might provide the 'competence' and 'leverage' for handling individual disputes.[93] The governmental agency could then aid that process by providing systematic information on the marketplace and seeking out general abuses.

I have perhaps overstated the case against mediation and underestimated its role as an inexpensive and informal means of solving a dispute, where independent expert knowledge can be applied. The government agencies are making a genuine attempt to reduce the transaction costs for the consumer in solving his problem. In addition, we must recognize that the small claims court may often perform a similar role to mediation or arbitration, except in a less expert fashion. Thus Sigurdson comments: 'Very often judges do not want to get involved in complex questions of fact or law and will encourage settlement, thus becoming in effect arbitrators. They do not try to play an active role because of the trivial nature, in their

90 Gulliver, supra note 86, at 16

91 See generally Silbey, supra note 88.

92 A useful account of the failure of pluralism in the public policy process is documented in Stanbury (ed) *Business Interests and the Reform of Canadian Competition Policy* (1977). While preparing this article, I attempted to obtain information on the mediation program under the Saskatchewan Consumer Products Warranties Act. The Department of Consumer and Corporate Affairs of the government of Saskatchewan was unable to produce any more than gross figures on the number of cases decided by mediation under the act. It is interesting to note that in the letter from a member of the department it was stated 'We have received excellent co-operation from the business sector in handling problems covered by the Act through the process of mediation and at this time we are not aware of any case law which would be of use to you' (correspondence on file).

93 See generally Cappelletti and Jolowicz, supra note 14.

eyes, of the matter and will often try to reach a compromise either by putting pressure on the parties or by making a 'saw-off' decision.'[94]

My general concern is that these alternative systems for delivering 'justice' to consumers might involve a significant watering down of consumers' rights to access to a judicial forum, and may simply result in a 'buffer' between the individual and the courts. If the purpose of recent consumer legislation is to provide consumers with new rights, then is there not a compromise of these rights involved in mediation? Might not the mediation process reinforce consumers' perceptions that the vindication of their rights is an expensive and wasteful process?

There is a further point. Ease of access to a potentially coercive institution such as a small claims court might provide useful bargaining leverage to a consumer. We do not judge a court's performance solely by what goes on in the courtroom, but also by its effect on bargaining and negotiations. Just as it has been argued that a moderate restriction on creditors' remedies could reduce creditors' leverage in forcing debtors into unfavourable settlements, so greater access to improved small claims courts and innovative remedies such as blacklisting retailers who did not respond to consumer complaints might enhance a consumer's bargaining power with a retailer.[95]

There is finally what Cappelletti calls 'the greatest danger' – 'the risk that streamlined, efficient procedures will abandon the fundamental guarantees of civil procedure – essentially those of an impartial adjudicator and of the parties' right to be heard'[96] and that 'the use of rapid procedures and inexpensive personnel will produce a cheap and unrefined product.'[97]

94 Roine and Sigurdson, supra note 4, at 49

95 See Whitford, A critique of the consumer credit collection system (1979) *Wis. L.R.* 1047. An example of the innovative use of Small Claims Courts was the action taken by the Canadian Automobile Protection Association in relation to the problem of certain automobile manufacturers' 'redating' cars. The association subsidized those consumers in Quebec with complaints by supplying jurisprudence, documentation, and free expert witnesses for the initial test cases. The association's president has argued that the APA's use of the small claims court put pressure on the automobile manufacturers to settle because '(1) A manufacturer's representative had to appear before each of the 84 Small Claims Courts in Quebec, (2) The judiciary was sensitized to the consumer's problems, (3) Journalists publicized extensively the consumer victories causing more lawsuits to be launched, (4) Consumers were encouraged to launch similar lawsuits after learning of other consumer victories, (5) Dealer representatives had to spend much time in court, (6) Customer confidence in imported cars' model year was weakened' (material presented at Small Claims seminar, Canadian Institute for the Administration of Justice, Toronto, Ontario, September 1980 by P. Edmonston, president, Canadian Automobile Protection Association). The association therefore provided the organizational competence for consumer claims and reduced the isolation of the individual complainant.

96 Cappelletti and Garth, supra note 3

97 Ibid, at 291

Another symbolic effect of legislation is its socializing and educative effect. It is possible that lawyers for business may play an important role in transmitting the values represented by the act to their clients.[98] The law may be able to serve what Laurence Tribe calls 'an educational channel for the transmission of advancing ethical demands.'[99] Such symbolic effects may be difficult to measure but should not be discounted.[100]

It might also be hypothesized that passage of this legislation will be regarded as a symbol of the success of consumer protection, especially by those who take an active interest in consumer affairs, complain about consumer products, and expect to obtain redress. The empirical studies suggest that these individuals may be disproportionately from higher socio-economic groups.[101] To this extent, the Saskatchewan legislation may be seen as legitimating 'the system' and vindicating their expectations of a society based on equality before the law. To others who have no such expectations of the system, it may be irrelevant. It is not surprising that studies have indicated that the desire to vindicate one's rights rather than obtain an expedient solution to problems varies directly with income level.[102] The paradox, therefore, is that this consumer legislation may legitimate the system to those individuals who are at present least disadvantaged.

There is thus the public and private face of this act. On one hand, it provides a set of rules which might be described as representing symbolic commitments. These are universal and uniform and provide an individual with remedies which in theory can be exercised in a court which is neither politically accountable nor subject to the lobbying or distortion of

98 See generally Macaulay, supra note 65.

99 Supra note 80, at 99

100 See Belobaba, supra note 2.

101 Macaulay, supra note 65, at 132, provides a useful example of this argument. 'We were told about a case where all of these difficulties were surmounted, and it can serve as an example of how rarely one might expect the consumer case to be taken as far as the complaint stage on the way toward litigation. A wealthy doctor ordered a $500,000 custom-made yacht from a boatyard. He refused to accept delivery, asserting that the boat was defective in many respects. He sued to recover his down payment, and also asked for a large sum as damages. His complaint reflected a high degree of creativity in the blending of traditional and newly developing contract and consumer protection theories. Only the wealthy can afford to pay for such creativity as well as the expert testimony that was called for. The example suggests that consumer protection law may most benefit an unintended population – the wealthy who can afford to pursue individual rights in dealing with the purchase of yachts and other luxury goods. The reformers may have aimed an inadequate weapon at the wrong target.'

102 See Steele, Fraud, disputes and the consumer: Responding to consumer complaints (1975) 123 *U. Pa. L.R.* 1107: Editorial (1978) 12 *Law and Soc. R.* 189. I have been conducting a study of debtors in trouble. The majority of debtors (who were from lower income groups) were not interested in vindicating their rights or contesting their debts but rather wanted an expedient solution to their problems. In addition, it was not surprising that our study indicated that debtor harassment is significantly higher than documented by reported cases or complaints to government agencies.

interest group politics. On the other hand, the overwhelming bulk of the act's everyday application will be potentially subject to the distortions of interest groups, compromise, and discretion. This distinction between the promise and the reality of this consumer legislation is admirably expressed in the following comment calling for consumer class actions. Each phrase seems dripping in irony when applied to the Saskatchewan Act: 'A federal class action law ... will put the power to seek justice in court where it belongs – beyond the reach of campaign contributors, industry lobbyists, or Washington lawyers – and it will put power in the hands of the consumers themselves and in the hands of their own lawyers, retained by them to represent their interests alone.'[103]

## CONCLUSIONS, SPECULATIONS, AND UNANSWERED QUESTIONS

Policy makers should attend carefully to the distinction between individual and group redress mechanisms. I have suggested that a perspective which concentrates primarily on improving individual case-by-case dispute resolution of consumer claims has a number of deficiencies. It is not surprising that an eminent student of comparative civil procedure should state that 'the conclusion seems inescapable that, in our mass production, mass consumption, and mass urbanization society, the days of civil litigation as a merely two-man battle are numbered.'[104] Moreover, informal private systems of individual complaint resolution, whether administered by business or government, may defuse a complaint and leave the consumer with the impression that his claim is trivial. The process may isolate the individual complainant, perhaps reinforcing both the belief that complaining is not desirable and the idea that individuals and not groups have problems and complaints. The few public causes célèbres in the law reports or the newspapers buttress the public opinion that it is only a small percentage of fly-by-night operators who smear the reputation of the vast majority of reputable businessmen. Consumer problems are therefore characterized as individual, not a pervasive aspect of the marketplace.[105]

I argued in the introduction that the key to successful consumer protection lies in measures which are able to 'reconceptualize little injustices as collective harms.'[106] Only if individuals become conscious that they suffer as a group is there likely to be the possibility of a change in the

103 Evidence by Ms Bess Myerson, commissioner of consumer affairs of the City of New York before the Consumer Subcommittee of the U.S. Senate Committee on Commerce, no. 91-48, at 172, cited in Australian Law Reform Commission *Discussion Paper No. 11: Access to the Courts – Class Actions*.

104 Cappelletti and Jolowicz, supra note 14, at 112

105 See Nader *The Great American Gyp* (1968).

106 Nader, supra note 8, at 1021

social perception of complaining and of accepting shoddy products as an inevitable part of life.[107] There may be difficult cultural and social barriers to the recognition of a group consumer interest. However, the aggregation of consumer claims and the mobilization of public opinion are important steps to the success of the resolution of individual problems.[108] Reforms must concentrate on the facilitation of sustained collective activity by consumers at all levels of government – legislative, executive, and judicial. Access at all these levels is access to power. Consumerism is an attempt to obtain a share of political power in a supposedly pluralistic society.[109] The consumer advocate and the class action are two important methods of developing this activity. Other methods of upgrading competence include membership organizations; interest-group sponsors; assigning rights to a third party (for example, a collection agency for consumers); clearing houses which establish a communication network (for example, the 'media ombudsman'); the use of specialized professionals; public-interest law firms; and finally governmentalization.[110] The disenchantment which many commentators have expressed over government enforcement of consumer rights suggests that reformers must seriously consider and study innovative alternatives such as collection agencies for consumer claims. We need to be constantly reminded of the old epigram 'Les derniers qui voyent clair les intérêts de la société sont pour l'ordinaire ceux qui sont payés pour les voir.'[111]

Reformers ought to be sensitive to the different layers of consumer dispute resolution and the relationship between the norms applied at these levels. It is unlikely that we would consider it desirable to channel all

107 Barrington Moore Jr in his work titled *Injustice: The Social Causes of Obedience and Revolt* (1980), explores at 77–9 the cultural and social reasons why people do *not* revolt against unjust and oppressive situations. He notes various mechanisms by which suffering is made to appear part of the inevitable order of things and indicates certain social processes which inhibit efforts to reduce collective pain or suffering: 1 / the extent to which the oppressed group represses any individual defiance through fear of retaliation against the whole group; 2 / the destruction of prior social ties and habits so that individuals are left without social support from other human beings; 3 / fragmentation of an oppressed group into competing groups. He comments that 'It is hardly necessary to add that effective action against the social causes of suffering must be collective.' These difficulties all appear in more muted form in relation to organizing the consumer interest. There are, of course, difficult problems in organizing the consumer interest. See generally Stanbury, supra note 92.

108 Thus, for example, Sigurdson quite rightly notes the central importance of government in changing social perceptions towards small claims court: 'How people think of the Small Claims Court must be changed by the actions of government assisted by aggressive consumer organizations' (supra note 4, at 3).

109 See generally Trebilcock, Winners and losers in the modern regulatory state: Must the consumer always lose? (1975) 13 *Osgoode Hall L.J.* 619.

110 Galanter, supra note 64, at 236–7

111 Pietro Verri *Pensées détachées*, quoted in Cappelletti and Jolowicz, supra note 14, at 13

consumer disputes into the formal system or expect that all resolutions of consumer disputes should apply the norms which a court would. The law may well have a more important indirect or symbolic effect on consumer disputing. Thus it is argued that law 'affects us primarily through communication of symbols – by providing threats, promises, models, persuasion, legitimacy, stigma, etc.'[112] This approach provides a wider and more realistic perspective than one which is solely concerned with 'getting disputants into court.'[113]

The importance of public perceptions in shaping individual decisions concerning consumer problems should make us wary of any policies which are premised solely on the argument that 'this is what most consumers want.' For example, those who argue for greater informal mechanisms suggest this argument, yet policy makers in this area must realize that there really is no such thing as giving people what they want. What a consumer wants depends, among other things, on what resources are available to him, what information he has, and what he perceives as either possible or 'the right thing' to do. These issues are all in turn affected by the position of government.[114] Existing consumer complaints and behaviour in problem solving are both a function of the existing system of informal complaint mechanisms and perhaps a widespread social perception that complaining is not a particularly praiseworthy activity. Approaches to consumer problems which stress mediation, conciliation, and arbitration might indeed be regarded as containing a latent value judgment that consumer claims are trivial or simple and therefore do not require full-scale adjudication. Yet it must be remembered that, through economies of scale, organizations have been able to use the courts to collect debts which might well be considered trivial in amount in the consumer context.[115]

Policy makers ought to hesitate before embracing wholeheartedly alternative consumer dispute-resolution mechanisms such as mediation or arbitration.[116] Mediation is particularly dependent both on the bargaining power of the parties involved and the values and interests of the third-party mediator. Those who point to the success of arbitration in fields such as labour law ought to note that it has been successful in this field not because of the inherent nature of the mechanism but 'because

112 Galanter, supra note 10, at 11
113 Ibid
114 See generally Smart and Williams, supra note 9.
115 This point was made in the United Kingdom Consumer Council study *Justice Out of Reach* (1970), at 5. Sigurdson, supra note 4, also noted at 73, 'I was struck by the number of professional firms who took advantage of the Small Claims Court to collect insignificant sums.'
116 See generally Tomasic, Mediation as an alternative to adjudication, supra note 11.

collective bargaining has established a rough equality and mutual respect between the parties.'[117] A pervasive problem, therefore, of all informal and market mechanisms is that they are significantly dependent on the continuing competence and power of the parties involved. While the studies of complaint handling indicate the potential for market mechanisms and complaints to solve individual problems, they also suggest that they are unlikely to be optimally effective unless this basic problem can be overcome.[118]

Greater access to a reformed small claims court system[119] might provide a consumer with more effective redress than mediation. It might also produce the greatest psychological satisfaction and reinforce a consumer's feeling of competence. It might also, notwithstanding what I have said above, be 'what a consumer wants,' since any consumer who is willing to take a complaint beyond a seller is probably not interested in mediation.[120] If greater access resulted in greater use, then the information on disputes gathered by the small claims court could provide a valuable input into regulatory activity. If greater publicity was given to the norms that are generated at this level there would be a significant development of legal doctrine which in turn might have an educative and political effect, particularly on lawyers. Moreover, if consumers had easier access to an institution with coercive power, then this might have an effect on two-party complaining. I have argued that a consumer at this latter level would have a more credible bargaining position in threatening to take legal action rather than simply threatening to go to the Better Business Bureau or governmental mediation.

It is also clear that government agencies must be more active both in seeking out those markets where complaint needs to be reinforced and identifying those market relationships where sellers have little incentive to prevent consumer mistakes. In addition, the defects of both market and legal redress mechanisms as methods of systematic quality control indicate that much greater attention should be paid by government to regulating specific product standards.

While lawyers have already played an important role in the consumer-protection movement, Macaulay's article suggests that reformers may be creating individual consumer rights 'without providing the means to carry them out. Grand declarations of rights may be personally rewarding to those who struggle for legislative and appellate victories, but, in practice,

117 Getman, Labour arbitration and dispute resolution (1978–79) 88 *Yale L.J.* 917, at 948

118 Ziegel, supra note 14, at 192

119 See Ison, Small claims (1972) 35 *Mod. L.R.* 18

120 Best and Andreasen, supra note 23, at 734

justice is rationed by cost barriers and the lawyer's long range interests.'[121] Consumer law must be made more economically attractive to lawyers, and those who practise in the consumer area may have to discard some of the traditional models of legal practice. Lawyers have skills in negotiating, organizing, and obtaining access to information. They may be able to play a key role not only in the courtroom but in acting as continuing aid to consumer groups. For example, reformers ought not to underestimate the potential socializing and educative effect of public-interest litigation which might act as a catalyst for change in other parts of the political process.[122] If an important goal of consumer protection is to change existing consumer perceptions of social reality, then lawyers might be well suited to accomplish this consciousness-raising role. The law schools also have an important responsibility not only to make consumer law a respectable branch of the law but also to sensitize students to the political and social context of consumer problems.[123] This brings me to my final conclusion.

There is a need in Canada for serious socio-legal research on the pathology of consumer disputes, on the roles of the actors involved, on the functioning of the various formal and informal redress mechanisms, and on the role of governmental regulatory agencies in this process. We know that existing data on consumer complaints collected by government and other third parties are inadequate. Yet we know little about the private decisions and behaviour which determine the nature and number of problems which are brought to public officials and institutions. For example, it may be extremely misleading to assume that the financial disincentives are the most important factor preventing consumers enforcing their rights.[124] The lack of any systematic socio-legal research in this and in other areas is a serious indictment of the Canadian academic legal profession. Without this type of research, it must unfortunately be concluded that policy making in this area, as in other areas of consumer protection, will 'remain what it has always been – at best an exercise in accidental wisdom.'[125]

121 Macaulay, supra note 65, at 161

122 See generally Handler supra note 88.

123 See, eg, (1977–78) 29 *Journal of Legal Education* 352.

124 Belobaba, supra note 2, at 363. Sigurdson, however, stressed the importance of public perceptions, and see also Ladinsky et al, supra note 11, at 6: 'The organized legal profession tends to explain channeling as one of differential access due primarily to cost barriers. From a sociological perspective that is a deceptively over-simple explanation.'

125 Trebilcock, The pathology of consumer credit breakdown (1975) 22 *McGill L.J.* 415, at 467

*Appendix A: Sampling – Edmonton Study*

247 businesses were randomly selected from 1204 businesses listed under 24 categories in the *Edmonton Business Directory*. Every department store listed was included in the sample, and in every other category approximately one fifth of the total number of listed businesses was included. This procedure was followed in order to ensure an adequate sample size for department stores which, it was felt, play an especially important role vis-à-vis the consumer.

Each of the selected businesses was sent a copy of the questionnaire reproduced in appendix B, together with a letter describing the study and requesting the co-operation of the store manager in filling out the questionnaire. A follow-up letter and a second copy of the questionnaire were sent out approximately three weeks later to each of the businesses which had not yet responded.

Altogether, 130 businesses responded by returning completed questionnaires. Of these, 24 were not usable because the businesses were not retail outlets but rather wholesale outlets or providers of services only. Thus the data analyses are based on a group of 106 respondents.

The 106 respondents were grouped into fifteen categories describing types of businesses or types of goods sold. The categories and the number of respondents in each were as follows:

| | |
|---|---|
| appliance | 3 |
| art and craft supplies | 2 |
| automotive supplies (including tires) | 6 |
| clothing and shoes | 18 |
| department stores | 11 |
| floors, wallcoverings, paint, draperies | 7 |
| furniture | 6 |
| hardware | 3 |
| jewellers | 4 |
| pharmacies | 11 |
| sound equipment, photographic equipment, musical instruments | 5 |
| sporting goods | 8 |
| perishable goods (health food stores, cigarette shops, confectioners, delicatessens) | 6 |
| stationery and book stores, music dealers | 4 |
| miscellaneous (eg, antiques, boutiques, fabrics, gifts, leather goods) | 12 |
| | 106 |

*Appendix B: Questionnaire*

1 / Name of store
2 / Are you part of a regional, national, or international organization?
3 / Gross sales per year (approximately)
4 / Do you allow customers to return goods for:
  a / a refund of the purchase price?
  b / a store credit?
  c / an exchange for another product?
5 / If so, what limitations do you place on the return of goods, eg:
  a / time limits?
  b / type of goods?
  c / proof of sale?
  d / must it be established that the goods are not satisfactory? Do you check the goods and come to your own conclusion?
6 / What other service(s) do you provide for dissatisfied customers?
7 / What do you do with returned goods?
8 / Could you estimate the percentage of sales returned?
9 / Please give a rough estimate of the cost to you of the service(s) you have described (including the refunding of the purchase price of returned goods).
10 / Are the policies that you have described in any way determined by your suppliers?

# [14]

Review Essay

## Who Speaks For The Consumer? Nader's *No Access to Law* and Best's *When Consumers Complain*

Susan S. Silbey

LAURA NADER, ed., *No Access to Law: Alternatives to the American Judicial System*. New York: Academic Press, 1980. Pp. xxiii + 540. Cloth $27.50; paper $12.95.

ARTHUR BEST, *When Consumers Complain*. New York: Columbia University Press, 1981. Pp. xi + 232. $16.95.

### Introduction

Consumer protection is not new; it dates from classical and medieval times, when trade regulation based on religious and social precepts was common. In the history of Western law, caveat emptor, the antithesis of consumer protection, is a relatively modern development of the market economy.[1] It embodies the dominant philosophy of both the Enlightenment and liberalism—a conscious abandonment of each individual to his/her own devices with a minimum of control, a minimum of fair practice standards, and a consequent maximum of individual autonomy. Caveat emptor incorporates the spirit of individualism into the law of market relations by expressing an ordinary rule of prudence: the consumer must use his/her own faculties to

**Susan S. Silbey** is Assistant Professor, Department of Sociology, Wellesley College. B.A. Brooklyn College, City University of New York; Ph.D. 1978, University of Chicago.

1. Caveat emptor first appeared in written works in 1534 in a legal discussion by Fitzherbert on horse trading. The sixteenth-century scholar wrote that "if he be tame and have ben rydden upon, then *caveat emptor*." *Quoted in* Walton H. Hamilton, The Ancient Maxim Caveat Emptor, 40 Yale L.J. 1133, 1164 (1931). Hamilton cites another passage where the same writer "cautions the buyer to make sure of the goodness of this bargain in horse-flesh while yet there is time, if the horse be sold without a warranty, it is 'at the other's peril, for his eyes and his taste ought to be his judges.'" *Id.* By the beginning of the seventeenth century, the maxim was well known, having twice been set down in treatises by Coke. The often-cited passage runs, "Note that by the civil law every man is bound to warrant the thing he selleth or conveyeth, albeit there be no express warranty, either in deed or in law; but the common law bindeth him not, for *caveat emptor*." The phrase was discovered in the law reports in 1601 as an aside in a case concerning the ravishment of a wealthy ward, Moore v. Hussey, Hobart 94, 80 Eng. Rep. 243 (1601), but it is in 1603, in the case of Chandelor v. Lopus, Cro. Jac. 4, 79 Eng. Rep. 3 (1603), that the principle of the vendor's nonresponsibility for his wares was formulated in such an authoritative manner that it has been cited as the foundation for successive decisions over the centuries. In this case, the purchaser of what turned out to be a worthless bezoar stone sought to recover in an action against the seller for deceit. A bezoar stone was thought to have magical powers to be used as an antidote against poisons. "[T]he bare affirmation that it was a bezar-stone, without warranting it to be so, is no cause of action; and although he knew it to be no bezar stone, it is not material; for every one in selling his wares will affirm that his wares are good, or the horse that he sells sound, yet if he does not warrant them to be so, it is no cause of action."

assess the worth and quality of the goods s/he purchases and must not expect remedies or protections against unsatisfactory, deceptive, or misrepresentative transactions.

By the end of the seventeenth century, caveat emptor was firmly established in English and American law, although never so absolutely as to deny the possibility of limited remedies against some market losses.[2] Private remedies at law for deceit and misrepresentation, *malum prohibitum* legislation, licensing and registration regulations, federal regulation of business, and assorted claims adjustment services provided a range of remedies for unsatisfactory transactions. Nevertheless, consumer advocates claimed that these private legal actions, mediating agencies, and public attempts at protective legislation did not effectively meet the needs of consumer protection. The costs were too high, the proof too difficult, the enforcement too inadequate, and the machinery of administration and judicial review too cumbersome.[3]

During the 1960s an active consumer movement demanded new approaches to consumer protection.[4] Ralph Nader began his campaign against unsafe automobiles and developed this interest into a sustained research and publicity effort aimed at exposing the mechanics of government regulation. In 1963, David Caplovitz's *The Poor Pay More*[5] was published as the first systematic inquiry into the plight of low-income consumers. In 1964, President Lyndon B. Johnson appointed a Committee on Consumer Interests to monitor and report on consumer problems. In 1966, Congress passed five consumer protection laws, having passed only two within the eight previous

2. Clarence J. Morrow, Warranty of Quality: A Comparative Survey, 14 Tul. L. Rev. 327 (1940); William H. Traylor, Consumer Protection Against Sellers Misrepresentations, 20 Mercer L. Rev. 414 (1969).

3. Samuel Williston, Liability for Honest Misrepresentation, 24 Harv. L. Rev. 415 (1911); Hamilton, *supra* note 1; K. N. Llewellyn, On Warranty of Quality, and Society, 36 Colum. L. Rev. 699 (1936); Samuel Williston, The Law Governing Sales of Goods at Common Law and Under the Uniform Sales Act (rev. ed. New York: Baker, Voorhis & Co., 1948); Rudolf Callmann, False Advertising as a Competitive Tort, 48 Colum. L. Rev. 876 (1948); Translating Sympathy for Deceived Consumers into Effective Programs for Protection, 114 U. Pa. L. Rev. 395 (1966); Richard J. Barber, The Government and the Consumer, 64 Mich. L. Rev. 1203 (1966); Developments in the Law: Deceptive Advertising, 80 Harv. L. Rev. 1005 (1967); Comment: Consumer Legislation and the Poor, 76 Yale L.J. 745 (1967); Note, State Consumer Protection: A Proposal, 53 Iowa L. Rev. 710 (1967); David A. Rice, Remedies, Enforcement Procedures and the Duality of Consumer Transaction Problems, 48 B.U.L. Rev. 559 (1968); Frederick Emerson Waddell, Consumer Action to Overrule Caveat Emptor: The Key to Quality, 4 New Eng. L. Rev. 89 (1969).

4. The late 1960s saw the third wave of active consumerism in American politics, following earlier campaigns during the Populist/Progessive and New Deal eras. What can be conceived of as constant pressure by consumers crystallized and solidified at certain periods to demand specific responses from government. Cf. Fred Block, The Ruling Class Does Not Rule: Notes on the Marxist Theory of the State, Socialist Revolution, May-June 1977, at 6; Mark V. Nadel, The Politics of Consumer Protection (Indianapolis: Bobbs-Merrill, 1971). The phrases, "public interest liberalism," "interest group liberalisms" (Theodore J. Lowi, The End of Liberalism: Ideology, Policy, and the Crisis of Public Authority (New York: W. W. Norton, 1969)), and "interest group representation" (Joel Handler, Social Movements and the Legal System: A Theory of Law Reform and Social Change (New York: Academic Press, 1979)) are used to describe this responsiveness of public policy to organized group demands. Groups pressure directly through political processes for specific legislative or administrative action and through the courts and legal system as a means of obtaining benefits from government. Cf. Karen Orren, Standing to Sue: Interest Group Conflict in the Federal Courts, 70 Am. Pol. Sci. Rev. 723 (1976).

5. David Caplovitz, The Poor Pay More (New York: Free Press, 1967).

sessions. Congress gave consideration to creating a department of consumer affairs, and Senator Warren Magnuson was conducting investigations into what he called the *Dark Side of the Marketplace.*[6]

The consequences of these efforts were to heighten public consciousness, mobilize interest group support for consumer protection, and focus political attention on two principal concerns: (1) the inability of consumers to purchase satisfactory products and services or to obtain redress for unsatisfactory purchases, and (2) the acute economic plight of less advantaged consumers—exacerbated by lack of shopping skills, of funds to make cash purchases or obtain favorable credit, and of access to alternative markets or to the legal system.

Fifteen years after this most recent wave of consumerism began, Laura Nader et al., in *No Access to Law,* and Arthur Best, in *When Consumers Complain,* tell us that the situation is not much improved. There is no access to justice, and consumers cannot get satisfaction when they complain. For both authors, consumer complaints are a sample of a larger universe of unarticulated legal problems that reflect a generalized but unsatisfied demand for justice.

Nader's book raises to highest priority consideration of the contradictions inherent in Anglo-American legal traditions. She challenges outright the individualistic assumptions of caveat emptor and the law of a market society. For Nader, the achievements of liberal legalism—minimum control and maximum autonomy—are problematic, demanding fundamental reconstruction of the basic principles of our legal order. This is an important and provocative book. It is a strong call for consumer justice, and as such offers an opportunity to discuss aspects of the "access to justice" movement in law and society research as well as research on consumer-initiated complaints.

Best covers similar empirical territory but is more narrowly focused on the process of consumer complaining than on the theoretical issues of social control generally. *When Consumers Complain* reports the histories of 132 consumer complaints, the difficulties in perceiving and voicing complaints, as well as the difficulties in obtaining redress for those complaints that are perceived and voiced. There is some overlap between the two books, although the Nader volume is clearly the more extensive presentation. I concentrate on the research and theses in *No Access to Law,* referring to *When Consumers Complain* (and additional literature) to elaborate and highlight points in Nader's analysis.

In section I of this essay, I present Nader's argument that the American legal system provides limited access to justice. Based on original empirical research and a review of the literature on internal complaint handling in a wide variety of settings and forms, Nader concludes that obtaining consumer justice requires systematic aggregation of consumer grievances, which will not be accomplished easily. The source of the problem is the inequality between

6. Warren G. Magnuson & Jean Carper, The Dark Side of the Market Place: The Plight of the American Consumer (Englewood Cliffs, N.J.: Prentice-Hall, 1968).

consumers and businesses rooted deep in the capitalist organization of production, distribution, and exchange and in the legal ideology supporting capitalism. Because consumers as individuals must confront corporations as collectivities, and because the relationship is face to faceless, a fundamental inequality exists. Pervasive inequality restricts consumers' ability to influence the production of reliable and useful goods and limits redress when goods are unreliable and unsatisfactory. Lacking collective identity, organization, and action, consumers are systematically disenfranchised. Moreover, the law perpetuates this subordination and relative powerlessness because it rests on the fiction that businesses and consumers are equals.

In response to the inadequacies of legal devices to remedy the consumer's dilemma, Nader et al. suggest a program of collective action, supported by changes in law to facilitate and encourage such action. Organized consumers can challenge the power of corporations by challenging individualistic legal ideology and complaint handling. The authors urge that consumer grievances be regarded as public rights rather than private claims and that the guardianship of these rights be the responsibility of specially created private organizations. Wishing to challenge not only traditional legal ideology but also the monopoly of social control by the state, Nader recommends a form of corporatism as an alternative to liberal legalism.

I generally share Nader's diagnosis and am sympathetic with her passion for social justice, but these proposals may rearrange rather than resolve matters. Although I agree that consumers have serious problems, this book, I fear, offers an inadequate analysis of the forces that create and sustain such problems and render them resistant to change. Its major strength, however, lies in its vigorous political and organizing statement.

*No Access to Law* seems to lament the loss of agrarian community life and makes a plea for the kinds of social interactions that prevailed in smaller more homogeneous communities of relatively equal members. Nader argues that our legal system is rooted in our agrarian past and must change because those communities no longer exist. But this argument has several conceptual and analytic flaws. One, our commercial law descends primarily from the merchant law of medieval towns, not from the customary law of agrarian communities. Two, the argument is idealist because the forms of law and grievance-handling mechanisms it advocates presupposes the existence of traditional social relations uncharacteristic of modern society. The analysis is generally ahistorical, abstracting the legal foundation of consumer problems—liberal legalism—from the social organization in which it grew and flourished. Consequently, the proposed solutions are unconnected to empirical social relations.

In section II, I examine the idealist framework underlying this argument and the questions it directs attention to: What constitutes access? What constitutes adequate response? Does the evidence support the authors' conclusions? From research on nine different grievance-handling mechanisms, the authors reject all but two, a media hotline and a grassroots consumer action group, on the grounds that only these organizations fulfill the criteria of their preferred model of responsive complaint handling. The authors contend that an appropriate and successful consumer agency would have the capacity for generalized and prescriptive remedies. Although the authors prefer participatory and accessible organizations, they advocate centralization in order to promote aggregation of claims and preventive solutions and reject conventional political office because of its susceptibility to corruption and particularism. It is ironic that the authors reject the most successful agency studied—a congressional office—because of its attention to constituency service and select as models organizations that have failed to provide higher rates of successful complaint resolution or even to sustain the organization itself. The authors' idealization of organization causes them to ignore the ambiguities and trade-offs inherent in different forms of organization and tends to obscure the recognition of similarities between the proposed reforms and existing structures.

The authors argue that an increase in complaints and disputes is a sign of both community disorganization and powerlessness; but it is unclear from the research that registering grievances tells us much about powerlessness or about community organization. Indeed, the evidence presented in these works and elsewhere suggests that complaining may be associated with higher socioeconomic status and therefore presumably with relatively greater social power. The analysis suggests but does not substantiate a link between consumer grievances and community organization and power by advocating a society in which grievances could be avoided and prevented. Nevertheless, the notion of a grievance-free society is not explored either theoretically or empirically.

Finally, in section III, I suggest that we are lacking a theory of complaint behavior necessary to answer questions about the relationship between consumer grievances, expectations, and fundamental processes of social control. I examine what Nader et al. provide or do not provide toward such a theory because of the limitations of their framework. Here, I draw upon Best's work to elaborate aspects of the analysis. I argue that we need to know more about what consumers expect when they engage in market transactions in order to develop conceptions of satisfaction, grievance, remedy, and right for a theory of complaint behavior. Consumer expectations develop within and emerge out of the culture of buying and selling and the use practices that organize our commercial and private lives. Without this context, it is not possible to assess the responsiveness or adequacy of existing mechanisms of redress.

## I. No Access to Justice

The research reported in the Nader et al. and Best volumes grew directly from Nader's earlier work among the isolated villagers of Oaxaca, Mexico. Intrigued by her observation of the interdependence of modes of formal and informal social control among the Zapotec, Nader began inquiries into functionally equivalent institutions in other cultures.[7] She began to study American culture when, as she states, an image began to form in her mind of a legal system that seemed to have no place for "most people's legal problems" (at xvii). Nader and a group of researchers from the Center for Responsive Law submitted a proposal to the Carnegie Corporation to establish a research center concentrating on existing grievance-handling organizations. It was the sixties; "old and new institutions. . . were developing as alternatives to a legal system that was unresponsive to legal problems" (at xviii). More than merely seeking to understand the legal system and its alternatives, Nader wanted to participate actively in changing these institutions.

*No Access to Law* and *When Consumers Complain* are both products of this research. Nader provides a full description of the research framework and an analysis of the results in two introductory chapters, one of which is coauthored by Christopher Shugart.[8] This constitutes 20% of the text; the remaining portion, written by Nader's students and associates, is divided between two chapters describing the content of consumer complaints and nine detailed examinations of particular complaint-handling agencies.

Nader's thesis is simple:

> An ideal complaint-handling system would, with speed and fairness, resolve grievances and would be part of an early alert to head off future similar complaints by providing public agencies with data with which to do their jobs better. An ideal system would also disclose aggregate patterns of abuse or injustice and would provide people with a competitive number of private and public avenues and forums within which to pursue just treatment. It would work for prevention an deterrence. (At 28)

Our legal system fails to meet Nader's ideal because, she claims, it was developed in small-scale agricultural communities and is no longer adequate or appropriate for an industrial society of "strangers of unequal power" (at 29).

Limited access to law is a social deficiency, according to Nader, only if there are no alternatives. Following Nader's earlier work identifying a variety of grievance-handling mechanisms in Zapotec society, the researchers sought to locate similar alternatives for resolving consumer grievances in American society. Research was conducted in a wide array of complaint-handling forums, confirming observations made elsewhere that consumer protection has taken the form of nongeneral, noncumulative, case-by-case resolution of individual complaints. Agencies are often passive, relying on consumer initiative to combat systematic product and service failures, as well as organized fraud and deception.[9]

7. Laura Nader, An Analysis of Zapotec Law Cases, 3 Ethnology 404 (1964); Choices in Legal Procedure: Shia Moslem and Mexican Zapotec, 67 Am. Anthropologist 394 (1965); Talea and Juquila: A Comparison of Zapotec Social Organization, 48 Am. Archaeology & Ethnology 195 (1964); Styles of Court Procedure: To Make the Balance, *in* Laura Nader, ed., Law in Culture and Society (Chicago: Aldine Publishing Co., 1969); Powerlessness in Zapotec and U.S. Societies, *in* Anthropological Studies, Raymond D. Fogelson & Richard N. Adams, eds. (New York: Academic Press, 1977).

8. Laura Nader & Christopher Shugart, Old Solutions for Old Problems, *in* Nader, at 57.

9. See Iain D. C. Ramsay, Consumer Redress Mechanisms for Poor-Quality and Defective Products, 31 U. Toronto L.J. 117 (1981); Philip G. Schrag, Counsel for the Deceived: Case Studies in Consumer

The grievance-handling mechanisms studied fall into one of three stages of "the disputing process": (1) internal complaint handling by sellers, (2) non-binding third-party review and binding third-party arbitration (including law enforcement agencies),[10] and (3) service and informational organizations (e.g., Better Business Bureaus and media complaint managers),[11] congressional offices,[12] individual businesses,[13] as well as trade associations,[14] labor unions,[15] and grassroots consumer groups.[16] Few of these organizations meet Nader's criteria for the ideal complaint-processing forum. Moreover, the availability of levels of complaint-handling systems "ensures that consumers are not too suddenly and unambiguously confronted with their powerlessness" (at 39). Nader reiterates the insight of an earlier generation of social critics that mechanisms of redress and responsiveness diffuse claims of denied access and injustice, in this case exacerbating and masking the relative powerlessness of consumers vis-a-vis businesses.[17]

Following a review of the literature on internal complaint handling, non-binding third-party mediators, arbitration, and adjudication, Nader concludes that although systematic aggregation of consumer grievances is required for consumer justice, this will not be accomplished easily. The source of the inequality between consumers and business is rooted deep in the social organization of production, distribution, and exchange and in the legal ideology supporting it.

Nader and Shugart note that because the individual consumer must confront the corporation as a collectivity, and because the relationship is face to faceless, a fundamental inequality has developed. Although legal fictions attempt to mask this inequality, the fact remains that while the consumer does not individually negotiate the terms of his/her transaction (e.g., the prolif-

---

Fraud (New York: Pantheon Books, 1972); Eric H. Steele, The Dilemma of Consumer Fraud: Prosecute or Mediate, 61 A.B.A. J. 1230 (1975); *id.*, Fraud, Dispute, and the Consumer: Responding to Consumer Complaints, 123 U. Pa. L. Rev. 1107 (1975); William C. Whitford & Spencer L. Kimball, Why Process Consumer Complaints? A Case Study of the Office of the Commissioner of Insurance of Wisconsin, 1974 Wis. L. Rev. 639; Susan S. Silbey, Case Processing: Consumer Protection in an Attorney General's Office, 15 Law & Soc'y Rev. 849 (1981); *id.*, The Consequences of Responsive Regulation *in* Keith Hawkins & John Thomas, eds., Enforcing Regulation (Boston: Kluwer Nijhoff, 1984); Susan S. Silbey & Egon Bittner, The Availability of Law, 4 Law & Pol'y Q. 399 (1982).

10. David Serber, Resolution or Rhetoric: Managing Complaints in the California Development of Insurance, *in* Nader, at 317.

11. Marian Eaton, The Better Business Bureau: "The Voice of the People in the Marketplace" *in* Nader, at 223; Michael C. Mattice, Media in the Middle: A Study of the Mass Media Complaint Managers, *in* Nader, at 485.

12. Angela Karikas, Solving Problems in Philadelphia: An Ethnography of a Congressional District Office, *in* Nader, at 345.

13. Angela Karikas & Rena Rosenwasser, Department Store Complaint Management, *in* Nader, at 283; David I. Greenberg, Easy Terms, Hard Times: Complaint Handling in the Ghetto, *in* Nader, at 379.

14. David I. Greenberg & Thomas H. Stanton, Business Groups, Consumer Problems: The Contradiction of Trade Association Complaint Handling, *in* Nader, at 193.

15. Elaine Combs-Schilling, Grieving and Feuding: The Organizational Dilemma of a Labor Union, *in* Nader, at 461.

16. Gregory Wilson & Elizabeth Brydolf, Grass Roots Solutions: San Francisco Consumer Action, *in* Nader, at 417.

17. Compare Herbert Marcuse, One Dimensional Man: Studies in the Ideology of Advanced Industrial Society (Boston: Beacon Press, 1964); Robert Paul Wolff et al., The Critique of Pure Tolerance (Boston: Beacon Press, 1969).

eration of contracts of adhesion), he/she must individually grieve any dissatisfaction deriving from the transaction. "Relations are no longer between groups, nor are they between individuals; rather they are between a social group on the one hand and an individual on the other" (at 48). Nader and Shugart identify seven ideological concepts that control and weaken the impact of laws and efforts on behalf of consumers: caveat emptor, custom treatment of complaint cases, equality before the law, confidentiality, deviant status of complainants, the state as legal guardian of public rights, and the fiction of the corporation as a person (at 61–70).

The collective argument in *No Access to Law* is that consumers must organize in order to challenge the power of corporations; this must be accomplished by challenging the premises and organization of our current complaint-handling processes, especially individual handling of consumer complaints and the individualist legal ideology. Because the sources of consumer grievances and adequate remedies are beyond the particularities of individual complaints, the authors suggest that consumer grievances should be regarded as public rights, rather than private claims. Moreover, they argue, the guardianship of these rights should not be left to public agencies, because such agencies have not been responsive to consumer problems as a public issue. The heart of their proposal for reform calls for the establishment of private organizations to protect public rights. It is time, Nader et al. argue, to challenge not only traditional legal ideology but also the monopoly of social control by the state that supports and is in turn supported by this ideology.

Only through bloc organizing of consumer interests can consumer representatives gain the advantages that go with repeated involvement in the legal system.[18] "Because organizations are better equipped to become repeat players, consumers, by organizing, can deal with corporations on a more equal footing" (at 88). A restructuring of legal relations could, in turn, challenge the ideological and doctrinal sources of inadequate remedies for consumer grievances—such as the legal fiction of the corporation as person.[19] Greater equality between business and consumer could result in delegalization of disputes, mutual accommodation, and structural change in the judicial system. The final and preferred outcome of aggregate actions on behalf of consumers would be preventive sanctions: publicity, "capital punishment" for seriously offending corporations,[20] and positive legal duties attached to specific corporate roles. This can be accomplished, the authors argue, through the aggregation of claims, such as class action suits, that would be used to pierce the corporate veil.

18. Marc Galanter, Why the "Haves" Come Out Ahead: Speculations on the Limits of Legal Change, 9 Law & Soc'y Rev. 95 (1974).

19. Compare Christopher D. Stone, Where the Law Ends: The Social Control of Corporate Behavior (New York: Harper & Row, 1975); *id.*, Stalking the Wild Corporation, Working Papers for a New Society, Spring 1976, at 17.

20. Some consumer protection statutes now provide for the dissolution of business enterprises that are shown to be habitual violators of the law. Studies of enforcement practices suggest, however, that it is unlikely that the ultimate sanctions under the law will be applied. See Silbey, Case Processing, *supra* note 9; Silbey & Bittner, *supra* note 9; Silbey, Consequences of Responsive Regulation, *supra* note 9.

By her attention to organization as the key to restructuring legal relationships, Nader makes a significant contribution to the study of consumer protection. Nader is aware that piecemeal solutions have been tried and failed; thus she suggests that her proposed solutions "are now begging to be dealt with at once rather than serially" (at 99). Although the recommendations she suggests are largely within the realm of law, she believes that lawyers will be inadequate to the task of fashioning reforms because they are too preoccupied by disputes and differences. The solutions to consumer problems will "need to be fashioned by professionals at ease with prevention" (at 49). Nader cites China and the Hopi[21] as examples of societies where avoidance and prevention are common; these agricultural societies of face-to-face relationships, she argues, can provide models for the reform of our own laws. Nader concludes that despite the fact that consumer grievances are symptoms of larger societal problems, "[s]olving the consumer complaint problem will allow people to stop focusing their discontent on this level and allow them to move on to grapple with the more fundamental questions" (at 102).

## II. An Ideal Complaint-handling System

*No Access to Law* includes the kind of rich descriptive studies necessary for general theoretical analyses. Moreover, because the research covers an extensive variety of public, private, and voluntary organizations, the authors offer several valuable observations about the systemic problems of complaint handling. The criticism of consumer protection as disaggregated, encumbered by a constricting legal discourse, private where it should be public (consumer grievances), and public where it could be private (enforcement), is well taken. Consumers are in a predicament. They complain in order to redress their immediate losses; at the same time, they have an interest in general solutions for consumers as a group. It is difficult to quarrel with this assessment, or with the observation that the consumer's predicament is compounded by features of consumer agencies and the structure of existing remedies. The authors are right to point out that there are no quick fixes for conflicts that emerge from fundamental structural sources.

Ironically, the strengths of *No Access to Law* lay the foundation for its weaknesses. The authors suggest that an appropriate response to consumer grievances would be generalized, organized, centralized, and professionalized, and would obliterate the distinction between public and private. Although, according to the authors, the legal system has failed to provide access to law or justice, they nonetheless envision solutions involving more law. These reforms might recreate the exact problems the authors seek to remedy.

The source of this confusion—as to what access means in a liberal legal structure—seems to lie in the idealism that frames the analysis. Nader begins with an a priori definition of an ideal complaint-processing system and re-

21. Bruce Alden Cox, Law and Conflict Management Among the Hopi (Ph.D. diss., University of California, Berkeley, 1968); Victor H. Li, Law Without Lawyers: A Comparative View of Law in China and the United States (Stanford, Cal.: Stanford Alumni Association, 1977).

ports the discrepancy between reality and the ideal.[22] As such, it makes nonproblematic what is actually quite problematic in legal practice—how people (consumers, lawyers, and businesses) construct legal systems through their interactions. The framework of idealism leads to a circularity in the argument; the analysis begins with assumptions about fairness, justice, the rule of law, and the universe of grievances and concludes by arguing that grievances are universal and unremediated, which is neither fair nor just but which is solvable through a revised notion of the rule of law. Nader argues that we should work to realize the ancient maxim of equity, "Every right should have a remedy." But legality is not a matter of remedies inferred from rights; it is exactly the reverse. Rights exist only insofar as remedies are provided by law.[23] The issue of legality in general, and consumer rights in particular, is thus transformed by Nader from an empirical and problematic phenomenon to a policy preference.

The desire to forge a general solution for consumer grievances is laudable, as is the desire to build these solutions from the bottom up. But Nader's picture of successful complaint management seems to be based on reified and idealized notions of organization and community as well as of the legalities involved. The solutions are premised on a different social order than what we in fact have. Thus, the conditions under which consumers do or do not have remedies, and therefore rights, is inadequately examined in this book. Ideal ahistorical conceptions of organization, community, and law lack measures to apply to the study of complaint mechanisms and complaint behavior. Moreover, it is difficult to measure access when access to justice itself may be a political ideology.[24] In short, the idealist framework weakens the work's significant observations of the relationship between the social organization of production, processes of social control, and the structure of legal practices and ideology.

### A. Ideal and Reified Organizations

*No Access to Law* contains studies of nine different redress mechanisms,

22. Although the authors emphasize the discrepancy between theory and practice, the work is not a typical "gap" study. Many empirical studies examining "the 'gap' between the *ideal* of law and the *actual* practices" do not specify legal goals or ideals but view them as self-evident and nonproblematic. See Malcolm M. Feeley, The Concept of Laws in Social Science: A Critique and Notes on an Expanded View, 10 Law & Soc'y Rev. 497, 497 (1976). Best and Nader both specifically delineate an ideal, albeit without much explication or justification, and without much attention to whether this ideal has any empirical referent in this or any other culture. The research is an examination of the gap between what is truly an "ideal" grievance-handling procedure and the behavior of real grievance-handling mechanisms. Thus the finding that reality is deficient is hardly surprising. See the discussion of idealized conceptions of law and legal systems in Christine B. Harrington, Delegalization Reform Movements: A Historical Analysis, *in* 1 Richard L. Abel, ed., The Politics of Informal Justice 35 (2 vols. New York: Academic Press, 1982, 1983). Further, the appropriate role of evaluative statements in the sociology of law is the subject of intense debate. See, e.g., Donald J. Black, Review *of Law, Society, and Industrial Justice*, by Philip Selznick, Philippe Nonet, & Howard M. Vollmer, 78 Am. J. Soc. 709 (1972); *id.*, The Boundaries of Legal Sociology, 81 Yale L.J. 1086 (1972); Philippe Nonet, For Jurisprudential Sociology, 10 Law & Soc'y Rev. 525 (1976).

23. E.g., Oliver Wendell Holmes, Jr., The Common Law (Boston: Little, Brown & Co., 1945).

24. See, Harrington, *supra* note 22, and generally Abel, *supra* note 22.

which are evaluated by the respective authors, and by Shugart and Nader, in light of a preferred model that emphasizes aggregation and collective action. Nader et al. reject all but two of the nine, a media hotline and a grassroots consumer action group. The authors claim that these mechanisms provide the broadest possible access, self-help, capacity for aggregation, and possibilities of politicization and mobilization of consumers. At the same time, however, the complaint-handling agencies that are rejected are evaluated not by these standards but by the criteria of formal organizations, favoring centralization, hierarchy, differentiation of tasks, and generalizability of practice. The idealization of the virtues of organization per se leads the authors to ignore the ambiguities and trade-offs inherent in particular forms of organization and response. For example, traditional individual economic action (department store complaint management) and politics (congressional district office) are among the few examples of successful complaint handling examined in the volume, but they are criticized by the authors because they are not centralized and bureaucratic.[25]

Although the authors argue that consumer protection requries organization and political action, they reject the model of the most successful agency studied, the office of Congressman William Aloysius Barrett of Philadelphia. Karikas writes that Barrett provided accessible, flexible, and responsive service for his constituents. Moreover, by seeing over 50,000 voters per year, he was speaking personally with approximately 10% of his constituency on matters of direct personal relevance. Yet his office cannot be considered an ideal complaint-handling forum according to Karikas and Nader, because it misdirected Barrett from his "real" functions in Washington,[26] was based on the unique position of one man, and rested on his ability to trade political favors. "[W]hen Barrett leaves, the entire system he has spent over 30 years in building will disappear with him" (at 375).

Karikas claims that Barrett's style and effectiveness were atypical and nontransferable, although the standard literature on congressional behavior indicates that constituency service is one of the most dominant characteristics of the job and that Barrett's activities are not atypical.[27] Although Barrett's trading seems to benefit his constituents directly, it "fails simply because it does not provide for lasting change and improvement. The Congressman's organization is a responsive voice mechanism, but it resolves problems on a

25. Nader supports a counterpart movement to the early twentieth-century public health movement, but a "movement in the law . . . that would center on the individual's ensured access to legal institutions, on simplified law, on techniques of dispute avoidance, and, most important, on a scheme to prevent or get at the source of legal controversies" (at 49). But, the literature on the public health movement certainly does not state that the public health movement is responsible for the improvement in health and medical care in the United States. See Paul Starr, The Social Transformation of American Medicine (New York: Basic Books, 1982); George Rosen, A History of Public Health (New York: MD Publications, 1958); Thomas McKeown, The Role of Medicine: Dream, Mirage or Nemesis (Oxford: Nuffield Provincial Hospitals Trust, 1976).

26. Karikas puts 'real' functions in quotation marks possibly suggesting a criticism of this criticism, but she does not elaborate on it (at 373).

27. Cf. David R. Mayhew, Congress: The Electoral Connection, (New Haven, Conn.: Yale University Press, 1974).

case-by-case basis only. . . . he has no incentive to make structural changes that would eliminate those politically valuable complaints'' (at 375).[28] If trading in political favors is the stock-in-trade of politicians, and constituency service one of the primary occupations of congressmen, why should complaint handling for this district cease with the next occupant of the position? Of course politicians are susceptible to pressure from wealthy constituents, who often help them get elected, but Congressman Barrett seemed to walk a fine line between the pressures of wealthy and more needy constituents. Nevertheless, this patronage model of consumer service based on reciprocity and local community is rejected (as nongeneralizable and corruptible) in favor of a centralized model of generalized and unspecified access.

Another type of mechanism rejected because it is decentralized is complaint management by department stores. Karikas and Rosenwasser acknowledge that consumers are generally satisfied and successful when they complain to department stores (at 312). Nevertheless, they suggest that ''[a] centralized office for the management of all complaints is a practical and desirable alternative to the current practice'' (at 315). Although it ''will not automatically turn the grievance procedure . . . into effective complaint channels for the public'' (at 316), centralized complaint management would better inform the consumer, make it easier for the store to keep records, offer more consistent responses, and help the public to express stronger, collective opinions. Of course, it would be the store rather than individual consumers that saw the individual complaints as part of a collective voice. Although such offices typically develop screening mechanisms that may actually reduce the number of resolutions in the consumer's favor, the authors again prefer a more bureaucratized and centralized solution.

Nader and Mattice claim to have found two successful grievance mechanisms: mass media complaint managers and grassroots organizing. The media managers studied generally resolved between 58% (KABL Call for Action) and 80% (Ombudsman Service) of the complaints received, within an average two-month period (at 514–15). Moreover, media managers represent the revival of ''a very important social-control mechanism that has been decreasing in mass societies'' (at 28)—publicity and information, often taking the form of gossip and scandal.[29] Mattice argues that media complaint-managers hold great promise because ''[f]ew other organizations can marshall such evidence of the weak points in our bureaucratic society as they see every day, and only they are prepared to broadcast their findings'' (at 519). Nevertheless, their performance offers meager evidence of substantially greater success than many traditional agencies. Because media hotlines are commercial operations relying on the support of subscribers and advertisers, audience ac-

28. The clear implication of this line of reasoning is that an adequate complaint mechanism would eliminate all current and prospective grievances and that there would not be other or different grievances that would occupy political representatives under a structurally revised system.

29. Sally E. Merry, Toward a General Theory of Gossip and Scandal, *in* Donald J. Black, Toward a General Theory of Social Control (New York: Academic Press, 1984).

quisition is their primary goal. Mattice admits that hotlines are unlikely to concentrate on complaints which lack mass appeal: repetitive complaints and most common problems seem to have little appeal and receive less attention. Nor is an action line likely "to be granted the substantial staff and equipment required for the greatest effectiveness in complaint management" (at 518). Cost consciousness inhibits research and investigation; therefore complaint resolution relies on straight referral, occasional telephone calls, and some interviews. Staff members work on those cases that are easiest to resolve; the more intractable complaints remain unresolved.[30] If an action line costs too much, threatens too many advertisers, or fails to attract a large audience, it is unlikely to be supported. Despite the fact that the media share serious shortcomings with other complaint handlers—reliance on economic support and attention to the easiest cases—Nader and Mattice (at 28, 519) argue that they have great potential because "[t]heir powers virtually equal those of government" (at 519).

The authors claim that grassroots mechanisms also work because they consist of consumers acting on their own behalf. The San Francisco Consumer Action group began in 1971 as a local outgrowth of a statewide consumer organization. Designed as a volunteer community service organization to handle individual consumer grievances, it evolved into a community action organization handling group complaints and promoting "a sense unity among consumers" (at 24). It produced informative and useful publications, lobbied government forums, trained residents to use the courts and exercise their rights there and elsewhere, and picketed as well as negotiated with businesses. Although the case load was small in comparison to that of formal consumer complaint handlers, it claimed a success (or partial success) rate of 78% for the cases it resolved (at 448), which is consistent with most complaint agencies. The consumer action group worked on the basis of local committees and sponsored five other committees by the end of its fourth year; they empowered consumers by organizing them.[31] Despite the enthusiasm and potential of the consumer action committees, as well as the real contribution they have made to improving the position of consumers, "[a]s of March 1980, SFCA was no longer handling consumer complaints. Affected by a shortage of resources, it is presently an organization dedicated primarily to consumer education and regulatory effort" (at 457). Nevertheless, the SFCA is cited by the authors as the most successful consumer organization studied despite the fact that it ceased to handle consumer complaints and has assumed the form of a traditional consumer lobby.

30. Cf. Silbey, Case Processing, *supra* note 9.

31. The committees operated by five general principles: (1) when evaluating whether a consumer has been treated unfairly, there is a strong bias toward the consumer's account of the situation; (2) committee assistance in resolving complaints is intended to supplement not substitute for the consumer's own efforts; (3) the committees are willing to use dramatic and unorthodox means of pressuring businesses to accede to consumer demands; (4) "consumer complaint assistance involves a series of judgments to be made collectively, not individually, though the individual consumer is the one who must finally decide whether to accept a particular settlement offered by the merchant"; and (5) "committees are seen by core members as having the potential for organizing consumers and involving them in a larger movement" (at 454).

The idealization of organization tends to obscure the recognition of similarities between the proposed reforms and existing structures. For example, Combs-Schilling, in her chapter on unions, suggests that unions create alternative forums within their organization to hear the grievances of union members against their unions. "By developing an alternative forum for workers that is not connected with either the management or the union hierarchy, it should be possible to solve some of the problems we have addressed" (at 482). The model is a traditional third-party complaint handler, but lacking structural, political, or economic supports necessary for such a mechanism to be effective.

*B. Organized, Grievance-free Communities*

The collection's basic argument suggests a preference for a society in which grievances would be avoided and prevented. "As an anthropologist I believe that an increase in complaints and disputes is a sign of disorganized communities, a situation that cannot be fixed by arbitration boards, improved small claims courts, CAP organizations, and so on" (at 29). The use of the word "disorganized" is unfortunate because of the legacy of social disorganization theory. The statement is reminiscent of the explanation in the 1930s for the distribution of crime in urban areas. According to Greshman Sykes, much of the writing about social disorganization in the period between the two world wars "did little more than reflect the distaste for the modern world of industry and large cities on the part of the textbook authors who looked back with nostalgia to their own rural and small-town antecedents."[32] Does Nader's emphasis on disputes and complaints as signs of disorganization reflect a preoccupation, not with the small-town America of the 1930s sociologists but with the anthropological model of the small-scale society?

By disorganization, Nader may mean that business and consumers used to have close ties because of the simplicity and connectedness of an earlier social life. Now there are few direct bonds, so that products and services are of lower or less reliable quality and consumers have problems that are often not easily rectified. However, this diagnosis of the consumer's predicament assumes, rather than demonstrates, that an organized social world is grievance free and that there has been a breakdown of social order.

Nader also argues that grievances are an index of "endemic powerless-

32. Greshman M. Sykes, Criminology 254 (New York: Harcourt Brace Jovanovich 1978). Sykes is drawing upon the work of C. Wright Mills, The Professional Ideology of Social Pathologists, 49 Am. J. Soc. 165 (1943). Mills writes that "The notion of disorganization is quite often merely the absence of that *type* of organization associated with the stuff of primary-group communities having Christian and Jeffersonian legitimations." *Id.* at 175. Quoting from T. V. Smith on Cooley, he goes on, "There is reflected here . . . what is highly common in our culture, an ideal of intimacy short of which we do not rest satisfied where other people are concerned. Social distance is a dire fate, achieved with difficulty and lamented as highly unideal . . . . In order to have social relations, we must nuzzle one another . . . . The aim to preserve rurally oriented values and stabilities is indicated by the implicit model which operates to detect urban disorganization; it is also shown by the stress upon *community* welfare. The community is taken as the major unit, and often it sets the scope of concern and problematization." *Id.* It is possible that anthropologists may be biased to the rural by inclination or training; of course, Mills said that sociologists of 'disorganization' were biased by virtue of class, he did not discuss training in any detail.

ness" (at 41) suggesting that disorganization equals powerlessness. If the characterization of communities with grievances as disorganized is not to carry elements of bias, I assume Nader means that members of these communities have less resources than members of communities she would characterize as organized. And because complaining consumers turn out to be "those with less economic need,"[33] the resources they apparently lack are not material but organizational—thus leading to powerlessness.

This provocative argument raises interesting questions. If grievances are a sign of powerlessness, are they not also a measure of power? If consumers have had problems with products and services for years and only recently have begun to act on them, this is a positive sign, not a negative one. It indicates that consumers are becoming active in their own interests. If, however, the number of grievances, negative experiences, and formal complaints has increased over the years, voiced consumer grievances may be the negative index that Nader suggests. But again, the increase in consumer grievances would need to be demonstrated rather than assumed. And, are all grievances, or just unresolved grievances, an index of powerlessness and disorganization?

Rather than pursue an analysis focused on social disorganization, the work would benefit from an examination of consumer grievances as an index of the relative inequality in resources between consumers and businesses, and the organization of consumers rather than of communities. I am suggesting that Nader et al. examine the distinction between general forms of social organization (ways in which social interactions are patterned) and particular patterns of interaction, such as formal organizations (lobbies, business firms, voluntary organizations). It would then be necessary to look at the specific organization of consumers that has relegated them to a subordinate position vis-a-vis the organization of business. Nader's analysis suggests not only a preference for a society without grievances but also one where remedies for grievances are pursued through orchestrated struggle between organized groups, a corporatism of sorts. Thus, the analysis cries out for attention to the role of organized interest groups in the political struggle for legal protections and rights, and the grounds on which satiation of organized political demands are determined.

Certainly the history of social reform in the United States belies any claim that consumers are without a political voice. The Sherman Anti-Trust Act, the Pure Food and Drug Act, the Federal Trade Commission Act, as well as a host of other social and economic regulations, were not gifts of altruistic businessmen or professional adovcates. In the same way, "the new deal didn't

33. "The very fact that people of all socioeconomic brackets write these letters [complaints about consumer transactions] is an indication that they are motivated to write by a sense of injustice rather than by pure and simple economic need" (at 8). In a footnote to this statement, Nader writes that "complaint letters seem to be written more often by those with less economic need" (at 8 n.3). Citing the research of Liefeld, Edgecombe, and Wolfe, she states that "[t]he average complainer turned out to be middle-aged, well-educated, affluent, and in the managerial-professional occupational strata" (at 8, n.3). Compare J. P. Liefeld, F. H. C. Edgecombe, & Linda Wolfe, Demographic Characteristics of Canadian Consumer Complainers, 9 J. Consumer Aff. 73 (1975).

come because FDR was such a great guy . . . it came from the streets because there were hollerers and dissidents,"[34] what William Douglas called the "thunder on the left." Of course these reforms may not have achieved all that their supporters fought for, but not because consumers did not organize on behalf of their interests. Consumers have organized, but business is better organized for the particularistic and instrumental character of American politics. Policy emerges out of a struggle in which consumer interests are at a distinct disadvantage, partially because of the diffuseness and generality of their concerns, and partially because of the society's dependence on business's confidence and investment.[35] Nader's demand for a society in which individual consumers are bonded into organized interest groups would be enriched by a historical analysis of organized group conflict.

The authors argue that our present social organization is incompatible with perfect consumer satisfaction. The vision of the organized and grievance-free society inevitably raises questions about who shall get what and how shall we decide. If, at present, legal rights and protections are the outcome of an imperfect pluralism, is the alternative perfect pluralism? It is unclear; Nader et al. simply argue that consumers should get what they want because at present they rarely do. But, what consumers want, what consumer grievances represent (power or powerlessness), and what constitutes complaint behavior, are empirical questions left unanswered by this research.

### C. *An Inappropriate Legal System*

Nader claims that our present system of consumer protection fails to meet the ideal pattern "not because of the absence of norms and legally recognized rights and duties but because of poor application, nonaccessible forums, and a refusal to recognize that our law, rooted in a small-scale agricultural period where face-to-face relationships predominated, is no longer appropriate in an industrial society where most of the real and potential complaints are between strangers of unequal power" (at 28–29).

Nader touches briefly on aspects of legal development but dismisses what is the heart of the problem for both legality and for consumers by suggesting that the contradictions in legal development are merely the ideology of an outmoded legal doctrine. For Nader, the principles of individualism—embodied in the doctrine of individual treatment of cases, equality before the law, and confidentiality and privacy, and constituting achievements of modern law—are removed from their sociohistorical development and dismissed as placing unnecessary limitations on the "ideal development and function of complaint processes" (at 61). But these ideologies are not merely excess baggage; the history of legal development attests to the fact that these doctrines symbolize concrete, albeit ambiguous, processes that lie at the

34. Studs Terkel, quoted in the Boston Globe, Mar. 3, 1983, at 3.

35. Grant McConnell, Private Power and American Democracy (New York: Alfred A. Knopf, 1967); Mancur Olson, Jr., The Logic of Collective Action: Public Goods and the Theory of Groups (Cambridge: Harvard University Press, 1965); Block, *supra* note 4.

heart of what we mean by legality in the modern world. They constitute the object/subject of inquiry for students of the sociology of law. The ahistorical and idealist framework ends up separating liberal legalism from the social organization in which it grew, thereby undermining the cogency of the critical analysis.

Our legal system is not the product of a singular line of development from an agricultural past; rather it is a melange of various elements, some of which of course trace to an earlier and distinct form of social organization. It is an eclectic mix of indigenous social norms, elements of Roman jurisprudence, a dose of canon law, and a large infusion of the law of medieval towns and fairs. The image of the homogeneous rural world in which indigenous norms govern face-to-face relationships, out of which formal state law developed, may be consistent with the history of New England villages; but the law that emerged was the law of interpersonal dispute resolution, vices, squabbles, and crime. It did not form the basis of the commercial law that now governs consumer transactions. Our commercial law is a more direct descendant of the law of the medieval towns, which formed islands of privileged immunity in the midst of medieval rural society. Although portions of this law relied on known and fixed relationships, a large measure rested on and promoted relations among strangers.[36]

The major achievement of bourgeois law was the creation of a sphere of individual autonomy within a rationalized legal system. It eschewed the tradition of ordeals, duels, and oaths administered by judges drawn from the local population and using local custom to

> regulate the relations of men living by the cultivation or the ownership of land . . . . [This] was inadequate for a population whose existence was based on commerce and industry. A more expeditious law was necessary, means of proof more rapid and more independent of chance, and judges who were themselves acquainted with the professional occupations of those who came under their jurisdiction, and could cut short their arguments by a knowledge of the case at issue. Very early, and at latest at the beginning of the eleventh century, the pressure of circumstances led to the creation of a jus mercatorum, i.e., an embryonic commercial code. It was a collection of usages born of business experience, a sort of international custom, which the merchants used among themselves in their transactions. Devoid of all legal validity, it was impossible to invoke it in the existing law courts, so the merchants agreed to choose among themselves arbitrators who had the necessary competence to understand their disputes and to settle them promptly. It is here undoubtedly that we must seek the origin of those law courts which in England received the picturesque name of courts of piepowder (pied poudre), because the feet of the merchants who resorted to them were still dusty from the roads. Soon this ad hoc jurisdiction became permanent.[37]

36. Henri Pirenne, Economic and Social History of Medieval Europe 49–57 (New York: Harcourt, Brace & Co., 1925); Max Weber, The City, trans. & ed. Don Martindale & Gertrud Neuwirth (Glencoe, Ill.: Free Press, 1958).

37. Pirenne, *supra* note 36, at 51–52.

Bourgeois law created freedom to come and go, to sell goods and to do business, powers not enjoyed by serfs and without which trade was difficult. It not only certified and created the conditions of trade, it formally acknowledged the emergence of the individual, freed both from manorial serfdom and from the group bonds constituting social and legal identity. "Freedom became the legal status of the bourgeoisie, so much so that it was no longer a personal privilege only, but a territorial one, inherent in urban soil just as serfdom was in manorial soil. In order to obtain it, it was enough to have resided for a year and a day within the walls of the town. 'City air makes a man free' (*Stadluft macht frei*) says the German proverb."[38]

If the development and pressure for an individualistic and rational law was not a linear development,[39] neither was it an unalloyed good. The freedom of not being treated as a member of a category or group, of being subject to rational rather than irrational criteria of proof and general rather than particular rules, was a long time in coming. It represented a major achievement and struggle[40] that cannot be easily ignored or dismissed by pleas for retribalization and group identity for consumers vis-a-vis the modern corporation. It is difficult to disagree with Nader and Shugart's observation that the legal rights of consumers deriving from the ways in which people sued one another in the eighteenth and nineteenth centuries do not help consumers secure satisfaction for deficient products and services in the twentieth century. But the source of this problem is neither identified nor explained by saying that our contemporary legal system is an anachronistic remnant of our agricultural past. The consumer's predicament arises directly out of the contradictions of modern liberal legalism that developed in a struggle with that agricultural world, a struggle to be rid of confining group statuses and identities. The dilemmas of modern legal systems arise from the contradictions between formal legal statuses, that is, the right to be treated as an individual and not as a member of a group, and social statuses not individually determined but which nevertheless encumber individuals with obligations and liabilities.

Perhaps the contradictions in the Nader and Shugart analysis—the image of a perfectable social life and the ahistorical analysis of the development of modern legal systems—derive from the repeated comparison to small-scale societies and to what Nader calls the anthropological paradigm. The model of face-to-face relationships, characteristic of agricultural societies, is invoked at critical junctures, and the essays assert that much can be learned by comparing our legal system to the social control systems in small-scale agricultural societies (e.g., at xvi, 234, 317). There is a certain truth to this classic assertion.[41] But Nader does not simply say that something useful can be

38. *Id.* at 51.

39. Weber, *supra* note 36, at 183.

40. Compare E. P. Thompson, Whigs and Hunters: The Origin of the Black Act (London: Allen Lane, 1975).

41. E.g., the dispute-processing literature emphasizes alternatives to traditional courts, and adjudication emphasizes the value of comparative analyses: Richard Danzig, Toward the Creation of a Complementary, Decentralized System of Criminal Justice, 26 Stan. L. Rev. 1 (1973); Richard L. Abel, A

learned from looking at small-scale societies; she argues that our legal system fails to provide access to justice because its roots are in small agricultural communities and it has not developed to meet the needs of a modern industrial society (at 29). Nevertheless, she suggests that if we are serious about providing consumer protection and access to law, we would do well to adopt aspects of these "inappropriate" models for the reform of our modern industrial legal system (at 49). It is unclear how Nader reconciles these inconsistencies, although it is clear that she wishes to recreate the kinds of relations that prevailed in more traditional premodern societies. The authors' analysis finally reifies the concept of society, abstracting it out of the material forces and relations of which it is constituted at the same time rejecting modernity and suggesting a preference for another earlier social form.

## III. A Theory of Complaint Behavior: The Connection Between Grievances and Social Structure

Nader and Shugart state that "consumer complaints are symptoms of fundamental and systemic problems" affecting "production, management-labor, distribution, equity, and law in a democratic society" (at 101–2). They also state that "[s]olving the consumer complaint problem will allow people to stop focusing their discontent on this level and allow them . . . to grapple with the more fundamental questions" (at 102). Although this analysis suggests why change is so difficult—because citizens are paralyzed with small injustices and grievances and cannot attack the real structural sources of those grievances—the analysis fails to either resolve its own contradictions or to link the individual concerns of consumers to the broader underlying structural issues. If consumer complaints are symptoms of more fundamental structural problems, and if Nader's primary argument is that piecemeal solutions do not work, how can complaint-handling mechanisms, even ideal ones, do more than simply nurse the symptom—consumer complaints? Why will complaint mechanisms resolve the problems of management-labor, distribution, equity, or law? Or, more important, how will the resolution of consumer grievances direct attention to these problems?

A theory of complaint behavior is necessary to make the link between individual consumer grievances and fundamental social structure. The Nader volume shold be explored for its possible contributions to such a theory. At present, however, it lacks a comparison between complainers and noncomplainers; moreoever, there is no way of knowing what a consumer complaint consists of because there is no conceptualization of rights, grievances, or

---

Comparative Theory of Dispute Institutions in Society, 8 Law & Soc'y Rev. 217 (1973); William L. F. Felstiner, Influences of Social Organization on Dispute Processing, 9 Law & Soc'y Rev. 63 (1974); Richard Danzig & Michael J. Lowy, Everyday Disputes and Mediation in the United States: A Reply to Professor Felstiner, 9 Law & Soc'y Rev. 675 (1975); Eric A. Fisher, Community Courts: An Alternative to Conventional Criminal Adjudication, 24 Am. U.L. Rev. 1253 (1975).

complaints.[42] It is not possible to assess the adequacy and responsiveness of existing mechanisms of redress without a context within which to "discover" the meaning of consumer complaints. What does the universe of consumer grievances look like? How do existing mechanisms deal with this phenomenon? Are consumers indeed paralyzed by small grievances? Is a complaint to the seller or a third party the latest move in a continuing series of unsatisfactory interchanges? How are the circumstances prompting a consumer complaint different from ongoing unsatisfactory circumstances, such as living with a toaster whose thermostat is erratic and therefore frequently burns bread? Is cost a determining variable?[43] Is it the frequency or the uniqueness of the problem that impels complaint?

These are empirical questions the authors could explore further. Although at present the research provides only limited answers, it offers a rich and critical argument. Nader et al. argue that the universe of consumer complaints is quite large but that grievance-handling agencies see only a small part because consumers are socialized to accept shoddy products and to see themselves as deviant if they complain. This argument generates important questions about the relationship between consumer grievances, expectations, and fundamental processes of social control.

### *A. The Universe of Consumer Complaints*

What does the universe of consumer complaints look like? Unfortunately, there is no victimology in the Nader volume. The two chapters describing the substance of consumer complaints are based on 300 complaints received by Ralph Nader between November 1969 and December 1971 and a single case that went through General Motors' complaint process. These letters are a subset of 5,000 such letters received by the Nader organization.[44] Complaints come from every region, more from married than single persons, more from urban than rural areas, and more from employed or retired than unemployed persons. But there is no information on the variation in the letters with regard to the characteristics of the general population and there is often more missing than codeable information. Moreover, we do not know whether these letters represent all those who have suffered unsatisfactory transactions or a subset of them. In fact, we learn very little about who complains and what consumers do about unsatisfactory transactions, because we do not know what these complaints are a sample of. Is this "the tip of the iceberg"

42. Compare Jack Ladinsky & Charles Susmilch, Conceptual and Operational Issues in Measuring Consumer Disputing Behavior, Disputes Processing Research Program Working Paper 1981-83, (Madison: University of Wisconsin Law School); William L. F. Felstiner, Richard L. Abel, & Austin Sarat, The Emergence and Transformation of Disputes: Naming, Blaming, Claiming . . . , 15 Law & Soc'y Rev. 631 (1980-81); see vol. 15, issue nos. 3, 4 of *Law and Society Review* generally.

43. There is some evidence that suggests that higher cost items are more frequently subjects of complaint, but the average loss is still relatively low. E.g., Best, at 109-10.

44. The 300 letters were "sampled, at random, 100 letters each in the categories of food, medical and appliance problems" (at 115) from the 5,000 in Nader's collection. "Among the letters available for study were many dealing with subjects other than complaints about products and services; we focused on product complaints letters however as the most directly linked to an understanding of the remedy system" (at 115 n.6).

(at xviii), as the authors assert, or is this the majority of consumers with complaints?

The Best volume attempts to provide an answer to this question. Chapter 6, "Surveying Consumer Troubles and Obstacles to Redress," is largely a reworking of the Best and Andreasen article that appeared in *Law and Society Review* in 1977.[45] Basing their analysis on a survey of over 2,400 households, the authors conclude that consumers are dissatisfied with nonprice aspects of their infrequent purchases 20% of the time and dissatisfied with both nonprice and price aspects of frequent purchases about 33% of the time. The authors estimate that approximately ten million households experience at least one unsatisfactory transaction per year due to cheating or deception. They estimate that the losses range from $1 to $3,000, with the average loss estimated to be $142. The survey also revealed that consumers routinely do not complain about losses and therefore the sample of complaints that are received is indeed a small sample (one-third) of unsatisfactory consumer transactions. Moreover, the complaints voiced are not representative but are biased in favor of simpler high-cost problems experienced by more affluent households. Therefore, data suggest that the affluent, not the powerless, complain.[46]

Despite his own evidence, however, Best argues that the universe of consumer complaints is potentially limitless because perceived consumer problems are merely a subset of all the problems consumers actually experience. This includes products that do not live up to the claims made for them and products that do live up to the claims but that OUGHT to be better. Best offers the example of cheaper energy and better cars as examples of the unavailability of practical alternatives; he discusses whole and term life insurance as an example of consumers not knowing their best interest. If consumers knew the difference, "they would no doubt consider themselves consumers with grounds for complaints" (at 10). "To purchase any of these products [which could be better], is to become, in a sense, a consumer with a problem" (at 6). Best concludes that consumers do not and cannot know the quality, safety, or durability of the products and services they buy and will not demand or purchase superior products even when they are informed about them; consumers do not act in their own best interests. Therefore, we need to improve complaint-handling mechanisms to ensure that consumers are treated "fairly," even if they do not choose to help themselves.

Thus, the Nader work is unable to illuminate the meaning of consumer

45. Arthur Best & Alan R. Andreasen, Consumer Response to Unsatisfactory Purchases: A Survey of Perceiving Defects, Voicing Complaints, and Obtaining Redress, 11 Law & Soc'y Rev. 701 (1977); see also Alan R. Andreasen & Arthur Best, Consumers Complain—Does Business Respond? Harv. Bus. Rev., July-Aug. 1977, at 93.

46. "The data indicate that the third-party complaint-handling mechanisms, as they now operate, disproportionately serve the better educated, better informed, and politically more liberal households." (Best at 127). Consumers are more likely to voice complaints about infrequently than frequently purchased products, about higher than lower cost products, and about expensive rather than inexpensive problems. The alternative to complaint is to exit; this is easier and more effective for repeated frequent purchases, which tend to be less expensive. (Best at 125).

complaints, and the Best work rejects its own evidence of consumer complaining.[47] Despite this lack of theory and uncertain evidence, the authors assert that the complaints received by sellers, nonbinding third parties, or binding third parties, are the tip of an enormous iceberg of aggrieved consumers. The argument runs in circles. It begins and concludes with the same undemonstrated assumption: if there are so many consumer complaints being processed, there must be that many more that are never voiced or even perceived. This is a central argument of the access-to-justice movement that begs to be empirically tested.

There is some contrary evidence from Best and others that sellers and third-party complaint handlers process numerous consumer grievances and that these complaints probably constitute a sizeable proportion of consumer problems. Several studies report data indicating that the universe of unvoiced complaints is not large and that what is seen is most of what there is.

In a study of the consumer problems of older Americans, McGuire and Edelhertz report that few respondents in two major metropolitan areas experienced repeated problems and that most of their consumer problems involved repairs and bait-and-switch tactics. Furthermore, "[t]he majority of respondents . . . who indicated experiencing consumer abuses suffered neither a lengthy delay in the delivery of repair services nor a very large or unanticipated monetary loss."[48] Of the respondents who had consumer complaints, 60% sought a private remedy, 10% sought a public remedy, and 30% took no action.

The Milwaukee Consumer Dispute Study showed that during a single year, only 9% of consumers (in 1,269 households) reported problems with their purchases of products or services. Of those experiencing a problem, 75% filed claims against the manufacturer or firm to try to get the problem resolved. Of those having problems with services, 81% filed claims, while of those experiencing problems with a product, 73% filed claims. Twenty-five percent of the sample were identified as "lump-its," consumers who don't like what they get but take no action. This evidence suggests that most of the iceberg is above water.[49]

47. There is a confusion in the Best work between consumer behavior, that is, complaints and grievances due to experience of faulty products or misrepresentation and a generalized desire for more efficient and effective products. These represent two different types of consumer problems and may derive from very different economic, legal, and structural sources. The author conflates the two and thus weakens his own argument. Because Best speaks of disadvantage consumers are not aware of, evidence of complaining or non-complaining is not relevant and cannot possibly substantiate Best's claim that there is a vast volume of unremedied consumer grievances.

48. Mary V. McGuire & Herbert Edelhertz, Consumer Abuse of Older Americans: Victimization and Remedial Action in Two Metropolitan Areas, *in* Gilbert Geis & Ezra Stotland, eds., White-Collar Crime: Theory and Research 266, 281 (Beverly Hills, Cal.: Sage Publications, 1980).

49. Ladinsky & Susmilch, *supra* note 42. Best found that only 39.7% of consumers who perceived a problem took any kind of action; it is possible that increased public attention to consumer problems has changed consumer behavior and that discrepant findings are merely the result of patterns evolving over time. Best conducted his survey in 1975, McGuire and Edelhertz in 1977, and Ladinsky and Susmilch in 1980–81. In my research in the Massachusetts Attorney General's Office of Consumer Protection I found that the volume of consumer complaints continually increased with time. Silbey, Case Processing, *supra* note 9.

There is, however, debate in the literature as to whether taking action and complaining lead to consumer satisfaction. Most studies report that consumer complaints, when voiced, are usually resolved to the consumer's satisfaction. Some of the studies report satisfaction rates as high as 80%. In the Nader collection, Mattice reports a range of 58–80% successful resolutions of consumer complaints by ombudsman services and media organizations (at 515), while Wilson and Brydolf report a 78.5% success rate for the grassroots organization they studied (at 448). Ramsay reports "consumer complaint and two-party negotiations between buyer and seller might play an important role in protecting the consumer against defective and poor-quality products" because "the overwhelming majority of retailers . . . had a policy of accepting returned merchandise."[50] Only 1 of 106 businesses studied would accept no returns at all. Although not all consumer complaints were resolved to the consumer's satisfaction, the "retailer's perception of the customer as a repeat player and the market advantages gained by satisfied consumers communicating their satisfaction to potential customers" led to a general policy of the customer being "usually" right. The Karikas and Rosenwasser chapter on department stores (at 283) confirms Ramsay's research. And Ladinsky reports from the Milwaukee study that of the consumers who complained 60% had "full success in getting what they wanted, 9% got part of what they wanted, and 27% abandoned the process after the initial complaints failed to bring about satisfactory results." The rate of success for complaints about services was 41%, while complaints about products was 70%.[51]

Although Best and Andreasen reported that only about one-third of all complaints to third parties were resolved satisfactorily, when they looked at resolution rates by the type of problem rather than the role of third parties, they found success rates above 50%, with the variation accounted for by the type of purchase more than the type of problem.

> In general, the principal discrepancy between perceived problems and voiced complaints is the underrepresentation of complaints requiring the consumer to assert a difference of judgment, e.g., about the selection of materials, design durability, and ease of use, and the overrepresentation of complaints about defects that can be proved objectively and easily, e.g., clerical errors, furnishing incorrect items or services, and breakage and loss of customers' property. [At 129]

Complaints based on the consumer's judgment had a lower satisfaction rate than objective complaints—only 50% led to satisfactory resolutions.

However, the McQuire and Edelhertz[52] survey found that only 41%–42% of consumers who took action received satisfaction, but 14%–18% of those who took no action also obtained some remedy. Whitford and Kimball found that only one-third of the cases reported to a state insurance office

50. Ramsay, *supra* note 9, at 127.
51. Ignoring Complaints Can Hurt a Business, Milwaukee J., June 14, 1983, at 1.
52. *Supra* note 48.

were resolved to the benefit of the complainant and closed as complainant satisfied.[53]

Consumers respond to unsatisfactory transaction, with a wide variety of strategies, of which complaining is only one. The idealist premises of these works inhibit the authors from taking account of other responses, including exit,[54] self-help,[55] and even crime and retaliation,[56] and from exmaining the consequences of these alternatives. Throughout the analyses there are unstated assumptions about the meaning of "fairness" or "justice." These concepts are neither defined nor subjected to empirical exploration, although consumer complaints and the consumer-complaint process are evaluated in terms of their justice and fairness (e.g., Best at 135, 197; Nader at xix). Boycott, stealing, and self-help are reasonable and possibly economical consumer responses, but they are overlooked because they do not fit the authors' preconceptions.

*B. Expectations and Social Control*

There is a giant leap in the Nader and Best works from the description of petty claims to the conclusions that unresolved consumer grievances represent a breakdown of the social order and threaten the stability of our society. The connecting thread is woven through a description of the role of processes of social control in regulating consumer expectations. The authors identify conflicting expectations between consumers and businessmen to be the heart of consumer complaints and suggest their structural significance by noting the sociopolitical consequences of failed expectations. The attempt to place the study of consumer complaints within a general theory of social control raises the Nader work above usual discussions of consumer protection.

Although the concept of social control is nowhere specifically delineated, it is invoked in each article in the collection.[57] Nader et al. and Best argue that consumers have expectations for justice and good products but that the regu-

53. Whitford & Kimball, *supra* at note 9.

54. Albert Hirschmann, Exit, Voice and Loyalty: Response to Decline in Firms, Organization and States (Cambridge: Harvard University Press, 1970).

55. Suzann R.Thomas Buckle & Leonard G. Buckle, "Doing Unto Others," "Bringing Justice Home" delivered at the Law and Society Association annual meeting Madison, Wis. June 1980, and "Self-Help Justice," delivered at the Law and Society Association annual meeting, Amherst, Mass., June 1981.

56. Cf. Donald Black, Crime as Social Control, 48 Am. Soc. Rev. 34 (1983).

57. To differentiate such control from ordinary interaction, I assume that an adequate definition would take account of whether social control is necessarily intentional, who and what is subject to it, who exercises it and by what means, and its goals and consequences (Jack P. Gibbs, Norms, Deviance, and Social Control: Conceptual Matters (New York: Elsevier, 1981)). For my purposes, social control is not ubiquitous and synonymous with all social interaction, it covers only the ways in which we extract conformity to behavioral patterns: "the processes and procedures which regulate behavior, in that they exert pressure on persons and groups to conform." Ronald M. Berndt, Excess v. Restraint 11 (Chicago: University of Chicago Press, 1962). Cf. August B. Hollingshead, The Concept of Social Control, 6 Am. Soc. Rev. 217 (1941); Paul H. Landis, Social Control: Social Organization and Disorganization in Process 7 (rev. ed. Philadelphia: Lippincott, 1956); Edward Alsworth Ross, Social Control: A Survey of the Foundations of Order, (1901 reprint; Cleveland: Press of Case Western Reserve, 1969). Ross was particularly concerned with individual adherence to social rules, and the theme of his work was to confirm that men "in their collective capacity" do "find a means of guiding the will or conscience of the individual member of society" (at 59). For Ross, social control meant inducing conformity and deterring nonconfomity on the part of the individual (*id.* at 395).

larly inadequate responses to consumer complaints systematically lower consumer expectations so that consumers learn to accept shoddiness and see themselves as deviant if they complain. The repeated denial of access to a remedy for consumer grievances teaches consumers not to complain and is thus a form of social control. It is the combination of failed with systematically lowered expectations that suggests to the authors that consumer grievances represent a very serious threat to the social order.[58]

Best states that social disillusionment grows from disappointed expectations undermining "confidence in our economic system and method of producing and marketing goods and services" (at 5). Nader states, "I discern that Americans have certain expectations with regard to their business transactions that are not being met." "Beyond the sense of powerlessness and the loss of trust, the very advertising techniques and packaging devices that companies use to sell their products are the source of expectations of justice and also of widespread disillusionment and lack of faith" (at 8).

It is difficult to accept the argument that experience is teaching us to accept shoddiness; the authors' own evidence and arguments suggest otherwise. There is no evidence of declining expectations, especially since there is no information about those who "lump it" and do not complain. Rather, the complaints reported in these books demonstrate that although we rarely deal with business people we know personally, we nevertheless normally expect good faith, safety and durability, competence and expertise. And although complaint mechanisms do not work efficiently or effectively to aggregate complaints and provide structural responses, consumer complaints are often resolved satisfactorily. Therefore it is also difficult to argue that consumers are socialized not to complain. This argument again rests on the assumption that voiced complaints are the tip of an iceberg.

By attaching significance to consumer expectations, these authors confirm how important it is to see that social life is predicated on shared understandings and social norms. I would certainly agree that consumers attach certain expectations to particular roles, as well as products and services, without which they could not live or interact with others—it is these expectations that often lead to consumer dissatisfaction. Any discussion of consumer expectations, however, requires attention to the culture of buying and selling and the use-practices that organize our commercial and private lives. We need to know more about this culture to develop conceptions of satisfaction, grievance, remedy, and rights. Niether book develops a theory of complaint behavior that shows the connection between consumer satisfaction and dissatisfaction on the one hand and socially generated expectations on the other. The authors instead ignore this connection by insisting that we hold expectations for consistently high performance without also holding socially gen-

58. Best offers at least eight reasons why consumers do not routinely complain about unsatisfactory products and services: the difficulty of determining facts, the difficulty of defining rights, the fact that problems change over time, the costs of complaining, intimidation and retaliation, confusion, lack of information and power, and lack of access to law.

erated understandings that sometimes things do not work out properly or exactly as we expect. Idealist conceptions again weaken the analysis, thus calling for elaboration of the socially constructed and contradictory nature of consumer transactions and expectations.

Where do consumer expectations come from? The authors suggest that they come from a world that no longer exists and in which remedies existed that no longer suffice. This is an inadequate explanation; expectations come from our experience as members of society. Consumer expectations are generated by the habits and practices of production and distribution; how we routinely buy, sell, and use goods and services establishes concepts of what constitutes adequate service or performance. As socialized beings, we learn of what the world consists, and our own role in it, by exposure and involvement; these interactions come to constitute our definitions of normality. Thus marketing practices, as well as complaint-handling practices, constitute forms of social control because they not only frustrate but also generate and form normative patterns and associated expectations. They become aspects of their own regulation and legitimation. Existence is its own justification.

Consider the following case:

> Mr. Smith arranged with a contractor to build a patio in his yard. A verbal agreement was arrived at as to the price, materials, location, and date of the work's expected completion. As the work began, it became apparent that Smith expected the site to be leveled. The contractor explained that the price did not include leveling. The consumer protested that this was mentioned from the beginning, "How ridiculous to have a patio that was not level." An additional charge for leveling was added to the price. The site was leveled with sand fill, but without supporting constructions of any kind to retain the sand. Smith complained that it was not possible to build a patio on an unlevel site without retaining walls, since it was most evident that it would wash away in the rain. The contractor agreed reluctantly that this might happen, but insisted that the cost of supports would have to be added to the price. Smith insisted that it must be included, as the patio could not be built without them, that it was intrinsic to the construction of the patio. After considerable haggling, the contractor agreed to build the walls, absorbing the price of the least expensive construction he could manage. With the first rain, the sand began to seep through the loose boards the contractor used to hold up the sides; the patio was definitely sinking. Until it was ultimately supported by a surrounding landfill, at additional cost, the patio was in constant need of repair.[59]

This illustrates not the ineptness of Mr. Smith but rather the commonplace and fundamental character of his problem. In hiring the contractor, he did not incorporate his desires and expectations for the completed work into a written contract; moreover, a written contract would not have helped. Mr. Smith could not describe the construction of the patio until it was going up. He was continually faced with escalating costs for reasons lying at the heart of consumer problems and the structure of social relations: he relied on his

59. Susan S. Silbey, Consumer Justice: The Massachusetts Attorney General's Office of Consumer Protection 1970–1974, at 288 (Ph.D. diss. University of Chicago, 1978).

socially generated perception of what a contractor is. The contractor was not a fly-by-night operator; his trucks and his name had been visible around town for a long time. Smith assumed that because the contractor was a known member of the community, he was therefore knowledgeable about building patios and would build one properly. Smith believed his role as consumer was to tell the contractor what he wanted in shape, color, placement; the engineering of the construction was the responsibility of the contractor. Smith acted on his expectation that the contractor possessed the expertise appropriate to his role.

This case may seem unusual and avoidable but the evidence in the Best and Nader volumes tell us that it is not. Consumers continually rely on unspecified expectations that people will behave in ways characteristic of their positions, and unless the general public begins to believe that no businessperson is to be trusted at his/her job, some will inevitably place trust in oral agreements.[60] Nevertheless, even when written agreements are made, consumers' incomplete understanding of the conditions of their transactions include a range of circumstances that can never be exhaustively defined but only progressively narrowed through experience.[61] Disagreements arise as to the quality of the service or product described by that agreement. How durable should sofa fabric be? How well has the car been tuned? Regardless of the agreement's formality, the issue is the worker's or manufacturer's skill and competence to perform the contracted job at the level the consumer accepts as satisfactory and reasonable. In what ways and to what standard of performance can purveyors be held accountable for the quality of their goods and services? Is this not THE basic question of consumer protection? Should not the consumer have a right, in some legally relevant sense, to expect workers, manufacturers, or professionals, to have some objective and verifiable competence at what they are supposed to do? Is there a right to expect that the patio contractor knows more about laying patios than the consumer?

Both authors claim that at present consumers have no protection for such expectations or such faith. Consumers cannot expect that record players will not destroy records, that stoves will not set houses on fire, or that contractors will know how to build patios. To have such expectations leads to disappointment and mistrust. Freedman, in his chapter on complaint letters, writes that despite the enormous variation in the form and content of the letters they express a "common theme—a loss of trust" (at 161). Experience with incompetent plumbers, dishonest professionals, derelict and corrupt officials, deceptive advertisers, and unresponsive merchants has sapped consumers' confidence in the market and eroded their previously held assumptions that most people and most organizations can be presumed to be con-

60. Of course, it is not a matter of trust but of accountability, which can be assured through written agreements; contract and trust are opposite activities. Stewart Macaulay, Non-contractual Relations in Business: A Preliminary Study, 28 Am. Soc. Rev. 55 (1963).

61. It should be noted that increasing use of standard form written agreements further undermines and frustrates the consumer's opportunity to incorporate interests and wants into market transactions.

cerned and responsible and able. Too often disappointed in their dealings, they now "recognize that our educational, political, and economic systems have done little to provide consumers with the knowledge and resources they need" (at 161).

Thus, the details of hundreds of consumer complaints describe more than picayune and petty grievances. They go to the heart of our political and social structure. In the end, we face the problem of putting faith and trust in the working of society. By this I do not mean the trusting relations between individual debtors and individual creditors, but trust in the arrangements that make performance possible.[62] Unresolved consumer grievances undermine not simply confidence in the market as a particular structure of production and distribution, as these authors explicitly state, but confidence in the reliability of the social order. The breakdown of trust signifies the breakdown of the social order itself. Thus consumer problems are not private grievances; they are a social problem demanding a general solution.

Because there is a systematic lack of attention in both the Nader and Best volumes to any consumer response other than active formal complaining, it is possible and certainly not unreasonable to conclude that disillusionment, disaffection, and possibly serious social alienation follow failed expectations. But this does not accord with what we know about social interactions, including those that generate consumer complaints.

What evidence do we have that consumers believe that 100% of their purchases will turn out to be exactly what they wanted or that when they are not 100% satisfactory consumers believe that it is unfair? We have no evidence that citizens routinely believe and act as if the world ought to be a world of perfect relations; in fact, these books provide much evidence to the contrary. The complaints reported in these volumes repeatedly indicate that consumers believe that sometimes repair services misplace items brought in, that sometimes purchasers must go through several personnel levels to find someone with the authority to refund money, or that differences of judgment about the durability of materials are not easy to resolve. Indeed, we expect to be taken sometimes and generally live with limited trust. Moreover, consumers develop strategies for assessing the reliability of transactions and adjust their expectations according to the particular situation.

We have many examples of how citizens hold, and interact on the basis of, mixed expectations and limited trust. Citizens are adept at balancing and coping with imperfect relations. The legal culture literature indicates that citizens believe that courts are crowded, overburdened, and often biased against poor and minority populations. Nevertheless, they are regarded in high esteem and seen to generally provide reasonable justice. Similarly, at one and the same time, citizens increasingly rely on professional expertise

62. "One of the bargains men make with one another in order to maintain their sanity is to share an illusion that they are safe even when the physical evidence in the world around them does not seem to warrant that conclusion." Kai T. Erikson, Everything in Its Path: Destruction of Community in the Buffalo Creek Flood 234 (New York: Simon & Schuster, 1976). See generally the section The Illusion of Safety, at 234.

and increasingly distrust expertise in general. Perhaps an appropriate question to ask would be whether consumers question expertise itself or their own ability to identify expertise. The evidence indicates that citizens voice approval for particular institutions or processes but deny the relevance or utility of those same processes for themselves. Consumers distance themselves from and cope with mixed experiences and possibly failed expectations by having mixed expectations, none of which impels the conclusion that society or its institutions are to be mistrusted.

If advertising and ordinary practices, even "unfair" practices, generate expectations, government intervention also creates assumptions about what is fair and to be expected. And what is to prevent disillusionment from periodic or even routine failure to meet these new expectations? Do organizational and governmental responses not bring their own problems, creating entirely new sources of grievances? If consumer problems are pervasive small injustices and errors, miscalculations and insufficiences that are often unpredictable and sometimes irremedial, is the ideal of providing perfect redress and complete satisfaction of the complaining consumer protecting the ongoing organization of business and services? Are we engaged in an ever escalating cycle of increasing expectations, the major beneficiaries of which are those whose occupation it is to provide remedies and services for the victims of failed expectations? Some would argue that the consumer is not the obvious beneficiary of these efforts.

## Conclusions

The consumer movement has reached a watershed in American politics; recent innovations on traditional legal remedies and third-party grievance mechanisms seem to have failed once again to provide efficient and effective responses for unsatisfactory transactions within the existing market. *No Access to Law* and *When Consumers Complain* document the latest efforts in this struggle. Their insights need to be examined carefully and mined for what they can contribute to an agenda for a new consumer movement. Any future work on consumer protection will have to take account of the critical questions and issues raised in these works.

# [15]

# STRUCTURING CONSUMER PROTECTION LEGISLATION TO MAXIMIZE EFFECTIVENESS†

WILLIAM C. WHITFORD*

Consumer protection legislation has burgeoned over the past fifteen years. Much of the literature that has considered the effectiveness of this legislation has emphasized its limited impact. Two principal reasons tend to be given for the limited effect. Some commentators have emphasized the limited ability of law to affect consumer transactions because of the influence on those transactions of other economic and social forces.[1] Other commentators, drawing on theories of political economy, argue that most consumer protection legislation was not intended by its drafters and promoters to have much impact on transactions. According to this view the purpose of enacting the legislation is largely symbolic. Symbolic legislation is designed to appear to help consumers, in order to legitimize the current political and economic system, while simultaneously failing to alter significantly the power and economic relations between merchants and consumers.[2]

There is, beyond doubt, a good deal of validity to the views described above. In this article, however, I make the assumption, no doubt also valid, that consumer protection legislation has some effects. The purpose of the article is to propose hypotheses about the relationships between these effects and both the structure of consumer protection legislation and the sanctions for its violation.[3] By structure of legislation I mean a number of details

---

† I am grateful for helpful comments on an earlier draft from my colleagues Professors William Clune and Stewart Macaulay. Nicholas Zeppos and Terrence Webb provided me valuable research assistance. A one semester award of a Smongeski Research Professorship provided me with much of the time I needed to prepare this article.

* Professor of Law, University of Wisconsin; B.A., 1974, J.D., 1977, University of Wisconsin; LL.B., 1964, Yale University.

1. *See* Macaulay, *Lawyers and Consumer Protection Laws*, 14 LAW & SOC'Y REV. 115 (1979), for a good example of this approach.

2. Professor Murray Edelman is a leading advocate of this viewpoint. *See, e.g.*, J. M. EDELMAN, THE SYMBOLIC USES OF POLITICS (1964).

3. These hypotheses take account of available published information, but unfortunately reliable, empirical information is often unavailable about the effects of consumer

about the legislation which can be varied without significantly altering the manifest or stated purpose of the legislation. Sanctions for violation can also often be varied without altering the stated purpose of the legislation.

Establishing the scope of this article requires that two definitional issues be resolved initially. One issue concerns the distinction between manifest and latent purposes. Legislation can have many purposes and some of the less visible, or more latent, purposes may in fact have had the greatest influence on the drafters of the legislation. For example, if a latent purpose is that legislation be merely symbolic—that is, to appear to benefit consumers without doing so in fact—presumably there would be an effort to structure the legislation so as to minimize impact. Because latent purposes are nearly impossible to discover empirically, however, I will ignore them here.[4] The structure of legislation will be considered consistent with its purposes if the structure is consistent with the legislation's stated purposes.

The other definitional issue to be addressed preliminarily concerns what I mean by the effects of legislation. In this article I will be primarily concerned with the extent of compliance with legislation. Compliance is the effect that is most readily ascertained. An attempt to ascertain all effects of legislation would necessarily become mired in factual uncertainty. For example, with respect to legislation requiring automobiles to be manufactured to particular safety standards, it would be necessary to estimate not only compliance by manufacturers but also the effects of the legislation on the level of foreign imports, on the price of cars, on the level of petroleum imports, and what have you.

## I. The Structure of Legislation

### A. *Legislation Without Meaningful Standards*

Some legislation considered to be protective of consumer in-

---

protection legislation. Often, therefore, I have relied on personal impressions about the effects of legislation gained over several years of teaching and researching consumer protection issues. It needs to be emphasized that this article only hypothesizes relationships between the structure of legislation and its effects. It goes without saying that further empirical research on the effects of legislation is sorely needed.

4. Anytime consumer protection legislation is ineffective, a latent legislative purpose that the legislation be merely symbolic could be inferred. If such a purpose is inferred, there is no way the structure of the legislation can be altered to increase effectiveness consistent with the purposes of the legislation. I avoid this conundrum by considering only the manifest purposes of legislation.

terests is essentially admonitory, providing no meaningful standards by which to assess the propriety of a consumer transaction. A good example is the unconscionability provision in Article 2 of the Uniform Commercial Code.[5] With respect to such statutes the question of compliance is almost meaningless. With this one type of legislation, therefore, to inquire at all about the effects of legislation, one has to look to effects other than compliance.

It is a fair conclusion that vague, admonitory legislation usually has little impact on the general character of merchant-consumer transactions. Certainly that would be an appropriate conclusion respecting the unconscionability provision. It is possible to argue, of course, that almost anything is unconscionable. But it has proven very difficult to obtain a judicial precedent about the meaning of unconscionability that has a substantial impact on a large number of transactions. This is partly because the unconsionability section, in its only really clear message, provides that a court must consider all the surrounding circumstances before deciding whether a contract provision or practice is unconscionable.[6] As a result it is nearly always possible to distinguish any precedent on the ground that some circumstance or another is different.[7] Furthermore, in litigation to establish a principle of potential general application in unconscionability cases, a merchant stands to be affected in many transactions, while a consumer litigant will be benefited in only one or a few. Merchants can generally justify greater expenditures on the litigation than the consumers, therefore, which probably causes decisions to be more favorable to merchant interests than they would be if each side invested equally in the litigation. For the same reason a merchant can more easily justify the expense of circumventing any undesirable precedent that is established by attempting to distinguish it in future cases.[8]

Though vague, standardless legislation is not likely to have significant effect on the great mass of transactions, it can have a conclusive, yet often unrecognized, effect on the outcome of particular litigation. Because there is always some argument that a

5. U.C.C. § 2-302 (1978).

6. U.C.C. § 2-302(2) (1978).

7. Arthur Leff developed this line of argument in his typically erudite and convincing way. Leff, *Unconscionability and the Crowd—Consumers and the Common Law Tradition*, 31 U. Pitt. L. Rev. 349 (1969).

8. *See* Galanter, *Why the "Haves" Come Out Ahead: Speculations on the Limits of Legal Change*, 9 Law & Soc'y Rev. 95 (1974).

transaction is unconscionable, it is virtually always possible for a plaintiff to impose some risk of losing a lawsuit on a defendant by raising an issue of unconscionability. More important, since nearly everything is relevant to a determination of unconscionability, interjecting the issue into a lawsuit may make available an opportunity for extensive discovery, with all the expense that can impose on the defendant. A consumer plaintiff, however, usually must make a considerable investment in legal resources to seek extensive discovery. As a consequence, this litigational ploy tends not to be used, except where legal resources are inexpensive or costless to the plaintiff, such as when the consumer is entitled to legal aid of some type.[9] Moreover, jurisdictions vary in the availability of extensive discovery in small actions; others have restricted discovery in unconscionability actions where the consumer is unable, prediscovery, to make a prima facie showing of unconscionability.[10] Where the discovery ploy is available and used, a common outcome is a settlement in which the merchant agrees to satisfy all or most of the particular consumer's claim, but in a way that does not establish a precedent for other claims,[11] and the consumer withdraws all discovery requests.

In sum, vague admonitory legislation is probably mostly symbolic in its effects, having little impact on the general situation of consumers. It can provide a useful tool for obtaining a favorable litigation result by a consumer with access to low cost legal services. Ironically, the more vague the legislation the more useful it may be in this respect, since increasing vagueness may increase the kinds of information reachable on discovery. There are already many vague principles available to consumer litigants,[12] however, so that any additional legislation of this type may not have even the limited marginal impact of enhancing the individual consumer's litigation position.

---

9. Another situation in which conditions are ripe for interjecting an unconscionability claim into litigation is when the consumer personally possesses the necessary legal skills. The consumer's direct costs for interjecting the claim *pro se* will be low, though in particular cases the opportunity costs will be high because of the time needed to develop an unconscionability theory.

10. *E.g.*, Patterson v. Walker-Thomas Furniture Co., 277 A.2d 111 (D.C. 1971).

11. For example, the merchant might agree that the merchandise delivered was shoddy, but for idiosyncratic reasons—such as mishandling by the delivery person.

Evidence that the unconscionability provision can be and is being used in this way has been gained from conversations with legal aid lawyers having sizeable consumer caseloads.

12. In addition to unconscionability, the common law doctrines of fraud and duress are often thought to be malleable enough to afford a remedy in virtually any situation.

### B. The Importance of Being Specific

My first proposition respecting the structure of consumer protection legislation is that as the conduct prescribed or proscribed is defined with greater specificity, there will tend to be a greater effect on the voluntary behavior of those regulated. By voluntary behavior I mean action which is not compelled by injunction or similar legal process, even though the action might be motivated in part by fear of legal sanction if it were not taken.

Stated more intuitively, this proposition asserts that if legislation directs merchants to do something particular, many will do it, almost regardless of the provisions for sanctioning violations. Compliance will result from such motives as a general belief in law abidingness and a fear of bad publicity.[13] On the other hand, standardless legislation is unlikely to have much effect on voluntary behavior, because merchants are likely to give themselves the benefit of the doubt in deciding whether their existing practices violate a vague standard, such as unconscionability.

Debt collection is regulated in Wisconsin by a set of rules that can be used to illustrate this proposition. The Wisconsin Consumer Act, which became effective in 1973, contains the following provision pertaining to the harassment of debtors by frequent telephone calls:

> [A] debt collector shall not . . . [c]ommunicate with the customer or a person related to him with such frequency or at such unusual hours or in such a manner as can reasonably be expected to threaten or harass the customer.[14]

The federal Fair Debt Collection Practices Act, which became effective in 1978, contains a similar provision:

> [A] debt collector may not communicate with a consumer in connection with the collection of any debt . . . at any unusual time or place or a time or place known or which should be known to be inconvenient to the consumer.[15]

The federal Act goes on, however, to provide:

---

13. It has also recently been argued that private litigation by a consumer alleging violation of a specific legislative prohibition is cheaper and more likely successful than litigation alleging violation of a vague prohibition. Pettit, *Representing Consumer Defendants in Debt Collection Actions: The Disclosure Defense Game*, 59 Tex. L. Rev. 225, 288-89 (1981). Fear of sanction, therefore, may be another reason specific legislation is more likely to have concrete effects on merchant behavior.

14. Wis. Stat. § 427.104(1)(g) (1979-80).

15. 15 U.S.C. § 1692c(a)(1) (Supp. IV 1980).

> In the absence of knowledge of circumstances to the contrary, a debt collector shall assume that the convenient time for communicating with a consumer is after 8 o'clock antimeridian and before 9 o'clock postmeridian, local time at the consumer's location.[16]

The proposition asserted above predicts that the more specific federal legislation has more substantial immediate effect on the voluntary behavior of debt collectors than the state legislation, even though the sanctions for violation of the state legislation are more severe than the sanctions for violation of the federal legislation.[17] This difference in impact would be obtained even though the manifest or stated purpose of the two enactments is essentially the same.[18] The difference in the enactments lies in what I have called their structure.

One implication of this proposition is that a statute should contain many specific propositions. At the same time, however, a statute ought to attempt to state its ostensible purpose in generalized terms—as both statutes discussed above have done—since it is highly likely that circumstances will arise that are unforeseen or so idiosyncratic as to be unworthy of specific legislative provision.[19] As a general rule, therefore, statutes should state

---

16. *Id.*

17. The strongest remedial provision in the state legislation provides that damages "shall include damages caused by emotional distress or mental anguish with or without accompanying physical injury." Wis. Stat. § 427.105(1) (1979-80). The federal Act has no counterpart provision. Otherwise the two enactments are similar in their provisions setting sanctions for violation.

18. It is the general impression of persons in the debt collection business in Wisconsin with whom I have discussed this matter that the two Acts have the differential impact on behavior I predict. It has not been practical to test the proposition empirically, however. An empirical test of the impact of the two Acts could be based on the different scopes of the two statutes. The Wisconsin Consumer Act applies to virtually all forms of debt collection, while the Fair Debt Collection Practices Act applies principally only to persons, other than attorneys, collecting debts on behalf of another (mostly collection agents). *Compare* Wis. Stat. § 427.103(3) (1979-80) *with* 15 U.S.C. § 1692a(6) (Supp. IV 1980). The proposition could be tested by contrasting the collection behavior of collection agents in Wisconsin with that of large institutions doing a good deal of collecting on their own behalf, such as banks, both in Wisconsin and elsewhere. The proposition would predict a variance in the behavior between collection agents and the large institutions, with the former much less likely to telephone outside the specified hours. It would also predict little variance in the collection behavior of large institutions in Wisconsin and elsewhere, even though the non-Wisconsin institutions might not be governed by any collection practices legislation at all. Difficulties in obtaining reliable information about collection behavior render this research design impractical, however. Debt collectors are not likely to reveal voluntarily information indicating behavior that might be regarded as harassing. Any other ways of acquiring information—for example, from consumers themselves—are difficult and expensive.

19. Suppose, for example, to the knowledge of the collector a debtor works at night

their principal purposes in general terms, followed by a number of specific applications.

A second implication of the proposition is that a generalized statement of purpose is likely to have more impact in the long run if the legislation provides a relatively easy way to specify its application in particular circumstances. Although a legislature can always amend legislation to specify its application, consumer protection legislation rarely receives such attentiveness from legislatures. Provision for rulemaking is normally desirable, therefore.[20] It is worth noting that the Fair Debt Collection Practices Act, discussed above, specifically prohibits rulemaking by the administrative agencies charged with enforcement responsibility.[21] The proposition asserted here implies that this provision, if it has any effect at all, can only inhibit the overall impact of the Act.

### C. *The Effects of Cost on Compliance*

My second proposition, almost tautological, is that where costs of compliance to the regulated merchant decrease, compliance tends to increase. Costs of compliance consist of two types: (1) direct costs—the costs of adjusting business practices to conform to the regulation; and (2) opportunity costs—the benefits of non-compliance, other than saved direct costs, that are foregone by compliance. An example of an opportunity cost would be profits from extra sales that are lost as a result of compliance with some regulation.

One implication of this proposition for the structure of consumer protection legislation is that effectiveness can be increased by minimizing the direct costs of compliance, to the extent possible consistent with the manifest purposes of the legislation. The proposition also implies that there will tend to be high compliance with regulation that has little impact on the economic position of consumers, for the opportunity costs of compliance with such regulation are likely to be low. There are numerous examples of the latter implication. For example, there

and sleeps in the daytime. Under federal legislation, only the general provisions could be used to sanction the collector for telephoning at 11 A.M.

20. An alternative to rulemaking, perhaps as effective for these purposes, is provided in the Federal Trade Commission Act. That Act subjects a merchant to financial penalties for "knowing violation of case law"—that is, engaging in an act or practice with actual knowledge that in another case it had been determined unlawful in similar circumstances. 15 U.S.C. § 45(m)(1)(B) (1976).

21. 15 U.S.C. § 1692(1)(d) (Supp. IV 1980).

is high compliance with legislation requiring health warnings on cigarette packages.[22] While no doubt there are several reasons for the high compliance level, one reason probably is that the warnings do not deter cigarette consumption, and hence there is a low opportunity cost to compliance.

Another example where low opportunity costs may explain high levels of compliance concerns the Truth in Lending Act.[23] It is commonly reported that there is a high level of substantial compliance with that legislation.[24] Later in this article I will suggest that some of the sanctions for violation of this Act are an important factor in this high level of compliance. It is generally recognized, however, that there are few opportunity costs to compliance with Truth in Lending, as the various required disclosures have proved to have little impact on consumer buying behavior.[25] These low opportunity costs may partly explain the high level of compliance with this legislation.[26]

One corollary of the proposition concerning costs of compliance is that usually larger firms will have a higher level of compliance since they can realize the economies of scale that typically exist with respect to the direct costs of compliance. Compliance typically involves some investment—for example, in legal resources for redrafting a standard form contract—and as the number of transactions affected by this investment increase, the cost per transaction will be less. Consistent with this reasoning it is the common experience of administrators of consumer protection legislation that small firms have the highest levels of non-compliance.

## II. Sanctions for Violation

One way to induce compliance with legislation is to provide sanctions for non-compliance. Potential sanctions can be divided

22. 15 U.S.C. § 1333 (1976).

23. 15 U.S.C. §§ 1601-1665 (1976).

24. This has been the consistent message of the Federal Reserve Board's Annual Report on the Truth in Lending Act. *See, e.g.*, Board of Governors of the Federal Reserve System, Annual Report to Congress on Truth in Lending for the Year 1978 10 (1978). *But see* Landers, *Some Reflections on Truth in Lending*, 1977 U. Ill. L. F. 669, 676-83.

25. *See* Whitford, *The Functions of Disclosure Regulation in Consumer Transactions*, 1973 Wis. L. Rev. 400, 405-20.

26. It must be recognized, however, that the direct costs of compliance with Truth in Lending are sometimes substantial, as the complexities of the legislation can make difficult the drafting of a complying disclosure form. *See* Landers & Rohner, *Functional Analysis of Truth in Lending*, 26 U.C.L.A. L. Rev. 711 (1979).

into three categories: private, hybrid, and public. Private sanctions are those initiated by an individual harmed by non-compliance and provide mostly for compensation to the extent of the harm. Hybrid remedies, as I use the term, are also initiated by individuals, but they are designed to fulfill a private attorney general theory of enforcement. They provide benefits which go well beyond compensation for any harm to the initiator of the sanction, commonly benefiting directly the entire class of consumers the legislation is designed to protect. Public sanctions are initiated by public agency. Typically, but not always, they are prospective remedies, seeking to prevent future statutory violations.

### A. *Private Remedies*

Most, though not all, consumer protection statutes establish a cause of action for compensatory damages in favor of a consumer injured by non-compliance with the statutes. Compensation for the injured person is one purpose for extending such remedies. Private remedies are often seen as a technique for inducing compliance as well. Where the costs of compliance to merchants are less than the projected claims for compensatory damages caused by non-compliance, the availability of private actions for damages will provide an economic incentive to merchants to comply.

Experience has shown indisputably that consumers simply do not utilize private compensatory remedies with sufficient frequency to provide any meaningful incentive for compliance with the vast majority of consumer protection legislation.[27] In the literature two reasons are commonly given for the low level of consumer utilization of private compensatory remedies. First, it

27. Exclusive reliance on private compensatory remedies is sometimes seen as an ideal strategy for obtaining compliance, because this strategy provides merchants a choice between compliance and non-compliance together with payment of damages to those injured. Merchants could be expected to choose the latter course of action where the costs of compliance exceed the likely losses to consumers resulting from non-compliance. Non-compliance in this situation would be regarded as socially desirable by the dominant utilitarian value systems in vogue today as tending to maximize resource allocation efficiency. In a sense, the availability of a non-compliance option can be seen as a useful check against excesses in the consumer protection legislation. *See generally* Stigler, *The Optimal Enforcement of Law*, 78 J. POL. ECON. 526 (1970).

The low level of utilization of private remedies by consumers means that, even in terms of neo-classical value systems, exclusive reliance on private compensatory remedies cannot be seen as an ideal sanctioning scheme. So many of the injuries caused by non-compliance go uncompensated, because unclaimed, that such sanctioning schemes provide excessive incentives for non-compliance.

is argued that consumers are typically unaware of their legal rights and remedies. Consequently they do not take whatever steps are necessary to initiate an available remedy, such as contacting a lawyer.[28] Second, it is widely asserted that, because violation of consumer protection legislation rarely visits extensive injury of a tangible, provable nature on any consumer, the amount of damages available under compensatory remedies is usually insufficient to render it economical for a consumer to initiate legal action for a purely compensatory remedy.[29] The costs of initiating legal action are typically significant, because for most consumers it is a practical necessity to hire an attorney in order to claim successfully a compensatory remedy.

Statutes fixing product quality standards are one potential major exception to this general conclusion that private compensatory remedies have little effect on levels of compliance. Although many statutes in this area do not provide for private compensatory remedies,[30] and there is little evidence of significant consumer use of private statutory remedies even where they do exist,[31] the common law of products liability may provide a significant incentive to comply with the standards fixed in the product quality legislation. Any product violating a statutory quality standard is likely to be considered defective in a products liability lawsuit. Since product liability lawsuits are initiated with regularity, a manufacturer choosing non-compliance as a course of action faces the prospect of claims for substantial damages if the non-complying product feature can cause serious personal injury.

Two qualifications must be made to the suggestion that the availability of private compensatory remedies under the common law of products liability significantly induces compliance with legislation establishing product quality standards. First, although there is a good deal of products liability litigation, prod-

28. *See* Macaulay, *supra* note 1, *passim*.

29. *See, e.g.*, Pettit, *supra* note 13, at 280-81; Note, *Private Enforcement Under the Fair Debt Collection Practices Act*, 28 Case W. Res. L. Rev. 710, 716-20 (1978).

30. *E.g.*, Federal Hazardous Substances Act, 15 U.S.C. §§ 1261-1274 (1976 & Supp. IV 1980); Poison Prevention Packaging Act of 1970, 15 U.S.C. §§ 1471-1476 (1976); Flammable Fabrics Act, 15 U.S.C. §§ 1191-1204 (1976 & Supp. IV 1980).

31. The Consumer Product Safety Act establishes a right of action for compensatory damages and permits a court, in its discretion, to award attorney and expert witness fees to the consumer. 15 U.S.C. § 2072 (Supp. IV 1980). The annual reports of the Consumer Product Safety Commission regularly discuss efforts to achieve compliance with Commission rules and orders, but the reports never mention the exercise of private remedies.

ucts liability claimants are not distributed randomly throughout the population. Specifically, a disproportionate number of product liability claims arise from injuries at the workplace. Commonly, the plaintiff first contacts an attorney in order to present a workmen's compensation claim and the situation is only later defined, by the attorney, as raising a products liability claim. Consumers injured in the home are much less likely to present a products liability claim.[32] As a consequence, products liability law may provide a lesser incentive to compliance with product quality legislation affecting products not used in the workplace than might first be assumed.

Second, though much is made in the theoretical literature about the kinds of impacts products liability has on product design and manufacturing quality control procedures, there is a dearth of empirical evidence specifically validating such a link.[33] Given the amount of products liability litigation and the size of judgments, it would be highly surprising if there were no impact at all, particularly with respect to products that present a substantial risk of costly injury. It is likely, however, that the impact is different from that which would be predicted if manufacturers' decision-making effectively maximized firm profits. Decision-making by many manufacturers is simply not well organized or efficient. More important, decision-making in many corporations is likely to be systematically biased in favor of the self interests of decision-makers (managers), where they diverge from the best interests of the firm. There is not yet a well-developed theory about how the potential conflict of interest between corporate managers and their firms affects particular decisions. It is possible, however, that the career interests of corporate managers are heavily influenced by the short-term profitability of the operations under their control, causing them to favor short-run gain, such as avoidance of extra manufacturing costs, over long-term loss, such as extra liability or higher insurance premiums in the future.[34] If so, products liability deci-

32. For one study showing the very low frequency of products liability claims arising from household injuries connected with use of consumer products, see Republic Research, Inc., *Claims and Recovery for Product Injury Under the Common Law*, in III SUPPLEMENTAL STUDIES TO THE FINAL REPORT: PRODUCT SAFETY: LAW & ADMINISTRATION 237 (Legal Taskforce of the National Commission on Product Safety, ed. 1970).

33. For one effort to test the existence of a link, see Whitford, *Products Liability*, in III SUPPLEMENTAL STUDIES TO THE FINAL REPORT: PRODUCT SAFETY: LAW & ADMINISTRATION 221 (Legal Taskforce of the National Commission on Product Safety, ed. 1970).

34. *See generally* O. WILLIAMSON, THE ECONOMICS OF DISCRETIONARY BEHAVIOR: MANAGERIAL OBJECTIVES IN A THEORY OF THE FIRM (1964). For a suggestion that account-

sions will have a lesser impact in promoting manufacturer investments in product safety than is commonly supposed.

Outside the product quality area private compensatory remedies, without more, have not provided significant incentives for compliance with consumer protection laws. A common legislative response has been to couple a right to a private compensatory remedy with rights to some additional compensation as well. Most commonly the statutes provide for the recovery by a victorious consumer litigant of a modest amount of punitive damages, typically between $100 and $1,000, and of reasonable attorney fees.[35] Sometimes the statute explicitly states that the reasonableness of the consumer's attorney fees should be ascertained with reference to the difficulty of the matters at issue and the time devoted to them, and not solely with reference to the amount of damages claimed.[36]

Allowance of these extra recoveries can be justified solely from the perspective of compensation to the injured consumer. As noted above, attorney fees are often a practical necessity if a claim is to be successfully litigated. And the limited punitive damages, often called exemplary damages, can be viewed as rough compensation for the time and energy the consumer must personally devote to any matter that is litigated, as well as compensation for the mental anguish that commonly accompanies consumer injury.

Whatever the legislative intent, one effect of the extra recoveries is to make a lawsuit more financially attractive to the injured consumer.[37] The availability of these extra recoveries has

---

ing practices can also introduce a systematic bias favoring short-term gain over long-term loss, see McNeil & Miller, *The Profitability of Consumer Protection: Warranty Policy in the Auto Industry*, 20 Ad. Sci. Q. 407 (1980).

Another factor blunting the impact of products liability litigation on manufacturing processes in the inability of the insurance industry to discriminate very clearly between different degrees of risk in setting products liability rates. *See* Denenberg, *Products Liability Insurance: Its Impact on Safety and Its Implications for the Consumer*, in III Supplemental Studies to the Final Report: Product Safety: Law & Administration 247 (Legal Taskforce of the National Commission on Product Safety, ed. 1970).

35. *E.g.*, 15 U.S.C. § 1692K (Supp. IV 1980) (Fair Debt Collection Practices Act). Sometimes these statutes permit recovery of the limited punitive damages in addition to provable actual damages. Other times the punitive damages are allowed only in lieu of actual damages.

36. *E.g.*, Wis. Stat. § 425.308(2) (1979-80) (one of the consumer's remedies under the Wisconsin Consumer Act).

37. Inducing compliance by stimulating private litigation is often considered a purpose for authorizing exemplary damages. *See generally* Pettit, *supra* note 13; Rice, *Exemplary Damages in Consumer Transactions*, 55 Iowa L. Rev. 307 (1969). At the time of the enactment of Truth in Lending, many believed that private litigation, stimulated by

not usually stimulated sufficient extra claims for compensatory remedies to have a significant impact on compliance, however. A common explantion for this lack of effect is that merely providing the extra recoveries does nothing to inform consumers of their enhanced litigational position. Consequently, most consumers still fail to take the steps necessary to initiate a claim, such as contacting an attorney. Furthermore, it is reported there is a widespread belief among attorneys that courts will not really award attorney fees commensurate with the time and effort involved where the amount in controversy is small.[38] As a consequence attorneys themselves, believing it is not possible to make money representing consumers, have not made extensive efforts to inform consumers of their rights in an effort to stimulate legal business.[39]

These conclusions about the usual ineffectiveness of allowing exemplary damages and attorney fees must be qualified somewhat when discussing experience under the Truth in Lending Act. Some commentators have concluded that the right of action for individual damages, which under the Act includes the right to exemplary damages and reasonable attorney fees,[40] has not been a significant factor in inducing compliance.[41] Other commentators, however, have noted the reasonably high incidence of litigation under the Truth in Lending Act, as well as the recovery of substantial fees by a number of victorious consumer attorneys. These commentators point out that it often is reasonably easy to use the Truth in Lending Act to establish a defense to an existing debt. A cause of action under Truth in Lending does not require development of difficult factual issues, the disclosure form and the written contract often being the only evidence needed. These commentators believe that creditors may make greater efforts to comply with the Act in order to avoid a Truth-in-Lending based defense to a debt, which the

---

the availability of exemplary damages and attorney fees to the victorious consumer, would become the principal means of enforcement. *See* Landers, *Some Reflections on Truth in Lending*, 1977 U. Ill. L. F. 669, 686 n.41.

38. This belief is not supported by judicial decision; such authority as exists tends to go in the opposite direction. *E.g.*, Welmaker v. W.T. Grant Co., 365 F. Supp. 531 (N.D. Ga. 1973); Ljapya v. M.L.S.C. Properties, 353 F. Supp. 866 (N.D. Cal. 1973).

39. The most extensive account of the workings of these statutes is Macaulay, *supra* note 1.

40. 15 U.S.C. § 1640(a)(3) (1976).

41. Note, *Private Enforcement Under the Fair Debt Collection Practices Act*, 28 Case Res. L. Rev. 710, 720 (1978); Note, *Recent Developments in Truth-in-Lending Class Actions and Proposed Alternatives*, 27 Stan. L. Rev. 101, 104 (1974).

consumer disputes or has not paid for some reason unrelated to the Truth in Lending Act.[42]

This ambiguous assessment of the effects of private remedies on compliance under the Truth in Lending Act suggests that a strategy of inducing individual claims for damages through financial incentive, although usually ineffective, is not necessarily so. Historically, attorneys have not welcomed consumer claims,[43] but perhaps a strategy of offering fees to attorneys that are commensurate with their efforts can change this attitude. If enough consumer claims are stimulated as a result, at least some effect in inducing compliance can be expected. Precisely such thinking led to the establishment in 1970 of a government funded program in the State of Washington which had as one purpose teaching attorneys about their ability to collect reasonable fees, from merchants, by taking on meritorious consumer claims under a local consumer protection statute. For undetermined reasons the program met with only limited success in increasing the bar's receptivity to consumer claims.[44] Certainly the unfamiliarity of the local bar with the substance of consumer protection legislation could have deterred active solicitation of consumer claims.[45] Professor Pettit has recently emphasized the importance of being able to prove Truth-in-Lending defenses with relative ease in generating a substantial volume of litigation under that Act.[46] Perhaps when litigation is

42. Pettit, *supra* note 13, at 294-95; Landers, *supra* note 37, at 676-86. It is worth noting that the incidence of litigation under Truth in Lending has apparently increased over time, perhaps as lawyers become more familiar with the statute and gain confidence in their ability to earn reasonable fees under it. *See Qui Tam and Federal Reserve Board Procedures, Hearings on S. 3008 Before the Subcomm. on Consumer Affairs of the Senate Comm. on Banking, Housing and Urban Affairs*, 94th Cong., 2d Sess. 2 (1976) (opening statement of Senator Biden).

43. *See* Mayhew & Reiss, *The Social Organization of Legal Contacts*, 34 Am. Soc. Rev. 309 (1969).

44. My information on this program, which was funded by the Office of Economic Opportunity, comes from correspondence with the Consumer Protection and Antitrust Division of the Office of the Attorney General, State of Washington. The statute which established the right to collect a consumer's attorney fees from a merchant found to have violated a consumer protection statute is Wash. Rev. Code § 19.86.090 (1978).

45. Macaulay has advanced this explanation for the lack of litigation under consumer statutes. Macaulay, *supra* note 1, at 146-47. The State of Washington program discussed in the text anticipated this problem and established a procedure, through the Office of the Attorney General, by which private attorneys could get technical assistance without charge on substantive law questions. Apparently this was not enough to guarantee the experiment's success, however.

46. Pettit, *supra* note 13. Professor Pettit's article is specially insightful in discussing the practical aspects of Truth-in-Lending litigation, including the dynamics of settlement negotiations.

likely to be factually complex, exemplary damages and attorney fees alone are insufficient to induce enough litigation to provide substantial incentive for compliance. On the other hand, an ever increasing supply of lawyers may ultimately generate enough economic need for new legal business to induce members of the bar to master the substance of consumer protection legislation and attempt to generate reasonable fees by taking all types of consumer claims, where exemplary damages and attorney fees are available.

A very different approach to stimulating claims for compensatory remedies, so that such claims can have an effect in inducing compliance, has been to lower the costs of asserting such claims, rather than enhancing the rewards for successfully asserting them. Costs could be lowered the most by establishing institutions for entertaining claims where it is not a practical necessity for the consumer to have an attorney. Small claims courts were established with this idea in mind, and it is well known today that they have not succeeded in attracting any significant amount of consumer claims.[47]

In the past ten to fifteen years there have been extensive efforts to establish viable informal consumer complaint mediation and arbitration systems, in the hope of achieving what small claims courts have not. A variety of such systems has been established, some within particular business corporations,[48] some by trade associations affiliated with business interests,[49] and others by diverse government agencies.[50] Both the purposes and procedures of these different programs vary widely.[51] Most com-

47. *See* Yngvesson & Hennessey, *Small Claims, Complex Disputes: A Review of the Small Claims Literature*, 9 LAW & SOC'Y REV. 219 (1975).

48. *See* Whitford, *Law and the Consumer Transaction: A Case Study of the Automobile Warranty*, 1968 WIS. L. REV. 1006, 1023-24.

49. The consumer complaint activities of Better Business Bureaus, sponsored by Chambers of Commerce, are the best known examples of such systems.

50. *See* Steele, *Fraud, Dispute, and the Consumer: Responding to Consumer Complaints*, 123 U. PA. L. REV. 1107 (1975); Whitford & Kimball, *Why Process Consumer Complaints? A Case Study of the Office of the Commissioner of Insurance of Wisconsin*, 1974 WIS. L. REV. 639.

51. A number of programs that are receptive to consumer complaints make no effort to resolve particular disputes. Rather they treat complaints as data about trade practices. In these programs a significant number of consumer complaints of a similar nature is considered suggestive of a possible abusive practice requiring some type of public remedy. A field investigation is likely to ensue if resources permit. A number of programs combine this approach to complaints—that is, treating complaints as data about practices—with an attempt to resolve disputes through mediation. *See* Bernstine, *Prosecutorial Discretion in Consumer Protection Divisions of Selected State Attorney General Offices*, 20 HOW. L.J. 247 (1977).

monly, the program limits its efforts to establishing communication between the consumer and merchant, hoping to resolve disputes that result from misunderstandings.[52] Some programs have the capacity to resolve disputes where the parties cannot come readily to some settlement. To have such capacity the program must be able to devote considerable attention to the particular details of a dispute. Where such capacity exists, it has been reported that individual consumers complain with considerable frequency,[53] with undetermined effects on the merchant's incentives to comply.

In summary, there is very little evidence that private compensatory remedies have ever had substantial impact in inducing compliance, with the possible exception of legislation fixing product quality standards. It is nonetheless appropriate that consumer protection legislation provide such remedies, for if nothing else they can offer a means of obtaining compensation for injury by the occasional consumer who asserts a claim. There also remains a possibility that in the future coupling private compensatory remedies with a right to attorney fees for the successful consumer claimant will have some effect in inducing compliance, though heretofore this approach has apparently had little effect. Finally, the establishment of informal dispute settling mechanisms to which the consumer can practically resort *pro se*, desirable in any event for a number of reasons, may abet the ability of private compensatory remedies to play some role in inducing compliance.[54]

### *B. Hybrid Remedies*

As I use the term in this article, hybrid remedies are initiated by an individual, but the relief obtainable is defined by the needs of the public, rather than by the harm visited on the plaintiff by non-compliance with the consumer protection legislation. These remedies are designed to implement the private at-

---

52. *See, e.g.*, Whitford & Kimball, *supra* note 50.

53. For such a program to be successful in resolving contested disputes, it may be necessary that the program have some kind of leverage over the merchants, in order to insure their participation. This leverage is often the power to initiate public remedy proceedings against the merchant where an abusive practice is suspected. *See* Steele, *supra* note 50.

54. For a generally favorable view of the desirability of establishing informal dispute settling mechanisms as a means of encouraging compliance, see FEDERAL TRADE COMMISSION OFFICE OF POLICY PLANNING, POST-PURCHASE CONSUMER REMEDIES 92-106 (1980).

torneys general theory of enforcement. One hybrid remedy is an injunction. Another is punitive damages. The most prevalent hybrid remedy is the class action, an action initiated by one or a few consumers but in which damages are measured by the harm caused to a large group of consumers to whom the recovery is distributed.

Absent special statutory authorization, consumers cannot ordinarily sue to enjoin non-compliance with consumer protection legislation. Continuation of the non-compliance will not usually cause the individual plaintiff irreparable injury, since the plaintiff, being aware of the merchant's conduct, can typically avoid harm simply by avoiding transactions with the merchant. On general principles, therefore, any individual consumer with sufficient awareness to initiate a claim will lack standing to seek an injunction. Sometimes an individual consumer can seek injunctive remedies by suing as a representative plaintiff in a class action. In this context injunctive remedies may lie since many members of the class will be unaware of the merchant's non-compliance. But there are many practical barriers to the initiation of class action litigation, as will be more fully discussed shortly.

The only statute of which I am aware that has specially authorized an individual consumer to sue for an injunction is the Consumer Product Safety Act.[55] There are no reported cases in which a consumer has initiated such a suit, and no available information about unreported claims. If this means, as I suspect, that the provision has had little impact on compliance, probably one reason lies in the fact that there is little other than altruism to motivate a consumer to initiate such a claim.[56]

Punitive damages, other than the exemplary damages noted in the previous section, are rarely authorized for violation of consumer legislation. One of the few exceptions is contained in the Truth in Lending Act. Under this Act whenever a lender takes a security interest in real estate that is the borrower's residence, the borrower has a three day "cooling off" period in which to rescind the transaction without liability.[57] The lender is required by the Act to provide the borrower with extensive no-

55. 15 U.S.C. § 2072 (1976).

56. Ironically, it has been held that a competitor—who might truly benefit from an injunction—is not permitted to initiate an injunctive action under this provision. Plaskolite Inc. v. Baxt Industries, 486 F. Supp. 213 (N.D. Ga. 1980).

57. 15 U.S.C. § 1635 (1976). First lien, purchase money security interests are exempted from the right of rescission.

tice of this rescission right[58] and is subject to a punitive remedy for failure to do so. Specifically, if this notice is not timely given, the three day period does not start running until the notice is given.[59] Consequently, where the required notice is not given, the borrower can rescind the transaction long after it has commenced and the borrower has received credit, without any showing that the borrower was harmed or misled by the non-disclosures. The punitive nature of this remedy is indicated by holdings that the borrower is without obligation to pay interest, even for the potentially extensive period that credit was in fact extended.[60]

This Truth-in-Lending section is generally believed to have had substantial impact in insuring that appropriate disclosures are promptly made where a security interest is taken.[61] This impact no doubt derives from both the substantial burden that rescission long after a loan is made can impose on merchants and the incentives to consumers to invoke the remedy because of the windfall recoveries to be gained. The failure to provide remedies of this nature more frequently in consumer protection legislation probably stems in part from a fear that the availability of windfall recoveries will stimulate too much litigation. Particularly

---

58. 12 C.F.R. § 226.9(b)(1980).

59. 15 U.S.C. § 1635(f)(Supp. IV 1980). The right of rescission in most cases expires three years after consummation of the transaction whether or not the required disclosures are made.

Recent legislation amended this section, effective April 1, 1982, in a way that will limit somewhat the availability of this remedy. 15 U.S.C. § 1602 (1976 & Supp. IV 1980). For a discussion of this legislation see Pettit, *supra* note 13, at 272 & n.88.

60. *See* Sosa v. Fite, 498 F.2d 114 (5th Cir. 1974); French v. Wilson, 446 F. Supp. 216 (D.R.I. 1978).

The remedy provided by the Truth in Lending Act, which I have here characterized as punitive, should be distinguished from the usual three day cooling off period, now provided by consumer protection legislation in a variety of circumstances. *See, e.g.*, FTC Regulations on Cooling-Off Period for Door-to-Door Sales, 16 C.F.R. § 429.1 (1980). The usual right of rescission cannot be considered a punitive recovery. It exists as a matter of right and is not conditional on a violation of the underlying legislation by the merchant. Furthermore, it does not typically provide the consumer a windfall recovery in the form of extensive use without charge of the property of the merchant. The right of rescission discussed in the text, on the other hand, comes into existence only if the merchant fails to make required disclosures, and it can provide the borrower free use of the creditor's money for up to three years.

61. Though this conclusion about impact is widely shared by those familiar with the area, I know of no empirical evidence validating it. Perhaps some inference can be drawn from the extensive consideration given to this provision of Truth in Lending in trade publications. *See, e.g.*, 1 CONSUMER CRED. GUIDE (CCH) ¶¶ 1800-1880R (Aug. 10, 1981). It is worth noting that even the limited three day right of recission available where proper notices have been given is credited with discouraging the taking of security interests in real estate altogether.

troublesome are the risks of a strike suit—litigation designed to pressure a defendant to agree to a small settlement in order to avoid the costs of protracted litigation and the possibility of a much larger judgment later, even though there is not a substantial argument that the defendant has violated the legislation. The pressure on the defendant to settle a strike suit increases when legislation defines the substantive obligation in vague and ambiguous terms, since the defendant then can not be certain that the litigation, if pursued to final judgment, will lead to denial of punitive damages.[62] Consequently, substantial punitive damages are probably appropriate, if at all, only where the substantive obligation is stated with considerable specificity.

The most successful of the hybrid remedies in inducing compliance has been the class action. Class action procedure is designed to permit efficient adjudication of a large number of small claims raising a number of identical issues by providing for a single determination of those common issues. Since merchants typically establish routine ways for dealing with consumers, class actions are often thought to be ideally suited for consumer transactions; if the rights of one consumer are violated, it is likely the rights of others are violated in the same ways. In fact, however, class actions have proven to be not useful in most consumer situations. In most situations there are some issues for which it is not possible to make a common determination of the rights of all consumers affected by the merchant practice. Damages typically present an issue of this nature, since they so often depend on the actual injury incurred by the consumer. It is technically permissible to maintain a class action even though not all issues can be determined in a common way,[63] but the necessity of making individual determinations on even some issues typically prevents the class action from achieving the economy in legal costs that is its main attraction.[64]

---

62. An analogous problem arose with exemplary damages under the Truth in Lending Act. Certain provisions of Truth in Lending were previously drafted in such a way that it was often difficult to determine what compliance required. In such circumstances even the modest exemplary damages recoverable under that Act were considered unfair. *See* Pettit, *supra* note 13. Recently the Truth in Lending Act was amended to limit the availability of exemplary damages to situations where the violation is considered serious and in any event the requirements for compliance are clear. Pub. L. No. 96-221, § 615(b), 94 Stat. 181 (1980) (current version at 15 U.S.C. § 1640(a) (Supp. IV 1980)).

63. FED. R. CIV. P. 23(b)(3) requires only that "questions of law or fact common to the members of the class *predominate* over any questions affecting only individual members." (emphasis added).

64. *See, e.g.*, City of Detroit v. Grimmel Corp., 356 F. Supp. 1380, 1388-89 (S.D.N.Y. 1932), *modified on other grounds*, 495 F.2d 448 (2d Cir. 1934); Boskes v.

A second major difficulty in maintaining consumer class actions in most jurisdictions is a procedural rule requiring the person initiating the action—called the representative plaintiff—to finance the mailing of a notice of the class action suit to all locatable members of the consumer class.[65] If the class action succeeds, the cost of this notice can be assessed to the defendant, but frequently the cost of the mailing is so great that no representative plaintiff can or will undertake the expense pending the outcome of the litigation.

The Truth in Lending Act presents a situation in which class actions have greater potential viability than they do under most consumer legislation. The great advantage for class actions under the Truth in Lending Act is that all consumer rights are defined formally—that is, in a way unrelated to the actual understanding of or the actual injuries to participants in the transaction. Thus, under Truth in lending, violations are defined in terms of failure to include certain information on a form; it does not matter whether the failure misled any consumer. Since merchants inevitably use a standard form for disclosure, it follows that the liability issue will necessarily be common to all consumers receiving the form. Furthermore, under Truth in Lending any consumer with a cause of action is entitled to damages of at least $100, without proof of any actual injury.[66] This damages provision was originally intended as an exemplary recovery, designed to encourage individual litigation as a way of stimulating compliance.[67] It has made class actions more practically available by providing a method for assessing damages in dependent of the individual circumstances of each consumer's transaction. Finally, the cost of providing notice to the class can often be minimized in a Truth-in-Lending class action because the merchant defendants, being in the credit business, are likely to be sending monthly statements to most members of the class. Courts have sometimes been willing to order defendants to include the required notice in a monthly statement mailing, thereby greatly reducing the initial investment required of a rep-

General Motors Corp., 59 F.R.D. 589 (N.D. Del. 1933).

65. For the federal rule, see Eisen v. Carlisle & Jacquelin, 417 U.S. 156 (1974). The decision is an interpretation of the Federal Rules of Civil Procedure and not a constitutional decision. Consequently states may be free to adopt a different procedure for financing notice to the class.

66. 15 U.S.C. § 1640(a)(2)(B) (Supp. IV 1980). This provision now limits a merchant's total liability in a class action to $500,000 or to one percent of its net worth, whichever is less. *See* note 71 *infra* and accompanying text.

67. *See* notes 41-42 *supra* and accompanying text.

resentative plaintiff in order to maintain a class action.[68]

Largely because of the many litigational advantages, a great number of class actions have been filed under the Truth in Lending Act. Originally only a small proportion of these class actions were actually certified as proper class actions.[69] Courts perceived an injustice in entering a class judgment against a merchant defendant for an enormous amount when the unlawful conduct consisted of an unintentional, technical omission on a disclosure form that caused few if any consumers actual injury. Faced with this sense of injustice, courts have been ingenious in finding technical obstacles to the maintenance of class actions.[70] More recently, Congress has responded to the problem by setting upper limits on recoveries in Truth-in-Lending class actions where damages are measured by formula rather than by actual injury.[71] Although only a small portion of the class actions initiated have led to class recoveries, it is widely accepted that the always very plausible threat of a class action has played an important role in encouraging merchants to comply with the Truth in Lending Act.[72] In this sense Truth in Lending has shown that the availability of a potentially maintainable class action can be an important tool in inducing compliance.

One reason for the filing of a substantial number of Truth-in-Lending class actions is the fees that an attorney for the representative plaintiff can earn if the suit is successful. Whereas in an individual action under Truth in Lending an attorney would very much want his or her fees based on the complexity of the suit and the time spent on it, in a class action it is in an attorney's interest to have fees based on size of the recovery, which is likely to be large if the suit is successful. Courts have considered

---

68. *See* Katz v. Carte Blanche Corp., 53 F.R.D. 539 (W.D. Pa. 1971), *rev'd on other grounds*, 496 F.2d 747 (3rd Cir.), *cert. denied*, 419 U.S. 885 (1974).

69. *See* Note, *Class Actions Under the Truth in Lending Act*, 83 YALE L.J. 1410, 1412 (1974).

70. The leading case is Ratner v. Chemical Bank New York Trust Co., 54 F.R.D. 412 (S.D.N.Y. 1972).

71. 15 U.S.C. § 1640(a)(2)(B) (Supp. IV 1980). The limit is $500,000 or one percent of the defendant's net worth, whichever is less. This amendment has created new technical problems in certifying a Truth-in-Lending class action. *See* LeValley & Walker, *Truth-in-Lending Class Actions Under Amended Section 130*, 24 KAN. L. REV. 471 (1976); Comment, *Truth in Lending and the Federal Class Action*, 22 VILL. L. REV. 418 (1977).

72. *See* Garwood, *Truth-in-Lending After Two Years*, 89 BANKING L.J. 3, 9 (1972); Garwood, *A Look at Truth in Lending Five Years Later*, 14 SANTA CLARA L. REV. 491, 511 (1974); Comment, *The 1974 Amendments to the Truth in Lending Act*, 53 N.C.L. Rev. 1259, 1262 (1975).

the size of the recovery in awarding attorney fees in class actions.[73] Aware of this, no doubt many attorneys have actively sought out potential representative plaintiffs. With class actions, as with individual litigation, the receptivity of the bar to this type of legal activity is most probably an important determinant of its incidence.[74]

In sum, under the Truth in Lending Act we have actual experience with a hybrid remedy playing an important role in encouraging compliance with consumer protection legislation by regulated merchants. Similar actual experience does not exist with respect to private remedies. It is not difficult to explain why hybrid remedies might be more effective than private litigation. Since hybrid remedies lead to much larger judgments than private remedies, a lower incidence of litigation will have a greater deterrent effect on merchants. In reaching a general conclusion about the utility of hybrid remedies, it would be useful if with respect to consumer protection legislation other than Truth in Lending there were experience with hybrid remedies inducing compliance, but to my knowledge there is not. This is especially unfortunate since, as argued earlier, there is reason to believe that a merchant faces low opportunity costs for complying with Truth in Lending. To some undetermined degree this fact must account for the reasonably high level of compliance with that legislation.

The explanation for our limited experience with hybrid remedies inducing compliance may lie in the fact that there are few statutes as ideally suited for maintaining class actions as the Truth in Lending Act. Though it is virtually always possible to provide for punitive damages consistently with the manifest purposes of consumer protection legislation, punitive damages hold out the possibility of windfall recoveries and the associated danger of strike suits. Class actions largely avoid these problems,[75] but their impracticality, unless virtually all issues can be litigated as common ones, has proved a major difficulty in relying on them as a technique for achieving compliance. Truth in

73. *See, e.g.*, Illinois v. Harper & Row Publishers, Inc., 55 F.R.D. 221 (N.D. Ill. 1972).

74. *See* note 43 *supra* and accompanying text. Concern has been expressed periodically that attorneys sometimes file "strike" suits under Truth in Lending. *See generally* Landers, *supra* note 37; text following note 61 *supra*.

75. The attorney for the class may stand to gain a significant amount, which accounts for the initiation of class action suits in many instances. *See* text accompanying note 73 *supra*.

Lending has illustrated an important statutory technique for making class actions more viable. In much consumer protection legislation it should be possible, consistent with the manifest purposes of the legislation, to provide a small exemplary damage as an alternative to actual harm as a measure of recovery, thereby making it possible to adjudicate the damages issue as a common issue.[76]

It may be more difficult to design legislation so that the question of violation is also standardized across a class of consumers, without doing violence to the manifest purpose of the legislation. Disclosure regulation, like Truth in Lending, defines what constitutes a statutory violation in ways naturally amenable to common determination in a class action. This results from the legislation's regulation of the contents of standardized forms given to many consumers. Legislation regulating product design has similar features, since manufacturers will produce many items according to a single design. Other legislation, particularly legislation concerning deceptive practices, presents difficulties, because of the tendency of merchants and consumers to act differently in the critical respects in each transaction that determine whether a violation has occurred.[77] Yet attempts to define the violation in ways that avoid the need for individual case by

---

76. There are other possible ways to establish a damages award that avoids the need for an individualized determination of damages. Under the Carter administration the Justice Department recommended legislation that would have permitted a representative plaintiff to sue for the amount a merchant gained as a result of a wrongful practice. Any portion of the recovery that could not be distributed to affected consumers as compensatory damages would have escheated to the government. H.R. 5103, 96th Cong., 1st Sess. 1979); *see* Comment, *Manageability of Class Actions Under S.3475: Congress Confronts the Policy Choices Revealed in Rule 23(b)(3) Litigation*, 68 Ky. L.J. 216 (1979-80). The Bill has been reintroduced in the current session but the position of the present administration is not known. H.R. 13, 97th Cong., 1st Sess. (1981).

77. The unusual facts of one well known case sustaining the availability of a class action in a deceptive practices situation tends to confirm the correctness of the text. In Vasquez v. Superior Court of San Joaquin County, 4 Cal. 3d 800, 484 P. 2d 964, 94 Cal. Rptr. 796 (1971); the California Supreme Court sustained a class action complaint alleging violations of the common law of misrepresentation in personal sales pitches because the complaint alleged that defendants' sales people memorized their pitches. If the latter allegation could be proved, the court held there was sufficient commonality to permit a class action. It must be an unusual situation, however, in which a plaintiff could establish a memorized sales pitch.

Where misrepresentations occur in media advertising, it may be possible to establish a substantive violation on a common basis. It would aid maintenance of class actions, however, if a statute established a right to damages without proof of actual damages or even of reliance on the misrepresentation. Otherwise these elements of the common law cause of action for misrepresentation could raise issues lacking commonality, perhaps inducing a court not to certify a class action and in any event making the litigation cumbersome.

case determination are likely to involve an altering of the manifest purpose of the statute.

A good example of this problem is presented by the fact situation involved in the case of *Kugler v. Romain.*[78] The Attorney General of New Jersey initiated the action under a statute authorizing that official to seek public remedies to protect consumers from fraud. The relief sought in the case included cancellation of all consumer contracts made by the merchant defendant and restoration of money paid under them. The litigational difficulty presented was that, while it was easy to show that the defendant made many misrepresentations in any sales presentation about which information was available, the specific misleading statements varied from transaction to transaction. Consequently, it was not possible to establish the existence of a specific misrepresentation in transactions involving consumers not before the court, a problem analogous to the difficulty of establishing commonality in a class action. The New Jersey Supreme Court avoided the problem by concluding that the price charged for the merchandise was unconscionably high and holding that unconscionability was the equivalent of fraud. Since the price charged was standardized across transactions, it then became possible to enter class relief. In the process, however, legislation directed at misrepresentation and fraud was interpreted to set a maximum markup at which merchandise of a particular market value could be sold, an interpretation that many would regard inconsistent with the manifest purposes of this legislation.

### C. *Public Remedies*

Virtually all consumer protection legislation today provides for public remedies. This may be seen as representing a consensus that private remedies are inadequate in themselves to achieve compliance, a conclusion clearly ratified by our past experience. There is a wide range of public remedies that can be made available to an enforcement agency. Probably most common is some form of injunctive remedy, typically effectuated through an administrative cease and desist order. Other public remedies include criminal and civil penalties, and public actions to require merchants to compensate consumers for injury.[79]

It is very difficult to make any judgment about the relative effectiveness of these different remedies. Experience teaches

78. 58 N.J. 522, 279 A.2d 640 (1971).

79. *See* Bernstine, *supra* note 51.

that the commitment of the agency to enforcement of the legislation is far more important in determining levels of compliance than the enforcement powers of an enforcing agency. A good example of this proposition is our experience under the Flammable Fabrics Act, first enacted in 1953. For about twenty years the primary enforcement agency was the Federal Trade Commission. The consensus of the various studies of that commission that were conducted around 1970 was that there had been little public enforcement activity with respect to the Flammable Fabrics Act, and that as a result there was a low level of compliance.[80] In 1973 enforcement responsibility for the Act was transferred to the Consumer Product Safety Commission. Little change was made in the public remedies available to the enforcement agency, but there was a significant increase in enforcement activity. Reports indicate a considerably enhanced compliance level,[81] no doubt largely because of the increased enforcement activity.

As important as the character and commitment of the agency is, unfortunately I cannot prescribe any formula for selecting an enforcement agency that will use public remedies in a way that maximizes compliance. I have suggested earlier that it is commonly useful for an agency to have rulemaking power. Such power permits the agency to specify the obligations of the regulated class in as much detail as possible, thereby probably increasing the level of voluntary compliance.[82] Except in this respect, however, determination of the important characteristics of effective enforcement agencies must await other studies.

## III. CONCLUSION

One important hypothesis of this essay is that increasing the specificity of legislation tends to yield greater effects in voluntary changes in behavior. Consistent with this hypothesis,

80. E. COX, R. FELLMETH & J. SCHULTZ, THE NADER REPORT ON THE FEDERAL TRADE COMMISSION (1969); ABA COMMISSION TO STUDY THE FTC, REPORT (1969). *See also* Comment, *Dressed to Kill—The Flammable Fabrics Act of 1953—Twenty Years in Retrospect*, 4 CUM.-SAM. L. REV. 358 (1973); Note, *Flammable Fabrics Act Protection: Fire Resistants v. Industry Resistance*, 39 GEO. WASH. L. REV. 608 (1971).

81. This information comes principally from the Annual Reports of the Consumer Product Safety Commission. A slightly less sanguine view of current compliance levels is reported by the General Accounting Office. *See Compliance and Enforcement Efforts of the Consumer Product Safety Commission, Hearings on S. 3755 Before the Subcomm. for Consumers of the Senate Comm. on Commerce*, 94th Cong., 2nd Sess. 11-19 (1976) (statement of Gregory J. Ahart).

82. Notes 20-21 *supra* and accompanying text.

vague, standardless legislation, such as the unconscionability provision of the Uniform Commercial Code, is likely to have little direct effect on merchant behavior, though it may have other political effects, most likely of a symbolic nature.

Perhaps the most important hypothesis proposed is that private remedies play little role in achieving compliance, even when supplemented by exemplary damages, provision for recovery of attorney fees by the victorious consumer litigant, and the availability of informal dispute settlement mechanisms. What I have called hybrid remedies may have greater potential to induce compliance, though there are many circumstances in which it is difficult to fashion an appropriate hybrid remedy. In most instances, however, it would seem that provision for public remedies is crucial to any effort to achieve compliance.

This conclusion is not inconsistent with the current popularity of deregulation proposals. This study says nothing about when the economic marketplace, policed only by general rules of contract law, performs inadequately enough to justify corrective regulatory legislation. If corrective legislation is deemed desirable, however, this essay hypothesizes that privately initiated remedies should not be relied upon as the exclusive means of enforcement. The best available evidence indicates that what might be called the "legal marketplace" has been found wanting in our past.

# Name Index

www.ingramcontent.com/pod-product-compliance
Lightning Source LLC
LaVergne TN
LVHW081342011026
849161LV00013BB/2990
* 9 7 8 0 8 1 4 7 7 4 2 3 6 *